Asian Business and Environment in Transition

Selected Readings and Essays

Edited by

A. Kapoor
Graduate School of Business Administration
New York University

THE DARWIN PRESS
Princeton, New Jersey

Library of Congress Cataloging in Publication Data

Main entry under title:
Asian business and environment in transition.

1. Asia—Commerce—Addresses, essays, lectures.
2. Investments, Foreign—Asia—Addresses, essays, lectures. 3. International business enterprises—Addresses, essays, lectures. I. Kapoor, Ashok, 1940-
HF5349.A7A74 338'.095 73-20719
ISBN 0-87850-020-0
ISBN 0-87850-021-9 pbk.

A Darwin Book

Printed in the United States of America

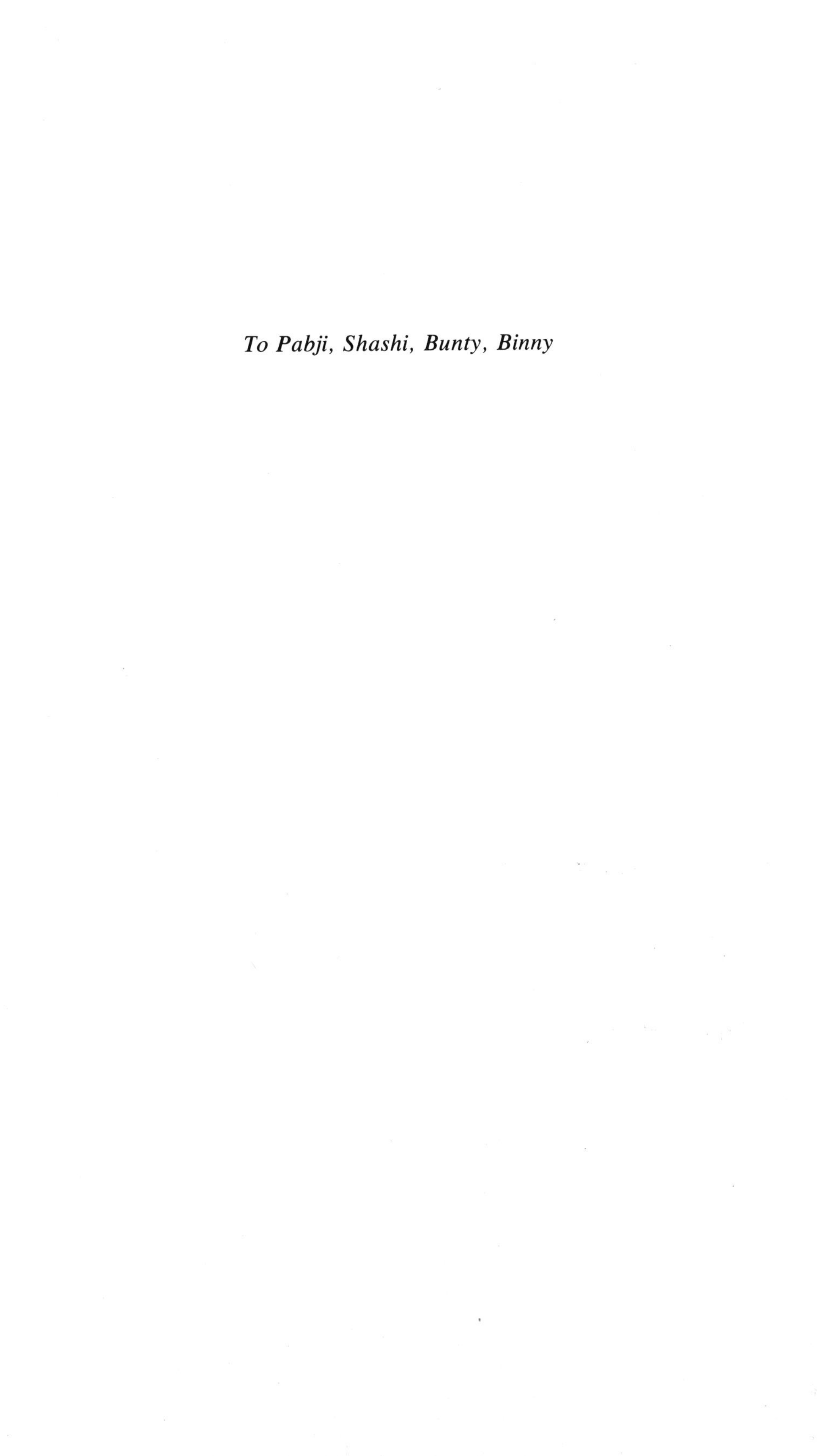

To Pabji, Shashi, Bunty, Binny

CONTENTS

CONTRIBUTORS

THOMAS W. ALLEN
National Investment & Development Authority (New Guinea)

DOLE A. ANDERSON
Michigan State University

ROBERT J. BALLON
Sophia University (Tokyo)

C. FRED BERGSTEN
Brookings Institution

A. BERTRAM
International Corporation Executive

MARTIN BRONFENBRENNER
Duke University

BUSINESS WEEK

CHARLES DRAPER
Editor, Economic Cooperation Center for the Asian and Pacific Region, Bangkok

PETER F. DRUCKER
Claremont Graduate School

ALEXANDER ECKSTEIN
University of Michigan

FAR EASTERN ECONOMIC REVIEW

KHODADAD FARMANFARMAIAN
Development Industrial Bank of Iran

ROBERT A. FELDMAN
Sophia University (Tokyo)

ARMIN GUTOWSKI
University of Frankfurt/Main

M. B. HOOKER
University of Singapore

THE JAPAN ECONOMIC JOURNAL

RICHARD TANNER JOHNSON
Stanford University

EUGENE J. KAPLAN
U.S. Bureau of International Commerce, Far Eastern Division

A. KAPOOR
New York University

NORITAKE KOBAYASHI
Keio University

LOUIS KRAAR
Fortune Magazine

VICTOR H. LI
Stanford Law School

WILLIAM W. LOCKWOOD
Princeton University

HIROSHI MANNARI
Kwansei Gakuin University

ROBERT M. MARSH
Brown University

ZUHAYR MIKDASHI
American University of Beirut

SABURO OKITA
Japan Economic Research Center (Tokyo)

WILLIAM G. OUCHI
Standford University

TERUTOMO OZAWA
Colorado State University

JEAN-LOUIS DU RIVAUX
Economist

ROBERT V. ROOSA
Brown Brothers, Harriman and Company

JIRO TOKUYAMA
Nomura Research Institute

YOSHI TSURUMI
Harvard University

UNITED NATIONS ECONOMIC AND SOCIAL COUNCIL

ARNOLD K. WEINSTEIN
University of Western Ontario

HOWARD F. VAN ZANDT
ITT Far East and Pacific, Inc.

CARROLL L. WILSON
Massachusetts Institute of Technology

ALEXANDER K. YOUNG
State University of New York

PREFACE

A large population base, growing purchasing power, an abundance of natural resources, historical involvement of Western nations with one or more Asian countries, attractive profit levels—these are some of the considerations attracting international corporations from the United States and elsewhere to participate in the development of the Asian region.

The Asian region is demonstrating changes in many dimensions, such as political orientation and structures, economic sophistication and ideology, a growing sense of national identity, and the gradual though still somewhat limited expression of a sense of regionalism. A central theme of the region is that business systems and the broader environmental context within which they function and with which they interact *are in transition*.

This book covers important dimensions of Asian business systems and the broader social-cultural-economic-political environments in which their interaction takes place. The articles discuss foreign investments in Asia, management, marketing, law, business-government relations including the dimension of negotiation, internationalization of Japanese companies, and the future evolution of the Asian region with reference to the Pacific Basin and Middle East, national resources, and the nature of interaction between the nation state and the international corporation. At times, the articles on the developing countries of Asia deal with one country. However, the issues discussed have relevance for other developing Asian countries.

A significant number of articles deal with Japan because of its importance to international companies, its major role in the political and economic affairs of the rest of Asia, and the emergence of Japan-based international corporations competing with U.S.- and Europe-based international corporations in Asia and elsewhere. The selected articles permit the reader to compare the Japanese business system with those of the developing countries of Asia.

The topics included in this book have relevance for other developing regions of the world, as well. The nature of Japanese management, business-government relationships, and internationalization of Japanese corporations are topics which are important for businessmen and host-government officials in Latin America entering into greater economic interaction with Japanese corporations. Also, the nature of conflict between the international corporation and the Asian nation state is relevant to the ongoing debate on the same subject in Latin America, Africa, the Middle East, and in some developed countries.

The articles have been written by Asian and Western scholars and practitioners and represent a diversity of viewpoints. Many of the issues are complex and controversial and must be seen from more than one viewpoint.

This book may be used at the graduate or undergraduate levels in courses covering Asia and developing countries and in courses placing particular emphasis on Japan. Additionally, the broad range of information and views will make the book an important source of information on Asia for businessmen and government officials.

I wish to thank students in the Asian Business course, academic colleagues in Asia and the United States for their support and encouragement, the journals for granting reprint rights, and the individuals who contributed essays for this book. As always, my family provided unfailing support.

Ashok Kapoor
July, 1976
New York City

1

Asian Triangle: CHINA, INDIA, JAPAN

William W. Lockwood

THE uncertain power balance created in Asia after 1945 by the defeat of Japan, the eclipse of European imperialism, and the weakness of newly independent nations drew the United States into commitments across the Pacific far beyond its original intentions or its long-run interests and capabilities. With the reduction of those commitments now in progress, what will be the shape of Asia's future as it takes charge more independently of its own destiny?

Abstracting from many complexities, this essay dwells upon the significance of the Asian triangle represented by China, the great land empire of East Asia; Japan, the industrial giant to the east; and India, the subcontinental realm southwest across the Himalayas. If Asia's destiny is to be decided increasingly by Asians, as it must be, then these three nations especially will dominate its future. On the wider world stage, meanwhile, their emergence will contribute still further to "the dwarfing of Europe, particularly of Western Europe, which is," says Max Beloff, "the major historical phenomenon of our generation." The United States may be included here, too, by the turn of the century, to judge by its declining share of world industrial and military power, and its return to a more inward orientation.

Strategically, of course, this focus on the Asian trio oversimplifies the multipolar complexities of the Asia-Pacific region. Certainly the United States and the U.S.S.R. are major participants, and lesser subregional roles are played by many others. The Soviet Union, indeed, with over half of its territory east of the Urals, can even claim to be an "Asian" nation. Moreover, Japan, for all her spectacular industrial achievement, has yet to translate her economic power once again into military strength. As for China and India, they are still only on the threshold of their industrial revolutions, a century or so behind present-day Japan and other advanced industrial nations in income level at their recent rates of growth. Indeed, two-thirds of their people still live in farm villages not far above traditional levels of poverty.

Nevertheless, the size and resources of the two continental giants—together they comprise a third of the human race—as well as the human capacities manifest in their long cultural heritage, suggest that they will play a decisive role in Asia's future, from the Yellow Sea to the Persian Gulf. This is true of Japan, too, as long as she possesses the bulk of Asia's industrial capacity within her island chain. Several smaller nation-states of the region may continue to lead in providing some of the better things of life at an early stage of development—political freedom, education, economic welfare. But the power balance is likely to be dominated increasingly by the three singled out here because of their strategic location, the weight of their resources, and their human potential.

A second reason for placing Japan, China and India in a framework of comparison is that they form a striking triangle of development models, embracing a wide range of modernizing ideologies and institutions. This adds

---

Reprinted by permission from *Foreign Affairs* (July, 1974).

its own dimension to their strategic relations and their influence upon their neighbors. No account of the "Asian drama" of the 1970s and beyond confronts realities unless it takes the measure of these alternative systems.

II

A point of departure is to note first that the contrasting patterns of development in the three nations cannot be explained primarily as inspired by radically different human ideals. Their leaders have sought legitimacy with their people through programs that differed widely in method and outcome. Yet all have articulated common aims: a prideful, independent nationhood; internal peace and security; modern technology applied to raising the level of life; and some popular sense of fair shares, social justice, and participation in the process of development.

It is the relative timing, sequence and emphasis of these goals as motor forces of modernization that vary. Japan, beginning a century ago, first displaced her ancient feudal order with a modern nation-state, legitimized with newly furbished nationalist-religious symbols of the Throne. Capitalizing on developmental forces already at work in the Tokugawa era, her new leaders now took her slowly but steadily down the path of industrialization, joining national ambition with personal incentives for wealth and power to transform her economic life. In time this led to the building of the economic and social infrastructures of a more democratic politics, too, until the crisis of the 1930s. Today, resurgent from defeat and devastation, Japan boasts the most developed democracy of the non-Western world, as well as an enterprise system that expanded its economic base at ten percent a year from 1952 to 1972. A salutary tension persists between state and society within the wider consensus of a strong national identity.

The circumstances of Japan's modern century thus permitted her to pass in overlapping sequences from nationalism to industrialism to democracy as animating values of social development. In this regard she emulated earlier historical experience in several Western nations, e.g., Great Britain. Nationhood and government legitimacy were well established before serious tensions began to grow over popular participation in politics, or over a more equitable sharing in the fruits of industrialization.

India and China, by contrast, entered upon their autonomous modernization in the twentieth century, not the nineteenth. These central aspirations for political and social development accordingly have arisen more nearly in conjunction with each other, and from this has come some of their more intractable problems, as well as some of their achievements. The two have, of course, pursued radically different paths. As recounted below, both have managed to achieve modest rates of economic growth over the past 15 years —somewhat above the rate averaged by Japan through the half-century before World War II. In China, however, this has been attended by a ruthless liquidation of old elites and a revolution in social institutions. Mass equalization of economic and social privilege has been achieved at the price of a pervasive social conformity—both consensual and coercive—in what proportions no outsider can say. Visitors are impressed with the evidence of personal compliance and a spirit of collectivity, or at least with the lack of evidence to the contrary, whether in the commune, the factory or the school.

India, her time margins lengthened by large-scale foreign aid, has made no such head-on assault against her traditional social order, partly transformed as it already was over a century of British rule. She continues in so doing to tolerate wide disparities in wealth and opportunity, finding it difficult to confront squarely the obstacles to reform within the parameters of her open, "accommodative" politics and her liberal, constitutional order. Great masses of her people continue to live at levels of destitution that are evidently a thing of the past in the People's Republic. By comparison with Communist China, however, hers has been thus far a more stable and continuous evolution. She has been spared the traumatic disorders and the harsh compulsions of Mao Tse-tung's efforts to consolidate his single-party, revolutionary dictatorship in order to usher in the new order that is his dream. By comparison with Japan's earlier experience, on the other hand, she is being committed far earlier and more seriously to social welfare programs than the modernizing elite of Meiji Japan found either necessary or desirable.

Despite these differences, the challenge to leadership in all three nations has been basically the same. Appealing to the aspirations of modernizing nationalism, they have had to generate pervasive forces for change. And they have had to do so within a framework of order that gave them purpose and direction, and enabled their peasant masses to move steadily into the modern world. How then to explain the radical contrasts in the three paths chosen toward these common goals? And are the divergences enduring?

III

One begins naturally with differences in social inheritance handed down in the three ancient cultures. Modernization must have been shaped by protean influences from the past; "no one can jump out of his skin." At many points, however, such cross-cultural analysis from history proves elusive.

Is it not paradoxical, for example, that of all Asian peoples it is the Chinese today who are the one great nation of Asia committed to a Communist pattern of development? Marx is singularly uncongenial to Confucius; no less are Lenin and Stalin. Given the pragmatic, secular and individualist (or familistic) orientation of the Chinese, with their relatively open, casteless society, their lethargic even if autocratic tradition of bureaucratic rule, their age-old attachment to private property, one might have looked here for something more like a capitalist industrial revolution, taking place within a rather permissive, cellular, decentralized order.

In Nationalist China of two generations ago, despite earlier decades of frustration, this was still a possibility—until its embryonic infrastructures were undermined and its hopes destroyed by the Japanese Army after 1937. Even as late as 1938 Mao Tse-tung was warning his fellow Communists of the inherent vigor of the Chinese middle class with its bourgeois outlook. The preceding decade had seen progress in national development, limited but substantial. Indeed, that was one reason why the Japanese struck. Some 20 years later, with uncommon frankness, Chou En-lai greeted a conservative Japanese politician in Peking by expressing gratitude to Japan for delivering China to communism.

If communism has triumphed in the interval, Mao's revolutionary genius in exploiting the opportunity created by China's long-aborted modernization was largely responsible. One's admiration for the Chinese leader only increases as he sees the ineptitude of latter-day "Maoists" elsewhere. They borrow his slogans but not his hard-headed realism in building a solid popular base for the seizure of power and the launching of a revolution. Even so, China's story is partly one of communism by default, seeming to defy a socio-cultural heritage that in different circumstances could have worked to a quite contrary outcome. To glimpse that "might-have-been" today, one need only look abroad to the spirit and capabilities of overseas Chinese in Taiwan, in Singapore, and in other expatriate communities of Southeast Asia.

As for Japan, no observer of the Asian scene in 1850 would have forecast that this island-nation could lead Asia's industrial revolution. With her meager resources, her remoteness from the dynamic centers of the West, her 250 years of self-enforced seclusion, her feudal constraints on merchant enterprise, she hardly looked the winner. Still more unlikely was it that these people—starting down the path of modernization under a paternalistic oligarchy, recruited mostly from a caste of military-bureaucrats—would emerge a century later as a parliamentary democracy. If it were the Japanese, and not the Chinese, who today found themselves secluded in an authoritarian, collectivist order we would all have easy explanations.

Modern India, too, is a nation where 25 centuries of history look down upon the present. Once again the observer of a century ago could hardly anticipate that the Indians, of all peoples, with their traditions of caste, personal despotism, and Mogul militarism—"the most rigidly hierarchical system in the world"—would be living today in a comparatively open political order, more democratic at least than most neighboring regimes, free of army rule, and with a development of private capitalism within a mixed economy such as the Chinese only found possible when they migrated overseas.

Thus, while traditions count, and especially in such ancient societies, they form part of a whole conjuncture of circumstances that can give them a surprising turn. What other forces, then, have contributed to these divergent outcomes, as we now look back with the advantage of hindsight? Reflecting on this intellectual puzzle, one would do well to begin with Jessamyn West's warning: "History is almost as much a work of imagination as our vision of the future."

IV

One set of historical circumstances bearing directly on the present was the weight and timing of Western aggression. On the Asian mainland it was India where the Europeans first arrived in force, and at a time when Mogul rule was in decay. Employing the tactic of divide-and-rule against a fragmented Indian elite, the British gradually subdued the continent, largely using Indian forces to create and maintain their "un-British despotism." Thereafter, India was ruled from London through a handful of British soldiers and civil servants, their task greatly facilitated by the weakness and delay in the rise of an all-India nationalism.

China's Manchu dynasty, too, like the Mogul, was moribund in the nineteenth century when Western diplomats, gunboats, traders and missionaries arrived on the scene. Its staying power was sufficient, nevertheless, to enable it to survive until 1911, too weak to rally the nation in defense after the T'ai-p'ing Rebellion (1851–65), yet strong enough to hang on for nearly 50 years. Western pressure on China, more than India, was limited by the constraints of distance and imperialist rivalry. The Powers even helped in some degree to shore up the bankrupt Manchu regime, which yet could never really modernize because to do so would undermine its own traditional supports and spell its doom. China could hardly have been conquered by a foreign power, once political nationalism began to develop, as the Japanese were to discover. But her humiliations over a century left deep scars that may continue to influence her relations with the outside world for years to come.

Japan, by contrast, lay at the end of the line of Western expansion in 1850. Here was only a remote chain of islands offering little wealth to attract the imperialists, occupied as they already were with commitments and rivalries elsewhere. Sir Stamford Raffles, the great British proconsul of the early nineteenth century, once tried to interest the British East India Company in a Japan venture. But his proposal fell on deaf ears. Any real intrusion into the islands would have rallied the Japanese in a fierce, nationalist resistance in any event. As it turned out, this was unnecessary, and the Japanese gained a valuable breathing spell. Thoroughly alarmed, nevertheless, they moved decisively to counter the external threat with the reforms ushered in after the Imperial Restoration in 1868.

Such contrasting responses to the Western challenge reflected differing social propensities, especially in the ideals and capabilities of emerging elites. The Japanese samurai, specifically a dissident youthful wing, met the West on its own terms in a remarkable feat of will and intelligence. Already, under the Tokugawa Shogunate, Japan was heading into an internal crisis of political renovation and economic change. Some 250 years of peace had largely converted its military elite into a clan-managerial bureaucracy. Commerce and the commercial classes were growing, and the male literacy rate had already risen as high as 40 percent. Thus key groups with access to power and with marked social learning capacity were "available for recommitment," and well connected by physical proximity and common tradition.

The external danger to Japan heralded by the arrival of Commodore Perry's "Black Ships" in 1853 reinforced emergent discontents and ambitions among the "outer" clans and progressive elements around the Throne. Overthrowing the semi-feudal order, and opening the door to Western ideas, they proceeded—"like Nehemiah . . . with sword in one hand and trowel in the other," says E. Herbert Norman—to build a modern nation-state on the foundations of growing industrial power. Their eyes fixed on the future, they moved forward step by step in a transformation that yet was steadily reinforced and legitimized by linkages with the past.

By contrast, the Chinese scholar-gentry, together with their Manchu overlords, failed tragically in the late nineteenth century to emulate the Japanese example of reform from the top down. Half free but half unfree under the unequal treaties, China had perhaps the worst of the three alternatives. She had neither the opportunity of an independent Japan, nor the constructive inputs of a British *raj*. The Manchu government, an alien regime, was the first target of rising Chinese nationalists led by Sun Yat-sen. Thus nationalism, a centralizing, integrative force in Japan, worked first in China to destroy the center of political power just when it was most needed. For a generation only a warlord anarchy was left across the face of the land. The Nationalist government formed in 1928 never got control of the country before it was confronted with the double challenge of the Communists and the Japanese army. Viewing this whole century, one is left to speculate what might have happened had the West arrived in the heyday of the Ming, a native dynasty, or even in the vigor of an early Manchu ruler like the great Ch'ien-lung (1736–1796).

India's experience under the British is something on which historians are far from agreement. "In some ways the most sterile period in Indian history" is the acid verdict of a distinguished civil servant, C. T. Garratt, hardly a fiery nationalist. Yet this is difficult to accept when one reads about eighteenth-century Mogul India, with its political fragmentation, its corrupt despotism, its human misery. On the other hand, no one would hail India's progress under the British in terms like those once applied by Thomas Carlyle to England's own colonial experience centuries earlier. Had it not been for the Norman conquest, he said, the English would have remained "a gluttonous race of Jutes and Angles, lumbering about in pot-bellied equanimity."

Britain's development goals in India were selective, favoring its own security and trade. To cite one illustration, as late as the turn of the present century expenditures to educate 240 million people amounted annually to one penny per head. Factory output rose six-fold in the last half-century of British rule, it is true. Even in industry, however, the whole tradition of the British in India was weighted toward investment decisions favoring imperial interests. Their laissez-faire, private enterprise model had to be radically altered, too, before it could suit the needs of an independent India. Here are obvious contrasts with Japan, developed by Japanese for Japanese—some Japanese, at any rate—and with a high sense of national purpose and civic responsibility.

Yet India in retrospect may be "thankful for what the British did, regardless of what they did not do," concludes one Indian scholar, D. P. Singhal. Devitalizing in some respects, the British presence was energizing in others. By comparison with China, India acquired an architectural framework of liberal institutions slowly maturing through the later colonial decades as the milieu for a creative independence movement that won her national freedom in 1947. This left her, after the trauma of partition, with a new spirit and structure of all-India unity, centered in a public-spirited elite already launched upon the tasks of building a democratizing, developing nation. "Western knowledge and techniques and a taste for the democratic way of life" is the way N. V. Sovani sums up the colonial heritage.

Today India is in the midst of that inevitable transition when she must assimilate her borrowings from the West more securely into her own tradition. This gives a latency, a sense of uncertainty, that will run through the 1970s at least, as it does throughout all of ex-colonial Asia. In a different context the same is true of the People's Republic of China since 1949. Here, too, Soviet models imported in the 1950s are going through an unstable adjustment to the realities of the Chinese environment, making it difficult to see clearly what lies ahead in the post-Mao era. By contrast, Meiji Japan, commencing a century ago, borrowed more voluntarily and defensively than India, more deliberately and selectively than Communist China, adapting all the while as she went along. Yet she too plunged into a great crisis in the interwar years 1920–1940, when the conservators of her traditions were brought to a final stand against the new order that they did not make and did not want.

V

As the century of Western domination recedes in history, other more enduring contrasts stand out clearly among these Asian societies. They include striking differences in geographical setting and nation-scale, affecting the concern for security and above all the design of the internal political system.

Geographic setting long ago gave rise to deep-seated differences, of course, that persist today. China was always the "wholly other" society of Eurasia, little exposed to invasion except by barbarian horsemen from the north, self-determined and culturally complacent, remarkably homogeneous across her enormous length and breadth. India, by contrast, was for centuries a crossroads of invasion and ethnic intermixture, generated by historic forces in Central Asia once attributed by Arnold Toynbee to "claustrophobia in the Oxus-Jaxartes basin." If the Hindu way of life remained nevertheless *un monde particulier,* owing little to the outside world, exposure on its flanks brought into the subcontinent that extraordinary diversity which is at once its fascination and its problem today. "The Chinese educated their conquerors by making them mandarins," says Sir Percival Spear; "the Indians embalmed theirs by making them separate castes." As others have put it, India's is an agglomerative culture. Political unity on anything like a continental scale has been historically the exception rather than the rule.

How different again was the historical experience of the Japanese, migrating from continental Asia in prehistoric times to their offshore islands, that cul-de-sac in the Pacific where they had to "fuse or perish." Shielded through their subsequent history from further invasion by the sea (until 1945), they were yet near enough to their great mainland neighbor to borrow selectively from Chinese institutions in the seventh century. Japan's cultural debt to the mainland, which still left her with a strong national identity, suggests analogies to that other offshore nation on the rim of Eurasia—"the Japan of the West." In both Britain and Japan the infiltration of foreign ideas, blending cultures, contributed to an instrumentalist, comparative habit of mind that has stood them in good stead. It showed itself strikingly in Japan after 1868, when once again she undertook a large-scale borrowing, this time from the nations of the West which she had now come politically to fear and technologically to admire.

From then on, with the sea no longer a barrier, Japan's prime worry as an island country has been this sense of external insecurity in a world where she finds herself flanked east and west by vast continental nations, and increasingly dependent on far-flung channels of world trade. India's political leaders, on the other hand, see her internal disunity, not external danger, as the prime threat to national progress. If Prime Minister Nehru's speeches on foreign policy used to evince a lofty sense of external security and moralistic nonalignment, this reflected India's sheltered position behind her sea frontiers and her Himalayan rampart. Such complacency is now somewhat eroded by the wars with China in 1962 and with Pakistan in 1965 and 1971. Yet Indians, despite concerns along their border, feel little of the apprehension with which the Japanese have looked out on their world, or the anxiety the Chinese now voice over their long and open frontier with the Soviet Union.

Boundaries are no guarantee of security, of course, wherever located. Recalling Japan's imperialist expansion from 1895 to 1945, Hilary Conroy quotes Lord Cromer's remark that the search for defensible frontiers "impelled the British to the barriers of the Himalayas and, when these had been reached, caused them to ask themselves whether even that frontier was sufficiently secure." In short, politics and technology are more decisive than geography in these matters. For both India and China a powerful Soviet presence in Asia today brings a striking reassertion of the importance of their inner Asian frontiers after a century of preoccupation with maritime approaches.

VI

Nation-size as a second physical variable, whether in land mass or population, shows up conspicuously in this triangle of Asian nations.

Differences in scale between China and India, on the one hand, and Japan, on the other, are differences in kind, not degree. This is especially true of the demands they make on large-scale organizational capacity, the scarcest factor in development. India crowds 575 million souls into an area one-third the size of the United States. (America would have 1.6 billion at the same density per square mile.) What is optimal size depends on the purposes at hand and the level of technology, of course. It is interesting to recall that France with 25 million people was the great power of Europe in 1789. England was then embarking on world empire with nine million. A century earlier Holland as a maritime power had staved off both Britain and France with a mere two million.

Today's Asian giants, vast agrarian societies of great cultural depth and complexity, confront problems of wholly different dimensions. To devise a system of political unity and a national market was one thing for Meiji Japan with her 35 million. To do so in a country of 600 or 800 million is something else. Japan proceeded after 1868 to build a new framework of national life within a few decades, aided as she was by her cultural unity and sense of nationhood. Her modest size, too, joined with her insular character, contributed to that defensive anxiety that afforded such powerful drives to her borrowing of new ideas. When Commodore Perry visited Japan in 1853, nothing fascinated his samurai hosts more than his Colt revolver and his miniature steam locomotive. By contrast, Chinese scholar-officials of the nineteenth century seem mostly to have been psychologically immobilized by a proud self-confidence (and self-interest), bred in an awareness of

China's ancient glory and sustained long after the Confucian tradition had lost its validity for the new era coming on. As late as 1930 R. H. Tawney could speak of China's urban development in her treaty-port areas as "a modern fringe stitched along the hem of an ancient garment."

What might China have become after 1850, had she consisted merely of the lower Yangtze valley, a nation of 35 million people accessible to the sea like Japan? The same question could be asked today of an Indian state like Maharashtra, with its 50 million extending back into the hinterland from the port and industrial center of Bombay. Singapore and Hong Kong impress one enormously with the achievement potentials of city-states of only two to four million people, especially when they are situated at a crossroads of world trade and their people are mostly Chinese. "We live by our wits," said a Singapore merchant. "What else do we have?"

In particular, the design of political systems appropriate to countries depends importantly on this factor of size, although tradition once again is bound to count heavily. China's record of imperial unity through the ages is an extraordinary one unmatched elsewhere in history. It was maintained for long periods by a closely indoctrinated, merit-oriented bureaucracy with built-in restraints on personal power. Essentially it was authoritarian rule through a balance of weakness within a self-renewing social equilibrium that changed only slowly. It was sustained politically by popular passivity and awe of government, as well as the usual instruments of coercion. The Center retained a minimal degree of national authority through devices that cut across and countered latent threats from local or regional aggregations of power. That was its chief objective, along with defense of the northern frontier. Absolutist in principle, it was yet quite permissive, certainly far from totalitarian. Such a limited concept of government once prompted Dr. Hu Shih to remark half seriously: "Lao Tzu anticipated Tom Paine by 20 centuries."

It seems ironic today that this country, with a population equal to that of North and South America and Africa together, should have been committed after 1949 to a constitutional design that looked so much to the omnipotent capabilities of a Communist party ruling from Peking. Not surprisingly, the turbulent history of the People's Republic in its second and third decades reveals an uncertain groping toward some more viable balance of forces, central and local. The problem is an old one: how to spread (and control) revolutionary initiatives throughout a vast nation within a national framework of discipline and order. Sharp lurches in policy like the Great Leap of 1957–59 and the Cultural Revolution a decade later exhibit once again the potentialities for disaster, as well as for achievement, in a one-party dictatorship lacking the checks and balances of a more pluralistic order. "Every seven or eight years," Mao is quoted as saying, "monsters and demons will jump up."

In the present rebuilding of China's political structures, there is an evolving equilibrium of factional and institutional groupings, civil and military, national and local, varying by region and functional sphere. Partly this is simply an erosion of a once-monolithic power exercised from the nation's capital—if indeed that was ever as complete as was once imagined. More positively it seems to be a calculated devolution of responsibility toward self-reliance and local enterprise in finance, farming, small industry, education and social services. If it manages to preserve a reasonable balance of benefits and costs, this aspect of the Chinese Communist model in the 1970s may well be a pioneering achievement. Significantly, except in certain strategic sectors of key importance, it is a movement in the direction of the regionalism, factionalism, and localism of the Chinese tradition.

The other horn of the modernizing dilemma, especially in these huge nations, is the danger of a decline of coherent authority at the center, to the point where no national policy can be pursued with force and continuity. In the short term at least, one wonders whether India has not reached such an impasse today under her quasi-federal constitution and multiparty system. Populist forces are eroding the legitimacy of the elites who have dominated the nation since independence. And a once-united Congress Party has been displaced by shifting intra- and inter-party coalitions varying from one state to another and from one year to the next.

In Prime Minister Nehru's day, national planners in New Delhi could pursue their goal of a middle-class, social-democratic revolution with fair rationality and dispatch under the political umbrella of the Congress. Now the whole process is increasingly the focus of bargaining and conflict within a widening political arena. At the extreme there is something ominous in a cry like "Maharashtra for the Maharashtrans," the party slogan of the Shiv Sena, violently regionalist, Hinduist, and anti-Communist. More constructively, many Indian states are moving to greater self-reliance in policies of development and reform, though nothing is being attempted here on the scale of China's decentralization of enterprise and finance. The need in both countries, it would seem, is to encourage such initiatives, while striving at the same time to strengthen national integration in those dimensions where unity and common action are essential to nation-building.

Compared with China, of course, the problem of unity in India is greatly complicated by diversity of linguistic, religious, caste and class groupings. Yet the very complexity of these plural divisions as they overlap and crosscut each other is a safeguard against the kind of bipolar confrontation that split Pakistan apart and threatens Ceylon and Malaysia. India's danger is rather the sort of leaderless drift and stagnation that is always the latent peril of coalition politics. It is doubly dangerous in a nation requiring massive revolutionary change.

The question now is whether India's "crisis of participation" can be successfully faced by a new leadership still operating within her liberal constitutional order with its free press and other civil liberties. This was the hope rearoused by Prime Minister Indira Gandhi's sweeping electoral victories in 1971–72. If the euphoria of those days has now faded, it is because her first years in power show only modest progress toward her goal of giving political freedom "its full economic and social content." Bangladesh and the refugees, drought and flood, inflation, strikes—all have handicapped vigorous policy thrusts such as would have been difficult enough in any event, given the necessity for broad coalitions of political support, inside and outside the Party. Fundamentally, though, it is a question of political will, pushing beyond rhetoric. "Democracy is on trial," the Prime Minister herself concedes. And the time is already late.

VII

It is on the economic front especially that the political issue in India may well be decided: Can she achieve acceptable growth with social justice within the parameters of her present political order, given all the difficulties of size and diversity mentioned above? Here it has been the habit of many observers to contrast India's growth capabilities unfavorably with China's. Grave disadvantages are seen in her "soft," gradualist approach. In this view China's one-party regime, whatever its constraints on political and intellectual freedom, is the efficient shortcut to an industrial revolution and a new social order.

Today, in the perspective of 25 years, such comparative judgments are still difficult to make; in the end they turn importantly on goals and values. Curiously, in statistical terms the overall scale of economic growth in India and China was probably not very different from 1957 to 1972, if we take this as a meaningful period for comparison. India managed to expand her total output at about 3.5 percent a year. The comparable figure for China is difficult to estimate. Weighted with prices typical of developing countries, it was probably a little over four percent, perhaps 4.5 percent a year—or a bit higher if we extend the span of time backward to cover the initial industrial upsurge of 1952–57. Both have achieved only modest rates of growth, it is fair to say, as compared with the performances of a number of their smaller Asian neighbors, most of which have been averaging five percent or better.

With populations growing as they are in both India and China, the gain in income per capita is minimal, needless to say. In neither country did consumption rise by more than 20–30 percent per capita over the entire period 1957–72. Probably the level of consumption was already somewhat higher in China, however, and had long been so. Now under Communist rule income is more equitably shared, and supplemented with social services improving security, health and education throughout the cities and the countryside. Today also a third contrast is beginning to appear as China's nationwide efforts to reduce her birthrate by contraception and late marriage are probably cutting population growth to two percent or less a year.

In manufacturing, both countries more than doubled their output from 1957 to 1972. China's industrial sector grew at something like seven to eight percent a year, with increasing dispersion through the countryside of small plants using "appropriate technology," i.e., capital-saving and labor-absorptive. Indian industry advanced more slowly, at about six percent annually. While avoiding the instability of the Chinese record, it has been plagued with raw material bottlenecks, power and transport shortages, strikes, cost inflation, and a none-too-efficient system of public management and control in a mixed economy. Efforts to strengthen and diversify small industry in rural growth centers have yet to attain much success. Here one suspects that India could learn much from China's new agro-industrialism—although one knows little to date about the inefficiency and waste that may result from the neglect of economies of scale and specialization in the Chinese pattern. In any event, it is these institutional foundations being built for the future that are important.

Slow progress on the agricultural front has handicapped both countries—a lesson each learned in the early years to its cost. Here India has done better since 1957. Her farm output is estimated officially to have grown at about 2.5 percent annually through 1972. The comparable figure for China over the 15 years is probably no more than two percent a year, hardly keeping pace with population. Again the Chinese record was marred by the collapse of the Great Leap in 1959–60 (worsened by bad weather), and the slow recovery that followed. Since then she has moved ahead more successfully, and her total output of food-grains is actually more than double India's, mainly because of higher yields. This means, of course, that India's potential for raising production may now be greater. Indeed, with the promise of the Green Revolution, both may be on the threshold of great gains in the 1970s, given the right combination of technology, peasant incentives and rural infrastructures.

One could go on with these comparisons, recognizing how sketchy are the data, especially from China, and how inadequate such macro-measures. At best they are only an introduction to closer study. Yet it is of great human significance that India, for example, has doubled her food supplies since independence and left behind the great famines of history, that she has tripled the number of children in school until they now approach 100 million, that she has improved health care to the point where life expectancy at birth has risen from 35 to 52, that her factories now provide her people with two million bicycles a year, that her newspaper press, one of the liveliest in the world, now reaches regularly some 20 million readers. Moreover, these changes have come about by peaceful means over a short span of 25 years, within a political order far more responsive to popular will than anything known in the past. We still need more humanistic indices of social progress, of course. One recent visitor to China, Leo A. Orleans, impressed with the simple well-being and satisfactions of life that he saw around him, suggests a new measure of development—a "degree-of-misery index." As a starter he proposes the formula: "average frequency of smiles, multiplied by the number of bicycles, and divided by the current crop of litchi nuts."

Even harder to assess than present progress, as remarked earlier, is the future potential of institutional patterns laid down over the past two decades, and the meaning of such potential for the kind of development that people want and will pay for—the true test of development. For example, China might have industrialized more rapidly had she, like India, calculated her foreign policy so as to assure a continuous inflow of foreign aid. In her leaders' view the political price was unacceptable once her break with the Soviet Union terminated assistance from that quarter in 1960. *Tzu li keng sheng*—"self-reliance"—became the watchword. A similar autarkic orientation has limited foreign trade to small proportions until recently. Yet China's difficulties have not resulted primarily from external isolation. And the lack of external aid has at least spared her certain disincentives to self-help that have shown up in India, where such assistance rose to an average of 3.2 percent of national income in the years 1960–66.

More serious for Peking has been the problem on the home front of devising structures of organization and incentives that are effective in the economic sphere and yet carry out with "creative obedience" Mao's convictions on mass mobilization as the motor force of progress. Erratic ups and downs in the economy over 25 years reflect this ideological pressure and institutional uncertainty. India's performance has been steadier, if lethargic in many respects. Certainly it has been marked with serious shortcomings in planning and administration. Indeed, food shortages and price inflation have now brought on a real crisis of confidence. In the longer view, however, one must still reserve judgment on such shortcomings in India's mixed system of state capitalism and private enterprise, as compared with authoritarian management in China's Communist order. Such a judgment must include the trade-offs, ultimately in terms of social and political goals.

Fundamental to the ideals of the Communist Party in China, and to its populist legitimacy, was its coercive redistribution of wealth and income after 1949, and its concern to spread widely the benefits of development. Substantial inequalities still exist among regions, localities and families, it is reported. But a floor has been placed under the lower levels of income, and a ceiling on top. In striking contrast is India, where the Planning Commission has had to concede failure to mitigate "in any significant measure" gross inequalities in income and wealth, for example with effective land reform.

China has also confronted sternly the problems of urban congestion and joblessness that plague all developing countries. She has sought to restrict urban growth, expelling millions of youths to villages or remote border areas, and seeking meanwhile to provide better amenities of rural life through community action. The problem basically cannot be very different from that of India, where new jobs must also be found somehow for 60 million or so new workers between 1974 and 1986, with only one in four likely to be found in urban areas. Yet India's slum-ridden cities are still growing every year, while in rural areas the better life is reaching but slowly to those massive majorities, "the young and the poor," in Indira Gandhi's phrase.

Finally, if the future rests with youth, it may well be decided in the realm of education. Both nations, of course, have achieved tremendous enrollment increases at all levels of schooling, with standards that are hard to compare. Peking's radical assault on the universities in the Cultural Revolution, with insistence that they become more mass-oriented in curriculum and admissions, may hold more promise in the long run than the conservative inertia of India's still elitist (even if overcrowded) campuses. China's leaders are showing imagination in taking education "down to the countryside" with programs directly related to the needs of daily life. After much trial and error new patterns appear to be taking shape on functional and equalitarian principles such as Asian leaders elsewhere acknowledge as desirable but are slow to implement. Meanwhile a high price must have been paid in the interruption of learning after 1966, in the constriction of teaching to what is deemed practically relevant and politically safe, and in the alienation of millions of students "sent down" to the countryside where their hopes to go on up the educational ladder seem at an end. And despite the Cultural Revolution the dilemmas of "redness" versus "expertise" still seem far from resolved, whether in the schoolroom, the factory, or the armed forces.

Chinese scientific and technological attainments appear to be at a high level in priority fields, nevertheless. The bomb and satellite are impressive achievements, for example, shielded largely from the trauma of political disorders. Western observers believe that China may already have medium-range missiles in place and is acquiring the technical capability to build ICBMs. Once again an authoritarian regime displays great capacity to arrange its priorities single-mindedly in terms of its goals. The costs of this nuclear weaponry must be formidable in the Chinese economy. But the results certainly inspire respect abroad. India is put under pressure to follow suit and Japan as well—both with substantial capabilities should they choose to apply them. Indeed, the former has already exploded one powerful nuclear device.

Given these challenges and uncertainties, it is hardly surprising that India and China in different ways should both enter upon a deep crisis of authority midway in the second decade of their autonomous development. India's progress thus far has been more orderly and more continuous. And it has been achieved within a framework of electoral choice and freedom of dissent that people prize—if its costs are not too great in other aspects of social advance. To be sure, there is today an ominous escalation of violence, prompted mostly by economic disorders. And the inability of her contending politicians and sluggish bureaucracy today to provide vigorous, coherent leadership in confronting her problems is spreading deep disillusion with the whole system. Yet despite her open political order—or because of it—India has yet to face anything like the convulsion of the Cultural Revolution or the uncertainties of the post-Mao political succession. One wonders how any Chinese bureaucrat or cadre can plan for the future, confident as to who will be in charge, when he looks back over the policy changes and factional ups-and-downs of 1949–1974. With Lin Piao, Mao's close comrade-in-arms, the latest figure to be denounced as a "renegade and traitor" preaching the "restorationist doctrines" of Confucius, who will be next in line, and what price is being paid throughout the whole institutional framework for this instability at the top?

The question remains, then, whether India's more gradualist approach will eventually endow her development with cumulative momentum, or with a set of unresolved dilemmas from the past such as Communist China has now forcibly broken through. If the one runs the risk of immobilism—too little and too late—the other, with its surges of mass mobilization, its leadership purges and rehabilitations, its romantic faith that "politics in command" can remake man in a revolutionary image, has yet to evolve an enduring design for political order and social progress in the next generation.

VIII

This overview of the two continental giants helps one to appreciate how nineteenth-century Japan, despite factors recounted above as seemingly in her disfavor, was able to override them with countervailing advantages of heritage and historic opportunity. The Japanese experience in turn affords useful perspectives on China's and India's problems and achievements thus far. "The greatest practical research laboratory of economic growth in our time," says *The Economist* of Japan.

First, it should be noted that Japan's poverty in natural resources was in some measure a blessing in disguise. Besides helping her escape colonial subjection, it turned her modern development outward from the beginning. To be sure, she was not wholly lacking in resources; like Britain, she was "built on coal and surrounded by fish." She made good use, too, of her limited cultivable lands, where her five million small farmers proceeded over two generations to double acreage yields by assiduous technical innovations. Mostly, however, she had to industrialize as the only path of development open to her, and this in turn meant a steady growth in foreign trade and urbanization. Such a pattern maximized the spread of modern ideas and technology through her cities and adjoining coastal plains where people were increasingly concentrated. Already by 1920 one could speak of an "urbanized peasantry," with schooling nearly universal at least through the primary grades. Finally, as noted earlier, Japan's relative size and external dependence probably strengthened those psychic drives to achievement that Frank Gibney once described as "a spirit, insular and protesting—a troublesome spirit, unsure of its place, but jealous of its station."

Even so, Japan's economic growth before the war was not rapid by modern standards. Many developing nations are doing better today. Over the half-century 1877–1927, and in most single decades, it was hardly three percent a year—certainly no higher than the rate maintained by India and China over the past 15 to 20 years. The significant difference here is that Japan's population meanwhile expanded annually at little more than one percent, permitting a yearly gain of nearly two percent in per capita income. India's population is growing at least twice the Japanese rate, reducing by one-half the gain in income level and creating huge employment demands on the farm and in the city. China has moved more decisively than India to restrict her increase in numbers, as noted above, but the problem is present there too, both as regards income and jobs.

The impressive thing about Japan's prewar economic progress was not any spectacular breakthrough. It was the fact that her advance was an incremental, all-round process virtually uninterrupted for 60 years. Her story is the story of the tortoise, not the hare—not great leaps but unflagging perseverance, decades of hard work and slow educational advance, and a skillful blending of indigenous and modern techniques in what the Chinese now call "walking on two legs." In no single decade was the achievement striking. Indeed, observers were commonly pessimistic about the future. And, contrary to what is often believed, growth was probably hindered, not helped, by long neglect of such problems as tenant farming, child labor, urban slums, and gross inequalities in the distribution of income and wealth. The Japanese just kept at it, nevertheless, "doing what worked" with unending patience and pragmatism. It was development from above, and development from below. In the end the leap was prodigious.

Even so, looking at China and India, it is well to recall that it took Japan

45 years (1880–1925) even to double her level of consumption per capita, and another 40 years to double it again. The implication is debatable, but it poses the question whether the continental nations can improve on this record, except to distribute the gains more equitably, and possibly avoid the drains of imperialism and war.

Japan's accelerated growth since World War II is another story, of course, though it continues to express the same basic propensities. Many factors have entered in: the loss of a burdensome armament and overseas empire; the displacement of other institutional constraints by wartime destruction and the Occupation's equalitarian reforms; the wider, competitive opportunities opening up for private enterprise, with the aid of high rates of savings, the spread of high-level education, and massive technological borrowing from abroad; and through it all the support and guidance of state ministries and banks within the relationship of "sponsored capitalism." Dynamic forces of growth have thereby been released in a new setting of stable, democratic politics at home and of guarantees from abroad of external security and boundless trading opportunities. Through the 1950s and 1960s the Japanese proceeded to double their standard of living each decade until it now is not far below that of Western Europe. Rising productivity, spreading welfare, and parliamentary politics have thus reinforced each other to a degree beyond the wildest hopes of a generation earlier, in the ruin of the war.

If there are clouds on the horizon today, as indeed there seem to be, they relate especially to growing frictions attending Japan's export expansion around the world, and renewed anxieties over her rising dependence on raw material imports, particularly oil, the lifeblood of her economy. These uncertainties abroad coincide with growing demands at home for the control of inflation and improvements in the "quality of life," e.g., cleaner air and better housing. Together they portend a marked slowdown in further high-pitched growth, at least for the present. Once again public goals and public policies, both at home and overseas, are assuming a more complex, ambivalent character than in the 20-year era just concluded. What may be the longer-term political implications of such a change it is too soon to say.

IX

Viewing this triangle of development models, one wonders if another decade will see some convergence in the Indian and Chinese patterns, whether or not they approach anything like the Japanese precedent. Here is treacherous ground, recalling the old adage: "Never prophesy anything less than ten years ahead; by that time no one will remember what you say."

Both great continental nations show the tendency already noted toward regional and institutional decentralization, and for basically the same reasons. The advantages are obvious in resource adaptability and ideological flexibility geared to the diverse realities of a vast countryside. On the other hand, the problem is posed of assuring minimal unity and discipline at the center to further national goals, even if the unitary leadership and discipline of the first generation can never be recreated. On this score Japan's problem was incomparably easier.

In another dimension of policy some measure of convergence may possibly be anticipated. Will the mixture of public and private enterprise in Indian industry move toward a widening of public responsibility and tightening of government controls, even though the glamor has pretty well gone out of the public sector? Or, after 25 years of experiment, will the balance shift toward a more permissive and coöperative blend of private initiative and public oversight such as proved so dynamic in Japan? One suspects that the latter may be essential, despite ideological pressures to the contrary, in order to relieve the resource constraints and lessen the political corruption that are handicapping growth today. Wide variations among states may be anticipated in any event.

In a different way China is caught up in a similar issue within her much more collectivist order. As her economy becomes more pluralistic and decentralized, it is inevitably less oriented to national planning, financing, and market controls, despite continuing stress upon socialist incentives and Party direction. A constant vigilance must apparently be exercised to check any inclination on the part of the peasant to turn his energies too strongly to private cultivation when he gets the chance. And there is evidently some problem in curbing the townsman's attraction to what Audrey Donnithorne calls "the lush undergrowth of private enterprise" in the urban world. But the "public sector" remains predominant, of course, with major functions still controlled from the center, even if much more of the actual decision-making is now left to provinces and localities than was envisioned in the "Stalinist" model of the 1950s. How far Mao's revolutionary socialism will sustain itself against bureaucratic tendencies to create a new mandarinate remains to be seen. The real change in people at the grass roots, too, is still uncertain.

Again, in such comparisons, one must recall that Japan industrialized in an era of Victorian economics, not Marxian nor even Keynesian. Nations today are in a hurry; governments are pressed by rising popular demands, as people look to the state for decisive action. "Time is not on the side of the slow-changers," says *Shankar's Weekly*, urging Indira Gandhi on. To make haste slowly may be a sensible policy. But it may not carry the day in politics.

More than that, the Japanese blend of public and private enterprise, increasingly private after the early years, required growing trust between business and political elites such as hardly exists in India today. The Meiji state led energetically in industrial pioneering at the outset. But it soon withdrew and left entrepreneurial responsibility largely to a private sector now maturing in capabilities—retaining only a pervasive administrative guidance and certain crucial controls in banking, foreign trade and a few strategic industries. There may be parallels in India, but the outcome is still indeterminate. One crucial difference, of course, is that Japan's joint, paternalistic elites in her pre-democratic era could tolerate and share in a concentration of wealth and privilege such as no Indian (or Japanese) leader seeking political legitimacy today can endorse.

Implicit here, as in all these issues, is the decisive role of leadership values and capacities in making the choices that shape national destinies. It would be hard to exaggerate the importance for China of the difference between

Chiang Kai-shek and Mao Tse-tung, or the contrast between them and Gandhi and Nehru. Both regimes will bear the stamp of these personalities far into the future.

By contrast, the very absence in modern Japan of such outstanding public personalities tells a lot about the structures of leadership and followership that built the nation. The pattern of authority in Japanese social groups is vertically strong, but collegial at the top. Decision-making tends to be consensual, making sometimes for stalemate and drift, but ensuring strong support up and down the line once a decision is reached. Happily, government and business have remained mostly in the hands of oligarchies of practical men of affairs who join institutional loyalty with personal drives to disciplined, pragmatic achievement. With the exception of the interwar crisis culminating in the Pacific War, the development process has been orderly but full of tension, incremental but never stagnant.

As for its representative character, one might describe the Japanese decision-making structure, say after the turn of the century, in much the same terms applied by Max Beloff to eighteenth-century England: "an oligarchy with certain popular elements, and with a blurring of public and private interests." Certainly a Messianic hero like Chairman Mao in his later stages of deification, or a charismatic statesman like Nehru, has never been conceivable in Japan. Yet from its early Meiji years this was a government that steadily legitimized itself because people accepted its structures, endorsed its principles, and mostly respected the personal qualities of its leaders.

To conclude this trilateral comparison of development experience across a century, one might pose the issue this way, at the risk of oversimplification: all developing peoples include among their growing aspirations three goals, however they vary in priority and emphasis. One is economic advance, whether for personal well-being, national power or other purposes. A second is some wider share in the making of decisions that directly affect their lives and fortunes. A third is greater economic and social equality, or at least a more favorable opportunity to rise in the scale of relative advantages and deprivations.

Japan's achievements in economic growth through the prewar decades were begun under a narrow oligarchy that only slowly widened itself as broader groups of people came to participate in politics. At the same time, throughout this era, great inequalities in income and wealth persisted long after remedies were at hand, had leaders chosen to apply them. The People's Republic of China, by contrast, has brought about a revolutionary equalization of income and opportunity since 1949, attended by gains in national output that compare favorably with Japan's early attainments, but with close constraints on freedom to differ and the right to protest and now an uncertain contest for power among the Party, army, and bureaucracy that is critical for the future. India, in the third dimension, is the one developing nation of the world today of great size, diversity and poverty to sustain over 25 years a "tutelary democracy" under civilian party leadership in an elective parliament, checked by vigorous criticism from professional and business elites, unions, and other organized groups. Her economic growth meanwhile compares favorably thus far with that of the others in output gains and institution-building. But the gains are distributed so inequitably that great masses of the common people have little to show for a doubling of the country's GNP through the period since independence.

The challenge of Asian development in the 1970s might be summarized as one of designing mutually reinforcing strategies to advance simultaneously toward all three goals—economic growth, social justice, and political accountability—in such measure as people themselves may choose to balance and pursue them.

X

Finally, among all the determinants of the future, none is more vital for these nations than the prospect for international security in Asia. While issues of war and peace must be largely left aside in this essay, their significance is obvious. As one illustration, India is now devoting over $2 billion a year to arms, or nearly four percent of her GNP. China's outlays are conjectural. With her border anxieties and her nuclear commitments, however, she is believed to be spending four or five times as much as India, perhaps even more.

Historically, it must be emphasized, nothing was more crucial for Japan's development after 1868 than that she managed to avoid any serious international conflict until the catastrophe of 1941–45. Her wars with China and Russia in 1894–95 and 1904–05 were no great drain; in some respects they even furthered her economic and political modernization. In World War I she was largely a spectator, profiting handsomely from the trading opportunities it afforded. To be sure, arms outlays were a continual drag on her economy, as well as a support to her military oligarchy. But not until World War II did she involve herself in a great tragedy of destruction. Whether the rest of Asia now grows at a pace approaching hers will depend heavily on the international milieu, political and economic.

Today's multipolarity in Asia presents a wide range of uncertainties, and a striking contrast between this region and most other parts of the world in its characteristics. Thus Europe's security problem since 1950 has centered upon its East-West division. Détente here means a relaxation of tension along this all-important bipolar boundary between two well-developed regions. Peace in the Middle East, too, hinges upon settling a bilateral Arab-Israeli conflict, interacting as it does with the wider East-West balance. International tension in Latin America, on the other hand, so far as it has any common frame, tends to relate to the unilateral dominance of one outside nation, the United States, and the reactions it generates across this gap in power and affluence.

In Asia no such bipolarity exists today, nor any dominant power. Instead, its two billion people display great diversity in national orientations, ideologies and capabilities. A wide North-South gap prevails in development levels, but it straddles an East-West gap in political affairs that is itself fragmented and blurred. Some 40 percent of Asian people live under Communist rule of one sort or another, and 60 percent under non-Communist. Most of them still wait for an industrial revolution to lift the burden of poverty off their backs. No single threat from outside, nor any single leading-nation, draws any large part of the continent together in an enduring alliance. Ethnic, religious and other historic divisions run across its length and breadth in great complexity. Any inclusive pan-Asian approach to collective security, economic integration, or political alignment is likely to come to little beyond rhetoric.

Central to this Asian reality is the lack of association among the three nations under consideration here, as well as the asymmetry of their relations with the outside world. Border disputes among them are minor, fortunately. There is the long-standing issue between China and India over their mountain frontier, and a dispute may develop between China and Japan over the potentially oil-rich Senkaku Islands, off the mainland coast. But these have been overshadowed by India's border quarrels with Pakistan, by Japan's claim on the northern islands still held by the Soviet Union, and above all by China's angry clash with the U.S.S.R. along their 4,500-mile frontier.

As for economic interdependence, commercial ties among them have yet to materialize on any scale. Trade between India and China is virtually nonexistent. Japan trades with India on a modest level, and has invested limited sums in Indian industrial development. More enthusiastically, Japanese business is now pushing into the China market, especially with sales of steel, machinery and equipment. Exchanges have risen steeply to a total exceeding $2 billion in 1973. But they are still of minor significance in Japan's total trade turnover now exceeding $70 billion a year.

In truth, Japan's economic orientation remains predominantly toward the West, as does her tourism, her cultural exchange, and the safeguards of her national security. In foreign markets and technological borrowing it is here especially that she has found the mainsprings of her spectacular postwar upsurge to become the world's third industrial giant. Her outlook abroad, therefore, is that of an "Atlantic" power, more accurately an Asian-Pacific power. It remains to be seen whether a sustained energy crisis will significantly alter this perspective in trade, in investment, or in politics. As yet all Asia contributes no more to Japan's trade than does the United States alone, though the Asian component approaches 25 percent and is expanding steadily. Asia accounts also for only 20 percent of her private direct investments overseas, again hardly more than the United States. Nevertheless, the smaller nations of the region are increasingly dependent on Japan economically—a relationship both sought after and resented. If "oilflation" now cuts Japanese fertilizer exports to Southeast Asia, for example, the area's food deficits will rise even further. By contrast, India's trade with the rest of developing Asia is comparatively small, and China's too, except for exports to Hong Kong. And their total foreign commerce is less than one-tenth of Japan's.

When one adds to these economic disparities the political complexities of the region, it is plain that a dependable estimate of realities imposes severe intellectual demands on policy-makers. The United States learned to its cost in Vietnam what penalties can follow from miscalculation. Still more recently Americans have seen the resentments aroused in both Japan and India by U.S. diplomacy during 1971–73, despite their stake in the viability and friendship of the two. Now the search for accommodation with China stretches ahead—a long and difficult road after the isolation and misperceptions of the past quarter-century. The euphoria of the first three years reminds one again of the swings of optimism and pessimism, of friendship and antagonism, that have marked America's dealings with Asian nations since the time of John Hay and Theodore Roosevelt.

The same point must be made as regards interrelations among China, India and Japan. They are radically different if not incompatible worlds, given their cultural traditions and experience over the past century. Only in Japan's approach to China does one see much public interest, or positive effort by mass media, or serious investment in research and education. Even here the younger generation no longer feels much cultural affinity or admiration for things Chinese, or sense of guilt over Japan's depredations on the mainland a generation ago. The general public is cool and inclined to be fearful, though a latent fund of goodwill is showing itself once again with the renewal of diplomatic and trade relations.

China, for her part, is still largely a closed society, and evinces openly little interest in Japan except for her industrial technology. It remains to be seen whether politics, both domestic and international, will now sustain the creation of a major trading relationship, or stand in its way. A hopeful sign is the initiation at last of discussions looking to a treaty of peace, following on the "normalization" of diplomatic relations in 1972. Meanwhile the *People's Daily* has lately muffled its attacks on Japan as a country of political repression, in bondage to a moribund U.S. imperialism, and hails the resumption of friendly contacts. By contrast, the Chinese press virtually ignores India, except to point to her occasionally as the victim of Soviet "revisionist" imperialism.

As for India's outlook to the east, the mountain barrier that divides the continent is matched by a culture gap equally formidable. There is little sense of mutuality between India and China, to say the least. In the wake of frontier disputes and the clash over Bangladesh, diplomatic relations are "frozen—not improving, not deteriorating," in the word of India's Foreign Minister. A feeling of apartness also separates Indians from Japanese on a personal level, despite Indian admiration for Japan's rise to affluence and a growing Indo-Japanese trade. In this sense the traveler who passes from Bombay to Peking, or from Tokyo to New Delhi, still crosses a great divide. "India is as different from China and Japan," remarks Guy Wint, "as Europe is from India." Characteristically a hairdresser in Tokyo, learning that a Japanese customer was going abroad, but this time to India not America, exclaimed with awe: "So far!" Even so, the Japanese are doing better today in Asia-wide mass-media coverage and academic studies than are the Indians. The mobilization of intellectual resources in South Asia for learning about East and Southeast Asia has barely begun.

Mutual understanding is never a guarantee of peace and friendship. But it is at least a necessary condition in a shrinking world. India, China and Japan, as coming leaders of Asia, need new avenues of intra-Asian communication about their common problems, their differences, their joint stakes in the future. One can think of few undertakings of greater significance for this half of the world in the next generation.

PART I:
Foreign Investments in Asia

2

Foreign Business in Japan

The Japan Economic Journal

I: FOREIGN CAPITAL

Foreign corporations are finally beginning to have their weight felt in the Japanese business and industrial fields.

The economic conditions surrounding the Japanese economy are now far from favorable, what with the aftermath of the oil crisis and the galloping inflation. Added to this will be another headache to the Japanese industry two years hence—the full liberalization of capital transactions.

Powerful foreign corporations, equipped with worldwide information and other networks, are now poised for serious activities in Japanese markets. Leading foreign firms have already firmly entrenched themselves in the administrative and industrial mechanisms here through the use of their famed "clairvoyance."

Most of them seem to have already acquired the knack of making the best of their operations here now that it is seven years since the partial capital liberalization.

As a matter of fact, a number of foreign-affiliated firms have already joined business and industrial organizations, reputed to be the most "Japanese" of all Japanese organizations. The voices of such firms are steadily gaining momentum.

Recently a minor problem presented itself in the august halls of Keidanren (the Federation of Economic Organizations) when Shell Sekiyu K.K., also a member of the Petroleum Association of Japan, expressed its hope of becoming a director of the organization. According to the Secretary of Keidanren, a director firm has access to "higher-grade" political and economic information brought up in directors' meetings than those obtainable by mere member firms which have access only to committee-level meetings. A director firm also is in a position to cultivate friendship with top executives of the nation's leading business and industrial organizations.

It is obvious that Shell Sekiyu was fully aware of such advantages when it put itself up for a director's seat in Keidanren.

Shell's application is now temporarily shelved on the technical ground that an addition of a non-Japanese-speaking foreign executive may impede proceedings.

In the meantime, eight foreign-affiliated firms are now members of Keidanren; they include IBM (Japan), Coca-Cola (Japan) and Nippon Goodyear. Of the eight, IBM (Japan) is a director, while seven other firms are quite active in committee levels.

Reprinted by permission of the *Japan Economic Journal*, from the May-August, 1974 issues.

Keidanren now follows an "open-door" policy for foreign-affiliated firms and admits that a growing number of such firms want membership and, in some cases, directors' posts in the organization.

The main objective of foreign-affiliated firms is quite obvious. They want to obtain various political and economic information at the earliest possible moment now that the economic conditions, within and without Japan, are rapidly shifting.

They also want to strengthen their ties with leaders of the Japanese business and industrial circles, know their true and unique prowess in its actual context and, at the same time, have their own opinions reflected in the administrative and industrial channels here.

Preparation of foreign-affiliated firms has been especially aggressive in Nikkeiren (the Japan Federation of Employers' Associations) which primarily deals with labor-management relations and problems.

Today, more than 120 foreign-affiliated firms are members of Nikkeiren and the membership is still growing.

Foreign members are also growing steadily in the case of the Japan Committee for Economic Development; they include Nippon Univac, Caterpillar Mitsubishi, and Amax.

Foreign-affiliated firms also are actively joining various industry-wide organizations in their hope of fostering cooperative relations with their Japanese counterparts.

NCR Japan, for example, is considering the possibility of joining the Business Machine Industry Association on the occasion of its standardization of its POS (point-of-sale) information systems.

Avon Allied Products, on the other hand, has recently joined the Door-to-Door Sales Cosmetics Industry Association.

According to a survey by the Ministry of International Trade & Industry, the sales share of foreign-affiliated firms is highest in the petroleum industry with 56.1%, followed by rubber with 16.8%, pharmaceuticals with 8.2%, ordinary machinery with 6.4%, non-ferrous metals with 5.8%, and chemicals with 5.1%. All these percentages (as of fiscal 1971) are considerably higher than the corresponding figures a few years ago.

The share for the entire industry, as a matter of fact, advanced by 0.5% to 3.5% in fiscal 1971 from the preceding fiscal year.

The total number of foreign investment cases in Japan stood at 756 in fiscal 1973 involving $167,260,000.

A MITI survey as of the end of June, 1972, shows that the total number of foreign investment firms which had advanced into Japan by that time ran up to as many as 1,364.

Advances of foreign companies into Japan, moreover, are expected to grow in the future. For one thing, the Japanese attitude toward foreign corporations has undergone a drastic change in the recent several years. The diehard xenophobia of some Japanese business executives has now almost entirely disappeared.

For another, foreigners' understanding of the Japanese way of doing things has incalculably increased in recent years.

Leading foreign corporations, whose top executives often had complained of the "strange mechanisms" of Japan, Inc., are now steadily muscling themselves into those very mechanisms.

II: JAPANESE MANAGEMENT

Coca-Cola (Japan) Co., Ltd., the Japanese subsidiary of Coca-Cola Co. of the United States, one of the most representative of "foreign interests" in Japan, has recently been bombarded by a series of telegrams from Atlanta, the headquarters of its parent firm, as well as by trans-Pacific flights in person by some of the parent organization's top executives—so urgent has been the parent firm's demands for the management formula of its Japanese subsidiary as well as those of leading Japanese corporations.

It was three years ago that Masaomi Iwamura ascended to the presidency of Coca-Cola (Japan) Co. as the first Japanese to have the distinction. At that time, Coca-Cola's Japanese subsidiary was seriously involved in a series of bottle explosion accidents.

Up to that time, Coca-Cola (Japan) Co. had faithfully copied the management processes of its American parent firm. Upon assuming the presidency, however, Iwamura immediately set about working bold changes in the conventional processes to meet the peculiarly Japanese situations. "There are great differences between the American way of management and its Japanese counterpart," Iwamura states with conviction. "The American way is individual-oriented, while the Japanese way is definitely group-family-situation-oriented."

Iwamura recruited Japanese management specialists from the nation's leading corporations and established the Corporate Planning Department, his equivalent of the President's Room which virtually masterminds management processes and programs in many Japanese firms.

Iwamura also added a new communications channel—the "bottom-to-top" route—to the company's organization in addition to the existing "top-to-bottom" channel. He also modified the company's wage and salary structure to combine the good points of both the American job-by-job system and the Japanese seniority system. He also introduced the annuity systems and the workers' stock holding system.

Marveled at the apparent success of Iwamura's "reform," the Atlanta head of Coca-Cola Co. has decided to make a go at the Japanese way of doing things. In line with this decision, the parent organization has added the Operation Board to its organization in addition to the conventional Policy Board. The Operation Board is similar in nature to the managing directors' council in many a Japanese corporation. It is also a sort of monument to the success of a Japanese top executive in a foreign-affiliated firm.

A growing number of Japanese is now ascending to the presidency of many foreign-affiliated firms in Japan.

Like Iwamura, Masamoto Yashiro made newspaper headlines when he was given the rein of Esso Standard Sekiyu K. K. He was acclaimed as the first Japanese president in a "major" international oil operation.

Other Japanese presidents of foreign-affiliated corporations include Iwao Shino of Pfizer Taito Co., Ltd., Yoshinobu Mitomi of NCR Japan Limited, Shio Omata of Nippon Univac Kaisha, Ltd., Yuichi Kato of American Express International Banking Corp., and Toshinao Morishige of Young & Rubicam K.K.

Among the long-time presidents of foreign firms are Sanae Inagaki of IBM Japan Limited and Hachiro Koyama of Johnson Co., Ltd.

Although their professional backgrounds are different (some are specialists in finances, others in engineering planning, labor relations, etc.), they are new-breed executives in their prime with extensive international experiences. They have invariably undergone rigorous training and apprenticeship within the organization of powerful international operations.

One of the special features of this new breed of executives is that they are by no means "yes men" to their parent organizations; they are depended upon to speak their piece when necessary.

Japanese top executives of international corporations are engrossed in taking full advantage of their firms' worldwide networks in their fierce bid to gain and expand their shares of the markets not only in Japan but also Southeast Asia as a whole. This has been particularly true in their strategies vis-à-vis new product development and marketing. Leaders of the headquarters of international corporations, on their part, have greatly changed their views of Japanese top executives.

"The reason for the growth of our voice in the final decision-making," opines President Inagaki of IBM Japan, "derives not only from successful operation of our own company here but also from the rapid expansion of the Japanese economy and industry as a whole."

Leaders of parent organizations are now not only letting Japanese managers of their subsidiaries have their own way in managing their companies but also trying to absorb what they think are good from them.

Although he is not a Japanese, W. S. Anderson, former president (present chairman) of NCR Japan, has become president of the parent organization and is now reportedly in brisk demand as an expert on the Japanese way of corporate management.

One of the good points about Japanese top executives of foreign-affiliated firms is their youth and bounding energy. This is in sharp contrast to leading Japanese corporations where old people still dominate the scene in spite of growing outcries against them. Rejuvenation is still very much a matter of hope rather than of reality.

It is true that there is some degree of truth to those who claim that Japanese presidents of foreign-affiliated firms are nothing to be amazed at and that there are plenty of equal talents in leading Japanese corporations.

There is no denying the fact, however, that the "talents" in Japanese corporations are not given enough rights and responsibilities that their counterparts in foreign-affiliated firms now enjoy.

"Now that acquisition of capable executives is the key to successful management of foreign-affiliated firms," states Masaaki Imai, president of Cambridge Research Institute, "appointments of Japanese nationals to the top posts show that the parent organizations of such firms have definitely started in a different direction than before."

Actions and policies of Japanese top executives in foreign-affiliated firms will have growingly important repercussions not only in Japan but also elsewhere in the world, including the home countries of the foreign interests.

Greater managerial opportunities are paying good dividends for foreign-affiliated firms in the fierce scrimmage for superior talents among corporations here.

"New university graduates are making little discrimination between Japanese corporations and foreign-affiliated firms," opine many executives in foreign-affiliated firms. "As a result, many superior people are now flocking to foreign-affiliated firms."

III: IBM JAPAN

Top executives of IBM Japan Limited, headed by President Sanae Inagaki, have organized an informal council of advisory staff comprising scholars, critics, and journalists.

The sole objective of this move is to monitor the people's sentiments and plan strategies for ideally meeting the company's social responsibilities.

IBM Japan, in other words, is determined to be fully prepared for the rapidly changing economic environments, including the rising tide of consumerism and strong moves for environmental protection. The first concrete move that IBM Japan has taken in its new community relations program has been the disclosure of its financial conditions. Although the disclosure has, for the time being, been limited to its balance sheet, IBM Japan has finally revealed its august financial stature for the first time in history.

The figures presented are truly formidable—more than ¥150,000 million (Approximately $500 million) estimated annual sales, ¥22,300 million (approximately $74 million) after-tax profits and the exalted net worth ratio of 74.8%.

"Non-disclosure has been the rule for IBM's overseas subsidiaries," admits President Inagaki. "In some special cases, as in West Germany and Canada, however, financial affairs of IBM subsidiaries have been made public. We at IBM Japan have decided to disclose our financial matters in the firm belief that non-disclosure may lead to serious misunderstanding here."

IBM Japan is the first wholly-owned foreign subsidiary in Japan to have taken this crucial step—with a promise of highly favorable popular reactions. "The only way for us to regain our credibility in Japan," a certain Japanese executive of an international oil corporation which has earned widespread distrust throughout the world in the aftermath of the oil crisis, has been moved to state, "is to explain with figures—not with words."

Strong criticism against international oil corporations at one time threatened to spread indiscriminately to foreign companies as a whole.

IBM Japan had long foreseen such possibilities and had acted accordingly—by deciding to disclose its financial matters to the public. The action would have been virtually unthinkable for IBM Japan of the past. IBM Japan, as a matter of fact, is now striking out one "social reseponsibility measure" after another in rapid succession. The company, for example, is taking elaborate measures both in Tokyo and Osaka to combat industrial pollution and is giving extensive assistance to the nation's "greening" programs.

The company has also started training the blind people to become computer programmers and is studying the possibility of letting its workers engage in social work in Japan on company pay, as IBM is doing in some other countries.

The corporate income of IBM Japan stood at about ¥40,000 million (approximately $130 million) in 1973, a sharp gain of 2.8-fold over the performance five years ago. The figure is big enough to place the company among the ten largest corporate income earners in Japan. The company at present has four major plants—one each in Fujisawa, Yasu, Tokyo, and Osaka.

The company is now marketing its products not only within Japan but also is aggressively exporting them to many parts of the world, especially Southeast Asia and Latin America. Last year, the company exported ¥20,100 million (approximately $67 million) worth of products to various parts of the world and earned citations from the Japanese Government as an outstanding contributor to the nation's exports.

Not entirely content with its present success, IBM is now pushing ahead with further "Japanization" of its operations here. The company, for example, has recruited ranking bureaucrats from the Japanese Government and has started paving grounds for closer ties with the Japanese ministries.

IBM Japan also is studying the feasibility of creating an employees' stockholding system in preparation for the eventual listing of its stocks on the Japanese stock markets.

IBM Japan also has recently replaced the American director of its research institute with his Japanese counterpart, thereby further bolstering the development programs of Japanese technical experts' own initiative.

According to a survey by Fujitsu, Ltd., IBM's share of the Japanese electronic computer markets has dipped from 37% six years ago to the 29% level recently. This develoment must have been a humiliating experience for IBM which boasts of more than 60% of the world's entire electronic computer markets. This is all the more reason why IBM is now placing extra emphasis on its operations in Japan after the nation's projected full liberalization of the electronic computer industry.

Japanese electronic computer manufacturers are in full agreement that IBM's aggressive "Japanization" moves are perfectly geared to the post-liberalization period, and they express fears about the future tactics of IBM in Japan.

IBM's recent moves are also made in full recognition of the inevitable shifting of the Japanese society from the industrial to post-industrial phase.

IV: WAGES AND SENIORITY

"Demands, demands, demands, nothing but demands," sighs a manager of the Tokyo branch office of a leading Southeast Asian banking institution. He has been bombarded by wave after wave of demands from the labor union. "When we opened the branch office two years ago," he continues with a long face, "our wage standards were not at all bad. Then came this infernal inflation. Big wage level increases of about 30% may be all right for big Japanese corporations. But, for us, it's virtually out of the question."

As it is only a very short while since its establishment, the branch office of the commercial bank is not yet operating at a reasonable profit. The trouble, however, is that the galloping inflation engulfs not only booming corporations but also their struggling counterparts.

ABILITY ALONE SHUNNED

The labor union of the commercial bank is now demanding a monthly starting pay of ¥81,000 (approximately $270) for an 18-year-old, ¥15,000 (approximately $50) of food allowances (instead of the current ¥7,000, or approximately $22), ¥10,000 (approximately $33) of housing allowances and ¥15,000 (approximately $50) of family allowances. These are by no means too steep a demand by this year's standards of wage and fringe benefit increases here.

"The truth is," the manager of the bank goes on explaining, "that the outlays of our corporation's overseas branch offices are controlled by the annual budget of our head office. To make the matter worse, we are not yet chalking up enough results. The head office will never swallow such big wage increases. The people at the head office won't even understand what housing and other special allowances are. I relayed the demands to the head office anyway . . ."

"Such troubles come from the still limited experiences of the corporation," analyzes an executive of the labor union of Chase Manhattan Bank's Tokyo office. "Top executives of the head office must be still far from fully understanding the Japanese situation. We ourselves have constantly fought for our rights since the end of the war, and succeeded in reinstituting discharged employees. Our present objective is to boost our wage levels up to those now maintained by leading Japanese city banks."

As to wage systems, even IBM Japan Limited, often referred to as the American "ability-first" policy reincarnated, went so far as to completely revise its wage system at the end of last year and incorporated much of the traditionally Japanese seniority system. According to the company, the average monthly wage level increase at the end of last year stood at ¥20,500 (approximately $68), excluding special allowances. Of this total, ¥13,500 (approximately $45) was awarded to every employee irrespective of ability and actual business performance.

The company at the same time created housing allowances for the first time in its history—¥10,000 (approximately $33) for a bachelor and ¥13,000 (approximately $43) for a family man. The housing allowances, moreover, were boosted to ¥15,000 (approximately $50) for a bachelor and ¥20,000 (approximately $66) for a family man as of last May.

IBM Japan explains that its new move was not exactly intended for seniority effects but was brought about by the fact that the ability standards of its employees were now so elevated through within-the-company training that there was little ability gaps among them.

A certain adviser to a foreign-affiliated firm, a former bureaucrat at the Ministry of International Trade & Industry, however, has a different view. Says he: "The move is a sign that IBM has finally realized that the American ability-first policy, which premises that men have widely different ability levels, is not only meaningless but also harmful in Japan."

CREATING ATTRACTIONS

Pfizer Taito Co., Ltd., one of the earliest-established of post-war foreign-affiliated firms, has already followed for some time a unique wage and salary system which is a combination of ability and seniority systems. In other words, the company gives enough elbow room and excellent pay for those who have enough ability and willingness to work. The company also does not neglect those who are less endowed with ability; it provides reasonable wages to such employees, too.

For a long time, foreign-affiliated firms enjoyed popularity among Japanese workers for their high wage standards and five day week system. Recently, however, such "attractions" are rapidly losing magic as Japanese corporations are now rapidly catching up with them both in wages and working conditions. Many foreign-affiliated firms, therefore, are now engrossed in creating new "sales points" to attract Japanese employees. One such "attraction" is the three-day week system inaugurated by Texas Instruments Japan Limited last year. It is noteworthy that the company has brought the newest of U.S. working systems right into Japan without modifications.

According to a survey announced last spring by the Ministry of Labor covering the labor-management relations in foreign-affiliated firms, only about 7% of all the foreign-affiliated firms polled retained complete controls of personnel and labor affairs. The survey was conducted in the summer of 1973. "Even if Japanese workers seem to be drinking coffee all the time," a Labor Ministry official who participated in the survey states, "they somehow have their work done by next morning. As long as work is done, it does not do any good to carp on the processes in which they are done. The smarter the foreign executives the sooner they realize this fact and let the Japanese do their work in their own way."

A few years ago, a specialist group of OECD conducting a survey on labor-management relations in Japan found that "the seniority system which more or less assures life employment for the workers is the secret for the spectacular growth of the Japanese economy." "Our wage and allowance levels are just about the same as those of a purely Japanese corporation," opines a young worker at Nippon Unicar Co., Ltd. "The atmosphere in our company is no different from any one of purely Japanese corporations. I feel as if I got employed at a Japanese firm—not a foreign-affiliated company."

The day seems to have already dawned in Japan when foreign corporations do not strike the Japanese with "foreign-ness."

V: SALES SYSTEMS

Levi's jeans are now proving an explosive success with Japanese youngsters who want, above all, to look "great" and "chic." "Perhaps it is because of its worldwide fame," gloats (with reason) Edwin G. Gibson, general manager of Levi Strauss (Far East) Limited, Japan Branch.

Primarily responsible for the spectacular success of Levi's jeans has been the unique development process of new sales routes followed by the U.S. jeans manufacturer. In the first year of its entry into Japan, Levi Strauss tentatively followed the conventional distribution process of supplying its products to retail shops through sales agent. One of the minus points of this sales process is that the company's controls of retail shops are necessarily limited. This, together with the necessity of giving proper guidances to retail shops in creating jeans corners, etc., in order to take full advantage of the prevailing boom in jeans, the Japanese branch of Levi Strauss added a sales department to its organization at the beginning of 1972 and started making direct deliveries to retail shops without the aid of sales agents.

At present, the Japanese branch of Levi Strauss has as many as 1,500 "direct deal" retail shops all over Japan. "Direct deals" with retail shops have long been the dream of Japanese textile goods manufacturers but they have met only scanty success so far. Levi Strauss, however, has succeeded, with apparent ease through the full use of its powerful Levi's brand name, in creating a powerful nationwide sales network of its own in a surprisingly short period of time—and far ahead of its Japanese competitors.

The Japanese people have long been used to see sales strategies of foreign corporations with a sort of jaundiced eyes and believed that they would disrupt the Japanese distribution systems by bringing in new products, creating their own sales networks, and bypassing the existing sales channels. The Americans, on the other hand, have long contended that the Japanese distribution systems are too complicated and have to be reworked and simplified. However, the age of criticism, on both sides of the Pacific, apparently has ended and many foreign corporations have already integrated themselves into the Japanese society and have successfully become "insiders" of the Japanese distribution systems, which once were considered to be virtually impenetrable for outsiders.

Some foreign corporations, moreover, have completely digested the workings of Japanese distribution systems and, on the basis of their full understandings of such systems, have successfully created their own distribution channels.

Olivetti Corporation of Japan, the Japanese sales subsidiary of Olivetti of Italy, is now steadily expanding its "direct deal" sales systems with Japanese retailers.

General Foods Ltd., a wholly-owned subsidiary of General Foods Corp. and maker of Maxwell instant coffee, on the other hand, has met with success in a different way. For some time, it accumulated a great deal of deficits because of unexpectedly dull sales of its products. In order to cope with the situation, the company parlayed Ajinomoto Co. into forming a joint venture —Ajinomoto General Foods Ltd.—last August. Ever since it started using Ajinomoto's powerful sales channels, the Maxwell coffee started selling extremely well and the company's sales increased from ¥6,700 million (approximately $22 million) in fiscal 1972 to over ¥10,000 million (approximately $33 million) in fiscal 1973. As a result, the company was able to write off a great majority of its accumulated deficits.

Fuji Xerox Co. for a long time followed the American system of letting each salesman handle only a single line of its products. Recently, however, the steady increase in the number of products has necessitated each salesman to handle more than two product lines and, as a result, more than one salesman has come to deal with the same customers and clients. In order to cope with the situation, the company has formally switched to the Japanese sales system of letting salesmen handle all product lines.

Coca-Cola (Japan) Co. has so far expanded its business through the use of its own route sales system in which the salesmen directly deliver the products to retail shops and directly collect accounts due from them. Recently, however, the company's sales started levelling off in the face of strong sales campaigns of Japanese manufacturers of soft drinks. In order to cope with the situation, Coca-Cola (Japan) has started experimenting a new sales system in which salemen are assigned only to give guidance to retail shops as well as to develop new sales outlets.

Often jokingly referred to as the "dark continent," the Japanese distribution systems have long been believed to be impregnable by foreign corporations. This myth, however, has been virtually exploded.

Many foreign corporations have come to have a deep understanding of the Japanese systems of merchandising, added their own time-honored traditions and experiences to them, reorganized their sales channels, and are now on the point of launching truly formidable sales campaigns in the Japanese markets.

VI: JAPANESE INDUSTRIAL POWER

"We are perpetually in search of opportunities to tie ourselves up with Japanese business partners in order to secure our presence in Japan in all our business fields," states President R. Howard Annin of General Electric

Japan, Ltd., the Japanese beachhead of the world's largest electric machinery firm—General Electric Co. of the U.S.

GENERAL ELECTRIC

Of 57 business sections under General Electric's 9 products and services divisions, 15 have already advanced into Japan in the form of joint ventures or business tie-ups.

One of the special features of General Electric's tie-up policy is that it does not choose its partners if it is convinced of success. As a matter of fact, General Electric now has tie-ups with 12 Japanese partners in such diverse business lines as electric machinery, automobiles, chemicals, foodstuffs, and advertising.

President Annin holds Japanese industrial technology in high esteem. It is nothing but his strong confidence in Japanese technological and financial prowess that resulted in the U.S. electric machinery firm's call to Japanese corporations to participate in its development project for a centrifugal process of enriched uranium production.

General Electric's confidence in the Japanese way of marketing, on the other hand, resulted in the 50% capital participation by the Toyota group (Toyota Motor Sales Co., Toyota Motor Co. and Nippondenso Co.) in General Aircon, Ltd., a GE subsidiary.

This does not mean, however, that GE's confidence in Japanese economy and corporations is unlimited. On the contrary, President Annin expresses concerns about the prevailing inflation and believes that the energy crisis will deal the most damaging blow to Japan. He also has a most guarded view of the future potentials of the Japanese market.

It is because of this cautious view that General Electric limited its co-operation to Eye Lighting System Corp., established last year by Iwasaki Electric Co., only to technological assistance for the time being. The contract is that General Electric will make a capital participation "in the next 5 years."

Capital participation in Yukult General Housing Co., on the other hand, was made only last spring—well after the strong growth potentialities of unit housing in Japan were ascertained.

ITT

International Telephone & Telegraph Corp., another representative multinational corporation, has a different view of Japanese companies. "Our management strategy," states Chairman Harold Geneen of ITT, "is to herd in independent industry groups throughout the world and make a system out of it." The company has infinite confidence in its overall management capacity firmly based on extensive experience.

When it comes to business mergers, in which ITT excels, however, a top ITT executive admits that mergers are very difficult in Japan and that creation of joint ventures would be a better solution.

ITT, as a matter of fact, established a joint venture—Mitsubishi Rent A

Car Corp.—in 1972 in a tie-up with Mitsubishi Corp. and another joint project—ITT Niles Co.—in cooperation with Niles Parts Co., an affiliate of Nissan Motor Co.

The company, moreover, is now negotiating with several electronic machinery makers for establishment of joint ventures.

CORNING GLASS

Corning Glass Works, on the other hand, is a business tie-up with Asahi Glass Co. and made a capital participation in Iwaki Glass Co., Ashahi Glass' subidiary, in 1965. An Asahi Glass executive states that his company imports all new Corning Glass products in the first place for local distribution and, when—and only when—it is assured of enough local demands, it assigns production and sales of such new products to Iwaki Glass.

The same executive goes on to extol his company's highly successful division-of-labor arrangements with its U.S. business partner by saying that Corning Glass takes care of the technological side, while his own company handles the local marketing.

Corning Glass Works also sponsors creation of a joint venture with Asahi Glass when its IC-making subsidiary—Signetics Corp.—enters into the Japanese market. Business multiplication moves by foreign corporations are especially active in the fields which are subject to wild business fluctuation.

BRUNSWICK

Nippon Brunswick Co., a joint venture of Brunswick Corp. of the U.S. and Mitsui & Co., in the field of bowling equipment, is a case in point. In order to cope with the prolonged slump in the bowling field, Nippon Brunswick is now engaged in development of its own antipollution equipment. The company also is engaged in imports of car washing machines from West Germany as well as in local production of game machines and indoor golf systems originally developed by its U.S. parent firm.

PHILIPS

Philips of the Netherlands has finally embarked upon establishment of a nationwide sales network for small home electric appliances in Japan in the hope of eventually bringing all its products into the Japanese market. Although the company has so far provided technologies on its Philishave electric razors to Matsushita Electric Works for local production, it has decided to distribute the electric razors of its own production in the Japanese market.

Ever since 1952, when it established Matsushita Electronics Corp. in the tie-up with Matsushita Electric Industrial Co., Philips has freely provided its technologies to Japanese corporations, thereby contributing toward the spectacular development of the Japanese home electric machinery industry. It has, however, changed its policy and has decided to market its own products to the Japanese market instead of limiting its interest in the Japanese market only to royalty incomes.

VII: TODAY'S JAPANESE ECONOMY

It is now a full year since Japan in principle lifted controls on the entry of foreign capital into this country. In other words, most foreign corporations are now in a position to advance into Japan if they *really want to.* It is only natural under the circumstances that many foreign "giants" have started taking advantage of many of the weak points of the Japanese economy, such as the oil shortages, tightening antipollution measures and the galloping inflation, and are muscling into the Japanese markets with use of their superior technologies and massive financial power.

One of such "giants" is Dow Chemical Co. of the U.S. which is now bent on entering into the soda industry. The Japanese soda industry is presently in the process of replacing the conventional mercury process of soda production with the new diaphragm process in order to cope with the mercury poisoning cases which broke out last summer.

Japanese soda makers are scheduled to complete 60% of their process conversion plans by September, 1975.

DOW CHEMICAL

The soda industry, in which as many as 56 plants of 40 individual companies are in cutthroat competition, is one of the least modernized of all Japanese major industrial sectors.

The change-over from the traditional mercury production process to the diaphragm method alone is estimated to cost the industry some ¥480 billion. To make the matter worse, almost all Japanese soda companies have to rely on foreign technologies for the conversion. The decision of Dow Chemical, which has the most advanced of diaphragm technologies, to enter Japan, therefore, has been a serious blow to the Japanese soda industry. "Dow Chemical is well aware of the extremely vulnerable position of the Japanese soda industry," admits President Fukashi Hori of Asahi-Dow, Ltd.

Dow's entry proposal is a determined one. It wants to enter the Japanese market with establishment of a fully-owned subsidiary and without making its superior technologies available to Japanese soda firms. It also plans to establish a huge plant with an annual production capacity of 300,000 tons, nearly 10% of the total soda demand in Japan. To crown everything, this is only Dow's first-stage entry program; it will certainly expand its facilities in the future.

The fact that the Japanese soda industry is diametrically opposed to its entry does not faze Dow Chemical one iota. "I cannot see any ground for opposition," coolly opined Chairman Carl A. Gerstacker of Dow Chemical when he visited Japan last April. "Japan has lifted controls on foreign capital entry, hasn't it? There is no change whatsoever in our company's original entry plan."

GOODYEAR

Goodyear Tire & Rubber Co. of the U.S. also is looking for a chance to enter the Japanese market on a serious basis. At present Goodyear's presence in the Japanese market is in the form of a wholly-owned subsidiary, Nippon Goodyear K.K. This subsidiary is solely engaged in marketing part of the products which the parent corporation has consigned for production to the Bridgestone Tire Co., with which it has tie-up relations. Goodyear executives, however, are repeatedly stressing production on its own in Japan, according to Managing Director Noboru Imamura of Bridgestone Tire Co.

MANAGERIAL CONTROL

Moves are also quite active among foreign corporations, which have so far been content with 50% capital participation in Japanese firms only because of foreign exchange controls and the "notorious" administrative guidances of the Ministry of International Trade & Industry, to obtain controlling shares of their Japanese affiliates. "Dow is perpetually demanding to up its share of our company by 1% to 51%," states President Hori of Asahi-Dow, "with the full knowledge that we won't accept such a proposal—ever." This is only one example of foreign corporations' "obsession" for majority control in their affiliates.

Some time ago, Hohnen Lever Co. made the newspaper headlines as an example of foreign domination of a joint venture when one of its parent firms—Unilever Co.—increased its share from 45% to 70%.

Recently, a similar case came up in the form of Procter & Gamble Sunhome Co., a U.S.-Japanese joint venture in synthetic detergents. This joint venture was established in 1972 through a tie-up with Procter & Gamble of the U.S. and three Japanese corporations—Dai-Ichi Kogyo Seiyaku Co., Asahi Electro-Chemical Industry Co., and C. Itoh & Co. This firm has been plunged into serious managerial trouble from the end of last year through this year because of sharp rises in raw materials and other troubles.

Taking this event as a cue, Procter & Gamble proposed a 2.5-fold capital expansion for its Japanese joint venture. The American chemical firm's plan is to put up a great majority of the funds needed for the capital expansion and get hold of the managerial right of the firm. The plan, however, ran into trouble as the Ministry of International Trade & Industry refused to approve it on the ground that the capital expansion was "inappropriate." There is a possibility that the capital expansion will be limited to 50%.

100 PERCENT CONTROL

In the field of ICs, one of the most advanced of modern industries, two U.S. giant firms—Motorola, Inc. and Fairchild Camera & Instrument Corp.—already operate 50% joint ventures here. Many industry informants believe that these two firms will try to turn their Japanese joint ventures into wholly-owned subsidiaries in and after next December, when controls on capital participation are completely lifted. Another U.S. firm—Texas Instruments, Inc.—operates a wholly-owned subsidiary here.

VIII: EUROPE IN JAPAN

Sweden has recently been very active in advancing into the Japanese market. Last year, the country sent a major industrial survey mission to Japan under the leadership of Prince Bertil. During its stay, the team members met Japanese Government and industrial leaders, including International Trade & Industry Minister Yasuhiro Nakasone, President Satoshi Sumita of the Export-Import Bank of Japan and the members of the Committee on Industry Technology of the Japan Federation of Economic Organizations (Keidanren), as well as the Emperor and the Empress.

In February, 1972, the spectacular Swedish Technical Week was held at a leading Tokyo hotel under the sponsorship of the Swedish Export Council and the Swedish Embassy in Japan. A total of 37 leading Swedish firms, including AB Svenska Kullagerfabriken, famous maker of ball bearings, Asea, a leading manufacturer of heavy electric machinery, Fagersta AB, an iron & steel manufacturer, and Sunds AB, a maker of wood products participated in the show. Most of the top executives of all these firms, moreover, appeared at the large-scale industrial exhibition and earnestly conducted sales campaigns for their products.

REASONS FOR ADVANCE

What, then, are the major reasons for the enthusiastic interest that Swedish industrial corporations are showing toward the Japanese markets? One answer can be found in the case of Hiab-Foco AB, the most representative crane maker in Sweden. It was only in 1972 that the company established a sales firm in the Swedish Building at Tokyo's Roppongi area and started marketing its products there. In a matter of only two years, however, the company apparently has succeeded in accounting for as much as 10% of Japan's entire crane sales.

Personnel costs in Sweden are now prohibitively high. In order to cope with the situation, Swedish industrial firms are putting far greater efforts on labor-saving and rationalization practices than their Japanese counterparts.

It may be only natural, therefore, that the cranes made in Sweden should have many labor-saving and efficient features and strongly appeal to Japanese users who are beginning to seriously suffer from sharply rising personnel expenses. "The Japanese market is really vast," opines President Bengt Hokby of Hiab-Foco AB. These words reflect confidence in the superiority of his company's products.

Recently, another Swedish firm—AB Svenska Flakt-fabriken—created a joint venture with Takasago Thermal engineering Co. for production of air treatment equipment.

It is especially noteworthy that the strength of the above-cited two Swedish firms lies in the very fields in which the Japanese industry is now desperately trying to catch up with advanced nations of the world—labor-saving and environmental protection.

ICI, HOECHST & BASF

It is not Swedish companies alone that are taking advantage of the rapidly changing trend in the Japanese industry. From about last fall, visits to Japan by top executives of European chemical corporations have been unusually frequent.

In November, 1973, for example, Chairman E. J. Callard of Imperial Chemical Industries Ltd. came to Japan, followed by similar visits in last May by Vice President Kurt Lanz of Farbwerke Hoechst A.G. of West Germany and Dr. Bernhard Timm of BASF A.G., also of West Germany. The latter came to Japan along with Dr. Matthias Seefelder who replaced Dr. Tim as the company's president from last July 1. It must be noted in this connection that all these visists were of a merely ceremonial nature. But a number of concrete moves have emerged in the wake of such visits. BASF, for example, recently inaugurated a joint venture—Mitsui Badische Dyes Ltd.—in a tie-up with Mitsui Toatsu Chemicals, Inc. ICI, on the other hand, has created ICI Pharm K.K. in cooperation with Sumitomo Chemical Co. for distribution of pharmaceuticals here.

U.S. *v.* EUROPEAN FIRMS

Although European companies are latecomers to the Japanese scene in comparison with the U.S. counterparts, their entry has been quite smooth and swift. One reason is the wealth of high added-value products which European companies are in a position to offer to Japan and the other is their superior technologies in the field of labor-saving and environmental protection fields. Through the use of such products and technologies, many Euorpean firms have almost unnoticeably eased themselves into the framework of the Japanese economy. This is the most important difference between European firms and their American counterparts which have virtually "stormed" the Japanese markets on the strength of their sheer financial prowess and managerial expertise.

Advances into Japan are by no means limited to Swedish and West German firms. Many companies from other European firms have already successfully entered Japan. They include Dutch firms (in foodstuffs and metal products), Danish companies (transportation, warehousing, and electric machinery), Swiss enterprises (fine chemicals and precision machinery), Norway (ship paints and furniture) and French companies (fashion and sporting goods).

All these firms are now steadily expanding their operations here successfully taking advantage of the rapid shift-over in the Japanese economy from quantity to quality.

IX: NEW GROWTH MARKETS

The Japanese economy grew on the basis of such "mass production" industries as steel and petrochemicals during the 1960s. Many agree, however, that the 1970s are for such "front-running" industries as antipollution equipment, leisure, electronics, fashion goods, etc.

It is only natural, therefore, that foreign corporations should be particularly interested in such new fields in planning their advances into the Japanese markets.

NUCLEAR POWER

In the field of nuclear power, the entry into Japan of General Atomic Co. of the U.S. was finalized. General Atomic Co. is the manufacturer of high-temperature gas cooled reactors which are often referred to as the "nuclear reactors for the 1980s."

As for electronics, many leading U.S. manufacturers of ICs are following the example of the "Big Three" IC makers—Texas Instruments, Inc., Motorola, Inc. and Fairchild Camera & Instrument Corp. They are seriously trying to muscle into the Japanese markets.

"Japan is a really big market for semiconductors, equal in scale to Europe," opines President R. S. Carlson of Microelectronics Group, Rockwell International Corp. "The rapid growth of Japan's industrial prowess is highly appetizing."

Some American firms find the slight technological gaps between the U.S. and Japan a big chance to get a foothold in the Japanese markets. "There still is a technological gap of about two or three years between the U.S. and Japan in the field of ICs," says President Marshall G. Cox of Intersil Inc. "It is brand new companies," insists President Charles E. Sporck of National Semiconductor Corp., "that have spearheaded the technical advances in the field of ICs."

LEISURE

Leisure is another field in which advances of foreign corporations are very active. "The idea of family-centered leisure time activities is still not fully developed in Japan," states President Marcel Guillaume of Trigano Vacances, a leading sporting goods manufacturer in France. "As the Japanese grow richer and have greater spare time, however, the situation will be different."

In the recent few years, a growing number of foreign companies are advancing into Japan in the field of leisure time goods, hotels, etc. Some of the most noteworthy of foreign ventures in such fields include Bridgestone Spalding Co. (joint venture between Questor Corp. of the U.S. and Bridgestone Tire Co.), Wilson Sports K.K. (joint venture between Wilson Sporting Co. of the U.S. and Pacific Overseas Inc.), Trigano Leisure Japan Co., Ramada-Chori Japan Inc. (a joint venture between Ramada Inns of the U.S. and Chori Co.), and Inn Keepers Supply of Japan Co. (joint venture between Holiday Inns, Inc. of the U.S. and C. Itoh & Co.).

In addition, Club Mediterranée of France is slated to make capital participation in Club Mediterranée of Japan within the current year.

Is Japan really ready for such a brisk influx of foreign leisure-time industries, then? "Leisure-time development in Japan will take time," admits an official of Club Mediterranée of Japan. "But there is no doubt that the leisure-time habits of the Japanese will gradually shift to the European pattern with strong emphasis on long-term sojourns at resort places."

"We have for some time limited our sales activities here to golf-related products alone," opines an official of Bridgestone Spalding. "But we have started marketing tennis goods, too."

Foreign leisure time corporations find great future potentials in the Japanese markets.

FASHION GOODS

"When we first came to Japan," wrily reminisces an official of IFG Triumph Co., a subsidiary of International Foundation & Garment Co. of West Germany, "we often ran into trouble in advertising in railway trains from the standpoint of the code of ethics." At present, however, electric car coaches are virtually inundated by bold advertisements for colorful undergarments and similar other items.

The Japanese mode of living has undergone an almost revolutionary change in the recent 10-year period.

Consumers also have become highly selective in buying fashion goods. Taking advantage of this development, the world's leading fashion designers, such as Pierre Cardin, Yves Saint Laurent, and Jonathan Logan, have been making strong onslaughts on the Japanese markets. Now that the nation is face to face with the energy crisis and the Japanese people are making an overall review of their mode of living, there is no way of knowing what developments are in store in this sector in the days to come.

ANTIPOLLUTION EQUIPMENT

In the field of antipollution equipment, several leading makers have already advanced into Japan. Neptune International, for example, is already operating a wholly-owned subsidiary here under the name of Nichols Far East, while Westinghouse Electric Corp. is operating a joint venture—Ebara-Infilco Co.—in cooperation with Ebara Mfg. Co. Union Carbide Corp. also operates a joint venture—Showa Unox K.K.—in a tie-up with Showa Denko K.K.

As to future work, Ebara-Infilco notes that as to the drainage system the dissemination rate now runs only to 19% but the Construction Ministry intends to build this up to over 50% in 1985 at a cost of ¥12,000 billion. This means that this field as well as others are still wide open for large growth, it says.

X: RAW MATERIALS SHORTAGES

It was in March, 1972, that Eastman Kodak Co. came up with the new pocket camera in the U.S. market. Only half a year afterwards, the U.S. manufacturer brought the epoch-making camera into the Japanese market.

The new pocket camera is a result of Kodak's tireless efforts in seeking the ultimate in compactness and simplicity of a camera as well as in developing a wholly new system in the photographic process covering sensitized materials as well. Kodak tried and succeeded in obtaining, in the new camera and the photographic process, an extra big enlargement ratio and high-temperature, short-time development quality of a film.

The U.S. camera manufacturer had sold 250,000 units of its new pocket cameras by the end of last September and has ever since been selling its product at a monthly rate of 20,000 units in the Japanese market.

PRICE REDUCTIONS

As the total sales of domestic cameras reach about 2,400,000 units per annum, Kodak's new pocket cameras have already come to account for more than 10% of the domestic camera markets. Kodak's entry, moreover, has "re-vitalized" the Japanese camera market as a whole, which had at the time been in a levelling-off period.

Kodak's Japan strategy has been very clever. It has successfully turned the prevailing materials shortages to its own advantage. Up to about three years ago, the price difference between Kodak's film roll (20 exposures) and its Japanese counterpart stood as much as ¥120 (approximately 40 cents). On the occasion of the tariff reduction in April, 1971, however, Kodak cut the difference by as much as ¥60 (approximately 20 cents) at a stroke. Ever since, Kodak has stuck to the new price even in the face of the yen revaluation and channeled the foreign exchange profits arising from the revaluation into internal reserves. "We will change the film prices only once a year, calmly observed Managing Director Tokutaro Shigeta of Nagase Co., the Japanese sales agent for Eastman Kodak, at the time, "and that in full consideration of future outlooks. We won't adjust prices every time the foreign exchange rate fluctuates a little."

When the tariff rate dropped to the 16% level in April, 1973, however, Kodak carried out a ¥50 (approximately 17 cents) price reduction on the ground of the tariff reduction and the fat foreign exchange profits, thereby cutting the price difference with Japanese film rolls to only ¥10 (approximately 3 cents). Then came the sharp price rises in raw materials at the beginning of this year, and domestic film makers were forced to mark up their film rolls to ¥480 (approximately $1.60). The price of Kodak's film roll, as a result, came to stand at ¥50 (approximately 17 cents) lower than its Japanese counterparts.

In carrying out the price hikes, Japanese film manufacturers believed that Kodak would have to follow suit because of the bearish movement of the Japanese currency in the international market.

As it actually turned out, however, Kodak stuck to its sales price. Moreover, the U.S. film manufacturer stopped production of its old films in the United States in April and put on the market the Kodacolor II, a new color negative film tied in with its new pocket camera. The per roll price of the new film stands at ¥490 (approximately $1.60), only ¥10 (approximately 3 cents) higher than the conventional Japanese film roll.

SWIFT REACTION

Kodak is by no means the only foreign company to have swiftly risen to an emergency development. Johnson Co., a joint venture of S. C. Johnson & Co. specializing in production and marketing of wax and detergents, swiftly formed a "Raw Materials Procurements Special Committee" within its organization in August, 1973, in the belief that a series of explosion accidents at petrochemical industrial complexes would certainly lead to a serious supply shortage of raw materials for its products. The U.S. parent firm of Johnson Co. also reacted swiftly to the emergency situation and held in the United States a meeting of those engaged in materials purchases in 39 countries of the world last fall. The company followed up with a similar meeting in Europe last spring.

QUICK RESPONSE

The problem was not so urgent and immediate for Japanese corporations some time ago when the communications between parent organizations in foreign countries and their Japanese "outposts" were not as complete as they are today and when their responses to economic changes were not as quick as they are now. Today, Japanese affiliates and their foreign parent organizations react as quickly or even more quickly than Japanese corporations. In some cases, foreign corporations are taking a definite head start on their Japanese counterparts because of their extensive international networks and resultant easier access to vital information and data.

Foreign corporations see the current turbulent international situations as an advantage—rather than a minus factor—in taking firm root in the Japanese markets. "We have formed a new organization called the Export Committee within our organization to take full advantage of the powerful Siemens group of West Germany," states Vice President Takamichi Kasaba of Fuji Electric Co.

Siemens, with which Fuji Electric has close relationships, has 115 subsidiaries in 50 countries of the world. By closely tying these overseas subsidiaries with Fuji Electric's seven overseas subsidiaries and representatives in as many countries, the Japanese electric machinery firm is trying to form an organic supply route of raw materials, etc. As a matter of fact, Fuji Electric and Siemens already have held two international meetings of representatives of both of their overseas subsidiaries.

Many Japanese industrialists ascribe the past sharp upswing in commodity prices to clever maneuverings of some powerful foreign corporations, headed by major oil firms. Although there is as yet no delving into the final truth of the matter, it cannot be denied that foreign corporations cut domineering figures in every international crisis. They seem to believe strongly that drastic changes in the international scene are the best opportunities to create new and favorable market mechanisms for them. Their tactics—which can best be described as taking advantage of the "muddy waters"—have certainly paid off so far and seem destined to perpetuate.

XI: THE FOREIGN BANK RUSH

Foreign banks' entry into Japan has greatly increased in recent years. As of now, 74 branch offices of 50 different foreign banks are already operating in Japan and 71 more banks have representative offices here and are trying to elevate their offices to branch status.

Ever since 1972, foreign banks have been advancing into Japan every year and have turned Japan into a virtual showcase of foreign banks of all nationalities, ranging from American and European to Asian and Latin American.

It was in 1902—some 72 years ago—that First National City Bank of New York opened its office in Japan to win the distinction of being the first foreign banking institution to advance into Japan. Ever since, foreign banks gradually have entered into Japan but never have the advances been as aggressive as they are today. Both Japanese government circles and banking circles simply are awed by the speed with which foreign banks are now opening their offices in Japan.

There are several major reasons for the "foreign bank rush" that Japan is now experiencing, according to Vice President Tatsuo Umezono of First National City Bank of New York. One naturally is the rapid development of the Japanese capital market and the other is the growing "open door" policy of the Japanese capital and securities markets. The third reason is the growing activation of overseas advances by Japanese corporations and the resultant fund demands on an international scale.

The securities industry is another field facing the aggressive entry of foreign corporations. It was only a couple of years ago that Merrill Lynch, Pierce, Fenner & Smith Inc. established a branch office in Japan as the first foreign securities firm to do so. In last April, Loeb, Rhoades & Co. had its Tokyo representative elevated to the status of a full branch office.

Foreign companies in such intellectual services as consulting, advertising, and information are also in the process of taking firm root in Japan in tie-ups with multinational manufacturing enterprises already operating in Japan. It must be pointed out in this connection, however, that foreign corporations in money and knowledge-related industries are meeting difficulties and restrictions almost unthinkable in the case of their manufacturing counterparts.

It is true that through the institution of full capital liberalization, foreign banks are now subject to the Japanese banking law and are in principle permitted to operate here as freely as their Japanese counterparts. Nevertheless, 50 foreign banks now operating in Japan account for only 0.9% of all the deposits and 1.5% of the industry's loans. "This poor performance," opine many foreign bank executives, "is simply due to the discriminatory attitude of Japan's Ministry of Finance which strictly limits new establishment and expansion of branch offices."

Even First National City Bank, which boasts of a longer history than Japanese banking institutions themselves, is restricted to only four branch offices—one each in Tokyo, Osaka, Nagoya, and Yokohama. No approval is forthcoming for new establishment of additional branch offices. The bank, as a result, has virtually no means to pipe up deposits from the general public in Japan and is always hard put how to raise enough yen funds.

Foreign securities firms and insurance companies also are meeting similar difficulties. When the "oil crisis" suddenly hit Japan and the nation's international payments situation instantly turned for the worse, the Japanese Government lost no time in clamping down restrictions on overseas investments, thereby robbing Merrill Lynch of its biggest specialty.

AIU (American International Underwriters) at one time handled all marine cargo insurance immediately after World War II and did pioneering work in spreading automobile indemnity insurances in Japan. The company's business performances, however, are way behind its Japanese counterparts and its share in the Japanese non-life insurance industry is steadily slipping.

When it comes to consulting, advertising, etc., the difficulties faced become all the more serious as such sectors directly touch upon nationalities, modes, customs, and other subtle phases. "The Japanese system of management has many good points—especially in finance, personnel, and wage systems," stresses President James C. Abegglen of Boston Consulting Group, who has a deep understanding of Japan and things Japanese. "Western corporations simply cannot bring their own ways of management directly from their home land without causing a lot of friction."

"Differences in 'soil' between Japan and other foreign countries are very big," concedes President Toshinao Morishige of Young & Rubicam K.K., a wholly-owned subsidiary of the American advertising agency. "Straight imports cannot bear fruit successfully."

3

Policies of ASEAN Countries Toward Direct Foreign Investment

Thomas W. Allen

INTRODUCTION

Direct foreign investment has played a major role in the efforts of the ASEAN (Association of Southeast Asian Nations) countries to develop their industrial structures.[1] This is reflected not only by the extent of direct foreign investment in these countries (variously estimated to be between $U.S. four to six billion for the ASEAN region as a whole), but also by the perceived efforts of the countries to attract foreign capital through such means as the offering of guarantees against nationalization and expropriation, assurances for the repatriation of capital and profits, the offering of financial and protective incentives, and the establishment of specialized investment promotion and control authorities.

In recent years, there has been a trend in the ASEAN countries toward defining more clearly the fields of industrial activity in which foreign investment is welcomed or encouraged and in specifying more explicitly the terms and conditions for the registration of such investments. This more controlled approach has arisen not so much because of the fear of foreign domination and a disenchantment with the extent of the contribution of foreign investment toward the development goals of the ASEAN countries (although these factors have been of some significance), but mainly because the countries now have a clearer picture of what they want to achieve, enabling them to be more explicit, on the basis of lessons learned in the past, as to the role they want foreign investment to play.

This paper attempts to explore the reasons for and the effects of the foreign investment policies being pursued by the ASEAN countries, placing particular emphasis on the changes currently taking place. The topics to be discussed will include:

basic industrial strategies;
present broad policies toward foreign investment;
policies toward ownership and control;
operational restraints on foreign enterprises;
investment incentives and guarantees; and
economic cooperation among the ASEAN countries.

The discussion draws extensively on recent studies made by the author of the motivations underlying direct investments of foreign enterprises in

This paper was originally presented at an Ad Hoc Seminar sponsored by the Southeast Asia Development Advisory Group (SEADAG) of the Asia Society, New York, on "Multinational Corporations in Southeast Asia" held at La Jolla, California. December 12-14, 1973, and was subsequently published as SEADAG Paper 74-4. Reprinted with the author's express permission.

Southeast Asia and the characteristics of these investments. This is because it is difficult to explain the changes currently taking place in the policies of the ASEAN countries without reference to the characteristics of foreign industrial enterprises already established and an assessment of the extent to which such investments have been contributing toward the development goals of the countries concerned.

BASIC INDUSTRIAL STRATEGIES IN THE ASEAN COUNTRIES

Even before investment incentives became a central feature in their investment legislation, countries within the ASEAN region (with the exception of Singapore) had pursued policies of development biased toward the protection of existing and new industries. These policies, based mainly on tariff protection and exchange controls, reflected the desire of the countries of the region to industrialize through the process of import substitution. As a result, investment during the 1950s and 1960s was heavily concentrated in locally-oriented industries such as food and beverages, consumer disposable products, and assembly of consumer durable products. Where resources were available, emphasis was also placed on their exploitation both for the local and export markets.

Only recently have the ASEAN countries turned from import substitution as a central theme of their industrial strategies to export promotion, with the emphasis on encouraging further processing of local raw materials and the development of "nontraditional" exports. This has involved not only the encouragement of existing and new local market-oriented enterprises to enter the export field (a policy made difficult by the distorted cost structures in certain industries as a result of high protection and "overcrowding" during the import replacement stage of development), but also the encouragement of enterprises to use more fully the resources of the country or to take advantage of the low labor costs for the processing of products for export to overseas markets. In addition, efforts are being made to induce multinational corporations to develop regional bases for their organization and to complement (through horizontal and vertical linkages) their existing activities in the various countries and in the ASEAN region as a whole.

The extent to which the pursuit of these strategies has affected the pattern of foreign investment in the region can be gleaned from an examination of the motivations underlying the investments of foreign enterprises in industrial projects in the ASEAN countries, for these reflect both the basic elements underlying the investment decisions of the multinational corporations and the development policies and strategies of the countries concerned.

PATTERN OF FOREIGN INVESTMENT IN THE ASEAN REGION

The motivations underlying the decisions of multinational enterprises to invest in industrial projects in the ASEAN region, though not at all clear-cut, can be categorized as follows:

1. the securing, maintaining, and/or developing of overseas markets—in many cases this also ensures channels for trade or other products and components produced or handled by the corporation so motivated;
2. the securing, maintaining, and/or developing of raw material supplies, including their subsequent primary processing;
3. the development of overseas lower cost bases for export purposes, necessitated by competitive forces in the home and international markets;
4. the securing, maintaining, and/or developing of regional bases, mainly to serve nearby markets;
5. the necessity or desire to complement other activities of the organization on a local or regional basis; and
6. such diverse motives as the capitalization of know-how, the protection of patents abroad, pollution control in the home country, and the like.

These categories correspond to the broad strategies of the ASEAN countries. For example, in a country pursuing an import substitution strategy, one would expect the bulk of foreign investments to be motivated by the desire to secure, maintain, and/or develop overseas markets (Category 1), given a favorable investment climate and market size in the country concerned. Similarly, strategies reflecting export promotion would, given the right investment climate, induce the establishment of enterprises searching for low-cost bases for export purposes (Category 3).

To obtain a measure of their importance, the motivations underlying the establishment of over four hundred primary and manufacturing projects in the ASEAN countries by United States, Japanese, and European corporations has been examined by the present author.[2]

The dominant consideration appears to be the *local market motive*, which accounts for around 52 percent of the total number of projects in the sample. The bulk of these, according to the companies interviewed, were implemented in order to prevent the loss of a local market for products in a specific country to another foreign firm contemplating the establishment of facilities in that country behind tariff barriers, import restrictions, and exchange controls. Some companies were established simply because it was cheaper to produce in a specific country than to export to it, or because market penetration is more effective if there are operations in the country concerned. The necessity to adapt products to foreign demands, a shortage of dollars for imports into the host country, and poor performance by local distributors are other examples of factors cited by companies as underlying this motive.

What is also of importance is the fact that some of the projects in this category were implemented with continued trading possibilities in mind, either through the supply of components and raw materials (the export of finished goods being replaced by exports of components and materials from other company plants) and/or the provision of needed machinery and equipment to establish the enterprise.[3] The latter factor, however, was less important for European or United States corporations than for Japanese firms.

The *raw material motive*, which includes the securing, maintaining, and/or developing of supplies such as iron ore, copper, timber, oil, sugar, shrimps, and the like underlies about 20 percent of the projects. This motive has major significance for Japanese enterprises in the ASEAN countries because of the few natural resources of the extractive type found in Japan. Executives of the companies interviewed stressed that involvement in projects in countries where such raw materials are available has been necessary to guarantee supply.

Approximately 15 percent of the projects were established because of the desire to develop *low-cost bases* for export purposes.[4] This motive has been of particular importance to United States companies which have been experiencing labor shortages, high labor costs, and (as stated by the executive of one company) considerable disruption to production because of labor union activities in their developed country plants. These factors have meant that a considerable portion of the United States and overseas markets for goods such as televisions, radios, electronic apparatus, textiles, and so on was being lost to producers in lower cost countries, mainly Japan. In order to overcome this loss, United States companies have found it necessary to set up facilities in low-cost locations. Similar considerations apply to European multinational companies, although the extent of their involvement in the ASEAN countries has been fairly limited to date.[5] The increasing importance of the low-cost base motive for Japanese companies reflects not only capacity and cost restraints in Japan, but also the increasing competitiveness of the United States and European enterprises which have facilities in the lower-cost developing countries.

The *regional base motive* accounts for only about 7 percent of the projects established in the ASEAN countries, noting that its importance to Japanese companies has been insignificant, mainly because of Japan's proximity to the region. The bulk of projects in this category are located in Singapore which is being used as a regional headquarters base for a number of companies; as a regional servicing and warehousing center for the supply of spare parts and after sales service; for the training of dealers, technicians, and maintenance and repair crews in Asia; as a base for the manufacture of equipment and products for the regional market for off-shore oil exploration, mineral, agricultural and forestry development, and construction projects in the area; and as the launching site for establishing manufacturing operations in other parts of the region.

The *complementation motive* is particularly important to the multinational companies where the scales of operations associated with the production of their various end products and components require careful consideration of the complementarity of production operations in various areas (for example, passenger cars, trucks, and earth-moving equipment).

TABLE 1

Motives Underlying a Sample of Existing Foreign Equity Investments in Primary and Manufacturing Projects in the ASEAN Countries *by Investing Companies*

Motive	United States	Japanese	European	Total
1. Securing, maintaining, or developing an overseas market	134	65	32	231
2. Securing, maintaining, or developing raw material supplies	40	30	19	89
3. Competitive forces necessitating low cost bases	45	11	12	68
4. Securing, maintaining or developing a regional base	21	1	8	30
5. Complementation of activities	2	1	1	4
6. Others	17	3	2	22
TOTAL	259	111	74	444

SOURCE: Data supplied by companies on their overseas investments in ASEAN countries.
NOTE: The statistics refer to enterprises established over the 1955-70 period (for Japan, 1960-70).

TABLE 2

Motives Underlying a Sample of Existing Foreign Equity Investments in Primary and Manufacturing Projects in the ASEAN Countries *by Host Countries*

Motive	Thailand	Malaysia	Singapore	Indonesia	Philippines	Total
1. Securing, maintaining, or developing an overseas market	82	40	21	12	76	231
2. Securing, maintaining, or developing raw material supplies	17	27	5	21	19	89
3. Competitive forces necessitating low cost bases	4	1	45	2	16	68
4. Securing, maintaining, or developing a regional base	4		21		5	30
5. Complementation of activities	1		3			4
6. Others	3	2	7		10	22
TOTAL	111	70	102	35	125	444

SOURCE: Data supplied by companies on their overseas investments in ASEAN countries.
NOTE: The statistics refer to enterprises established over the 1955-70 period (for Japan, 1960-70).

It is of minor significance in the ASEAN context at the present time, accounting for under 1 percent of projects in the sample.

An examination of the growth of activities of many of the large United States multinational companies in Europe offers a good example of the operation of the complementation motive in conjunction with the regional base motive where individual plants in different countries belonging to the same organization complement each other, product wise or process wise. It is difficult to repeat the same in the ASEAN context because of the barriers to trade among the constituent countries. The successful development along similar lines to that of Europe will depend to a large extent on the removal of these barriers; complementation programs can then be implemented, whereas at the present time many of the large corporations have only sales outlets or assembly facilities in these countries.

The *diverse motives* are also insignificant. They constitute a residual category which do not necessarily operate by themselves and are uncommon as an initiating force for overseas investment.[6]

The country-by-country bias in the foregoing motives is apparent, reflecting the investment conditions in the individual countries and the strategies and policies adopted for industrialization. Singapore recognized early the extent of international competitiveness for such investment and thus made an all-out effort to ensure an investment climate conducive to these activities. The Philippines, Thailand, and Malaysia, on the other hand, have received mainly projects with the local market in mind, such as food items, consumer durable assembly, chemicals and pharmaceuticals, and beverages (all final products), although a number of projects have concentrated on intermediate goods (batteries, tires, and metal components), and building materials (galvanized iron and cement, for example). This reflects the strong bias in their development strategies toward import replacement, although recently there has been a growth in foreign export-oriented activities as these countries have shifted to export promotion through export incentives, free trade zones, and the like. Resource development projects remain important, although there has been a move toward the further processing of raw materials.

Indonesia is attracting mainly raw material-oriented projects, but the number of local market projects established during the 1960s suggests that its potentially large market is attracting a number of investors. Indonesia still appears to be pursuing a resource development and import substitution strategy. It has, however, tightened up considerably on import substitution and light manufacturing industries with a high import content.

EFFECTS OF BASIC STRATEGIES ON THE INDUSTRIAL STRUCTURE AND DEVELOPMENT PROSPECTS OF THE ASEAN COUNTRIES

The pursual of an import replacement policy by some of the ASEAN countries has resulted in the establishment of a number of industries which, under a nonprotectionist policy, would probably not have been set up. This has resulted in dollar savings, employment generation, and other benefits to the economy. However, it has not been without costs.

First, the fear of allowing monopolies to establish themselves in still relatively small markets has meant that production has become fragmented with less than optimum high-cost plants being established (or optimum plants operating well below full capacity) in a number of highly protected industries. This, in addition to resulting in higher prices (and/or lower quality) to the local consumers for these products, has made it difficult for the industries to compete on the international market—a difficulty which applies not only to the protected industries themselves but also to other local industries dependent on them for supplies. The dilemma is that under such circumstances, it is not easy for the country to lower the level of protection as this would certainly, in the short run at least, lead to unemployment and cause considerable problems to the industries in readjusting their productive structures.[7]

Second, the bulk of the foreign investments in these fields have been in the production of relatively simple products which do not have complex process production requirements. These include many of the food products, simple chemicals and pharmaceuticals, and rubber products which are mainly "single or continuous process" type activities. For only the assembly operations have been carried out, with the companies relying on imports for their component needs. The small size and fragmentation of the markets have contributed toward preventing any effective vertical integration on the part of the companies (although some of these companies would prefer to keep it this way to ensure markets for the components produced in company plants in other countries), so reducing the overall impact on the balance of payments and employment creation.

The extent to which simple process products and the assembly of complex products for locally-oriented foreign projects has dominated more complex process products with at least some degree of vertical integration, to be seen in Table 3. This table classifies some three hundred and thirty industrial projects of Japanese and United States enterprises in the ASEAN countries according to product and process structure and market served.[8] A number of interesting points emerge:

- Simple process products account for about 60 percent of the projects, the majority of which are dominant single process plants. The proportion is higher for locally-oriented projects.
- Metal based projects reveal a much higher proportion of complex process products than other products, with over 70 percent of the projects being of a complex nature. The proportion is lower for locally oriented projects in which around 65 percent of the metal based projects are of a complex nature; however, the bulk of these are assembly projects.
- The importance of final product assembly plants (based on imports) and of simple single or continuous process plants for locally oriented activities implies that horizontal and vertical linkages have not been of great significance in many projects where local raw materials are used for the major inputs.

- The proportion of multiproduct projects is surprisingly small, with these accounting for under 30 percent of all projects.

There are of course differences from country to country and according to the nationality of the investor. The country to country differences are explained mainly by the motivational pattern of investments, while a classification of projects according to nationality of investor reveals that the United States investments contain a higher proportion of multiple and complex process plants than do the Japanese investments.

The dominance of simple process and assembly projects implies that the development of the skills of the local work force to a high grade has not been extensive overall and, as suggested above, that horizontal and vertical linkages have been minimal. This has reduced the potential for self-inducing growth. On the other hand, the lack of a skilled work force along with the lack of a well-developed industrial structure (which could support complex-type activities) may have been major factors in determining the structure and type of projects, and thus a "chicken and egg" situation exists. Of particular interest is the fact that there is some potential for the development of more integration. This has been hampered in the past, as explained previously, by the distorted cost structures of industry in these countries, although the lack of vertical integration of many of the complex product export-oriented projects suggests that this is not the only factor.

Third, the import replacement strategy has also encouraged a heavy concentration of "enclave" industries in the major population centers (normally near ports), serving to contribute toward the considerable disparities in income and employment opportunities within the ASEAN countries. This has led to a "dualist" structure being developed which has caused great concern to policy makers in recent years.

Fourth, evidence suggests that high protection of final products coupled with tariff and taxation concessions on capital equipment has resulted in the adoption of capital intensive techniques of production; a strategy biased toward export production would seek to ensure that the major comparative advantage of the ASEAN countries, a surplus of employable labor, is made use of by encouraging labor intensive techniques of production. The extent to which this does not hold has been debated at length. Some argue that there is, in effect, considerable technological fixity with very little flexibility in the substitution of labor for capital, especially in modern manufacturing. Others hold the reverse to be the case. There is no doubt that in certain areas of industry more labor intensive techniques of production could be adopted—farm machinery and textiles are examples. Moreover, many companies have installed modern transfer lines and support facilities which have unnecessarily displaced labor in the relevant operations. For industries such as cement and flour milling, however, the economic possibilities of using less capital intensive techniques are limited. But as these points are discussed below, suffice it to note here that in the author's opinion the import replacement strategy has encouraged investments in those fields which

TABLE 3

Classification of Products, Markets, and Processes of Sample of Enterprises in the ASEAN countries with United States and Japanese Equity

PRODUCT/MARKET CLASSIFICATION	PRODUCT NUMBERS		SIMPLE PROCESS PRODUCTS					COMPLEX PROCESS PRODUCTS					
	Single	Multiple	Dominant Single Process	Multiple Process			Total	Dominant Single Process	Multiple Processes			Total	TOTAL PROJECTS
				Inte-grated	Some Processes	Assem-bly			Inte-grated	Some Processes	Assem-bly		
LOCALLY ORIENTED													
Extractive - minerals	2	-	2	-	-	-	2	-	-	-	-	-	2
- other	3	-	3	-	-	-	3	-	-	-	-	-	3
Basic - metals	2	1	-	-	-	-	-	1	1	1	-	3	3
- other	7	-	5	1	-	-	6	1	-	-	-	1	7
Intermediate - metals	10	10	6	-	-	-	6	2	1	4	7	14	20
- other	32	5	25	-	6	1	32	4	-	1	-	5	37
Final Product - metals	43	18	13	2	4	4	23	2	1	10	25	38	61
- other	53	23	58	2	7	2	69	2	-	2	3	7	76
Total	152	57	112	5	17	7	141	12	3	18	35	68	209
EXPORT ORIENTED													
Extractive - minerals	16	-	16	-	-	-	16	-	-	-	-	-	16
- other	16	-	16	-	-	-	16	-	-	-	-	-	16
Basic - metals	2	1	-	-	-	-	-	2	-	1	-	3	3
- other	13	-	11	-	-	-	11	2	-	-	-	2	13
Intermediate - metals	22	9	3	-	-	-	3	3	2	6	17	28	31
- other	10	-	6	-	1	-	7	3	-	-	-	3	10
Final Product - metals	10	10	4	-	2	2	8	-	-	2	10	12	20
- other	12	1	10	-	3	-	13	-	-	-	-	-	13
Total	101	21	66	-	6	2	74	10	2	9	27	48	122
Total All	253	78	178	5	23	9	215	22	5	27	62	116	331

are, by and large, more capital intensive. Therefore, in looking at the implications of the import replacement policy one ought to consider the industries in which investment has taken place rather than the type of technology adopted within particular industries.

The move toward export promotion and the further processing of resources in Thailand, Malaysia, and the Philippines[9] thus reflects not only the diminishing opportunities in the import replacement field, but also the desire to correct distortions apparent in the industrial structure as a result of pursuing an import replacement strategy.[10] This changing emphasis will serve to ensure that competitiveness and quality consciousness are developed in local industry where this is both possible and desirable; considerably more scope for foreign exchange earnings and employment generation is also a likely consequence of promoting those industries which can use the comparative advantages of the ASEAN countries. As a "corollary," vertical and horizontal integration and regional dispersal are being encouraged. However, the desired changes cannot be achieved by simply readjusting tariffs to encourage a more competitive situation; this would cause too much upheaval. Other means have to be sought to supplement the slow adjustments which can be made and these may be of a permanent nature (for example, ASEAN complementation programs) or of a temporary nature (for example, export incentives or bans on exports of unprocessed raw materials).

Considerable reliance will still have to be placed on foreign investments to achieve the foregoing aims. The access provided by foreign companies to their marketing outlets throughout the world and the technology they possess are both necessary elements in a concerted drive to restore balance of payments deficits quickly and to generate employment. An export promotion strategy also fits in with the desire of multinational companies which are placing more emphasis on the development of low-cost export oriented bases overseas, a trend that was already apparent from the flows during the late 1960s.[11] These "export oriented" investments, however, are more flexible from a locational viewpoint than the projects which result from other motives—in other words, the comparative investment climates of the various possible locations (both within and outside ASEAN) will become increasingly significant since the projects are not limited in their location by raw materials or local market considerations.[12]

It is also important to note that multinational companies are beginning to consider the securing, maintaining, or developing of a regional base in ASEAN countries as a major step. Again, as the emphasis of these multinational companies turns toward Asia and Africa from Europe and America, regionalization and complementation will pay an even more significant role. However, to achieve the full effects of these moves, the companies feel that the ASEAN countries will have to give due emphasis to improving the climate for investment and take steps toward evolving a common market of complementarity programs.

PRESENT BROAD POLICIES TOWARD FOREIGN INVESTMENT

In order to implement their basic industrial strategies, the ASEAN countries are using a wide range of policy tools. Foreign exchange controls, price controls, credit lines, tariffs, and financial incentives all play their parts. In controlling foreign investment, however, considerable reliance is placed on the agencies which have been established in all of the countries for the purpose of implementing the laws and regulations governing foreign investment and incentives.[13] These agencies are now assessing more carefully the overall social and economic impact of foreign industrial projects, which not only involves guiding foreign investment into desirable industrial fields where the investment can contribute effectively to development, but also determining the conditions under which this investment will be accepted. Moreover, since effective and sensible control (and effective and sensible policies) requires an appreciation of the operations of business, the factors which affect market mechanisms, as well as an understanding of economics, sociology, and government, more business oriented technocrats are becoming involved in these agencies.

MAJOR LAWS RELATING TO FOREIGN INVESTMENT

The major laws pertaining to foreign investment in the ASEAN countries and the agencies given the responsibility of implementing them are summarized in Table 4. While there are other laws which affect foreign investment (including special laws to cover, for example, the operations of free trade zones) and policy objectives which are outlined in various development plans, the body of the legislation governing the operations of foreign enterprises and investment incentives is contained in the laws listed in the table.

The laws as set out are of varying degrees of complication. The Economic Expansion Incentives Act of Singapore, for example, is fairly simple and straightforward. The situation in the Philippines, on the other hand, is complicated with differential incentives for industries, varying limitations on foreign equity, and the like. Further, some laws which in theory appear simple and nonrestrictive are complex and somewhat restrictive in application; such is the case in Malaysia, for example. Thus, in interpreting the laws, their application should be considered as well as the written word. Further, the laws should be construed in their environmental context.[14]

The key element in all of these laws is the control they provide over the inflow of foreign investment. All of the ASEAN countries have restrictions on the fields in which foreign investment can enter and conditions which must be met before a foreign enterprise can be established. While the benefits of foreign investment are appreciated (the provision of capital, entrepreneurship, and managerial know-how, technology and training facilities, export market access and experience, stimulation of the local business/industrial environment, bias toward industrial rationalization, taxpaying orientation, and so forth), the recipient countries want to ensure that these are maximized and various "malpractices" minimized (the excessive importing of raw materials, insufficient orientation toward export or unfair market sharing, uneconomic transfer pricing in dealing with overseas affiliates, failure to share equity with local entrepreneurs, inadequate employment and training of local personnel, lack of local research or adaptation of technology to local needs, absence of local philanthropic activities and identity, and the like).[15] What the foregoing means in sum is that foreign investment is being subjected to closer scrutiny than in the past, with recipient countries realizing that this should not be done in a way to give the impression that foreign investment is not welcomed or encouraged. After all, a "joint venture" is involved, requiring understanding between the host government and the investor.

PRIORITY AREAS FOR FOREIGN INVESTMENT

Most of the ASEAN countries have set certain industrial priorities either in the form of a plan or through promotional efforts. All the countries have also specified certain areas of industrial activity which are reserved for foreign nationals or the local government, allowing no foreign government investment into these fields. With regard to the areas closed to *any* foreign investments,[16] it is sometimes difficult to differentiate permanent from temporary restrictions. However, areas related to national defense (all countries)

TABLE 4

Major Laws Relating to Foreign Investment in the ASEAN Countries

PHILIPPINES

MAJOR LAWS

R.A. 5186 Investment Incentives Act, 1967 (as amended by Presidential Decree No. 92 in 1973)—with the objectives of accelerating the sound development of the economy in consonance with the principles and objectives of economic nationalism; the achieving of a planned, economically feasible and practical dispersal of industries under conditions that will encourage competition and discourage monopolies; and the channeling of investment into preferred areas.

R.A. 5455 Foreign Business Regulation Act, 1968 (as amended by Presidential Decree No. 92 in 1973)—with the objectives of regulating foreign investment in all fields of activity in the Philippines and preventing alien entry into fields adequately exploited by the Filipinos.

R.A. 6135 Export Incentives Act, 1970 (as amended by Presidential Decree No 92 in 1973)—with the objectives of actively encouraging, promoting, and diversifying exports of services and manufactured items from domestic raw materials to the fullest extent possible and developing new markets for Philippine products.

AGENCY RESPONSIBLE

Board of Investments, involving also Department of Finance, Central Bank, Mariveles Free Trade Zone Authority, National Economic Development Authority, and other Government agencies.

TABLE 4 (continued)

THAILAND

MAJOR LAWS

Announcement No. 227, October, 1972 (revised Promotion of Industrial Development Act of 1962—with the objective of promoting investors whose businesses are of economic and social importance to the country.

Alien Business Law (Announcement No. 281, 1972)—with the objective of restricting majority-owned foreign enterprises in various fields of activity.

AGENCY RESPONSIBLE

Board of Investments, involving also Ministry of Industry, Ministry of Interior, and other Government agencies.

MALAYSIA

MAJOR LAWS

Investment Incentives Act, 1966 (amended 1971)—with the objective of channeling foreign investment into less familiar fields, and attracting foreign investment in new enterprises. Specific emphasis is given to export-oriented industries. (See also Income Tax Act, 1967).

AGENCY RESPONSIBLE

Federal Industrial Development Authority and Ministry of Trade and Industry, along with Malaysia Industrial Development Finance Berhod, Malaysia Industrial Estates Berhod, and other Government agencies and departments.

SINGAPORE

MAJOR LAWS

Economic Expansion Incentives (Relief from Income Tax) Act, 1967 (amended 1970)—with the objectives embracing a free enterprise system with growth maximization. The Government's policy toward private investors—foreign and local—combines maximum assistance with liberal incentives.

AGENCY RESPONSIBLE

Economic Development Board, along with Jurong Town Corporation, Ministry of Finance, and other Government agencies.

INDONESIA

MAJOR LAWS

Foreign Capital Investment Law, 1967 and other decrees designed to state the basic principles governing foreign private capital investment, and both to encourage and regulate that kind of investment.*

AGENCY RESPONSIBLE

Foreign Investment Board (recently reorganized) and other Government departments.

* The Indonesian Government in January of 1974 announced further changes in the law to reflect increasing nationalist feeling. These changes are not included in this paper since details were not available at the time of writing.

and public utilities (all countries except the Philippines) are permanent areas of restriction, mainly monopolized by the local government.

The Philippines has also prepared a list of "overcrowded industries" in which no new investment is allowed, neither domestic nor foreign. This list, revised from time to time, is determined on the basis of capacity of existing industry in relation to the size of the domestic market. However, projects in these areas geared for the export market may be allowed to be established. Such temporary exclusions are also common in the other countries although lists may not be published. Malaysia, for example, will not register new foreign investment in industries regarded as "overcrowded"; however, a list of these industries is not published—mainly because a project could be approved in an "overcrowded" area under certain conditions (for example, if principally geared for export). Rather than deter an investor, the Federal Industrial Development Authority of Malaysia would prefer to have the opportunity to talk him into investing in the field if it would be useful to do so. The purpose of refusing to register further investment in these areas is to insure that overinvestment does not lead to the development of considerable excess capacities and that foreign exchange is conserved by avoiding unnecessary duplication of capacity and inputs, as was characteristic of the early import replacement phase of development.[17]

The availability of incentives and the extent of foreign equity participation allowed are closely related to the priority areas of investment in the ASEAN countries, although the form in which such priorities are declared differs widely, ranging from the listing of specific products in the Philippines to a broad "high technology" categorization in Singapore.

The Philippines, for example, prepares an annual Investment Priorities Plan which lists the preferred areas of investment open to both foreign and domestic investors. Such listing is on a product-by-product basis (for example, asbestos, nylon fibers, primary steel, and sorghum) with a specified measured capacity for each representing local market potential—investors can register capacity in these fields until the measured capacity has been "filled." The preferred areas (of which there are approximately one hundred at present) are divided into "pioneer areas" (that is, those that involve the production of goods not produced in the Philippines on a commercial scale or that use a technology new and untried in the Philippines) and a "non-pioneer area," the former offering more liberal incentives and less restrictive conditions on foreign ownership and control. In determining the preferred areas, the criteria used include the possibilities of import substitution, the extent of further processing of raw materials, and the possibility of exports, as well as the necessity for a project to be economically, technically, and financially sound, and to provide a high rate of return to the national economy.

In addition to the Investment Priorities Plan, the Philippines also prepared an Export Priorities Plan, listing products and services for which incentives are available to existing as well as new entities engaged in exports, and a Tourism Priorities Plan, listing services for which incentives are available to existing as well as new entities engaged in providing services to foreign tourists. Under certain conditions, foreign investors can register in these fields. Foreign investment is also allowed in other fields of activity outside these plans (without incentives) provided: such projects do not conflict with national objectives and other laws affecting the scope available for foreign investment; are in areas not adequately exploited by Filipinos; and would provide tangible benefits to the Philippine economy.

The "shopping list" impression conveyed by the Investment Priorities Plan in the Philippines (the first plan was prepared in 1968) still reflects the import substitution phase with incentives being offered to compensate for a distorted tariff structure and to attract investment into the listed fields.[18] This is now changing, with the Board of Investments attempting to prune the list (one reason being to avoid giving incentives to industries that do not really require them—a topic to be discussed in a later section of the paper), placing more emphasis on industries which also have potential for export and for the further processing of raw materials.[19] The Export Priorities Plan serves to supplement this change (the Export Priorities Plan was first prepared in 1970 and the Tourism Priorities Plan in 1973).

Malaysia has no fixed criteria for granting pioneer status (those projects for which incentives are available) although local equity participation, market and employment prospects, and integration with existing industries are all favorably considered in arriving at a decision about a particular application. However, special incentives and relaxation on equity involvement are given for export-oriented investments and priority products: Over fifty priority products, ranging from food canning to ball bearings, are at present recommended by the review committee on investment incentives.

Thailand also prepares a list of "promoted" industries eligible for registration for incentives; there are considerable restrictions in foreign investment in areas outside these activities. Labor intensity, potential foreign exchange earnings or savings, extensive use of indigenous raw materials, and potential forward and backward linkages (as well as technical, financial, and economic viability) are among the criteria for choosing priority areas. While there is still a strong element of import replacement apparent in the list of promoted activities (which includes fishing, processing of agricultural products, petrochemicals, mechanical and electrical components, textiles, and certain services), the desire to promote exports and upgrade existing processing is apparent.

Singapore has now also become selective in the projects it will encourage. It has a strong preference for those with a high technology content serving world markets, such as electronics. The Economic Development Board does not publish a list of such industries, although there is no doubt it has an indicative list for its own use and actively promotes investment in these fields through contact with relevant manufacturers throughout the world. For this purpose, Singapore has a number of offices abroad, solely for the purpose of investment promotion.

Apart from restrictions on the extent of foreign investment in certain industries, Indonesia has not prepared any list of priority industries. With opportunities numerous in all fields of activity, the government has left it to the private sector to search these opportunities out and then apply for registration to obtain incentives and negotiate the conditions for the project. However, the recent reorganization of the Foreign Investment Board suggests that Indonesia may also start determining priorities on its own accord.

Thus, while the extent to which priorities are specified varies, all of the ASEAN countries seem to be concerned with establishing priorities either in a plan, and/or specifying the characteristics of preferred projects. While priorities can be overdone (as in the Philippines to some extent), they do serve a number of purposes. They let the investors know what opportunities are open for negotiation, thus saving the time and expense a general search would require. They assist the ASEAN countries to achieve more effective coordination of their plans and the activities of the various government instrumentalities. They ensure that a country has at least explored the opportunities available to help facilitate a more effective channeling of foreign investments into desirable fields and to provide a basis for negotiating and determining conditions for their establishment. And they enable a country to determine whether or not incentives, tariff protection, finance, and the like are needed. Other advantages of having a system of priorities could also be listed, noting that the opportunity still exists, however, for foreign investors to propose other fields they would like to enter. To the extent that this is the case, investment priority lists are more "indicative" than final; they are related to the overall industrial strategies of each of the countries.

Before concluding the discussion on investment priorities, three further points of significance should be made. First, the author anticipates a determined effort by some of the ASEAN countries not only to diversify their industrial base and develop certain industries as key areas of specialization, but also to diversify the nationality base of foreign investment to avoid too much reliance on the investments of one or two nationalities. For example, we may see the Philippines promoting certain projects in Europe to reduce reliance on United States investment (which now accounts for well over 80 percent of the total foreign investment in the country); Japanese (and to some extent Chinese) investments will not require considerable promotion. This will not, of course, involve discriminatory policies. Second, while United States, Japanese, and European companies will continue to invest mainly within their respective "spheres of influence," the author envisages greater investment by these nationalities in ASEAN countries which do not constitute their "normal" areas of investment; for example, more Japanese investments in the Philippines than in Thailand (or Taiwan), more British investments in ASEAN countries other than Singapore and Malaysia, and more American investments in countries outside of the Philippines—a broadening which should be more rapid for United States and Japanese investments than for the more "conservative" British. Thirdly, the author foresees an increase in investments from one ASEAN country to another and from other nearby countries such as Hong Kong and Australia. Hong Kong, for example, is now experiencing cost increases and labor shortages and so is hiving off less sophisticated production such as cheap textiles and certain electrical goods for manufacture in other countries, concentrating on the more sophisticated end of the production of these products. Australia is also now starting to hive off production of products with a high labor content.

POLICIES TOWARD OWNERSHIP AND CONTROL

All of the countries in the ASEAN region prefer joint ventures of foreign and domestic capital to fully-owned foreign enterprises, although such a preference is enforced only in certain fields of activity. Even in such areas where it is enforced (mainly in raw material and certain local market-oriented projects), it is doubtful whether this causes considerable concern to the bulk of the foreign investors unless they are placed in a position of having to accept minority interest and control where this is detrimental to the effective management of the enterprise or gives access to markets and specialized technology acquired by the foreign corporation at considerable cost.

The extent of foreign control of enterprises varies among the ASEAN countries. For example, in enterprises with foreign capital established over the 1959-69 period in Thailand, approximately 13 percent of the registered capital was accounted for by 100 percent foreign-owned firms and 75 percent was accounted for by 50-100 percent foreign-owned firms.[20] Recently, however, there has been strong pressure to reduce the extent of foreign-owned and controlled firms, and the above percentages have been considerably reduced.

In Indonesia, fully foreign-owned projects accounted for more than 25 percent of the number of approved foreign enterprises established over the 1967-70 period, with the bulk of the remaining approved foreign enterprises having over 60 percent foreign capital.[21] The high proportion of ownership and control by foreign enterprises in Indonesia, compared to the other ASEAN countries, reflects to a considerable extent the relative lack of local capital and suitable joint venture partners and management skills in Indonesia. It should be noted, however, that as a condition of registration, progressive increases in local participation are normally required. Under current conditions in Indonesia, local capital is unlikely to contribute significantly to equity requirements in industrial ventures, although in common with the other ASEAN countries, Indonesia wishes progressively to increase the extent of local participation in industrial activity.

REASONS UNDERLYING THE DESIRE FOR JOINT VENTURES BY THE ASEAN COUNTRIES

At least seven arguments have been advanced for requiring local participation in certain projects.

(1) There is the emotional argument that a country has a right to participate

in locally-based ventures in order to meet the national objectives of increasing indigenous ownership and control over the key areas of economic activity. The experience of many countries has shown that this is a strong argument. Some countries which have been liberal toward foreign investment find, on looking back, that by not encouraging local participation in projects as they were established, the proportion of key sectors of the economy under foreign ownership has increased quite dramatically. Nor have their expectations that the financial and employment contributions of the foreign companies would compensate been fulfilled. The development of indigenous activity has nearly always proved slower than expected. A political "hot potato" can result, rightly or wrongly; to expect "economic rationality" to prevail under such circumstances[22] is like expecting the leader of a trade union to negotiate for a wage decrease to combat inflation!

(2) There is a fear that the concentration of ownership of key productive assets in foreign hands would jeopardize national interests, especially if the economy is heavily dependent on the activities involved and most of the investment is from investors of one nationality. This could take a number of forms: Policies pursued by the home country of the investor in its own national interest could have repercussions on the host country; policies pursued by the foreign investors may be contrary to the policies of the host country; political pressure could be brought to bear on the host country through the medium of the foreign enterprises. Other possibilities could be mentioned; it is, however, difficult to tell the extent to which the argument that foreign investment could compromise national interest is or has been applicable to the ASEAN countries.

(3) Local ownership and control of an enterprise puts the government in a better position to influence the activities of the company through various fiscal and monetary measures. A majority-controlled foreign enterprise is much more independent of host-country measures than a locally-controlled company.

(4) It is argued that the country is providing an asset (in some form or another) to the foreign enterprise establishing in the country; otherwise the former would not invest. This argument is applied particularly to the resource and local market-oriented projects.

(5) Foreign investment normally moves into highly profitable fields in the country. There are thus potential financial gains for the local population in involvement in the enterprise. While there are alternative means to direct equity (that is, through taxation and other financial policies) for obtaining such gains, the "accounting" practices followed by many of the multinationals make this approach difficult, especially where there is collaboration by corrupt officials in the host country.

(6) There is concern that foreign capital with better know-how and greater access to resources will dominate certain fields. And when domestic local entrepreneurs or groups have developed sufficiently to enter such fields, it may be too late.

(7) Many foreign investors actually prefer to enter joint ventures with host-country partners.[23]

There is no wish to get involved in the pros and cons of the foregoing arguments. They have been listed here because they are reasons which have been advanced in the ASEAN countries for preferring joint ventures. It should be stressed, however, that their strength varies from country to country; in general, their applications are less harsh than popularly believed.

POLICIES RELATING TO LIMITATIONS ON FOREIGN OWNERSHIP AND CONTROL OF ENTERPRISES IN THE ASEAN COUNTRIES

Table 5 summarizes details of the policies in the ASEAN countries which relate to ownership and control of industrial enterprises. As the table is self-explanatory, the discussion is limited to comments on a few points of significance.

Only in the Philippines does the law itself specify the extent of foreign control in some of the areas open to foreign investment. However, *in practice*, all the ASEAN countries have some form of restrictions. In Malaysia, for example, companies which depend entirely on the local market for their sales are generally required to have at least 51 percent Malaysian equity participation. If the company does not depend entirely on the domestic market, the ratio is negotiable. A similar situation is found in Thailand and Indonesia. The interesting point is that all of the ASEAN countries have similar policies for nonresource export-oriented activities; roughly, the greater the proportion of export, the greater the proportion of foreign equity participation allowed. It is only in local market-oriented and resource-oriented projects that the countries become more stringent on foreign ownership and control and even for some of the projects in these fields, majority ownership and control by foreigners is accepted (at least for a period) if significant benefits to the economy can be shown to exist, including technological transfer.

As implied by the foregoing, the continual comparison of the "restrictive" policies toward foreign ownership of the Philippines, Malaysia, Indonesia, and Thailand with the "open" policies of Singapore is not a valid comparison. Singapore has no natural resources or local market of significance,[24] and it is only in these areas that the other ASEAN countries are stringent on foreign ownership and control. Probably if Singapore possessed either of these factors, it too would pursue policies similar to the other ASEAN countries. If we compare the policies toward export-oriented industries, there is very little difference among ASEAN countries, except for the requirement in the Philippines[25] that local ownership and control be achieved within a thirty- to forty-five year period (even longer in some cases)—surely a long enough period in the eyes of all parties. Similarly, for the ASEAN countries with significant local markets and resources, foreign ownership and control requirements are also similar.

A second point to be made is that even when majority ownership and control is not permitted, the ASEAN countries are quite willing to allow

TABLE 5

Limitations on Foreign Ownership and Control of Enterprises In the ASEAN Countries

---

PHILIPPINES

AREAS CLOSED TO ANY FOREIGN INVESTMENT

Permanent: Rural banks, mass media, retail trade, rice and corn (may be open in certain instances), and certain military goods.

Temporary: "Overcrowded industries" are closed to any new investment unless the product is to be exported or the location of the enterprise would promote regional dispersal. These products include air conditioners (room), G.I. sheets, nails, pencils, radios, and matches. There are at present forty industries on the overcrowded list.

AREAS SPECIFICALLY RESTRICTED IN PROPORTION OF FOREIGN EQUITY

Banking institutions (0 percent)* except new banks established by consolidation of branches or agencies of foreign banks in the Philippines; savings and loan associations (60 percent); public utilities (60 percent); domestic air commerce and/or air transportation (60 percent); financing companies (60 percent); fishing vessels (61 percent †); marine mollusca and other fishing activities (61 percent†); permits or leases for tapping or utilizing geothermal energy, natural gas, and methane gas (60 percent); natural resources (60 percent); certain educational institutions (60 percent); land (60 percent); and coastal trade (75 percent†).

POLICY ON OTHER AREAS OPEN TO FOREIGN INVESTMENT

For areas listed in the Annual Investment Priorities Plan (which can vary from year to year) the policy is as follows:

Preferred

Pioneer Areas: Up to 100 percent foreign ownership and control may be allowed, but within thirty years it has to be reduced to 60 percent Filipino ownership and control (if exporting at least 70 percent of production, this is extended to forty years). These periods may be extended ten more years in special circumstances. Examples of present pioneer areas are copper metal, primarily steel, asbestos, foundry coke, polypropulene, small gasoline engines, and interisland shipping.

Non-Pioneer Preferred Areas: Up to 40 percent foreign ownership and control is allowed. However, if the measured capacity is not realized within three years after its first listing on the Investment Priorities Plan, the areas become "liberalized" and up to 100 percent foreign ownership and control is allowed, subject to conversion to 60 percent Filipino ownership and control within the time periods as specified above for Pioneer preferred areas. Examples of present non-liberalized, non-pioneer preferred areas are palm oil, copper ore, glass containers, palay threshers, perlite, and feed yeast. Liberalized areas include barges and tugboats, coconut oil, fruit and vegetable processing, pumps, fishing boats, pulp, and paper.

---

* The figures in parentheses indicate the minimum local ownership control of equity capital. The † symbol after some of the percentages means that this amount can be Filipino or American capital, a provision applying until the expiration of the Laurel-Langley Agreement in 1974.

TABLE 5 (continued)

For Areas Listed in the Export Priorities Plan as open for investment by new enterprises (List B), a similar pioneer/non-pioneer categorization to the investment priority plan exists. The ownership and control requirements are the same, except that foreign enterprises (that is, where foreign equity is above 40 percent) may register under the Export Priorities Plan even in the non-pioneer areas if exporting at least 70 percent of production. Examples of present Pioneer export industries are activated carbon, furfural, rice bran oil, pliers and wrenches, electronic parts and components. Examples of present non-pioneer export industries are (note there is no non-liberalized areas) essential oil, blockboard and blockboard cover, garments, footwear, processed vegetables, and food. (The 60 percent ownership and control requirement for the non-pioneer areas may be waived and these may be treated as pioneer areas if regional complementarity is involved. Note also that a 10 percent "public participation" in the equity of all enterprises receiving incentives is normally required.)

For Areas Listed in the Tourism Priorities Plan. Up to 100 percent foreign ownership and control may be allowed, but within thirty years this has to be reduced to 60 percent Filipino ownership and control; this period may be extended ten or more years in special circumstances.

For all other areas up to 100 percent foreign ownership and control may be allowed, but when above 30 percent such investment must be approved by the Board of Investments. Authority for such investment will be granted unless the proposed investment:

- would conflict with existing constitutional provision and laws for regulating the degree of required ownership by Philippine nationals in the enterprise; or
- would pose a clear and present danger of promoting monopolies or combinations in restraint of trade; or
- would be made in an enterprise engaged in a field adequately being exploited by Filipinos; or
- would conflict or be inconsistent with the Investment Priorities Plan in force at the time the investment is sought to be made; or
- would not contribute to the sound and balanced development of the national economy on a self-sustaining basis.

THAILAND

AREAS CLOSED TO ANY FOREIGN INVESTMENT

Public utilities, savings banks, rural banking, insurances, and certain military goods.

AREAS SPECIFICALLY RESTRICTED IN PROPORTION OF FOREIGN EQUITY

Aliens doing business are subject to the Alien Business Law which restricts the participation of non-Thai nationals in certain fields of business activity. These are classified in three categories as follows:

Category A. This category includes business activities which are reserved for Thai nationals or enterprises which are majority owned (that is, at least 51 percent) and controlled by Thais. Aliens engaged in activities in this category as of November 26, 1972, are given until November 26, 1974, to wind up their operations. Category A includes the agricultural areas of rice farming and salt farming; the commercial areas of internal trade of agricultural products and trade in real

TABLE 5 (continued)

property; the services of accountancy, law, architecture, advertising, brokerage, auctioneering, haircutting, hairdressing, beauty treatment, and building construction.

Category B. Existing foreign-owned and controlled business activities under this category which were operating in Thailand as of November 26, 1972, will be allowed to continue to operate for an indefinite period. However, no new majority-owned foreign enterprises will be allowed to establish; that is, at least 51 percent Thai ownership and control will be required. The areas included in Category B are the agricultural areas of farming, fruit and vegetable farming, livestock, forestry and fishing; the manufacturing areas of rice milling, flour, sugar, beverages, ice, medicine, cold storage, wood processing, products from gold and other exotic minerals, lacquerwares, woodcarvings, matches, lime, cement and by-products, stone blasting and crushing, garments or shoes except for export, printing, newspaper publications and silk products; the commercial areas of retailing (except those specified in Cateogy C), sale of mining products and food and beverages (except those specified in Category C), and sale of antiques and works of art; the service areas of tour agencies, hotels, businesses defined by law as service premises; photography and printing, laundry and tailoring; and internal transportation by land, water, and air.

Category C. As with Category B, existing foreign-owned and controlled businesses in Category C may continue to operate indefinitely. Further, the formation of new companies majority owned and controlled by foreigners, may be allowed under certain conditions. However, for enterprises under this category (and Category B) existing as of November 26, 1972, production or sales in subsequent years are limited to 30 percent of the quantity produced or sold in 1972; for new enterprises under Category C, the maximum growth is subject to negotiation. The areas included in Category C are the commercial areas of wholesaling (except those specified in Category A), export of all types of products, retailing of machines and tools, and sale of food and beverages for the promotion of tourism; the manufacturing and mining areas of animal feeds, vegetable oil, embroidered and knitted products, glass containers and light bulbs, crockery, writing and printing paper, rock salt mining and mining; all other services not specified under Category A and B; and other constructions except those specified in Category A.

POLICY ON OTHER AREAS OPEN TO FOREIGN INVESTMENT

Joint ventures are encouraged in all fields. However, in addition to Category C products, foreign-owned and controlled enterprises may be allowed in the promoted areas which do not fall in Categories A and B. These cover a wide range of fields including certain activities in agriculture, minerals, metals, ceramics, chemicals, mechanical and electrical equipment, construction materials, textiles, services, and other products. Incentives are available for these promoted activities.

MALAYSIA

AREAS CLOSED TO ANY FOREIGN INVESTMENT

Public utilities, domestic air transport, and certain military goods.

AREAS SPECIFICALLY RESTRICTED TO PROPORTION OF FOREIGN EQUITY

No areas specifically restricted.

TABLE 5 (continued)

POLICY ON OTHER AREAS OPEN TO FOREIGN INVESTMENT

A high degree of flexibility exists, although companies which depend entirely on the Malaysian market for their sales are generally required to have at least 51 percent domestic participation in the equity. If fully export-oriented, up to 100 percent foreign ownership may be allowed. Companies whose export performances fall between these extremes can negotiate with the Government and Malaysia investors concerned on the percentage of equity. In certain instances, flexibility also exists for high technology products.

SINGAPORE

AREAS CLOSED TO ANY FOREIGN INVESTMENT

Public utilities, domestic air transport, and certain military goods.

AREAS SPECIFICALLY RESTRICTED IN PROPORTION OF FOREIGN EQUITY

No areas specifically restricted.

POLICY ON OTHER AREAS OPEN TO FOREIGN INVESTMENT

Generally, Singapore prefers local collaboration, but is very flexible in its policy in this regard.

INDONESIA

*AREAS CLOSED TO ANY FOREIGN INVESTMENT**

Industries which are vital fucntions for defense, including arms and ammunitions, explosives, and war equipment.

In the field of mining, foreign investment must take the form of "work-contracts."

Sectors of trading and distribution business are also closed to foreign investors, particularly domestic retail trade and exporting and importing unless coupled with domestic manufacturing. From time to time regulations are issued by Ministers to restrict certain types of investment because the industry is "overcrowded" or could readily be exploited by Indonesians. Some forty industries in the light engineering field are on this "temporary" restricted list.

POLICY ON OTHER AREAS OPEN TO FOREIGN INVESTMENT

Officially, a capital investment owned and controlled 100 percent by foreigners may be permitted but there is a general requirement that, at some suitable time, domestic capital will be brought into the venture (or if the arrangements under which the enterprise is put into operation involved establishment of controls by the Government). An investment permit has a thirty-year maximum validity. (This may be renewed.)

---

* The January 1974 Amendments are not reflected in this table.

management and technical assistance contracts to be drawn up between the multinational company and the host-country enterprise. This is quite a common occurrence, allowing the multinational corporation to have effective control over the management of the enterprise.

A final significant point is that many of the businesses in which foreign direct investment is restricted to under 50 percent of total equity in both Indonesia and Thailand are recent additions to the restricted list. In

November, 1972, for example, Thailand revised its Aliens Business Law to specify, among other things, certain areas where majority-owned foreign enterprises would not be allowed unless permitted by Royal Decree. Where such already exist, they were given two years in which to disinvest.

What, then, are the views of the multinational corporations on these policies? To answer this question we now turn to a consideration of the ownership policy of multinational corporations.

OWNERSHIP POLICY OF MULTINATIONAL CORPORATIONS

Japanese investors appear to have accepted joint ventures much more readily than United States and United Kingdom investors who have not been as prepared to enter joint ventures or have been less willing to accept minority interests. Approximately 60 percent of the projects of Japanese investors in the ASEAN countries, for example, involved an equity percentage of 50 percent or less, and studies by the author of the projects of other investing countries revealed considerably lower percentages.

Although most of the executives of Japanese companies interviewed said that they would prefer the options for ownership to be wide, in nearly all cases they would still opt for joint ventures,[26] for the following reasons:

(1) Local companies are much more familiar than the Japanese companies with local conditions. Their greater knowledge can assist in getting a project off the ground; overcoming liaison problems with suppliers, outlets, and government; overcoming language barriers; and so forth.

(2) The risk is spread—although it has been found that in many cases the risk carried by the Japanese company is higher than that of the local company because of the latter's inability to raise capital. In a number of the projects studied, for example, it was found that the Japanese partner had to lend finance to the local partner in order that the latter could contribute its share of equity. In many cases, the loan/equity ratio was considerably higher for the Japanese partner than for the local partner.

(3) In a large number of cases, the joint venture was initially proposed by a company which was already tied to the outside partner as a customer or selling agency.

(4) There is more acceptance of the project in the host country if local partners are involved.

(5) The motives for investment may not necessitate complete ownership or even majority holding. For example, the supply of certain raw materials may be ensured with only minority participation in a particular project, supplemented with suitable long-term contracts.

(6) The market or source of supply may be controlled by local investors and thus it is necessary to enter into a venture with them.

(7) The local partner may possess the necessary supplementary skills, knowledge, and the like, essential to the project.

For these reasons, joint ventures appear to be more acceptable to the Japanese companies and this affects their investment motives and the kinds of plant they become involved with. In marked contrast to American and European investors, those factors which work against joint ventures (especially the disclosures of secrets and know-how—until recently Japanese companies were using Western know-how, contributing very little original research) have not been normally applicable to Japanese investors. In terms of control, however, there appears to be stronger preference for majority control (that is, 51 percent or more of equity), especially over the initial stages of the project. Again, this varies depending on the type of project, but where it appears that the investors have little to contribute, where a large amount of funds is involved, or where technology and management are important, majority control tends to be desired. Many non-ASEAN companies stressed the desire to have control over the initial stages of projects. This was reflected in their comments that if ultimate majority control is required by the host governments for its investors, then "fadeout" equity participation should be considered, or a 40 percent foreign equity, for example, should be coupled with strong management agreements and government-backed local funds for the local joint venture partners.

While United States and European companies still have a marked preference for control, changes in the motivational pattern underlying their investment in the ASEAN countries is beginning to alter the picture. Where preference for majority control still exists, the willingness to enter joint ventures varies substantially with the underlying motives.

For the local market investments, there has been a relaxation of attitudes toward having full control or ownership simply because the laws of many countries are now enforcing joint ventures and if the company is unwilling to enter a joint venture, it loses the opoortunity to someone else. The competition from countries such as Japan during the 1960s (whose companies reveal a desire to enter joint ventures, especially in Southeast Asia) has reinforced this. The question then becomes one of extent of control. One company interviewed, for example, stated that its policy during the 1950s was complete ownership: "We have had to change our attitudes on this, otherwise we would have lost the markets in certain countries to companies willing to enter joint ventures . . . but we still insist on majority control."

For the resource-oriented investments a similar picture emerges, although the exploration aspect of many of the investments necessitates separate considerations, especially where contracts-of-work are involved. For the low-cost, export-oriented projects, on the other hand, many of the United States companies do not appear so flexible and maintain a 100 percent ownership policy. The main reasons for this stance are that joint venture partners normally have little to offer in such projects and because possibilities for this type of project mean that a company can always find suitable locations which allow it 100 percent ownership.

The reasons many of the large multinational companies advance for their stringent application of the majority control principle relate to their argument that most ventures are but a "cell" in their overall organization and that decisions by that "cell" where it is a joint venture may go against the interests of the organization; for example, the "high production, low profit margin" principle is frequently not acceptable to a joint venture partner. Where joint ventures are necessitated, the degree of autonomy given to the local affiliation (if it is majority owned by the United States company) is normally minimal; if the affiliate has only a minority interest of the United States company, then the contribution of this company to technology transfer, market development overseas and the like, is stifled to some extent.[27]

In addition to the reasons listed above, the desire to have complete control over, and to reap full benefits from, the activities of the subsidiary, the inability of joint venture partners to contribute anything additional to the venture, the unsuitability of joint venture partners, and the fear of divulging know-how and technology developed over many years to other persons were also frequently mentioned in support of the argument for 100 percent ownership or majority control. The last reason, the question of technology and know-how, was especially singled out.

As suggested above, the preference patterns of the overseas investors are modified by the laws of the various ASEAN countries. Extractive investments are often subject to stringent ownership conditions as outlined earlier. In the case of manufacturing investment, it could be argued that more flexibility is allowed simply because national sentiment in the developing countries is directed more to land and resource ownership questions. Where there is such flexibility, factors such as the existence of suitable local partners become significant. This is important because the existence of a suitable, reliable joint venture partner will determine whether a project will go ahead or not in a country where foreign equity participation is restricted as well as (if it is approved) the form and rate of build up of the project. It was apparent from our data that there is a tendency for some companies to enter new projects with local investors with whom they have already had associations; "since reliable partners are hard to find,"[28] it is felt desirable to maintain relationships which have proved successful. (This does constitute a possible danger in some of the ASEAN countries where concentration of industrial wealth may be further encouraged if companies continue to work with the same, proved reliable, partners.) In implementing legislation, this factor should be carefully considered—not so much by restrictive policies but by encouraging the participation of companies in joint ventures.

It is of interest that many multinational companies have found difficulty in finding suitable joint venture partners in the ASEAN countries. They suggest that the governments should give due emphasis if the legislation involves minority interest on the part of the foreign company. Overall, however, the shifting industrial strategies of the ASEAN countries and the motivational pattern of investments of foreign corporations do seem to be moving in the same direction and this has considerable implications on the ownership and control questions. The growing importance of the low cost base and regional base investments of the multinational corporations (investments in which they appear less willing to enter joint ventures, especially if minority interests are involved) meets the needs of the ASEAN countries now wishing to attract such investments. These countries, in turn, appear more willing to allow foreign ownership and control in these fields, at least for a long enough period to allow the multinational corporations to reap sufficient benefits from investments. Still, in all of the ASEAN countries, resource-oriented and local market-oriented investments are subject to fairly stringent local participation requirements—their extent depending on expected exports, the sophistication of the technology in-involved, and in some cases, the location.[29] The more a foreign corporation can contribute to these development objectives, the less stringent the conditions on local ownership and control. Most multinational corporations now accept, and are willing to enter into, joint ventures on this basis.

OPERATIONAL RESTRAINTS ON FOREIGN ENTERPRISES

This paper has thus far outlined the areas open to foreign investment in the ASEAN countries and indicated the ownership and control regulations affecting investment in these fields. Probably even more significant to the achievement of the industrial goals of the ASEAN countries, however, are the operating restraints placed on foreign investment. It is through the conditions placed on the operations of foreign enterprises that a country is able to ensure some form of control over their activities and derive maximum benefit from their presence.

The operational restraints range from restrictions on the ownership of land and the employment of foreign personnel to agreements relating to the phasing in of local content in the manufacturing operations. They can be grouped, for convenience, into three categories:

1) General restrictions relating to such factors as employment of foreign nationals and exchange controls.
2) Industry restrictions relating to industry guidelines covering local content, the technology to be adopted, and so on.
3) Specific restrictions relating to the terms and conditions, in addition to the above, applying to a specific enterprise.

Table 6 summarizes and compares the important general restrictions applicable to foreign-owned (and in some cases locally-owned) firms in the ASEAN countries. As it is not possible to present industry and specific restrictions in such a table, certain aspects of these restraints will be discussed after a brief look at the general restrictions.

GENERAL RESTRICTIONS ON THE OPERATIONS OF FOREIGN ENTERPRISES

While there are general restrictions, incorporated company, commercial, and other laws which apply to all enterprises, foreign and domestic, only two of these regulations shall be discussed here: the employment of foreign nationals and financial controls.[30]

TABLE 6

Important General Restrictions on the Operations of Foreign-Owned Firms in the ASEAN Countries

Area	Philippines	Thailand	Malaysia	Singapore	Indonesia
Land Utilization for industrial purposes	Lease of public lands may not exceed 2,500 acres per firm (applies also to local firms). Land can only be owned by companies with at least 60 percent Filipino equity. Lease on industrial estates and free trade zones.	Foreign owned and controlled companies are not allowed to own land. In other cases (below 50 percent foreign equity) limited to 10 rai (1 rai=1,600 square miles). Promoted industries with approval can own more if incorporated in a country which has a treaty with Thailand concerning land ownership. Lease on industrial estates.	Unrestricted. Lease on industrial estates and free trade zones.	Appears to have no restrictions. Lease on industrial estates.	No foreign enterprise can own land. Foreigners may lease land for up to thirty years (can be extended for a further twenty years at the Government's discretion).
Company management (applies also to local enterprises)	Management control by Filipinos is usually required whenever Filipino majority is also required. However, management contracts are allowed.	Management control by Thais is usually required whenever Thai majority ownership is also required. Management contracts are allowed.	Management control by Malaysia is usually required whenever Malaysian ownership is also required. However, management contracts are allowed.	Unrestricted	Unrestricted
Employment of nationals	Firms receiving incentives may not employ aliens in any capacity after the first five years of operation. Within the five year period, alien employment in supervisory, technical, or advisory positions is limited to 5 percent of firm's total such employment. For pioneer areas, the time period can be extended and	Certain occupations restricted to Thai nationals (some thirty-nine occupations listed). Work permits required. Thai workers must be trained.	Foreign companies are required to maximize employment of nationals (especially Malays and to plan for replacement of expatriates by Malaysians. Training program is required.	Employment of foreign nationals in technical and professional positions. Local workers must be trained.	Employment of foreign nationals in managerial and technical positions that cannot yet be filled by nationals. Foreign enterprises are required to organize and provide systematic

TABLE 6 (continued)

Area	Philippines	Thailand	Malaysia	Singapore	Indonesia
Employment of nationals (contd.)	the restriction does not apply by category of employment. Also when majority foreign owned, positions of president, treasurer, and general manager may be retained.				training and educational facilities with the aim of gradually replacing foreign employees with nationals.
Exchange controls -- remittances of profit	Generally unrestricted.	Unrestricted except in cases when required by the Central Bank for balance of payment purposes.	Unrestricted	Unrestricted	Unrestricted
Exchange controls -- remittances of royalties	May not exceed 50 percent of royalities earned during that year. (This is not a permanent restriction.)	Unrestricted	Unrestricted	Unrestricted	Unrestricted
Exchange controls -- repatriation of capital	For export oriented firms, annual repatriations may not exceed firm's yearly net foreign exchange earnings. For BOI registered firms engaged in export or import substitution industries, repatriation limited to annual net foreign exchange earnings beginning one year after start of operations, or three annual dollar installments after one year of liquidation.	Unrestricted, but capital freedom is guaranteed only for that investment capital derived by the promoted person from a foreign country.	Unrestricted	Unrestricted	Allowed, but such repatriations will not be granted as long as the exemption or concessions concerning taxes and other levies are in effect.

TABLE 6 (continued)

Area	Philippines	Thailand	Malaysia	Singapore	Indonesia
Exchange controls -- repatriation of capital (contd.)	For other BOI registered firms and firms which have not availed of domestic credit, repatriation in four annual installments after one year of liquidation. For all other firms, repatriations are limited to installments ranging from five years ($250,000 or less) to nine years ($500,000 and above).				
Debt/equity ratio access to local finance	Normally limited to 70/30.	None specified	None specified	None specified	None specified
Access to local finance	Restricted to some extent.	Unrestricted	Unrestricted	Unrestricted	Unrestricted
Import restrictions (applies also to local enterprises)	Imports are restricted in varying degrees to protect domestic industries and conserve foreign exchange.	Imports are restricted in varying degrees to protect domestic industries and conserve foreign exchange.	Imports are restricted in varying degrees to protect domestic industries and conserve foreign exchange.	To a limited extent only.	Imports are restricted in varying degrees to protect domestic industries and conserve foreign exchange.

TABLE 6 (continued)

Area	Philippines	Thailand	Malaysia	Singapore	Indonesia
Fixing of royalties and technical fees (applies also to local enterprises)	Subject to authorization	Left to negotiation between licensee and licensor.	Left to negotiation between licensee and licensor.	Left to negotiation between licensee and licensor.	Subject to authorization.
Joining local trade associations	May be permitted	No compulsion	No compulsion	No compulsion	No compulsion
Capital issue control (applies also to local enterprises)	No laws	No laws	No laws but timing determined by Central Bank.	No laws	No laws

All of the ASEAN countries have some restrictions on the *extent* of employment of foreign nationals, with policies varying according to the extent of availability of manpower possessing the required in each country. The Philippines, for example, limits the employment of foreign nationals to a certain percentage of total work force and even then these normally have to be replaced within a period of five years. The Philippines is able to adopt such strict regulations because of the ready availability of a wide range of managerial and work force skills in the country. Indonesia, by contrast, has a limited number of local personnel qualified for managerial and technical skills and is thus more liberal, although the Foreign Capital Investment Law provides that foreign enterprises must use Indonesian workers in all types of occupations if and when qualified personnel are available. Similarly, Thailand has listed a number of occupations in which foreign personnel are not allowed to be engaged.

Associated with restrictions on the employment of foreign nationals[31] are the conditions placed on foreign enterprises with respect to labor training. In most of the ASEAN countries, foreign investors are required to submit a program for such training which, in the case of the Philippines, is subsidized through a tax credit on training costs. Thus, while each country recognizes the need for foreign nationals to be involved in industrial projects, there is a concerted effort to ensure that the employment and training of local personnel is maximized. This enables the skills of the local work force to be developed and the transfer of technical and managerial know-how to be more effective.

The *financial controls* on foreign investment vary, incorporating such areas as restrictions on the repatriation of capital and income, debt to equity ratios, and access to local finance.

Broadly, the position of capital and income repatriation is that income transfers of dividends, royalties, interest, and wages and salaries are freely allowed while capital repatriation is subject to a number of conditions. In addition, there are certain taxes which may be applicable to income transfers. Many of these transfer conditions, however, are the subject of guarantees by the host countries and/or incorporated in bilateral agreements with capital-exporting countries.

The proportion of debt to equity associated with foreign investment has received varying treatment by the ASEAN countries, but the usual practice is to allow the enterprise itself to decide. In fact, the Philippines is the only ASEAN country (to the author's knowledge) which operates under a fairly strict rule in this regard: All registered enterprises are required to have a maximum debt to equity ratio of 75/25 and only in special circumstances is this allowed to be exceeded. This requirement hurts Japanese enterprises more than any other since they are accustomed to working with high-gearing ratios. There is, however, concern in some of the other ASEAN countries that foreign investors working on high-gearing ratios can exert considerable influence on the operations of ASEAN enterprises in which the foreign investors have minority equity investment; also, considerable strain could be placed on the balance of payments situation with the early amortization of the loans.

Access to local finance is regarded as very important by foreign enterprises. Over 60 percent of Japanese enterprises, for example, use local host-country banks as one of their main sources of both long-term and short-term finance after establishments (if branches of Japanese banks in the host countries are also considered, the figure rises to over 80 percent).[32] Increasingly, however, the ASEAN countries (apart from Singapore which aims to become the financial capital of Asia) are restricting the access of foreign companies to local funds and encouraging the companies to use other sources. The Philippines, for example, restricts the access of majority foreign-owned companies to local savings and rural banks, mainly to ensure that such funds are channeled to Philippine companies which do not have ready access to overseas funds.

INDUSTRY RESTRICTIONS ON THE OPERATIONS OF FOREIGN ENTERPRISES

The investment agencies in the ASEAN countries are given considerable leeway to determine the types of conditions which should be placed on foreign investment in certain industries.[33] These conditions relate to operational aspects such as the scale of operations and the proportion of capacity devoted to exports; the location of an enterprise; and its local content, horizontal and/or vertical integration, and the technology adopted.

In certain cases, the ASEAN countries specify the *scale of operations* of a plant in a particular industry, whether minimum in nature (a minimum economic-sized plant) or maximum (with capacity installed not to exceed a certain amount). In the Philippines, for example, the Investment Priorities Plan specifies a measured capacity for local market-oriented projects for the various products; and firms, in applying for registration, request for a certain allocation to them of this measured capacity.[34] In an effort to avoid monopoly situations, any one firm is not normally allowed to take up the entire measured capacity; on the other hand, it must be above a certain minimum economic size. Such an approach does cause problems, especially when multiproduct operations are involved—it does, however, work rather well and the Board of Investments can be fairly flexible in applying the principle. Similar criteria, though not published, appear to be applied in Malaysia, Thailand, and, in some limited instances, Indonesia.

Specifying a *proportion of capacity to be devoted to export* seems to be becoming more common in the ASEAN countries and fairly definite guidelines are being evolved for the purpose, especially when incentives are involved.[35] The purpose is not merely to increase export earnings, but to force companies to operate on efficient scales, competitive in the world market, and to ensure that quality standards are maintained. The latter is one of the main reasons for the Philippines' recent decision to allow the expansion of textile manufacturers (previously declared an "overcrowded" industry) only if they agree to export at least 50 percent of the increased output, and/or locate outside the Greater Manila area.

Locational considerations are also becoming increasingly significant, reflecting the ASEAN countries' (other than Singapore) desire to encourage the establishment of industries outside the major existing concentrations. Apart from using incentives as a means to achieve this (which is treated more fully in the next section of this paper), direct controls over location are extensively used. Indonesia, for example, is not allowing additional pharmaceutical plants to establish in the Jakarta area; the Philippines has allocated measured capacities for certain industries on a regional basis; all the ASEAN countries limit the areas in which resource-oriented facilities can be located (and, in certain instances, pollutant activities). Of particular interest is the use of industrial estates as a vehicle for dispersal. Malaysia has set up a number of industrial estates in strategic areas throughout the country. Indonesia, Thailand, and the Philippines appear to be following similar courses, though not on a scale comparable to Malaysia.

Local content and horizontal or vertical integration are closely related and so are discussed together. They constitute one of the most significant areas of operational restraints on foreign enterprises. To avoid the establishment of purely assembly facilities, the ASEAN countries lay down guidelines for increasing the local content of production in certain industries. This can take the form of specifying that the foreign enterprise has to introduce gradually further processes over time either forward (for example, mining and later smelting) or backward (for example, assembly of pumps and later making the castings), or increasing local content by subcontracting out certain components or parts to already established local companies. In many instances, a combination of both vertical and horizontal integration arrangements are required.

The car manufacturing programs of Thailand and the Philippines are good examples of local content requirements, although the form taken by each differs. Briefly, Thailand has allowed any number of manufacturers and models, but has specified that each reach a certain percentage of local content by a certain time period. The Philippines (on the basis of "competitive bidding") allowed only five manufacturers with a limited range of models: The five selected were those offering the best "deal" to the Philippines while at the same time agreeing to minimum local content conditions. What is of particular importance in the Philippines is that local content has been defined to include component export, paving the way for ASEAN complementarity.[36] One of the major aims of progams such as these is to use large international companies as a means for transferring technology and quality standards to local small scale industry.[37]

SPECIFIC RESTRICTIONS ON THE OPERATIONS OF FOREIGN ENTERPRISES

To understand the specific restrictions pertaining to foreign enterprise, one has to have an idea of the registration process in the ASEAN countries. Generally, the investor first discusses the proposed project with the investment agency which will outline the type of general and industry conditions to be placed on the project. The investor may then be asked to complete an application form and a project study which is submitted to the investment agency for evaluation—these will vary for each country and according to area of registration. The submission will then be evaluated by the appropriate agency by checking the qualifications of the applicant, whether or not he can adhere to the general and industry restrictions, the soundness of the project, and so on. In addition, at this stage the agency will determine whether additional specific restrictions will be placed on the applicant before registration. If there are any, the investor will be informed and when and if he agrees to the additional conditions (or some compromise is reached) his project will be registered.

The specific restrictions can take a number of forms. They may relate, *inter alia*, to the sources and terms for overseas funds, the process and product mix, the terms and conditions of technical assistance or management agreements, quality control, or pollution restrictions. An investor thus has to be prepared for such conditions to be imposed—being qualified to set up facilities is not enough, a fact which many lawyers, especially, fail to appreciate.

Of course, restrictions are useless if the host countries cannot ensure their enforcement. This is normally no problem as incentives can be withdrawn, access for foreign exchange and local finance withheld, penalties imposed, and the like. Elaborate supervision procedures have been installed by the ASEAN investment agencies to monitor projects.

INVESTMENT INCENTIVES AND GUARANTEES

In an effort to overcome some of the natural and artificial barriers to investment in their countries, all of the ASEAN nations offer some form of investment incentives and guarantees. The natural barriers relate to the lack of work force skills, undeveloped industrial support services and facilities, language and custom differences, and the like. The artificial barriers include (in some of the countries) distorted tariff and exchange control structures and apparent economic and financial instabilities.

The basic guarantees are relatively straightforward and concern guarantees against nationalization and expropriation, freedom to repatriate income and capital, patent protection, and other measures to make the investor feel "more at ease." It is difficult, if not impossible, of course, for any government to speak for future governments, and the ASEAN nations are certainly no exception to this rule. Even the freedom to repatriate income and capital is generally qualified with such phrases in the legislation as "except in extreme cases of balance of payments strain where the Central Bank may limit the extent of repatriation for a short period." However, investors do look for guarantees along these lines and all of the ASEAN nations have made efforts to ensure that these are given. Table 7 summarizes the guarantees as applicable to each of the ASEAN countries.

The desirability and applicability of the various types of incentives has

TABLE 7

Basic Guarantees to Foreign Enterprises in the ASEAN Countries[1]

Area	Philippines	Thailand	Malaysia	Singapore	Indonesia
1. Patent Protection	Yes	No	Yes	Yes	Yes
2. Freedom from expropriation and requisition	Yes[2]	No	No	No[11]	Yes
3. Freedom from nationalization	Yes	Yes	Yes[8]	No	Yes
4. Guarantee of national treatment	No	Yes	No[9]	No	No[12]
5. Repatriation of investment and convertibility in foreign currency	Yes[3]	Yes[7]	Yes	Yes	Yes[13]
6. Remittance of earnings and convertibility in foreign currency	Yes	Yes[7]	Yes	Yes	Yes
7. Remittance to meet payments of foreign loans and contracts and convertibility to foreign currency	Yes	Yes[7]	Yes	Yes	Yes
8. Remittance of amount corresponding to depreciation of fixed capital assets	No	No	No	No	Yes
9. Nondiscriminatory application of laws	No	Yes	Yes	Yes	Yes
10. Employment of aliens (Restrictions apply to local and foreign firms)	Yes[4]	Yes	Yes[10]	Yes	Yes
11. Company management by aliens (Restrictions apply to local and foreign firms)	Yes[5]	Yes	Yes[10]	Yes	Yes
12. Access to all investment incentives	No[5](40)	Yes	Yes	Yes	Yes
13. Access to all export incentives	No(40)	Yes	Yes	Yes	Yes
14. Access to loans from host government financial institutions	No	Yes	Yes	Yes	Yes
15. Access to loans from local private financial institutions	Yes	Yes	Yes	Yes	Yes
16. Access to awards for host government public work contracts	No(25)	Yes	Yes	Yes	Yes
17. Access to awards from host government supply contracts	No[6](40)	Yes	Yes	Yes	Yes
18. Freedom from government ment competition	No[5](40)				

[1] For privileges not extended to wholly-owned firms, the figures in parentheses indicate the maximum percentage of foreign ownership permitted in order to be eligible for each privilege.

[2] Freedom from expropriation is subject only to right of eminent dominion and convertibility in foreign currency. Freedom from requisition may be waived in case of war or national emergency and convertibility in foreign currency in cases where payments are received as compensation for requisitioned property.

[3] See Table 6, and the earlier discussion on operational restraints.

[4] Limited. Must ultimately be replaced by locals.

TABLE 7 (continued)

[5] If pioneer preferred, yes.

[6] This varies; for example, public works must be 70 percent Filipino or American capital.

[7] Except in cases when required by the Central Bank for balance of payments purposes. Capital freedom is guaranteed only for that investment capital derived by the "promotion person" from a foreign country.

[8] In 1966, however, the Malaysian Government took over the cables of Overseas Telecommunication on a negotiated basis.

[9] Guarantee (as regards nationalization) with the United States and Germany; open to other countries also.

[10] Limited. Must ultimately be replaced by locals.

[11] An investment guarantee agreement exists between the United States and Singapore with 100 percent political risk and guarantees against losses from expropriation, war, revolution, insurrection, non-convertibility of foreign currency, and 75 percent guarantees for political and business risk.

[12] Guarantee valid for thirty years. Guarantee to American investors (bilateral agreement) against losses due to nationalization, war, and inconvertibility of currency.

[13] Repatriation shall not be granted as long as the exemptions or concessions concerning taxes and other levies are still in effect.

[14] Remittance of earnings or profits after subtraction of taxes.

---

been the subject of considerable debate. Many commentators have argued that financial incentives in the form of taxation exemption are not important to enterprises in their investment decisions and thus the developing countries are unnecessarily subsidizing industry or diverting their financial resources from more important attraction factors such as infrastructure and education facilities. Others argue that countries are competing for scarce capital and so financial incentives are important. Before commenting on these and other "debates," it is desirable to outline the form taken by investment incentives in the ASEAN countries so as to put the arguments for and against incentives in context.

FORM OF INVESTMENT INCENTIVES

It is very difficult to compare the incentives offered by various countries simply because the non-incentive taxes, infrastructure, and climatic investment base differ. For example, one country may allow liberal income tax incentives but have a high base rate of tax; another country's tax incentives may not be so liberal but this is offset by a low base rate of tax. One country may give taxation concessions for capital gains while another offers none simply because capital gains may not be taxed anyway. Similarly, one country may put more emphasis than another on infrastructure development as opposed to taxation incentives. These differences make it difficult to judge one set of incentives as "better than" another. This could only be determined by simulating a plant in the countries being compared and assessing the overall impact of all incentives and certain factors of the economic base. The answer is bound to differ from project to project. In this paper, therefore, no attempts are made to compare incentives on this basis.

Investment incentives in the ASEAN countries mainly take the form of taxation incentives—exemptions from certain taxes (for example, import duties on capital equipment or income tax holidays for a period of five years) or certain deductions from the taxes to be paid (for example, deductions from income tax labor training expenses). Special incentives are also given to export industries. Non-tax benefits include, for example, tariff protection and industrial sites.

Table 8 summarizes the incentives available to various groups of industries in the ASEAN countries. The incentives are categorized as follows:[38]

- income tax exemptions and deductions, and tax credits;
- import duties and tax exemptions and deductions;
- exemptions from other taxes; and
- other benefits.

It can be observed from Table 8 that incentives can take a multitude of forms. Thus, in the Philippines a complicated pattern of deductions, exemptions, and tax credits is apparent—although this requires more administrative control, it has been necessitated by many of the "antiquated" fiscal and monetary policies. The Singapore system, on the other hand, relies on straight-out exemptions, which administratively simplifies dealings with investors.

It is apparent that the ASEAN countries are more often using incentives to achieve their economic and social objectives rather than simply as straight attraction mechanisms for foreign investment. This is clearly seen in the Malaysian legislation which structures incentives so as to encourage exports, the location of enterprises in less developed areas, and the input of local content in the manufacture of priority products. Under the provisions of the special incentives for export-oriented industries, tax relief is allowed for periods ranging from four to seven years compared to the relief period of three to five years for other pioneer industries. Similarly, a company locating its factory in a less developed area producing a priority product and having more than 50 percent local content can be granted a maximum tax relief period of eight years.

The Philippines incentive laws present a parallel situation with added incentives for exports, preferred industries, and the use of local raw materials and labor. Recent changes in the expansionary reinvestment allowance (which accounts for the bulk of the tax credits claimed by registered enterprises) have given fuller flexibility to the Board of Investments to use varying rates depending on labor intensity, exports, and regional dispersal.[39]

The foregoing changes reveal a realization that incentives can be manipulated to influence the structure and location of a project, and to contribute more effectively to the overall economic and socal aims of a country. In addition, it has been realized by the ASEAN governments that by giving

TABLE 8

Comparison of Investment Incentives in ASEAN Countries

INCENTIVE	Philippines			Thailand	Malaysia			Singapore			Indonesia
	Pioneer Preferred	Other Preferred Philippine Enterprises	Registered Export Products		Pioneer	Non Pioneer	Registered Exporters	Pioneer	Expanding Enter-prises	Export Enter-prises	
I. INCOME TAX EXEMPTIONS AND DEDUCTIONS AND TAX CREDITS											
Complete exemption from income tax				Yes[3]	Yes[4]	[4]		Yes[5]		Yes[5]	Yes[6]
Reduced income tax rate for a period according to a formula			Yes				Yes		Yes		
Income elements excluded from taxable corporate income											
Special deduction for export income			Yes[2]	Yes							
Concessionary rates on interest accrued on savings deposits								Yes	Yes	Yes	
Concessionary rates on royalty payments								Yes	Yes	Yes	

TABLE 8 (continued)

INCENTIVE	Philippines			Thailand	Malaysia			Singapore			Indonesia
	Pioneer Preferred	Other Preferred Philippine Enterprises	Registered Export Products		Pioneer	Non Pioneer	Registered Exporters	Pioneer	Expanding Enter-prises	Export Enter-prises	
Capital gain from stock issues	1	1	1		Yes	Yes	Yes	Yes	Yes	Yes	
Capital gain from sales of securi-ties	1	1	1		Yes	Yes	Yes	Yes	Yes	Yes	
Capital gain from revaluation of assets					Yes	Yes	Yes	Yes	Yes	Yes	
Income from in-vestment in other enterprises											
Special exclusions from taxable corpo-rate income and tax credits											
Organizational preoperating expenses	Yes	Yes									
Expansion re-investment	Yes	Yes	Yes								
Credit for taxes withheld on in-terest payment on foreign loans	Yes	Yes									

TABLE 8 (continued)

INCENTIVE	Philippines			Thailand	Malaysia			Singapore			Indonesia
	Pioneer Preferred	Other Preferred Philippine Enterprises	Registered Export Products		Pioneer	Non Pioneer	Registered Exporters	Pioneer	Expanding Enter-prises	Export Enter-prises	
Necessary infra-structure works			Yes[7]								
Double deduc-tion of export promotion ex-penses					Yes	Yes	Yes				
Additional de-duction for la-bor training expenses	Yes	Yes	Yes								
Allowance on do-mestic purchases of capital equip-ment	Yes	Yes	Yes								
Allowance for cost of raw materials used for export pro-ducts (or special tax credit)			Yes								
Allowance for ex-penditures on plant equipment				Yes		Yes		Yes			Yes
Accelerated de-preciation	Yes	Yes					Yes	Yes	Yes	Yes	Yes

TABLE 8 (continued)

INCENTIVE	Philippines			Thailand	Malaysia			Singapore			Indonesia
	Pioneer Preferred	Other Preferred Philippine Enterprises	Registered Export Products		Pioneer	Non Pioneer	Registered Exporters	Pioneer	Expanding Enter-prises	Export Enter-prises	
Carry over of net losses	Yes	Yes	Yes		Yes	Yes	Yes				Yes
Reduced income tax for exports based on local raw material and labor usage	Yes	Yes	Yes								
Labor utiliz-ation						Yes	Yes				
Double deduc-tion of trans-portation, elec-tricity, water supply				Yes							
II. IMPORT DUTIES AND TAXES, EXEMPTIONS, AND DEDUCTIONS											
Complete exemp-tion from import duties and taxes	Yes	Yes	Yes	Yes	Yes	Yes	Yes	Yes	Yes	Yes	Yes
Other imports			Yes		Yes	Yes	Yes	Yes	Yes	Yes	
Partial exemption from import duties and taxes											

TABLE 8 (continued)

INCENTIVE	Philippines			Thailand	Malaysia			Singapore			Indonesia
	Pioneer Preferred	Other Preferred Philippine Enterprises	Registered Export Products		Pioneer	Non Pioneer	Registered Exporters	Pioneer	Expanding Enterprises	Export Enterprises	
Other imports				Yes	Yes	Yes	Yes				
III. COMMODITY SALES TAXES, EXEMPTIONS, AND DEDUCTIONS											
Exemptions for exports	Yes	Yes	Yes	Yes				Yes	Yes	Yes	Yes
Other exemptions	Yes		Yes[8]	Yes				Yes	Yes	Yes	Yes
IV. EXEMPTIONS FROM TAXES OTHER THAN INCOME AND COMMODITY/SALES TAX	Yes		Yes[8]	Yes	Yes		Yes	Yes	Yes	Yes	Yes
V. OTHER BENEFITS											
Postoperative tariff protection	Yes	Poss.	Poss.	Yes	Yes	Yes	Yes	Yes	Yes	Yes	
Anti-dumping protection	Yes	Yes	Yes	Yes	Yes	Yes	Yes	Yes	Yes	Yes	
Industrial estates	Yes	Yes	Yes	Yes	Yes	Yes	Yes	Yes	Yes	Yes	

TABLE 8 (continued)

INCENTIVE	Philippines			Thailand	Malaysia			Singapore			Indonesia
	Pioneer Preferred	Other Preferred Philippine Enterprises	Registered Export Products		Pioneer	Non Pioneer	Registered Exporters	Pioneer	Expanding Enter-prises	Export Enter-prises	
Export processing zones or free port facilities	Yes	Yes	Yes		Yes	Yes	Yes	Yes	Yes	Yes	
Export assistance fund	Yes	Yes	Yes								

NOTES: 1. Allowance available to Philippine national investors. However, could also be allowed to foreigners under certain conditions.

2. If in "special" area then only one of these -- special deductions or carry over lossess -- are allowed.

3. For new industries, from three to eight years; 50 percent tax allowance for further five years.

4. The tax relief period varies from three to four years (basic) and to eight years if located in a development area, if a priority product, and if more than 50 percent Malaysian content (one year for each). Dividends from exempt income are not subject to tax. For export industries, tax relief from four to seven years is standard.

5. Available for five years. Extendable up to fifteen years depending on capital intensity.

6. The basic term is two years, but the exemption can be extended up to six years depending on foreign exchange savings, location, infrastructure spending, and the like.

7. If located in special area.

8. If in pioneer area for some of these.

incentives to enterprises, much more control can be placed over their operations and easier cooperation can be obtained.

DESIRABILITY OF INVESTMENT INCENTIVES

The debate over the use of investment incentives has centered on a number of issues. The two most important are whether or not incentives are a major attraction factor for foreign investment and whether or not the way in which incentives are used distorts the industrial structure in a manner contrary to most country's aims.

INCENTIVES AS AN ATTRACTION TO FOREIGN INVESTMENT

In the author's surveys of motivations underlying the establishment of foreign industrial projects in the ASEAN countries, companies were asked to assess the importance of various investment-climate factors in their investment decisions. The results representing the comments of twenty-six major Japanese, United States, and European international companies are summarized in Table 9. The conclusions were not surprising. The factors considered to be very important by the majority of the companies were:[40] political and economic stability; stable labor force; access to local finance; ready availability of foreign exchange; stable currency value; existence of a good joint venture partner; government incentives, especially taxation; and duty free imports.

One interesting fact emerging from interviews is that taxation incentives appear to have been made into an important factor by the developing countries themselves. If taxation incentives did not exist, it is unlikely that the volume of investment in the ASEAN countries would be reduced significantly. Taxation incentives become important in assessing relative climates simply because they exist—which is more important for the low-cost export base investments (for which alternative locations exist) than for resource and local market-oriented investment (for which alternative locations may not exist).

Services normally provided by government development agencies, such as assistance in feasibility studies, arranging joint venture partners, and provision of data bank facilities are not normally regarded as extremely important. Nor are infrastructure and availability of sites on industrial estates of great importance, although such factors rank highly for certain types of projects such as large chemical and metal-working projects.

Overriding all other considerations is the political and economic stability of a country and the stability of its work force. Nearly all companies consider these to be very important factors, and give them heavy weighting in assessing relative investment climates and in determining whether or not to invest. These factors will, *inter alia*, be reflected in a stable currency value, the ready availability of foreign exchange, a good overall economic policy, and a healthy interest by the host country toward the investor—all factors on which the companies place considerable emphasis. Most of the ASEAN countries realize the relative importance of these factors in attracting in-

TABLE 9

Factors Considered by Multinational Enterprises in Assessing the Investment Climate of a Country

Factor	Very Important	Important	Not Important
1. Overall economic planning policy	11	3	2
2. Government incentives			
Taxation	15	10	1
Grants	9	5	12
Duty-free imports	13	10	3
Tariff protection	10	12	4
3. Political and economic stability	26		
4. Existence of planned industrial estates		8	18
5. Assistance by country in feasibility studies	1	6	19
6. Assistance in arranging JV partner	3	7	16
7. Assistance in providing data on locational information	2	16	8
8. Existence of data bank in country	1	9	16
9. Assistance by country during and after establishment	2	16	8
10. Overall interest of country toward investors	9	15	2
11. Existence of training facilities for workers	4	11	11
12. Existence of support facilities	7	15	4
13. Access to local finance	16	9	1
14. Developed manufacturing base		15	11
15. Ready availability of foreign exchange	18	7	1
16. Stable currency value	21	5	
17. Experience of country in high-technology industries	1	9	16
18. Infrastructure			
Ports	11	15	
Roads	10	15	1
Railways	8	16	2
Power	9	17	
Communications	11	15	
19. General living conditions	3	19	4
20. Stable labor force	26		
21. Red tape	6	18	2

vestments and attempt (some successfully) to project an image of stability. They also realize that, overall, incentives become important by their very existence, that is, unless general agreement could be reached (not only among the ASEAN countries but with competing countries outside the

ASEAN region as well) to reduce incentives, competitive forces necessitate their maintenance, especially with the current moves toward export-oriented project promotion. To some extent, the ASEAN countries are attempting to overcome this dilemma by using incentives more selectively. As explained earlier, some are using them in a fashion more applicable to overall social and economic objectives (by emphasizing priorities) as well as to control more easily the operations of local enterprises and to ensure their closer co-operation with the Government. The future should bring an acceleration of the trend in this direction.

INCENTIVES AS A DISTORTING INFLUENCE ON THE INDUSTRIAL STRUCTURE

The argument associated with the distorting influence of incentives on the industrial structure relates mainly to the use of incentives which are biased toward the use of capital-intensive techniques of production while the requirements of the developing countries are for more labor-intensive operations. The main "culprits" in this regard are the tax-free importation of capital equipment, and the accelerated depreciation and reinvestment allowances. The capital-intensive/labor-intensive debate involves complicated issues; the discussion which follows is limited to a few observations on some of the points raised in the debate.

Essentially, those proposing the capital-intensive bias thesis argue that the three incentives cited above are in fact a form of subsidy on capital: They encourage the use of capital-intensive techniques because such techniques become cheaper relative to labor costs (a process which is further enhanced in those countries—such as the Philippines—which set minimum wages and fringe benefits for workers above their true "equilibrium costs"). Further, such policies also discourage the development of a local capital goods industry. While acknowledging that a capital-intensive bias does exist and that perhaps the countries concerned should reduce the subsidy-provided capital to some extent, this author does not believe that the results of such a policy would lead to substantial changes for the following reasons.

First, in Helen Hughes' words, "The choice between capital and labor is not, in the main, in production processes, but in products and industries, and the relatively low employment generated by foreign investment is due (mainly) to its concentration in capital intensive industries encouraged by high protection."[41] In other words, the question is more one of priorities than of the character of projects.

Second, and here again the point has been made by Hughes: "In modern industry there is very little room for the substitution of labor for capital except in preparation and finishing, and here the substitution of labor for capital is common." Hughes goes on to say, "The greater productivity of capital intensive techniques generally exceeds the savings of relatively low labor costs in labor intensive processes, and raw material utilization tends to be much more economic with modern processes. Where products have competition from imports, or are wholly or partly exported, quality requirements frequently impose modern techniques. Labor intensive techniques generally make much heavier demands on skilled and supervisory labor than capital intensive techniques and such labor is usually in acutely short supply."[42]

Third, the question is not always one of prices. There are many examples where companies have imported equipment knowing that they could get the equivalent more cheaply locally because the credit terms offered by the overseas supplier outweighed the price disadvantage, even where the overseas equipment was more sohpisticated and less labor intensive in use. The implication is that attention should be paid to improving the credit position of local suppliers.

Fourth, in some cases equipment of a more capital-intensive nature than might otherwise be used is important because the machinery is familiar and spare parts and servicing are or are believed to be easier to obtain. Considerably more research is thus required into appropriate technologies for the ASEAN countries. Also, more information should be disseminated concerning the local facilities available for constructing equipment and providing spare parts and replacements.

The above points are by way of emphasizing the author's opinion that the capital- vs. labor-intensity question cannot be "solved" by imposing duties and taxes on capital equipment imports and dropping the other incentives which contribute toward use of imported capital-intensive techniques, although it would contribute to some extent. Partial steps are being considered by some of the countries (for example, imposing duties on capital equipment imports with the duties paid over a period of, say, three years), but a much more concerted program toward investigating appropriate technologies and developing the local fabrication industry is required.

Another area of debate relates to the possible "over subsidization" of industry by allowing tariff protection along with taxation incentives. Again, this issue will not be discussed here except to note that one of the reasons for the use of the tariff relates to the relatively slow implementation of anti-dumping protection; if the means could be provided to ensure quick response of the latter device to the requirements of industry, then tariffs could be reduced. The fear of many manufacturers in some of the ASEAN countries is that by reducing tariffs too much, they become more susceptible to "dumping" and, in most cases, the procedures for implementing anti-dumping legislation are too slow.

AGREEMENTS WITH OTHER COUNTRIES RELEVANT TO FOREIGN INVESTMENT

In closing the discussion of incentives and guarantees, it should be pointed out that a number of bilateral agreements have been concluded by the ASEAN countries covering not only taxation agreements, but also general treaties to promote trade and investment. With respect to general bilateral treaties, two main types are found: the comprehensive treaty of friendship, including special provisions on the position of foreign investments; and the specialized treaty exclusively covering the promotion and protection of foreign investment.[43] The United States, Japan, and the United Kingdom, for example, have used the comprehensive treaty exclusively, while West Germany and Switzerland have used both but have been putting increasing emphasis on the specialized treaty.

Relief from double taxation may be given "unilaterally by the capital exporting or the capital importing country, or through bilateral agreements. Such agreements either divide the field of taxation between the two countries, or provide for tax credits on double taxes income.[44] While there are few such agreements in ASEAN countries (with the agreements relating to income and profit taxes, generally providing that non-residents will be taxed only on the income tax in another country), double taxation is not widespread since most countries unilaterally provide some relief.

Of particular importance is the fact that a number of ASEAN countries have ratified the international agreements on Settlement of Industrial Disputes worked out by the United Nations, the World Bank, and others. This agreement came into force in 1966 and an international Chamber of Commerce handles trading disputes between foreign private companies and governments. Also noteworthy is the growing cooperation between some of the Asian countries in the investment field. An example is the ASEAN complementation program currently being mooted. Although no agreement has yet been reached for any specific program, there appears to be great promise for cooperation on this basis. This paper now turns to a discussion of the potential for economic cooperation in ASEAN.

ECONOMIC COOPERATION IN ASEAN

The possibilities for economic cooperation among the ASEAN countries has been explored by a United Nations Study Team over the last three years. Their final report has recently been published. Some of the findings of the report will be highlighted below as it is, in this author's view, one of the most significant studies to emerge in the last few years. Some of the comments made by the multinational corporations on the possibilities of achieving cooperation within the ASEAN region will also be presented, for while these comments were made before the final report of the U.N. Team was published, they still have applicability.

The case for cooperation rests primarily on the advantages of an expanded market and the subsequent larger scales of production in bringing costs in the ASEAN region to levels comparable with those in Western countries. Such developments would allow a potentially larger product/activity mix within the ASEAN region—as a result of the production of goods for the larger market which could not have been economically produced in a fragmented market. It would also allow a reduction in the reliance of the ASEAN countries on imports from other countries and increase their potential to have competitively priced exports. The U.N. Study Team realized, however, that in the ASEAN context, "though the extent of effective cooperation may increase significantly during the 1970s, there will not be as yet a preparedness to accept very close and complete integration in the form of a complete free trade area, a customs union of a common market. It may legitimately be assumed on the other hand, in the light of many economic and political forces working in favor of cooperation, that there will be a welcome for a limited trade liberalization scheme, covering a number of carefully selected commodities and a limited scheme for cooperation in the development of new industrial projects, supplemented by a number of other cooperative measures of a more direct character in the monetary and financial fields, in the provision of agricultural services, in shipping, in tourist facilities, and in other similar forms."[45]

For industrial development, the Team recommended three separate but related techniques for cooperation:[46]

Selective trade liberalization, to be negotiated on a product-by-product basis and gradually applied progressively on a wider scale through a series of annual or biennial negotiations designed to enable the individual countries to reap the advantages associated with the exchange of commodities in which they have a comparative advantage, to allow a movement toward specialization within each country, and to ensure balanced trade among the countries;

A system of complementary agreements, involving the preparation of schemes of specialization for the manufacture of different products within an industry (or in related industries) in each of the countries and their subsequent exchange—the entrepreneurs themselves are encouraged to prepare these schemes;

A system of "package-deal" agreements, involving the negotiation of the governments of the ASEAN countries for the establishment of (principally) new large-scale projects for a limited period in specific ASEAN countries—the necessary tariff and other assistance would be incorporated in the agreements.

The U.N. Team recommended that the industries on which selective trade liberalization should be focused are those which principally compose small- and medium-scale enterprises with underutilized capacity. Each country would prepare a list of selected products in these fields for which it would like concessions, and a list of products for which it would be willing to grant concessions. Initial negotiations could cover such items as textiles, garments, footwear, certain chemicals and pharmaceuticals, selected foodstuffs, household equipment, and other consumer durables.

For the complementarity agreements, large-scale enterprises with "divisible" operations should be involved. The Team suggests that the initial discussions cover three to ten industries from, for example, the fields of appliances and apparatus, rubber products, road motor vehicles, other vehicles, agricultural machinery, pharmaceuticals and cosmetics, electric and nonelectric power generating and distributing equipment, building materials, dry cell batteries, processed foodstuffs, leather products, clothing textiles, and handicrafts.[47] "Package deal" agreements on the other hand should be limited (according to the Team) to the introduction of new large-scale industries or branches of industries not at present established in the ASEAN countries because of the fragmented market. The initial projects considered (twelve to fifteen are recommended) could include nitrogeneous and phosphatic fertilizers, basic chemicals for the man-made fiber industry, sheet glass and newsprint, steel ingots, scaled compressors and other mass-produced electrical items, small diesel engines, typewriters, and similar light engineering products.

To implement effectively such programs, a spirit of cooperation has to evolve within the ASEAN countries. There are beginning signs of such cooperation, with the initial moves on a bilateral basis and the hope of expansion to a regional level. The move toward complementarity arrangements, for example, has taken its first steps in the form of the car manufacturing programs in the Philippines[48] of Ford, General Motors, Toyota, Chrysler, and Volkswagen in which certain components are being produced (engine blocks, transmission units) which will form part of their future ASEAN programs. At present, no overall regional car manufacturing program exists, although there have been initial talks between manufacturers on how such a program can be evolved. In the author's view, regional cooperation must come, but it will be a slow, evolutionary process. In this regard, it is of interest to note the views of the multinational companies and institutions whose executives were interviewed on this matter in the early part of 1972.

VIEWS OF MULTINATIONAL CORPORATIONS ON ECONOMIC COOPERATION FOR ASEAN

According to the executives interviewed, there is no doubt that an ASEAN Common Market (along the lines of the European Common Market, albeit more limited in scope) would be extremely beneficial to the countries involved and would lead to much more rapid growth for the region as a whole. Investment could be rationalized, plants could be operated on more satisfactory scales, intra-regional trade would be encouraged, and a more satisfactory monetary situation vis-à-vis the rest of the world would result. Other likely benefits could be cited (such as the gradual reduction in income disparities), but the above-mentioned appear to be the most important from the capital exporting country's viewpoint. However, all of the interviewees felt that the possibility of such an ASEAN common market in the next ten to fifteen years was extremely limited. Several reasons were given for this belief. The most common were: the problem of determining which countries should be included in the common market, with some companies feeling it should be limited at first, consisting of the present ASEAN countries and others feeling that it should incorporate Australia, Japan, South Korea, and others not now members of ASEAN; the disparities in the economic, social, and political structures of the ASEAN countries would make it too difficult to evolve a satisfactory policy; that most countries need to industrialize to employ their unemployed or underemployed workforce and to raise living standards—under such conditions, where competition for industry and funds would be strong, each would want to gain advantage relative to the others; the fact that some countries in the region are doing much better than others and may not at this stage be willing to give up their position—a point related to the two foregoing ones; and difficulties in having other common laws and codes besides tariffs, incentives, and the like which would be essential for an effective economic union—administration might in itself pose insurmountable problems.

Thus, while a common market was deemed desirable, there was a consensus among the sample interviewed that it is not achievable in the near future. The differences among the countries are so great as to make it difficult to find common ground to bring them together (a difficulty faced even in Europe where the disparities are not nearly so pronounced). Only when development is more equalized and the social and political problems of the various companies more manageable, will a common market become a realistic possibility. However, this is not to imply that the Japanese investors consider it impossible to begin the process toward a common market by achieving cooperation in various fields. The gradual evolvement of *complementarity* programs in the industrial sector is one such possibility which companies have examined and in which they see opportunities.

While officials of the companies and institutions interviewed feel that many of the difficulties cited above would still hinder the evolution of a complementarity program for industrial development in ASEAN, they nonetheless believe that a carefully planned program could be implemented in certain fields. For a number of the companies, however, no particular advantages would accrue to them from such a development. These are companies which do not handle or manufacture products which would lend themselves to such a program, except in the case of "product-swapping" by countries, that is, where one country produces one product, another country a different product, and so on, with appropriate tariff structures to allow such exchanges. Economies could certainly be achieved, but it is doubtful that a satisfactory program on this basis is attainable at the present time. There would even be arguments as to which products a country should have, what is regarded as satisfactory operating scales as opposed to minimum economic scales, the role of the future growth of allocated plants on allocations in later years, and so on. A number of the companies interviewed also stressed that "product-swapping" would cut across the considerations of companies in choosing locations for their enterprises. Their fear is that they may be forced to locate their plants unsuitably. This particularly applies where the differences in plant types adopted by enterprises of the advanced countries to produce certain products are marked.

The two major areas where it is felt complementation programs could and should be implemented are: large-scale indivisible projects such as petrochemical complexes, where economies of scale and/or proximity of activities are necessary; and large-scale divisible projects, such as car manufacturer and assembly where economies of scale are pronounced but proximity of activities is not necessary. The former, by their very nature, would imply only one of a few locations and some product-swapping would be involved. The latter, however, could readily be dispersed and while component swapping would be involved, it would be on a manageable scale.

It is not the purpose here to determine how the companies interviewed would suggest the manner in which a complementation program could be implemented and the forms it could take. Thus, the points discussed related mainly to the determination of the industries which the investors feel would lend themselves readily to such programs and some of the factors which need to be considered by the countries involved in constructing these.

The large-scale indivisible projects would include petrochemical complexes, steel rolling mills, and other basic processing. The difficulty with such industries is that each country would like to possess the base activities itself and this would not be possible. To a considerable extent, the desire of each country to have its own steel mills, petrochemical complex, and the like reflects the belief that these will enourage the development of related activities. This is true to some extent; but in the metal-working field, for example, it is apparent that thc attraction mechanism is now working from the final product end, with the advantages of proximity between intermediate units (such as foundries and forges) and principal units (final producers) the significant factor. Obviously, there are advantages in having all the related activities together, but it is certainly not essential. Also, the location of the appropriate raw materials would be a limiting factor in the location of these basic activities and this would mean that some countries would lose out completely unless a careful policy framework was formulated which enabled adequate "compensation" to these countries—a most difficult task. Thus, the companies do not see significant agreement among ASEAN countries for such large-sale indivisible projects to be part of a complementarity program, although from the investors' viewpoint they constitute the most desirable fields for cooperation.

The large-scale divisible projects are, on the other hand, fields where agreements could be reached. Car manufacture and assembly is being mooted at the present time. Other possibilities include ship building (but not for some components), farm machinery and equipment, telecommunications equipment, motor scooter and cycles, commercial vehicles, and other fields which require mostly standard components for their manufacture. However, a fragmented approach should be avoided if possible, and a number of these industries (with the exception of cars) would require considerations on a regional basis. These would have to include the following factors:

1. A careful evaluation of the market is essential. For some products, the market in ASEAN as a whole is still not sufficient to support the most economical size plants for components. Toyota, for example, stated that even in Australia where the market for cars is five times that of the combined Southeast Asian market, certain of the components are produced at a cost considerably higher than in Japan because full economies cannot be achieved. Markets outside the ASEAN region may thus have to be taken into account.

2. It is necessary to select the goods to be produced carefully and in some cases it may be necessary to influence the purchasing patterns of the population. For example, the customers for cars in ASEAN are normally the richer sections of the area's population, and they tend to prefer individualized cars as opposed to an "Asian car." This is possible to overcome to some extent. It would nonetheless affect the components which could be standardized. It is accepted by the Japanese that assembly, "one-off" compo-

nents, and some components produced on machinery used for other products and components, could be produced in each country.

3. Related groups of products would have to be considered in many cases. The components which could be produced in separate plants would then have a number of outlets making the economies of large-scale production operational. This would even apply to car and commercial vehicle assembly —some components are common to each and joint consideration would enable economic-sized plants for certain components to be achieved which may not be feasible if only one of these outlets could be relied on.

4. Parallel conisderation would have to be given to quality control and standardization, probably through some kind of regional body. British standards, for example, apply in some countries and United States standards in others. Much of the standard purpose equipment adopted for certain components is not flexible between these measures of standards. The companies place considerable emphasis on the problems of quality control, even in their existing ASEAN plants where quality varies considerably. The countries involved in a regional program would thus have to ensure that some mechanism is established which enables regular quality checks so that adequate control is maintained, although large companies could handle this themselves.

5. A mechanism to enable synchronization of establishment of the units and the free-flow of components among countries is essential, especially if different companies are involved. Many of the problems which would arise would be minimized if one company was controlling all, or most, of the plants, but this may not be desired or feasible.

6. The governments should, in the planning stages, involve relevant manufacturers so as to obtain their ideas and gain familiarity with the likely problems (as recommended by the U.N. Team). The companies certainly demonstrated a willingness to help in this way.

The presence of problems, as outlined by the companies, should not be taken to mean that a complementarity program for ASEAN is not, in their view, feasible. On the contrary, they feel it is feasible, and a number of companies have already been considering some of the possibilities. But the foregoing are serious problems which the companies feel have to be faced in evolving workable programs.

CONCLUDING REMARKS

This paper has attempted to provide an overview of the ASEAN foreign investment policies as these relate to the objectives and development strategies of the countries concerned. Certainly there are differences among the various countries, but each regards foreign investment as a means to an end rather than an end in itself. Thus, their concern to pursue policies that will guide foreign investment into fields where it can contribute most to national objectives, noting that careful evaluation is made not only of the overall costs and benefits of foreign direct investment in certain projects, but also on the costs and benefits of obtaining technology, markets, and the like through such other means as technical assistance agreements, "turnkey" contracts, the use of consultants, and so on. In the past, the ASEAN countries have often given special privileges to foreign direct investments where the same technology and management skills could have been readily and more cheaply obtained by, for example, the use of consultants or technical assistance agreements. The "package" nature of equity investments (incorporating know-how, finance, and markets, for example) is recognized, however, and such packages are difficult to obtain by other means of know-how transfer than direct foreign investment.

As for the multinational companies, they have a role to play in the development of the ASEAN region. If they have an understanding of the philosophy behind the laws and regulations of the ASEAN countries and are willing and able to compromise their "internationalism" with the host countries' "nationalism," where required, then a happy "marriage" can result.

NOTES

1. Throughout, the terms "direct foreign investment" and "foreign investment" are used interchangeably to refer to *equity investments* in industrial projects. The ASEAN region constitutes the countries of Thailand, Malaysia, Singapore, Indonesia, and the Philippines.

2. Comments by officials of the parent corporations, of ranking executives in the region headquarters, and of the executives of some of the ASEAN-based companies, provided basic data for the study.

3. The provision of machinery and equipment as a trading consideration for establishing an overseas affiliate, important during the 1960s, appears to be decreasing in importance.

4. Note that investments of Japanese, European, and United States enterprises in Hong Kong, Taiwan, and South Korea (not included in the figures for Tables 1 and 2) are heavily concentrated in low-cost base activities. Among the ASEAN countries, this motive has only been important in Singapore.

5. British investment in Singapore and Malaysia is an exception here, although few of these have been because of the desire for lower cost overseas bases.

6. Pollution, of course, is now an important problem in the developed countries, and their governments are imposing heavy penalties on activities regarded as generating pollutants. Many companies are now searching for sites in developing countries for such activities, putting the developing countries in the position of having to reassess their own policies toward pollution.

7. See Helen Hughes, "The Assessment of Policies Towards Foreign Investment in the Asian-Pacific Region" for a more detailed discussion of these points. (Paper presented at the Third Pacific Trade and Development Conference, 1970.)

8. The information was obtained during the course of the surveys referred to previously.

9. Indonesia is still putting emphasis on resource development and import substitution, while Singapore is placing considerable stress on "upgrading" the technology of existing (mainly export-oriented) industry by encouraging more component production and the introduction of more sophisticated products and processing techniques. It is, in effect, trying to become the "Switzerland of Asia"—a strategy it has to pursue to survive without resources and with small markets. Would Singapore's strategy have been different if it had a large market and/or resources?

10. This is not to say that the import replacement strategy should not have been adopted. It has served to start the industrialization process, which may have been difficult to achieve with other strategies. After all, balanced growth does not seem possible; it may be that a "series of disequilibria" is part and parcel of the growth mechanism.

11. By the late 1970s, the desire for low-cost export-oriented bases will probably be the most important motive for multinational investments. It was also apparent from interviews that considerable emphasis during the next few years will be placed on resource-oriented investments (especially by Japanese companies) to ensure that adequate raw materials are available. The companies envisage, however, a slow-down in resource-oriented flows by the end of the 1970s since adequate sources should have been developed by then and the retained earnings of the overseas operations should have grown sufficiently for the self-financing of many of the projects.

12. Also, host countries will have to be more careful as the interests of the multi-national companies are more "company" than "country" oriented.

13. The investment agencies do not always act in isolation. They may serve as initial contact and coordinating agencies involving other ministries and departments in various aspects of investment regulation.

14. Without discussing the complexities or procedures for project approval, it might be noted that these also range from simple straight-forward procedures as in Singapore to complex and frustrating procedures as in Indonesia (the latter have been improved somewhat with recent administrative changes).

15. See Charles Draper, "Benefits Foreign Investment Can Provide: Issues," *Economic Cooperation Bulletin 1*(ECOCEN: January, 1973).

16. There are also areas in which the extent of foreign ownership and control is restricted, as discussed later in the paper.

17. See Table 5 for an indication of the areas in the ASEAN countries closed to foreign investment.

18. In the early Investment Priorities Plan, considerable reliance was placed on the private sector for determining priorities.

19. The development of industry sector programs represent a new attempt in the Philippines to integrate industrial priorities more fully.

20. Source: Board of Investments, Thailand.

21. Foreign Investment Board, Indonesia.

22. The very assumption that economic rationality can be determined in such circumstances is debatable.

23. This point is discussed in greater detail later in the paper.

24. For the local market Singapore does possess, it has not found it worthwhile to be extremely stringent on local ownership and control, simply because it is insignificant as an attraction factor for investment. This attitude may change as more "inter-mediate" and service industries develop.

25. Indonesia requires reapproval of projects after thirty years, presumably in the direction of greater local participation. All of the ASEAN countries encourage gradual local participation, where no restrictions exist.

26. For the trading companies, controlling interest is even less important, unless an associated Japanese manufacturing company is also involved in the venture. The main concerns of trading companies are trading relations and ensuring adequate management and marketing for their projects.

27. Investments of many of these large companies in Japan, however, have been on a fifty-fifty basis (and in some cases, a minority basis). Thus, "special" markets are sometimes exempted from the strict application of the majority-owned principle.

28. This remark was made by one of the executives interviewed.

29. For example, host countries might prefer investments in rural areas or depressed area locations. It should be noted that restrictions on land ownership do not seem to cause much concern to investors.

30. Other general restrictions listed in Table 6 are not discussed, as the table is self-explanatory on these. Not listed in the table are the general restrictions incorporated in company, commercial, and other laws which apply to all enterprises. The mining and petroleum laws do, however, require detailed explanation, but this is not attempted in the present paper.

31. Regulations concerning the issuance of work permits, registration of aliens living in the countries, and so on, while concerns related to the question of the employment of foreign nationals, are not considered in the present discussion.

32. The Export-Import Bank of Japan, "Japanese Private Investment Abroad: Survey," 1972. Local banks account for 41 percent of the funds for establishment; the figure is 62 percent if local branches of Japanese banks are included.

33. Many of these conditions also apply to local investment.

34. If firms agree to export, they can have a greater capacity.

35. Care is also taken in scrutinizing project agreements relating to franchise arrangements.

36. Initially, most of these components (engine blocks, transmission units, car bodies) will be exported to Japan, Australia, and the United States.

37. The question of type of technology to be adopted is of extreme importance, and obviously is closely related to local content. However, it is only touched on briefly in the following section of the paper on "Desirability of Investment Incentives."

38. It was too cumbersome to include all the qualifications for each incentive in the various countries.

39. It is of interest to note that the proposed legislation for Papua New Guinea (outside the ASEAN region, of course) reflects the desire to use incentives to encourage enterprises to export and locate in less-developed areas rather than as an attraction *per se* for foreign investment.

40. These exclude such basic motivation factors as market size and resource availability, which are "preconditions" for considering investment.

41. Hughes, *op cit.*, p. 24.

42. *Ibid.* It is interesting to note the views of Swiss industries on this point. In interviews with Swiss companies it was stressed that it is dangerous to take the concept of labor intensiveness too far at the plant level; that by adopting lower technologies not only is quality sacrificed, but the developing country would find the technology gap becoming even wider, as Swiss research and development concentrates on capital-intensive techniques (because in Switzerland labor is in short supply). In other words, the gap would widen between the technology adopted in the developing country and the technology being adopted in other parts of the world, and competitiveness of the former would suffer. It is thus important, the Swiss say, for developing countries to use the latest techniques and look to growth as a supplier of employment opportunities (and, to some extent, to horizontal as opposed to vertical integration) rather than labor intensiveness in the production of specific commodities.

43. See M. Sakurai, "Review of Laws and Practices Covering Foreign Investment in Developing Countries of the Region and Measures to Improve the Investment Climate in Them." (ECAFE: Asian Conference on Industrialization, September, 1970), pp. 33-35.

44. *Ibid.*, p. 27.

45. "Economic Cooperation for ASEAN" (*Report of a United Nations Team, 1973*), p. 29.

46. *Ibid.*, Part VI: "Summary of Principal Recommendations."

47. Some of the items on this initial list of the U.N. Team are surprising—for example, handicrafts and clothing.

48. The Philippines has defined local content to include export of components, with the ASEAN program in mind.

4

China's Trade Policy and Sino-American Relations

Alexander Eckstein

IN June 1971, a month before Henry Kissinger's secret trip to Peking, the United States lifted the trade and payments embargo that had been in effect on the Chinese People's Republic ever since 1949. The move followed a number of lesser measures of relaxation taken from 1969 onward, and of course set the stage for the Kissinger visit and President Nixon's trip in February 1972. In the Shanghai Communiqué, the two nations agreed "to facilitate the progressive development of trade between their two countries."

Roughly four years after these dramatic events, it is a good time to take stock of the trade aspect of the Sino-American relationship. For it has followed a course few, if any, would have predicted in 1971. On the import side, to be sure, there has been the slow and gradual upward trend that seemed logical, from both political and economic standpoints, for the trade pattern as a whole. But U.S. exports to China have been a different story, rising much more rapidly in 1973 and 1974 than anyone had forecast—so much so that America became, next to Japan, China's most important supplier. Then, in the current year of 1975, exports have been dropping back so sharply that it now looks as though total trade both ways will be less than half the levels of the two previous years. As shown in Table I, these divergent export and import trends have also produced very wide fluctuations in the Sino-American trade balance, which rises from a 2:1 ratio in our favor in 1972 to almost 12:1 in 1973 and then (based on current projections) reverts to less than 2:1 in 1975.

TABLE I

U.S.-CHINA TRADE, 1971–1975

(in millions of U.S. dollars)

	1971	*1972*	*1973*	*1974*	*1975*
U.S. Exports	0.0	63.5	739.7	820.5	250
U.S. Imports	4.9	32.4	63.9	114.7	150
Total Trade Turnover	4.9	95.9	803.6	935.2	400

SOURCES: The data for 1971 to 1974 were obtained from *U.S.-China Business Review,* March-April 1975, p. 19. 1975 figures represent U.S. Department of Commerce projections developed in William Clarke and Martha Avery, "The Sino-American Commercial Relationship," *China: A Reassessment of the Economy,* Joint Economic Committee, 94th Congress, First Session, Washington: GPO, July 1975, pp. 500–534.

Why these drastic fluctuations? Are we seeing here the renewed impact of political factors, especially on the Chinese side? Or are there serious disabilities, partly political and partly economic, that account for the United States being only a residual supplier of grain to China, and only a minor source for the industrial plants that China has been purchasing since 1972?

These are central questions for the current and future state of Sino-American relations generally. But before one can provide reasonable answers one must look at the foreign economic policy of the People's Republic as a subject in itself. For the cumulative evidence of the last four years clearly shows that in this period China has not only embarked on a major shift in her foreign policy, including the separate rapprochements with the United States and Japan, but has adopted far-reaching changes in her trade policy and indeed in her whole outlook toward close economic relations with foreign countries. The nature, depth, and permanence of these changes are vital elements in any estimate of the future policies of China under the successors to Mao Tse-tung and Chou En-lai.

II

The fall of Lin Piao in September 1971—and his death in an airplane crash between China and Russia—marked the culmination of a period in which the role of the military in China had been very much enlarged. With the virtual disintegration of the Party apparatus during the Cultural Revolution (1966–68), the Army was called upon to perform many Party roles and to serve as the cement holding the polity and economy together.

This enlarged political role of the Army was reinforced by rising Sino-Soviet tensions, aggravated by the enunciation of the Brezhnev Doctrine and the Soviet invasion of Czechoslovakia in 1968. The perception of a grave Soviet threat apparently spread and gained increasing credibility in China thereafter. The accumulated tensions then exploded in the Chenpao (Damyanski) Island incident of March 1969, leading to large-scale border clashes between Soviet and Chinese troops along the Amur river border. All these developments combined seem to have then prompted a rapid rise in military outlays between 1969 and 1971.

However, during 1971, it appears that the Chinese leadership must have engaged in a fundamental reappraisal of its internal and external policies. In part, of course, this reappraisal must already have been under way, as shown by Mao's interview with Edgar Snow in December 1970 in which he indicated that Nixon would be welcome to visit

China "either as a tourist or as President."[1]

Perhaps most notably, the steep rise in military expenditures was not only halted but reversed, so that since 1972—according to analyses recently published—Chinese military expenditures may have declined by as much as 25 percent measured in constant dollars.[2] Never formally announced by the Chinese leaders, the reasons for this abrupt change can only be surmised: one, quite possibly, was that the perception of a Soviet threat seemed less acute. With the reopening of relations with the United States virtually assured after the Kissinger trip, Chinese policy-makers may have begun to rely implicitly and tacitly at least on American deterrence to check incipient or overt Soviet expansionist tendencies in Asia.

Internal needs and developments must also have contributed to the shift in the allocation of resources. As the Party was being reconstituted in the post-Cultural Revolution period, it was once more bidding for supremacy of control over all institutions including the Army. Shrinking military expenditures would necessarily involve some reduction in the Army's control over resources. At the same time, the Cultural Revolution-engendered disruptions had led to a decline in the nonagricultural sectors of the economy, and there was also an accumulated backlog of investment forgone during this period. These deficiencies had been made more critical by the 1969–71 subordination of economic requirements to military claims on resources.

It seems probable that debate on these issues was acute while Lin was still alive and in good standing, and that he himself was deeply involved. Whether his fall reflected or triggered a denouement we shall perhaps never know. In any case, the full thrust of a new line of policy began to emerge after his death.

Basically this new line raises the priority ranking assigned to sustained and long-range economic development. It has been evidenced in the decisions taken by the Chinese leadership and in the large number of new projects launched since early 1972, and was most clearly, explicitly, and authoritatively enunciated recently in Premier Chou En-lai's Report on the Work of the Government delivered at the National People's Congress in January 1975. In this speech he sketched out his hopes for China's future economic development, speaking of turning "a poverty-stricken and backward country into a socialist one with the beginnings of prosperity in only twenty years

[1] *Life*, April 30, 1971.

[2] Sidney H. Jammes, "The Chinese Defense Burden, 1965–74," *China: A Reassessment of the Economy*, pp. 459–466.

and more." Before the end of the century, China "is to accomplish the comprehensive modernization of agriculture, industry, national defense and science and technology so that our national economy will be advancing in the front ranks of the world."[3]

The full sweep of actions under the new development policy need not detain us here. From the standpoint of foreign economic policy, the key point is that the leadership appears to have recognized from the outset that the central elements in the new policy—increased investment, stress on more fertilizer production and other agricultural assistance, and advanced technology generally—inevitably called for increased imports of capital goods and even of some capital. And the leadership could not proceed very far along this road without coming into conflict with the more or less autarkic Chinese foreign trade policy that had dominated the 1960s.

Since 1949 Chinese policy-makers have in effect pursued three different foreign trade policies. In the 1950s they followed an open and active foreign trade orientation. China's foreign trade grew at an average annual rate of 15 percent (in real terms) between 1952 and 1959, much faster than GNP, so that in a literal sense the Chinese economy was becoming more rather than less foreign-trade oriented.[4] Foreign trade was leading growth in an economy in which it necessarily constituted a quite small sector. And, in particular, the Chinese economy became heavily dependent on the Soviet Union; foreign trade expansion meant primarily a rapid growth in commercial exchanges with the U.S.S.R. and Eastern Europe.

About 1960 this trade policy was reversed, and the Chinese turned to a policy of "self-reliance," interpreted at that time as import minimization. The triggering event was, of course, the rising Sino-Soviet tension that led to the sudden withdrawal of Russian technicians in 1960. A number of complete plant projects had to be left standing in an unfinished state for years, and there was a significant delay in the Chinese nuclear program and a disruption in the weapons procurement process. Faced with these consequences of the Soviet withdrawal, the Chinese apparently resolved not to become dependent again on any foreign country.

The withdrawal of Soviet technicians happened to coincide with the onset of a deep economic depression (1960-62) in the wake of the failure of the Great Leap Forward. This depression forced the Chinese to cut back exports, thus reducing their earnings of foreign

[3] "Report on the Work of the Government," *Peking Review,* No. 4, January 24, 1975, pp. 23–25.

[4] Alexander Eckstein, "China's Economic Growth and Foreign Trade," *U.S.-China Business Review,* July–August 1974, p. 16.

exchange. Therefore imports had to be curtailed sharply. At the same time the economic decline led to large cutbacks in investment and to an attendant shrinkage of machinery and equipment imports. Concurrently, the scarce foreign exchange had to be husbanded for financing grain imports needed for filling part of the gap left by a succession of poor harvests. Thus China's economic growth rate was significantly reduced in the 1960s, and the combination of slow growth and autarkic trade policy naturally produced a stagnation in foreign trade levels.

TABLE II

THE FOREIGN TRADE OF THE CHINESE PEOPLE'S REPUBLIC, 1950–74.

(in millions of U.S. dollars)

Year	*In current prices*		*In constant 1963 prices*	
	Exports	*Imports*	*Exports*	*Imports*
1950	620	590	NA	NA
1951	780	1,120	NA	NA
1952	875	1,015	795	1,005
1953	1,040	1,255	995	1,295
1954	1,060	1,290	930	1,345
1955	1,375	1,660	1,295	1,715
1956	1,635	1,485	1,560	1,555
1957	1,615	1,440	1,530	1,380
1958	1,940	1,825	1,940	1,825
1959	2,230	2,060	2,315	2,085
1960	1,960	2,030	1,920	2,070
1961	1,525	1,490	1,540	1,520
1962	1,525	1,150	1,585	1,180
1963	1,570	1,200	1,570	1,200
1964	1,750	1,470	1,685	1,435
1965	2,035	1,845	2,005	1,785
1966	2,210	2,035	2,155	1,915
1967	1,945	1,950	1,930	1,840
1968	1,945	1,820	1,920	1,735
1969	2,030	1,830	1,920	1,690
1970	2,050	2,240	1,865	1,890
1971	2,415	2,305	2,180	1,880
1972	3,085	2,835	2,570	2,115
1973	4,895	4,975	3,000	2,760
1974 (preliminary)	6,305	7,410	2,765	3,165

SOURCE: Nai-ruenn Chen, "China's Foreign Trade, 1950–74," in *China: A Reassessment of the Economy*, p. 645.

As may be seen in Table II, China's foreign trade peaked in 1959 and thereafter exports and imports fluctuated around a more or less stable level until 1972. Foreign trade lagged behind growth so that the economy was becoming less foreign-trade oriented. The trade share of GNP dropped from an estimated 8 percent in the 1950s to perhaps around 5 percent for Chinese exports and imports combined. This compares with 7 percent for the United States, 15 percent for India, 18 percent for Brazil, and 22 percent for Japan, with much higher ratios for small countries. Thus even by the standards of the large continental economies, China's trade ratio was (and still is) low.

This autarkic policy of the 1960s was apparently relaxed, on present evidence, in 1971 or 1972. While the Chinese continue to speak of "self-reliance," more and more it has become evident that the slogan has been reinterpreted. Apparently, it no longer means minimizing imports. On the contrary, it implies a much more open foreign-trade orientation. To the extent that "self-reliance" still has any of its old meanings, this may be in the sense of seeking to minimize the country's foreign *financial* dependence. The Chinese have repeatedly stressed that they are not interested in foreign credits, and are not prepared to accept these. China's foreign trade must be self-financed and, in principle, should be constrained by the country's ability to export and earn foreign exchange. We shall see later whether even this principle has been strictly followed in actual practice.

III

China's new international economic policy became visible in several quite dramatic ways. Foreign trade was expanded very rapidly, a large program of importing complete plants was launched and a most substantial expansion of oil production and exports was decided upon. At the same time, major commitments have been made to developing the whole foreign trade infrastructure, that is, port facilities, shipping, pipelines, railways and aviation.

As noted before, China's foreign trade contracted very sharply in the early 1960s, reaching its low point in 1962. It then nearly recovered to 1959 levels by 1966, only to experience a setback due to disruptions engendered by the Cultural Revolution. By 1971 foreign trade not only started to recover once again but was clearly following a vigorous expansionary path. As a result, former peak levels were finally exceeded in 1972. This was followed in 1973 by a dramatic 35 percent rise in imports and a 15 percent increase in exports, representing a sharp spurt in total trade turnover, all expressed in real terms. The marked rise—particularly in imports—resulted from greatly stepped-up purchases of capital equipment, industrial materials and grains, to fuel the invigorated development program on the one hand and to fill the food supply gap on the other. The last was an emergency action probably outside the original plans; we shall come back to this in the context of Sino-American trade relations.

An ambitious plant import program was initiated in late 1972, with the first contracts signed in December of that year. This involves sales to China of complete factories and power plants, with the buildings constructed by the Chinese. Machinery and equipment are transported to China, to be installed with the assistance of foreign technicians, who also help in the training of engineers and other operational personnel charged with running the plant. Between December 1972 and the spring of 1975, the Chinese entered into approximately 45 contracts for the purchase of about 100 complete plants valued at around 2.2 to 2.5 billion U.S. dollars.[5]

This is clearly a very massive program which will greatly augment China's present production capacity, particularly in steel, petrochemicals, chemical fertilizer and electric power generation, the industries in which most of the purchases are concentrated. The scope and importance of the program can perhaps best be gauged in comparison with plant imports from the Soviet Union and Eastern Europe in the 1950s. Building on foundations previously laid and representing the core of the first five-year plan, that earlier program went a long way toward creating China's present industrial base; in terms of 1973 prices it was a three-billion-dollar program first conceived about 1950 and executed over the period roughly from 1953 to 1960, at an average annual rate of delivery of about $430 million. By comparison it now appears that virtually all the plants bought between late 1972 and early 1975 will be put in place over a three-year period, between 1975 and 1978, representing an annual delivery rate of about $700 to $800 million. Therefore on an annual basis the present program is much more intensive than the complete plant imports of the 1950s, although in the aggregate it is still about 25 percent smaller.

If the program of importing complete plants bears a significant resemblance to Chinese undertakings in the 1950s (except, of course, as to source), the second striking feature of post-1971 trade policy—China's increasing role as an oil exporter—is entirely new and original in Chinese economic history. Until the 1960s it was generally thought that China was poorly endowed with oil resources. Indeed, Chinese crude oil production was quite small and the country was dependent on imported supplies of petroleum and its products, mostly from the Soviet Union. As part and parcel of the self-reliance policy and to free themselves from dependence on the Soviets, the Chinese then embarked on a most active program of geological exploration.

[5] Based on "Plant Sales to China," *U.S.-China Business Review*, No. 1, Vol. 1, pp. 36–38; No. 2, Vol. 1, p. 10; No. 3, Vol. 1, pp. 38–41; No. 5, Vol. 1, pp. 8–15; No. 6, Vol. 1, pp. 8–9.

As a result, sizable deposits were discovered in North and Northeast China, the Pohai Gulf, and offshore along the continental shelf.

Although the Chinese have said little to this day about the scope of these discoveries, their impact became apparent in a small way even in the mid-1960s when the Chinese ceased to have to import oil. By the early 1970s China was exporting small marginal quantities, and the leadership must have been aware that it had, in oil, a major potential asset that could transform China's capacity to earn foreign exchange. It is intriguing to speculate on the weight this revelation may have had in setting the new overall policy; what is clear is that the Chinese have for some years been making the heavy investments—in exploration and drilling, and now in shipping—required to develop and sell their oil in quantity abroad.

Thus, in recent years, we have seen a dramatic rise in Chinese oil production and especially in exports. Total output, a mere 5 million tons a year in 1961 (or 100,000 barrels per day), has now been estimated at 54 million tons in 1973 and 65 million tons in 1974. (By comparison, Indonesia's 1974 production was 70 million tons.) And in 1974 exports of oil first became a substantial entry in the Chinese trade ledger; between 5.5 and 6 million tons were exported, and the return to China was around an estimated $500 million, or approximately 8 percent of China's total export earnings. The bulk of the 1974 shipments went to Japan, about 500,000 tons were destined for the smaller countries of Asia, and 1 to 1.5 million tons went to North Korea and North Vietnam.[6]

The best present estimate is that in the current year, 1975, Chinese oil exports will rise to 10 million tons (or 200,000 barrels per day). Japanese energy planners, perhaps the best-informed foreigners on the subject, currently project Chinese oil shipments of 30 to 50 million tons to Japan by 1980. Should these materialize they would provide about 10 to 15 percent of Japan's oil import requirements.[7]

Actually in projecting China's oil export capabilities and Japanese purchases of this oil over the next five to ten years, a number of complex factors must be taken into account. As indicated above, China's 1974 oil production was estimated at 65 million tons (or 1.3 million barrels per day). There seems to be a fair degree of consensus among oil industry and energy specialists who have followed Chinese developments that 200 million tons may be a reasonable production estimate for 1980. This is projected on the assumption that output will grow at

[6] Bobby A. Williams, "Chinese Petroleum Industry: Growth and Prospects," *China: A Reassessment of the Economy,* pp. 228, 239–40.

[7] Based on interviews with Japanese economists, government officials and businessmen in April and May 1975.

an average rate of 20 percent per year and that virtually all of it will come from fields in which drilling is already under way.

These fields are preponderantly onshore, with some drilling anticipated in the shallow waters of the Pohai Gulf, close to shore. To attain these production levels will require additional investment in drilling facilities, pipelines, and harbor facilities so as to get the oil transported. On present indications, these investments do not seem to be beyond China's capabilities either in terms of the resources or technology required.

This process could be greatly accelerated if the Chinese wished to commit themselves to rapid development of offshore drilling. Correspondingly, it could be slowed down if the necessary investments for further expansion of onshore drilling and for transport were not sustained. At present the development of oil production is clearly assigned top priority along with food and steel, as was underlined again this spring by Vice-Premier Teng in a meeting with a group of American newspaper editors. One can of course never rule out the possibility that these priorities may be altered, but barring a major political upheaval or economic disaster this is not too likely over the next few years.

Quite powerful economic and foreign policy considerations converge in support of a high priority for the development of the petroleum industry. Rising oil exports can greatly augment China's foreign exchange earnings. At the same time they can minimize Japan's inducements to invest in the development of Siberian oil resources, thus also diminishing Japan's interest in seeking closer economic and political links with the Soviet Union. However, China's interest in the development of her oil resources has at least up to now not gone so far as to encourage a large-scale program of offshore exploration and drilling. Given the highly complex technology involved, such a program would require some form of technical assistance by major international oil companies, apparently on terms which are not compatible even with China's liberalized self-reliance policy. Therefore, on the basis of present indications, the Chinese prefer to embark on this effort by themselves, purchasing the drilling rigs, other equipment and technical assistance abroad as needed but managing the whole enterprise themselves. This will necessarily be a slower development, but in the light of the considerable potential for onshore exploitation in the next five years at least, there is no great pressure on them to accelerate the offshore program.

This analysis of China's oil export potential has thus far only considered factors bearing on supply availability. What about the character of demand and markets for this oil? Given Japan's geographic proximity and almost total dependence on imported oil, she can be justifiably viewed as the most natural or logical outlet for China's surplus. Nevertheless, there are a number of conflicting considerations that must be taken into account in assessing China's prospects in the Japanese oil market.

First of all, Chinese oil has certain peculiar characteristics. Some of it is of low quality (e.g., Shengli oil), primarily suitable for burning as fuel. This does not apply to most of the exported product, which has a low sulphur but high wax content and leaves a heavy residue after refining—quite similar to Indonesian but different from Middle Eastern oil. Since Japanese refineries are largely geared to processing Middle Eastern oil, Chinese oil presents special problems and requires special refining equipment or devices. Therefore the market for this type of oil is limited and must be shared with Indonesia.

Since the Japanese have a strong interest in maintaining close links with Indonesia, they consider it most important to continue importing sizable quantities of oil from there. Necessarily this then constrains the demand for China's oil in Japan. The problem is further complicated by shipping bottlenecks—specifically the inability of Chinese ports to accommodate large tankers so that most of the oil has to be shipped in smaller bottoms which drives up the transport costs. However, there are several counteracting factors at work. Viewed from the perspective of the Japanese government, an important national objective is to diversify the country's sources of oil supply and thus minimize the risks attendant upon primary dependence on Middle Eastern oil. Therefore from the standpoint of long-run energy policy, there is a strong incentive for the Japanese government to subsidize the importation and refining of Chinese oil, and in fact various schemes designed to accomplish this are under active consideration.

There is also a serious concern that unless the Chinese can find an outlet for their products, they will not have the purchasing power required to buy Japanese machinery, equipment and other products. In these terms, too, Chinese oil imports are much more welcome than textile shipments which compete directly with Japanese textile manufactures. Finally, political considerations reinforce the economic factors cited. There seems to be a strong and deep commitment in Japan today to develop closer links with China and to use trade as perhaps the most important avenue for building a long-term relationship between these two neighbors.

Thus, what may be emerging in China's foreign trade is a new pattern. As Table III shows, until recently China has been selling agricultural products (including rice) and textiles, the proceeds of which are used to purchase wheat, some other grains, chemical fertilizer, machinery and a variety of other products. However, the Chinese have experienced increasing difficulties in placing their cotton textiles, silk and some other products in recent years, and this in turn has placed definite constraints on the level of trade.

Viewed from this perspective, China's rapidly rising oil production

TABLE III

COMMODITY COMPOSITION OF CHINA'S TRADE, 1966 AND 1973

(in percentages)

Imports	1966	1973
Foodstuffs, of which	26	20
Grains	(20)	(17)
Crude materials, fuels and edible oils, of which	17	20
Rubber	(4)	(3)
Textile fibers	(7)	(8)
Chemicals, of which	12	9
Fertilizers	(8)	(4)
Manufactures, of which	45	50
Textile yarn & fibers	(2)	(1)
Iron and steels	(11)	(19)
Nonferrous metals	(3)	(8)
Machinery and equipment	(22)	(17)
Other	1	1
Total, in percent	100	100
in millions of dollars	2,035	4,975

Exports	1966	1973
Foodstuffs, of which	28	33
Animals, meat & fish	(10)	(10)
Grains	(7)	(11)
Fruits & vegetables	(5)	(5)
Crude materials, fuels and edible oil, of which	22	18
Oil seeds	(4)	(2)
Textile fibers	(5)	(6)
Crude animal materials	(4)	(3)
Chemicals	4	5
Manufactures, of which	42	44
Textile yarns & fabrics	(14)	(16)
Clothing	(8)	(6)
Iron and steel	(4)	(2)
Nonferrous metals	(2)	(1)
Other	5	1
Total, in percent	100	100
in millions of dollars	2,210	4,895

(Components may not add to totals shown due to rounding.)

SOURCE: Nai-ruenn Chen, "China's Foreign Trade, 1950–74," in *China: A Reassessment of the Economy,* Tables A.2 and A.3, pp. 646 and 647.

and exports provide an opportunity for breaking away from the old constraints on her trade. In effect, the new oil exports pave the way for a continued high level of imports of plant and equipment. Since these developments are quite recent they do not yet show up in the figures presented in Table III but may be expected to appear clearly in China's export and import data for 1974 and 1975. If this is in fact to be the pattern at least for the next few years, its significance is very great indeed.

Certainly this transformation in China's trading pattern must pose some political dilemmas. It could significantly augment China's involvement in the international economy, and thus expose the Chinese economy to the vagaries and uncertainties of the world market—as we shall see was amply demonstrated in 1974. An enlarged international sector may also entail more contact between foreigners and Chinese businessmen, officials, technicians, scientists and others. One of the prime avenues for extensive contacts is provided by the complete plant program. For instance, the construction of the large steel complex in Wuhan—being jointly installed by DEMAG and Nippon Steel—will require the presence of 20 German and 200 Japanese technicians in China and a six-month stay for training by Chinese in Japan. There will be approximately 250 to 300 Americans engaged in the installation of eight fertilizer plants, with perhaps a maximum of 100 to 120 present at any one time for periods ranging from two to fifteen months. It has been crudely estimated that a total of 2,000 to 3,000 foreign technicians will be stationed in China between 1974 and 1977. This then may not only bring with it transfer of foreign technology, but transfer of foreign ideas, approaches and influences.

These issues have clearly been debated in the top ranks of the leadership—as evidenced by occasional attacks on the policy in the Chinese press and by periodic rebuttals and counterattacks. They have almost certainly constituted one of the foci of policy conflict between the contending groups in the leadership. Nevertheless, the course that took shape in 1971 and 1972 seems to have been followed quite consistently since, apparently with the full backing of Premier Chou and with the probable blessing of Chairman Mao.

The development of oil resources and the rapid expansion of foreign trade imposed very heavy strains on China's port and shipping facilities. In 1973 and the first half of 1974, the China trade was replete with complaints of port congestion, long turnaround time for ships, shallowness of ports so that large tankers could not use the harbors, and poor bulk loading and unloading facilities. Given the character of Chinese ports, Chinese oil is shipped in 20,000- to at most 30,000-ton freighters rather than 100,000- to 200,000-ton tankers. This necessarily raises transport costs and reduces somewhat the competitiveness of Chinese oil as compared with other sources of supply available to Japan. At the same time, lack of container port and bulk handling facilities has slowed down the delivery of grain, iron ore and a number of other products.

Against this background, Chinese planners have allocated substantial resources to correct this situation. A major effort is under way to deepen the ports, and in this connection large orders for port dredging equipment have been placed abroad. The Chinese are also building a major container port near Tientsin and possibly in one or two other harbors, and an offshore oil loading facility is being built near Dairen which will accommodate large tankers. An oil pipeline network is under construction in North and Northeast China, with a long spur from the Taching oil field to the port of Chinghuangtao and another running from this port to a refinery on the outskirts of Peking completed recently.

Finally, as part and parcel of this effort to create the necessary infrastructure for the support of a foreign trade expansion program, the Chinese have invested heavily in expanding their merchant marine. Since 1971 or 1972 they have added about 1.5 to 2.0 million tons to their shipping fleet, about 1.1 million of which consists of 64 secondhand ships mostly bought from Japan, Norway, Poland and Yugoslavia.[8]

IV

China embarked on her new foreign economic policy at a time when the world economy was experiencing a boom. The opening of relations with the United States, the entry of the People's Republic into the United Nations, and the normalization of relations with a number of countries, all occurred while the world economy was rapidly expanding. In these circumstances—and even before oil came into the picture—the climate was favorable for a significant increase in China's traditional exports which then could be used to finance the increasing imports needed to meet new development priorities.

Expansion of imports was also facilitated by China's readiness to accept what were in effect intermediate-term credits—typically up to five years. These took the form of deferred-payment schemes, through suppliers' credits financed by commercial and government banks and in most cases government-guaranteed. Willingness to accept these forms of financing was another manifestation of the more open economic posture since 1972, although the Chinese had entered into similar arrangements on a much more modest scale with West European manufacturers in the early 1960s.

The advent of the world recession and the concomitant "slumpflation" in late 1973, however, confronted the Chinese with an entirely new and unprecedented situation. In the 1950s, when China's trade

[8] Based on information provided by Japanese shipping and commercial sources in interviews with the author in April and May 1975.

was likewise growing very rapidly, it was expanding primarily within the context of guaranteed markets, defined through bilateral agreements between the Soviet Union and East European countries on the one hand and the People's Republic of China on the other. Then, in the 1960s, when China started to reorient her trade after the Sino-Soviet break, China's total trade was sluggish, while the world economy and world trade were expanding rapidly. Therefore, the Chinese had no difficulty in finding markets for their goods. Moreover, during the 1960s world market prices were reasonably stable so that Chinese planners could pretty well forecast their foreign exchange earnings and requirements. They could then plan for a balance-of-payments equilibrium, usually with a small surplus.

As world inflation gained momentum in the early 1970s, the prices of China's imports were rising along with the volume of imports and thus the total import bill was increasing rapidly. For a time this was compensated both by higher prices that could be charged for the country's exports and by the quantitative increase—as noted earlier, the volume of exports rose by about 15 percent (in real terms) in 1973.

However, in 1974 the world situation became one of widespread and deep recession linked with double-digit inflation. As a result, Chinese trading corporations found it quite difficult to place their traditional exports. This was most pronounced in textiles, but by no means confined to it. Thus, Chinese sales to Hong Kong in 1974 were about 22 percent below 1973 levels if one adjusts for price increases. And while total Chinese exports to Japan rose in 1974 with the surge of oil, non-oil exports declined by about a quarter.[9] Since about 30 percent of China's exports go to Japan and 20 percent to Hong Kong, the impact was serious.

All told, China's exports may have declined by about 10 percent in 1974 if expressed in real, quantum terms. On the other hand, import schedules designed in 1972 had created a momentum which carried forward well into 1974. Complete plants began to be delivered in 1974, and the demand for imported industrial materials was steadily rising. Furthermore, grain imports, greatly stepped up in 1973, continued at almost the same rate in 1974 in order to build up domestic reserves badly depleted following the inferior 1972 harvest.

Chinese planners could not and almost certainly did not anticipate the seriousness of the world recession or the resulting decline in Chinese sales. Consequently they apparently did not slow down the pace

[9] The Hong Kong data are based on official statistics published by the Census and Statistics Department. The estimates for Japan were derived by the author from detailed statistics of Sino-Japanese trade in "General View of Japan-China Trade in 1974," *JETRO China Newsletter*, No. 7, April 1975, pp. 1–10.

of import orders until the latter part of 1974. Thus, in spite of belated corrective measures, the 1974 trade deficit turned out to be about one billion U.S. dollars, by far the largest incurred by the People's Republic in its 25-year history.

However, this may be expected to be a short-term phenomenon. In 1975 and 1976 Chinese planners may be expected to scrutinize imports more carefully than they did in 1973 and 1974. But a sizable share of imports are based on advance commitments, and there are strict limits to how far purchases from abroad can be curtailed without slowing down domestic investment and the pace of development. As the world economy gradually pulls out of the recession, China's traditional exports—mostly agricultural and textile products—may once more find somewhat readier markets. Most importantly, year by year China's oil exports are rising very rapidly and this will almost certainly reestablish the country's trade balance while providing greatly enlarged foreign exchange resources.

V

In the meantime how are the Chinese financing their trade gap? The measures taken perhaps represent the clearest illustrations of the new and reinterpreted self-reliance policy. One of its most explicit formulations is the following statement by Vice-Premier Teng Hsiao-ping in October 1974: "Only self-reliance is a sure-fire method. Why is there world inflation, with only the Renminbi [People's currency or yuan] not likely to be affected? Because of our reliance on our own resources. We now also accept installment payment terms for machinery from abroad *but only in the knowledge that we are capable of making regular payments.* We must remain free from debts, both at home and abroad, and go not further than that."[10]

Clearly short-term and medium-term indebtedness is considered compatible with the self-reliance policy provided it is not labeled credit and in its overt form comes from a commercial supplier in the form of deferred payment rather than a bank or a government finance agency. In implementing this policy, the Chinese have used a number of expedients to cover the large trade deficit of 1974 and a smaller deficit in 1973. In this process, the Bank of China has greatly expanded its operations in recent years and has become very active in international financial markets.

A whole variety of devices have been used either to defer payments for goods received or to obtain foreign exchange to pay for them.

[10] Teng made this statement at a reception of Overseas Chinese in Peking on October 2, 1974; quoted in *U.S.-China Business Review*, No. 1, Vol. 2, p. 34.

These range from quite short-term 30-day suppliers' credits to 5-year deferred-payment schemes linked to complete plant deliveries. Even during the 1960s, when a quite strict self-reliance policy was pursued, the Chinese purchased grain on 12- and 18-month installments from Australia and Canada respectively. More recently, the massive purchases of grain from the United States in 1973 and 1974 were financed by 12- to 18-month credits extended in large part by American banks operating through foreign or multinational banks.

This spring a contract was signed for the purchase of 1.5 million tons of steel from Japan, to be delivered within six months and paid for over a 12-month period. This was the first time that a deferred-payment scheme was used for steel shipments to China. In the last year or two the Chinese have also greatly stepped up their reliance on short-term financing of deliveries in virtually all commodity categories. These involve commercial credits ranging from 30 to 180 days. In addition, a number of West European and Japanese banks have been invited to place foreign currency deposits in the Bank of China. Apparently these deposits are for periods up to one year, renewable year by year. They are placed at Eurodollar rates or at rates approximating these, and they may have totaled several hundred million dollars in 1974. They could be considered as loans in disguise.

There are unconfirmed reports that the Chinese have sought and obtained a large three-year loan financed by an international banking consortium. There have also been occasional rumors that Iran and possibly one or two Arab countries may have extended substantial and rather long-term credits to the Chinese. While this cannot be ruled out, it is improbable since it would represent a radical departure even in terms of recent Chinese policy and practice, at least in form and principle.

Will the Chinese relax their practice on foreign credit still further? Or may they swing in the opposite direction, tightening up and reverting to past standards? At this writing there is little evidence or basis for judgment, though one can sense that the steadiness of recovery in major Chinese markets will weigh heavily in deciding the direction of Chinese policy, as will the future direction of the country's foreign and domestic policies as a whole in a post-Mao/Chou era. The Chinese will not lightly repeat the 1974 experience, but with the growth of oil exports there is little reason to anticipate that they would need to run that risk, unless the world demand for oil is drastically curtailed or the OPEC cartel collapses within the next five years. Barring these contingencies, Chinese earnings should be adequate to finance a substantial development program, at least by past

Chinese standards. If there should be a significant expansion in foreign borrowing, it would suggest a whole new degree of commitment to a markedly accelerated program of domestic economic development and a complete abandonment of the self-reliance policy—with far-reaching internal political implications.

VI

It is time now to come back to Sino-American trade and to the questions that surround it. It was purely fortuitous that a foreign policy reorientation, the crystallization of a new foreign economic policy, and the opening of relations with the United States coincided with a poor harvest year in China. Yet this particular combination of circumstances goes a long way toward explaining the peculiar pattern of Sino-American trade referred to at the outset.

China's new foreign policy and the opening of Sino-American relations were a necessary precondition for Chinese imports from the United States. These would have been precluded as long as our China policy was based on containment and isolation. The absence of any trade served both as an illustration and as an embodiment of our China policy between 1951 and 1971. Concurrently China's new foreign-trade policy, a more relaxed attitude toward credits and deferred payments, and the generally more active foreign-trade orientation discussed in preceding sections may have encouraged Chinese planners to permit the accumulation of sizable trade deficits if need be—something they would have tried to avoid at all cost in years past.

With these considerations in mind, Chinese foreign-trade planners had apparently very little reason to hesitate in placing purchase orders in the U.S. market once a clear need could be demonstrated. In these terms, the sharp rise in U.S. exports to China in 1973 and 1974, and the subsequent drop in 1975, can be explained summarily as follows: whereas U.S. trade benefited very greatly from China's need to remedy the effects of the bad 1972 agricultural harvest, the United States from the outset had only a very limited share in Chinese purchases of capital goods, especially complete plants. And, when the boom in U.S. farm exports broke, not only was there no steady rise in industrial exports to take up the slack but even in the agricultural area the United States found itself relegated to the role of a residual supplier not needed in normal times.

Take first the situation in sales of complete plants. Out of the approximately 100 complete plants purchased by the Chinese between late 1972 and mid-1975, only eight are American, and these account for $200 million out of a total program of about $2.5 billion.

Therefore the U.S. share is about eight percent in terms of both numbers and value. By far the largest supplier is Japan, followed by the West European countries as a group. The same picture presents itself in relation to machinery and equipment purchased by China outside the complete plant framework. It is not surprising therefore that in 1973 and 1974 only 10 to 15 percent of our sales to China comprised industrial materials and equipment.

Needless to say this has been contrary to all earlier forecasts and expectations, which suggested that the United States would become a major supplier of capital goods to the People's Republic. How can one explain the poor performance of our capital goods sector in the China trade? No doubt the Japanese enjoy certain advantages in terms of geographic and cultural proximity, a long experience of trading with the P.R.C., perhaps a more aggressive pursuit of the China market, and certainly in some fields at least a competitive edge in terms of costs. However to this list must be added another most important factor which distinguishes the Japanese and U.S. situations: there is no obstacle in Japan to complete plant sales on a five-year deferred-payment or credit basis.

These credits are directly or indirectly Japanese Export-Import Bank financed at a six percent rate of interest.[11] In effect this means it is government-financed at subsidized interest rates. Under present circumstances this type of financing could not be pursued in our case for several reasons. There are institutional, corporate and individual claims by Americans against assets confiscated by the P.R.C.; correspondingly, Chinese holdings in the United States were frozen at the time of the Korean War. There is some evidence to suggest that though the United States has sought to resolve these claims-assets issues separately, the Chinese may wish to tie their settlement to full normalization of relations. In turn, until the claims-assets question is settled, U.S. Export-Import Bank financing is probably barred by law. In this sense, then, the absence of formal relations places U.S. exporters of machinery, equipment and complete plants at a disadvantage.

Given the slow growth of our capital goods exports to the P.R.C., the volatility of our trade—dramatic rise followed by sharp curtailment—is entirely due to the marked fluctuations in our sales of farm products to China. The rise in our China exports from about $63 million in 1972 to $740 million in 1973 was due preponderantly to in-

[11] In reality the Ex-Im Bank only finances up to 80 percent of the sales value while the remaining 20 percent must be obtained from the commercial banks. Typically the Ex-Im Bank lends these funds either to a commercial bank which then finances the supplier, or it lends it directly to the latter. In either case, the Chinese deal only with the supplier of the complete plant.

creases in agricultural sales—both in 1973 and 1974 about 80 percent of our exports to China were agricultural. Why are these then dwindling in 1975? This question can only be illuminated through a brief analysis of China's grain import demand.

Through the 1950s China was a net exporter of grains, primarily rice. This trend was reversed under the impact of the acute agricultural crisis between 1959 and 1962. Consequently China began importing large quantities of grain in 1961, primarily from Australia and Canada and secondarily from France and Argentina. At first they imported about 6 million tons of grain annually, mostly wheat. This then declined somewhat and since the mid-1960s purchases have fluctuated between 3 and 5 million tons. At the same time they resumed rice exports, although these did not match the grain imports in terms of quantity or value. Then, in 1973, China's grain imports (wheat and corn combined) increased from 3.4 million tons in 1972 to a record of 7.3 million tons, dropping back only slightly to 6.9 million tons in 1974. They are now expected to drop to 5.5 million in 1975. In 1973–74 the Chinese also stepped up their imports of other farm products, notably soybeans and cotton, again reflecting harvest fluctuations.

Canada and Australia had been China's traditional suppliers of grain. However when China rapidly raised her requirements just at a time when U.S.-China relations were opened, she looked to the United States to meet the greatly increased demand; in a tight world grain market it is improbable that Australia and Canada could have provided the additional quantities. Then, when import orders were curtailed following a good 1974 harvest, China reverted to her traditional sources of supply in 1975, treating the United States as a residual supplier of agricultural products and thus sharply reducing purchases here.

However, this account does not appear to explain fully why, when China curtailed her farm import orders, the whole burden of reduction was shifted to the United States, and not equally distributed among Canada, Australia and the United States. There is no question that there were quite serious quality problems with the wheat, corn and soybeans supplied by the United States. Moreover, China has three-year wheat import agreements with Australia and Canada and not with the United States. Yet, these considerations do not seem an adequate explanation, nor do they apply at all to the 1975 cancellation of raw cotton orders from the United States, particularly since China continued to import cotton from other sources. Therefore it would not be unreasonable to assume that the lack of formal diplomatic recognition constituted an additional reason for the cancellation of contracts. It is more than probable that, in anticipation of President Ford's visit later this year, the Chinese wished to indicate to the American government and business community that full normalization of diplomatic relations is a necessary precondition for wholly normal and sustained trade relations.

The experience of other countries may be instructive in testing this proposition. As shown before, China's foreign trade rose rapidly after about 1970 under the combined impact of domestic development and a more open foreign trade orientation. This was also the period during which a number of countries established formal diplomatic relations with Peking. For 14 of these there are continuous trade figures including the period since 1970. If one takes for comparison the level of exports in the year preceding diplomatic recognition and then in 1974, in the case of Canada, Japan, Germany, Italy and Spain, exports to China did not increase more rapidly (in some cases less rapidly) than total non-communist world exports to the P.R.C. over these intervals. On the other hand, nine countries exhibited appreciably faster trade growth with the P.R.C. following recognition than the non-communist world as a whole for equivalent periods. This phenomenon was particularly pronounced in the case of Australia, Belgium, Iran, New Zealand, Nigeria, Turkey and Peru. It was somewhat less so for Argentina and Mexico.

Clearly, even in these purely descriptive terms, the relationship between recognition and rate of export growth is far from conclusive. A number of complex economic and political factors govern the course of exports between any one country and China. Therefore one cannot simply pick out a single variable such as diplomatic recognition and ascribe to it alone decisive importance. However it is impossible to avoid the inference that political factors have played an important role in many cases.

The case of Australia may be of particular interest. Australian exports to China were quite significant throughout the 1960s, ranging between $100 and $200 million, largely due to wheat exports, and were around $130 million in 1970. They then dropped below $30 million and $50 million in 1971 and 1972 respectively. After the new Labor government in Australia extended diplomatic recognition to the P.R.C. in December 1972, however, exports nearly trebled in 1973 (to $140 million) and rose very sharply again in 1974, to $320 million. The inference seems plain, that the Chinese cancelled their grain purchases in 1971 and 1972 as a way of exerting pressure, reinstated them in 1973 after relations were normalized, and kept on expanding trade to other fields and commodities as well, which accounts for part of the marked increase between 1973 and 1974.

Turning to other factors, the claims-assets and Ex-Im Bank financing problems—both linked to normalization—are not the only practical obstacles to a sustained expansion of Sino-American trade. Another barrier is the absence of most-favored-nation treatment (MFN), so that a full tariff is levied on Chinese goods entering U.S. markets. According to several tentative studies, it would seem unlikely that our imports from China would increase by more than 25 percent even if the MFN barrier were removed—in 1975 from a projected level of $150 million to less than $200 million; our imports from China would still be quite low, ultimately because our market for the kinds of products the Chinese export is quite limited.

But if a change in MFN status in and of itself could be expected to have only a marginal effect on our China trade, the political significance of MFN is still substantial as a symbol of discriminatory treatment and thus of less than completely normal relations. Paradoxically, under the stipulations of the recent trade act, it would be easier to lift the MFN restrictions on Russia than on China. This act not only includes the Jackson-Vanik Amendment but a number of other stipulations, the most crucial of which makes MFN treatment conditional upon a government-to-government trade agreement. If the Russians chose to relax their emigration barriers—and thus satisfy the requirements of the Jackson-Vanik Amendment—they could reinstate the 1972 Moscow trade agreement and become eligible for MFN treatment. However, in the absence of a similar formal intergovernmental trade agreement, the Chinese would not be eligible even if they were to meet the emigration requirements of the Amendment or even if they were exempted from its requirements by the Act of Congress now proposed by Senator Mansfield. And it seems most improbable that the necessary trade agreement can be concluded in the absence of formal diplomatic relations.

In sum, a careful analysis points inescapably to the conclusion that the lack of diplomatic relations is a more serious obstacle to the further development of trade than is generally recognized. Financing problems, the claims-assets issue, and the lack of MFN status or of a formal trade agreement—all these barriers can be traced back to the question of full normal relations. And the evidence of Chinese import selectivity toward the United States underscores the point. Unless and until this basic problem is cleared up, Sino-American trade will necessarily be erratic, sharply fluctuating and devoid of a firm, systematic, and fully institutionalized footing.

5

Australasians Approach Southeast Asia

Charles Draper

Australian and (*a fortiori*) New Zealand investment in Southeast Asia is very small both absolutely and relative to that of Japan, the United States, and even the minor EEC powers. This reflects the two Commonwealth countries' traditional economic ties with the United Kingdom, Western Europe and, in recent years, the United States; their preoccupation with the import of capital; the emphasis in their economies and exports on agriculture rather than the development of industries which might have led to overseas investment in the pursuit of markets, lower production costs, structural rationalization, etc.; a propensity to define "aid" in the strict sense excluding private direct investment; the operation of exchange controls preventing portfolio and inhibiting direct overseas capital flows; and the ownership of a considerable proportion of their industry by international capitalists and much of the rest by small operators for whom the investment of Australian or New Zealand capital overseas has held little attraction.

But recent political, economic, and monetary developments have affected most of these factors, and produced at least a propensity for a considerable expansion to occur in Australasian investment overseas, and particularly in Southeast Asia (including Papua-New Guinea, now in its last days as an Australian dependent). Moreover, a few traditional characteristics make Australia and New Zealand likely candidates for the role of overseas investor, although in a less dominating form than that often adopted by a larger nation. Among these are: their long history of trading externally on a significant scale (New Zealand's exports total a quarter of its gross domestic production); their similarity to Southeast Asian states in the small size of their domestic markets (Australia's population is 13 million, New Zealand's almost 3 million) and their approach to industrial development; and their basic sympathy with small nations seeking to replace colonial ties with cultural, political, and economic independence.

Although available statistics are too sparse to enable a complete picture of Australasian investment in Southeast Asia to be drawn, a rough outline can be sketched. *Australian* private overseas investment over the past decade has been concentrated in Papua-New Guinea, New Zealand, North America, and the United Kingdom, leaving a flow of only \$(U.S.)27.4 for "other countries" in 1971-72. This represents 17 percent of that year's total outflow of \$164.4 million, of which 78 percent was "direct." Full stock

---

Reprinted by permission of the Economic Cooperation Center for the Asia and Pacific Region, from Study No. 7, February, 1974.

figures are unavailable, but the sum of the annual direct outflows plus reinvestment for the eight years 1971-72 was $647 million; and the income receivable from all overseas investments except portfolio reached almost $86 million in 1971-72 bringing the total for the eight-year period to $476 million. Individual recipient country figures for Indochina are not available at the time of writing, but the 1971-72 flows to Southeast Asia's ASEAN countries included the Philippines $0.8 million, Malaysia $2.0 million, Singapore $2.1 million, and Indonesia $4.3 million, with Thailand negative at $0.1 million.* Not even this type of information is available for *New Zealand* at present, but the outflows of capital to the region have clearly been very small.

The statistics indicatc the low level of Australian investment in the region, but they belie the interest in activity beyond pure trading which is being shown. *Australian* operations in Thailand already include producers of glass, containers, Ford vehicles, reconstituted dairy products, food canning, plasterboard, gases, feathers, and adhesives, with a steel foundry and a galvanizing plant currently being established; meanwhile, factories with Australian interests in Malaysia include producers of batteries, steel products, drugs, glass, and containers; interests in Indonesia are considerable and include gases, TV assembly, drugs, engineering equipment, and dairy products; and there are also some interests in Cambodia, the Philippines, and elsewhere. In most of these operations the Australian equity share is substantial, although sometimes there are other foreign interests involved too. *New Zealand's* present or forthcoming interests in the region include refractories, geothermal energy, sawmilling, construction, and consultancy in Indonesia; refractories, dinnerware, drainage pipes and paper in the Philippines; plastic and electrical hardware in Malaysia; and abattoir-construction in Laos. Although some production activity is involved in these fields, licensing and minority positions are often used, and the main component of the New Zealand interest remains the supply of expertise and materials and the organization of projects to build roads, shopping complexes, drainage systems, water supply operations, etc. The emphasis of both New Zealand and Australian activities has been concentrated on marketing and, more recently, the supply of services in infrastructural development: The new focus of attention should be on production facilities to help satisfy Southeast Asian desires for development through industrialization.

A MORE ACTIVE APPROACH TO INVESTMENT OVERSEAS

Each of the principal factors which have been inhibiting investment abroad is currently subject to an important change in both countries. The traditional ties with the West have been undermined by Britain's move into the European Economic Community, a development which will have a profound effect on the dairy and meat export-oriented New Zealand economy (and which has

* See Reference 1. Statistics amended by reference 2. (January 1974) using an average conversion rate of (A)$1 equal to (US)$1.191. All figures in this chapter in United States dollars unless otherwise specified.

affected Australia too). This "British entry" has stimulated both a more vigorous search for new markets for traditional products, and more serious attempts to bring about structural changes in an economy which can no longer take the risk of remaining fairly undiversified. Along with Japan, Southeast Asia has become an object of considerable attention as new trading partners are sought. The new focus of attention on Australia's "near north" has been sharpened also by the coming to power of Labour Party governments in both countries late last year. This has coincided with an increasing recognition of the importance of commerce in international politics—spurred perhaps by significant recent examples of trade and friendship arrangements being conducted without the seal of diplomatic propriety, by the example of Japan's "great power" status achieved through trade, by the renewed spirit of internationalism in the West, and by the need to assist "stable" neighbors in the national interest.

Both of the countries have established diplomatic links with the main Asian country, the People's Republic of China, strengthened ties with Japan, and are developing associations with Asia's other socialist governments. At the same time, increased attention is being paid to their more immediate neighbors in the South Pacific and (in the case of Australia) the ASEAN and other Southeast Asian states. Indeed, the Australian Prime Minister has discussed widely various approaches toward Asian regional cooperation, and some form of association between Australia and the fledgling ASEAN grouping is currently under consideration. The New Zealand Prime Minister has confined his attention a little more closely to the South Pacific, but the association of Indonesia with the expanding regional arrangements in the Pacific is being studied. The greater involvement in the affairs of their neighbors which these various moves imply is likely to be reflected also in the commercial sphere. Not only wider but also more intensive relationships can be anticipated, with investment complementing trade and technical assistance.

INDUSTRIAL DEVELOPMENT AT HOME

Meanwhile diversification and industrial development proceed apace although, in New Zealand at least, the small local market, only partly expanded by the trade agreement (NAFTA) between the two countries, inhibits the emergence of a strong industrial export sector. For *New Zealand*, the proportion of physical exports sold to the United Kingdom, Western Europe, and the United States fell from 82.1 percent in 1964 to 63.2 percent in 1971, while the proportions sold to Australia, Japan, and other countries each doubled to 8.6, 9.2, and 18.9 percent respectively. Over the decade to 1971 the value of all non-agricultural export quadrupled to $(NZ)380.5 million while overseas sales of agricultural products rose by only 82 percent to $(NZ)980.9 million. During the decade ending 1972/73, *Australia's* proportion of exports going to the United Kingdom and Western Europe dropped from 36.9 to 23.3 percent, while the importance of sales of Japan almost doubled to account for nearly a third of total exports and those to the five ASEAN states rose from 4.1 percent in 1962/63 to 6.3 percent in 1972/73. Processed primary exports and manufactures each now account for almost 20 percent of Australia's total merchandise sales abroad, and this diversification is likely to continue during the current decade.

A number of significant Australian and New Zealand businessmen interviewed by the present author in 1973 have referred to the role which investment overseas might play in *restructuring* aspects of this diversification process. And Japan provides an example of an increasing consciousness of the way in which a shift of some labor-intensive industries to Southeast Asia can assist in industrial reconstruction at home. To meet new export markets more cost-consciousness is necessary, both in lines which lend themselves to mass production techniques and in those which are more specialized and craft oriented. In some, rising freight costs are eroding the profit margin formerly derived from producing at home-plants for overseas markets. A large portion of the traditional manufacturing sectors in Australia and New Zealand is using scarce financial, entrepeneurial, and human resources to pursue activities which are probably inappropriate for advanced economies with small labor forces, high labor costs, and limited home markets. Indeed, some industries (such as simple textiles) require considerable tariff protection to sell at home and there is often an *a priori* economic case for their replacement by imports to capture lower production costs. There may sometimes be a complementary case for investment by Australasians in such Southeast Asian production lines. Although technology in these traditional industries is relatively simple and widely available from other foreign sources, Australasian involvement could ensure the use of Australasian supplies and the meeting of home-market needs.

More important are those areas in which Australasians do possess *special expertise*: They should be identified and, especially where the opportunity cost of applying domestic production resources to them is high, they could be "helped abroad" by home governments. Such areas include product lines developed in Australia or New Zealand to suit local production and market conditions which in some ways (skilled labor shortages, rugged physical circumstances, relatively small markets, etc.) are similar to Asian conditions. They include also lines which might have been developed anywhere but for which the most appropriate technology happens to be held by Australasians. A number of products in the light machinery, sportsgear, plastics, and other fields could be cited in this regard. Thirdly, they include industries which may incorporate production or assembly but which emphasize skills, techniques and creativity. Included in this group are such activities as "one-off" engineering, adaptation for specialized markets, project coordination and the organization of "task-force" expertise, specialized construction, etc. Often it may be more convenient to operate such business from permanent Southeast Asian locations than from Australia or New Zealand.

On economic grounds, of course, imports should replace local production in less efficient lines even if Australian and New Zealand producers express no interest in investing abroad. In the real political world, however, consumers' interests are not sovereign, and the governments may need to seize the opportunities provided by potential investors in order to proceed with the restructuring process at all. Theoretically, this argument is "weak," since the amount of industrial change directly attributable to investment overseas will probably be fairly small, at least in the first instance. But in the presence of other pressures for increasing efficiency, the investment argument must help rather than hinder the political forces favoring economic rationality over protected production.

Two current factors which could boost businessmen's propensity to invest abroad (and enhance the promotion of investment overseas as an explicit measure at this time) are rapid domestic inflation and export surpluses which are causing reserves to burgeon. Continual *cost inflation* is making the need to rationalize industry in the search for high productivity more urgent, and thus improving some Australian and New Zealand businessmen's perception and acceptance of the case for relocation of some industries in lower-cost offshore areas by making it applicable to more industries. Meanwhile, the *export surplus* has caused a further revaluation of the Australian dollar, and could invite slackening of the export drive. In the latter regard, the new Australian government has declared its continued interest in assisting exports, but the "export incentive scheme" will henceforth take the form of grants to subsidize new market development expenditure.[2] The export of capital to finance profitable ventures overseas would provide a desirable complement to such measures. Moreover, if the phasing out of the incentives, coupled with raising of tariffs in Southeast Asian markets, do cause Australian exports to slacken, an alternative reason is provided for transferring production facilities into those customs areas. Thus, whichever stance the Australian government adopted to deal with its overseas exchange transactions situation, the encouragement of investment in Southeast Asia by Australian businessmen could be a helpful part of the policy package. This pressure is considered to be less intense in New Zealand, but the argument applies to some extent there as well.

The traditional preoccupation with the *import* of capital is being eroded, too, although the two economies (especially New Zealand) remain both dependent on and attractive to substantial inflows in spite of recent measures to exercise more control over them. The increased public awareness of capital flows (stemming from the concern about inflows which produced the measures referred to), and the rapid rise in business being transacted overseas by manufacturers and other potential investors, have combined to dispel the feeling that net capital-importing countries should not expect to be capital exporters as well. Indeed, the present very high level of overseas exchange reserves held by both Australia and New Zealand provide a fund of capital which both businessmen and aid lobbyists seek to use for transfers to the developing countries. Recent measures by the Australian and New Zealand governments to restrain some types of foreign inflows into their own countries should not be overemphasized, although they could be extended sufficiently to have a macro effect. However, if some *diversion* does occur as a result of limiting short-term capital inflows into Australia, then Southeast Asia could benefit from it. This is especially likely if international liquidity conditions encourage outflows from America and elsewhere to continue at their recent rate, if the multinational companies turn to Southeast Asia instead of to Australia for the establishment of regional bases, and if the concept of regional industrial cooperation becomes implemented.

NEW ATTITUDES TO AID

A further evolution observable in Australian and New Zealand attitudes which might promote investment overseas is a lessening propensity to define *foreign assistance* strictly as grants and loan-subsidies (*"which we cannot afford in significant quantities"*). It is now frankly recognized that for most donor countries in the foreseeable future, the "one percent aid" target relates to total flows of financial resources, including export credits and private commercial investment. Even so, only four countries have reached the target, but Australia is not far from it with a total flow of 0.95 percent in 1972, including 0.62 percent on the strict definition. New Zealand expects to meet the 1 percent total, 0.7 percent strict targets in 1975-76. Increasing awareness of the need for capital injection into developing countries with small savings and smaller ability to mobilize them into productive channels (and, for some perhaps, awareness of the opportunity to "make charity pay") also have had their impact in these two wealthy, trade-oriented countries whose interests (and conscience) will be served by economic growth, developing markets, and less conspicuous poverty in Southeast Asia.

Indeed, the connection between aid and investment is taken still further by enterprising New Zealanders who are putting into practice their nation's new-found identification with Southeast Asia. For reasons discussed elsewhere in this essay, New Zealand's capacity for investment overseas in production facilities is very limited, but this is compensated for by a significant effort to export project-services accompanied by some capital involvement and organization. Although some of these "investment" ventures are now usually commercial, the experiment has been enhanced substantially by a disturbingly close association between the suppliers of services (and sometimes merchandise) and the aid flows of the New Zealand government. A significant proportion of the country's commercial activity in Southeast Asia (particularly Indonesia) will be based on the experience gained in these quasi-official operations. There is a threat to recipient countries implicit in excessively close ties between international businessmen and their home governments, and this should be mitigated by good relationships between home and host governments and by strict self-discipline on the part of the source country. In the imperfectly competitive international market for servicing aid projects, some official promotion of the supply of commercial investment funds to the developing countries may be necessary until reputations are established; however, tampering with the projects should not be resorted to.

Coupled with the changing atittude to aid is the opinion which many Australians and New Zealanders have of *Southeast Asians' attitudes* toward their southern neighbors. This is often seen to be favorable and some Oceanic entrepreneurs feel that their "forthright style," their distrust of expensive, time-consuming feasibility studies, and the absence of a threat of "economic imperialism," make them relatively welcome with investment promoters and aid receivers in the region. This argument can be taken too far, of course, as it is by those who see "a common attitude among countries which have thrown off colonial fetters." The discrete desire of some Southeast Asian policy-makers to create a countervailing influence to the dominant positions maintained by the economic giants, Japan and the United States, could be an important factor in raising the level of Australian and New Zealand (as well as EEC and "other Asian") investment in the areas. Overt discrimination is an unpopular and possibly expensive concept, however, and the main effect to the desire for balance will probably be psychological.

Changes occurring in *Southeast Asian policies* also are making investment there more attractive and necessary—although accompanying changes may be making it more difficult also, especially for Australia in the face of strong Japanese competition for good investment opportunities. The main short-term factor likely to encourage investment in local production is the anti-trade tariff imposed to protect the countries' infant manufacturing sectors and to raise further revenue to finance social, military, and developmental expenditure. In addition, industrial development itself is reducing the region's dependence on many import lines. Australian exporters to Southeast Asia are already responding to the threatened loss of markets by establishing joint ventures, licensing arrangements, and other forms of local production. Early action is encouraged by the promotion and restriction system operated by most countries of the region. This gives prompt investors in an industry significant tax advantages over late-comers, who in some cases may be barred from majority ownership or from entry altogether unless it can be shown clearly that existing producers cannot supply the market. These are relatively short-term considerations, however, perhaps overshadowed by a more fundamental change which is occurring in the region. This, of course, is the process of economic growth and development, which will expand the region's *potential market* a great deal faster than the growth in the population (at present about 250 million in the five ASEAN and four Indochina states). Australians and New Zealanders are aware that they possess the technology and expertise to secure a share in this market. But the need to contribute to the market's development (through generating employment, etc.), and the protective tariff arrangements adopted for the same purpose, will ensure that for many products the share secured will depend more on investment than on exports from Australasian production locations.

CURRENT MEASURES TO FACILITATE INVESTMENT

The new *Australian* government has continued to welcome the interest of its nationals in private direct investment overseas. The principal arguments used to commend it to the Government appear to have been the buoyant reserves situation and the desire to reduce net inflows. The desirability of joint ventures and the need to invest in accordance with host countries' national aspirations and development priorities and to use local raw materials have been emphasized by the Department of Overseas Trade and the developing countries of Southeast Asia and the Pacific specified as a key investment sphere. Concrete measures to encourage this process include:

- ready approval for exchange outflow wherever investments involve significant Australian managerial participation, the export of managerial and technical skills, the promotion of Australian exports, or the protection of existing investments;
- provision of government-backed overseas investment insurance through the export payments insurance corporation, EPIC;
- spread of information through departmental studies of host countries investment climates, organization of survey missions, and dissemination through seminars and other publicity;
- allocation of $(A)100,000 for investment promotion in the 1973 budget;
- availability of advice and assistance in host countries through the trade commissioner service; and
- treaty arrangements with Southeast Asian countries which include "best endeavors" clauses on investment in trade agreements and (currently under negotiation) investment guarantee agreements.

Meanwhile, the *New Zealand* government's favorable attitude toward investment overseas, not yet translated as clearly into policy, appears to be based mainly on the desire to achieve the target of "one percent aid" (non-strict definition) by 1975-76, the current plentiful reserves position, a continuing wish to promote New Zealand exports, and some recognition of the need for internal industrial restructuring. Even compared with Australia's stance, the New Zealand policy is only weakly reflected in concrete measures. These are restricted largely to:

- support for overseas commercial operations through the official aid program;
- more willingness by the central bank to approve outward investment propositions which facilitate the export of goods or skills and which promise an early return; and
- provision of Government-backled overseas investment insurance through the export insurance corporation, EXCO.

Each of these Australian and New Zealand measures is discussed briefly in this section. The question of whether further, more direct official encouragement or assistance is desirable is treated later in the paper following consideration of impediments to increased investment abroad.

AUSTRALIAN MEASURES

The Australian Central Bank's *exchange control* is liberal toward the supply of funds for external equity investment, with no restriction on amounts, types of venture, or direction of outflows. Dividends and profits, apart from those required for "ploughback," are required to be repatriated promptly, however, and authorization for reinvestment must be secured. Some association of an investment with exports from Australia is necessary, unless its object is to protect an existing investment. But exporters are defined liberally to include management and expertise so the stance is not as narrowly oriented toward export promotion as it might appear to be. Furthermore, the restraint on outward portfolio ("indirect") investment has been eased, with new annual limits of $(A)10,000 for an individual and $(A)1 million for a company investing in shares or property (but not loans or other securities). It would seem that Australia's exchange control offers only a mild deterrent to investment overseas, and the "currency" criticisms voiced in interviews with a dozen major investors mainly concerned approval by EPIC rather than by the Bank, and revaluation.

The export payments *insurance scheme* was extended to cover investment eight years ago, in recognition of the need for exporters to invest to retain their markets. As EPIC acts as agent for the government in investment and other "national interest" insurance, the scheme's considerable export orientation will continue until the government is persuaded that expertise should count as goods for the purposes of the export condition imposed on EPIC's operations. The Export Development Council, the Department of Overseas Trade and other parties have supported the view that alternative circumstances should be permitted, and indeed, it is to be hoped that Treasury and the other ministries which act for the government in the scheme will recognize the non-export arguments for promoting investment—aid, financial returns, "flag-waving," helping to restructure home industry, etc. At present insurance on even a semi-export oriented investment, motivated by the desire to protect a market from a potential threat, could be refused if its short-term effect was to decrease sales from Australia and perhaps cause importation from a new plant overseas. However, Australia's reduced need to promote its own exports vigorously and the increasing consciousness of the development needs of Southeast Asia in the fields of management and project expertise may produce liberalization of the insurance scheme. The inexperience and wariness of most Australian industrialists with respect to investment abroad, and the slow development of machinery to provide guarantees against expropriation and exchange restrictions at the official treaty level make proper investment insurance very necessary.

EPIC maintains an extensive bank of information and cooperates with the Berne Union and OECD in sharing information relevant to investment risks, although strict confidence is maintained in the interests of clients. Information on host countries will probably be maintained also by the proposed Export-Import Bank and there could be scope for some association to pool such facilities. EPIC offers cover against expropriation, non-transfer of exchange and war damage to Australian companies, and encourages joint ventures with local capitalists. Insurable investments may take any form and, although the export of capital without management or technology is not usually insured, the extension of the scheme to cover short-term loans is under consideration. By the end of June, 1973, business written on the government's account with respect to overseas investments totaled a contingent value of $(A)46.7 million, spread among 36 investments in Southeast Asia and elsewhere. Four of these investments with a value of almost $(A)4 million had been written in the last six months of this period.

The main activities undertaken so far by the Australian government itself in the spread of *information* to assist investors are the preparation of investment climate studies and the organization of joint official-private survey missions. A mission visited Indonesia, Malaysia, and Singapore late in 1972 and has since been reported, while another has now surveyed Thailand and the Philippines. A comprehensive investment climate study of Indonesia was in its final draft form by mid-1973 and eleven others (including Malaysia and Singapore) were in preparation. Unfortunately, detailed coverage of Thailand and the Philippines has yet to be undertaken, reflecting the scarce resources available for this work and the cautious approach by Australians toward parts of the region which are less well-known or geographically close. Meanwhile, the private sector is beginning to stimulate the spread of information on the region, notably through the formation of groups such as the Australian-Indonesian Cooperation Committee. More could be done by both official and private groups to overcome those elements of Australians' hesitation to look abroad which stem from lack of knowledge and mistrust of the unknown, but the arrangements so far are likely to become more used and extended as interest in overseas investment increases.

The Trade Commissioner service, which Australia has established somewhat more distinctly from the normal diplomatic posts than has (say) New Zealand, appears to be generally well thought-of by Australian businessmen operating in the region. But a few of those interviewed, perhaps thinking of the closer identification practices by some investing countries, called for more vigorous action by the service to promote Australian commercial investment in the context of the country's diplomatic (and defense) goals.

Treaty arrangements referrring to investment between the Australian and Southeast Asian governments are beginning to occur. The trade pact with Indonesia includes a "best endeavors" clause on the subject and the new government plans to have such clauses in agreement with all ASEAN states. Trade and investment are being linked in official communiques. Furthermore, the negotiation of investment guarantee agreements is underway and models used by more active investor countries are being studied. Australia wishes only investments approved by the host government to be guaranteed, and agreements to be made in a spirit of cooperation (rather than, for example, under threat of withdrawal of investment insurance in their absence). If such attitudes continue to govern Australia's relationships in the region, these new arrangements should provide a good base for the expansion of constructive Australian investment there.

NEW ZEALAND MEASURES

As indicated in an earlier section, the New Zealand government's principal encouragement of activity overseas apart from traditional physical exports has been provided by the use of the *foreign aid progam*. Official support for ENEX, a group formed by engineering consultants, manufacturers, and others to sell New Zealand skills and supplies overseas, has encouraged activity of the technology- rather than offshore-production-type. Meanwhile, those manufacturers who do wish to invest in production in Southeast Asia are proceeding with little concrete encouragement from their government. Whatever the merits (inexperienced investors are reassured by the government covering the risk, etc.) and demerits (the charge of "tying," etc.) of hoping that aid will promote commercial spin-off (following the use of New Zealand factors to lower aid's foreign exchange cost), a policy based on this approach has the considerable limitation that New Zealand's aid vote is necessarily very small and much of it is directed toward the emergency relief and consumer assistance rather than productive projects. Consequently spin-off would need to be considerable if a significant amount of investment was to occur as a result of the aid stimulus alone.

Like its larger neighbor, New Zealand has been massing substantial exchange reserves, and a liberalized policy toward outflows has been adopted by an *exchange control* which has traditionally placed severe limits on investment overseas. Portfolio investment continues to be inhibited by the central bank, but funds are made available for direct investment which facilitates the export of goods or skills. Although the government's foreign aid policy is said to be followed in the imposition of conditions regarding repatriation of capital gains, dividends, and other earnings, investors are generally expected to repatriate their original investment quickly. Given the aid-orientation of New Zealand's approach to investment overseas, it would be appropriate for the authorities to avoid restrictions of this nature. The interest of host countries may be ill-served by investors of the type who wish (or are expected) to get their money back within three years or so.

Investment insurance—handled by EXCO but reinsured with the government as "national interest" risk as in Australia—is more closely integrated with the central bank system than it is across the Tasman. Insurance is sought after exchange approval has been granted. Little real investment has been insured so far through EXCO, although the latter's officials are keen to encourage it. One technical difficulty which has occurred is EXCO's practice of insuring on letters of credit whereas sight terms are necessary in dealings with countries like Indonesia. As in Australia, an EXIM Bank is being proposed for New Zealand. In the interests of economy and efficiency the merger in this institution of the half-hearted Overseas Trading Corporation, and some formal association between EXIM and EXCO, have been suggested.

FACTORS STILL INHIBITING INVESTMENT OVERSEAS

The measures just discussed are reinforcing the more general economic and political trends favoring investment abroad. But many factors continue to inhibit rapid expansion of this form of Australasian interest in Southeast Asia. Some of these are treated in this section in the contexts of "home-country" and "host-country" problems. We begin with those associated with the Australian and New Zealand governments' policies on investment abroad and deal with criticisms both of the present policy stance and of the lack of constructive measures to support the more favorable stance which is developing. In treating the broader issue of the governments' policies on industry, reference is made to some of the difficulties involved in restructuring, removing protection, identifying industries deserving of support, and releasing resources to them. Apart from the inadequacies of official policies, investment is inhibited by certain characteristics of the Australasian industrial sectors. These include: a large proportion of foreign ownership, an orientation toward "servicing" rather than mass production, a tendency to think of investment largely as an extension of exports, a relatively small industrial base, and current "boom" conditions at home. This situation is compounded by the countries' relative poverty of experience in the specialized financial fields, and the shortage of investment experience and human resources which can be spared to initiate and supervise overseas activity and interests, especially industrial joint ventures in more alien cultural systems than those to which Australasians are used. This last consideration leads into host-country problems. Finally, in this section we discuss the main aspects of the Southeast Asian investment climates which appear to bother present Australian and New Zealand investors or to deter potential ones.

INVESTMENT POLICY PROBLEMS

In spite of the increased official interest in investment abroad, a primary impediment at the present time appears to be the lack of a well-defined, comprehensive policy by the home governments. This may be understandable in view of the recent political changes in both Canberra and Wellington, but in the meantime it is reflected also in promotion measures which many see as half-hearted. The Australian government's policy on investment overseas is clear enough in principle and, as described above, some measures to put it into effect are underway. There has been unresolved discussion in Canberra, however, on whether further encouragement is appropriate. While manufacturers and some officials argue that more positive incentives will be necessary to coax many industrialists to adopt a new attitude to overseas operations, some consider that the private sector should respond to the climate already created through EPIC and the liberal exchange policy.

The view is fairly widely expressed among Australian and New Zealand businessmen that their governments should appreciate more clearly the role of commerce in modern politics. According to this argument, as expressed in Australia, governments and businessmen (also ministries of foreign affairs and of trade) should work more closely together since current political circumstances in Southeast Asia dictate a commercial approach to relations between countries of this region and Australia. It is suggested that Australia's abilities (such as experience in small-scale production operations, and the possession of available capital and relevant equipment) can meet Southeast Asian needs—but government support for the private sector is necessary to bring the two together. Thus, constructive aid for the region would be given through assistance to private Australians doing business there. Critics point to the closer association apparently practiced by Japan, the United States, and even New Zealand. But in the latter country, also, businessmen see a diplomatic case for increased official backing for their hesitant advances toward overseas investment in the region. The aid program, it is said, is inadequate to bring about a desirable level of activity abroad on the part of a private sector used to looking to the government for leadership, protection, and incentive. As well as promoting investment to further Australia's diplomatic and other interests, it is argued that more effort should be put into establishing good official relations to further commercial interests in the region.

Present inadequacies which could be remedied by governments wishing to follow up a favorable investment policy stance with constructive measures include:

- the unavailability of sufficient suppliers' credit to back a switch in emphasis from finished exports toward machinery-supplies related to investment projects;
- the lack of double taxation avoidance agreements, which makes some potential investments unprofitable, causes others to be routed through Hong Kong subsidiaries, and removes the value of tax incentives offered by host governments at considerable cost to themselves;
- the lack of financial incentives, such as tax subsidies, either on a general basis, or to facilitate particular aspects of investment—such as training of local labor and technicians;
- the lack of assistance with the high cost of pre-operation expenditure or even the conduct of feasibility studies to help indicate whether investments might be worth considering;
- the maintenance of export incentives, which permit the export of goods when the outflow of technology, capital, and enterprise would be more consistent with underlying economic costs in some cases (although some businessmen argue that the incentive scheme is not a deterrent as it does not have a larger effect on home costs anyway);
- the present lack of government-to-government arrangements to provide sufficient guarantee of repatriation to permit EPIC to offer insurance cover on extended finance, or bankers to make finance available in cases where deals are not covered by the guarantees offered by host countries on the equity finance of promoted investments;
- a failure to advocate foreign investment to manufacturers sufficiently

well (in particular by suggesting it as an alternative to export from home rather than merely an extension of the "export drive" dependent on the latter's success) to provide adequate specific information on investment opportunities and conditions overseas, or to identify and then stimulate manufacturers with the potential to invest abroad:

- some inability on the part of trade commissioners in the field and trade and industry officers at home to provide vigorous support and back-up expertise in the absence of a clear policy by their governments; and
- a failure by governments to call sufficiently on those services which private financial institutions can provide to an overseas investment drive, and to coordinate them with the official efforts.

At another level, aspects of the operation of the investment policies of Australia and New Zealand may be inhibiting the more desirable type of investment—desirable at least from the recipients' points of view. Leading examples are the export-orientation and the procedures (which are sometimes inconsistent with those of foreign governments) of Australia's investment insurance; and the "early repatriation" approach of the New Zealand Reserve Bank. As well as being unhelpful in the cause of promoting constructive investment flows to the mutual advantage of both source and recipient countries, such elements would seem inconsistent with the overall attitudes of the new governments and with the wide range of reasons for investment abroad based in the present economic needs of their countries. The New Zealand emphasis on direct aid (rather than the indirect concept of assistance through commercial ventures mentioned above) also poses some difficulties. For example, the rationale for "strict-definition" aid may be difficult to reconcile with a businesslike approach toward joint ventures, now the accepted investment form in Southeast Asia. Also, aid available as a "pipe-opener" is limited in amount and might be better spread more thinly to provide initial stimulus to more ventures. And finally, the emphasis raises questions of objectionable "tied-aid" even though its use so far has been restricted mainly to services rather than to supplies.

INDUSTRY POLICY PROBLEMS

Industrial conditions at home could be an important political element in the move toward overseas investment by Australasians. Rapidly rising labor, freight, and other costs, the limitations of small domestic markets, the need to build strong manufacturing sectors rigorously based on comparative advantage and high productivity, and the consequent urgent need to allow the restructuring of industry in order to export (where appropriate) skills, techniques, and enterprise rather than finished goods, have been referred to elsewhere in this paper. In spite of the *a priori* case for it, however, such restructuring can be a slow and (without care) socially painful process, usually difficult to execute at times when it is most needed and almost as hard to bring about when boom conditions breed complacency. Industrial and technological revolutions are never easy, even in a country where the expansion of capital-intensive manufacturing and labor-intensive services are occurring simultaneously.

Industrial development policy has long provided the arena for serious debate rather than determined action in Australia and New Zealand, and the recent changes in government appear to have complicated rather than clarified the situation at the present time. The previous trend toward less protection of domestic industry is being halted and/or redirected, regional policies discussed, and new mechanisms for considering industrial development introduced. The powerful lobby among manufacturers which has long resisted vigorous moves to "throw inefficient sections of industries to the wolves" has welcomed the change of administration in the expectation of more sympathetic policy toward the existing industry structure, and the representatives of organized labor might look forward to a more understanding attitude toward any temporary redundancy or dislocation which a reorganization of resources could entail. In this context it is not surprising that definitive and progressive industry policy has failed to emerge—with consequent difficulty for the execution of overseas investment policy. Similarly, the governments' stances toward aid—in particular, the admission of imports from developing countries under the Generalised Scheme of Preferences, whether or not Australasian capital is involved in their production, is compromised by the need to protect the *status quo* at home.

The tariff structure comprises the prime visible element of the process of selecting industrial activity, and policy changes affecting it are necessary to allow the winds of international competition to assist the restructuring process. In addition, changes are needed to permit industries to go abroad if they wish to continue supplying their home markets. Some of the businessmen interviewed in Australia and New Zealand suggested that cost savings through producing in Southeast Asia, though positive, would be insufficient to enable them to "reimport" their output over high domestic tariff barriers or in the face of quantitative restrictions. Indeed, whatever the argument for protection, the invalidity of such a tariff stance is demonstrated when producers themselves recognize the advantages of imports over production in Australasia. In such cases both home-consumers and Southeast Asian factors of production might benefit from a lowering of Australasian protective barriers. One New Zealand producer had planned to manufacture in Malaysia for export to home and "third" markets (apparently with no reduction in home production), until the recent change of government reduced the threat of import licensing removal posed by the previous administration. As with many other investments, this plan involved some complementation between the output of home and overseas plants, and there may be scope for the home governments to facilitate such activity on a larger scale by initiating mutual tariff-reduction discussions with Southeast Asian governments. The difficulty of such an approach—as evidenced by the failure of the ASEAN states to achieve any progress among themselves and by the slow expansion of NAFTA's coverage—does not detract from its desirability in the interests of creating markets of a viable size and locating facilities more efficiently. An urgent need is for the Oceanic countries' tariff boards to consider the needs of domestic industry far more in a context of international trade and investment. Institutional lethargy should not be allowed to override economic sense (especially when the latter is accepted by the interest groups concerned, and policy changes in the boards' terms of reference seem necessary to enable proper consideration of Australasian production in its international context).

In spite of the above argument, examples abound of manufacturers who can both invest abroad and export vigorously from their Australasian bases, but who still claim to require substantial protection in their home market against international oligopolists. But it is interesting that one such, increased protection for whom provoked heated public discussion in New Zealand earlier last year, expressed the view to the present writer that . . . *"manufacturers who receive protection in the domestic market are thereby obliged to 'get up and go' on exports and investment overseas."* Fortunately, such attitudes are not common, except perhaps among the "public but still essentially sole-proprietor" businesses on the Australasian scene. However, the case illustrates the subtlety required to operate an industry policy of sufficient selectivity to avoid destroying relatively aggressive, possibly efficient firms in a restructuring process.

An example of the sociopolitical difficulty of dismantling an industry which seems a prime candidate for reconstruction, and some of whose members are already investing overseas, is the textile-garment industry. Efforts to deal intelligently with those parts of the industry which should release resources to more buoyant sectors of the economy seemingly conflict not only with the general goal of full employment, but also with the new governments' "decentralization" policies. Some uneconomic plants are sited in districts where they provide the bulk of employment for women whose relocation is not feasible particularly if their husbands are employed satisfactorily in the area. The trend toward equal pay for female labor is making such plants even less economic in the short-run, but the associated trend toward the employment of women in traditionally "male" occupations may bring a solution in the longer term. Government stimuli to efficient industry to move to slow-growth areas should help also, provided such relocation occurs on the basis of planning which allows for the relevant long-run considerations, and provides for the transfer of these elements of the industry not well suited to Australasian conditions.

The successful transfer abroad of some production lines—like other apects of proper restructuring—will depend on the vigor of training and retraining programs, increasing managerial competence and efficiency in the distribution sector, and the other above-mentioned elements of a clear policy on industry- and resource-use. The two main problems of industry-policy are insufficient attention to identification of "good industries" in an environment which has eroded the ability of the market's "invisible hand" to identify them, and insufficient action on promoting the flexibility and mobility of resources. It is not argued here that investment abroad itself will cause these modifications to occur generally. But it should do so in some key cases —perhaps the worst examples of excessive protection—and thus assist the more general arguments for an efficient industrial structure.

INHIBITING INDUSTRIAL CHARACTERISTICS

Apart from their propensity to seek protection in order to overcome the basic disadvantages of high costs and low volumes, parts of the manufacturing sectors exhibit several other characteristics which could make investment overseas difficult to inspire. Perhaps the most important of these is the large proportion of foreign ownership or control through licensing of Australian and New Zealand industry. This could be a favorable factor, with American or other foreign principals using their Australasian affiliates to participate in Southeast Asian ventures and permitting them to gain some of the benefit therefrom. Alternatively, such principals could switch their regional bases from Australia to Southeast Asia in recognition of the latter's developing markets, or choose to define Pacific-Asia as the "sphere of influence" of their Australasian associates. One of New Zealand's largest companies benefits by the latter type of arrangement and is a prominent overseas investor in Southeast Asia, drawing on the help of its North American associate only when this is mutually desirable. However, more general support was expressed among interviewed manufacturers for the opposite view—that overseas parents or licensors would deny the right of overseas expansion to Australia and New Zealand. Industries whose investment overseas might be inhibited in this way include those in the important automotive, pharmaceutical, rubber, and petrochemical fields. Large sections of these industries are foreign-owned, as indeed are many less prominent ones. And even firms which are important domestic industrialists are often tied to their home markets with respect to products manufactured under license to Japan, America, the United Kingdom, or, in New Zealand's case, Australia. Several cases of this were cited to the present author in explanation of companies' failure to implement overseas investment potential. Even where agreements with foreign associates specifically preclude market restriction, it is suggested that a strong deterrent often remains.

Another industrial disadvantage is the emphasis which is placed on "service" as opposed to mass production. Some important Australasian industries are highly geared for follow-up work or for fabricating items more-or-less to order, and it has been suggested that such operations are difficult to transplant to foreign production units. On the other hand, the supply of short-run specialty lines from plants located on the spot might be one of the strengths of the overseas investment process as suitable partners and skilled labor are found in Southeast Asia.

A further inhibiting characteristic has been alluded to already in the context of official inadequacies. This is the tendency to think of investment purely as an extension of exports and it is to be found among manufacturers even more generally than among officials. Over-emphasis of this approach could impede the process of identifying suitable lines for investment since some producers may be unable to export satisfactorily for the same reason that they should produce abroad: high domestic costs. The export incentive policy should be designed to encourage such manufacturers to maintain and develop their foreign markets pending a shift in production to lower-cost locations.

In the case of New Zealand at least, the underdevelopment of heavy infrastructure—such as steel and petrochemical facilities, also largely absent from the Southeast Asian region—is a fourth possibly inhibiting factor. Successful investors from other source countries do not always draw on the vast output of Japanese or American heavy industry, however, and the need to import such materials need not preclude investment in lines New Zealand manufacturers can produce well. But enterpreneurs from the large investing countries do gain some advantage from the control of such international facilities being in the hands of their compatriots or even affiliates.

Australian and New Zealand financial, legal, and other services' relative lack of experience and expertise in dealing with overseas investment problems provide an unfortunate complement to the inhibiting paucity and the limiting industrial characteristics, as well as to the shortages of resources and investment experience (discussed below). A number of New Zealand industrialists and financial experts—and even some Australian businessmen who do invest abroad—have drawn the author's attention to the passive situation brought about when neither manufacturers nor their servicing consultants have a dynamic, confident approach toward investment abroad. It is suggested that *Australian* banks should be more active in Southeast Asia if they are to have the local knowledge to service investment there. In the absence of their own offices in the region, the banks must rely on their correspondents, usually banks domiciled in other investment source-countries. In addition to the banks' lack of enthusiasm for seeking overseas business actively on account of their relatively non-competitive situation at home, they are prevented from opening branches in countries which would expect a *quid pro quo* that cannot be given since Australia is closed to foreign banks. Critics point to the lack of a proper foreign exchange market in Australia, to the high costs of long-term credit, and to the shortage of expert financial advice. In addition, the legal profession is said to be inexperienced in anticipating pitfalls involved in investing in Southeast Asia, although experts in the legal interface are now emerging with respect to Malaysia and Singapore, as well as Fiji and Papua-New Guinea.

New Zealand, the basis of whose banking system consists of branches of three Australian and one British-based trading banks in addition to the larger Bank of New Zealand, suffers from the same if not greater problems than its trans-Tasman neighbor, although bankers claim to be ready to finance activities abroad, especially during recent conditions of high liquidity. But if investment overseas does expand, a move toward consortium banking will be necessary to provide finance and expert advice. Merchant banking, a relatively recent development on the New Zealand financial scene, does not appear to have made a substantial difference to the fund of enthusiasm for equity investment abroad, in spite of the foreign connections of some of the merchant banks. Plentiful investment opportunities in New Zealand over the recent inflationary period, and a concentration on portfolio finance in their dealings abroad, may account for the relative lack of interest in equities. There are more than enough merchant banks and finance houses to service New Zealanders' domestic needs, however, and increasing interest in foreign activity is to be anticipated. This should occur particularly if boom conditions lessen at home and if investing New Zealand firms place demands on them. It has been suggested that the trading banks with merchant bank wings and finance company subsidiaries could spearhead this in the organization of consortia. Further support for overseas investment could come from the Development Finance Corporation, a government-supported institution which the new government is expected to rejuvenate, and from the proposed Export-Import Bank. The traditional antipathetic attitudes by both official and private institutions are being eroded now as New Zealanders emerge from a period when inward investment was almost the only form of capital movement, but more effort will be necessary to produce the channels and expertise which potential investors overseas will require.

SHORTAGES OF HUMAN RESOURCES AND INVESTMENT EXPERIENCE

Shortages of entrepreneurial and technical human resouces, and of experience in offshore manufacturing, may be the most important of all deterrents to more rapid investment overseas. If the manufacturing sector had the enthusiasm, capacity, and confidence to invest abroad when such action was dictated by rational pursuit of maximum rates of return on capital, the lack of official incentives and inadequacy of services would cause problems but would not necessarily deter investors. The buoyant conditions at home over recent years have not only attracted attention away from overseas activity; they have also placed heavy demands on Australian and particularly New Zealand scarce management and technical talent. Examples can be cited of firms which have persevered with overseas investment recording relatively poor performances at home, and some observers allege a connection between the two aspects. In other cases, investment prospects have been lost because the appropriate personnel could not be spared from other activities to provide the supervision and training required in foreign ventures.

This shortage of manpower to supervise and service investment abroad may be an important reason for Australasian investors' general preference for licensing arrangements and joint ventures when suitable partners can be found, in spite of the loss of control these cause. Few organizations have divisions specifically concerned with foreign activity and, where these exist, the emphasis is usually on exports. Sometimes it is the difficulty of living overseas, particularly in Indonesia, which reduces the availability of technical and commercial staff who might otherwise be available. And to some extent it is a problem of distribution associated with imperfections in the market. Enthusiastic investors are often medium-sized firms which are fully extended while more powerful, domestically-oriented employers may be able to retain vital staff; or firms which possess the technological genius to make them potential investors may be weak in administrative and commercial capability. Although shortages of financial resources and technical advantage were said to be major constraints by some interviewed executives, a more fundamental limiting factor seems to be the human one.

Nevertheless, even this difficulty could be overcome in many cases if Australasian firms were sufficiently oriented toward investment abroad to ring the necessary changes in their employment, promotion, personnel allocation, and training policies. The underlying cause of their lack of motivation is often lack of experience. In spite of the heavy trading posture of the Australasian economies, insular attitudes and fears of foreign conditions are observable at all levels. Some of these fears will be reduced as an increasing number of firms "blaze the trail," as the home governments provide more information and support, and as ventures are diversified to more developed parts of Southeast Asia than Indonesia, which now absorbs a large proportion of Australasian interest in the area. However, note should be taken by the ASEAN and Pacific governments of the difficulties expressed by present and potential investors from Australia and New Zealand, for three reasons: (1) many of the problems are faced by investors from other source-countries as well, (2) it seems to be considered desirable to increase Australasian interest in the region in order to diversify foreign investment sources and to acknowledge the association of interests between Australasia and its developing neighbors in other fields, and (3) the difficulties expressed by current investors have affected their choice of host country.

SOUTHEAST ASIAN DIFFICULTIES DETER INVESTMENT

Most of the chief executives and highly-placed observers of investment overseas, interviewed during the ECOCEN mission to Australasia in mid-1973, volunteered one or more "host-country" difficulties said to be real deterrents to Australian and New Zealand investors. The responses were based on actual experiences or investigations, although the respondents were asked also to nominate factors which would inhibit potential investors in general. More than half of the constraints named referred to various problems concerning the political stability of the countries of the region, their *governments'* policies toward foreign investment, frequent changing regulations, red tape and procedural difficulties, or corruption in the bureaucracies. A quarter of the factors related to infrastructural inadequacies, including finance, or to shortages or inadequacies of *factors of production*, including labor productivity, the availability of reliable joint-venture partners with access to needed resources, or to the high non-wage costs of operating in the region. About 10 percent of the responses concerned the high *tariff barriers* which preclude regional production—making all or part of an item at one location for marketing throughout the ASEAN area. A fourth category of factor mentioned is the fear of Japanese *competition*—on account of Japan's economic strength and prominence in the region—or of dumping there by other countries.

GOVERNMENT PROBLEMS

Excessive red tape and procedural delays stand out as the major complaint in the government category. Almost all of those who raised this point alluded specifically to Indonesia, although examples were cited of difficulties experienced in dealing with the authorities in the other ASEAN states (except Singapore, which is generally rated as "efficient"). The chief complaint concerns the long time it takes for a company to become incorporated, attributed mainly to a shortage of staff at the level at which decision-making is concentrated. Also mentioned were the large number of copies of documents required, and the difficulty of finding out requirements in advance. A second aspect of government to attract considerable criticism is the attitude toward foreign investments as reflected in laws and restrictions affecting aliens. Most of those interviewed claimed to be highly sympathetic to Southeast Asian efforts to avoid domination by foreign business, but some complained of the "rules being changed during the game," while others outlined disadvantages of holding minority positions. (Australasian businessmen probably lack the experience of exercising control from such positions, by contrast with the nationals of larger investing countries—in spite of the extent to which Australian and New Zealand partners are themselves subject to such external controls.)

Dislike of corruption—or, rather, unfamiliarity with systems of prebendalism—clearly disturbs the businessmen interviewed; although some expressed the view that they might "come to live with it," especially since the "cut" was an increasing phenomenon outside the developing world as well. Others, however, seem to have avoided recourse to bribery altogether. The number mentioning this factor was about the same as the number expressing doubt about the political security of the region or particular countries within it. Australian and New Zealand businessmen are uncertain of the stability of what they tend to describe as "military juntas" or "police states," but one experienced investor in the region pointed to the different types of strong rule in the Philippines and Singapore as a favorable factor. He also summed up some of the others' views when he observed the difficulty of assessing whether a country's investment climate is good or bad: "The Philippines has martial law *but* 40 million bright, intelligent, hardworking, relatively homogenous people; Indonesia has major problems of graft and underdevelopment *but* a large population and strong future; Malaysia has a healthy economy and good institutions *but* incipient racial disharmony . . . ." and so on.

FACTORS OF PRODUCTION

The main single difficulty described in the factors of production category was that of finding reliable joint-venture partners, but this includes questions of the various factors which the partners might be expected to supply. Furthermore, some of the more vigorous New Zealand operators had experienced little difficulty in forming suitable partnerships. It is interesting too that New Zealanders spoke of joint ventures more often than Australians: sometimes they were thinking in terms of Japanese or North American partners, but more often indigenous businessmen—reflecting the concept of investment as an extension of licensing or trading arrangements. But investors from both countries spoke of the need for partners with local knowledge, marketing contacts, ability to mobilize local resources, and "connections." Although resource shortages usually lie behind the joint-venture partner difficulty, sometimes the problem is that entrepreneurship is oriented toward trading rather than production.

Various infrastructural inadequacies were mentioned, among them the "very crude" financial system in some countries of Southeast Asia. The Australia-Indonesia Cooperation Committee has suggested the latter as a topic for a study financed by the Australian government. Other particular difficulties of producing in the region include:

- the need, at least initially, for expensive expatriate staff, because of the unavailability of local workers in fields such as accountancy, the shortage of skilled process-workers, and high training costs;
- inferior production results due to mechanical breakdowns, less efficient production-line planning, and an unwillingness to accept responsiblities;
- high costs of local materials and (for most countries) of imported materials not for re-export; and
- the absence or high cost of utilities, especially outside the metropolises.

Difficulties of this nature occur in all of the ASEAN countries, although Indonesia and, to a lesser extent, Thailand appear to have particular reputations among Australasians for some of these constraints.

TARIFF ARRANGEMENTS

A problem which is really a regional marketing issue, although it has serious implications for economic scales of production, is the absence of tariff arrangements between the Southeast Asian states. Apart from the special interest in Indonesia's huge potential market and undeveloped resource base, many Australian and New Zealand businessmen tend to think of the ASEAN region as a whole. Their limited resources for operating overseas interests preclude the establishment of a plant in each customs area even if the economics seem to justify that course. In many cases the economics do not do so, of course, and manufacturers find it profitable to continue exporting from the Australasian plants in spite of tariff, freight-cost, and labor-cost barriers. And the latter constraints may not be too severe in lines which are capital intensive or which are benefiting by the integration of the Australasian market through the NAFTA trade agreement or which are already large-scale exporters. Many recognize that this may be short-sighted, however, since other foreign investors or domestic entrepreneurs will begin production of competing commodities, will seek and receive additional protection from the Southeast Asian governments, and will capture the markets now served by imports from Australasia and elsewhere.

Where this is likely to happen, it behooves Australian or New Zealand manufacturers to think seriously about offshore production, and to turn the absence of integration among the many Southeast Asian customs areas to their advantage by exploiting their experience in producing reasonably efficiently in small, protected markets. Even if markets are not threatened by local production, manufacturers may find it more profitable to jump the tariff barriers from low-cost locations in neighboring countries than to export from home—provided they can spare or create the managerial resources to guard their interests in these locations. The latter is the constraint most mentioned by the interviewed businessmen who raised this point, and it probably applies even more strongly to domestic businessmen in Southeast Asia for whom also managerial resources are too scarce to spread wastefully around many high-cost, low-scale plants.

Another tariff complaint used to explain the preference of Australasian entrepreneurs for export from the home plants concerns high duties on imported inputs. Some who already produce in the region referred to small margins between the tariff rates on inputs and final goods, which deter such production. Such margins may be small because of the desire to protect high-cost local producers of the inputs. Where these are reasonably competitive with imports, the cost inflation caused by the tariff may be a necessary part of the "price" of industrial development. Obviously it would be an excessive price if it actually deterred as much local production as it created, or if it were being paid to protect products which were improper substitutes for the imports. Some Southeast Asian states execute formulae covering price and quality of local substitutes in the setting of import levies, but such execution can be cumbersome and unsatisfactory in the bureaucratic environments referred to earlier. Such problems are very important to Australasian entrepreneurs with the potential to invest in the region, not least because many are motivated by the desire to substitute intermediate or raw-material exports for the sale of final goods to the Southeast Asian markets. It must be both economic and convenient for them to do so before they will overcome their inhibitions about operating abroad. Dumping was another tariff problem mentioned, but only in the context of EEC surplus dairy products. With this possible exception the threat of dumping is one with which the Southeast Asian authorities are normally well equipped to deal.

SUGGESTED MEASURES TO PROMOTE EXPANDED INVESTMENT

An increase would seem desirable in the amount of capital and associated technology and management flowing from Australasia to Southeast Asia. Present flows are now becoming significant and there is considerable scope for them to be expanded, spread further in the region, and oriented toward projects with greater benefit to the host countries. Whether or not the Australian and New Zealand governments wish for a greater political association with their northern neighbors, and *vice versa*, a number of measures should be considered to validate the present policy-stance and to recognize the interrelationship between commerce, investment, aid, and sociopolitical connections. In this paper we have been dealing with private direct investment and much responsibility rests with the private sectors to build the necessary economic arrangements; but some stimulation and facilitation from the governments is both necessary and, if not "desirable," at least consistent with the general levels of social involvement in business and industry. Possible steps which have arisen from the discussion in the earlier sections are listed summarily here.

Collective measures which might be taken by both the governments of Australia and New Zealand, on the one hand, and the Southeast Asian governments, on the other, to facilitate Australasian investment abroad include:

- double taxation avoidance agreements between each pair of governments, including clauses to provide for tax exemption under foreign inducement statutes (on account of priority status, promotion certification, etc.) to be treated as paid by the investor's home government;
- the more prompt concluding of treaties between each pair of governments to guarantee Australasian investments made with the approval of the host governments against expropriation, withdrawal of remittance rights, etc., including provision for recourse to a forum such as the Court for International Settlements in the event of a dispute;
- discussion between home and host governments on ways to make private capital and associated flows greater and more beneficial, on investment rules and codes (as an alternative approach to the imposition of arbitrary restrictions), on the exchange of statistics and information, and on investment opportunities;
- official support for the development of joint business committees (such as the Australia/Indonesia Cooperation Committee) and other forums for private sector contact—perhaps by the provision of funds for industry or commercial research and information, and for frequent meetings between businessmen of the region; and
- movement toward mutual tariff reductions to enable Australasian goods needed for Southeast manufacturing units to be traded with the output of Southeast Asian factories more readily and cheaply for consumers on both sides.

This fifth suggestion is rather more than one collective measure, of course. It probably presupposes the involvement of the Australian and New Zealand governments in a wide range of negotiations on tariff reductions, trade payments, and industrial cooperation with their Southeast Asian, as well as Japanese and possibly South and East Asian counterparts. Whether such discussions take the form of bilateral government-to-government talks, or that of multilateral regional and subregional arrangements, it is difficult to foresee rapid progress occurring without unusually strong initiatives being taken by Australia and New Zealand.

Australian and New Zealand official measures might include some clarification of present policy on investment abroad, some improvements in related policy areas, and some direct assistance. Specifically, the two governments might:

- think through the relationship between commerce and politics, perhaps with a view to recognizing their interdependence and to clarifying such a view to private sector participants in the exercise;
- think through the desired relationship between foreign aid and private investment or other commercial activity in developing economies, perhaps with a view to redirecting some aid to prime private entrepreneurs to make a greater contribution to development than the aid could alone, and to directing more aid toward the provision of infrastructure necessary to avoid delays and bottlenecks in the private sector (including financial administrative and physical infrastructure), but also to avoiding an association between aid and investment which reduces the value of the former by tying it to inefficient forms of the latter;
- review more vigorously the immigration, education, and other policies which affect the many aspects of cultural prejudice still to be found in Australia and New Zealand, to minimize the incidence of both official and popular discrimination which inhibits friendly relations with Southeast Asian peoples and prevents Australasians making rational economic choices;
- devote more resources to speed up investment climate studies, and to provide for their continual revision, for the inclusion of information on investment opportunities in Southeast Asia, and for their ready availability to Australasian entrepreneurs (there may be scope for Australia-New Zealand cooperation here);
- further liberalize exchange controls to remove expectations of early repatriation, in order to encourage investors willing to identify their interests with the Southeast Asian region over the longer term;
- amend the policies covering investment insurance to permit EPIC and EXCO to maintain requirements consistent with the needs and procedures of the Southeast Asian countries, and (in the case of Australia) to permit the export of managerial or technical expertise and the making of short-term loans associated with investments to be insurable; perhaps also to associate EPIC and EXCO with the export-import banks which are in the process of being established at least in the pooling of information;
- improve the supply of long-term suppliers' credit, cooperate with private sector financiers of foreign investment, and encourage an "overseas outlook" in the financial sector generally, perhaps by offering assistance in arranging training in special fields (such steps could be taken, especially

in cases where the financial institutions' activities are partly controlled by the states' monetary policies and have adequate facilities to deal with domestic needs);

- consider the admission of Southeast Asian banks into Australia and New Zealand on a *quid pro quo* basis to help local banks gain experience in Southeast Asia, or, if local banks cannot provide necessary services, the use of foreign banks might be encouraged to gain access to relatively cheap international long-term finance;
- provide funds for investment overseas in special cases through the (New Zealand) Development Finance Corporation, and, more generally, by the pooling of expertise and credit in consortia with the ability to service investment abroad;
- offer tax or other subsidies to encourage investors to operate desirable training programs in Southeast Asia, in their home plants and through educational institutions, and to assist with the costs of preinvestment and feasibility studies; and
- develop clear and integrated industry, regional manpower, merger, export, foreign ownership, and other related policies which will hasten and facilitate industrial restructuring and resource flexibility in order to:
  —transfer production overseas where appropriate,
  —put protection of industry in a long-term international trade and investment perspective,
  —avoid deterring offshore production for reimport, promote investment overseas and/or exports as a *quid pro quo* for a protected home market,
  —identify the characteristics of Australasian manufacturers with the capacity for successful investment abroad,
  —marry technological advantages, investment skills, and other factors into units which can undertake such investment,
  —ensure that export incentives promote the best forms of overseas commercial activity, including the export of skills and services, and
  —encourage local control of Australasian firms to free them to sell or manufacture in Southeast Asia.

Finally, the *Southeast Asian governments* who wish to encourage Australian and New Zealand entrepreneurs to bring capital, technology, management, etc. to the region on a basis at least as favorable as that of the larger investor countries might take steps to:

- provide the information and assurances which hesitant investors require if they are to operate in an alien environment;
- assist the matching of investors with satisfactory joint-venture partners; improve, streamline, and (where possible) reduce corruption in the bureaucratic machinery;
- create (with the help of foreign aid where necessary) the transport and other physical infrastructure necessary for reasonably efficient industrial production;

- emphasize education, vocational training, and manpower planning to enable maximum use of local human resources in joint ventures without loss of efficiency;
- avoid excessive protection, especially of inefficient local industries supplying essential inputs; and
- move faster toward the development of customs unions, or at least progressive tariff reductions to create a larger market.

Attention to the problems for which these suggested measures provide some solutions should increase desirable private investment flows from Australia and New Zealand to Southeast Asia. The two source countries are unlikely to become major suppliers of capital in the near future. Their own development needs are too great and their potential as a channel for international funds is limited. But their entrepreneurs are realizing the offshore investment opportunities which Southeast Asia presents, and their governments are recognizing the importance of private capital in achieving the objectives of foreign assistance programs for countries seeking their economic independence and pursuing vigorous and non-socialist industrial development. Australia and New Zealand possess valuable technology and industrial experience of particular relevance to Southeast Asia, and private capital flows can be expected to play a key role in transferring them profitably but in a spirit of cooperation and mutual interest.

REFERENCES

1. Commonwealth Bureau of Census and Statistics: *Overseas Investment 1971-72*, Tables 25, 26, Canberra 1973.

2. Department of Overseas Trade: interviews with officials (April, 1973), correspondence with ECOCEN (January, 1974), various papers and tables, Canberra, 1973 (mimeo).

FURTHER REFERENCES
(not included in footnotes)

3. Commonwealth Treasury: *Overseas Investment in Australia*, Treasury Economic Paper No. 1, Canberra, 1972.

4. Reserve Bank of Australia: Three Studies of Private Fixed Investment.

5. Commonwealth of Australia: *Export Payments Insurance Corporation Act, 1956-66*.

6. Export Payments Insurance Corporation: *Annual Report, 1972*, Sydney.

7. Norton, W. E. (ed.): *Three Studies of Private Fixed Investment*, Reserve Bank of Australia Occasional Paper No. 3E, Sydney, 1971.

8. "The Investor": *Australia in Thailand*, special report, Bangkok, March, 1972.

9. Brash, Donald T.: "Australia as host to the International Corporation," in *The International Corporation*, a symposium edited by C. P. Kindleberger, M.I.T. Press, 1970.

10. Reserve Bank of New Zealand: *Exchange Control, RBEC 3, 4, 18, Wellington, 1968-69*.

PART II:
Selected Functions

MANAGEMENT

Management

6

Understanding the Japanese:

PREPARATION FOR INTERNATIONAL BUSINESS

Robert J. Ballon

How pleasant it is to dream that 100 million Japanese consumers are standing on the piers of Yokohama and waiting for our shiploads of goods to sail into harbor. The reality, from the Western point of view, is far less agreeable; too many consumers are standing on the piers of Hamburg, London, and New York waiting for ships laden with Japanese goods.

Is there a strategy for achieving some balance between reality and dream? Perhaps some answers can be found in an examination of Japan's relationship to world business, as competitor or partner. Since the past and the present are known and can be learned from, we will look at Japan first as a historical, social, and economic continuum. We will then examine Japanese behavior in the industrial setting (the business enterprise), and, finally, describe some attitudes of both Japanese and foreigners in the context of international business.

THE JAPANESE CONTINUUM

According to Japanese mythology, Amaterasu O-mi-kami, the Sun Goddess, created Japan. Since that day, there has always been a spot on the map of the world called Japan (or some equivalent name) inhabited by Japanese. No other industrialized country can claim such a long and continuous history. Today's Japan and its inhabitants cannot be understood without keeping in mind this continuum, which is historical, social, and economic in nature.

THE HISTORICAL CONTINUUM

The Western concept of "nation" applies to a reality three or four centuries old at best; "Japan," on the other hand, has existed since the dawn of history. Anyone concerned with the domestic and international policies of Japan should consider how they are affected by its concept of nation.

Unity has been characteristic of Japan during its entire existence. It has enjoyed geographic unity (four islands off the mainland of Asia); ethnic unity (the aborigines, the Ainus, never really challenged their successors); and cultural and linguistic unity (amazing when compared to most other countries). Such continuity, unmarked by interruption, is rooted in ancient times and is expressed by the myth establishing an unbroken line of rulers. How can all this be adequately described by the usual concept of nation? The West has no comparable concept.

Reprinted by permission from *Business Horizons* (June, 1970).

Japan, more than any other country, enjoys a deep sense of identity; there is a clear-cut distinction between what is Japanese and what is not. But this identity, however, strong it may be, would not have survived the test of twenty centuries and more if it had not always been ready to react to circumstances. Japan guaranteed it permanency, its continuity, by always being ready to change, to adapt to new conditions.

Fifteen centuries ago, Japan decided to adopt Chinese civilization, and did so, but not at the cost of becoming Chinese. Japan assimilated the Chinese heritage in order to remain Japanese. A century ago, Japan decided to adopt Western industrialization, and did so, but not at the cost of becoming Western. Again, it was in order to remain Japanese in the context of new circumstances created by the presence of Western powers in Asia. The changes seen today in Japan are called Westernization by the Westerners; to the Japanese, who feel responsible for such changes, they are signs of modernization, the way for Japan to remain Japan in the modern world. The Westerner often feels that there must be conflict between tradition and change; to the Japanese, tradition has always meant change.

THE SOCIAL CONTINUUM

Historians have insisted that the Meiji Restoration (1868) was not a revolution, but was rightly called a restoration. At that time, Japan opened to Western trade and prepared to begin the process of industrialization. One generation later, it was clear that the nation had reaffirmed its continuity with the past; changes had occurred, but they were in Japanese style.

In the West, industrialization was initiated by rugged individualists who turned their energies to industrial (or colonial) pursuits; they were children of the future, rebelling against the prevailing order of their still agricultural society, and forcing their ambitions on the people and the State. Japan followed an entirely different course; the government took the lead. The private sector was familiar only with commercial activities and was not anxious to embark on the untested process of industrialization. Only by the mid-1880s did the private sector show an interest in industry, and the government gladly turned it all over (except for military establishments).[1] Since then, industrial initiative has been in private hands, but the origins of industry are never denied.

The traditional agricultural society, for its part, reacted to the challenge of industrialization by providing, through silk and tea exports, most of the foreign exchange needed to purchase industrial know-how from the West. In addition, the agricultural sector increased productivity in order to keep up with the increase in population, and contributed a diligent and industrious work force to industry.

Generally speaking, the industrializing process was extraordinarily smooth from the social viewpoint, because it did not upset the more basic relations:

> The natural community (the extended family) greatly helped the industrial commitment of the rural workforce.

The local productive community had been for centuries the village community; its set of values was now progressively transferred to the industrial enterprise.

The national community was strengthened by a sense of emergency (successively, the threat of invasion by the Western powers, the lack of natural resources required by industry, the pressure of population, and the perennial problem of balance of payments).

The industrial society that emerged is today surprisingly homogeneous, a characteristic greatly enhanced by the high degree of education of the masses. The affluence of recent years is reflected in the *sarariman* (Japanese pronunciation for "salary man" or wage-earner).[2] The *sarariman* epitomizes the postwar transitional style of living that steadily moves up the average income without really widening the spectrum of income distribution. This modern Japanese man is not yet the powerful consumer of, say, the American economy, but he is moving rapidly toward that stage. He does not feel, however, that he is a member of a privileged class; he is simply the typical member of a society that depends for its success on the success of its members, the 100 million Japanese. Western observers have tended to overemphasize Japan's dependence on exports. The truth of the matter, however, is that present-day Japan's success is based primarily on the expansion of its domestic market; it would be more to the point to consider the exports as the means of paying for the imports.

The traditional lack of concern for individualism reinforces the collective dimension of society, today as much as yesterday, and produces an overwhelming communal motivation. At no time has the individual been an outsider who may or may not join the group; no Japanese has opted for Japan—he was born there! In fact, he would not be Japanese without Japan; conversely, there would be no Japan without Japanese! One result of this identification with nation is that Japan so far has suffered little from the brain-drain that bleeds many other nations, developed and developing alike.

Social change in the West is usually understood as the replacement of some outdated institution by a new one, but in Japan the change takes place by adding the new to the old in an uninterrupted process of growth. It is likely that for a while the old and the new will stand in seeming contradiction, but the community views it is a manifestation of the dynamism of life.

THE ECONOMIC CONTINUUM

It is to be expected that the prevailing unity of Japanese society will affect the economic sector.[3] At one end of the economic spectrum is the industrial enterprise; at the other, the state. Between these two extremes are found all possible forms of cooperation and integration, as well as what the Japanese call excessive competition, indicating that the total system should not be considered as monolithic, but rather as highly flexible.

In social life, a person's family name is preferred; his first name is practically never used. Similarly, in economic life, the identity of an industrial enterprise is not expressed as often by its individual characteristics (capital, management, and so on), as by its relations, its family name. Bearing an average ratio of 80 percent debt capital and 20 percent equity capital or worse, the Japanese firm would soon collapse without its participation in the web of relations, financial and personal, that make up the business world. The grouping of enterprises takes many forms; the most specific are the grouping of small firms around a large one, and the grouping of several large firms. The first form is called *oyagaisha-kogaisha* or parent-firm (*oya* meaning parent, and *gaisha* meaning company) and child-firm (*ko* meaning child). It may express vertical division of labor or diversification or sub-contracting. Usually, former managers of the parent-firm are found on the board of the child-firms. Under the impact of rapid technological progress and labor shortage in some sectors of the labor market, such family ties tend to grow. Japanese management believes that this satellite system leaves more flexibility than a single mammoth corporation or outright amalgamation.

The other major form of industrial grouping involves several large firms. In prewar years, this was known as *zaibatsu* and referrred to firms like Mitsui and Mitsubishi. The term has come to be misleading, however, insofar as it seems to indicate a repetition of the prewar grouping; it would be more accurate to use the term *keiretsu* (alignment). The prewar *zaibatsu* operated under highly centralized family control through holding companies; the *keiretsu* consists of a number of corporations aligned by common interests usually sponsored, but not necessarily controlled by, one of the large city banks.[4] Such alignment materializes through swapping of shares, products and managers, credit preferences, favored access to supply sources, and so on. A trading house is often included; it does not, however, monopolize supplies and sales of the group, but its own volume of operations requires the backing of a large industrial group. The trading house plays also an important credit role, especially in regard to the smaller firms in the group.

Another meaningful instrument of cohesion is the trade association. Its main function is to serve as a communication channel between the government and the private sector; for example, most industrial statistics are compiled by these trade associations for use primarily by the government. The association is only one instance of the close relationship between government and business. The Japanese have not been conditioned to such an assump-
and business. The Japanese have not been conditioned to such an assump-
tion. They would rather think of the coin called "Japan, Incorporated," of which one side is the government, and the other is business.[5]

The Japanese continuum—historical, social, and economic—can be compared to a tree, which lives by feeding on its environment, soil, air, rain, sun. It does not lose its identity by this dependence; furthermore, it grows, adding one more ring to its trunk every year. Branches and leaves are as valuable as the trunk, since all contribute to the life of the whole tree.

The lesson is that no understanding of the tree will be gained by looking only at one leaf or one branch. In regard to the Japanese continuum, foreign firms considering a Japanese counterpart commonly overlook the total reality. Business is never conducted with one particular firm, notwithstanding appearances; business has always to do with the whole economy, with Japan, of which some immediate manifestations are government regulations, distribution complexities, employee motivation, and business outlook and practices.

As a result, despite foreign investment controls, it is much easier to start business in Japan than to stay in business; staying in business requires foreign interests to face the test of being part and parcel of the continuum. Two decades ago, it was easy for DuPont to sell its nylon technology to Toyo Rayon for a price that was more than the capitalization of the purchaser, but today the Japanese company is one of the top producers in the world. The greatest challenge of the foreign corporation is to keep up with Japan.

THE ENTERPRISE AS MICROCOSM

Foreign investment in Japan must carefully consider what an industrial enterprise is in Japan, rather than to assume that it is the same as it is at home. It is commonly assumed that "K.K." after a company's name stands for "Inc." or "Ltd."; that is true only so far as the dictionary and the law are concerned. It should be understood that the context is different and that the internal reality of the enterprise is also different.

The Japanese industrial enterprise is a microcosm of Japan, a kind of reduced version of the total reality of social and economic life. Japanese scholars in the field of industrial organization describe the Japanese enterprise as more a *Gemeinschaft* than a *Gesellschaft*, person centered rather than job oriented, and more a human community than a mere economic organization. In today's Japan, the company, as exemplified by the large corporations, has three human dimensions that have made it one of the most highly motivated socioeconomic organizations we know.

DIMENSIONS OF EMPLOYMENT

Shoku-ba ("place of work")—When a child is asked, "What is your father doing?" the answer in the West is usually given in terms of the father's occupation. In Japan it is always given in terms of the company that employs the father. The Westerner is afforded security by his occupation or skill; the Japanese expects security from the company, whatever his job may be at any given time. Social psychologists have traced that value back to the importance of the *ba* (place) associated with an agricultural civilization. The lack of occupational pride explains the ease, even the eagerness, with which the Japanese—the individual employee as well as his labor union—adopt technological innovation. Little obstruction, if any, is found concerning automation, change of job, retraining, or transfers, since they are all for the good of the real industrial dimension that counts—the place of work, the company.

The Japanese labor union also derives its existence and identity from the place of work. The organization is almost always an enterprise-wide union, including only—but all—the permanent employees (up to, but excluding, the chief of section). For example, a labor union in a university will include, in the same union, university professors, cafeteria counter-girls, laboratory assistants, boilermen, drivers, and so on. Collective bargaining will not include any outsider. Employment regulations (which take the place of individual and collective labor agreements as well as of work rules) and welfare programs are of little concern to the union; they are considered to be a specific responsibility of management. An employee who is dismissed (a rare event) or quits has lost his membership in the union. Such a union concentrates its energies on the protection of lifelong employment and the remuneration system.

The Japanese sense of identification with the company applies equally to management. The average manager is not so much a manager by some individual talent that he could exercise anywhere, but a manager primarily because of his employment by this company. This view has a far-reaching consequence: Managers and employees—and sometimes the union—feel that they almost equally represent the company.

Shushin koyo ("lifelong employment")—Whenever feasible, employment in Japan is for life, in the sense that the employee is hired at the time he leaves school and will stay with the company until retirement. The employer will not fire him (except for some extraordinary reason), and the employee will not quit (unless he wants to expose himself to financial loss and social blame.)

This rather uncommon practice is not a matter of legislation; it was established by custom and is now protected by the enterprise-wide union. Not all firms, however, can afford the system in its entirety, and some employees cannot stand it. As a result, labor will move not from a large firm into another large firm and not from a small firm into a small firm—but from a large firm into a small firm, and from a small firm into another small firm.

Lifelong tenure offers the employee the much desired security at the place of work. Of course, it supposes that the enterprise is somehow "eternal," as in the case of the large firms. The durability of the firm is, therefore, the employee's main concern; he has an invaluable motivation for work. The soundness of the firm is also desired by the labor union; unions are thus found almost exclusively in the large firms where they organize only the permanent employees. Technological innovation in the West is often seen as a threat to occupation and security, but in Japan innovation is seen as a means of strengthening the enterprise and bolstering the security it provides. The labor union will not object, as long as innovation does not result in lay-off.

Nenko joretsu ("merit years")—The employee of a Japanese firm will "grow in age" with the enterprise on which he depends for his security. As years go by, he acquires more and more experience with the firm as a human organization; his experience is based on daily contact and familiarity with all the facets of the firm's activities and of the people involved. *Nenko* is not accurately translated as seniority; it is rooted in personal devotion to the company as manifested by length of service. It is the key to development and promotion; promotion is less related to the individual than it is to his membership in the organization. Japanese employees as well as managers are, therefore, more generalists than specialists. Their best skill, their best chance, and their best security are not related to some technical talent, but to a human dimension—how to best fit in, and contribute to, the whole enterprise now and in the future.

MEANING FOR MANAGEMENT

These three dimensions of Japanese employment require, of course, a special type of remuneration.[6] Rather than to speak of wages or salary, it would be more specific to speak of a guaranteed life income paid out in installments. This income is not measured by one's contribution to production but by one's living and social needs, and incorporates an elaborate system of savings through deferred wage payments, such as the bonus and the retirement allowance. It all amounts to a substantial financial stake in the enterprise. At present, remuneration based on performance and efficiency is awarded in standard Japanese fashion—by simply being added to the existing wage system.

Some Japanese scholars condemn these values as "remnants of feudalism," but they have nothing to do with feudalism. They are up-to-date expressions of the familism pervading Japanese society, and form a system of employment that was institutionalized only in postwar years with the successful backing of the labor unions. Managers may lament about its cost (for all practical purposes the labor cost is fixed), but they capitalize on the resulting growth of the enterprises and of the economy.

The management-labor relationship is similar to the government-business relationship described earlier; there is no true gap between the two. The enterprise is like a coin, of which one side is management and the other is labor. Management is never labor, and labor is never management; the only reality is the enterprise. Employment could then be summarized in one word—participation. What the West is now expecting from the techniques, if not almost ideologies, such as "management by participation" and the like, already exists in Japan's participative employment. One of the most difficult aspects of the Japanese system, however, is that the principle of "equal pay for equal work" cannot really apply.

But what about the small enterprises? They represent more than 90 percent of the firms and employ well over half of the labor force. Participative employment is the ideal that small firms strive for; if it were not for the progressive wage system, they would succeed. About the age of 35, the salary flattens out, and the employee often starts to drift from one employer to the other. Furthermore, small firms in Japan are not usually meant to become large and are looked at, in the national economic context, as expendable; it is not that the economy could do without them, but while small firms can disappear, large firms are "eternal." The small firms give the total economy the required flexibility that large firms cannot provide. In recent years, the growing concentration of small firms in the parent- and child-firm system as well as the growth from small to medium size are changing the traditional picture to some extent.

Japan's labor shortage has been much discussed, but how can one speak of a labor shortage in overpopulated Japan? As in all industrial countries, Japan suffers from an acute shortage of managerial and technical talents because of the fantastic expansion of the business sector, as well as the absence of imported labor. On the other hand, it must be remembered that Japan has one of the most widely educated populations in the world. At present, the labor shortage that hurts most is that of new entrants into the labor force. This has to do with lifelong employment and the wage system based on "merit of years" that keeps firms from hiring middle-aged employees. When new employees fresh from school are hired in large numbers, they bring down the average age and thus the average salary in the enterprise. But there is no absolute shortage of middle-age workers. In order to tap this labor reservoir, a greater flexibility is slowly being incorporated into the wage system.

If the Japanese enterprise is this complicated and unfamiliar, it is legitimate to wonder whether foreign investment in Japan is at all possible, however many liberalization rounds the Japanese government is considering. Foreign operations in Japan, whatever their size, are considered by the Japanese as large firms, and, therefore, should accommodate the three dimensions of industrial employment that have been described. To fall short in any dimension will have to be paid for in loss of motivation, and, perhaps, by labor unrest. The reason is not so much that the Japanese employee suffers from prejudice, but that he does not find in the foreign firm the expected relationship. Psychologically, the most upsetting experience to him is not the presence of foreigners, but the fact that foreigners come and go, and, while around, manage the enterprise in disregard of what a Japanese enterprise essentially is, a human organization. Personnel administration is the most demanding task of the foreign business executive in Japan; most regrettably, it is also the task for which the home office allows least time.

INTERNATIONAL BUSINESS AND JAPAN

"If you can't beat them, join them!" seems to describe the mixed feelings of international business toward the phenomenal success of Japan's domestic market and exports. Any businessman's mouth waters at the thought of a growingly afluent market of 100 million consumers; he may be less enthusiastic about the inroads of Japanese exports onto his own market. Some business executives ponder the advantages of using Japan as a beachhead for an assault on Asian markets. The general feeling is that, for many years to come, Japan will keep growing at the rate of at least 10 percent annually in real terms, or two or three times the rate in the West.[7] International business has no choice; it must take a position in regard to Japan. Some die-hards still predict doom and wish for ways to strangle such a growth; most observers, however, fall into two groups: those who look for business *with* Japan, and those who look for business *in* Japan.

BUSINESS WITH JAPAN

The most basic problem for international business determined to do business with Japan seems to be that of establishing a long-term position; this is often interpreted as asking for short-term leniency in regard to Japan. Not at all! A long-term position almost always requires foregoing quick returns for greater returns later. This is especially difficult in Japan because of the fast tempo of economic growth. It could be compared to an attempt to jump on a fast-moving vehicle; the safest way is to run along at the same speed and then jump. Economies outside of Japan grow at rates of 2 to 4 percent in real terms; this is not fast enough to jump safely onto the Japanese economy that grows at 12 to 14 percent in real terms! Yusuke Kashiwagi, vice minister of finance, stated recently that monetary and fiscal policies are usually of the stop-go type; in Japan, they are at best of the walk-run type!

Another related aspect is that in the West business is, by and large, the affair of an individual firm, with the government playing (hopefully) the role of traffic policeman. In Japan, business is essentially a communal affair. The result is a difference in outlook that can be best understood by looking at planning. Western corporations and Western economies consider planning as essential; targets are established in the future we do not really know, and the driving force then becomes the pull of the future. The Japanese do not know the future anymore than we do, but it seems to inhibit them less than us; their driving force is the push of the past. Asked recently to comment on planning in his company, the president of an internationally well-known Japanese corporation stated in essence that: "Planning is not the point; flexibility is what counts!" This attitude may explain why the Japanese feel immediately familiar with innovations.

Another upsetting aspect of doing business with Japan is what is in our eyes scandalous waste and inefficiency. In Japan, the annual national total spent for business entertainment (the so-called company expense accounts) is higher than the government budget for social security! No Japanese will ever do anything alone, whether it is a business transaction, a business decision, a trip, or anything else. In addition, foreigners are prompt to accuse the Japanese of being exasperatingly slow in making decisions. But the Japanese often accuse foreigners of being slow in making decisions.

What is the problem? In a Japanese organization, a decision is never taken by one man; a proposal generated at the lower levels of management is discussed endlessly at all levels, slowly moving up the management hierarchy.[8] When finally it is endorsed (not really decided) at the top, the entire organization is ready for *immediate* execution. The process may have taken, say, six weeks, but at the end of these six weeks, everybody is poised for action and highly motivated. In a Western organization, let us imagine that one morning the president wakes up with a bright plan and starts issuing orders (or it may be that his representative in Japan has just cabled that the Japanese have agreed to a proposal). Six weeks are now needed to translate these orders into execution, possibly haphazardly and totally lacking in motivation. The difference between decision making in the West and in Japan is not found in the time dimension, but in the motivation of the entire organization!

On the other side, the greatest handicap of Japanese business at the international level is its lack of experience in dealing with foreigners on a reciprocal basis. It is as difficult for the Japanese to deal with foreigners as it is for foreigners to deal with Japanese. When the Americans point at the opportunities given to Japanese business on the American market, and request "equal opportunity" for American business on the Japanese market, the Japanese are puzzled: "Equal opportunity? Does this mean opportunity between equals?" Their reaction is then to fall back on mere commercial considerations, at a time when business (between people) means much more than trade (of goods).

This attitude has earned a Japanese Prime Minister the label of "transistor salesman," and provoked developing countries to call the Japanese businessmen "economic animals." Such a psychological complex is most harmful because business, particularly at the international level, does not make sense outside of the human relations on which it rests. At this point of history, it is not clear yet whether the long history of the Japanese continuum is an advantage or a handicap in regard to internationalization. There is hope, however, because the continuum has always proved to be dynamic and resilient.

BUSINESS IN JAPAN

For international business, the true experience of doing business with Japanese will be found in Japan. It is a most traumatic experience. Generally speaking, foreign interests would prefer to go at Japan alone (an expected expression of Western individualism). The reason given is that one is then able to control directly all the elements of the experiment. Is that so? the difficulty with this approach is that the experiment does not take place in a vacuum; it takes place in Japan. And how do you achieve control? Furthermore, one may wonder whether a decision taken for reasons of control is always the best business decision.

Business in Japan necessarily means business with the Japanese. The most common form, and the one favored by the government, is the joint venture.[9] As might be expected, a marriage between a Japanese and a foreign business is not necessarily blissful. In a joint venture, the human dimensions are the most meaningful, and the foreign partner is often guilty of some common shortcomings.

First, when establishing a joint venture with the Japanese, foreign interests display an almost blind faith in the written word of the contract, as they also do for ordinary business contracts. They should remember, however, that Japan has only 8,000 practicing lawyers (the United States has over 300,000 for twice the population). In Japan, the gentlemen's agreement that backs the written word is much more important; it is impossible to put daily business partnership agreements on paper.[10]

Second, shortsightedness by the home office often causes innumerable difficulties, because it judges too readily Japanese operations on the basis of financial figures. Japan has about 4,000 certified public accountants, of whom only about half are active in business. Tremendous efforts are now being made to bring Japanese accounting standards up to the international level, but how can the figures of one firm properly account for the continuum explained previously?

Another problem with the home office is the endless stream of questions originated at headquarters. The foreign representative in Japan must waste the best of his limited energies answering questions from the home office, rather than managing Japanese operations. Another set of difficulties results from the attitude of the foreign manager to whom Japan is not a specific challenge, and whose first concern remains with promotion at the home office. These difficulties and many more are piled on top of the fundamental difficulty of developing a feel for Japanese idiosyncracies, as well as that of keeping up with a faster growth rate.

Shortcomings on the part of the Japanese partner are no less dangerous.[11] Almost all of them can be reduced to a basic one: that he will consider the joint venture, once and for all, as a child-firm, owing its life and subsistence to the Japanese parent. This danger should be discussed at length between the two potential partners before any agreement is signed. The only valid angle from which to tackle the problem is the personnel policy of the Japanese partner in regard to the joint venture. Regrettably, most of the negotiation time is spent discussing capital contributions and the amount of control they command.

The international businessman has no choice but to work hard for a transition from Japan as a competitor to Japan as a partner. During the twentieth century, American business has expanded to dominate the economic scene; Europeans called it *Le Defi Americain*.

If asked to state in one word the reason for the American "success," many would answer, "Pragmatism." But in my experience, many Americans are most dogmatic about their pragmatism. If the Trojan horse of international business is pragmatism, then the situation is hopeless, because the Japanese are pragmatic about pragmatism! The purpose of this article was precisely to learn from "Le defi Japonais."

NOTES

1. See Johannes Hirschmeier, *The Origins of Entrepreneurship in Meiji Japan* (Cambridge: Harvard University Press, 1964).

2. See Ezra F. Vogel, *Japan's New Middle Class* (Berkeley: University of California Press, 1963).

3. For a discussion of the economic continuum, see Robert J. Ballon, ed., *The Japanese Employee* (Tokyo: Sophia-Tuttle, 1969), Chapter 1.

4. See Iwao Hoshii, *The Dynamics of Japan's Business Evolution* (Tokyo: Orient West, 1966).

5. James C. Abegglen, ed., *Business Strategies for Japan* (Tokyo: Sophia-Britannica, 1970).

6. *The Japanese Employee*, Chapter 6.

7. *Business Strategies for Japan*, Executive Summary.

8. Robert J. Ballon, ed., *Doing Business in Japan* (Tokyo: Sophia-Tuttle, 1968), pp. 158-78.

9. Robert J. Ballon, ed., *Joint Ventures and Japan* (Tokyo: Sophia-Tuttle, 1968).

10. J. Toshio Sawada, *Subsequent Conduct and Supervening Events* (Tokyo: University of Tokyo Press, 1968), pp. 199-200.

11. See Herbert Glazer, *The International Businessman in Japan* (Tokyo: Sophia-Tuttle, 1968).

7

American Businesses in Japan:

A NEW FRAMEWORK

Robert A. Feldman

SUMMARY

A large number of the business problems and personnel problems which American firms now face in operating in Japan are the result of inadequate procedures for screening and selecting representatives. The selection at present, judging from results, fails to consider some factors very important to success in Japan, while overestimating the value of others. The factors considered important in candidates for Japan are generally the same as those considered important in candidates for posts in America; thus, in many cases, the vital consideration of the different cultural environment of business in Japan is being virtually ignored.

This paper is an attempt to establish a new framework for personnel selection for posts in Japan. It is hoped that through applying this new framework, American firms will be able to select personnel particularly adaptable to the environment of Japanese-American business. The framework consists of three parts: (1) a theory of Japanese society which defines many of the situations to which American businessmen have to adapt, and also provides rules for understanding what is acceptable and what is taboo in Japan, (2) a theory of expatriate American society in Japan which illustrates the different reaction patterns which different groups of Americans have to Japanese society and evaluates each group in terms of its business effectiveness in Japan, and (3) a series of individual personality traits and situations in life which are important in determining, first, a candidate's adaptability to Japanese society and, second, the particular group of expatriate society he is likely to enter.

The theory of Japanese society presented here is basically that of Professor Chie Nakane of the University of Tokyo, as disucssed in her books *Japanese Society* and *Tekiō no Jōken*. It describes Japanese society as one which forms interest groups (e.g., enterprises, schools, intra-office cliques) on the basis of where people are rather than of what they do, a system of interest group formation radically different from the one Americans are used to. The rules for forming and preserving these interest groups are described below, and then some of the implications this way of organizing society has for American business in Japan are discussed.

The members of expatriate American society are separated into four groups in this paper, each group being characterized by its members' reactions to Japanese society. The four groups are (1) those simply not concerned with cultural problems, called the Not-Concerned (NC) group, (2) those who

---

Reprinted by permission of the Nomura Research Institute, from the May 15, 1974, issue of the Nomura Investment Report.

want to Americanize the social and business systems in Japan, called the Americans Abroad (AA), (3) those who feel that compromise with Japanese social and business ethics is the best way to handle cultural problems, called the Americans in Japan (AJ), and (4) those who have adopted Japanese methods for their operations in Japan and thus turned the system to their own favor, called the Relative Americans (RA). The traits of each of these four groups are described, and the latter two are recommended as effective and useful for assignment in Japan while the former two are not.

Among the individual personality traits and situations in life discussed are optimal age for assignment in Japan, the need for almost saintly patience, how one's wife must be included in the evaluation process, and linguistic ability. These factors, and others, must be considered in selection of representatives for Japan. The latter, linguistic ability, is particularly important because it not only is essential to adjustment to the environment, but it is also the indicator by which effectiveness in all other fields is measured. If a man has no linguistic talent, he cannot be an effective representative in Japan.

INTRODUCTION

Very few American businesses today choose their representatives for Japan on the basis of an evaluation of how well they will fit in with Japanese society. Unfortunately, a man's success in an assignment in Japan cannot be predicted by how well he has done in past assignments. Personal, linguistic, and political abilities play roles in the world of international business in Japan very different from those which these traits play in America, so that the man with a magnetic personality and consummate office political ability in New York may end up in Tokyo as an isolated, arrogant outcast, whom Japanese employees may wish to keep far from their own lives. Certainly not all Americans sent to Japan have such harsh experiences. But at the present time, whether or not a representative fits in with Japan is often a case of hit or miss; in other words, the reasons a man fails or succeeds are seldom the factors considered in selecting him for his post.

Such a hit or miss state of affairs may have been unavoidable at one time because of lack of widespread experience by American companies in choosing representatives for Japan. Today, however, it is quite avoidable. There have been enough success stories of Americans in Japan to be able to isolate distinctive characteristics of the people involved.

Japanese sociologist Professor Chie Nakane of the University of Tokyo has said that "In every society, a man's social life is carried on within the holes between the threads in a complex social fabric" (*Tekiō no Jōken*, p. 10). This statement is just as true for business life as for social life in general. In light of this, it can be said that the successful Americans in the Japanese-American business world are those who are capable, through linguistic, political, and personal abilities, of identifying and then adapting to the new "threads" which define the freedoms and constraints of dealing with Japanese colleagues.

In order to choose the right man for Japan, the person in the home office who does the selecting must have conceptions of both Japanese society and American expatriate society in Japan, as well as an idea of what specific traits are helpful in adapting to Japan. Moreover, he must know his own corporation's objectives, and must be familiar with the career objectives of the men he evaluates. Some corporate objectives, such as short-term profits, are not deemed worth pursuing by many Japanese, and thus a company with such objectives will never be able to attract Japanese employees or satisfy the ones it already has. Moreover, the man who leaves the U.S. to seek the promotion sometimes brought by the status of having been stationed abroad is not likely to be well received by Japanese employees. Going abroad to enhance one's position at home is not necessarily disastrous to a foreign branch; but the short-term nature of such assignments and the "here-today-gone-tommorow" attitude that sometimes goes with them can be basic causes of the all too frequent wide gaps between Americans stationed in Japan and their Japanese colleagues.

Management techniques and ideas of what constitutes success are often transferrable to Japan. The American who has succeeded at home at fostering respect among his juniors through keeping his distance or by being an idea man himself is not likely to get along with Japanese employees. The latter consider aloofness impersonal and egotistical, and the higher a man climbs in an organization, the more he is supposed to rely on juniors for ideas (or at least let them think he relies on them). Nor will the man who can measure success only in profits be able to represent his company effectively in Japan. Japanese simply do not measure success in profits, but rather in the size, stability, and prestige of a firm, along with the level of harmony in intra-company politics.

This paper will attempt to discuss some of these topics in light of theories of both Japanese society and also American expatriate society in Japan. By understanding these two societies, the traits that fit into them, and the implications they have for business, it is hoped that those choosing men to represent their companies in Japan will be able to capitalize on the lessons to be learned from both the successes and failures of the past, and be able to choose Americans more apt to fit in well with the Japanese-American business world.

A DEFINITION OF SUCCESS

Differing conceptions of what constitutes corporate success was one basic problem mentioned above which contributes to friction in the Japanese-American business world. This problem is a classic one, in that virtually every American company operating in Japan faces it. Thus, it can serve as an excellent example of the type of problem many have in dealing with Japan, and illustrates better the three aspects of correct personnel selections.

The basic result which Americans often look for from a business is profitability. A firm which yields a return on capital of 10 percent is considered more successful than one which yields only 9 percent, other things being equal. Stability is another factor of importance. While a company may be cyclical, its long-term average profits are held to be quite important in evaluating it. Size, whether measured by market share, sales, production capacity, or what have you, is not always considered important by Americans. A small company is not necessarily a second-class one. While working conditions and the satisfaction of employees are sometimes deemed quite important by certain managers and executives, they are not always considered essential to a successful business. As long as the unions are happy enough not to strike, business is not considered much hindered by employees' dissatisfaction. In other words, the American idea of a successful company revolves around the concept of profitability.

Japanese consider some of the same factors when evaluating the success of a business, but their order of importance is quite different, and other factors enter as well. The primary factor is that of ranking. In every industry, there is severe competition for ranking. Rank is assigned by size (measured by sales, number of employees, number of branch offices, market share, production capacity, etc.), and by prestige. Profitability is not considered too important; often firms will sacrifice profits in order to expand capacity to be the biggest in their field. The harmony of internal politics in a company is also an important measure of success. A firm in which juniors and seniors have close personal relationships is considered more successful than one were the two groups are not close, even if profitability is unaffected. In short, success depends on constructing a solid interest group based on personal relations, one which can compete for rank with other groups (other companies) similar to it. Profitability, while useful as a tool for making the firm stronger, is not considered essential.

Every American business which operates in Japan inevitably runs into trouble in the area of defining success. American representatives sometimes complain that Japanese just do not understand profitability, while their Japanese colleagues complain that the Americans are deaf to concerns of improving or defending the firm's ranking. The Japanese may think the Americans are greedy, while the Americans may feel that the Japanese do not understand the object of business. The clash here is not, at base, a question of business philosophy or management philosophy, but rather a cultural problem; success means different things to the people from these two cultures, even though both have chosen industrialism to achieve their own types of success. And because the problem of defining success is cultural, it cannot be solved once and for all in favor of one side or the other no matter how much patience and time are invested.

In light of this, then, one realizes that an American representative in Japan must be a person who can learn to live with insoluble differences, not just enduring them and waiting to be sent home, but realizing the appropriateness of Japanese methods, given the cultural expectations Japanese have of companies. At the same time, there will inevitably be clashes with the home office back in America, so another necessity for the representative in Japan is to win enough confidence among his Japanese colleagues to gain both a sympathetic hearing of the home office's views and also compromises suitable to it.

Winning the confidence of Japanese colleagues in order to gain the leverage needed to represent the home office effectively involves basically three factors. First, one must understand the structure of Japanese society, one's Japanese company as a subset of it, and the actions and attitudes one should expect from one's Japanese colleagues because of that situation. For example, it would be unrealistic to hope for a firm to break off relations with its trading company simply because the distribution system in Japan is uneconomical in many ways. Breaking off relations would destroy all trust in the firm, render it unable to get loans from banks, and brand it as antisocial, not to mention the possibility of certain stores refusing to handle the goods of a company so unethical as to break away from its trading company. An understanding of Japanese society will keep one from trespassing taboos, and thus foster a closer relationship with Japanese partners.

Second, wining confidence means that one must be the type of American who reacts well to Japanese society. There are definite patterns of reaction to Japan among Americans which have definite corresponding counter-reactions by Japanese. For example, if one is fascinated by Japan, stays for many years, and learns the language, one is likely to be completely accepted by Japanese colleagues. This reaction and counter-reaction pattern exists, though it is not seen often, and finding a man who will fit into it can be the best thing possible for an American company operating in Japan.

Third, winning confidence means that the representative must have certain skills of adaptability, some of which are inborn. For example, the man with no language ability will never be able to understand the structure and internal politics of a Japanese company because the places where one finds out about such things (after hours meetings at bars and clubs) are places where some Japanese must be used.

To understand the first problem more clearly, we must now turn attention to the problem of what the basic structure of Japanese society is, and what are the implications this structure has for the Japanese-American business world.

JAPANESE SOCIETY

There have been many attempts to describe Japanese society, the most famous in English being, of course, Ruth Benedict's *The Chrysanthemum and the Sword*. Unfortunately, this book, though a classic, is quite dated now, and is considered by some to be irrelevant to much of what goes on in Japan today. Benedict's book has been superseded by another description of Japanese society, that of Professor Nakane (quote above), called simply *Japanese Society*. Professor Nakane discards the concept of class in analyzing Japan, and arrives at a new type of society, one which she labels "vertical society."

At the core of Japanese society is the institution of the "frame," a place of business, a school, an office, etc. around which the people who frequent it form an interest group. The chief criterion for entrance is not occupational, but rather situational; simply being there, no matter what one's job, makes one part of the group. Thus, in any one company, everyone from the president to the janitors belongs first to the company. A janitor from Company A has more in common with the president of the company than with another janitor in Company B. To put it another way, the managers, scientists, and workers in Company A will socialize with each other, but not with the managers, scientists, or workers of Company B.

All societies have established means of forming interest groups. In India, occupational groups (castes) are the accepted way, and in America as well, managers often socialize with other managers, scientists with scientists, and auto workers with auto workers. The interest group is formed by members with a similar attribute or job, so society is horizontal. But in Japan, function or attribute is not the prime factor in group formation; frame or situation is the primary factor, so society is vertical.

In such a vertical society, and in the vertical subsets of it as well, it is taboo to say that one part of the group is more important than another, since that might create divisiveness in the group and leave members with no place to go should the group fall apart. (Why one cannot join other groups is explained below.) Likewise taboo is giving the impression that any one person or job is too much more important than any other. For example, there cannot be a special managers' coffee break; there must be a coffee break for everyone or for no one at all. It is not proper to construct a hierarchy inside a group according to attribute or function.

However, some order and some hierarchy are obviously necessary lest anarchy reign and nothing at all get done. In place of horizontal society's hierarchy by function, groups in Japan's vertical society give themselves hierarchy based on seniority within the group and on personal relationships of friendship, duty, and obligation. When a man joins a group, he enters on the lowest rung on the ladder. (Thus, movement from one group to another is seldom beneficial since the social capital built up by membership in one group is not transferable to another.) The only way to move up is to wait and gather seniority. Age, while sometimes important, is not so important as the number of years of service to the group.

However, seniority is not enough to give order to an interest group. The personal relationships between those in a group often set definite limits to who is permitted to do certain jobs or to receive certain honors. There relationships usually assume a senior-junior character, with the senior treating the junior to free liquor after work, and advising the junior on personal matters. These senior-junior relationships are very strong, and to transgress them is considered a formidable sin. Even within an interest group, one will not go outside the channels of personal relationships in trying to do anything, even for the good of the whole group.

Horizontally structured societies often see strong and even excess competition between the horizontal groups; e.g., workers will hold a strike or management a lock-out to the detriment of both. The same sort of competition takes place in Japan, and with all the same severity and dis-economy, but between vertical groups. Widget manufacturers will make exactly the same kinds of widgets, glutting the market, and neither will stop since it is important for their groups' ranking in society to make a full line of widgets. One cannot be first in one's industry without doing everything one's competitors do. Competition between groups thus can become very intense. (However, on the other side of the coin, competition sometimes, though not often, will disappear as firms settle into a situation of "peaceful coexistence" in their industry.)

With such a society, attempts at friendly contact between the members of different groups can take on a character of treason. While it is not forbidden, for example, for the presidents of trading companies Mitsui Bussan and Mitsubishi Shōji to talk to each other, too much togetherness would not be welcomed by their respective employees, or by the firms associated with the two. Indeed, many groups are quite cold toward all people outside their own particular group and those other groups with whom they have close relationships. It must be pointed out that not all groups other than one's own are treated coldly. Often groups will be related through personal relations of their members or through business ties, and so will be on quite amicable terms. For example, often enterprises depending on a certain bank for most of their loans will form a super-group and get along well. But firms grouped with another bank will be treated as outsiders.

In summary, then, the most basic difference between Japanese society and American is the method of interest group formation. While America has a horizontal society, Japan has a vertical one.

IMPLICATIONS FOR BUSINESS

This vertical principle has many implications for Americans doing business in Japan, because it runs counter to what Americans are accustomed to in economics, personal relations, and integrity. Thus, Americans will often characterize Japanese methods as "illogical," "irrational," or "feudal" when frustrated with having to deal with a society organized along lines different from their own. Americans, as mentioned before, are children of a horizontal society, and they naturally try to apply their horizontal methods, even when in vertical Japan. Hence, they are apt to break unknowingly taboos such as those against contact with non-related interest groups and against creating an impression of hierarchy by function, thus inviting the indignation of Japanese colleagues. What, then, are some of the elements of this vertical society against which Americans often run afoul, and what can they do to avoid these snags?

One of the most important things of which Americans must be aware is the role of personal relationships of friendship, duty, and obligation. First, it is absolutely necessary to know who considers whom junior and senior. Much of the work inside a company is distributed along these lines, and who will do what job is often decided by them. Just looking at the organization chart is not enough to find out who is senior and who is junior; such charts do not always reflect reality. One needs to learn enough Japanese to understand who addresses whom as junior and senior. Knowing the forms of language Japanese employees use in addressing each other is an almost failsafe way of finding out who is on the top and who is on the bottom. A junior will address his boss as "—*san*" (e.g., Tanaka-*san*), while a senior will address a junior as "—*kun*" (e.g., Tanaka-*kun*). In other words, understanding a company's organization means that one must learn not only the organization chart but also enough Japanese to know how different people demonstrate the personal relationships between themselves and others through their language.

A second part to understanding the personal relationships of Japanese colleagues, both in and out of the office, is to know who is friends with whom and who has duties and obligations to whom. Having gone to the same university is often a very strong tie between Japanese. Knowing who arranged whose marriage, and whose brothers were on the same tennis team in high school, etc. can often lead to very important business contacts. Moreover, getting things done through connections is not considered in any way improper or lacking in integrity. Rather, it is an essential part of getting business done between vertical interest groups which under normal conditions have no non-treasonous way of contacting each other. One must know the web of personal relationships of one's employees and colleagues in order to work effectively.

Another important implication the Japanese social system has for Japanese-American business is that it disrupts Americans' traditional patterns of making friends, and limits the number of people available to become acquaintances. Most Japanese choose their friends largely from their own interest group. Thus, an American, on entering a group, is expected to do the same to an extent. It is considered very egotistical to search outside the group for all one's friends; and since life can become very difficult for those considered egotistical (such as people suspected of disloyalty to the interest group), it is best in many cases to socialize as much as possible with those in the group to prove one's loyalty. Japanese society is given order by people's participation in interest groups, so to deny the group's validity by closing oneself up in the American community is to give oneself the status of an exile and to ask for corresponding treatment.

One more serious implication that vertical society has for Japanese-American relations concerns the time frame of personal and business relationships. In a horizontal society, a man can move into a group to do a particular job, then move on to another group when that job is done. Because relationships are functional, the time span one stays in a certain job can be fixed for relatively short periods (one or two years) without disrupting the group's social structure. However, in a vertical society such as Japan's, where relationships inside firms are based not on function but rather on seniority and personal ties, no such mobility is possible. A man cannot be sent as chief to a new department where he has no personal ties and conduct business there with any authority. His new subordinates still retain their ties to their old boss, ties which they will not transgress should there be any conflict between the new man and the old. Thus, when a man is sent to a new post, a long time passes before he is able to win the loyalty and enthusiasm of his new subordinates.

The implication for the American businessman is that very little can be accomplished in an assignment of less than three or four years. Any assignment of a shorter term, except for purposes of study, is likely to be much less than 100 percent effective. In other words, a man only begins to be 100 percent useful after several years in Japan. It takes that long to make the friends and find the contacts needed to do business. It is indeed unfortunate that the average length of stay of American business people in Japan is only two and a half years; the Americans seem to stay in Japan just long enough to build the social capital needed to *start* in business before they return to America. Sending people to Japan for terms of less than three years is often a total waste of time, and the longer a stay continues, the more effective the representative becomes. Any candidate for a post in Japan can serve his firm best by preparing to stay in Japan a long time.

EXPATRIATE AMERICAN SOCIETY IN JAPAN

So far this paper has concentrated on describing Japanese society and some of the points where Americans are likely to conflict with it. Certainly, measuring prospective representatives against the demands which Japanese society creates is a process indispensable in evaluating them. However, there is another society against which candidates should be measured, that of expatriate Americans in Japan. One can reach an accurate conclusion as to a candidate's suitability for Japan by determining which sector of expatriate American society he is likely to enter.

Expatriate American society in Japan is comprised of four groups, each of which is different in its attitudes toward Japanese society, in its average level of linguistic accomplishment, in the level of intimacy of its members with individual Japanese, in the reaction it evokes from Japanese, and (for the business community) in its level of acceptability for assignment in Japan. Through the following description of each of these groups, it is hoped that the reader can obtain a clearer idea of whom to choose to represent his company in Japan.

There is one group of Americans in Japan with absolutely no interest in things Japanese; this group shall be labeled the "not-concerned" group or NC group. Though unfortunate, it is true that some American companies sometimes use their branches in Japan as places to send people whose presence is no longer appreciated at the home office. In a sense these people are exiles, and many realize this to be so. Because of their position, they are

Diagram of Expatriate American Society in Japan

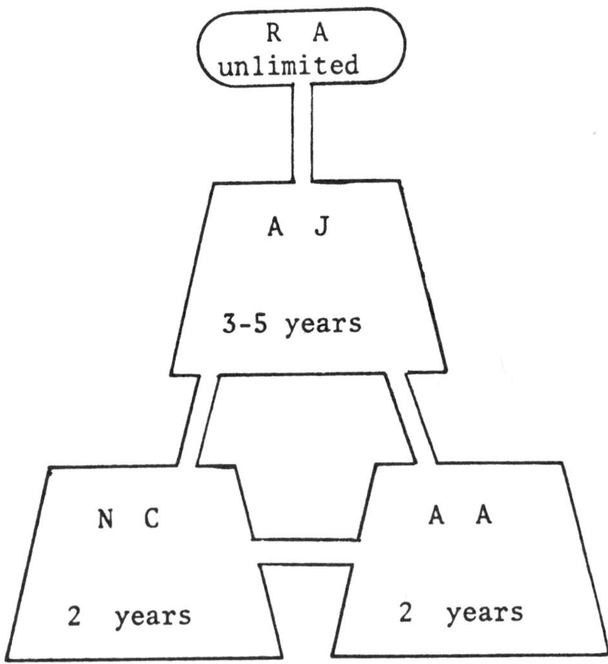

merely marking time in Japan waiting for retirement or to return to America. Usually they do not try to make any friends, much less try to learn the Japanese language. Life in Japan under such circumstances can be quite embittering, since one does not join Japanese groups (not wanting to do so). It is obvious that those isolated in this way are, in a sense, prisoners of their own lack of interest in Japan, confining themselves to the American community. Thus, they have not the slightest chance of helping the home company establish the all-important personal relationships with the Japanese members of the firm which are so essential to business in Japan.

Many companies realize that sending such people to Japan as representatives is one of the worst things that can happen to a business relationship. Luckily those likely to enter the NC group are relatively easy to identify, so that they can be eliminated from consideration before disaster strikes. One way to identify latent NCs is to determine whether or not a candidate really wants to go to Japan. If not, it is usually counterproductive to send him since those who do not want to go in the first place are the most likely to fall into the NC group. Secondly, one can look at the range of interests a man has outside his job. Someone with few outside interests is not likely to have the will to learn about things Japanese. Those with many interests can always acquire more, but those with few rarely can. Also, apathetic types such as those who have not read a book since graduating from college are prime candidates for the NC group. The NCs simply do not think that understanding culture is important to running a business well. Sending such people to Japan should be avoided if at all possible.

The other three groups of expatriate Americans all recognize the importance of culture as a background for business. Nevertheless, there is still considerable variation among these groups, since simply recognizing the importance of the cultural environment of business and turning that recognition into action are two entirely different things.

The barriers between recognition and adaptability are basically three: linguistic, psychological, and chronological. Language is obviously a tremendous problem, but not just one of having the time to learn; while time to learn is certainly necessary, having the motivation to learn is undoubtedly more important. Those who have the will to learn will usually make time to do so. The psychological barrier involves developing a sense of relativity about even the most basic principles. For example, as mentioned above, Americans often consider a man who uses his contacts to get things done as somewhat lacking in integrity, but Japanese do not look at contacts in this way. This is one example of the many psychological barriers which must be overcome. Finally, the three groups differ in the average lengths of their stays in Japan, the number of years for each group being marked on the preceding diagram. The names of these other three groups, in increasing order of usefulness to the home company, are the Americans Abroad (AA), the Americans in Japan (AJ), and the Relative Americans (RA).

The Americans Abroad derive their name from the fact that they do not seem to be particularly aware that they are in Japan, as opposed to, say, France, Argentina, or Tanzania. For them, the world is subdivided essentially into two parts, America and "everywhere else," and the sub-units of "everywhere else" are judged good or bad depending on how closely they seem to resemble America. In a sense, the AAs are missionaries of American culture, believing in the universal applicability of American ideals and business methods and striving to convert the world to what they consider "rational," "logical," or "modern" ways of operating. The AA will often struggle with life in Japan, but he will sometimes console himself since he thinks he will be vindicated in the end in his struggle to Americanize Japan.

The basic belief behind the AA attitude is that American culture and business methods should be universal. The AAs often think that English should be universal as well, and thus refuse to learn any Japanese. This, of course, handicaps them seriously in trying to deal with Japanese, and even in getting basic information about their own company. The frustrations of the language problem as well as other aspects of the AA life often build up quite rapidly, so that an AA will be exhausted after only one or two years. After this period, the AA either changes his attitude about the universality of American culture or is forced to return to America.

The reaction of Japanese to the AA has two aspects, one being respect for his dedication to his principles and the other anger at his arrogance. Unfortunately, the respect, while sincere, tends to decrease in direct proportion to the length of time spent working with an AA and proximity to him. Since the AA puts his principles above all (while Japanese owe loyalty to the interest group itself rather than to the way it is run), there is bound to be conflict between the two. In other words, the AA often turns out (along with the NC) looking like an ugly American. No such type of person can construct the personal relationships mentioned above which are so essential to do business in Japan. AAs have little to offer the Japanese-American business world; they are not the people to choose as representatives for Japan.

So far, the picture for Americans in Japan seems rather grim. Both the AA group and the NC group have been found unacceptable for assignment in Japan. From now on, however, the picture will brighten, since the remaining two groups can be of great value to companies in dealing with Japan and Japanese.

The Americans in Japan (AJ) is a large group of Americans, some of whom have moved into the AJ group from the AA group, who have realized the limits of their culture and come to working compromises with Japanese colleagues on business methods. Some have achieved a moderate fluency in Japanese, and enough knowledge of Japanese operating methods to know which suggestions will be ignored from the start, and which ones have a chance of being accepted. In other words, the AJs have achieved an understanding of the need to compromise on operating methods and a certain level of understanding of the unique cultural setting of business in Japan. The time span of an AJ's stay in Japan is usually three to eight years.

The basic philosophy behind the AJ's attitude toward dealing with Japan and Japanese business methods is that compromise is necessary since changing the system is impossible. Thus, some American companies will offer some housing allowances to Japanese employees, but refrain from providing company housing. They realize that one must offer the allowances in order to attract talented people, but they are still unwilling to go into the housing business. Also, rather than trying to recruit new employees by sending interviewers to colleges, they realize that going through contacts will be more effective.

However, most all of the AJs still complain of having a hard time knowing what their Japanese colleagues are thinking. This, of course, makes compromise difficult since the AJs do not know what their counterparts want. Thus, in an effort to make the process of compromise go more smoothly AJs will often try to communicate through Japanese who have spent several years in the United States, and who can guess what Americans are thinking. The AJs presume that such Japanese can explain in words what their countrymen are thinking, but this is not always the case. By relying on Japanese to explain to them in English what other Japanese are thinking, the AJs remove themselves a step from the communication process and thus increase their chances of misunderstanding. In other words, information is guaranteed to go from Americans to Japanese, but not necessarily from Japanese to Americans. While the AJs have accomplished a great deal, information is still going directly only one way. In this sense, the AJs are not really listening directly to Japanese, so there is still room for improvement. However, it must be recognized that the AJs represent a considerable improvement over the AAs, in that the AJs realize that listening to Japanese colleagues is important.

Japanese tend to accept and admire the AJ in direct proportion to the amount of concern he has for compromise and how much he tries to understand things Japanese. American businessmen in Japan are often quite pressed for time, and their Japanese colleagues often understand and sympathize with the AJs' inability to find time for study of the cultural problems of business. This means that any effort an American does put in is doubly appreciated and respected by Japanese. Many AJs seem to understand that time is more precious than money, and they use this knowledge to establish respect for themselves by giving time to study things Japanese and to building personal relationships with Japanese. A man likely to fit into the AJ group linguistically, psychologically, and chronologically can be of much value in operating an American business or a joint venture in Japan.

The remaining group in the expatriate American community in Japan is the Relative Americans (RA). One can identify an RA by his linguistic accomplishments: The RA can read, write, and speak Japanese with a high level of fluency. This language ability is certainly worthwhile in itself, but it signifies much deeper accomplishments, both psychological and chronological. First of all, since learning Japanese takes several years, fluency means that a man has had a fair amount of experience with Japan, and thus has a broad knowledge of general conditions. Secondly, achieving fluency means having to talk with many Japanese over the years. This implies that almost anyone fluent must have a fair number of contacts—contacts which can be put to good use in business. Thirdly, the amount of cultural exchange necessary with the Japanese people during the learning process means that a person fluent in Japanese has been able to cross the psychological barriers that make the AA and sometimes the AJ look arrogant. One simply cannot help but develop a relativity about one's values after so many conversations with Japanese. Hence the name Relative Americans.

This does not mean that the people in the RA group have turned into Japanese; they have not. But they have realized the relativity of all their American values, even while they still hold to them. Thus, they know that Japanese values and operating methods are not irrational, illogical, or feudal in any way when applied to the society they spring from. While the AAs try to change the system, and while the AJs try to compromise with it, the RAs adopt it while working in Japan and turn it to their own ends. In other words, the RAs have achieved a level of super-adaptability, working under the rules of a system different from the one into which they were born. In a sense, the RAs are chameleons, changing to fit their environment.

Japanese react extremely well to the RAs, because of respect for their diligence and their caring enough to learn Japanese, and also for having the maturity necessary to learn to live by a different set of rules. Any company who can claim an RA is likely to be highly ranked among foreign firms in Japan, and, along with the RA himself, achieve a high level of exposure and fame.

There are, however, two unfortunate aspects to the RA group. First is, of course, that there are so very few members. Those with the desire to learn Japanese are very few among Americans, first, since business can be carried on fairly well by depending solely on Japanese to learn English, and, second, since most Americans do not want to stay in Japan long enough to learn. But there is also an institutional factor which works against the development of more RAs. Because of the time factor involved in becoming an RA, those who choose that path are virtually cut off from all others. In other words, Japan is almost a dead-end assignment if one goes about doing business seriously. Contacts are important in America too, so that anyone who spends time cultivating the contacts for business in Japan almost necessarily cuts himself off from contacts in America. Therefore, some RAs either quit or are forced out of their American companies because of lack of political leverage in the home office. Thus, the companies sometimes squander a precious resource, and even fewer Americans want to become RAs.

In the diagram of expatriate American society, and in the paragraphs describing each of the groups in this society, each group is assigned a time frame. While these numbers indicate a rough average length of stay for each group, they have another meaning as well. They also represent, in a sense, upper limits to judge the *mobility* of a man from one group to another group more useful to the home office. For example, a time span of two years is put on the NC group. This does *not* mean that every American businessman who comes to Japan spends his first two years as an NC. Rather it indicates that anyone who falls into the NC category for reasons of personality or situation will either (1) be out of it after two years at most, or (2) likely not get out at all. Likewise, few AAs will stay in that group for over two years. Either they will return to the U.S. or move up into the AJ category. Also, any AJ who has not learned enough Japanese after five or so years to become an RA will likely never learn at all.

PERSONALITY AND SITUATION

This paper has dealt until now primarily with systems and men's places in them rather than with individual traits. While it is true that virtually any kind of personality is permitted inside a vertical interest group in Japan, one must also realize that certain traits take well to vertical groups and make entering them easier. There are other traits which make life just a bit easier if one has them. Moreover, people in certain situations, such as being the father of teenage children, have to devote large amounts of time to affairs other than business and thus will be at a relative disadvantage to those in different situations. This paper will now attempt to deal with some of the personality traits and situations in life from the standpoint of personnel selection for Japan.

The most important single personality trait a foreigner in Japan needs for success—by any standard—is patience. There is not a single American businessman in any of the four groups who does not continually stress the need to hold one's temper and go back and try again when things do not go properly. There are many reasons for things not being done the way one hopes they would have, such as language or conceptual problems. Certainly losing one's temper over honest mistakes is bad for business, even in America.

However, losing one's temper in Japan has a far deeper meaning than it does in the U.S. First of all, losing one's temper embarrasses the person scolded, thus creating enemies within an interest group, and leading to factionalism. No one in Japan takes kindly to any action which destroys the cohesiveness of his group. Secondly, the ability to control one's temper under stress is a virtue highly admired by the Japanese, and the inability to do so is despised. While Americans use temper as a tool to get work done better or more quickly when efficiency sags, applying the same method in Japan can only bring disaster. This point cannot be overstressed. Anyone without patience approaching that of a saint will have serious problems in doing business in Japan.

Another personality trait of great use is that of seeing oneself as an onlooker rather than a major player in events, but without being dull. Professor Nakane echoes this when, in describing those best suited to foreign contact, she says that "it goes without saying that a bright personality that takes in all it hears is preferable to an introverted, dark one. Rather than the exhibitionist who wants to be bathed in footlights on stage, the type who wants to be in the audience is better" (*Tekiō no Jōken*, p. 84). The reason this applies to Japan in particular is that one of the major defense mechanisms Japanese use to protect themselves individually is making the group responsible for everything, both failures and successes. Trying to be a "star" disrupts this most basic of Japanese values, and is certain to invite trouble.

In the United States, managers often use the "star system" to improve performance by offering employees credit for successes while taking the blame themselves for failures. An offer like this, which seems like the best of all possible worlds to an American, is likely to be refused outright by Japanese, because the latter do not want the credit. Taking credit would elevate a man above the other members of his group and possibly cause a rift, something which no one wants. The best way to avoid creating a situation where this might happen is not to send a representative from America who believes in the "star system," either for himself or for anyone else.

Another two traits that are virtual necessities are sensitive powers of observation and second-guessing. It is well known that Japan is a nation that is ethnically homogeneous, so that simply the suggestion of certain circumstances or facts automatically indicates a certain conclusion. This conclusion is not necessarily the one which would be drawn by someone raised outside the system even from exactly the same facts. In ethnically varied America, such tacit communication does not occur frequently, but it is a way of life in Japan. Thus, the American sent to Japan must be able to piece together bits of information to find out what is going on. For example, if a man comes back to Japan from an assignment abroad and goes to lunch with everyone in the office once, he is simply renewing acquaintances. But if he continues to make the rounds, gradually concentrating on certain people, one knows that he is trying to create his own personal following in preparation for some sort of intra-company political move. These subtle actions are an integral part of business in Japan, and the ability to understand them is essential to doing one's job.

Language skills have been mentioned above as necessary for understanding the organization of the office, and for the politics of getting oneself accepted as a full member of one's group. Language ability is certainly in part a question of heredity, but, as also stated before, the desire to learn is more important than hereditary linguistic ability. However, to find the representative who is capable of learning Japanese, one must go still one step further and ask why certain people have the desire to learn a foreign tongue while so many others are content to remain monolingual.

One important factor is having had significant contact with foreign language while still under twenty years of age. Those who have lived in situations where their lives depended on the ability to speak a foreign tongue realize that learning is not impossible; moreover, they know how much easier their lives become by speaking the vernacular of the place in which they live. A second factor is how well one speaks one's own language. Those who speak precisely and succinctly, who change their language according to the situation, are likely to know how closely one's language is tied to one's values and one's life. From this, it is only a small step to realizing all the implications that go with learning the language of the country in which one lives. Both of these factors depend largely on the environment of one's childhood. That Americans in general are poor linguists compared to Indians in general does not mean that Americans are not as intelligent, but rather that the environment in the United States does not make speaking a foreign language necessary while that in India does. Those Americans who have been lucky enough to have been raised in situations stressing linguistic accomplishments are apt to be better choices for Japan than those who have not.

Age is another factor which affects one's ability to be an effective representative in Japan. Those in the stage of life where their children are in junior high school or high school often have troubles finding schools. Most Americans send their children to one of the several international schools in Japan, though others feel that this is a waste since a few years of experience in a Japanese school is often far more educational for the children than being put into an international school much like American schools. But no matter which school one chooses, there are bound to be problems. From a company's point of view, the costs of tuition (which are usually borne by the company) and the time the father has to devote to his children instead of business contacts can amount to considerable losses for the company, though this is not always the case. For those not at the top of an organization, it is usually best for the company to send younger men, since this affords them the chance of making friends among younger Japanese whose circle of contacts is not yet firmly established. Thus, sending younger men often can help the company build contacts for the future. In summary, then, it is advisable in most cases to send men to Japan who are under 35 or over the age when their children are still in school.

Another situation which must be considered in evaluating a man's suitability for Japan is what sort of person his wife is. It has long been known that a wife's happiness greatly affects a man's performance at the office. The better off she is, the better his performance will be. Almost all American businessmen agree that wives have harder times adjusting to Japan than do husbands. This is because the latter often have translators and can go through a business day much as in America, while the wives must do all the things they did at home, but under radically different conditions and without translators. Prices of food and other goods destroy all ideas of proportion in the family budget, and getting steady help around the house is quite difficult. In a sense, the wife confronts Japanese culture far more directly than does the husband, so if she is not the outgoing type of person who likes discovering new things and doing things in new ways, then life will be extremely difficult.

One piece of evidence that wives become more deeply involved with Japanese culture than do their husbands is the fact that wives often become far more accomplished in the Japanese language. While it is certainly part of American culture to consider foreign language study "girl's stuff" while men are supposed to study "solid" subjects like mathematics and finance, the wives' accomplishment does not spring totally from this role playing. In everyday life, the wives feel a far greater need for the Japanese language and thus feel a stronger motivation to learn. The true meaning of the higher level of wives' accomplishments in learning Japanese must not be overlooked in choosing the right man to send to Japan. Choosing the right wife is an integral part of choosing the right man.

These are only a few of the important traits and situations in life one must consider in choosing a representative for Japan. While there are many others, listing and discussing them would take many pages. One way to discover some of these others is to talk to Americans with experience in the business community in Japan and ask what their problems were. One must be cautious since the advice of those who have returned from Japan is not always correct, especially if it comes from someone in the NC or AA groups. But, in choosing a new representative, identifying the reasons for failures can be at times even more useful than knowing the reasons for successes.

PARTING WORDS

This paper has approached the problem of finding the right man to represent an enterprise in Japan from three points of view: those of the demands of Japanese society, the demands of expatriate American society in Japan, and of several individual traits and situations in life which are important in adapting to Japan. It must be stressed that these three points of view are merely different roads to the same destination; one cannot use one viewpoint to the exclusion of the others and still make a satisfactory selection. Indeed, one must approach the problem from all angles.

The process is not at all simple, especially if those doing the selecting have had little experience with Japan. In such cases, it is best to give major attention to determining which section of expatriate society a candidate is likely to enter and select one from those likely to become AJs or RAs. The reason this shortcut will work is that the groupings of expatriate society are defined not in terms of American values, but rather in terms of Americans' reactions to Japanese society. Since certain patterns of American reaction to Japan evoke certain counter-reactions from Japanese, one can predict a man's usefulness by predicting his reaction to Japan, i.e., which group of expatriate society he will enter.

While it is next to impossible for Americans without some years of experience to judge directly the characteristics which make a man suitable or not to Japanese society, finding characteristics which will put one man into one category of expatriate society and another man into another is easy. Selecting representatives with emphasis on what category of expatriate society they are likely to enter is essentially a process of Americans judging other Americans. In other words, one determines a candidate's characteristics just as one would if evaluating him for any job in America, but then one must choose which characteristics are valuable by a new set of rules.

It is said that the state of the Japanese economy at any time can be roughly determined merely by looking at the balance of payments situation. In a similar way, the indicator of how well an American businessman is doing is his degree of accomplishment in learning Japanese. Certainly language is only one of the elements in doing business, and even a secondary one in a direct sense, since almost all businessmen use translators no matter how good their Japanese. However, most all of the other factors Americans need to do business in Japan are tied closely to accomplishment in learning Japanese, factors such as access to information about Japanese markets, understanding the psychology of business in Japan, ability to make contacts, etc. Just as success for the Japanese economy lies in how well it manages the balance of payments problem, success for an American businessman in Japan depends directly on how well he handles the language problem.

8

A New Look at "Lifetime Commitment" in Japanese Industry

Robert M. Marsh and Hiroshi Mannari

The Japanese case is strategic in the literature on economic development because Japan is the major, if not the only, non-Western society to have reached high levels of industrialization, and the society with the highest sustained economic growth rate in the postwar world. An even more compelling reason is that, according to a widespread view, Japan's industrial productivity has developed within a paternalistic, particularistic, diffuse, and nonrationalized form of social organization, common in large, technologically advanced companies. In this viewpoint Japan is seen as either a "special case" or as a disconfirmation of earlier sociological theory concerning "the logic of industrialism" and modern rational bureaucracy.

Central to this different social organization in Japanese industry, according to Abegglen,[1] is the pattern of "lifetime commitment" (*shūshin kōyō*),[2] defined as the practice of entering into employment in a firm directly from school and remaining in the same firm until retirement. The pattern is supported by Japanese beliefs in "the firm as one family" (*kigyo ikka*), "familistic management" (*keiei kazokushugi*),[3] and the seniority system (*nenko joretsu seido*).

The controversy over the *extent* to which there is lifetime commitment in Japanese industry has continued for over a decade now. Several Japan specialists[4] have argued that Abegglen exaggerated the prevalence and

* The authors are professors of sociology at Brown University and at Kwansei Gakuin University, Nishinomiya, Japan, respectively. The research reported in this paper was partially financed by research grants from the John Simon Guggenheim Memorial Foundation and the Ford Foundation.

[1] James C. Abegglen, *The Japanese Factory* (New York: Free Press, 1958).

[2] *Shūshin* means "lifetime, lifelong, permanent," and *kōyō* means "employment."

[3] Hiroshi Hazama, "The Logic and the Process of Growth in the 'Familistic Management in Japan,'" *Shakaigaku Hyoron* 11 (July 1960): 2–18.

[4] Koji Taira, "Characteristics of Japanese Labor Markets," *Economic Development and Cultural Change* 10 (1962): 150–168; Ken'ichi Tominaga, "Occupational

Reprinted by permission of the University of Chicago Press, from *Economic Development and Cultural Change*, Vol. 20, No. 4, July, 1972.

persistence of lifetime commitment. To the present writers the most important questions raised in this controversy are: First, what are the actual rates of interfirm mobility in Japan and in other modernized societies? Second, if the Japanese rate is lower than the American—as Abegglen claimed—is this due to the norms and values Abegglen incorporated into the concept of lifetime commitment, or to other causes? Third, rates, norms, and values concerning interfirm mobility can be seen as resultants of structural pressures, some of which act mainly to maintain commitment to one firm, while others weaken this commitment. In the language of functional analysis in sociology, some structural factors have functional consequences and others have dysfunctional consequences for lifetime commitment; it is also possible that the same structure has both functional and dysfunctional consequences. The first two of these questions were analyzed in a previous paper, which we shall review briefly here. The main thrust of this paper, however, concerns question 3. Data from published sources and from our own field research in Japanese factories in 1969–70 will be presented.

Rates, Norms and Values

Our previous paper[5] analyzed data on interfirm mobility, which show that from 1959 to 1968 the Japanese employee was considerably less likely than the American to leave his firm (see table 1).

TABLE 1

AVERAGE MONTHLY SEPARATION RATES FOR WAGE AND SALARY EMPLOYEES, MANUFACTURING SECTOR

	1959	1960	1961	1962	1963	1964	1965	1966	1967	1968
Japan	2.0	2.1	2.5	2.4	2.3	2.6	2.3	2.2	2.4	2.3
U.S.A	4.1	4.3	4.0	4.1	3.9	3.9	4.1	4.6	4.6	4.6

SOURCE.—Japan: Rōdō sho rōdō tōkei chosa bu, *Rōdō tōkei yoran* (Tokyo: Okura Sho, 1969), p. 63, table 42; U.S.: Department of Labor, Bureau of Labor Statistics, *Monthly Labor Review* 92 (August 1969): 98, table 15.

NOTE.—For both countries rate includes regular and temporary workers, transfers within a company, retirements, voluntary quits, and discharges. Rate for voluntary quits alone is not available in comparable terms. U.S. data are for firms of all sizes; Japanese, for firms with thirty or more employees. Rate is computed by dividing the number of separated employees during a month by the total number of employees at the end of the previous month, and then averaging the twelve monthly rates.

Mobility in Japanese Society: Analysis of Labor Market in Japan," *Journal of Economic Behavior* (Japan) 2 (April 1962); M. Tsuda, *The Basic Structure of Japanese Labor Relations* (Tokyo: Society for the Social Sciences, Musahi University, 1965); Robert E. Cole, *Japanese Blue Collar: The Changing Tradition* (Berkeley: University of California Press, 1971); and Bernard Karsh and Robert E. Cole, "Industrialization and the Convergence Hypothesis: Some Aspects of Contemporary Japan," *Journal of Social Issues* 24 (1968): 45–64.

[5] Robert M. Marsh and Hiroshi Mannari, "Lifetime Commitment in Japan: Roles, Norms and Values," *American Journal of Sociology* 75 (March 1971): 795–812.

For Abegglen, "lifetime commitment" refers to more than the mere behavioral fact of staying in one firm: it means staying *because* one holds certain beliefs and has internalized certain norms and values. Abegglen described a tightly reciprocal set of obligations between the company and the employee: the company will not discharge the employee except in the most extreme circumstances, and the employee, in return, will not quit the company for employment elsewhere. Abegglen's discussion suggests to us that there are two levels or layers of reciprocal obligations: (1) The employee will not leave the company because the company will reward his loyalty, over the years, by an accumulation of pay increases, bonus and fringe benefits, paid vacations, promotions, and in general by a steadily advancing status in the company. We have called this the *status enhancement* type of lifetime commitment norms and values. (2) The second, deeper level of commitment is suggested by Abegglen's claim that "the worker, whether laborer or manager . . . is bound, *despite potential economic advantage*, to remain in the company's employ" and "a system of shared obligation [takes] the place of the economic basis of employment of workers by the firm."[6] Thus, the first level refers to the economic and other status advantages the worker can derive by commitment to one firm; the deeper level means that the employee owes the company loyalty as such and should stay in one company because it is morally right to do so, independent of how much status enhancement the firm gives him over the years. The second type is referred to as the *moral loyalty* type of commitment values, reinforced by moral sanctions.

Data were gathered on these two types of commitment norms and values in a major electrical appliance firm and a leading shipbuilding and heavy machinery firm in the area of Osaka-Hyogo prefectures. Field work in one branch factory in each firm was carried out from July 1969 to February 1970, by means of company personnel records, observation, interviewing, and a questionnaire distributed to all production, staff, and managerial personnel. Salient characteristics of the units studied—which we shall call "Electrical Company" and "Shipbuilding Company"—are given in table 2.

Our data suggest (1) that the reciprocity between the Japanese employee and his company exists, but its symmetry is both less than and different from what Abegglen claims; (2) employees who stay in one firm (lifetime commitment role behavior) often do so for reasons extraneous to both the status enhancement and moral loyalty types of commitment; and (3) insofar as employees stay in one firm because they have lifetime commitment norms and values, these are much more likely to be of the status enhancement type than of the moral loyalty type. For example, employees who profess lifetime commitment and who perceive others as also committed tend to be male, older, with more seniority and higher

[6] Abegglen, p. 17, italics added.

TABLE 2

CHARACTERISTICS OF THE COMPANIES AND BRANCH PLANTS STUDIED

Characteristics	Electrical Company	Shipbuilding Company
No. of employees in company, 1969	13,500	18,000
Characteristics of plant or division studied:		
Main products	Electric motor, electric fan, vacuum cleaner	Diesel and turbine engine, industrial heavy machinery
No. of employees	1,200	780
Percentage completing questionnaire	85%	76%
Percentage male employees	50%	96%
Average age of employees	22	34
Average length of service in company	4 years	11 years
Quit rate during previous year	7%	5%

pay, rank, and job classification—all of which can be subsumed under status enhancement reasons.

Now we wish to approach the problem of lifetime commitment from a different angle. Which structural factors are functional, that is, maintain or strengthen lifetime commitment, and which factors are dysfunctional, that is, weaken commitment? Only as we understand these conflicting elements can we hope to predict future trends in lifetime commitment in Japan.

Structural Factors Which Maintain Lifetime Commitment

Seniority

By far the major factor which maintains lifetime commitment is the seniority (*nenko joretsu*) system. The amount of pay a Japanese employee receives is determined primarily by his education and length of service in the company. The slope of pay increase rises more sharply with seniority than it does in the United States. Base pay, fringe benefits, and retirement pay are scaled in such a way as to increase steadily with one's seniority. Given the assumption of lifetime employment in one firm, the employee is paid on a lifetime basis, as it were: relative to his skill and performance, the seniority system underpays him in his early years and overpays him in his later years in a company. Data in table 3 show that employees with maximum seniority (reaching retirement age) generally receive four or five times as much monthly pay as those with minimum seniority (just out of school), in manufacturing in general and in the two industries studied, electrical and shipbuilding. These ratios are considerably higher than in the United States.[7] Moreover, in Electrical Company, the seniority

[7] The most comparable data for the United States that we know of are found in U.S. Bureau of the Census, *U.S. Census of Population: 1960. Subject Reports.*

TABLE 3

Amount and Ratio of Monthly Pay of New and Retiring Employees, by Education and Status, Japanese Industry, 1967

Education and Work Status: Males*	Beginning Pay† (1)	Pay at Age 55‡ (2)	Ratio of (2) to (1)
College graduates—clerical, white-collar:			
All manufacturing	28,964	136,615	4.7
Electrical manufacturing	27,895	144,406	5.2
Shipbuilding	28,943	144,813	4.0
High school graduates—clerical, white-collar:			
All manufacturing	21,189	110,722	5.2
Electrical manufacturing	20,214	119,323	5.9
Shipbuilding	22,173	110,147	5.0
High school graduates—manual, blue-collar:			
All manufacturing	21,260	90,928	4.3
Electrical manufacturing	19,193	94,678	4.9
Shipbuilding	22,714	63,470	2.8
Junior high school graduates—manual, blue-collar:			
All manufacturing	16,977	79,654	4.7
Electrical manufacturing	15,204	83,269	5.5
Shipbuilding	14,960	61,512	4.1

Source.—Tōyō keizai, *Tōkei geppō* (December 1967).

* Data for females given only through age 35; ratios somewhat lower than those for males to age 35.

† In *yen*.

‡ Normal retirement age in Japanese industry.

system works in such a way that two female assembly line workers in their mid-fifties with over twenty years' seniority receive more than twice as much pay as young girls with low seniority, performing exactly the same jobs on the assembly line. Insofar as one's seniority is not transferable to another company, there is strong pressure making for long service in the same firm.

Characteristics of the Job Itself

In Japan as elsewhere, the degree of interfirm mobility is negatively related to such characteristics of the job as its skill, variety, and interest.

Occupation by Earnings and Education, Final Report PC(2)-7B (Washington, D.C.: Government Printing Office, 1963), table 1. Data are for mean annual earnings in dollars, 1959, for the experienced civilian labor force. The closest age comparisons are between: (1) the age group 25–34 years old (U.S.) and "beginning pay" (Japan) (2) 45–54 years old and 55–64 years old (U.S.) and "pay at age 55" (Japan). The U.S. ratios of earnings at age 25–34 and either age 45–54 or 55–64 are consistently and markedly lower than the Japanese. U.S. ratios are: (1) college graduates, managers, officials, and proprietors except farm, 1.9 for 45–54/25–34-year-old groups, and 2.3 for 55–64/25–34; (2) college graduates—clerical and kindred, 1.3 and 1.2; (3) high school graduates—clerical and kindred, 1.5 and 1.1; (4) high school graduates—craftsmen, foremen, and kindred, 1.1 and 1.0; (5) eight years' schooling—craftsmen, foremen, and kindred, 1.1 and 1.1; (6) high school graduates—operatives and kindred, 1.1 and 1.0; and (7) eight years' schooling—operatives and kindred, 1.1 and 1.1.

The cumbersomeness of the parts worked on in Shipbuilding Company is sometimes mentioned as a negative aspect of the job (although for other workers the heaviness is more positive, because it is "masculine" work, and the heaviness may be offset by the skill and variety of work on diesel engines). The main point in the present context is that since the skill demands of a job are inversely related to its quit rate, and since substitution of machines for human labor tends to eliminate the least skilled and most heavy work, this will have the effect of *strengthening* lifetime commitment.[8]

Social Relationships on the Job

In Japan as elsewhere, the social relationships of the work group influence quitting rates. One aspect of this is the relationship between workers and supervisors. In Shipbuilding Company, a first-line foreman attributed the low quit rate among his young workers (normally the group with the highest turnover) to "the good group atmosphere at work. I have kept my section's [*han*'s] quit rate quite low by being an 'elder brother' or 'father' to my workers. It's only workers with psychological loneliness who quit." Other data from our questionnaires in Shipbuilding Company and Electrical Company indicate that Japanese workers strongly prefer a section head "who sometimes demands extra work in spite of rules against it but, on the other hand, looks after you personally in matters not connected with the work." Thus, primary-group ties between superiors and rank-and-file workers have the function of reducing turnover.

Apart from supervisor-worker relationships, commitment to one firm is also maintained by strong social solidarity among workers. As one Shipbuilding Company employee put it, "I stay at this company because human relations are good. We have leisure activities, such as hiking, together. All workers in my section [*han*] take turns working on the machines. Also, my section has mostly younger workers, so we have better teamwork." Similarly, when asked why the quit rate in one section was lower than in another in Shipbuilding Company a worker replied that the lower-turnover section had better human relations.

Another aspect is how relaxed the work pace is. This is to some extent positively correlated with more skilled jobs in which the work pace can be determined by the workers, rather than by the machines. In Shipbuilding Company one worker reported that although the pay was higher in another shipbuilding company, "the work situation is more relaxed here. Workers tell me supervisors are more strict in other companies. Here we can talk, take time out to smoke, etc." His statement was corroborated by our observation. Workers could be seen talking and relaxing in small groups, gathered around a stove, or seated near their machine, while it

[8] Robert Blauner, *Alienation and Freedom* (Chicago: University of Chicago Press, 1964), chaps. 6–7.

performed automatic operations, or while they waited for the overhead crane to bring them the next parts for engine assembly.

Structural Factors Which Reduce Lifetime Commitment

The Labor Shortage

As a result of the declining birth rate, the higher levels of educational attainment, and the increase in the number of jobs in manufacturing, Japan is now experiencing, perhaps for the first time in a period of peace, a significant labor shortage, particularly with regard to young workers.[9] This is probably the single most important factor making for greater interfirm mobility and less lifetime commitment. There were many signs of this change in Shipbuilding Company. Until recently, the company's main source of recruitment was directly from school; now, as a personnel officer told us, "the emergent demands of the labor market require us to hire about half *chūto saiyo* [workers with experience elsewhere]." "In 1961, when I quit the small firm I was working for," said a worker, "there was still a labor surplus, so that company didn't care if I left." His implication is that now a company cares much more.

A personnel director in another leading electrical firm recalled that he used to have a surplus labor force from which to hire. His task then was to screen which of the many candidates he wanted, and most of his time could be devoted to training them in the company. The labor shortage now compels him to spend more energy recruiting than training workers.

School Recruits and Chūto Saiyo

In Japanese industry there is a basic distinction between (1) employees recruited by a company directly from school, who are "brought up" by the company and remain in it, and (2) *chūto saiyo*, literally, "halfway or midway employment," that is, employees recruited with previous

[9] According to a Japanese Ministry of Labor survey in 1969, the ratio of job vacancies to job seekers leaving school in March 1970 would be 6.9 for junior high school graduates and 4.5 for senior high school graduates (*Japan Labor Bulletin* 9, no. 2 [February 1970]: 2). "In the Tokyo Metropolitan area, there were 140,000 job openings for junior high school graduates and 240,000 for senior high school graduates, giving rise to an acute labor shortage" (*Japan Labor Bulletin* 9, no. 3 [March 1970]: 2). Two further items indicate that the labor shortage is not limited to new graduates. "The number of effective job-offers in the period from July to September 1967 for other than new school graduates registered a substantial increase of 53 per cent on an annual basis over 1966. . . . Meanwhile, the number of job-seekers continued its downward trend, with the ratio between effective job-offers and effective job-seekers being reduced to less than one to one" ("The White Paper of Labor, 1967," *Japan Labor Bulletin* 7, no. 10 [October 1968]: 5). A Ministry of Labor "Survey of Labor Economics Trends" in 1969, based on data "from 3,300 establishments with more than 100 employees in the case of manufacturing industries. . . showed that . . . the establishments which have idle machines and equipment due to the labor shortage amounted to about 5 per cent of the total" (*Japan Labor Bulletin* 8, no. 6 [June 1969]: 2).

occupational experience.[10] This distinction is seen in published statistics on labor and in company personnel records, as well as in the conversation of employees. Does it have consequences for the lifetime commitment pattern? If lifetime commitment norms and values are strong, we would expect *chūto* workers to be regarded as "outsiders," given a lower informal status than the school recruits, and subject to prejudice and discrimination. If this is the case, we should expect workers to be less mobile, for they would fear negative sanctions in the new firm. Conversely, if lifetime commitment norms and values are weaker, and if *chūto* employees are not perceived by school recruits as a threat, prejudice and discrimination would be minimized, and there would be greater willingness to change employers. Another general expectation we might have is that if the *chūto* worker is subjected to prejudice and discrimination, he would experience more of it in the beginning and less as he becomes a longer-tenured *chūto* worker in the company. Let us examine these expectations in terms of the data from Shipbuilding Company.

To the extent that negative attitudes toward *chūto* workers exist, their source varies as between management and workers. Management in Shipbuilding Company would prefer to hire all personnel directly from school and train them within the company, but because of the present labor shortage it has to resort to *chūto*. In 1969 the company was able to hire only 130 from school and had to recruit another 130 from *chūto* applicants. One reason for management reluctance to hire *chūto* workers is that about 30 percent of them leave the company within the first year, in contrast with only about 3 percent of those hired from school. (During their first five years with the company, about one-third of the school recruits leave.) Management also feels less safe with *chūto* employees because they are more likely to be recruited through the impersonal mass media (newspaper job ads, etc.) than through the traditional, preferred means of personal recommendations. Thus, on management's side, negative attitudes toward *chūto* workers arise from problems of their loyalty and the reduced social control the company has over their recruitment.

Among workers there is a different source of possible resentment against *chūto saiyo*. Shipbuilding Company has a rule of equal pay for experienced *chūto* recruits and for those originally hired directly from school, of the same age and education; this rule applies in principle until

[10] In prewar days employees hired directly from school were called *yoseiko*, "brought up workers." More recently they are called either *kunrensei*, middle school graduates, given a three-year training program in the company; *minarai*, graduates of polytechnic high schools; or *kenshusei*, general high school or university graduates, given a four months' training program in the company. Now at Shipbuilding Company all school recruits are *kenshusei*; the three-year training program has been replaced by the four-month program. Most school recruits are *teiki saiyo*, hired at a stated time, typically every March and April, when the school year ends. The important point is that *yoseiko*, *kunrensei*, and *kenshusei* are all in a separate category from *chūto saiyo*.

the age of forty. Thus, a man who changes employers at the age of thirty-nine (only sixteen years from retirement in this company, as in most large companies) is in principle not handicapped in terms of pay. School recruits regard this rule as a violation of strict seniority payment, and as a denial of rewards they feel the company owes them for their longer loyalty.

Several *chūto* workers spoke of the difficulties they faced in becoming integrated into the network of human relations in the new company. The smallest formal work group in Shipbuilding Company is the *han*, consisting of from ten to twenty workers, including a foreman (*hanchō*) and an assistant, the *boshin* (Japanese rendering of the naval rank of boatswain or bosun). The *boshin* and one or more of the workers are the informal leaders of the *han* work group. The new *chūto* worker must adapt not only to the technical aspects of the job but also to the informal social relations and preferences of the leaders and workers in his *han*. Some adaptations can be learned; others are ascriptively beyond his control. For example, two or three men may use the same machine at different times. Seniority in the *han* is an important criterion in this area, and younger workers of longer seniority are more likely to be team leaders or "second *boshin*" than are older workers with less seniority. It is said that if a *chūto* person lasts two years, he will be integrated into his *han*; but, as we have seen, some workers do not survive this informal initiation period. It is possible that an experienced *chūto*, who enters at the same pay level as school recruits of the same age and education, would experience particular difficulties in this initiation period. This, it would appear, is one cause of the *chūto* personnel's higher quit rate.

In practice, however, most *chūto* recruits have not had precisely equivalent job experience in their former place of employment. Most come to Shipbuilding Company from smaller machinery firms, and even if they had worked on the same kind of machine or job, it was on a smaller scale. *Chūto* recruits also tend to come to Shipbuilding Company after a few years' prior experience and are in general little more skilled than amateurs or recruits just out of school, with regard to the relevant skills and knowledge concerning diesel engines. Those workers in other firms who would most fully meet the "equal pay for equal experience" rule—such as men who had worked for ten or twenty years in another large shipbuilding company, on a similar job—would have little incentive to change employers, for they would probably not significantly increase their overall economic position. In fact, *chūto* recruits in their thirties, especially their late thirties, have often spent only the recent half of their work life in a comparable firm and job, and the first half on a farm, in a barber shop, or in some other irrelevant work.

For these reasons, most *chūto* recruits initially receive less pay. A high school graduate now twenty-five years old, who has worked for Shipbuilding Company for seven years, has a base pay of ¥755 per day.

A *chūto* recruit of the same age and education, but without the same occupational experience, would start at 5 percent lower pay. When *chūto* recruits' experience and skill cannot be precisely determined at the beginning—which is commonly the case—the company's practice is to wait until the *chūto* worker has been in the company four to six months before formally deciding his pay. At that point, the *chūto* worker may find himself channeled into a lower rung of the pay hierarchy than he initially expected. This is another reason for the higher quit rate of *chūto* workers during their first year.

Thus, the majority of *chūto* recruits do not pose a threat to employees of longer standing or to the strict seniority basis of wages. This being the case, prejudice and discrimination by longer-tenured workers against the *chūto* workers is minimized, and therefore a potential obstacle to interfirm mobility is also minimized. It is said that if a *chūto* worker has merit, he can catch up with the pay of his school-recruit age-mates after a period of five to ten years in Shipbuilding Company. By that time, it is likely that a man's social definition as *chūto saiyo* will have become blurred and partially forgotten. This means that by the time most *chūto* employees have achieved the same level of pay as school recruits, the onus of their being "outsiders" will have been greatly reduced. Again, our conclusion is that the distinction between *chūto* and school recruits is not a major support for the pattern of lifetime commitment; that is, it is not a major hindrance to a man who—for whatever reasons—wants to change firms.

Our more direct evidence supports this structural argument. There is no single set of informal attitudes toward and treatment of *chūto* employees. There are isolated instances of alleged discrimination. A foreman (*hanchō*) said he makes no invidious distinctions between *chūto* and school recruits, but that his own immediate superior (a *sagyochō*, or second-line foreman) "always picks out a school recruit for further training in the company" (and thus greater opportunity for advancement); he saw this as a kind of discrimination. Another foreman admitted that he preferred *kunrensei* (company-trained workers) over *chūto* workers because he can train the former in his own way, whereas the latter, especially if they are older, may be intractable. This suggests that even the isolated instances of discrimination may have some justification. A staff person in personnel said that a *chūto* worker in his twenties can adapt to the new work setting, but those over thirty have more problems because they believe they deserve more pay, or because they may be older than their foreman.

As against these instances of disadvantage, our interviews indicated several examples of fair treatment. A *sagyochō* claimed, "As to *chūto saiyo* and those hired directly from school, I can't say one group makes better workers than the other. Many *chūto saiyo* are excellent." A new *chūto* employee, who might be expected to experience some hostility from the more long-tenured workers, told us, "I don't feel any discrimination. . . .

The [school-recruited] workers were kind to me while teaching me my job." Interestingly, however, he attributed this to the fact that "half of the workers here are *chūto*, like me." Thus, another factor militating against discrimination with regard to *chūto* personnel is their sheer social density in the company, which sets the tone for the prevailing group norms. Since workers under thirty are more mobile in today's labor market in Japan, the company has to resort to *chūto* recruits over thirty years of age. It has tried to cope with this situation by telling *hanchō* and other managerial personnel to try harder to integrate these older *chūto* workers into the human relations of the shop.

In conclusion, the distinction between *chūto saiyo* and school recruits is pervasive in Japanese industry, but it is not a major source of support for the practice of lifetime commitment. On the contrary, the distinction now has the function of increasing interfirm mobility.

Inducements to and Legitimation of Mobility

Increasingly, newspapers carry job advertisements (a quite recent phenomenon) which seek not only new school graduates but also older, experienced workers. These ads state the company's pay scale for given ages up to the age of thirty-five or forty. Shipbuilding Company ads publicize an entering pay scale which ranges from ¥29,500 (base pay) and ¥38,100 (with overtime) per month, for eighteen-year-olds, up to ¥43,900–51,900 (base pay) and ¥56,400–66,700 (with overtime) for forty-year-olds. It does not matter, in this context, that pay is still geared more to age than to job performance, nor that, as we have seen, many *chūto* recruits in fact do not have enough relevant prior experience to receive as much pay as their longer-tenured counterparts. The social significance of these newspaper ads, with regard to the future trend of the lifetime commitment pattern, is that major, pace-setting companies now openly—in principle, at least—violate strict company seniority as a basis of pay.

Another type of inducement to interfirm mobility is the practice of interviewing *chūto saiyo* applicants on Sunday, which enables people to search for a new job on their day off, without having to quit one company before looking for a new one.

The norms surrounding the kinds of inducements a company can offer to attract applicants are more restrictive in Japan than in the United States. Company *X* is expected not to raid company *Y* and not to offer a specific employee of another company a job. The employee must initiate the interaction, not the employer.

Size of Firm

The proportion of employees who leave a firm is lowest in the largest firms (see table 4). The basic reason for this is that larger firms are, in an

TABLE 4

SEPARATION RATES IN JAPANESE MANUFACTURING ESTABLISHMENTS, BY SIZE OF ESTABLISHMENT, 1963–67 (%)

Scale of Establishment (No. of Employees)	1963	1964	1965	1966	1967
500+	21.2	23.4	21.6	19.3	21.1
100–499	31.6	33.3	30.2	28.0	30.5
30–99	33.9	37.2	33.9	32.6	35.6
5–29	32.5	31.3	31.7	30.3	30.0

SOURCE.—Rōdō sho, ed., *Rōdō hakusho, 1968* (Tokyo: Okura Sho, 1967), p. 228.

NOTE.—The separation rate = number of separated employees during the year/total number of employees at the end of December of the previous year × 100. Note that the separation rates in table 1 are *average monthly*, whereas table 4's rates are cumulative for an entire year. Thus, the 21.2 rate for establishments with 500 or more employees would be 21.2/12 or 1.8 per month.

overall sense, more attractive places in which to work. Monthly wages generally are positively related to firm size, but this is only one difference. As a Shipbuilding Company worker told us, "Smaller companies are unstable. In a boom period they may pay higher monthly wages than a large company, but they don't have stable pay, bonuses, benefits, and so on." Another worker said, "I used to work for a factory employing under 100 people, which took orders for ship parts from larger firms. There was a lot of fluctuation in the number of hours we could work. While working, we could never stop a minute; sometimes there was no overtime." A common expression is, "to seek employment in a larger firm in order to stabilize [*anteisaseru*] my life." As one Shipbuilding Company *chūto* worker put it, "My brother-in-law told me to find a settled, stabilized company. This company, which was then recruiting, was larger, and had higher wages and better equipment. My fellow workers in the smaller firm felt the same way, and they quit for the same reason." It appears that the term a "stable, settled firm" is at times a euphemism for a firm offering higher pay, larger bonuses, welfare, etc., rather than referring to the firm's likelihood of failure or bankruptcy.

In 1967, of employees in all firms of five or more people who had changed firms, 15 percent were earning 30 percent or more pay in the new firm, 24 percent were earning between 10 and 30 percent more pay, 38 percent were making between 10 percent more and 10 percent less, 14 percent were earning between 10 and 30 percent less, and 6 percent were earning over 30 percent less than in their previous job. Thus, 39 percent had gained more than 10 percent in pay by moving, in contrast with 20 percent who had lost more than 10 percent.[11]

The desire to move to larger, more stable firms is found even among white-collar staff and managerial personnel, the group which is generally the most committed to lifetime employment in one firm. Employment

[11] Rōdō sho, ed., *Rōdō hakusho* (Tokyo: Okura Sho, 1969), p. 71, table 53.

agencies for executives are a growing phenomenon.[12] A personnel manager in a leading electrical appliance firm told us it is now not uncommon for middle managers, engineers, and clerical workers to seek to change firms, and that companies regard this behavior as legitimate when it reflects the desire to move to a larger firm. Such men are given an appropriate rank in the new firm, but not line authority until they have been with the new firm for some time. It is still quite uncommon for a man who is to direct many subordinates to be recruited from outside the company, especially in the case of larger firms.

Yet, despite the general desire to move to larger firms, objective factors operate to move many employees in the opposite direction. Table 5 shows

TABLE 5

NUMBER OF NEWLY HIRED EMPLOYEES IN MANUFACTURING ESTABLISHMENTS, BY SIZE OF PREVIOUS AND PRESENT ESTABLISHMENTS (IN THOUSANDS): JAPAN, 1967

		SIZE OF PREVIOUS FIRM				
SIZE OF PRESENT FIRM	TOTAL*	500+	100–499	30–99	5–29	1–4
500+	121.9	41.0	31.1	26.8	19.7	1.9
100–499	133.4	21.8	47.8	34.7	25.9	2.3
30–99	168.5	17.6	47.0	53.4	43.8	5.2
5–29	139.7	11.4	16.6	30.6	70.1	9.5
Total	563.4	91.8	142.5	145.6	159.6	19.0

SOURCE.—Japan Ministry of Labor, *Rōdō tōkei nenpō, 1967* (Tokyo: Labor Law Association, 1968), p. 33, table 20.

* Including unknown establishment size of previous occupations. Totals sometimes reflect rounding errors.

that in 1967, of *chūto saiyo* employees newly hired, as many as 145,000 (26 percent) had moved from larger to smaller firms (total of all cell entries to the left and below the main diagonal). One reason for this is lack of success in a larger firm, or an attitude that one must atone for a mistake by leaving the firm. There is also a practice whereby older workers, or those reaching the compulsory retirement age, in a large firm must accept employment in a smaller subsidiary company if they want to be employed at all. Table 5 also reveals that of the 91,800 newly hired employees in 1967 who had left firms of 500 or more employees, only 45 percent were able to enter firms in the same size category. To leave a large firm, then, generally means *downward mobility* in scale of firm—and in wages, benefits, etc. This partially explains why mobility is relatively low in large-size firms. Insofar as these conditions of differential attraction in firms of different size continue, there will continue to be structurally induced interfirm mobility: workers in smaller firms desiring to move to

[12] Masaaki Imai, *Tenshoku no susume* [Recommendations for changing your job] (Tokyo: Saimaru, 1968).

larger firms, and some in the latter being required to move to smaller firms. Differential attractiveness has the function of weakening lifetime commitment. There is, however, another structural factor—changes in the proportion of employees in firms of different sizes over time—which is relevant here. Assuming a continuation of the lower quit rate in large firms, the larger the proportion of the labor force employed in large firms, *the lower the national interfirm mobility rate will be.*

The proportion of employees in the manufacturing sector in firms of 500 or more has remained remarkably stable during most of the postwar period: 22.6 percent in 1951, 23.6 percent in 1960, and 23.4 percent in 1966. But within this size class there has been an increase in the number of very large firms. Thus, in 1966 there were 1,192 companies with 1,000–4,999 employees, and 217 companies with 5,999 or more employees.[13] It is likely that the proportion of personnel in very large firms will continue to grow. There has been a trend toward consolidation. A significant harbinger of this trend was the merger of Yawata and Fuji, two major steel companies, which created in 1970 the new Nippon Steel Corporation, Japan's largest firm (over 79,000 employees) and the world's largest steel maker except for U.S. Steel.

Thus, the factor of firm size is a two-edged sword. On the one hand, it encourages mobility between smaller and larger firms; on the other hand, the likely increase in the proportion employed in large firms may have the opposite effect—of reducing the overall interfirm mobility rate.

The Shift from Seniority to Job Classification

A number of recent developments in the Japanese economy have begun to weaken the prevailing seniority (*nenko*) system. The traditional assumption was that an employee's contribution to the firm increased with seniority. Under conditions of rapid scientific and technological change, older workers' knowledge and skills become obsolescent, and those with less seniority may in fact have the most valuable contributions to make. In response to the demands of younger workers for higher pay, and the rapidly rising market value of their labor, companies have been raising the pay of younger workers at a faster rate than that of older workers.[14] Table 6 shows that the ratio of wages at age fifty-five to beginning wages has been declining during the last decade, but the former are still four or five times larger than the latter. Note also that the absolute difference in pay between beginners and those of age fifty-five increased rather than decreased between 1958 and 1967.

The major institutional mechanism through which these changes are

[13] Ministry of Labor (Japan), *Rōdō Tōkei Chōsa Nenpō, 1951* (Tokyo: Ministry of Labor, 1952), p. 87, table IE2; Rōdō sho, ed., *Rōdō hakusho* (Tokyo: Okura Sho, 1968), p. 223, table 7; Office of the Prime Minister, Bureau of Statistics, *Nihon Tōkei Nenkan, 1967* (Tokyo, 1968), p. 82.

[14] *Japan Labor Bulletin* 5, no. 9 (September 1966): 7–8.

TABLE 6

Amount and Ratio of Monthly Wages of New and Retiring Male Employees, by Education and Status, Japanese Manufacturing Firms

Education and Work Status	Beginning Salary (1)	Salary at Age 55 (2)	Ratio of (2) to (1)
College graduates—white-collar:			
1958	14,149	80,879	5.7
1960	15,183	85,495	5.6
1965	24,746	116,831	4.7
1967	28,964	136,615	4.7
High school graduates—white-collar:			
1958	9,544	62,225	6.5
1960	10,145	66,289	6.5
1965	17,589	88,495	5.0
1967	21,189	110,722	5.2
High school graduates—manual, blue-collar:			
1963*	13,796	70,638	5.1
1965	17,605	82,230	4.7
1967	21,260	92,629	4.4
Junior high school graduates—manual, blue-collar:			
1958	6,827	43,475	6.4
1960	7,263	46,020	6.3
1965	13,892	68,488	4.9
1967	16,977	79,654	4.7

Source.—Tōyō keizai, *Chingin soran*, 1968 ed. (Tokyo, 1969), pp. 146–200.
Note.—See footnotes to table 3.
* Data for earlier years not given.

beginning to take place is some form of *job* or *skill classification* system. "Progressive firms are making deliberate efforts to move gradually toward a system that emphasizes merit, performance, and ability rather than the former criteria."[15] The firms we studied—Electrical Company and Shipbuilding Company—have moved in this direction. Electrical Company has gone further: its *shigoto-betsu chingin* system classifies all jobs in the plant according to four major levels of skill: Creative, Operative, Routine, and Training, with subdivisions of skill within each. In the future, pay will be based on job classification, rather than only on education and seniority. In Shipbuilding Company, although all job titles are classified, pay is not yet based on type of job. However, there are provisions for employees to advance in status and rank more on the basis of examinations and performance, and these will be less closely tied to seniority than heretofore.

Job classification and performance-oriented systems have not yet been widely incorporated into the salary structure of Japanese firms. But the trend now appears to be in this direction.[16] Moreover, as noted above,

[15] M. Y. Yoshino, *Japan's Managerial System* (Cambridge, Mass.: M.I.T. Press, 1968), p. 236.

[16] Yoshino, p. 240.

even some firms which hew to the *nenko* (seniority) system have modified it by offering equal pay to *chūto saiyo*, providing they have had equivalent prior work experience. Thus, we conclude that the strict *nenko* system is most functional for lifetime commitment, the modified *nenko* system is less functional, and the new job-skill classification systems are dysfunctional for commitment. The first type minimizes interfirm mobility, the second increases it somewhat, and the third makes for the greatest mobility. To the extent that a person can change employers in mid-career *without* having to sacrifice his seniority-related pay and other rewards, without having to "start over again," the lifetime commitment pattern is undercut, and interfirm mobility becomes more feasible.

Rationalization and Automation

Technological rationalization—the substitution of mechanization and automation for human labor—has developed rapidly in postwar Japanese industry. The wartime destruction of much of Japan's plant and equipment made the introduction of the newest technology after the war both necessary and easier. Technological rationalization has important consequences for lifetime commitment. One, already noted, is that it undercuts the earlier assumption that a worker's contribution to the firm increases with age (seniority). To some extent, rapid technological change makes it more valid to say younger workers make the greater contribution, while older workers suffer obsolescence. A second consequence is that automation increases the need for continuous operation of the costly capital equipment, and thus increases the probability that workers will have to engage in shift work. Since night shift work is more unpopular than day work, in Japan as elsewhere, it has the function of increasing interfirm mobility (from firms that require night work to those that do not). As a Shipbuilding Company worker put it, "At first I disliked the work here. I had to work nights and missed having recreation with my friends in the evening." In some of the interviews, dislike of shift work was a reason given for changing firms.

A third consequence can be stated only as a possibility: as employers and managers in Japan are compelled to take more seriously into account how to cut labor costs and avoid redundancy, their rationality with regard to workers may stimulate a more rational, pragmatic, instrumental attitude on the part of the worker toward the company. In the United States, redundant workers have been laid off. In Japan this has not been a serious threat thus far. When a company wants to decrease its personnel, one mechanism is simply not to replace those who retire, die, or leave voluntarily. Another adaptive mechanism is the distinction between regular and temporary workers.[17] The latter group—which comprised

[17] "Temporary workers" (*rinjiko*) should not be confused with part-time workers. A temporary worker works full-time for a stated period, in contrast with a regular worker, who works full-time until retirement.

5–6 percent of all manufacturing employees in 1967—can be discharged without violating the company's side of the lifetime commitment obligation, since this refers only to *regular* employees.

When a job is eliminated by technological advance, the worker can be absorbed by the company to fill other production needs, as long as economic development and the labor shortage continue. Objectively, given these conditions, technological unemployment is not a serious threat. Nevertheless, it is worth testing the hypothesis that when workers think they are viewed not as a "constant" but as a variable in terms of labor and production costs, they become both more detached from an attitude of lifetime commitment and more alert to the possibility of interfirm mobility.

Communication with "Significant Others"

A number of our interviews revealed that in the process of making a decision about leaving a company, the influence of specific other people with whom one interacts tipped the scales in one or the other direction. In the Japanese setting, a "significant other" may be one's (usually paternalistic) work superior. In Shipbuilding Company this person may be the *oyakata* of one's machine. (As noted above, of the two or three men who use a given machine, the most senior is the *oyakata*, and he is the one held finally responsible for the maintenance of the machine, training those who use it, etc.). Or, one's *boshin* or *hanchō* may be a "significant other." Another alternative is the person who recommended one for employment in the company. One Shipbuilding Company worker recalled that, for a variety of reasons, he was at one time considering leaving the company. "But when I told [the person who recommended me] I wanted to quit he said he'd lose face if I did. So I thought about it and decided to stay." The same worker said, "When I started here (1961) everybody came through personal recommendations, such as a relative in the company. So the quit rate was lower. Now more and more workers come through newspaper ads, without personnel introduction, *so they suddenly disappear from the company.*" Implied here is the function of significant others in deterring quitting—in this case the person who recommended one for employment in the company. Since those recruited through the more impersonal mass media do not have these obligations, they are more likely not only to quit but to do so without any warning.[18]

[18] A Shipbuilding Company worker described the social process by which he had severed his ties with a previous company. "I told my fellow workers I was going to quit. But in a small company like that, if I just talked with management about my plan to quit, they'd argue with me forever to make me not quit. So I told management in the form of a letter, saying I was returning to Kumamoto for farming work. I did this in [September 1968] and actually farmed for six months on my family's land. Then I decided that to stabilize my life I should get a job in a big company. When I went back to visit my old company, after quitting, half the workers and managers there had resigned themselves to my quitting, but half still tried to get me back."

Another way in which "significant others" may influence the decision to stay or quit is in the context of night school classes. The desire to complete high school (as well as more advanced education) is so strong among younger Japanese workers today that many who are compelled to enter the labor force after completing middle school (ninth year of school), enroll in night high schools, which meet from 5:30 to 9:00 six evenings a week. During one's four years in this program he meets workers from other firms, and the benefits of working in each firm are discussed. A Shipbuilding Company worker told us, "A lot of workers from [a leading nearby electrical factory] are in my night high school. I made friends with them and found out they get higher wages and higher bonus. But they told me their work is repetitive, assembly line type, and they don't like it too much." This man is therefore not inclined to leave Shipbuilding Company.

Summary and Conclusion

In the present and likely future situation of Japanese society and industry, the strength of the lifetime commitment pattern derives mainly from the following structural factors:

1. The seniority system, especially when it operates to make seniority or other aspects of status in one company less than completely transferable to another company.
2. Advanced technology eliminates the least skilled jobs and makes for job enlargement and greater variety, all of which factors tend to reduce quitting and thereby strengthen commitment to one company.
3. Strong primary group ties among employees, and between supervisors and workers, in a company.
4. An increase in the proportion of employees who work in large firms (since large firms have the lowest quit rates). This proportion is likely to increase in the 1970s.
5. To cope with the labor shortage, as well as for other reasons, management is strongly in favor of lifetime commitment.

The above-mentioned structural factors have the function of maintaining or strengthening the commitment of employees to long service in

---

This case highlights several structural elements that operate in the process of disengagement from a Japanese firm. (1) To avoid the situation in which such "significant others" as management could try to dissuade him from leaving, he resorted to impersonal communication, and made his letter present the decision to quit as a *fait accompli*. (2) The traditional cultural symbolism of agriculture as the root of all other productive activities, and the obligation to one's family of orientation, provide convenient means of legitimizing one's decision to leave an industrial job. (3) It is less embarrassing to the company if the worker who quits at first returns to the family farm, rather than directly entering another company. (4) Attitudes toward quitting, and the conditions under which it is the correct move, vary among both workers and managers; their sanctions are therefore mixed, some accepting the quitter, others trying to dissuade him. Negative sanctions are thus sporadic rather than uniform in their application by "significant others."

one firm. At the same time, several structural pressures undermine lifetime commitment and increase the probability of mobility:

1. The labor shortage, especially the shortage of young workers.

2. The shift of relative emphasis from seniority to job or skill classification systems as bases of pay and promotion.

3. The shift from strict seniority to modified seniority systems, whereby equal pay is offered for equivalent experience, whether in one firm or in different firms.

4. In general, insofar as *chūto saiyo* employees expect to receive and in fact do receive equal treatment, rather than prejudice and discrimination, from fellow employees and management in a new company, this obstacle to interfirm mobility is removed.

5. The public nature of inducements to change firms—newspaper advertisements and the like—legitimizes the practice of changing firms. A number of devices (e.g., Sunday job interviewing) facilitate the exploration of alternative jobs while still employed.

6. As long as there is differential attractiveness of employment in large *versus* small firms, there will be structurally induced interfirm mobility.

We have seen that some of the above factors have a highly contingent influence upon lifetime commitment; that is, their influence depends on their relationships with other factors. Consider firm size. Given size differentials in firms' attractiveness, lifetime commitment is supported by increases in the proportion of employees who work in the most attractive (the largest) firms; and it is undermined by decreases in this proportion. Alternatively, given the disappearance of size differentials in firms' attractiveness, variations in the proportion of employees in firms of different size will be unrelated to lifetime commitment and mobility rates. Put in another way, interfirm mobility could be kept at its present level (*ceteris paribus*) either (1) by reduced size differentials in firms' attractiveness or (2) by continued size differentials in attractiveness coupled with an increasing proportion of employees in the most attractive firms.

It should also be clear that the same factor may have multiple consequences, some functional and others dysfunctional for lifetime commitment. Advanced, automated technology is one of these. Since it offers jobs that are more skilled and varied, it decreases mobility. Yet automation also tends to increase the likelihood of night shift work, which, because of its unpopularity, tends to increase the quit rate.

Another factor which has both functional and dysfunctional consequences for lifetime commitment is communication with "significant others." Workers engaged in the process of deciding whether to leave a firm are influenced by specific interactions with and attitudes of significant others, and their influence may sway the person in either direction.

In conclusion, there are clearly factors that continue to operate so as to maintain and strengthen commitment to one firm, and the Japanese interfirm mobility rate is not likely in the immediate future to become as high as in the United States. Nevertheless, considering the net balance of functional and dysfunctional consequences, we concur with the judgment that "during the past two decades, at least some of the basic premises and values that have supported the paternalistic ideology appear to be eroding. There are indications that the well-entrenched paternalism is slowly but surely losing its viability and appeal to workers."[19]

To paraphrase Marx, the lifetime commitment system may contain the seeds of its own destruction. The more successful a company is in eliciting lifetime commitment, the higher the average seniority of its personnel will be, and the greater the company's direct and indirect wage and welfare costs will be. Therefore, the company will be compelled to modify its seniority basis of payment in the direction of a job or skill classification system. As it does this it may weaken the degree of lifetime commitment. Japanese industry applied liberalization (*jiyuka*) and rationalization (*gorika*) first to technology, then to marketing. It is likely that it will now increasingly extend these policies and practices to personnel administration.[20]

[19] Yoshino, p. 113.
[20] Imai, n. 12 above.

9
A Day in the Life of Li Sheng, Chinese Manager

Jean-Louis du Rivaux

Li Sheng belongs to that group of individuals who, in today's new China, are lumped together under the heading of "new managers spawned by the Cultural Revolution." Li Sheng was a technician in Shanghai's Number Seven Diesel Motor Plant in 1970 when, at a worker's general assembly, he was elected to membership in the company's Revolutionary Committee. His appointment was then approved by the higher authorities of both the Party and the State.

Li Sheng's metamorphosis into a "manager" has failed to bring about any far-reaching changes in his life style. No more so than did his former job as a skilled blue-collar worker, his new responsibilities entail no privileges over and above those of the bulk of the plant workers. His wages remain the same as before—52 yuan per month, slightly above the mean but less than those of certain veteran employees whose pay amounts to around 80 or 90 yuan.

Li Sheng lives in a workers' housing complex in Shanghai's southern suburb, in a two-room apartment that is a tight squeeze for the family, which consists of four people besides himself—his wife, two children, and his mother. The housing unit is located at a fairly considerable distance from the plant. Mr. Li therefore has to be up at the crack of dawn each day —by 6:30 a.m. at the latest. He and his wife gulp down a hasty breakfast of vermicelli soup and steamed rolls, after which he proceeds to the next door park area for his daily "constitutional," a set of physical exercises participated in by a group of local workers. A loudspeaker, retransmitting from a radio, blares out the various exercises. When this "sports" broadcast is over, Li Sheng listens to the news bulletin and then darts off on his bicycle. It's 7 a.m. by the time he disappears into the heavy crowds of cyclists who are already swarming along the highways and byways. His wife will leave the house a bit later; the textile mill in which she works lies nearby. Li Sheng has to pedal for a full hour before pulling up at the entrance to his factory.

His is a medium-sized company—2,000 blue-collar workers, around 300 technicians and engineers, and 300 white-collar employees in its administration (commercial department, statistical office, planning department, and bookkeeping), which used to be larger but is now considerably reduced since the campaign against bureaucracy launched during the Cultural Revolution.

Reprinted, by permission, from *European Business* (Winter/Spring, 1974).

THE REVOLUTIONARY COMMITTEE'S INNOVATIONS

The revolutionary Committee was formed at the end of the Cultural Revolution, in a move to replace, at the head of the company, the earlier "two-headed" executive machinery—the political and ideological management carried on by the "party cell," and the economic and technical management by a "committee of experts" assisted by a director. Even in those cases in which it did not spark conflicts, this dualism had instituted a distinction whose effects had been repeatedly decried in the past: in fact, completely apart from all political criteria, the plant had been run by the executive director and his committee on the basis of the purely financial criteria of "profitability" and by the methods that would have warmed the cockles of any capitalist entrepreneur's heart: parcelization of tasks, standardization of production, price policies designed to hasten recovery of investments and propitious for self-financing. Wages on a piece-work basis, the multiplication of bonuses (production bonus, technological development bonus, overtime bonus)—all these were geared to stimulate worker productivity. These were "economic" measures in which the political officers and party members did not always have a say, even though some of them were outspokenly against the sharpening of wage differences and the introduction of a new form of inequality between workers. In this motor manufacturing plant, the party cell failed to put up any objections. On the ideological level it administered a management chain of command whose methods and instruments were highly hierarchized. All this notwithstanding, the main company officers, most of them men who had worked their way up from the workers' ranks, had long since lost contact with manual labor.

With respect to this former system, the Revolutionary Committee represents an innovation from two points of view:

First, the distinction between "Red" leaders and white-collar "experts" has been wiped out. Although the party cell unquestionably retains its distinct existence, its main members are simultaneously members of the Revolutionary Committee, together with the workers, the technical and administrative staff, and the militiamen: In theory, it should not be possible for the Committee to adopt any decision that is not politically sound and economically and technically feasible.

It is perhaps inaccurate—and this is the second innovation—to speak of decisions by the Revolutionary Committee. Since Li Sheng has been a member—for nearly three years—this Committee has never voted. Unanimity and consensus are the rule. Before these can be achieved, long discussions are sometimes necessary in which the "masses"—i.e., the plant workers as a group—are free to speak their minds. At the outset, the masses participated in the proceedings of the Revolutionary Committee itself, in which they have representation: The Committee's 27 members include ten company executives, ten representatives of the "masses," and seven delegates from the military, only two of whom are members of the People's Liberation Army, the remainder being militiamen, i.e., workers trained in defense tasks.

For outstanding issues on which agreement is not reached by the Committee and, in any event, for all the most important matters, the base is consulted, either via the intermediary of the "Workshop Commission" or directly, via the convening of a "plant workers' general meeting."

Li Sheng has participated in several meetings of this kind concerned with a wide variety of topics: plant working conditions, safety regulations, ways of avoiding waste. Above all else, discussion has focused on the goals of the Plan, on the conditions requisite for achieving them, and there was recently a session devoted to summing up progress to date.

SPAWNING INNOVATION

Li Sheng has particular responsibilities on the preparation of the annual Plan; he heads a task force which, acting within the Revolutionary Committee, debates the selection of product items and recommends the launching of new products. It bears no resemblance whatsoever to the usual "innovation" or marketing department well known in capitalist countries.

For one thing, Li Sheng doesn't boast an office. During part of the day only, he holds forth in the Revolutionary Committee's study hall which, what with its blackboard and student desks, curiously resembles a classroom. The rest of the time he's "on the spot," i.e., in the workshops. He is convinced that this is where worthwhile ideas and projects are spawned, not in the ivory towers of bureaus of experts concerned with abstract research. Since the Cultural Revolution, one of the Revolutionary Committee's goals has been to encourage the masses' innovative capacity, since their practical experience is regarded as no less valid than the theoretical knowledge of the engineers and must in fact correct and complete such knowledge.

In many cases Li Sheng has known workers to come up with first-rate suggestions that have proven invaluable. One of them designed improvements for his machinery that enabled an 8 percent reduction in copper consumption. Two others set up a soundproofing system in their workshop that made working conditions more pleasant and fostered an increased output. The most dazzling example is that of the personnel in one workshop who, after duly poring over the motor they were busy producing, came up with a simpler design for a less powerful but sturdier and more economical motor. A few years earlier such a breakthrough would have been rewarded by an "economy bonus" or an "innovation bonus." Today such rewards have been done away with; it is not the lure of "filthy lucre" but rather their revolutionary consciences and their political reflection and practice that should spur the workers ever onward in their efforts toward ever higher achievement.

However, individual exploits are still rewarded in another way: This workshop has become a "pilot agency" to which all other workers have come for training periods, in groups. The two best workers have also been registered in night school before, perhaps, going on to a university.

Individual bonuses still exist in spite of the Cultural Revolution, but they are highly criticized. A factory which exceeds the Plan can use part of the surplus revenues for its welfare fund (housing, canteens, social equipment), which is of a collective nature. When a workshop or department is responsible for an innovation, it can receive pens, books, or even a small sum of money, roughly four to six yuans, that is, 10 percent to 15 percent of a monthly salary. Nevertheless, the current trend in 1974 is to fight against any individual bonuses!

Li Sheng meets with State Planning representatives at regularly-scheduled intervals. On these occasions, the representatives include the bigwigs of the Shanghai Municipal Planning Office (the motor plant is not one of the big "national interest" companies which, like the Shanghai automobile Works, come directly under central authority). On behalf of the Committee, he submits for the planners' consideration projects for manufacturing new items, which will not be approved until it has been shown that they would dovetail with the overall Plan—or, better yet, that they mean improved conditions for achieving the latter.

The Plan provides a wealth of detail on production goals and conditions, volume, total values, nominal product values, payrolls and mean wage scales, depreciation, and profits. For each type of motor it sets forth the technical specifications, selling price, and cost price. It is a delicate structure in the preparation of which the plant has participated. On occasion, Li Sheng may well wonder whether it is wise to challenge it by introducing innovations. There would seem to be no incentive to do so. There is neither concern with ensuring additional "outlets" for the plant's output, since the products are purchased and distributed by the State on the basis of the equipment plans of consumer enterprises (the market is both guaranteed and fixed); nor is there concern with swelling the plant's wealth, because if profits exceed the amount specified in the Plan, all excess reverts to the State (there is no such thing as corporate self-financing—except for what we have just said on the use of part of the "profit" for social purposes within the plant).

STRIVE, SAVE, SERVE

The worker's motivations are much stronger: a quasi-ethical imperative, a duty that is steadily dinned into him, the theme of every discussion and of all the revolutionary mobilization meetings that recur at stated intervals (during certain periods there is one meeting a day) in the factory. This imperative is pithily summed up in just three words: strive, save, serve.

Strive . . . to exceed the predictions of the Plan, naturally. Its goals have been defined by the plant workers and decision makers in accordance with the city and central planners, on the basis of realism and moderation, but with the understanding that they are to be considered as a minimum. All the production teams in each workshop strive to overreach their goals and, in so doing, to outdo their fellow workers. In Shanghai, Li Sheng's motor plant boasted a record for the first months of last year. It was given feature coverage in the press. Along with a few other representatives from factory 407, Li Sheng has undertaken an "exchange of experiences," meeting with a team that has become a "pilot" team. The slogan—"Catch up with plant Number Four and beat it!"—has become a byword with all concerned, scrawled in great sprawling red ideograms on eye-catching white banners displayed in all the workshops.

Save: in the motor plant as everywhere else, this duty has been assigned as a system. For Li Sheng, economy is perhaps the prime criterion for appreciating the value of the technological innovations submitted for his assessment. The best are the ones that make it possible to produce as much —if possible, more—while consuming less. A number of prominently-displayed signs indicate that the plant is in a permanent state of mobilization against waste. Underneath the electric switches there are posted exhortations reading "Comrade, save electricity!" Handwritten notices tacked up on the walls pinpoint errors that have been committed, or single out for special praise certain exemplary workers whose activities have been inspired by the concern with saving. One huge poster in one of the workshops cites as an example the attitude of a certain worker who, together with a few of his fellows during a recreation period, undertook to retrieve certain copper wastes from the plant residues, or describes another worker who developed a system for recovering the cantine's waste water and using it as a fertilizer in a suburban commune.

Serve: Another of Li Sheng's interlocutors is the consumer. Not the purchaser—not the Shanghai purchasing agency—but the actual final consumer, who consistently enjoys the right to address himself directly or indirectly to the factory (the manufacturer's name and references are always listed on a product) for the purpose of airing his views concerning such-and-such an item.

CONTACT WITH CONSUMERS

Factory Number Seven basically produces hydraulic pump motors and other agricultural irrigation implements. The users of such instruments (communes and brigades) are located throughout the country, sometimes at great distances—in the arid hinterlands of the northern plains or the furrowed Shensi plateaus where intensive hydraulic engineering projects are being carried out. Like industrial production units, one of the motor plant's guiding principles is to keep in contact with these consumers. Last year, Li Sheng performed a survey of the peasants in two provinces to check whether the equipment produced by his factory was giving satisfaction from the standpoint of quality, ruggedness, and technical features. The need emerged for a new, low-power model for certain isolated units that generate their own energy in small makeshift hydroelectric plants. Such a model had not been included in the product range offered by the plant. Research was begun on it. This phenomenon is in no way exceptional: It is now a "way of life," forming part and parcel of the "exchanges of experience" in which Li Sheng has participated concerning these methods of consumer consultation, to which each and every factory is endeavoring to give increased importance.

A few months ago a group of "foreign friends" visited the plant. Li Sheng greeted them on behalf of the Revolutionary Committee and escorted them on a guided tour of the workshops. He was asked a lot of questions about himself, his life and his work. Several visitors were amazed to behold this "manager" garbed in work clothes like everyone else, who obviously enjoyed a relationship of equality and comradeship with the other workers. "In the beginning, things weren't exactly like this," Li Sheng explained. "I began working here in 1965, after graduating from Futan University where, after three years of studying in the mechanics departments, I had received my diploma as a senior technician. When I first came here I behaved somewhat like a 'chief,' and, during the Cultural Revolution, I was reproached for my behavior. The workers organized meetings at which I was requested to think about my attitude and reconsider it. I stopped having foolish pride in my diploma, and I realized that I still had plenty to learn from the experience of both the workers and the peasants, and also that I myself had to acquire the practical experience that is derived from work, above all from manual labor. In 1968 and 1969, I did two stints in a 'Seventh of May' school of the Shanghai municipality. When I got back here, things became different."

At regular intervals (accounting altogether for about one month out of the year), Li Sheng resumes his manual work. Like all of China's executives today, he alternately wears the white collar and the blue collar: He is obliged to continue learning in the company of manual workers on the job, and to participate continuously in production.

10

The Indian Manager Looks at the American Technician

A. Kapoor

"Hari om'! Hari om'!" (Hallelujah! Hallelujah!") chanted the priest while the senior management of Ram Lall-Shyam Lall and Sons along with their families sat cross-legged around a holy fire in the factory premises on New Year's Day. The smell of incense was heavy and the smoke curled gradually through the production machinery. Ram Lall and Shyam Lall, in a tradition handed down by their grandfather, were seeking the assistance of the gods in the coming year.

The services had lasted for over three hours and before he finished, the priest took particular care to ceremoniously bless the company ledgers. This was an important day in the company's life. Not only did Ram and Shyam Lall believe in the efficacy of such a service, but so did their friends, relatives, and workers.

But the American technician had a quizzical grin on his face as he watched the ceremonies. It was a completely new experience for him, and such companies represent a different business world which the American technician must learn to understand if he is to be effective in his work in India.

This "different business world" has some important characteristics peculiar to India which can and do affect a foreign technician's performance. I will discuss some of the important ones.

Business Objectives: For all practical purposes, the Indian businessman runs his business for and by the family. Separation of ownership and management, except in some of the truly large Indian companies, does not exist. As reflected in Case One, the technician must recognize the strong family orientation of Indian business, for it has a strong bearing on what he can accomplish.

CASE ONE: WHERE IS THE ORGANIZATION CHART?

Ram Lall and Shyam Lall were brothers who had inherited a family business (less than $5 million in annual sales) from their father. Each brother had two sons who were married. Ram and Shyam, their wives, married sons and grandchildren lived together as a traditional joint family in a large house. They shared the same kitchen, eating together, socializing with a set of family friends, and in general spending most of their waking hours together. Ram, Shyam, and their sons ran the family business together and expected the grandsons to succeed them.

Reprinted by permission, from the July/August 1969 issue of *Worldwide P & I Planning—The Magazine for Multinational Management*.

In 1964, an American technician arrived in India to set up a plant and start operations under a collaboration Ram Lall-Shyam Lall and Sons had concluded with a medium-sized U.S. company. But he found his task to be impossible. Ram Lall-Shyam Lall did not have an organization chart. The distribution of authority and responsibility was highly fluid and changed among the family members almost weekly. The pace of work was highly relaxed.

The technician decided to "take the bull by the horns" and force the company to set itself up more efficiently. As the first step, he developed an organization chart along with a brief job description for various members of management, namely, Ram Lall, Shyam Lall, and their sons. The technician placed Shyam Lall's *younger* son as director of manufacturing and gave his *older* cousin (Ram Lall's younger son) a subordinate position.

Ram Lall's wife was furious that her son, who was older than her youngest nephew, had not been named director of manufacturing. She complained to her husband. On the other hand, Shyam Lall's wife felt *her* son should have the director's position because the American "expert" judged him competent. The conflict on this point between the families of Ram and Shyam Lall soon escalated and threatened to end the joint family relationship.

As the family elders, Ram and Shyam Lall were disturbed by this turn of events. They wanted to keep the entire family together and both expressed the sentiment "what is the business good for if it breaks up the family?" Therefore, they asked the American company to withdraw its technician.

The moral: *The American assumed certain things were business necessities —an organization structure, separation of ownership and management, delegation of authority and responsibility, separation of family from the business. But none of these assumptions was correct for Ram Lall-Shyam Lall and Sons. The owners gave the highest priority to family harmony, not organizational efficiency or project implementation. The implication for the foreign technician: In India, he must recognize the nature of the broader family context for its effect on the business and, therefore, his role in it.*

Personal relationships: In Indian society, relationships between individuals are always personal. There is no such thing as just a purely professional relationship. In fact, the ability to perform well at a job is largely conditioned by how intimately a person knows other members of an organization on a personal basis—a trait of Indian business life which the American technician must recognize.

CASE TWO: COULD YOU GIVE ME A RAIN CHECK?

An American technician arrived in India to advise on a manufacturing start-up project. Top management of the Indian company, including the director of manufacturing (an Indian), recognized his know-how and ability.

For the first two months on the job, the American worked very hard, arriving early and leaving late. He developed a thorough understanding of plant operations. He also received many invitations from members of top management, including the director of manufacturing, for cocktails and dinner at their homes. The technician declined all but one or two of these invitations on the grounds that he was too busy with his work at the plant.

By the end of the second month, he made a series of recommendations to the director of manufacturing, but the latter's enthusiastic support seemed to be missing. The technician was getting discouraged, and talked over his problem with another American, who remarked: "You ought to let them know you better as a person." The technician took the advice, spent fewer hours working on the machinery and more time mixing with the Indian management both at the factory and in their homes. He soon achieved greater receptivity and action on his recommendations.

The director of manufacturing wanted to know the entire person—the professional as well as the personal aspects of the man making recommendations which could have a significant bearing on the director's advancement. The director could not understand why the technician was such a recluse and wondered whether he was hiding something in his personal life. The American, on the other hand, thought his views would be accepted for their inherent professional soundness alone.

The moral: *The foreign technician should recognize that his ability to perform professionally in India will be significantly affected by his personal relationships, particularly with local management.*

Social responsibility: The Indian businessman views his social responsibilities in the following order of priority: the immediate family, the larger family, the clan, the community, the region, the country. And these social responsibilities condition his approach to business.

CASE THREE: NO CHANCE FOR ADVANCEMENT

All senior positions in a collaboration were held by American and British personnel. A number of Indians, particularly at junior and middle management levels, had joined the company because it was an American company and therefore would offer more rapid advancement than an Indian or British company. Indians in middle management were unhappy because they felt their progress was impeded by the foreigners who occupied the senior executive positions. The Indians presented their case to top management but received no satisfaction.

They informed top management that the company was discriminating against Indians, that the days of colonialism were over, that India was for the Indians, and that they would present their case to the newspapers and representatives of both the State and Central governments. These developments resulted in a sharp division and mutual distrust between Indians in management and the foreigners.

CASE FOUR: MR. BANNERJEE AND THE YOUNG PUNJABI

An American technician was in charge of manufacturing for a joint venture with a businessman (Mr. Bannerjee) from Calcutta in Bengal. The technician was anxious to hire a bright young Indian assistant who could hopefully replace him over the next three to five years. He passed the word to many of his friends in the Indian and American communities in Calcutta.

After interviewing a number of applicants, he settled on a young Punjabi (from Northwestern India). The technician told Mr. Bannerjee, the company president, of his choice and asked his approval. Instead, Mr. Bannerjee hit the ceiling. He said he eventually wanted the position of director of manufacturing for his son who would graduate next year from Cambridge with honors in English Literature. The technician objected on the ground that Bannerjee's son was not qualified. Bannerjee retorted that his nephew, soon to graduate from engineering college, would also be a good choice for the post. The technician held out for the Punjabi.

Finally, Bannerjee stated that if the American did not find his nephew suitable, he should consider applicants from the Bengali community. There was no need, in Bannerjee's opinion to "go outside."

The moral: *Family and community bonds are strong in India. Because of the high unemployment rate, a businessman will often willingly accept a "less-than-best" qualified person from a* professional *sense if he meets the* nonprofessional requirements *of caste, family, community, and so forth. Thus, to function effectively, the American technician must understand the reasons behind certain actions and policies of Indian management.*

Nationalism: The slightest difficulties in Indian business relationships with foreigners can bring out nationalism in varying degrees of intensity. As shown in Case Three and Case Five, local nationalism can often cause significant problems for American management in India.

CASE FIVE: THE AMERICAN SLAPS AN INDIAN

Workmen were unhappy with general economic conditions on a large project which employed several American technicians. The union had threatened several walkouts and there were frequent wildcat strikes and slowdowns.

In this potentially explosive situation, an American allegedly slapped an Indian foreman. The union leaders were incensed, and shortly after the incident, a crowd gathered in front of the American compound (living quarters) to which the Americans had retreated after the incident. The workmen shouted nationalistic slogans and demanded an apology from the accused American. At first, the Americans refused to offer an apology, but they agreed as the crowd became angrier.

Then the discussion turned to the method of the apology.

The labor leaders demanded that the accused American should allow the Indian foreman to slap him in return. The Americans refused. After more discussion, it was agreed that the accused American would extend his hand under the fence separating the American colony and touch the Indian foreman's feet. (Touching the feet of another person in the Indian tradition can either mean obedience, humility, respect, or, as in this case, it can be a sign of admitting defeat.) Allegedly, many of the Americans at the project were disgusted by the incident and threatened to quit in a body.

In Case Three, the push for rapid Indianization was bolstered by a strong feeling of nationalism which would be supported by the wider society (government, political parties, etc.), and resulted in a redefinition of the American technician's role. In Case Five, labor's discontent with its economic position and prospects was aimed at the company as it was the only visible, tangible object toward which grievances could be expressed. The American technicians, as part of the company, were exposed to the grievances.

Indian businessmen often maintain that the American technician will not disclose all that he should because his American employer tells him not to do so. Thus, the Indian senses a type of American nationalism in the technician's own attitude toward full disclosure. The American may feel disclosing all he knows to his Indian counterpart would jeopardize the security of his fellow craftsmen and indirectly that of his country.

The moral: *There are three implications for the American technician in these two cases: (1) He must be aware that the ever-present feeling of Indian nationalism can surface at any time; (2) Nationalism may be triggered by actions and policies which the American considers fair and neutral; (3) Nationalism may be due to circumstances not of the foreign technician's making and beyond his control.*

The technician's cost: American salaries are higher than what the Germans, Japanese, or British get, and are sky-high compared to the salary of an Indian in an equivalent position. The Indian businessman, concerned as he is with the high salaries paid to the American technicians, becomes even more so by the extra expenses he incurs on their behalf—expenses which may be the straws that break the camel's back.

CASE SIX: HELPING THE AMERICANS SETTLE DOWN

In a collaboration of several million dollars, a number of American technicians came to India with their families. In addition to his regular work, the Indian partner had to rent housing for all technicians, preferably in the form of an American compound separated from other residential areas. He had to furnish the houses with air conditioners, water heaters, and a range of other fittings. He hired servants who could speak English, and cooks who could turn out both Indian and Western cuisine. He provided information, and where necessary, arranged for the admission of the technician's children to private schools. He provided air-conditioned automobiles with driver, one for the technician, another for his wife and family. He helped wives get curtains and household items, and he provided imported items (such as Kleenex tissues) not available in India.

The Indian partner, at the time of the joint venture, knew he would have to help the Americans and their families settle down. But he discovered that catering to individual family needs was not only a source of friction, but also time-consuming.

The resolution: *The Indian partner decided that in future collaborations, he would ask the American company to appoint one of its personnel for liaison between the foreign families and the Indian partner. Under this arrangement, the liaison officer would be responsible for dealing with the American personnel while the Indian partner would deal only with the liaison officer–a marked improvement over dealing with a number of individual families.*

Disclosure: As state earlier, the Indian businessman often feels that the foreign technician limits his disclosure of knowledge to Indian technicians. Cases Seven and Eight reflect how Indian companies achieve maximum disclosure by the American technicians.

CASE SEVEN: MAKING THE UNDERSTUDY SYSTEM WORK

A growing Indian company had set up a number of joint ventures including some with American companies. The practice of the Indian company was to assign one of its personnel as an understudy to every technician it secured from the overseas partners. However, many understudies complained that a significant number of foreign technicians were not willingly disclosing information. This was important enough to be reported to the firm's president. The understudies, along with some members of top management, were convinced the president would admonish the technicians and inform their American employers of his dissatisfaction. But he did not.

The president called a meeting of all understudies and top management. He made it clear that he blamed the understudies for not being able to extract information from the American technicians. He emphasized that it was up to the understudies to learn all that the foreign technician could possibly teach them. He (the president) did not care how many hours the understudies stayed awake, or what the attitude of the foreign technicians was toward disclosure.

The president also changed the system of one understudy to one technician by assigning three or four understudies per foreigner. The understudies were instructed to become the shadow of the American technician from the moment he arrived to the time he left the country. The president made it clear that promotion and salary increases would be largely determined by how much and how effectively each one was able to learn from the American, regardless of whether the latter was willing to disclose information or not.

In this way, the president introduced understudy competition and also added a safety margin—at least one out of three or four understudies would be able to extract the information needed. Six months later there were hardly any complaints about lack of disclosure.

CASE EIGHT: WHO CONTROLS WHOM?

Another progressive Indian company was concerned with possible problems of inadequate disclosure, and in a broader sense, with the question of control over foreign technicians. The normal procedure for securing foreign technicians was for the American partner to assign one or more of its personnel for a period of time to the new company established for the collaboration. Though the technician worked for the Indian company (in which the American company always had less than a majority equity interest), he remained the employee of and was controlled by the American company.

The Indian company felt, since the foreign technician was to work for the Indian company, he should also become its employee. This arrangement would give the Indian company greater control over the foreign technician and hopefully result in a better disclosure relationship between the technician and the Indian company. An additional benefit would be that the foreign technician would not have a "dual obligation" in the sense of being an employee of one company and working for another.

The Indian company has since insisted on this arrangement with all foreign partners, and it is pleased with the results.

The overseas Indians: A large number of Indians are in the United States and other countries for advanced training in a variety of fields. While many return to India, others settle overseas and are a potential source for recruiting skilled personnel for assignments in India, as reflected in Cases Nine and Ten.

CASE NINE: A "THIRD CULTURE" MANAGER

One of the terms of a joint venture was that the American company would appoint the director of manufacturing. He would have the final say on all production matters and, in particular, on product quality. The Indian partner agreed to this requirement.

The American company was of the opinion: (1) that the success of its Indian collaboration would largely depend on how well the director of manufacturing could get along with the Indian partner; (2) that there would be many problems in the initial stages of project implementations; (3) that it was particularly important, from the very first, to maintain good relations with the Indian partner since friction with him at that time would probably adversely affect subsequent relationships; (4) that effective project development would depend less on the technical expertise of the director of manufacturing and more on his ability to understand and anticipate the Indian partner's requirements.

To achieve these four points, the American company appointed an Australian and an Indian as co-directors of manufacturing. The American partner hired the Indian in the United States. His dollar salary was equal to what the company would have paid an American for the equivalent position.

The Australian was to look after the technical aspects of plant operations. The Indian co-director was to be the liaison between the Australian and the Indian partner and between the American and Indian companies.

The Indian partner has been pleased with the co-director arrangement, and in particular, with the Indian for his effectiveness in maintaining good relationships between the two companies. The Indian partner attributes the Indian co-director's success to his being a "third culture" person—one who understands the language and motives of both the Indian and American partners. This attitude helped him anticipate and interpret views much more effectively than an American could have done.

However, the Indian partner was concerned about one aspect of the Indian manufacturing co-director—his salary. Since he was Indian, local management personnel became more conscious of the salary gap between them and the Americans in the project. This feeling would have been less acute if the co-director had been an American. Indians expect other Indians working in India to get a lower salary than Americans working in equivalent jobs.

CASE TEN: HIRING FOR GOVERNMENT RELATIONS

The negotiations with the Indian government leading to final investment approval had been long and tedious. The U.S. company realized the ability of its management in India to establish effective relationships with the Indian government would have a material influence on the project's development. The company felt that an Indian should staff the senior management position involving relations with the Indian government.

But many sensitive issues were at stake, and it wanted someone of unquestioned loyalty, familiar with the U.S. firm's worldwide operations, imbued in its business philosophy. The company selected a naturalized U.S. citizen of Indian origin, an employee for several years, who had held various overseas posts.

The American company has been pleased with the performance of this executive in dealing with the Indian government. As a side benefit, it attracted smart young Indians who were encouraged to join the Indian company by the presence of this executive at a senior post.

The moral: *The net observations suggested by Cases Nine and Ten: Overseas Indians can be a source of skilled personnel as long as the American company feels that they can adapt to both the Indian and the American ways of doing things.*

BEST MAN OR NOT?

Many Indian businessmen claim the American technicians they receive are not the best ones available. Their reasoning is as follows: The Indian venture is only a small part of the U.S. firm's worldwide operations. Therefore, the American company has only a peripheral interest in the Indian operations. Add to this the shortage of skilled multinational line management. Therefore, the American company would rather send its best men to a European subsidiary offering a greater contribution to overall profits.

(While Indians criticize U.S. management on this point, they themselves do not send their best personnel to their own foreign operations in Africa and Southeast Asia for the same reasons!)

In general, Indian businessmen feel the Japanese have a much better understanding of the Indian framework than do Americans because the Japanese social-cultural context is similar to the Indian. For example, as in India, the Japanese emphasize deference to age, to tradition, to group orientation, and as such are more in tune with the business policies and practices of Indian businessmen.

A major criticism by Indian businessmen of the American technician is that he does not understand the nature of Indian conditions—labor, suppliers, customers, dealings with the government, etc. For this reason, and for cost considerations, the Indian prefers to use the American for solving specific problems instead of for overall technical administration. The businessman argues that his relationships with his "publics" are highly unique and personal, and the presence of an outsider would be detrimental to the cultivation of such relationships.

For example, Indian businessmen argue, effective labor relations is of growing importance because of labor unrest. In an effort to control labor, Indian businessmen try to win over labor leaders through cash rewards, by promising employment to their relatives, or through other means. However, such relationships are established over time and they cannot be done by a foreigner. Indian labor leaders know how to deal with Indians on these matters, but would not know how to deal with a foreigner.

One point on which a growing number of Indian businessmen and American technicians agree is that the latter must understand the nature of the broader context—economic, political, social, cultural—within which he functions. Ability to do so results in better performance. Also, both agree that efficiency purely in the technical sense is not enough. The American technician must be more than that—he must also be a little bit of a psychologist, sociologist, political scientist, and anthropologist.

MARKETING

Marketing

11

Internationalization of the Japanese General Trading Companies

Alexander K. Young

"Action think tanks," "Japanese-type conglomerates," "mammoth traders handling 10,000 commodities from instant noodles to missiles," "modern monsters with worldwide communications networks rivalling that of the CIA," "Japan's new Zaibatsus," and "speculators in stocks, rice, land, lumber and other necessities" are all appellations used in characterizing the Japanese trading companies which have been the object of intensive interest and admiration abroad in the past few years while recently coming under attack in their home country.

A more adequate analysis is needed of the strategic responses of the ten largest trading companies to the changing world economy in the years between 1955 and 1973, just prior to the current oil crisis. Their importance is such that U.S. Secretary of Commerce Peterson called them the "world's most efficient international marketing channel."[1]

These ten largest companies, known in Japan as *Sogo shosha* (general trading companies), can be distinguished from small- and medium-sized firms and from firms specializing in just one or two commodity categories such as steel, textiles, or machinery. These ten are Mitsubishi, Marubeni, C. Itoh, Sumitomo Shoji, Nissho Iwai, Tomen, Kanematsu Gosho, Ataka, and Nichimen Jitsugyo. They represent less than one fifth of one percent of the approximately 6,600 Japanese trading firms, but their sales in the Japanese fiscal year 1972 (April 1 to March 31, 1973) totalled $94 billion or about 30 percent of Japan's GNP and slightly more than twice the size of the government budget (see Table 1).[2] Morover, they were responsible for 51 percent of total exports and 63 percent of total imports during fiscal 1972. The top six firms made the list of the top forty Japanese corporations in terms of earnings in the half year period ending March 31, 1973.

In 1973, the *Sogo shoshas* had over 800 offices worldwide and more than 5,000 employees stationed abroad. Mitsui & Company alone had about 10,000 employees working at 56 offices in Japan and over 3,000 Japanese and locally recruited non-Japanese at 123 overseas offices.

SERVING AS COMMISSION MERCHANTS, 1955-70

The strategies of the ten trading companies have clearly reflected national policies. The Japanese economy between 1955-70 was characterized by high growth rate revolving around the chemical and other heavy industries.

Reprinted by permission, from the Spring 1974 issue of *Columbia Journal of World Business*.

Table 1

Total Sales—Fiscal 1972
(Yen: 000,000,000 omitted)
(dollar: 000,000 omitted)

	4/72–9/72	10/72–3/73
Mitsubishi	¥ 2,386	2,796
	$ 7,747	10,550
Mitsui	¥ 2,278	2,678
	$ 7,396	10,104
Marubeñi	¥ 1,572	1,828
	$ 5,103	6,923
C. Itoh	¥ 1,460	1,714
	$ 4,738	6,469
Sumitomo Shoji	¥ 1,109	1,306
	$ 3,567	4,929
Nissho Iwai	¥ 1,065	1,328
	$ 3,456	5,011
Tomen	¥ 724	827
	$ 2,350	3,121
Kanematsu Gosho	¥ 543	650
	$ 1,762	2,453
Ataka	¥ 518	647
	$ 1,685	2,440
Nichimen Jitsugyo	¥ 508	656
	$ 1,648	2,476
Total	¥12,162	14,430
	$39,486	54,452

Source: **Yukashoken Hokokusho** (Securities Reports), 9/72 & 3/73
Notes: 1. Sales in U.S. dollars between 4/72 and 9/72 are based on the $1/¥308 exchange rate. Sales between 10/72 and 3/73 are based on a rate of $1/¥265 because of the difficulty in computing exact dollar values for each transaction occurring before the second Yen revaluation of 3/73 and because many trading companies used the latter rate from fall/72 to fall/73.
2. Strictly speaking, only the Yen figures are accurate bases for comparison because of the two Yen revaluations and the continuing float of major world currencies.

High growth was a cornerstone of government policy and received whole-hearted support from industry. New plant and equipment investment in the manufacturing industry averaged over 30 percent of GNP annually and the share of the chemical and heavy industries grew from 47.6 percent in 1955 to 59.9 percent in 1970, the highest proportion in the world.[3]

Spurred by active government financial and fiscal measures and by the opportunities in the U.S. market, Japanese exports expanded tenfold in 15 years to $19.4 billion in 1970. The role of the *Sogo shoshas* between 1955 and 1970 was that of serving as the trade vanguard of Japanese industry, i.e., that of commission merchants. They handled agricultural imports to feed the people. But their chief role was that of importing iron ore, oil, and other raw materials for industries and selling their manufactured products at home and abroad. In this process they made substantial contributions to the growth of the nation's economy and trade.

CHANGING THROUGH MERGERS AND DIVERSIFICATION

As international competition intensified in the 1960s, the trading companies made adjustments by concentrating on handling chemical and heavy industrial products and by becoming general trading companies through mergers and diversifications.

In 1954, Mitsubishi completed the amalgamation of its trading companies which had split from it by the U.S. Occupation authorities as part of the *zaibatsu* dissolution program. Mitsui merged in 1959 with Daiichi Bussan; Sumitomo Shoji absorbed Sanko Shoji in 1962 and Sogo Boeki in 1970. The other trading companies, which were non-*zaibatsu* in origin, engaged in similar mergers.

A diversification program centering around efforts to expand the share of chemical and heavy industrial products was pushed with special vigor by the non-*zaibatsu* firms. For example, Marubeni and C. Itoh, the third and fourth ranking *Sogo shosha* in terms of volume of sales, were formerly textile trading firms. This pattern of diversification into metals, machinery, and chemicals was followed by the other specialized textile traders such as Tomen, Sosho (now Kanematsu Gosho), and Nichimen Jitsugyo (see Table 2).

Aware of trends indicating that the role of the commission merchant would decline as the amount of direct exports by manufacturers expanded, the top ten firms engaged in strengthening their distribution and financing functions, branched into processing, packaging, and warehousing, extended credit supplies for import and export financing, and improved their position as risk buffer for the major city banks (i.e., *Sogo shoshas* extend loans, originally supplied by banks, to industries for manufacturing and trading purposes and assume whatever risks involved). These firms managed to maintain a 50 percent share in exports between 1960 and 1970 (see Tables 3 and 4).

1970s ENVIRONMENTAL CHANGES

By 1970, several changes in the economic environment began to have an impact on Japan. The values of the Japanese people gradually became transformed from one group work ethic to that of individualistic and private values, seeking greater services and leisure time. Serious water and air pollution problems along with a labor shortage resulting from a declining birth rate clouded the economic picture.

The awareness of the impact of these problems led to the development of Prime Minister Tanaka's Japan Remodelling Plan, which called for the decentralization of industry, communications, and services.

Table 2

Share of Total Commodities Sales

March 1961 v. March 1971

	Metals	Machinery	Textiles	Food	Chemicals
Mitsubishi	25%-35%	23%-20%	22%- 9%	19%-14%	10%-16%
Mitsui	28%-35%	15%-20%	10%- 8%	21%-13%	18%-12%
Marubeni	14%-27%	10%-24%	47%-21%	13%-12%	3%- 7%
C. Itoh	11%-15%	8%-16%	54%-34%	12%-14%	9%-12%
Sumitomo Shoji	58%-46%	11%-21%	3%- 4%	7%- 7%	8%-14%
Nissho Iwai	48%-44%	9%-18%	16%- 8%	18%-11%	4%-n.a.
Tomen	9%-23%	9%-22%	57%-26%	15%-17%	3%- 6%
Nichimen Jitsugyo	11%-23%	9%-14%	47%-28%	9%- 9%	5%-11%
Ataka	43%-33%	9%-11%	12%-12%	4%- 5%	11%-14%
Kanematsu Gosho	21%	15%	29%	(food + chemicals 35%)	

Source: Nikko Research Center, **Toshi Geppo,** 9/71.

Notes:
1. The 10 companies used slightly different commodity classification methods in the past and the Japan Foreign Trade Council is in the process of working out uniform standards.
2. Commodity breakdowns for Kanematsu Gosho are from the research department of C. Itoh and apply to 3/73.
3. Figures may not add to 100% because of rounding.

Table 3

Share of All Trading and Manufacturing Companies in Total Japan Trade

Fiscal 1960 to Fiscal 1972
(000,000,000 omitted)

	Wholesalers, Retailers, Dept. stores	Manufacturers, Others
	export-import	export-import
1960	80%-84%	20%-16%
1961	83%-84%	17%-16%
1962	80%-83%	20%-17%
1963	78%-81%	22%-19%
1964	75%-82%	25%-18%
1965	75%-82%	25%-18%

	Wholesalers, Retailers	Dept. Stores	Manufacturers	Others
	export-import	export-import	export-import	export-import
1966	72%-81%	0.1%-minimal	27%-19%	1%-0.4%
1967	72%-81%	minimal	27%-18%	1.7%-0.5%
1968	71%-81%	0.1%-0.1%	27%-18%	1.7%-0.6%
1969	71%-82%	0.1%-0.1%	28%-17%	1.4%-0.5%
1970	70%-81%	0.1%-0.1%	29%-18%	1.9%-1.0%
1971	69%-81%	0.1%-0.1%	30%-18%	1.2%-1.4%
1972	69%-80%	0.1%-0.1%	30%-19%	0.5%-1.3%

Source: Japanese Ministry of International Trade & Industry (MITI), **Boeki Gyotai Tokeihyo** (Foreign Trade Statistics), 13 vols, 1960–1972.

Notes:
1. Under MITI classification, trading companies are defined as wholesalers, retailers, and department stores that engage in foreign trade.
2. MITI statistics do not give detailed breakdowns until 1966.
3. Figures may not add to 100% because of rounding.

Table 4

Share of the 10 Trading Companies in Total Japan Exports and Imports

Year	Exports	Imports
1963	50%	62%
1964	52%	64%
1965	52%	64%
1966	52%	64%
1967	51%	65%
1968	51%	64%
1969	47%	63%
1970	48%	65%
1971	51%	62%
1972	51%	63%

Source: Research Department, Mitsui & Co.

The international economic environment has also been affected by changes in the basic structure of the world economy, such as the decline of U.S. international economic competitiveness, the parallel rise of Western Europe and Japan and the weakening of free world trade and the international monetary systems. The United States and Western Europe mounted pressure on Japan for greater trade and investment liberalization. Moreover, the developing nations, especially the oil producers, began to demand assistance in domestic economic development by industrialized nations in exchange for their natural resources.

RESPONSES OF THE *SOGO SHOSHAS*

The Nixon "shocks" of 1971 brought home the necessity for creating new economic and trade policies. The national leadership, including Prime Minister Tanaka and Kogoro Uyemura, President of the powerful Japan Federation of Economic Organizations, contended that Japan could not afford a zero growth economy and should pursue a high growth strategy with the new goals of improving the social welfare and the amount of international cooperation. It became imperative that Japanese industry shift its weight from the energy consuming chemical heavy industries to knowledge intensive industries, just as the former has earlier replaced the labor intensive industries.

The new environment required a shift in Japanese foreign trade policies from export promotion to export control and from uncontrolled concentration in a few export markets to orderly marketing overseas. The policy of import control should be discarded in favor of a policy of import promotion, energy source diversification, and importation of labor intensive industries.

The ten firms responded in seven ways:

New emphasis on the domestic market.
Premium on knowledge industries.
Social responsibilities.
Systems organizer function.
Nucleus of industrial groups.
New import-export posture.
Internationalization.

Table 5

Performance of the 10 Trading Companies—Fiscal 1972

	Sales	Sales/ Employees	Profits	Profits Growth	Profits/ Sales	Net Worth/ Total Assets	Profits/ Share
Mitsubishi	1	1	15	51	679	723	202
Mitsui	2	2	26	143	686	721	223
Marubeni	3	5	40	38	680	720	379
C. Itoh	4	4	18	17	667	717	168
Sumitomo	5	3	73	57	685	725	254
Nissho Iwai	6	9	90	47	688	722	380
Tomen	7	8	110	19	681	730	264
Kanematsu Gosho	8	6	191	50	689	733	256
Ataka	9	7	154	101	683	728	393
Nichimen Jitsugyo	10	10	149	24	682	718	288

Source: **Nihon Keizai Shimbun,** 6/4/73 and 6/30/73.

Notes: 1. These rankings are based on Japanese corporations listed on the 1st Tokyo Stock Exchange (banks and insurance companies are excluded).

2. While this article does not discuss the capital, debt and profit structure of the trading companies, it should be pointed out that these companies have long thrived on huge sales volumes, supported by enormous bank and other loans amounting to over 20 times their capital. However, these companies are recently becoming more interested in profits growth.

Table 6

Structure of the 10 Trading Companies-Fiscal 1967 to Fiscal 1972

	1967	1968	1969	1970	1971	1972
Exports	17%	18%	17%	17%	19%	17%
Imports	24%	22%	22%	21%	19%	18%
Domestic Trade	56%	56%	57%	57%	56%	57%
Overseas (Third Country Trade)	3%	4%	4%	5%	6%	8%

Source: Data for 3/67 to 3/72 from Giichi Miyasaka, "Sogo shosha no kaigai torihiki no tsuite" (On the Overseas Trade of General Trading Companies), **Kikai Yunyu Kyokai Geppo,** February 1973.
Figures for 4/72 to 3/73 from **Yukashoken Hokokusho** (Securities Reports), 9/72 and 3/73.

NEW EMPHASIS ON THE DOMESTIC MARKET

The changed goal and structure of the Japanese economy, the growing consumer and service economy, and the rising social capital investment, meant more spending by government, private business, and citizens. The ten *Sogo shoshas*, whose domestic sales averaged about 50 percent of their total sales between 1963 and 1973, perceived new opportunities. They expanded sales by forming ties with leading supermarket and department store chains and actively pushed the rationalization of Japan's hitherto extremely complex and feudal marketing system. This new strategy strengthened their position in the intensifying competition with foreign firms for the Japanese market. The sales of the ten firms grew from 55 percent in 1965 to 57.3 percent in March, 1973, a significant growth in terms of dollar value (see Tables 5 and 6).

PREMIUM ON KNOWLEDGE INDUSTRIES

The second response involved increasing the handling of the knowledge intensive industries such as computers, atomic energy plants, ocean development, advanced industrial plants, system engineering, high fashion clothes, and consulting work.

SOCIAL RESPONSIBILITIES

Long known for fierce competition and for a lack of unity, the trading firms exhibited rare unity (undoubtedly prompted by adverse public opinion) in issuing in Spring, 1973, the *General Trading Company's Code of Behavior* through the revitalized Japan Foreign Trade Council headed by Tatsuzo Mizukami. Although officials privately complained that much of the public's criticism was based on misunderstanding of the fact that it was worldwide inflation, rather than hoarding or speculation, that was the major cause of the spiral rise in the prices of soybeans, food, lumber, and other commodities, and that excess liquidity in the aftermath of the first international monetary crisis of August, 1971, was at the root of the firms' expanded purchases of stocks and land, the *Code of Behavior* stated:

> The general trading company shall ensure, through the strengthening of its internal auditing system, company personnel training and other systems, the constant self-recognition, throughout its entire organization, of its mission to society and shall control and regulate itself by the basic principle of social responsibility. Special care to ensure conformity to management philosophy and functions shall be taken in business dealings involving land, stocks, and goods related to the people's livelihood.[4]

Moreover, each *Sogo shosha* issued separate and more specific codes of behavior pledging to avoid speculation in rice, food, lumber, stocks, and land. On July 4, 1973, the Board of Directors of Mitsui & Company approved a plan to contribute between 2 to 4 percent of its annual profits before taxes to pollution control and to other social service projects. On July 19, President Fujino of the Mitsubishi Corporation declared that the firm would make contributions in the same areas as part of its annual plan.

He urged business and industry to become actively involved in projects wth long-term benefits for the people and to sacrifice short-term profits, if necessary.[5]

SYSTEMS ORGANIZER FUNCTION

The systems organizer function involves diverse products, industries, and firms, both in Japan and abroad, in contrast to single commodity transactions. The global information and organizational resources and talents of the trading firms place them in a far more strategic position than manufacturers or commercial banks in organizing such huge projects as natural resource developments, urban and regional development, and overseas investments. Large scale trading of commodities will continue, but the organizer function is expected to become the leading role for the firms in the future.

NUCLEUS OF INDUSTRIAL GROUPS

Each of the six largest *Sogo shoshas* has attempted to strengthen its position as the nucleus of its respective industrial group, although not limiting business dealings to the group as such, in order to meet domestic and international competition and to carry out the systems organizer function. Increased purchases of stocks of enterprises in the group and expanded loans to these enterprises were the chief methods used.

Purchases of stocks of both group and non-group enterprises by the ten firms increased by $837 million between April and September, 1972, and by $788 million between October, 1972, and March, 1973, with Marubeni, C. Itoh, and other non-*zaibatsu* firms showing special zeal in efforts to narrow the gap between themselves and the two giant *zaibatsu* firms, Mitsubishi and Mitsui.[6] The balance of long- and short-term loans and investment in group enterprises by the top six firms stood at about $4.15 billion at the end of March, 1973.[7]

Joint ventures, with top *Sogo shosha* officials serving as executive and board directors, were organized. Examples are the Mitsubishi Development Corporations, the Mitsubishi Research Institute, and the Mitsubishi Atomic Energy Corporation. Sumitomo Shoji, under Chairman Tsuda, organized group joint ventures as the Sumitomo Australia Development Company, the Sumitomo Petroleum Development Company, and the Sumitomo Ocean Development Company (see Figure 1). Mitsui & Company strengthened its position within the *Nimokukai*, the top policy-making body consisting of chairmen or presidents of 22 leading group enterprises (see Figure 2). Marubeni solidified its leadership in the Fuyo group, C. Itoh in the relatively new Daiichi Kangyo Bank group, and Nissho Iwai in the Sanwa Bank group. All in all, by 1973, the top six *Sogo shoshas* just about replaced the commercial banks, whose investments in a corporation are limited by law to 10 percent, as leaders of Japan's mammoth industrial groups.

NEW EXPORT-IMPORT POSTURE

C. Itoh ran full-page advertisements in *The New York Times, The Chicago Tribune*, and other United States newspapers in 1972 and 1973, offering to sell

Figure 1

The Sumitomo Ocean Development Company

Officers		*Position in parent company*
Chairman:	H. Tsuda	Chairman, Sumitomo Shoji
President:	T. Nishimora	President, Sumitomo Heavy Machinery
Executive Director:	J. Yasui	Manager, Office of Technology Development, Sumitomo Heavy Machinery
Executive Director:	J. Tamura	Manager, Department of Ocean Development, Sumitomo Shoji
Director:	S. Shimazaki	Manager, Marketing Department Sumitomo Metal Industries
Director:	S. Uematsu	Executive Director, Nippon Electric Co.
Director:	K. Higuchi	Manager, Business Promotion Department, Sumitomo Bank
Director:	R. Nosaka	Executive Director, Sumitomo Trust & Banking
Director:	T. Tsuchikata	Director, Sumitomo Chemical
Director:	H. Mizusawa	Director, Sumitomo Metal Mining
Director:	H. Oguri	Executive Director, Sumitomo Marine & Fire Insurance
Director:	K. Noguchi	Director, Sumitomo Coal Mining
Auditor:	K. Ito	Executive Director, Sumitomo Electric Industries
Auditor:	E. Tsuda	President, Japan Ocean Industries President, Ocean Machinery

Investors

1) Sumitomo Heavy Machinery, Sumitomo Bank, Sumitomo Metal Industries, Nippon Electric, and Sumitomo Shoji have each a 5.83% participation.
2) Sumitomo Trust & Banking, Sumitomo Electric Industries, Sumitomo Chemical, Sumitomo Metal Mining, Sumitomo Marine & Fire Insurance, and Sumitomo Coal Mining have each a 3.5% participation.
3) Kashima Construction 2.92%; Sumitomo Life Insurance 2.33%; Nippon Glass and Sumitomo Cement 1.75%; Sumitomo Construction and Kochigumi, each 1.46%; Sumitomo Warehouse and Sumitomo Real Estate each 1.17%.
4) Sumitomo Light Metal Industries and 40 other companies have each a .87% share.

Source: Sumitomo News, 7/73.

Figure 2

Members of the Nimokukai (Mitsui Group)

Mitsui & Co.
The Mitsui Bank, Ltd.
The Mitsui Trust and Banking Co., Ltd.
Mitsui Mutual Life Insurance Co.
Taisho Marine and Fire Insurance Co., Ltd.
Mitsui Shipbuilding & Engineering Co., Ltd.
The Japan Steel Works, Ltd.
Sanki Engineering Co., Ltd.
Mitsui Construction Co., Ltd.
Mitsui Toatsu Chemicals, Inc.
Mitsui Petrochemical Industries, Ltd.
Toray Industries, Inc.
Mitsui Mining Co., Ltd.
Mitsui Mining & Smelting Co., Ltd.
Hokkaido Colliery & Steamship Co., Ltd.
The Mitsui Warehouse Co., Ltd.
Mitsui Real Estate Development Co., Ltd.
Mitsui O.S.K. Lines, Ltd.
Nippon Flour Mills Co., Ltd.
Tokyo Shibaura Electric Co.
Mitsukoshi Department Store
Oji Paper Co.

Source: Keizai Chosa Kyokai, **Keiretsu no Kenkyu,** 1973, Daiichibu Joba Kigyohen.

United States goods to Japan. In August, 1973, Marubeni signed a contract with the Western Growers Association to promote exports of U.S. agricultural products to Japan.

The general trading companies had long been involved in buying United States agricultural and other primary products as well as small quantities of manufactured goods. Between Spring, 1972, and Fall, 1973, however, they actively promoted the sale of U.S. manufactured products, including consumer goods, to Japan. In exports, they became more conscious of orderly marketing strategies and of diversifying the export market. They turned their attention to areas of expansion such as Western Europe and the Communist bloc, especially the People's Republic of China and the East European countries.[8]

INTERNATIONALIZATION

The so-called third-country trade (i.e., offshore trade not directly involving Japan) was promoted. For example, Nissho Iwai sold unprocessed Indonesian wood to Western Europe and Mitsui & Company sold U.S. machines to Malaysia and Rumania. Such trade helped to reduce Japan's huge trade surplus which had caused complaints and to create goodwill both for the companies and for Japan. The ten firms' third-country trade increased annually 26 to 50 percent between April, 1967, and March, 1973. This market accounted for 7.7 percent of total sales in 1973 as compared to 3 percent in 1967.[9] Strikingly, Mitsubishi's trade between April, 1972, and March, 1973, increased by 83.8 percent; Mitsui's trade by 107.8 percent; and Marubeni's by 90 percent.[10] Hiro Hiyama, President of Marubeni, predicted that the share of third-country trade in terms of total sales of the *Sogo shoshas* would reach 10 percent by 1976.[11]

Overseas offices in advanced countries, which had been independent foreign corporations in name only, were granted greater autonomy and became more oriented toward the host country by gradually adopting such strategies as promoting local non-Japanese employees to top management positions. Overseas investments were also expanded. The cumulative total of Japan's overseas private investment grew from slightly over $1 billion in 1966 to $7 billion in 1973, still far smaller than that of the United States which amounted to $128 billion in 1972.[12] It was estimated prior to the oil crisis, however, that Japan's overseas investments would double to $15 billion by 1975 and to $30 billion by 1980.

Equally significant was the changing pattern of investment. Prior to 1972, most overseas investments in developing countries had been in natural resources development for exports to Japan and in labor-intensive manufacturing industries; while investments in advanced countries had been chiefly in commerce, finance, and insurance. However, investments in manufacturing industries and in real estate in advanced countries were expanded in 1972 and in 1973. Moreover, there was a shift in emphasis from loans to equity investments. Investments abroad, whose chief role was to support imports and exports, became part of Japan's multifaceted international economic strategy. Mitsui & Company, as of July, 1973, had the largest outstanding balance of investments, totalling $300 million.[13]

The *Sogo shoshas* began a program of promoting close links with major world enterprises. The example of C. Itoh's President Echigo whose motto is "C. Itoh covers the world," is typical. He promoted General Motors' 34 percent equity participation in Japan's Isuzu Motors and the business connections between Oscar Mayer and Prima Ham, between Procter & Gamble and Nippon Sunhome, and between Ford Motors and Kansai Paint Company. In 1972, C. Itoh signed a joint venture with Ente Nazionali Idrocaburi, Italy's giant state-owned conglomerate, for joint development and sales of oil, liquified natural gas, uranium, and petrochemicals, and with Holiday Inn for building a motel chain throughout Japan.

The final step toward internationalization was expanded financial operations abroad, especially in the United States and Western Europe. The *Sogo shoshas* expanded the offering of convertible debentures and the securing of impact loans abroad. The international capital market became increasingly important, and the ten firms have proposed being listed on the New York Stock Exchange.

Sekai kigyoka (Becoming world enterprises) and *Takokuseki kigyoka* (Multinationalization) are current phrases used by trading companies in describing their responses to the international economic environment. As this article has shown, their actions have corresponded exactly to their mottos. It is hoped that these companies will use their unique resources to further benefit the world economy and trade.

NOTES

1. Peter Peterson, *The United States in the Changing World Economy*, Vol. II, *Background Material*, U.S. Government Printing Office, December 1971, p. 66.

2. All financial figures are in U.S. dollars. Figures for August 15, 1971, and earlier are based on the old $1-¥360 exchange rate; figures for later August 1971 to early February 1973 are based on the $1-¥308 rate; and those for the period since mid-February 1973 on the $1-¥265 rate. Because of the two yen revaluations and the continuing float of major world currencies, only the yen figures can be a more accurate basis for evaluation and comparison.

3. The Japanese Ministry of International Trade and Industry (MITI), *Tsusho Hakusho, Soron* (International Trade White Paper, Vol. I), 1972, p. 213.

4. "Sogo Shosha Kodo Kijun," *Nippon Boekikai Kaiho*, No. 218 (June 1973), p. 14. Translation by Alexander K. Young.

5. One of the *Sogo Shoshas* that withstood the trying test of 1973 was Sumitomo Shoji. Although established since World War II and aggressive in expanding its operations, it had long emphasized the 400-year Sumitomo tradition of placing priority on trust and sound business and of frowning on speculation. Its Code of Business, framed and long posted in offices throughout the world, states: "Sumitomo shall be alert to the changes of time and be concerned with business profits and losses, but, whether in times of growth and success or in hard times, it shall not engage in speculation and other questionable acts for quick and undue gains." Translation by A. K. Young.

6. Kazuo Umezu, "Nippon keizai no katsuryoku ubau zatshoku shudan," *Ekonomisuto,* March 20, 1973, pp. 6-10. Also Choei Shioda, "Toki kigyoka suru shosha no mirai," *Ekonomisuto*, March 20, 1973, pp. 11-15.

7. *Nihon Keizai Shimbun*, July 14, 1973.

8. For Japan's trade with the People's Republic of China following President Nixon's visit to Peking, see Alexander K. Young, "Japan's Trade with China: Impact of the Nixon Visit," *The World Today*, The Royal Institute of International Affairs, August, 1972.

9. Giichi Miyasaka, "Sogo shosha no kaigai torihiki ni tsuite" ("On the Overseas Trade of General Trading Companies"), *Kikai Yunyu Koyokai Geppo*, February, 1973, pp. 44-48.

10. Department of Research and Information, C. Itoh & Co.

11. *Marubeni Monthly*, May, 1973, p. 3.

12. For Japan's overseas investments in recent years, see: Jetro, *Kaigai Shijo Hakusho, 1972: Waga Kuni Kaigai Toshi no Genjo* (Overseas Market White Paper: the Current State of Japan's Overseas Investments).

13. *Toyo Keizai Tokei Geppo*, September, 1973, p. 9

12

Japan is Opening Up for *Gaijin* Who Know How

Louis Kraar

From the flood of gloomy reports in American papers recently, U.S. businessmen might easily conclude that Japan's economy is tumbling into a crisis that will cripple opportunities for their companies in that promising market. But the impact of Arab oil cutbacks has been much exaggerated. The resilient economy has never been threatened with collapse. In fact, Japan has been receiving adequate energy supplies. Over the past few years a surprisingly wide range of U.S. companies have broken into the long-closed Japanese market, and nearly all of them are pushing ahead with expansion plans made before the Mideast erupted last fall.

U.S. executives on the scene plainly see rich prospects in Japan, though there are economic problems. The greatest is raging inflation. But one problem that used to be the most formidable—stubborn Japanese resistance to letting foreigners conduct business in their country—is rapidly receding.

The lopsided trade relationship that frustrated Americans for many years is no longer so lopsided. Not long ago, the Japanese were grabbing rich segments of the U.S. market (such as cameras, television sets, and compact cars), but American corporations couldn't gain equal access to Japan's consumers. Now that the country has opened its doors, many U.S. companies are making the most of it. A quarter of Coca-Cola's worldwide earnings flow from its subsidiary in Tokyo. And Brunswick Corp. receives 24 percent of its total net profits from a joint venture that sells bowling equipment in Japan.

"The Japanese market must be viewed as the largest overseas opportunity for U.S. business," says James Abbegglen, president of the Boston Consulting Group, which advises corporate clients about how to sell in Japan. "Most of the old protectionist barriers are down, and the rest are fast diappearing."

TOWARD A WESTERN LIFE STYLE

Only in the last year and a half has the Japanese government, under relentless international pressure, eased the major restrictions against foreign enterprises. A voluntary 20 percent across-the-board tariff cut on manufactured items put Japan's import duties roughly on par with those in the U.S. and Europe. Import quotas on non-agricultural products were largely removed. And the government adopted a sweeping liberalization policy that allows foreign investment in nearly all industries. The few notable exceptions, such as computers and pharmaceuticals, will be opened before the end of 1976, according to a precise timetable.

Reprinted by permission, from the March, 1974, issue of *Fortune*.

Consumers in Japan, who have attained buying power comparable to those in Western Europe, are especially ready for U.S. goods. After long years of self-denial to speed economic growth, they want to improve the quality of their lives. The Japanese, in fact, are moving toward a life style somewhat closer to the Western pattern. They eat an increasingly varied diet, pursue leisure activities with frantic zest, and are spending huge sums to improve and replace their generally shabby, cramped housing.

A SPIDER WEB THAT RESISTS OUTSIDERS

But the key to Japan's locked market was the ability of some U.S. corporations to perceive that doing business there requires considerably different techniques than in any other country. Companies that have accepted the unique environment and adjusted to it are doing well. They point the way for others to follow if they have the wit and patience to learn. The main business obstacle, often underestimated in the past, is the clannishness of the Japanese. In this homogeneous, tight-knit society, foreigners are not only called *gaijin*—outsiders—but are instinctively treated as such. The Japanese business system resembles an intricate spider web of personal and financial relationships. It is inherently difficult, though not impossible, for an outsider to enter.

U.S. businessmen face a costly, multilayered distribution system, bound together by credit arrangements and friendships, which is very difficult to crack. Salesmen since feudal days have enjoyed little status; even now they mainly take orders from wholesalers. Aggressive, hard-selling techniques clash with the overwhelming Japanese concern for harmony. Though competition is fierce, there is a tacit understanding that no company will abruptly take away too much of a rival's share of the market.

Ingrained corporate practices pose formidable difficulties. Japanese corporations recruit the best students right out of school, nurture them with paternalism and fat annual pay increases (20 percent last year), and keep them for life. As a result, foreign companies find it is so difficult to attract talented Japanese employees that few of them can operate independently. Though wholly foreign-owned ventures are now permitted in most fields, most companies find it necessary to take a Japanese partner.

SEARS MAKES A QUICK START

A new Sears, Roebuck venture illustrates the possibilities open to companies that adopt a deft approach. Without making any capital investment, the world's largest retailer offers virtually its entire U.S. line to Japanese consumers. The Seibu Group of Retail Enterprises, a family-controlled company with over $2 billion annual sales, serves as a sales agent on a commission basis. Already seventeen Seibu outlets have opened Sears mail-order centers. The Japanese have responded enthusiastically to the Sears way of merchandising and to Sears's prices. Though sales started only eight months ago, customers have snapped up 200,000 catalogues, and monthly volume in merchandise is about $1 million.

Sears owes its quick start mainly to the selection of an able local associate, which shares its aims. Seibu eagerly accepts the Sears policy of money-back guarantees on catalogue sales—far from the usual retailing practice in Japan. Robert Ingersoll, a Chicagoan and former business executive who helped arrange the Sears venture while he was Ambassador to Japan, points out: "They're really taking a market survey, and it will lead to much more later—even though Sears top management doesn't fully realize it yet."

COKE'S GIFT TO THE COMPETITION

Few foreign businesses have had more success in Japan than Coca-Cola—or had more troubles because of it. From the start in late 1957, the company avoided the cumbersome local distribution system. Instead, Coke followed its normal practice of franchising bottlers. They are controlled by powerful Japanese corporations, such as Mitsubishi and Mitsui, which have sufficient influence to defy the system and sell directly to dealers for cash.

But as sales skyrocketed toward their present 40 percent of the country's soft-drink market, disgruntled Japanese competitors counterattacked. Small local soft-drink bottlers charged that a "foreign invasion" was driving them into bankruptcy. The press widely publicized claims that large Coke bottles mysteriously exploded. Although the company says it has had no such complaints in any other country, it brought out new bottles reinforced with a double coat of epoxy resin. Even the Coke slogan—"It's the real thing"—was forbidden by Japan's Fair Trade Commission on grounds that it implied other drinks were somehow not genuine.

Finally, Coca-Cola turned to what was widely regarded as the major source of its trouble. The company appointed a Japanese as president; he arranged payment of $550,000 to the protesting local bottlers as a conciliation gift, a traditional gesture. The moves have calmed criticism and protected the company's dominant market position.

A "SOFT TOUCH" THAT SELLS COPIERS

Xerox found an extraordinary way to bridge the gap between American business methods and Japanese culture. Its joint-venture partner, Fuji Photo Film, completely manages daily operations without a single Western senior executive or board member in residence. The solid local image has helped to attract bright, young employees who readily adopt—and adapt—Xerox sales techniques. The company has held the lion's share of an expanding market for copying machines, despite intense competition recently. In the past seven years, sales have grown an average of about 40 percent annually to $200 million last year, and net profits have generally approached 10 percent of sales.

Fuji Xerox thrives by blending aggressive Western marketing with subtle Oriental touches. Signing up rental customers poses special problems in a land that has habitually looked down upon salesmen. So senior management looked down upon salesmen. And senior management not only advises new recruits that selling is the path to rapid promotion, but also rewards the best performers with prestige titles. "It means something socially, so we call them managers—even if there aren't many people reporting to them," says Yotaro Kobayashi, managing director and general manager for marketing.

At Xerox's urging, the company bucked custom by providing personal monetary incentives to salesmen. The difficulty is that Japanese regard group effort as more important than individual accomplishment. Moreover, most employees feel insecure working on a commission basis. "Our feeling at the beginning was that this was really against the Japanese grain," says Kobayashi, "but we really wanted better results." So Fuji Xerox set sales goals as team objectives. Salesmen collect regular salaries and benefits, but teams that exceed targets receive extra payments in the bonuses given all personnel twice annually. The system works.

One innovative Japanese approach to customers succeeded so well that Xerox is trying it in other countries. Fuji Xerox created a completely new job category, the customer-service officer (C.S.O.), and filled it mainly with attractive women college graduates. They regularly visit offices that already have the rented machines and offer advice about their use. The "soft touch from an intelligent woman," as Kobayashi puts it, helps to retain contacts and persuade customers to convert to more profitable newer models. The C.S.O.'s proved especially resourceful in countering a wave of cancellations two years ago, when rival machines were offered at lower prices. Nowadays, many of its customers call Fuji Xerox with requests to arrange marriages with C.S.O. women, for matchmaking is an enduring Japanese custom.

The U.S. company initially considered the C.S.O. system unnecessary. But as an American executive of Xerox explains: "We're smart enough to realize that there are lots of things about doing business in Japan that we really don't comprehend."

LEARNING TO LIVE WITH GROUP DECISION MAKING

The joint venture started in 1962 as a compromise, for Fuji wanted a straight licensing agreement and Xerox sought majority ownership. Each settled for 50 percent of the joint company. Fuji insisted on managing the venture, but its executives rely heavily on Xerox for advice and technology. Almost all the machines rented in Japan are manufactured locally. Major decisions, including introduction of new products and annual budgets, must be approved by a board on which both partners are equally represented; neither can act alone.

A major advantage of the setup is that Japanese employees and customers regard the corporation as one of their own. Fuji preserves such venerable practices as group decision making; a proposed policy or action plan is circulated among all connected with the problem and discussed until a consensus is reached. By Western standards, it is a lengthy process and often appears to dilute the authority of top executives. But Kobayashi maintains, "Any plan has to be backed up by those who carry it out. People tend to stay with a company here, so you don't want to make enemies of those you'll be working with for many years."

Fierce competition is putting the Xerox arrangement to a severe test. Ten rivals are wooing its customers with lower-priced copying machines. This is a common tactic in Japan, where companies invest heavily to increase market share even at the sacrifice of immediate profits. Even though it is the industry leader, Fuji Xerox is vulnerable because rising operating costs and profit-consciousness rule out price cuts. So the company is responding in other ways that draw on resources of both joint-venture partners. For the first time, Japanese engineers are participating in the design of new products in the U.S. so that Fuji Xerox can introduce them simultaneously. Previously, there was a year or more of delay because American machines had to be adapted for the larger standard paper sizes used in Japan.

A LOSS OF FACE

By contrast, Caterpillar Tractor oversees its joint venture with a large team of Americans. The resulting clash of cultures has caused plenty of management problems. For the past ten years, Caterpillar has politely but firmly "advised" Japanese managers to do things its way—and often succeeded. Says a Caterpillar senior executive, "It's working with independent U.S. dealers, who must be persuaded to do things but never forced." Half the company is owned by Mitsubishi Heavy Industries, which belongs to Japan's largest zaibatsu; it is known for strong-minded executives, too. Says one insider: "Mitsubishi people are very proud. When Caterpillar told them what to do, they felt a loss of face."

Initially, U.S. executives sharply questioned the relatively high salaries and fringe benefits of employees that Mitsubishi assigned to the joint venture from its other companies. But caterpillar had to accept them. As start-up costs mounted, it was Mitsubishi's turn to worry. Japanese companies plan ahead, but they don't make the highly detailed financial projections common in the U.S. Having carefully calculated the costs of building a huge plant outside Tokyo and establishing dealerships, Caterpillar expected a large cumulative deficit. Much to the consternation of Mitsubishi Group officials, the losses eventually reached some $38 million. It was early 1972 —right on the Caterpillar timetable—before profits erased the red ink.

IT'S HARD TO SAY "NO"

Caterpillar guides the company by means of a tandem management set-up that has become the talk of Tokyo. Twenty-two Americans sit close by Japanese executives who have precisely the same responsibilities; the Caterpillar men advise their counterparts, who give orders down the line. At every level, each official is supposedly coequal. But Caterpillar managers reinforce their influence by reporting to the chairman of the joint venture, an American. He takes the case to the president, a Japanese. "Above all, we avoid confrontations and adjust details to get results," insists E. J. Schlegel, who was chairman of Caterpillar Mitsubishi from 1970 through 1973 and is now a Caterpillar vice president in Peoria. "There are times that we say, 'Okay, we'll do it your way.' "

Getting the joint venture to adopt Caterpillar's manufacturing and sales methods demands long rounds of meetings that are often beset by snarled communication. Neither partner is completely fluent in the other's language. "Sometimes we come out with completely different impressions of what's been decided," says Schlegel. One reason is that in Japan both the ambiguities of the language and customary politeness make it difficult to express a blunt "no."

The most difficult task was persuading Mitsubishi to adopt the Caterpillar marketing system, which relies on sizeable dealerships to provide customers with parts and servicing. Normally in Japan, there's a much greater division of labor: manufacturers sell to trading companies, which in turn finance dealers, who have little capital of their own. Maintenance and repairs are left to small independent shops. The Caterpillar-type dealerships have enabled the joint venture to snare about 30 percent of the country's annual sales of earthmoving equipment.

Though the business relationship seems to be working, it has to be conceded that personal relations at Caterpillar Mitsubishi are somewhat tense. In the managers' dining room, one sees Caterpillar people choose tables on one side, while all the Mitsubishi men sit on the opposite side of the room. Few of the Americans have close personal relations with their Japanese associates, and turnover among the Mitsubishi executives has been high, because they prefer to go back to other divisions of the zaibatsu where they feel the atmosphere is more congenial. Profits hold the joint venture together.

HOW HEINZ GOT OUT OF THE SOUP

One of the most inviting opportunities for U.S. companies is the processed-food industry, which is increasingly receptive to Western products. But, again, the convoluted distribution system poses an implacable barrier to most outsiders who tackle it alone. Selling any brand involves pushing it through a maze of intermediaries into thousands of tiny retail outlets. When H. J. Heinz tried to buck the system, the result was a fiasco. To enter Japan, Heinz hastily took a minority interest in a joint venture with Nichiro Fisheries, which lacked both capital and broad distribution channels. Heinz ketchup, canned goods, and baby foods reached the Japanese market in 1963—and flopped. One problem: Nichiro's name on the label gave many housewives the false impression that the contents were fish-flavored.

As losses mounted, the partners argued bitterly over what to do about them; Heinz finally bought 80 percent of the joint venture in 1967 and began using American-style marketing. It bypassed primary wholesalers and sold directly to smaller ones; then it began dealing directly with large retailers. The whole Japanese food network banded together in a boycott of Heinz products.

To repair the damage, Heinz turned in December, 1970, to a gentle Japanese executive, Kazuo Asai. He had marketing experience in both countries (having worked for a Japanese trading firm), a degree from the Wharton School of Finance, and a willingness to leave his last employer, Dow Corning. Asai also has what counts most in Japan—an acute sensitivity for human relationships and good personal connections through his wealthy family. In a year as president of Nichiro Heinz, he turned the chaos into profit.

"My predecessors didn't understand the delicate situation here," says Asai. He put Heinz back into normal distribution channels through the sort of personal effort that most impresses his countrymen: He visited every major wholesaler and profusely apologized for bypassing them. "At first most of them wouldn't even listen and several said, 'Go to hell.' I kept going back until they were convinced we were sincere," he recalls. Asai purposely offered no additional monetary incentives to distributors. "No matter how much money you offer or how many big geisha parties you give, it makes no difference if people don't trust you. That was our problem." Within the company, Asai conducted a similar campaign of persuasion to restore morale, which had been shattered by high turnover of personnel.

Once harmony was restored between Heinz and Japan, the company's products gained increasing acceptance. Its market share of canned soups, for instance, has doubled, to 60 percent. In addition to regular retail outlets, Asai has developed substantial business with hotels and restaurants by carefully cultivating a relatively small group of specialized wholesalers. Heinz has also broadened its appeal by making products in Japan (among them curry-flavored ketchup) that cater to long-standing local tastes.

Since the Japanese president took over, sales have risen by an average of 30 percent annually, to nearly $4 million last year. Asai expects they will climb 50 percent this year and next because of a shift to an even more traditional distribution channel, Mitsubishi Corp., Japan's largest trading firm, now handles all Heinz products. The trader's extensive contacts and credit facilities will greatly increase outlets for Heinz.

DOING "THINGS WE NEVER DREAMED OF"

Unlike Heinz, Brunswick Corp. bet on the right strategy immediately when it came into Japan in 1961. It formed a joint venture to sell bowling equipment—and then shrewdly used its presence to develop ever widening business in other lines, ranging from boat motors to medical supplies. Each activity has enhanced Brunswick's ability to move into another.

Taking a long-range view of the potential returns, Brunswick asked for no royalties when it teamed up with Mitsui & Co., a major trading house. Instead, the company waited for profits from the fifty-fifty joint venture, called Nippon Brunswick. It overcame a sluggish start when the new Japanese bent for leisure brought on a bowling boom. The company has provided a third of the country's 130,000 lanes—and profited immensely. Among corporations with substantial foreign capital, its pretax earnings of $58.6 million were second only to I.B.M.'s, according to Japanese tax returns published last year.

From the start, Brunswick itself has also been expanding its activities through an independent Tokyo branch. One big reason the company has been able to do so successfully is that, unlike most American corporations, Brunswick keeps U.S. executives in Japan for long periods and expects them to learn the language. Garrett M. Flint, managing director of the Tokyo branch for nine years, speaks Japanese fluently. "Just because you're here leads to all sorts of other things—things we never dreamed of at first," says Flint. The Japanese mania for golf opened the way for MacGregor clubs and bags, which bring Brunswick $10 million in annual sales. In status-conscious Japan, golf is now the prestige game and name-brand clubs bestow extra cachet. By being on the scene, Brunswick spotted the trend early and built up volume gradually. The clubs are exported from America; the bags are manufactured in Japan by a licensee. Initially, the U.S. company sold through normal wholesale channels. But Flint saw that he could cut prices and raise margins by selling directly to retailers. That's a risky step in Japan, but the company made the switch in 1970 without stumbling.

"You can do things differently here if you know what you're doing and proceed the right way," says Flint. He bypassed distributors by working through Brunswick's Japanese staff. The staff concluded that the shift was feasible, recruited a larger sales force, and—most delicately—broke the news to wholesalers. Brunswick now provides credit to 300 mostly small retailers who were previously financed by wholesalers.

Brunswick uses its association with large corporations to good advantage too. In 1968 its own sales force started promoting products for Sherwood Medical Industries, a U.S. subsidiary that makes disposable hypodermic needles and syringes. But Flint found that it needed better contacts with Japanese hospitals. So Brunswick turned to Mitsui, which is in touch with every major industry through its own teams of specialists. Last year Brunswick and Mitsui formed a new company, Nippon Sherwood, to manufacture and sell the medical items.

"There's certainly a synergistic effect," observes Flint. "The more contacts you have the more power you have to get things done. I don't mean dictating, but skill in finding your way through the labyrinth of negotiations and achieving results."

THE SALESLADY HAS TO BE FORMALLY INTRODUCED

Business contacts normally begin with formal introductions through mutual friends and rarely occur in Japanese homes. In the face of these strong traditions, Avon has launched door-to-door sales of cosmetics. But the system it uses in seventeen other countries had to be modified to suit the sensitivities of Japan—as did many of its products.

Under its well-tested system, the company has found 20,000 housewives willing to become sales representatives on a commission basis. As elsewhere, each is called an "Avon lady." But the similarity ends there. In Western countries, Avon sales representatives routinely call on people they don't know and often obtain an order on the first visit. Japanese, on the other hand, regard their homes as sacrosanct, and any sales relationship is fraught with fear that one of the parties—buyer or seller—may lose face. Not surprisingly, as George E. Gustin, Avon general manager in Japan reports, "the Avon lady here is not as aggressive and outgoing as her counterpart in the West."

After much handwringing and experimentation, Avon started adapting its approach to meet these special challenges. Through friends and relatives, area managers around the country arrange formal introductions of Avon ladies to prospective customers. To help overcome the innate shyness of its sales force, the company appeals to Japanese group-consciousness; as it does nowhere else, Avon holds large "beauty class" meetings, where it dispenses product data and pep talks.

Even though Avon offers up to a 33 percent commission on sales in Japan, the company has discovered it can't be too blunt about monetary rewards alone; working only for money seems crass to most Japanese. Thus Avon inspires its Oriental ladies by discussing things of value they can buy with earnings, such as a TV set or refrigerator, and stressing what Gustin calls "pleasant objectives," such as helping make customers look better.

Average sales of a Japanese Avon lady still lag behind those in most other countries where the company operates. But each Japanese customer buys more. So far, Avon has garnered about 2 percent of Japan's cosmetics market, which has reached a wholesale volume of $1.2 billion a year (the world's second largest after the U.S.). If the company continues to overcome the social barriers, it expects to earn profits in Japan starting next year. It is showing its confidence by investing $5 million to build a plant near Tokyo to meet anticipated demand for the next decade.

Both the successes and the failures of American companies in Japan demonstrate that the only way to operate there is to accept the country's ways and adapt to them. Once the Japanese are met on their own terms, there is a lot of latitude for introducing fresh techniques in sales and management.

Above all, things get done through personal contacts, not just formal business transactions. Cultivating the essential friendships requires more time than the usual two- or three-year executive assignment. Most corporations would be better served by keeping men in Japan for five or even ten years. Top executives need not speak Japanese fluently, but some knowledge of the language not only smooths social relations but also affords valuable insights into the Japanese way of thinking.

Patience, grace, and the ability to communicate are especially important in Japan. Even a seemingly relaxed evening of entertainment, for instance, may be a crucial test to a Japanese of an American's compatibility. Smart U.S. executives never talk business at such gatherings.

When they do get down to business, always in the office, Japanese executives are just as interested in harmonious relations as in profits. Brisk Americans eager to sign contracts are likely to run into delays; the Japanese move deliberately and prefer to rely on overall understanding rather than legal contracts. There are few business secrets in Japan. As many U.S. companies have learned, anyone who discusses investment plans with a government ministry can expect the whole local industry to know about it, too. Thus it is usually best to meet Japanese competitors and tell them directly, for their acceptance is also vital. Avon, among others, did this before entering Japan.

NEW HELP FOR U.S. EXPORTERS

The Japanese themselves have belatedly recognized that their cohesive business system and insular customs remain formidable barriers. To prove that the old protectionism has ended, several of the nation's leading exporters have assumed a new role—helping U.S. companies sell in Japan. Sony is distributing through its own facilities about fifty products, including Shick Electric razors, Heathkit amplifiers, and Whirlpool refrigerators.

Still, the best starting point for many U.S. export items is a Japanese trading company. Some of the giant traders are already so busy handling rival products that they may give newcomers insufficient attention, but hundreds of smaller, specialized firms are eager to exploit Japanese enthusiasm for international name brands and unusual products. Some fifty companies expressed interest in teaming up with Sears for catalogue sales. "There are still a lot more opportunities here than American companies are aware of," says former U.S. Ambassador Ingersoll, "but first they must know more about Japan."

13

Development of an Advertising Industry in Asia

Arnold K. Weinstein

A simplified form of an advertising decision model could read as follows: *match the media and message to the market.* Completion of this matching process requires the collection and assessment of an almost infinite assortment of data. When reviewing his opportunity to advertise in Asia, the intelligent advertiser is going to study the environmental constraints of political, economic, technological, and cultural structures.

Some of the problems faced by the advertising agency business in eight Asian countries will be examined in this article. An effort will be made to show that there are specific patterns to the problems faced by these agencies. It is postulated that the problems faced by an agency in a particular country are tied very closely to that country's stage of economic development and to its more basic cultural characteristics.

Gordon E. Miracle suggests that eight factors strongly influence the appropriateness of an advertisement in a particular country: the type of product, the homogeneity or heterogeneity of markets, the characteristics and the availability of media, the types of advertising agency service available in each market segment, government restrictions on the nature of advertising, government tariffs on art work or printed matter, trade codes, ethical practices, and industry agreements and corporate organization of the advertisier.[1] Without taking exception to any of these factors, it can be demonstrated that most of the above factors vary in importance according to a country's stage of economic development and according to some very basic cultural characteristics.

For Asia in particular it is important to make the distinction between the type of problems postulated by Miracle and the association of these problems to the stage of economic development. Many Asian nations stand on the brink of either economic chaos or in the doorway of economic resurgence. To meet this economic challenge, the countries of Asia must simultaneously create political stability, productive capacity, consumer purchasing power, and an organized system of distribution and marketing. If we are to understand the role of an advertising industry in this evolution from agrarian, non-industrial country to industrialized nation, then an economic and cultural framework might be a most suitable frame of reference for the study of Asian advertising.

Arnold K. Weinstein, "Development of an Advertising Industry in Asia," pp. 28-36, *MSU Business Topics*, Spring 1970. Reprinted by permission of the publisher, Division of Research, Graduate School of Business Administration, Michigan State University.

All advertising agencies for which addresses were available in Ceylon, Hong Kong, India, Japan, Malaysia, the Philippines, Singapore, and Thailand were mailed questionnaires. Fifty-six returns were received from a sample frame of 290 for a response rate of 19 percent. It is apparent that small agencies did not return their questionnaires, yet they made up a significant portion of the sample; two examples will clearly demonstrate this point. Ninety-three questionnaires were mailed to India and eighty-two to Japan; these represented 60 percent of the total. Fifteen returns were received from India and fourteen from Japan for response rates of 16 and 17 percent respectively. Billings reported by the Indian agencies amounted to approximately 30 percent of estimated Indian billings in 1966-67.[2] Billings reported by the Japanese agencies accounted for nearly 35 percent of the 1966 billings reported by Dentsu.[3] The questionnaire covered each of the following subjects: employees retained on a permanent basis, international firms as clients, service arrangements, ownership arrangements, problems faced by the industry, services provided to clients, biographical data on key employees, billings, and number of years in business.

The author interviewed the heads of twenty leading Asian advertising agencies and these interviews supported the information previously collected in the mail survey.

SUMMARY OF PROBLEMS

Specific data for this article were generated by the question, "What do you see as the major problems facing advertisers and the advertising industry in your country?" Arranging the eight countries by level of economic development and then listing the problems stated in the replies from each country reveals a pattern that strongly suggests the overriding importance of economic development. A classification scheme developed by the Marketing Science Institute was found to be particularly relevant in ranking the eight countries involved in this study.[4] The "Regional Typology" system, which studies five groups of factors (the economy, health and hygiene, educational level, communications, and transportation) produces the following ranking going from the highest in development: Japan, Hong Kong, Singapore, Malaysia, the Philippines, Ceylon, Thailand, India.[5]

Each of the problems mentioned by a significant portion of the respondents from a particular country is indicated in Table 1. Group one includes the problems most evident in the truly underdeveloped countries. A second set of problems appears to be present until minimal industrial facilities are made available. A third group of problems, which show up in Malaysia, Singapore, and Hong Kong, emerges only after a considerable industrial base has been laid and the desire for true economic independence exists. Problems in group four seem to require complete industrial development of the type achieved by Japan before they disappear (see Table 1). Problems reported by Japanese agencies were unique to that country and could only emerge in Japan's atypical form of a highly developed economy. A final set of problems

TABLE 1

Summary of All Problems Reported

	India	*Thailand*	*Ceylon*	*Philippines*	*Malaysia*	*Singapore*	*Hong Kong*	*Japan*
Group One:								
1. Import restrictions and a shortage of foreign exchange	X		X					
2. High levels of taxation	X		X					
3. High taxes on imported advertising material			X					
4. High tax on advertising expenditure			X			X		
5. Government policy adverse to advertising	X		X					
6. No commercial television	X		X					
7. Few technical journals	X							
8. High printing costs	X		X					
9. Sellers' market conditions	X		X					
10. Local businessmen do not regard advertising as necessary	X		X		X	X		
11. Advertising not accepted as profession by the business community			X					
Group Two:								
12. High cost and poor quality of paper	X		X	X				
13. Poor facilities for color photographers	X	X	X	X	X			
14. Poor facilities for printing	X	X	X	X	X			
15. Poor facilities for 35 mm. moving picture production		X	X	X	X			
Group Three:								
16. Many firms tied to overseas principles					X			
17. High numbers of expatriate staff					X	X		
18. Poor production facilities for TV					X	X	X	
19. Lack of audited circulation figures							X	
20. Lack of a TV rating system							X	
Group Four:								
21. Lack of a strong advertising association	X	X		X	X	X	X	
22. Lack of trained advertising personnel	X	X	X	X	X	X	X	
23. Shortage of creative talent	X	X	X		X	X	X	
24. Lack of training institutions	X	X			X		X	
25. Lack of reliable marketing research	X		X	X	X	X	X	

TABLE 1 (continued)

	India	*Thailand*	*Ceylon*	*Philippines*	*Malaysia*	*Singapore*	*Hong Kong*	*Japan*
Group Five:								
26. Selling firms use their own staff to create advertising								X
27. Domination of print media by strong publishers								X
28. Selling firms use a multiplicity of agencies for different media								X
29. Domination of agency structure by one giant agency								X
30. Need to finance clients		X						X
31. Account executive system not developed								X
Group Six:								
32. Agencies just space brokers	X	X	X	X		X		X
33. Agency commission rebating and discounting		X	X	X	X	X	X	X
34. Rural nature of the economy	X	X	X	X				
35. Multilingual society	X	X	X	X	X	X	X	
36. Multiracial, multireligious society	X		X		X	X		
37. Copy restrictions imposed by government					X	X		
38. Low literacy	X				X			

which do not seem to fit any specific set of economic data might be called cultural and value system oriented. They also reflect some problems common to the advertising business throughout the world. The reader will note an anomaly in Table 1: Thailand, although less developed than Ceylon, does not seem to share problems with India and Ceylon. No explanation can be found to fully explain this phenomenon.

GROUP ONE PROBLEMS

Problems within group one are concentrated in Ceylon and India. These two countries are faced with the problems of taking their first real steps toward economic takeoff. The problems are:

1) *Import restrictions and a shortage of foreign exchange*
2) *High levels of taxation*
3) *High taxes on imported advertising material*
4) *High tax on advertising expenditure*
5) *Government policy adverse to advertising*
6) *No commercial television*
7) *Few technical journals*
8) *High printing costs*
9) *Sellers' market conditions*
10) *Local businessmen do not regard advertising as necessary*
11) *Advertising not accepted as a profession by the business community*

Import restrictions and a shortage of foreign exchange caused by chronic balances of payment deficits have created serious problems for most industries in Ceylon and India. Not only have imports of consumer goods been severely curtailed, but imports of capital equipment that would stimulate economic growth have been restricted. Advertising executives feel that these restrictions are slowing their country's growth of both market potential and buying power and therefore limiting the opportunities to sell advertising. A very real effect of import restrictions on the advertising of imported consumer non-durables has been to make advertising largely unnecessary. The unsatisfied demand for some imported goods makes it possible to sell smuggled goods at twice or three times their normal price.

The burdens of high levels of taxation on imported advertising material, high levels of taxation in general, and specific taxes on advertising expenditures are borne reluctantly by the advertising agencies in those countries where they exist. The resultant higher price of advertising is a less efficient investment for potential clients as, in some cases, the cost factor must be passed on rather than be absorbed. In this instance, the tax on advertising expenditure seems to be repressive.

It is difficult, on the other hand, to sympathize with complaints about taxes on imported advertising materials. A high tax on imported materials is meant to encourage the development of local industry. It is also a means of saving precious foreign exchange. In the author's opinion, the policy may be justified as being beneficial to the economy in the long run. Also, if one is allowed to import large amounts of advertising material from overseas, there is a temptation to use the material without adaptation to local conditions. Import restrictions could be a strong force in motivating the creation of advertising directly suited to local conditions.

It was interesting to note that in India and Ceylon, where the overall level of purchasing power was lowest, members of the advertising industry itself felt rather optimistic about its future. At a January, 1968, meeting of the Association of Accredited Advertising Agencies of Ceylon, the members seemed to think that there was great promise in their industry and that the country's economic problems would eventually be solved. The desire in India for many consumer goods is immense. Several Indian advertising executives mentioned that only small improvements in the average income level would bring large numbers of new customers into the marketplace.

The shortage of foreign exchange, which is causing slow industrial expansion, is also a root problem; there are few technical journals and no commercial television. It also creates high printing costs by forcing the utilization of old and obsolete printing equipment in Ceylon and India. Advertising agencies in Ceylon and India felt that exchange problems were being used as an excuse by governments that were not convinced of the value of advertising. Bureaucratic interference and go-slow policies in granting vital import licenses are felt to be a symptom of an unsympathetic government. Many Asian businessmen, especially those enjoying a sellers' market, do not feel advertising is necessary. Large portions of Asian commerce are conducted by very small firms. The people who own and operate the businesses are unlikely to spend large sums of money on advertising. It is undoubtedly true, nevertheless, that the relatively larger firms are becoming more convinced of advertising's value.

In Ceylon, advertising executives feel that the general business community does not regard advertising as an honorable profession. However, a majority of the advertising executives interviewed in India and Ceylon felt that this situation was changing and that in the near future the average businessman would regard advertising as an integral part of his marketing mix.

This feeling of confidence in the future of advertising is consistent with our hypothesis of problems changing along with economic development. In the most developed countries advertising is accepted and sellers' markets are disappearing. In Singapore and Malaysia it was always the *small* businessman who regarded advertising as unnecessary.

GROUP TWO PROBLEMS

Problems in group two seem to be very closely related to the previous group. These problems are:

12) *High cost and poor quality of paper*
13) *Poor facilities for color photographers*
14) *Poor facilities for printing*
15) *Poor facilities for 35 mm. moving picture production*

The poor quality and shortage of paper in Ceylon, India, and the Philippines cause high printing costs and poor reproduction. In India and Ceylon these problems result from the critical shortage of foreign exchange. The reported inadequacy of printing facilities in the Philippines and Malaysia came up in conversation with executives from these two countries. These executives had reached a level of sophistication where they were anxious to produce work of high quality in terms of world standards.

Poor production facilities in the area of printing and processing color photography stem from several sources. Equipment shortages cause most of the trouble. Knowledge, technique, and equipment requisite to production of 35 mm. films is absent in Malaysia, the Philippines, Ceylon, and Thailand. Color 35 mm. movie photography is a skill that seems to be lacking in much of Asia. Adequate processing facilities for 35 mm. film are not available in Ceylon, Malaysia, and the Philippines. India, although the most underdeveloped of the countries studied, has managed to develop a large size and active moving picture industry. The advertising industry has been able to draw upon this industrial base for the filming of advertisements.

The basic difference between the problems in group one and the problems in group two is a degree of expectation and sophistication. It seems that when a small industrial base has been established, the advertising agencies become anxious to quickly improve their capability to produce quality work.

GROUP THREE PROBLEMS

Concern about expatriate labor and the dependence on overseas firms for decision making reflects a gain in confidence by a country as it feels capable of managing its own future. Group three's problems are therefore an important part of demonstrating the basic premise of this article. These problems exist and are recognized in Malaysia, Singapore, and Hong Kong, but they were not reported in the lesser developed countries. The problems in group three are:

16) *Many firms tied to overseas principles*
17) *High numbers of expatriate staff*
18) *Poor production facilities for TV*
19) *Lack of audited circulation figures*
20) *Lack of TV rating system*

When overseas agencies opened local offices in Asia they were forced to bring in much expatriate executive labor. These people normally came on relatively short-term contracts which did not leave them time to train local replacements. This situation is slowly being overcome as a result of agency awareness to the problem and government action. Several of the Asian governments, Singapore in particular, are strongly encouraging staffing from local residents. Malaysia and Singapore seem to be aware and concerned about this problem. In the less developed countries there are still many expatriate advertising employees, but these people are regarded as a very necessary asset for industrial development.

The fact that many clients are tied to overseas companies and are not allowed to make independent advertising decisions is creating frustration. Although this problem is listed for Malaysia, it was brought up in conversation with agencies in Singapore, Hong Kong, and the Philippines.

Several Hong Kong agencies complained about the lack of a television rating system and audited circulation figures. This type of concern shows an increasing sophistication in the programming of advertising. The complaint about poor television production facilities is another manifestation of the feeling that arises when new capabilities are introduced into a country.

Agencies in Malaysia, Singapore, and Hong Kong are very anxious to improve television production facilities so as to use that medium effectively for advertising.

There is a significant factor to remember when reviewing the problems in group three. Although the problems were only reported in Hong Kong, Singapore, and Malaysia, they exist in some of the lesser developed countries. Perception rather than existence is the important factor in this group of problems.

GROUP FOUR PROBLEMS

With some minor exceptions, the problems in this group are spread across all of the countries studied except for Japan. It is the fact that the problems do not exist in Japan that demonstrates how economic development tempers the problems faced by an advertising industry. Each of the problems demonstrates that a fully developed economy has not yet emerged in these countries. They are the kinds of problems one would expect in a country that has not reached industrial and economic maturity. The list includes:

21) *Lack of a strong advertising association*
22) *Lack of trained advertising personnel*
23) *Lack of creative talent*
24) *Lack of training institutes*
25) *Lack of reliable marketing research*

A shortage of qualified personnel is the most pressing internal problem facing the advertising agencies studied. Complaints ranged from blanket statements that "there are not qualified local people available" to "there is a shortage of qualified creative talent."

The general shortage of trained personnel is a result of several factors. Lack of adequate training institutes means that agencies must do extensive on-the-job training. Most of the smaller agencies do not have the time or money available to carry on adequate "in company" training programs. The large agencies which carry on training programs find that they are simply training and providing personnel for their competitors. What might be called the immaturity or the youth of the advertising agency business in some of the countries studied is another reason why there is a shortage of qualified personnel. In Ceylon the problem is so acute that a newcomer to the industry can become an account executive handling important accounts in less than a year.

The most critical shortage seems to be in the area of creative personnel. Most agencies studied (both Asian and International) said that the indigenous population did not have sufficient creative talent. Agency executives were unable to give a better explanation for the phenomenon other than to say it was a cultural characteristic. Without a strong and active advertising association, it is unlikely that these problems will be solved. Many of the executives interviewed stated that they could see a need for such an association organizing training programs. They then added the qualification that they did not think the industry in their country was quite ready for that type of activity.

Marketing research is not yet regarded as an important part of the marketing mix in most of the countries studied. For this reason it is often difficult to contract high quality research.

GROUP FIVE PROBLEMS

Japan's industrial structure is unique among the countries studied; it also holds true that the advertising industry in the country has its own unique set of problems. Most of the problems are related to the high degree of concentration in all aspects of Japanese industry. The reader will note that with one minor exception, the group five problems are Japanese problems exclusively. These problems are:

26) *Selling firms use their own staff to create advertising*
27) *Domination of print media by strong publishers*
28) *Selling firms use a multiplicity of agencies for different media*
29) *Domination of agency structure by one giant agency*
30) *Need to finance clients*
31) *Account executive system not developed*

Large advertisers tend to produce all of their own advertising, using an agency as a space broker only. For this reason, some of the large agencies do not have fully developed creative staffs. Because of the strength of many publishers in Japan, an advertiser may have to use several agencies to get complete coverage. Publishers will not recognize nor accept advertising placed by an agency that does not place a minimum amount of advertising in their publication. Dentsu, the giant of Japanese advertising, controls a formidable percentage of media space available to advertisers. All other agencies seem to respect this power and "out and out" fights with Dentsu seem to be rare.

It is a characteristic of most Japanese businesses to pay debts with a promissory note. Advertisers pay their agency by note, but because of the very strong position of the publishers they are able to demand cash payments. This practice is a severe financial strain on the smaller agencies.

One of the few indications of a problem in Japan that might disappear with further growth was a reported deficiency in the development of an account executive system. This problem appeared to be closely related to the situation of manufacturers producing their own advertising, and therefore not requiring the complete services of an account executive.

It is important to re-emphasize that Japanese agencies did not report the same types of problems brought out in the earlier parts of this article.

GROUP SIX PROBLEMS

These are the seven problems listed in Table 1 as group six:

32) *Agencies just space brokers*
33) *Agency commission rebating and discounting*

34) *Rural nature of the economy*
35) *Multilingual society*
36) *Multiracial, multireligious society*
37) *Copy restrictions imposed by government*
38) *Low literacy*

It would appear that two problems mentioned in this group can be considered normal advertising practice. Agency commission rebating and discounting is common in many parts of the world. One would hope that the industry-weakening secret nature of this activity would disappear. This is not to say that competition among media is not wanted. What is desired is that the competition would be overt and hence of a more beneficial nature. Price should not be regarded as the only competitive factor in the marketing advertising services.

The other problem in this group, and perhaps the most frequently voiced complaint relative to the structure of the industry, was that "many agencies are just space brokers." It was felt that this condition lowered the overall standard of advertising and also created very stiff price competition. Space brokers seemed to be the most disliked because they claimed to be advertising agencies. Perhaps if they would call themselves "space brokers" or "media brokers," part of the animosity would disappear. The phenomenon of space brokers is not unique to Asia. In the United States we are witnessing the evolution of very sophisticated media brokers. There are also large numbers of small agencies that offer no real service other than the purchase of time and space.

The multiracial, multireligious nature of Ceylon, Malaysia, Singapore, and India compound the difficulty of advertising in these four countries. All of these socioeconomic characteristics are deeply interrelated and have interesting cross influences. The effects of multiracial, multilingual, multireligious interrelations are easy to predict. But, low literacy, combined with a rural economy in a multiracial, multilingual, multireligious environment, can cause the advertiser no end of frustration.

In Ceylon a problem arises in the existence of a large number of Indians who have not been completely assimilated. There is always a potential conflict, for instance, between the Tamil-speaking Indian Hindu and the Sinhalese-speaking Ceylonese Buddhist. This problem is made more complex by having significant Muslim and Christian segments in the population. One example of how religion has forced its way into Ceylonese business practice has been the adoption of a lunar week to satisfy strong Buddhist elements. The more widely recognized week of Sunday through Saturday has been replaced by a week beginning on Poya Day and continuing for one-quarter of the moon's cycle. This causes a week that varies in length from seven to eight days. Work days vary in length and there is little relationship between the occurrence of Poya Day (a legal holiday) and the Sunday holiday observed in other parts of the world.

Malaysia and Singapore are troubled by an undercurrent of conflict between their Chinese Buddhist communities and their Malay Muslim communities. While most advertisers would like to consider these two countries as one market, in actual practice this has become more and more difficult. The Singapore government's domination by a Chinese faction and the Malaysian government's domination by its Muslim faction make complete integration of advertising campaigns difficult.

The Muslim population in both Singapore and Malaysia is much more conservative in a Western sense than its Chinese counterpart. The cultural patterns of these two groups are very different, and each country has at least two distinct markets. Advertisers must reach the different segments with different languages and with different appeals. Interspersed between the Chinese and Malay populations are a large number of Indians and a small group of Europeans, further complicating the marketer's task.

Copy restrictions, especially in the press, exist in both Singapore and Malaysia. For instance, copy must be sent out for approval to a government censor before an advertisement may be placed in the local newspaper. These policies have prevented sections of the multiracial societies from offending each other, and in this way they do serve a purpose. But sending material to an outside agency can cause important delays which could completely negate the effectiveness of an otherwise well-timed current events-oriented advertisement. In an effort to promote its national language the Malaysian government has imposed some restrictions on language usage. However, at present, these do not appear to be a very severe handicap.

CONCLUSIONS AND IMPLICATIONS

The problems reviewed here seem to be sounding a warning. They say that once you have recognized and weighed the importance of economic evolution, you must then pay specific attention to the culture and society of the country in which you want to advertise.

There is evidence to support the hypothesis that the problems faced by an advertising agency in a particular country are tied closely to that country's stage of economic development and to its more basic cultural characteristics. It cannot be stated that the hypothesis is proved because of at least two factors: Several of the problems reported by the very underdeveloped countries still exist in the industrially mature countries of the world; ranking countries is a very difficult task and the ranking used in this article could be argued if other factors had been used in their development. Keeping these qualifications in mind we can say that the apparent existence of this relationship has important implications for the multinational firm.

It is common for large land areas, such as Asia, with many countries each at a different stage of economic development, to be the responsibility of one corporate division. The desire to simplify management procedures could easily produce one set of management standards for all countries within an individual area of responsibility. Much as the intelligent international advertiser now realizes that international advertising campaigns must be modified for local conditions, he must also recognize that agency performance will vary according to local conditions. Therefore the multinational firm's advertising control system should be sensitized to the relationship described in this article.

NOTES

1. Gordon E. Miracle, "International Advertising Principles and Strategies," *MSU Business Topics*, Autumn 1968 (East Lansing: Division of Research, Graduate School of Business Administration, Michigan State University), pp. 29-36.

2. S. Watson Dunn, *International Handbook of Advertising* (New York: McGraw-Hill Book Co., 1964), p. 575.

3. *Marketing Activities in Japan, 1968* (Tokyo: Dentsu Advertising Ltd., 1968), p. 24.

4. B. Liander et al., *Comparative Analysis for International Marketing* (Boston: Marketing Science Institute and Allyn and Bacon, 1967).

5. Ibid., pp. 92-93.

14

Developing National Markets:

THE THAILAND CASE

Dole A. Anderson

One of the crucial problems of our time is the acceleration of the process of nation building—that unifying or integrating into a viable organization of the people who reside within a country's boundaries. While this integrating process has political and social dimensions of great importance, our interest is in economic integration, as manifested by the spread in the use of money and in the exchange of goods across the nation's land area. The development of a national market is at the very center of the process of economic development.[1]

Three concepts from the literature of economic development have special reference in the development of a national market. *Dualism* refers to the coexistence of modern and traditional sectors in a society, and corresponds to the now commonplace observation of outsiders that a developing nation is not one but really two. Most apparent is the modern sector, usually centered on the capital city with its jet airport, international hotels, new factories, and Westernizing middle class. Only miles but often centuries away is the traditional sector, consisting of the remainder of the country's population, producing and consuming at the levels and by the methods of the past. This dualism has obvious effects on the size of the market and hence on the nature and organization of economic activity. Related to the concept of *dualism* is that of *incentive goods*—those attractive items such as a flashlight, transitor radio, ballpoint pen, or a motorbike which serve as a stimulus to the new consumer to rise above the subsistence level by increasing his output or diversifying into cash crops. Curiously, the realization of the essentiality of luxuries to people of developing societies occurs at the same time that we in the developed societies are disturbed by the side effects of our gadgetry. Finally, *import-substitute industrialization* is an important step of developing nations toward modernization. Local production of articles which formerly were imported takes advantage of a protected market of known dimensions and thus simplifies the immediate tasks of new industrialists by postponing the problem of developing the market. Clearly, the three concepts are interrelated and together are a key to the development of a national market; the strategy of import-substitute industrialization has a chance of success if incentive goods broaden the market by reducing the significance of dualism in the society.

Dole A. Anderson, "Developing National Markets: The Thailand Case," pp. 31-37, *MSU Business Topics*, Spring 1969. Reprinted by permission of the publisher, Division of Research, Graduate School of Business Administration, Michigan State University.

Although the Kingdom of Thailand has a long history as an independent nation, only recently has a substantial degree of integration of the national territory been achieved. Within the past two decades a program of road building, motivated more by national security than by economic development considerations, has spread the infrastructure for a national market system to a large part of the country, with revolutionary marketing results. It is our purpose to examine some of the effects of a developing national market, especially for consumer goods, in the Thai example.

ECONOMIC GROWTH IN THAILAND

If national income accounting had been practiced in the seventeenth century and international comparisons of per capita income had been available, it is likely that Thailand, then Siam, would have ranked among the more developed nations of the world. All we have from that period, however, are the reports of European traders expressing their amazement at the splendor of this Oriental kingdom. It was not only the extravagance of the gilded palaces and opulent courts that impressed them; the peasantry in this soft and pleasant land were living comfortably in comparison with their starving ragged counterparts in Europe. Today, three centuries later, revolution has pushed the European peasant far ahead of his Asian counterpart. No longer is a condition of mere survival with relative ease considered sufficient for a citizen of the modern world, and Thailand's per capita income ranks her among the least developed nations.

In 1855, during the reign of a modernizing king, the West forced open the doors of Siam to free trade and her isolation was broken. But she was, and continued to be an independent nation, adroit enough to maintain her freedom from Western colonialism and unique among her neighbors of the Indo-China peninsula (Burma, Cambodia, Laos, Malaya, Viet Nam, all of whom became independent nations only after the Second World War). And she was affluent enough, and concerned enough to offer military assistance to a friendly nation in the form of a herd of war elephants which King Mongkut thought President Lincoln might find useful in prosecuting the American Civil War.

Until recently, however, change came slowly, and economic progress slower still. Commentators writing during the latter years of the last century expected "progressive Siam" to achieve greater economic development than Japan, the only other independent nation. But the Thai continued to do what he liked most, planting rice and enjoying the amenities of village living; even at the present time about four-fifths of the population is employed in the agricultural sector. He works it by the proven methods of the past. If he has a surplus over the needs of his family and is close to good transportation facilities, he secures a cash income which makes possible the purchase of small quantities of imported goods. He was not interested in commerce although the ethnic Chinese were, and nearly all the distribution system has been concentrated in their hands. It is they who have broken bulk of a limited variety of consumer goods imports arriving at Bangkok and carried them upcountry. On the return, they have bulked the small rice surpluses of individual farm families into Thailand's principal export. Although products of agriculture, forestry, and fisheries account for 90 percent of foreign exchange earnings, recent diversification has brought down the relative importance of rice from one-half of total exports to only one-third.

Development efforts began late; the first economic development plan for the kingdom covered the period 1961-66. Growth during this period exceeded plan expectations, averaging about 7 percent annually in real Gross Domestic Product and about 4 percent annually in real per capita output.[2] Targets for the Second Plan period 1967-71 are slightly higher than the achieved rates for the First Plan period. This growth is reflected in the beginnings of a national market. Dualism is still extreme; the two Thailands consist of three million in the Bangkok metropolitan area, and 30 million elsewhere in the nation, of whom less than one-tenth reside in urban places. But the government's road building program, aided by heavy inputs of funds and technical assistance from the United States and others, has greatly increased the degree of mobility. The notes of a Thai interviewer evaluating the effect of a new road put it in picturesque fashion:

> At first the villagers of Ban Non Ta Saeng wanted the road cut around the village. It was cut through instead, but they seem enthusiastic because they have new experiences. When they grow vegetables, fruits, and raise chickens, they know where to sell them. *Everything can be changed into money*.[3] (Italics added.)

Indirect evidence of increasing monetization may be found in the spread of commercial banking; as late as 1950, three-quarters of the seventy-one provinces were without bank offices but by 1967 no province was without a bank.

THE MOBILITY REVOLUTION

A necessary, although not sufficient, condition for developing a national market is a modern transportation system that interconnects the inhabited regions of the country, including those regions with exploitable natural resources, whether currently inhabited or not. The historical process in Thailand, and the impact of highway building, the most recent and revolutionary stage, can be demonstrated by considering the proportion of the nation's land area which has been made accessible by facilities usable the year around. Thailand began with settlement around a river system. Until late in the nineteenth century when railroad building began, the nation was integrated (i.e., developed) only in the heartland centered on the rivers, with connecting canals, which emptied into the Gulf of Siam. This first stage of economic integration covered only 14 percent of the land area of present-day Thailand. While the inland waterway system was as "all-weather" or "hard-surfaced" as any alternative system might have been and offered lower-cost transportation than others, it integrated only a small part of the nation; elsewhere, with ox-cart, pack animal, or the backs of humans available, only an economy of near-subsistence level was possible since these forms offered neither low-cost nor all-weather transportation.

The second stage of national integration consisted of building a railroad system during the period from the late 1890s to the Second World War. This system opened an additional 14 percent of the nation's land area beyond the 14 percent which had already been integrated by the waterways, bringing a total of 28 percent of the nation within fifteen kilometers or about nine miles of low-cost, all-weather transportation. The railroads, while they did open up vast areas in the North and Northwest unfortunately were somewhat restricted in their developmental and integrative role. The treaties with Britain and other Western powers which imposed free trade on Thailand in the mid-nineteenth century forced the Thai government to search for revenue sources other than those based on foreign trade. By 1926, when Thailand finally regained autonomy over its fiscal affairs, income from the state railway system was an important source of government revenues. Thus, it is not surprising that for a long period the government's highway policy was to use roads as feeders to bolster railway revenues rather than as infrastructure for economic development.

The third stage of transport development, the highway system, has truly revolutionized the economic integration of the nation. Again using our rough measure of service area for illustrative purposes, the all-weather highway system has added 28 percent of the nation's land area not heretofore served by water or rail transportation. Of course, the highway system not merely extends beyond the older water and rail systems; in large part it also duplicates those systems, so that the all-weather highways serve a total of 56 percent of the national territory.

The number of motor vehicles in Thailand has, as we would expect, grown more rapidly than the road system. Wihle the national highway mileage increased six times during the fifteen-year period beginning in 1950, motor vehicles increased over ten times, to a toal of approximately one-quarter of a million, a third of which are two- and three-wheeled motorcycles. Of greater interest for our thesis of a developing national market, however, is the larger growth of vehicles outside of Bangkok during this fifteen-year period. Thus, the number of trucks registered in the Bangkok metropolitan area dropped from over one-half of the total in the kingdom to less than one-quarter. The private passenger car is found where the affluence is; thus, Bangkok had 87 percent of all these vehicles at the beginning of the period and fifteen years later still had 80 percent. The motorcycle, on the other hand, must be viewed as the minimum-investment modern wheeled vehicle for transporting persons and cargo. Even though TV advertising in Thailand pictures the Honda as a sports vehicle for a boy and his girl, it is more usually a utilitarian vehicle, piled perilously high with cargo, or with father taking the children to school or the entire family for an outing on the weekend. The motorcycle is transportation for the upward mobile, who have probably already moved up from a bicycle and who will trade up further from two wheels to four when finances permit.[4] During the fifteen-year period, the number of motorcycles in the kingdom increased from 1,400 to over 87,000. Significantly, 75 percent of the motorcycles in the kingdom were concentrated in Bangkok in 1950, but 15 years later, the proportions were reversed and 70 percent were outside the capital.

A number of results of the revolution in mobility can be identified; although there is overlapping, we may distinguish the effects of *reducing costs, creating alternatives*, and *diffusing change*. The growth of highway transportation in Thailand repeats the experience of other developing nations over the world. From a position of approximate equality in 1955 in ton-miles of inter-city freight hauled by road and by rail, rail traffic less than doubled in ten years while road traffic increased about five times. The higher quality and flexibility of the trucking service has reduced the total costs of transportation in Thailand as in many other countries.[5]

As a result of reduced costs of transportation from areas hitherto not served, alternatives have been made available to the rural sectors of Thailand. Beginning in the mid-fifties, new cash crops for export, such as maize, kenaf jute, and cassava root, began to be developed. The combination of an international demand for these products and the road system which made the farmer a part of the world market, even in areas not suitable for rice production, elicited a response from the traditionally conservative and unmaterialistic Thai farmer. Diversification of agriculture, the long-sought breakthrough for societies based on a system of monoculture, became a possibility. "Everything can be changed into money."

The diffusion of change is perhaps the crucial effect of the mobility revolution.[6] The isolation which is being broken by the road program is, of course, relative and not absolute. Opium from the farthest hills will always get out and the ubiquitous Singer sewing machine will apparently get in—everywhere. But the movement of items of high value in relation to their bulk or weight does not evidence an integrated national market. The itinerant peddlar has roamed every corner of Thailand for centuries, leaving behind after his occasional visits the small high-value trinkets from the factories of many nations. What has changed with low-cost accessibility is the frequency and variety of the intrusions from the outside on the peasant's world. In many areas, the principal agent of change is still the traveling middleman, with his small truck or Jeep, in which he leaves the improved road and strikes out across cart tracks or open country to the dispersed clusters of settlement. Lowering the cost of accessibility through road improvement increases the market area which the middleman can serve. For a particular village it increases the number of middlemen who reach it, the frequency of their visits, and the quantity of agricultural produce and cottage manufactures they can take out and the variety of consumer goods they can bring in. Studies of the impact of roads on formerly isolated Thai villages read much like the history of change in rural America. There has been a net gain of about 20 percent in the number of stores and an increase in the variety of items stocked after the road was opened; a few stores had to close because they were unable to compete with stores in nearby larger towns to which the villagers could now go to shop. The villager's response, when questioned on what has happened to his world and his ways, may sadden but not surprise us. He reacts favorably to the new experience of movies, ice, ready-made clothing, and beauty parlors, but he fears the dust and danger of passing vehicles and the development of expensive family tastes for new goods and services.[7]

THE CHANGING NATIONAL MARKET

A developing national market means the distribution of different goods to different consumers through a marketing structure which is inevitably different. The differences between the consumers of a largely self-sufficient economy except for the capital city and of a broadening mass market have already been described. We turn now to examine some characteristics of the different kinds of goods demanded by a developing national market.

Clearly, those articles which the new consumers want and can afford are inexpensive, attractive, and of reasonable quality. The trend toward cheaper imported consumer goods is illustrated by the case of wrist watches. Thailand imported nearly identical quantities of watches in 1956 and in 1966 —approximately 135,000 in each year. In 1965, the CIF value of these imports was 25.5 million baht (approximately U.S. $1.3 million) and 98 percent of these watches came from Switzerland. In 1966, the value of imported watches was 19.5 million baht or 26 percent lower, and 74 percent of the imports came from Japan, with Switzerland contributing only 25 percent. The following consumer goods, selected because of comparability in customs classification, are illustrative of the trend toward less expensive products for the growing middle- and lower-class markets, rather than representative of consumer goods in general:

Product	*Percent Change in CIF Value per Unit Between 1956 and 1966*
Toilet soap (tons)	+64%
Tires for motor cars	-5
Motorcycles	-9
Passenger cars	-13
Wrist watches	-26
Air conditioners	-27
Toilet paper (tons)	-29
Refrigerators and freezers	-43
Radios	-52
Television receivers	-56
Dentifrice (tons)	-58
Ballpoint pens	-92

The exceptional case of toilet soap, which increased rather than decreased in value per ton imported, reflects the effect of import-substitute industrialization; the quantity of imported soap dropped by more than one-half over the period and what came in was increasingly luxury items as local manufacturers took over the mass market. The other extreme case on the list, ballpoint pens, reflects the enormous growth in popularity of throwaway pens everywhere (Thailand imported 165,000 pens in 1956 and over 20 million in 1966) and may be considered a different product from that which was imported in 1956. To a degree, of course, other items illustrate this same tendency toward "different products" in the product mix, that is, smaller, simpler models as in automobiles and refrigerators.

This group of one dozen products illustrates another striking tendency, the capture by Japan of these markets. During the eleven-year period, Japan moved from a minor share of the market to domination (70 percent or more by quantity) on four products and to leadership over all other importers on five more products. Only in home air conditioners does the United States continue to dominate. The Japanese manufacturer's slogan "Asian cosmetics for Asian complexions" has obvious appeal, but so have a wide range of products characterized by their small size, simplicity, and adaptability to a developing national market.[8]

The promotion of industrialization began on a significant scale in the late 1950s. Because of Thailand's strong foreign exchange position, import-substitute industrialization was not forced on the government as is the case for most developing societies. Rather, the aim of industrialization has been to reduce the relative importance of agriculture in the economy, to utilize local raw materials, and to develop employment opportunities for the rapidly growing population. Promotion has consisted of granting tax exemptions and reducing duties on the importation of machinery and raw materials for a five-year period. Import controls on finished products have been used sparingly so that local manufactures generally compete with similar imported products. By the end of 1967, promoted industries in operation had a total investment of the equivalent of U.S. $282 million. Twenty percent of this investment was in an oil refinery and a cement company; of the remainder, 38 percent was in consumer goods industries including foods and textiles, 14 percent in services, mainly hotels, and about 28 percent in non-consumer goods including construction materials, chemicals, and intermediate metal processing.[9] Clearly, a significant start has been made toward industrialization; of the twelve consumer goods cited above, all but three are now produced or assembled locally. However, it is still too early to say whether this industrialization will develop goods, except for foodstuffs and textiles, which are adapted to local needs, at lower prices than the imported equivalent, and with adaptations to use local raw materials; as yet, this has not occurred to a significant degree.

Finally, we may note that the distribution structure changes as industrialization and a broadening of the market occur. In Thailand, Western trading houses continue in the tradition of the East India companies of three centuries or more ago; one such describes its current product line of imported goods as "from toothpaste to tractors, textiles to toilet tissues and flashlights to frozen food." A recent article in this journal has called attention to the difficulties of adapting a marketing system which evolved to distribute imported goods into a system adequate to serve domestic manufacturing.[10] In the past, the advice given Western manufacturers considering production in Thailand has been to use the existing networks of trading firms for distribution of their products; there is growing dissatisfaction with such arrangements, however. Increasingly, manufacturers find it desirable to control distribution of their products down to the retail outlet.

SUMMARY

We have examined some aspects of the process of development of a national market by reference to recent experience in Thailand. The case is highly specific, of course. War and instability on the Indo-China peninsula have given a high priority to rapid development of an infrastructure which would integrate the nation and enable the central government to counter insurgency in the least developed and isolated regions of the country. A by-product of this effort has been a lowering of the costs of moving goods and people throughout the country and an increase in the amount of such movement, both in the intensive and extensive dimensions. People respond, even in such a self-satisfied society as that of Thailand. A market develops for locally manufactured goods as well as for imports, but the goods for this new larger market must be attractive, inexpensive, and of reasonable quality. This is not to say that a developing economy needs only a low-cost year-around transportation system to achieve self-sustaining growth. There are other requisites and only time will confirm whether these are present or can be generated in the Thai society. But the important role of a developing national market in the process of economic integration is clear.

NOTES

This article is adapted from a forthcoming study, "Marketing Development in Thailand." The author gratefully acknowledges a grant from the Midwest University Consortium for International Activities, Inc. which helped make the study possible.

1. The role of developing national markets in the economic growth process has been described by W. W. Rostow in *View from the Seventh Floor* (New York: Harper and Row, 1964), pp. 132-44 and in "The Concept of a National Market and its Economic Growth Implications," in Peter Bennett, ed., *Marketing and Economic Development* (Chicago: American Marketing Association, 1965), pp. 11-20.

2. "The Second National Economic and Social Development Plan (1967-1971)" (Bangkok: Office of the Prime Minister, the National Economic Development Board, 310 pp. mimeographed.)

3. *Evaluation Report*, Second Joint Thai-United States Operations Mission Evaluation of the Accelerated Rural Development Project, July, 1966, II, V-B, 22.

3. In mid-1968, the relative Bangkok retail prices, for cash, in dollar equivalents, were: bicycle—$40, motor-bike—$100, motorcycle—$225 up, lowest-priced four-wheeled passenger car (Honda)—$1,600, Volkswagen sedan—$2,825.

5. Dan Usher has found that in hauling rice, the oxcart and the jeep were the most expensive because of their small capacities, and were used only for short distances where trucks could not get in because of road conditions. Trucks and rail were competitive on rates with the latter at a disadvantage on service. Where available, water is of course the cheapest transportation. "The Thai Rice Trade," in T. H. Silcock, ed., *Thailand, Social and Economic Studies in Development* (Canberra: Australian National University Press), 1967.

6. A recent study of economic, political, and social data for seventy-four underdeveloped countries suggested that the "underlying influences most conducive to transforming ideas and attitudes in low-income countries are the geographic linking together of the population through the creation of transportation networks and the economic integration of the country by means of the spread of the market throughout the nation." Irma Adelman and Cynthia Taft Morris, "An Econometric Model of Socio-Economic and Political Change in Underdeveloped Countries," *American Economic Review* (December, 1968), p. 1191.

7. *Evaluation Report, Op. Cit.*

8. A small part of the decline in value per unit is due to lower freight costs from Japan than from Western Europe.

9. Tabulated from listings of promoted firms in operation, as reported by the Board of Investment, Bangkok, 1968, mimeo. The investment of all enterprises granted promotion certificates, including those not yet operational, totalled nearly U.S. $700 million and were estimated to provide employment for 69,000 Thais. The majority of enterprises are joint ventures with twenty-four nations represented; in terms of registered capital, Thai investors account for 68 percent, Japan, 11 percent, and the U.S. and Nationalist China about 5 percent each of the total registered capital. "Investment Newsletter," Board of Investment, January, 1968.

10. A. A. Sherbini, "Import-Oriented Marketing Mechanisms," *MSU Business Topics*, Spring, 1968, pp. 70-73.

LAW

Law

15

The Japanese Notion of Law:

AN INTRODUCTION TO FLEXIBILITY AND INDEFINITUDE

Jiro Tokuyama

SUMMARY AND RECOMMENDATIONS

Given a limited amount of land on earthquake-prone islands, even the primitive inhabitants of what is now Japan had to be highly flexible in the face of climatic forces beyond their control. The historical traditions of flexibility and indefinitude fostered by these conditions have served Japanese well over the ages, enabling them to adjust to even non-climatic changes in their environment in ways such as to preserve their country. For example, the indefinitude and flexibility of the nature of the imperial institution enabled Japanese to adjust it to new geo-political situations both at the time of the Meiji Restoration in 1868 and at the time Japan was occupied after World War II, all the while preserving the institution itself, even though altering considerably its function. Without flexibility and indefinitude, Japan would long ago have disintegrated, and, indeed, modern Japan could never have been created.

The following chapters illustrate that the basic principles behind the Japanese notion of law are, as with other areas of Japanese culture, those of flexibility and indefinitude. These principles behind the legal notion are being utilized and given new meaning by the crowded realities of life in modern postwar Japan, as the country continuously seeks to readjust itself to changing world conditions. There are still too many conflicting interests in Japan in too little space to afford a combative notion of law such as held in Western countries. These two concepts of flexibility and indefinitude will, therefore, continue to be central to the Japanese legal notion, in spite of increasing contact by Japanese with Western legal notions.

These underlying concepts of flexibility and indefinitude naturally form the underpinnings of the central institutions of the Japanese legal notion *wakai* (amiable reconcilitation) and *chōtei* (patriarchal mediation), while the Western-like institution of *chūsai* (arbitration) is still less popular, especially in non-business relationships. The former two institutions are strongly characterized by the use of accommodation among parties without reference to contractual obligations, and even the process of *chūsai* retains considerable elements of accommodation. The use of accommodation as a means of structuring and conducting legal relationships can be successful only when all parties to a relationship hold the same basic values and cultural

---

Reprinted by permission of the Nomura Research Institute, from the December 13, 1973, issue of the Nomura Investment Report.

understandings as a tacit basis for settlements. Culture, therefore, rather than contract, is the basic reference point for Japanese-style legal relationships.

Bccause of the central role of culture as a reference point in the legal process in Japan, foreigners with values, morality, etc. (i.e., culture) differing from those of Japanese can seldom successfully participate in Japanese-style legal relationships. By the same token, Japanese often have rather bitter experiences when trying to deal with foreign legal systems. Though the point is obvious, it must be stressed that there exists a profound barrier between Japan and the rest of the world on the basic question of how to structure and conduct legal relationships.

What steps, then, can be recommended to parties to international legal relationships to help them pass through the cultural barrier? First, of course, must come generous amounts of patience and good will on both sides of the barrier. But patience and good will, though absolutely necessary, are not enough. In order to establish a basis for amiable relations, the parties must go beyond the need for mere patience or good will, and arrive at a deeper understanding of the cultural values that separate them. Only after creating such understanding can parties deal with each other successfully through the cultural barrier.

This paper has been written in the hope of helping to create such an understanding of one aspect of the cultural barrier, that of legal notion. In light of the fact that many volumes have been written on the Japanese legal system, this paper can be seen only as a short introduction to the subject. Nevertheless, it is hoped that the key concepts which have been introduced and illustrated below (i.e, flexibility, indefinitude, and accommodation) may provide an adequate framework which the reader may use to organize further observations on the subject, be they of a personal or of a scholarly nature.

INTRODUCTION

The feudal political system of the Tokugawa Shogunate came to an end in 1868 in what is called the Meiji Restoration. With this epochal upheaval ended the policy of national isolation pursued by a previous government, the Tokugawa Shogunate, over nearly three centuries. With a learner's enthusiasm, Japan began introducing into its own society elements of Western culture, and the European legal system in particular.

The Meiji Government first sought to copy British law which was in its heyday in the nineteenth century at the time of the Meiji Restoration. However, the Japanese lawmakers found the British law to be heavy with overtones of individualism, and thus unfit for the conditions of their own country. By and by they turned their eyes to the legal system of Germany which was at the time still unmatured as a capitalist country. Japanese leaders felt that Japan resembled Germany in many ways. For example, Japan was also on its way to a capitalist economy, and both countries had to catch up quickly with advanced capitalist nations under powerful centralized monarchal administrations. Thus, many Japanese leaders felt that German legal institutions might offer useful precedents for Japan.

Long and strenuous efforts to establish a constitution and laws bore fruit in the promulgation of the Imperial Constitution in 1889, the Civil Procedure Code and the Criminal Procedure Code in 1891, the Civil Code in 1898, the Commercial Code in 1899, and the Criminal Code in 1908. With some French influence these laws were, in the main, imitations of German statutes, transplanted from the land which was, after all, quite different in social foundation. Thus, one cannot say that Japanese laws were born of Japanese society or tradition.

Until the Meiji Restoration of 1868, under the influence of Chinese law and Confucianism, Japan knew little of systematic and comprehensive European law. The laws in force before the Meiji Restoration were of a patchwork nature, and they were designed mostly for the *samurai* (warrior-bureaucrat) class; they embodied and institutionalized Confucianism and feudalism which underlay the Japanese aristocratic spiritual tradition.

The leaders in post-Restoration Japan were much too intent upon studying and introducing a European legal system to work out their own legal system based on the traditional Japanese values. Moreover, in its endeavor to introduce the Western system, the Meiji regime surprisingly won all-out support from the people at large.

However, the reason for this support was more political in nature than sociological. In 1858, just before the dawn of the Meiji era, foreign powers had compelled Japan to sign treaties granting extraterritoriality to foreigners on the grounds that Japanese laws were not considered (by foreigners) civilized enough to permit their application to foreigners. The latter were certainly not willing to forfeit their much valued rights merely because of a change in locale.

Before the foreign nations were willing to release their right of extraterritoriality, they wanted assurance that Japan would treat foreign nationals in what foreign opinion considered a "civilized way." Japanese, both leaders and people, were quick to realize that the best way to convince Europeans of Japan's legal maturity would be to copy closely a European legal system in the construction of their own system. This realization of the unavoidable necessity of copying a foreign system as a step on the road to national autonomy was the main reason that the Meiji leaders' policy of introduction of foreign laws was widely supported in Japan.

Revision of the unequal treaties, including especially the withdrawal of the extraterritoriality, was at the top of the agenda of the nation's foreign as well as domestic policies. The treaty partners—advanced Western nations—time and again throughout the early Meiji era had declined Japanese revision requests.

Only after many years of onerous negotiations was Japan able to persuade them to withdraw extraterritoriality clauses on condition that Japan set up laws modeled after a modern European system. In 1894, Britain initiated a treaty revision move, and extraterritoriality had been entirely repealed by 1911.

Thus, the desire for treaty revision was the reason Japan worked out the five above-mentioned major laws in such a short period on the examples of German and French laws. Most of the new laws enacted against such a historical backdrop had heavy European overtones—in terminology, logicality, conceptualization, and ideology; only the family law within the Civil Code contained the native Japanese feudalistic family system of which modern European laws knew nothing. These imported laws, so different in nature from what the traditional Japanese social order required, functioned peculiarly in controlling Japanese society, and the Japanese people reacted to them peculiarly.

Westernization of laws, however, did not mean that contemporary Japanese life required such laws or that there existed the spiritual foundation for them. The political purpose of repealing unequal treaties was the sole reason for legal importations. Hence, these laws, in terminology and provisions, were in line with those of highly developed capitalist countries, whereas actual Japanese life retained a wide range of factors of backwardness. In fact, there was a wide gap between the grand system which these laws connoted and the actual lives of the general public.

This gap between law and reality, or that between the demands of law and the people's notion of law, has persisted over the one hundred years since the Restoration. Without understanding this gap between legal systems and social reality, it is almost impossible to grasp the Japanese notion of law with any measure of accuracy.

After World War II, under the direction of General MacArthur, Japan attempted to introduce concepts of American democracy. Of course, the Japanese intellectuals of the prewar period had understood the principle of democracy at least as a concept, and therefore they were capable of absorbing the idea conceptually. However, to the general public "democracy" was an alien concept, one quite inconsistent with their way of life.

The new Japanese Constitution enacted in 1947 and most of the laws set up thereafter in line with the Constitution were all based on American democratic principles. However, these postwar laws often ran counter to the everyday realities of people's lives, just as had the previous laws introduced so hastily by the Meiji Government.

Japanese concepts of law have changed markedly since the end of World War II. Reasons for success in rapid Westernization of the Japanese notion of law in recent years are the extraordinary digestive and absorptive capacities of Japanese, and more importantly the realization of the need to "catch up" with institutionally advanced European countries. Moreover, the popularization of higher education and frequent and closer contacts with Western culture after the War are also partly responsible for revolutionary changes in the Japanese way of thinking and their sense of law.

For instance, many major Japanese companies have learned bitter lessons through negotiations with foreign companies, and thereby changed their notion of law. Rational processes of thought—an outcome of higher education—also have enabled the general public to accept Western views of laws without much difficulty. These are but two examples of many radical postwar changes in the Japanese notion of law.

It would be best to repeat, however, that despite such changes in the Japanese view of law, there persists a strong non-Western notion of law in the Japanese mentality. This imbalance in legal notion is more conspicuous in rural communities than in cities, and more so among elderly people than among young people.

This article shall attempt a general survey of the notions of right and law of the Japanese people who have their own time-honored background as well as attempting a review of how such notions are embodied in major legal areas such as contract, ownership, commercial transaction laws, litigation, and family law. It shall also attempt to look into how these notions contradict, or react to, those laws received from abroad, and then to find out what foundation has created such notions and how they will change in the future.

Before going into details, the term "the notion of law" held by the Japanese people as referred to in this article must first be defined. This term shall mean the notion of how to settle arguments that the Japanese people harbor somewhere within their mentality in the course of their daily lives before they feel the need to resort to the court of law. This consciousness of the people serves as the background which produces law and right, and thus must be considered the foundation of Japanese legal consciousness.

Generally, legal notion does not pose any problem in Western society where laws develop from the people's actual lives. Western notions of law hardly contradict the provisions of law. Just as we take air matter-of-factly, so do Western people take their notion of law; they do not feel the need to take the trouble of studying the legal notions that underlie their legal and right systems.

By contrast, the traditional Japanese view of law developed against a historical and social background quite different from that of the modern European laws which Japan has introduced. Naturally there are perceptional gaps. The reception of European laws has helped Westernize, to some extent, the Japanese notion of law, which, fostered over the ages, will not change overnight. Tokyo, after all, was not built in a day.

In brief, "the notion of law" referred to herein means that notion fostered in the people's extrajuridicial daily lives through long history and through the process of Westernization under the influence of the laws received from abroad.

THE JAPANESE NOTION OF RIGHT AND DUTY

The underlying concept of modern Western law is "right." Usually the wording of a law goes as follows: "The people, a judicial person, or the government is granted the right to do so and so." Social life may be divided into two aspects; one has nothing to do with laws and the other is the "legal relationship" where laws are called for. Under modern Western laws, legal relationships are based on the concept of right. Therefore, one may also call legal relationships "right relationships." The German and French laws that Japan adopted in the late nineteenth century are, of course, based on right and most of their provisions concern the rights of the people. One may recall with interest that "recht" in German and "droit" in French both refer to either "law" or "right." The implication is that law and right are synonymous.

This Western way of thought contrasts sharply with Japan's traditional lack of the idea of right. All the pre-Restoration social norms under the feudalistic system were based on duty. The term "right" itself was not in the intrinsic Japanese vocabulary when the country adopted the Western legal system. As a result, opinions varied as to how to translate properly the term, "regt," or "recht," into Japanese. The absence of the idea of "right" at the time of the creation of Japan's modern legal system still significantly influences the actual functioning of modern Japanese law.

Even in pre-Restoration days there were highly developed trade and commerce relationships among merchants, between merchants and feudal lords or samurai, and between merchants and other classes of people. For instance, a money lender could demand repayment of the lessee, and individual persons could own land or houses. Therefore, the Japanese people in those days must have had an idea which filled the role which right played in Western nations. Nevertheless, it is very interesting to note that the Japanese concept of "right" failed to assume Western connotations.

As mentioned above, the Japanese legal system before the Meiji Restoration was keynoted by duty. But the "duty" was quite different from that of Western people. Under the modern Western law, "duty" must be qualificatory and quantifiable. Let us suppose that a person A owes another person B ten thousand dollars. A's obligation to B is limited to the act of repaying the money and the interest thereof. The amount of repayment must be no more or no less than ten thousand dollars; likewise, the interest paid must be at a rate no more and no less than contracted.

This is the legal quantification of duty. Under modern laws, right and duty usually represent the obverse or reverse that make up the same thing, whereas under feudal legal systems only duty and obedience exist.

The qualification and quantification of duty naturally entail qualification and quantification of right. However, the traditional Japanese notion of law has had little if no such qualification and quantification of duty since pre-Meiji days. This notion of law has prevailed fairly strongly in the daily lives of the people ever since the introduction of modern Western laws. The concept of right faces the same situation as illustrated in the following areas.

First is the traditional notion of right and duty regarding employment.

Since the end of World War II, these notions have undergone a major change and come closer to those of Westerners. Nevertheless, the traditional notion still remains in many places. In the traditional Japanese concept of employment, the employer has the "power" over the employee, but this does not comprise the "right to demand labor." Conversely, the employee does not think that he has the "right to demand wages" from the employer. Instead, he is humble enough to think that he is "allowed to work for, and receive wages from, the employer."

This power relationship pattern entitles an employer to "order" his employees but saves him from having to face demands for rights from them. Thus, the legal relation between the employer and employee is not that of right and duty, but that of order and obedience. To the employee, the opportunity of working for, and receiving wages from, the employer does not compose a right based on labor contract, but rather amounts to a "favor" granted by the employer.

Such a way of thinking makes up the core of the traditional Japanese notion of employment. As a result, it is utterly out of the question that employees could ever demand payment of wages or organize labor unions, or go on strike. The employer, on his part, extends some benevolent gestures to his employees such as voluntary raising of wages and solatia for deaths, injuries, or diseases of the family members of his employees.

This patriarchal relationship works to facilitate smooth relations between management and labor. This means that the Japanese regard the management-labor relationship not as one of commodity exchange—the commodity being labor offered—but as a sort of patriarchal or family relationship. This is a precedent established during Japan's feudal past and in ingrained social value which has prevailed for over three hundred years.

This traditional notion of employment has radically changed since the end of World War II. The new Japanese Constitution guarantees the workers' right to work in Article 27, and the right to organize in Article 28. These provisions led to the enactment of the Labor Relations Adjustment Law in 1946, and many other derivative labor codes.

The series of labor laws helped workers win the right to unite and to strike, and the right to demand better working conditions. The frequent recurrence of strikes after World War II may be attributable to this change in the management-and-labor relationship. The conventional order-and-obedience relationship has now been replaced with a right-and-duty relationship, and this change has prompted workers to negotiate, or launch strikes, for wage hikes or to protest "undue" discharge.

However, despite a surface Westernization as seen in modernized terms of labor laws enacted after the war, as well as played-up news reports on labor problems, the traditional concept of employment still persists when one investigates more closely the Japanese mentality.

For example, Japanese companies offer, by custom, bonuses twice a year, apart from regular wages. However, it is left completely to the discretion of management whether or not they will give and how much they give. The employee is in no position to demand a bonus as a right. Bonuses are nothing more than an expression of an employer's benevolence or good will, but still are designed to complement regular contracted wages. Moreover, the higher the wages, the higher the retirement allowance which has to be paid by the employer. In order to avoid paying relatively high retirement allowances, therefore, many companies have made it custom to pay higher bonuses and hold down regular wages. In a nutshell, the Japanese bonus originating in the concept of employer's benevolence, has become what the employee can demand as a right.

This dualism in the custom of paying bonuses apparently contradicts thc quantification of right and duty. Moreover, there are other non-obligatory customs in some Japanese customs which are of a nature similar to indirect wages of the bonus type, e.g., free lessons in tea ceremony and flower arrangement for female employees. This indirect and non-contractual manner of remuneration is accepted by workers partly because of the high level of job security in the nearly universal lifetime employment system, under which an employee is rarely dismissed without serious or gross misconduct. These practices are, however, a far cry from the modern concept of employment in other advanced countries.

Another peculiar employment practice in Japan is that both management and labor tend to avoid specifying employment terms when concluding an employment contract. The employee hesitates to demand the wages he wants, though wages are one of his most important concerns; he only expects the would-be employer to offer him a proper amount. The employer, on his part, does not like to be demanded by the applicant to fix wage terms in detail; he rather would prefer that the employee rely upon his sound judgment. Nor will the employer specify the exact number of working hours expected or other conditions; he tends to leave these considerations to the employee's discretion or to accepted practice.

Today, it is common practice among big companies to formalize the contents of employment contracts, and enter into detailed contracts. However, small companies have been slow in adopting such practices. Even in big companies, however, individual employees in practice more or less retain the traditional concept of employment.

Another example of Japanese aversion to detailed written agreements concerns loan contracts. In the Civil Code, a lessor can demand repayment of money from a lessee at the end of the term of a loan. However, by custom, both parties tend to expect an extension of the term. If the lessor immediately resorts to law for his money, he may be branded as coldhearted or merciless. Such a reputation will almost certainly rebound against the lessor in the future, not only socially but in business circles as well, since he might find it difficult to find customers willing to be obligated to a man of bad reputation. Thus, the preference for flexibility in legal agreements enforces itself through social pressure. This example attests to the contradiction between, on the one hand, the quantification and qualification of right and, on the other hand, the Japanese lack of insistence on repayment of the stipulated amount of money within the prescribed term.

The same sort of phenomenon often occurs in traffic accidents. While driving on American roads, one will notice road signs saying "Yield Right of Way" or simply "Yield." These signs entitle a car driving along a broader road the right of way over a car moving in from a narrower road. The rationale is that there arises a relationship of rights between the cars. The Japanese Road Traffic Control Law stipulates similarly (Article 36, Clause 3) that a car driving in from a smaller road must yield the right of way to a car driving on the larger road. However, the similarity between Japanese and American law ends here. The Japanese law is based on duty relations; it says that the car driving in from the smaller road "shall not interfere" with the procession of the car driving along the larger road.

Suppose an accident takes place. A truck drives from a narrower road onto a wider road, interrupting the procession of a small passenger car on the wider road, and the former strikes the latter. Under the Traffic Control Law (Article 36, Clause 3), the truck is naturally to blame. The provisions of the law do not require the small car to be prepared to decelerate. Rather, the small car has the right of way.

In an actual court case of this nature, however, the Tokyo District Court decided that the passenger car was at fault because it failed to prepare to stop at a moment's notice by decreasing its speed. In this ruling, the right of way of the small car was not acknowledged. The result of the case was tantamount to a negation of the legally bested right or duty.

These are only a few of many examples of the contradiction between law and custom that Japanese encounter in their daily lives. To foreigners, the Japanese notion of law in these cases may look quite underdeveloped. The fact is, however, that the legal rulings are more influenced by Japanese social and racial structures and the traditional way of thinking than by the letter of the law. The problem is not one of relative advancement or relative retardation of culture; rather, it is one of lack of agreement between society and law. A separate chapter will elaborate on what has caused the aforementioned Japanese notion of right (see "Cultural and Social Bases for the Japanese Notion of Law," p. 289); here it will suffice to point out some characteristics of the notion.

Despite the totally non-Western nature of the Japanese notion of right, however, legal problems which are brought to courts or to law offices for action, or even to law schools for case study, tend to be treated according to basic principles in compliance with the law in question. The traditional Japanese concept of law is completely ignored unless it identifies specifically with the provisions of the law. This situation poses a big problem for Japan. Strictly speaking, the Japanese notion of law *on the level of court* differs from that outside the court. Here again, an understanding of the dualism of the Japanese concept of right is essential in appreciating the general Japanese concept of law. The reasons and background for the dual notion of right shall be treated later.

THE JAPANESE NOTION OF LAW

The above observations regarding the Japanese notion of right also applies to the Japanese notion of law. The Japanese concept of indefinitude of law must be viewed from two points. One is the Japanese notion of the "indefinitude of contents" involved in law. The other is the Japanese notion of the "indefinitude of the norm itself" of statutory provisions.

INDEFINITUDE OF THE CONTENTS OF STATUTORY PROVISIONS

Laws stipulate important contents regarding people's rights and duties, and, therefore, their contents must be precise and clear. This means that people's interests are protected to a definite degree and also that the framework of governmental power enforced upon the people is clearly fixed. Were this not the case there might arise disputes or improper protection of people's rights.

Preciseness and clarity are essential for full functioning of the law. Unless the contents of a law are definite, it is impossible to have a "prescience" regarding a legal issue. We can have the prescience regarding the repayment of lent money under prescribed terms only because the law expressly stipulates that the money must be repaid at a certain time. Prescience of a legal issue accorded us by law is one of the most important of its functions. For this reason, in Western countries and in Japan alike, specific legal terms are employed for their distinctiveness and for avoiding confusion with everyday terms.

However, people's values and the nature of their social lives often change. If the contents of law and the meanings of legal terms are irrevocably fixed, they may depart from changing reality and leave law outdated. Hence arises the need to "adjust" the meanings of legal terms. The adjustment in this context is called the "construction of law" in Western countries and Japan as well. However, the Japanese attitude toward construction is quite different from that of Westerners.

Western peoples have a strong conviction that the meanings of legal terms should be definite and fixed. Consequently the interpretation of the meanings of legal terms is limited. Interpretation should be within the construction of the legal terms. If disagreement begins on the understanding that the standard for judgment is covered in the meaning of the legal term, but then bogs down, it is agreed that the law itself must be revised or there must be employed a secondary legal norm (e.g., customary law or reason).

Japan has introduced this theory on the sources of law, at least in an abstract form. But few lawyers actually apply reason and customary law in rendering decisions or use these secondary norms as standards for legal judgment. Moreover, the law is rarely readjusted to changing social conditions. How then do Japanese lawyers fill up the gap between law and the actual social conditions? They do so through radical "construction";

they construe legal terms to include in the meanings the original standards for judgment.

An example might be of value here. The Civil Code defines in Article 85 that a "chose" (one of the objects of right) is a piece of corporeal property. Literally speaking, electricity and gas are not corporeal properties. Yet, they have economic value. Naturally, gas companies and electric power companies must claim the ownership and other rights for them. In the Japanese Civil Code the objects of ownership fall under the category of "chose" and, therefore, gas and electricity must be "chose" or corporeal properties, if they are to be the objects for ownership.

Common sense tells us that electricity and gas are intangible, and it is unreasonable to include them in corporeal properties. Therefore, the Civil Code must be modified to include those intangibles in the objects for ownership. Westerners may very well modify their laws. Japanese lawyers and lawmakers will not. Instead, they simply *construe* electricity and gas to be included in chose or corporeal properties. However, even lawyers are aware that this interpretation is, in essence, incompatible with our normal concept of corporeal property. What they do then is as follows: They further *construe* the corporeal property as referred to in Article 85 of the Civil Code to include even the intangibles as far as they have some economic value and are under human control.

Lawyers contend that the concept of corporeal property in physics cannot be the same as that in law, and that both comprise a specific legal conception is sufficient only for the purpose of law. Of course, since revision of law cannot be viewed lightly, as it might lead to legal instability, Western peoples attempt to improve insufficient provisions and adjust them to changing times or changing social conditions by means of as free a construction as possible. However, when Western lawyers construe law, they understand that the meanings of legal provisions are definite and qualificatory.

While studying in the U.S., Japanese jurists and practitioners of law often have an impression that American law schools do not spare much time for detailed construction of the provisions of law. They feel that their American counterparts "read" law much less than do Japanese. Hence, Japanese lawyers, especially jurists, accustomed to sophisticated construction of provisions, often have some misgivings about American jurists' ability to construe law and have a mistaken notion that American lawyers study improperly. Many Japanese jurists, after a relatively short stay in the U.S., have returned home with such a mistaken impression. The reason for this misunderstanding lies in the ignorance of the difference in the construction of law between the two nations.

A capable lawyer, by Japanese standards, must be a man who can construe any provisions quite freely to apply them to all phenomena and can construe any difficult problems within the framework of an existing law. This definition tolerates some degree of deviation from common sense or the plain meaning of the terms.

However, foreign lawyers do not seem to follow this line of thinking. What American law students learn first in legal process is the technique for detailed construction of written laws and the plain meaning of a term or its ordinary meaning. Only when this process proves insufficient is the legislative purpose or legislative history called for in construing the law.

In other words, American lawyers seem to place a greater emphasis on definitude and qualification of legal terms and minimize the allowance for construction, in an attempt to avoid unexpected implication of law resulting from different interpretation. Without understanding this difference, American lawyers' attitudes and American law education may sound unsatisfactory to Japanese lawyers.

It is true that Japanese lawyers' skill for elaborate interpretation enables imperfect laws to bring intricate social phenomena under control. Construction assures the ability to change an imperfect legal system into a perfect one. But in the process the Japanese lawyer seems to be more fascinated with how beautifully and perfectly he can reorganize the law than with how he can ensure the retention of prescience or the original meaning of the law. Law interpretation thus seems to have turned into philosophical aesthetics.

This tendency results in a great disadvantage to the ability to fulfill law's fundamental function—prescience. Detailed interpretation is most likely to give an interpretation outside the plain meaning of law and thus weaken the prescience of law as well as the degree of definitude of legal terminology.

In this respect, too, the Japanese notion of law differs from the Western notion from the very starting point. Westerners contend that the meaning of law should be definite, whereas the Japanese basically hold that the terminology of law should be indefinite and variable.

INDEFINITUDE OF THE "NORM" OF LAW

The Japanese people also differ greatly from Western peoples in the degree of strictness with which they regard the norm of law. In the traditional American and Western thinking, the norms of law are always put in contraposition against each other, and "legal process" exists in a relationship of tension between "that which ought to be" (*Sollen*) and "that which actually is" (*Sein*). This dualism of ideal and reality is not peculiar to law; it underlies the European religions (absolute separation of God from Man) and moral (of which Kant's moral philosophy is typical). Dualism regarding law is but one aspect of this current of thought.

In this dualism, *Sollen* and *Sein*, or law and social reality, are in contraposition against each other, and the *Sollen* of norm becomes definite. This dualism in law finds a most impressive expression in the saying *Fiat justitia pereat mundus* (Let justice be done, though the world should perish).

The basic principle of dualism is that, as far as law is acknowledged as effective, man should work on reality by means of law and that there must be no compromise between the two. One of the most pertinent examples is the U.S.'s Volstead Act of 1919. Though the ban on alcoholic consumption was extremely unrealistic, the Government continued an ineffectual fight against brewing and sale of liquor, once the law had been enacted.

It is true that even Western society, morality or law, when unable to counter the pressure of the reality of society, often adjusts itself in compromise. This is an unavoidable phenomenon. Nevertheless, in people's consciousness and thought, the dualistic correlation between *Sollen* and *Sein* is absolute, and a compromise with, or an adjustment to, reality does not take the form of piecemeal concession as in Japanese society. Rather, the process of compromise seems to be continual, accompanied by varied processes in creating confidence in the justifiability of such compromise, but only after confronting resistance.

Japan has little or no tradition of such dualism in which ideal and reality are in strict contraposition. God is not an existence that transcends the human being; man becomes god or Buddha when he dies. A temple or shrine is often built to the memory of a prominent dead person. For example, Tōshō-gū Shrine in Nikko, north of Tokyo, is dedicated to the first Tokugawa Shogun, who established the Tokugawa Shogunate. Tōgō Shrine is dedicated to Admiral Tōgō Heihachirō who crushed the Russian Fleet in a battle in the Japan Sea in one of the crucial showdowns of the Russo-Japanese War in 1904-5. In prewar Japan, emperors were revered as living gods, and even today the heads of certain religious sects are "living gods" for their believers.

By the same token between moral *Sollen* and law, or between human spirit and the reality of social life, there exists no relationship of absolute opposition. Compromise between the two is presupposed. Strict application of social norms in the name of law or moral code to their opposite number—the reality of social life—is criticized in Japan as an uncompromising act or a cruel attitude that shows little consideration for more human sentiments. Popular and prominent judges in Japanese history are those who have displayed humane pliability in rendering decisions. This pliable attitude appears in many legal processes. Perhaps some examples can clarify the concept of pliability.

When disputes arise between two parties regarding right and duty, they are settled through *wakai* (amicable reconciliation) in most cases in a way somewhat different from Western practice. In a dispute between A and B over the ownership of a certain tract of land, for instance, the land must belong to either A or B in the eyes of the law, and the court must decide which is to be the owner. However, in actual court cases the judge often intervenes between A and B to force a compromise. Such amicable reconciliation is often strongly recommended even when the land is obviously the possession of one party.

In the Western dualistic thinking, the court must award the case to the party who is judged to be the owner, and that party must be able to claim his property. In Japan, however, a claim to total ownership is often regarded as exceptionally covetous; the party to whom the case is awarded is forced to concede to some degree even if he is obviously the rightful owner.

In disputes over leased land or rented housing which account for the greatest percentage of all postwar cases, the legal norm has often been watered down in actual legal process. For example, even when a lessor can demand eviction due to the non-payment of rent on the part of the lessee, the dispute often winds up in compromise through strong recommendation of the court, and the lessee can continue to occupy the house, or evacuate upon receipt of a considerable amount of compensation for removal from the lessor.

In a strict application of the legal norm, the lessor has no obligation to pay compensation for removal or renew the once-terminated lease contract. It is true that this situation more or less reflected the dearth of housing during postwar years. Yet, the housing shortage does not explain the whole story. Undeniably, such a method of settlement largely reflects the unique Japanese notion of law. Even when a house or land is illegally occupied, the owner has had to pay compensation for removal, or has been forced to renew the contract, through conciliation.

Such a phenomenon takes place in executing the traffic control laws as well. Designed to prevent physical danger to both body and life, such laws should be strictly followed. However, strict observance and rigid punishment of infringements are seen only during the traffic safety week. During other weeks, control is relatively lenient. To put it more bluntly, regular weeks virtually turn into "traffic unsafety weeks."

What is common among these phenomena is the fact that people or even judges and police do not regard the legal form as determinate. Undistinguished from reality, the legal norm is forced to compromise with the reality of social life to a great extent. The Japanese regard with disfavor the strict application and execution of law by rote as they feel it to be unrealistic and too rigorous.

In Japan, law is often compared to a treasured sword handed down from generation to generation in a family. The sword is not for killing; it is rather an item used for decoration or as a prestige symbol. Likewise, law is not for controlling social life; it is a mere decoration. This analogy illustrates how the Japanese law, even though elaborately systematized, fails to make its influence felt in actual social life.

CULTURAL AND SOCIAL BASES FOR THE JAPANESE NOTION OF LAW

It is hoped that the foregoing chapters have helped clarify the historical and social background of the Japanese notion of law and right. This chapter will summarize that background in three categories of causes.

First is the influence of Tokugawa-era values (feudalism) that prevailed throughout the country over nearly three centuries before the Meiji Restoration. As stated before, Japan underwent a rapid Westernization after the Restoration in 1868 and emerged as a modern state at least as far as education and military systems as well as economic, political, and legal institutions are concerned.

The fast introduction of alien culture did help wrap Japan with the robe of a modern nation, but alien influence was slow to penetrate to the core of national life. Moreover, alien culture often runs up against influence of the feudal system with its vertical and order-and-subordination human relationships, which during the Tokugawa era penetrated every nook and corner of the nation. A family was composed of a head and his dependents, including wife, children, and other members. In the employer-and-employee relationship, the employer was in a patriarchal position holding absolute predominance over his employees.

In the social structure, a caste system with four ranks—warriors, farmers, artisans, and tradesmen—was firmly established. In the nation's political structure, an order-and-subordination system took root.

At the dawn of the Meiji era the Japanese people had been accustomed to such a class system for nearly three centuries. Small wonder that the introduction of a modern Western legal system based on right into an order-and-obedience-oriented society did not succeed fully.

Employment relationships were perceived in terms of order-and-subordination rather than right. Wages came not as a right which employees could claim but rather from the employer's benevolence. To offer labor was something the employee had the honor of being permitted to do by the employer.

Such a notion was especially strong in continuous contracts for employment, land and house rental, or tenancy, as well as in family relationships. The deeper-rooted Tokugawa-era notion was one of the major causes of the Japanese double legal notion, i.e., the disparity between law on the level of court, and law on the level of actual life.

Concepts of American democracy introduced in the wake of Japan's surrender in World War II have drastically changed the Japanese legal notion and democratized, in particular, people's legal notion in the aforementioned continuous contracts and family relations. Under the stringent surveillance of the state, workers' claims to wages and better working conditions have been strengthened.

Since the right to strike has been legalized, labor unions have been organized in most large and medium enterprises and national federations formed. Workers have awakened to the strong sense of right, and have become less hesitant to act according to their perception of it. Thus, Japan's labor scene has developed into a condition similar to that in the United States. This new pattern is a significant departure from the typical prewar labor relationship which smacked heavily of Tokugawa-era values.

A change has also taken place in the areas of land and house rental and tenancy as well as in family life where husband and wife together have taken over the family "headship," in the development of the nuclear family.

What is most responsible for Japan's ability to make these radical changes is the fact that in the process of taking in modern Western civilization over the seventy-seven years after the Meiji Restoration, Japan had a cultural foundation strong enough to absorb the foreign influence of American democracy. The all-out compulsory education system, widely diffused college and university education, and vigorous absorption of, and assimilation to, alien culture helped build up the foundation during these nearly four scores of years. Rapidly increasing exchanges with foreign countries in postwar years have also facilitated the changes.

Also responsible for the major changes in the legal notion is the fact that ever-growing Japanese enterprises have reached a point where conventional paternalism in management-and-labor relationships is no longer sufficient. Nevertheless, deep-rooted values have not been completely wiped out; they continue to occupy a part of the Japanese notion of law as exemplified in the lifetime employment system—an embodiment of the feudalistic paternalism—and the bonus system which is not a right in the strict sense.

The second main influence on the development of the Japanese type legal notion lies in the Japanese tradition of giving priority to non-legal social norms. Of course, law is not omnipotent in controlling social life, as indicated in a legal saying to the effect that law is the minimum of morality, or, in another saying, "A good lawyer, a bad neighbor." However, Japanese tend to pay greater respect to non-legal norms than do Western peoples, and Japanese also tend to feel ashamed of directly resorting to law in deciding their actions. This tendency partly explains why the Japanese notion of law may seem lukewarm by Western standards and why there has formed a dualistic legal notion.

The Japanese tradition of valuing non-legal social norms has been created by many causes:

The first is the influence of Confucianism as the spiritual mainstay of Japanese feudalism. Confucian thought values autonomy and obedience and has made the Japanese people view with contempt the heteronomous legal norm.

The second reason for Japanese non-legal social norms is that of Japanese racial unity. Living in a limited space, on islands quite surrounded by seas on all sides, the Japanese people have spontaneously developed a common morality, customs, and language as well as common patterns of thought. This homogenous situation well befitted Japan's actual life style. In contracts or in other legal relations, people could expect—tacitly—a common conclusion or result, without taking the trouble to stipulate minutely contracts or laws.

The third cause is related to racial unity. Unlike Western societies, the Japanese sociey lacks, comparatively, the long history of bloody and savage struggles. The necessity for right or law is not so keenly felt without the catalyst of life-and-death strife. Among different races or even within a single race, law makes the only common basis for adjustment or prevention of conflict when people are belligerent. The Japanese happily had the choice to be less belligerent thanks to the relatively mild climate and comfortable environment of the Japanese islands.

These three factors are the reasons why the Japanese have had few opportunities of coming into contact with, or little necessity for, legal norm in their lives; these factors have been offered to explain in depth the second influence in the development of the Japanese legal notion, priority given to non-legal norms.

The third influence on the formation of Japanese legal notion lies in the construction of the Japanese language. As pointed out before, the Japanese notion of legal norm is "indefinite." The Japanese linguistic construction does not engender clear-cut expression. One of Japan's literary giants, Tanizaki Junichirō (1886-1965), once compared a passage from the original *Genji Monogatari* (The Tale of Genji) with the translation (6 vols., 1923-33) rendered by Arthur D. Waley (1889-1966). As Tanizaki wrote in his comparison:

> . . .six lines of the original Japanese passage have been extended to thirteen lines in the English. No wonder the English version has many explanatory words that are missing in the original. . . . In other words, the English version is more precise and has little ambiguity. The original leaves unspecified the points that can be understood without elucidation, whereas the English translation attempts to be more specific even in such points which are clear enough (to Japanese). . . . The English way of expression does clarify the meaning, with the result of limiting and shallowing it. . . . Therefore, our men of letters spare such useless efforts and intentionally use implicative words that can connote more than one meaning. They supplement the rest with sensory elements. . . tones, type face, or rhythms. . . . In other words, relatively fewer suggestive words stir up readers' imagination, urging readers to complement what is missing. The writer's pen works only to stir readers' imaginations. The Western manner of writing is to pin down meanings as much as possible, allowing no shadows and leaving no room for readers' imagination.*

This explanation helps shed some light on what has been described as the indefinitude of the Japanese legal notion. The Japanese writing does not convey definitely restricted meaning and content. Rather, by the use of the words that express the central idea, it suggests other meaning and content, and, as a result, the surroundings of the expressed words become obscure and changeable depending upon the recipient of the message.

This is what is called *ganchiku* (implication or suggestiveness). Writings which use ganchiku are highly regarded, as the Japanese writers often attempt to use this implicit style. As Tanizaki pointed out, articles without ganchiku, as penned by Western writers, are branded as poor in quality. This characteristic of the Japanese language cannot possibly be consistent with legal wording which gives utmost priority to clarity and qualification. Articles written by lawyers have often been criticized as examples of bad writing.

One example of this criticism was seen in the case of the lawsuit about the Japanese version of *Lady Chatterley's Lover*. Japanese writers unanimously criticized not the translation, but rather the wording used in the indictment

---

**Bunshō Tokuhon* (Reader of Composition) from the Collected Works of Tanizaki Junichirō, Vol. XXI, page 42 ff., Chūō Kōron Sha, 1958.

written by the prosecutor. The reason for the criticism is obvious from Tanizaki's comparison of styles.

This linguistic habit of ganchiku is closely related to the way the Japanese perceive social norms. Usually, Japanese grasp the core of a social norm relatively clearly and recognize the surroundings as being unclear and indefinite; and, they determine their behavior accordingly.

Thus, to summarize, these three influences of Tokugawa-era values (feudalism), the priority given to non-legal norms, and the Japanese language, have been instrumental in creating the indefinitude which pervades the Japanese notion of law.

THE JAPANESE NOTION OF LAW IN MAJOR LEGAL AREAS

LEGAL NOTION OF CONTRACT

A contract is an agreement made among more than two persons to form, modify, or eliminate right and duty among themselves. The contract system presupposes legal equality between parties concerned and is based on the private property system. In other words, modern contract law presupposes that formation, modification, or elimination of private property rights among equals are effected only when the parties agree of their own accord.

As capitalistic economy is possible only with the exchange and distribution of commodities, a contract is an indispensable factor in its successful function. Today, contracts are the major source of almost all kinds of rights and duties and have highly varied aspects. As the source of change (formation, modification, and elimination) of right, a contract is the main medium for capitalistic transactions. Naturally, the most important requirement of modern law—clarification and definitude of right and duty—applies to contracts. Hence, the "prescience" of the contents of right and duty involved in a contract becomes an indispensable requirement for their success.

This paper will now explore the questions of what notion the Japanese people have of the act of concluding contracts in their social lives, and what notion they have of the contents of the rights and duties arising therefrom.

Japanese notion of the act of concluding contracts. From the standpoint of modern contract law, it is necessary to specify when and how a contract is made, and to clarify whether the contract is in effect or not. This should be preceded by another process—clarification of whether there has been an agreement between the parties.

Contract law allows only the alternatives of whether or not the contract has been effected—"all or nothing." It allows no intermediate ground and no ambiguity. Contract laws of many countries stipulate many means to specify and minimize any possible uncertainties. Based on modern concepts, Japanese contract law is no exception. It allows only the alternative of whether or not the contract in question has been effected. However, in many cases, Japanese people do not perceive contracts only in terms of this alternative. Hence, more often than not, there arises a considerable discrepancy between their notion of contract law *in social life* and their basic notion of contract law as law. There are many examples of this discrepancy in everyday life.

One example concerns the method of transactions between publishing companies and their wholesalers and retailers. The conventional method is called "sale on consignment" (in which actual sales are settled later and unsold copies can be returned to the publisher); the stocking of a store at the risk of the wholesaler or retailer, as practiced in other ordinary transactions is quite the exception in the book business. One reason for this practice is that book wholesalers and retailers cannot afford sufficient inventory. Another reason is that neither side objects to the fact that purchase-and-sale contracts for the merchandise in question (books) are not totally binding.

A similar indefinitude exists in the relationship between department stores and wholesalers. It is said that department stores employ three major methods of stocking goods from wholesalers. The first, called ordinary stocking, is an ordinary "buying up" (purchase of goods at the buyers' risk). Stock in trade becomes an asset of the department store; the store has no right to return unsold articles and has to bear losses including decrease in quantity or number of articles.

The second method is called stocking on consignment. The goods become an entire possession of the department store as is the case with ordinary stocking. The store bears the losses from decrease in quantity or number, but it can return unsold articles.

The third method is called "consumption stocking," or "sales stocking," in which stock in trade belongs to the wholesaler and the department store pays for sold articles only. The losses from decrease in quantity or number are shouldered by the store.

Though these three methods of stocking are clearly distinguishable from each other, actual stocking contracts made by the department stores are not so definite. When goods arrive, the department store only issues a slip of receipt, with the seal of receipt stamped. It appears to be an unconditional purchase, but in reality the store can return unsold articles in most cases through negotiations with the other party. This means that there is an uncertainty as to whether the articles are sold or consigned.

Though the situation has been rapidly changing lately, such uncertainty remains in the transactions of even major companies involved in international trade. In many transaction contracts among big companies the parties are not always clearly aware when a contract has actually been effected. In one example, two major trading firms once brought suit against each other, the issue being the time the contract in question was effected, i.e., if the time was when the parties reached the agreement or when they documented the results of the agreement. On this issue the Civil Code is explicit; a contract is effected at the time of the agreement unless otherwise specified, and there is no need to render the contract in writing. However, the parties in this case entered the contract without even considering this provision.

This case illustrates the peculiar Japanese notion of contract. Japanese social life does not perceive the formation of a contract in terms of "alternative" as demanded by the Civil Code. Herein lies the gap between legal notion from the *judicial viewpoint* and legal notion in people's general *social life*.

Japanese legal notion of contents of a contract. Next comes the question of Japanese legal notion of the contents of a contract. Again there exists a similar gap. A typical example of the gap can be seen in a construction contract. Fundamentally, a construction contract calls for the contractor to have a definite duty to complete the contracted work at the contracted cost. More often than not, however, the work is delayed and construction expenses are increased. It seems as if the contractor takes the postponement for granted. If the client should turn down the contractor's demand for an increase in construction expenses, the work is left half completed. The client anticipates a demand for an increase in cost as well as a delay. This is an example of the indefinite Japanese legal notion of the contents of a contract.

The contents of many Japanese contracts for construction or other projects are highly simplified. Foreigners often wonder whether simple terms so prevalent in Japanese contracts can cover complicated contents. But, Japanese tend to disfavor detailed contract terms, and Japanese lawyers are no exception. One of the difficulties a young lawyer faces when he starts practicing law is the gap between the concept of contract he learned as a law student or as a legal trainee and the actual method of writing contracts. The young lawyer naturally attempts to work up a detailed agreement but his client and his senior partner are not likely to approve that kind of contract. Why is this the case?

One reason may be the Japanese preference for simplicity. The greatest reason, however, is the desire to leave room for construing the contract in whichever way is most advantageous in case of a dispute over the terms of the contract. A definite and detailed contract does not allow for flexible interpretation when a dispute takes place. Therefore, an attempt is made to include the fewest possible terms in any set of circumstances. This attempt is motivated not only by the above-mentioned calculations but also by linguistic habits mentioned earlier.

No matter what the reasons, the Japanese notion of contract makes the contract terms highly indistinct. The terms become ambiguous, and are not always explicit as to which parties have what rights. This, then, summarizes the general Japanese way of making contracts.

What do Japanese do when a dispute arises from an indistinct contract? Customarily, a Japanese contract ends with a clause, "Should a dispute arise from this contract, the parties thereto shall settle the dispute in accordance with the principle of good faith." Instead of directly resorting to the principle of modern Western law provided in the Civil Code, the parties desire to settle the dispute according to many non-legal ethical codes. This is a manifestation of the aforementioned Japanese tendency to respect the non-legal social norms. Though this is a laudable custom in itself, it is far removed from the principle of modern contract law.

An outcome of the high respect for the non-legal social norm may be a serious disadvantage to a party to a contract among urban residents who have less personal contact with each other, and hence less common ground to settle disputes on terms of good faith, especially when the other party abides by the original contract principle. Such a dispute, when unsolved by the good faith clause, is settled by lawsuit. In this case, the court handles the case according to principles different from the legal notion the parties hold in their social lives. This discrepancy is one more feature of the Japanese legal notion regarding the contract terms. (Yet, there is room for the Japanese legal notion in social life to be put to work in means of mediation even at the stage of lawsuit, as elaborated later in ''Legal Notion in Civil Litigation,'' p. 298).

Undoubtedly, Americans are likely to feel quite uncertain if the contract terms (right and duty) are indefinite, and if the terms of a contract are to be decided later through negotiations. The Japanese people do not feel uneasy; to them it sounds more uncertain to make a contract definite and inflexible from the outset. Japanese regard it as safer to leave room for a modified interpretation of the contract on the basis of good faith of the parties concerned because of the changeability of social conditions even after the contract is concluded.

This way of thinking is the result of Japanese ethnic homogeneity and the resultant confidence that there will be little difference in value judgments among the parties because of common custom and common cultural understandings. Again, they expect much from extrajudicial social norms which are above legal norms. This expectation of conformity to social mores is only rarely betrayed in the contracts in force among Japanese. A few exceptions to this practice are insurance contracts or banking contracts which place emphasis upon uniformity; they are usually made in the detailed American manner.

However, since the end of World War II, the singularity of the Japanese legal notion has resulted in bitter experiences for Japanese businessmen transacting with American corporations. The American notion of law, in a diametrical contrast with the Japanese notion, demands that a contract should be rendered in detail and the terms thereof abided by most strictly. No amicable settlement with the slightest deviation from the terms is allowed. However, because of the Japanese habit of resolving disputes with ''good faith,'' the Japanese used to enter contracts with Americans without fully studying the contract terms and thus the Japanese parties often found themselves forced to meet strict contract terms in cases of dispute, and often ''suffered considerable damage.''

Many years of bitter experiences have made Japanese companies particularly cautious about international transactions. They have developed a practice of asking experienced attorneys to prepare and examine the contract terms beforehand and prepare themselves to meet the contract terms from the outset.

In domestic transactions, however, the traditional notion of contract still prevails, but major companies, with few exceptions, have come to hire attorneys and seek their professional opinions in advance. Small- and medium-sized companies, however, cannot always afford their own attorneys because of lack of financial strength. They are now learning the same lessons large companies have learned in dealing with American companies and the American legal notion.

LEGAL NOTION OF OWNERSHIP

The Japanese ownership system introduced after the dawn of the Meiji era is the private property system based on principles of "modern ownership." Modern ownership is characterized by granting the right "to control the property absolutely and exclusively" to the possessor of the property. If a house belongs to A, for instance, the ownership of people other than A cannot simultaneously cover the house, and any act by others that may infringe A's ownership can be absolutely excluded.

This principle is acknowledged by the Japanese Civil Code. However, the notion of ownership held by Japanese in their social life is not one of absolute control. Since the end of the war, there have been many instances of eviction from houses or lands, and removing the evictee usually has cost the owner much time and trouble. Moreover, the police avoid interference in such civil cases. Cases which have been brought to the court have often taken more than ten years to settle.

Willingly or unwillingly, the owner of a house or a piece of land pays compensation for removal to the evictee, who then uses the money to rent or buy another house or land in another place. From the point of view of the principle of ownership, compensation for removal of an evictee is quite out of the question. This phenomenon of the Japanese eviction process is quite difficult to understand for Americans, who are usually quite sensitive about trespass of private property, but it is partly explicable by the dearth of housing immediately after the war. No matter how opaque to Americans, however, this phenomenon certainly illustrates that the Japanese perception of ownership is not one of absolute control.

If a land- or houseowner demands eviction of a tenant in accordance with law, he is criticized in society as covetous and therefore is put to shame publicly. On such occasions, the Japanese notion of law requires a solution between the tenant and the landlord or houseowner which is of a patriarchal nature. In other words, priority over legal norm is given to paternalism. (Here, the paternalism is forced by the tenant, and is not a normal representation of the Japanese legal notion.)

Such phenomena also take place in the relationship between the management of Japanese companies and their shareholders. A company is certainly not owned by its executives; the management only administers the company in trust for the shareholders. The fact is, however, that the executives often capitalize on their position and spend company money on meals, drinks, and trips with the plausible excuse of "perquisite." In so doing, they do not feel guilty, and take their actions almost for granted. The shareholders, on their part, do not pay much attention to the executives. On the contrary, shareholders who take an interest in management are often regarded as nosy, and are shunned as a nuisance to the company. It seems as if the executives are the real owners of the company. This is another example of the indistinctness of the Japanese notion of law.

Until such acts by executives surface as exposure of tax evasion or other legal issues and until the executives are prosecuted for embezzlement or breach of faith, they fail to realize what they have done. It is often the case with medium- and small-sized companies that personal property is quite indistinguishable from company property. This points out the fact that the Japanese have a notion of ownership as if all were members of a family.

LEGAL NOTION IN CIVIL LITIGATION

Civil lawsuits aim at solving disputes over rights in private law between individuals or between individuals and public organizations (including the state) in compliance with legal norms. There is little room for extrajudicial social norms to work. Consequently, the results of the solution by the court often deviate from the notion of law which Japanese hold in their daily lives.

Decisions in civil lawsuits are absolute—all or nothing; the plaintiff wins or loses. However, as described before, the Japanese tend to dislike such absolute decisions. Even in civil lawsuits, the Japanese tend to seek intermediate solutions, which are not recognized by judicial norms—solutions through friendship, paternalism, obligation, and faith. This notion of law in society exerts a great influence upon the Japanese civil lawsuit system.

By tradition, Japanese resort to *chōtei* (mediation) and *wakai* (amiable reconciliation) to settle disputes. Though referring to legal norms, these practices call for an amicable settlement of disputes through mutual concession by the parties. The minimal requisite for this type of solution is an agreement between the parties. Only when an agreement has been reached can a solution contradictory to legal norm be tolerated. Japanese prefer this means of solution. Opposition to solution by this method may be criticized as merciless, with the same social loss of face as alluded to previously.

As this means of solution does not depend upon the legal norm (all or nothing), its basis is nothing but the extrajudicial social norm that is applicable to the parties. When a solution is difficult, a basic Japanese thought—truth exists in the middle—goes to work for a fifty-fifty solution. Undeniably, this manner of solution has been popularized and encouraged by the Japanese notion of law that has been referred to so often. In the United States, it is not a popular method of solution. Though they seem to avoid courtsuit if possible, the Japanese usually do resort to arbitration.

The Japanese have little notion of *chūsai* (arbitration), and some Japanese do not distinguish *chūsai* from *wakai*. Even professionals occasionally confuse these two ideas. Arbitration is conducted by the state-designated judges, whereas mediation assures the same solution as that by the state courts, except that decisions are made by private "judges" and the procedure is more autonomous than an ordinary court decision.

A solution by arbitrators calls for "all or nothing" as is the case with a court decision, and is reached according to legal norm. It does not seek an intermediate solution as mediation does. The reasons why mediation (*chōtei*) and conciliation (*wakai*) are often resorted to in Japan and why arbitration (*chūsai*) is hardly used in domestic disputes lie in the Japanese distaste for court-like solutions by arbitration. Arbitration is resorted to only in the case of international transactions and then only because there is no better way of settlement.

Apart from the aforementioned points, the reason why the Japanese prefer solutions by mediation and conciliation to solutions by civil court decisions lies in the patriarchal sentiments that continue to cling to the value system in Japan. By custom, Japanese regard it as laudable to place emphasis on obligations, to save the face of mediators, and to agree to whatever settlement the mediators have worked out for them. In many cases, mediators are family heads, landlords, community leaders, seniors at the office, or benefactors of the parties, and thus it is virtually impossible, because of social pressure, to reject the mediator's decision. This is in contrast to judicial mediation in which the court appoints a mediator irrespective of personal relationships, so that the force of social pressure is not used to help solve the dispute.

The title "mediator" in Japanese carries a patriarchal nuance, indicating that mediators settle disputes from the point of view of patriarchal considerations. Parties to mediated disputes feel obliged for the trouble to which the mediators have gone and agree to whatever solution is reached. The ingrained nature of these values is seen in the fact that problems of this means of settling disputes are often taken as themes in Kabuki plays and not infrequently move audiences to tears.

Moreover, even though judicial mediation is quite free from such personal connections, it more or less involves the traditional Japanese feeling toward mediators.

Even in administrative lawsuits (which are treated as a special form of civil litigation in Japan), the state often takes the legislative position of preferring mediation to lawsuit, with the result of frequent use of mediation. Even in this kind of lawsuit, however, the bureaucrats often demonstrate a measure of the patriarchal attitude toward the people.

The flexibility of the Japanese system of mediation is certainly one of the commendable aspects of Japanese social inclinations, but at the same time feelings of obligation to mediators often supress the free exchange of opinions so necessary to modern decision making.

LEGAL NOTION OF FAMILY LAW

The traditional Japanese notion of law remains most influential in the realm of family law. When Japan adopted German family law after the Meiji Restoration, the new laws met with tough opposition. Though the new laws were a portion of the Civil Code, the family law came to be accepted and enforced much later than the other laws. Even then, the family law which was put into effect assumed a Japanese coloring as it underwent major revisions to enable it to retain the Japanese family tradition.

For instance, the family law retained the ideas of "family head," and the "family register system," institutions of the Tokugawa era. Only after the introduction of American family law after World War II did things begin to change markedly. The American system helped establish the system for sharing property between husband and wife, and insured the wife's position of equality even in the home, all as a part of a marked democratization of family life.

At the same time, primogeniture was rescinded and replaced with the equal succession system. The grounds for divorce have been strictly stipulated by law, and divorce by a husband's mere whim is prohibited. A wife's right to demand solatia and alimony and her right to raise children on the occasion of divorce have been reinforced. These improvements represent a considerable departure from the prewar situation.

However, compared with other legal areas, family law has been unquestionably the slowest in changing and still retains heavy overtones of Tokugawa times. Though the reasons for divorce have been set by law, the system of divorce by agreement has often resulted in great disadvantages to the wife. Indeed, Japan has been called by some the husband's paradise for divorce. This unfortunate situation is partly attributable to wives' general lack of legal knwoledge.

Divorce is also decided in other cases by mediators designated by the Family Court in what is called divorce by mediation. However, this type of divorce, though intended to protect wives' interests, is not always as protective as is purported by the system. There are two main obstacles to the effective functioning of the divorce mediation system. One is that mediators often force upon the wife divorce conditions that are favorable to the husband.

The other obstacle is that women mediators designated for a case to protect the wife's interests are, in most cases, elderly women who began their married lives in, and still retain, prewar values. By contrast, wives who seek divorce are usually much younger people who have undergone their spiritual development in democratic post-war years. There is a great difference in values between these two generations of women.

Female mediators sometimes go so far as to allow themselves the sport of boasting to the frustrated young couples how happy their own married lives have been. For these reasons, the rights of the wife in divorce cases cannot be said to be fully protected.

The same situation applies to solatium and alimony. The amounts granted in Japan are quite small when compared with those of the United States.

Until a few years ago, the Japanese men could obtain divorce for only about one thousand dollars, and in most cases the payment was made in installments. What is more, there is no punishment for the failure to pay solatium or alimony. The means for collection of such monies in Japan are quite imperfect.

The system of sharing property between husband and wife has also been legalized. The law stipulates that the property owned by the wife before marriage belongs to her and the property acquired after marriage is to be shared equally by the couple. However, a tendency still prevails toward regarding even the premarital property as the husband's, to say nothing of postmarital property.

Primogeniture has been rescinded, but, especially in non-urban areas, the equal succession system is not followed as closely as it should be. Even in cities, a guilty conscience often accompanies the claim for equal succession.

This kind of gap between family law and the general public's legal notion is very wide. This is why the Japanese notion of law remains to be radically changed, with much to be improved in the legal area of family law.

16

The Relationship between Chinese Law and Common Law in Malaysia, Singapore, and Hong Kong

M. B. Hooker

THERE is a considerable body of literature on the relationship between common law and various systems of personal laws especially in the Asian context. My only excuse for adding yet another account is this: A technical legal description of this relationship, focusing on such topics as marriage, divorce, inheritance, and so on, adds a real and important dimension to the study of culture contact. Except in Hong Kong, common law is no longer the dominant political system; it has become, with local variations, "government law" in the territories under consideration. Since law is the instrument most often used in the implementation of new government policies affecting family matters, for example, it seems important that some attempt be made to describe the techniques of interaction and to set out the present law as accurately as possible. Hopefully this essay will serve as skeleton reference material on the relation between these two systems of law. To accomplish this aim I will: (a) describe the ways in which the common law has been adapted so as to take account of Chinese law, (b) state the "principles of Chinese law" which the courts have formulated in the course of this adaptation, and (c) note the points at which the respective courts in the three territories have differed in their interpretation regarding the content of Chinese law.

The materials on which this paper is based are the relevant statutes and judicial decisions of the territories, plus, in the case of the former Straits Settlements, a report on Chinese marriages (1926) and, in the case of Hong Kong, a report on Chinese law and custom (1953). A cautionary note needs to be inserted here with respect to Singapore and Malaysia. These states, as now constituted, share a legacy of common law but the respective histories of this law are dissimilar. Singapore and the present states of Penang and Malacca in Malaysia were once part of the colony of the Straits Settlements. The states of Perak, Pahang, Selangor and Negri Sembilan were once part of the Federated Malay States. The remaining states of Malaysia were part of the Unfederated Malay States. The present federal states of East Malaysia, Sabah and Sarawak, were once the colony of North Borneo. The judicial histories of these areas vary and where the variation is relevant it is pointed out in the body of this paper.

The Legal Bases of Chinese Law

The Straits Settlements (Singapore, Penang and Malacca). These three settlements which came under the control first of the East India Company, later of the India Office, and finally of the Colonial Office were provided with a series of charters known as Charters of Justice. The Charters (dated 1807, 1826, and 1855) provided for

Reprinted, by permission, from the *Journal of Asian Studies*, Vol. XXVIII, No. 4, August 1969.

the setting up of courts and a judicial service: they also provided that the law in each of the settlements was to be English law and was to apply to Europeans and to natives in "so far as the several religions, manners and customs of the inhabitants will admit." This interpretation of this phrase and the decisions as to how far English statute applied in the colony have resulted in a series of cases which are well-known and need no further comment here.[1]

In addition to the provisions in the Charters, Chinese law has received a basis for its application through the use of private international law principles.[2] This is mainly illustrated in cases involving polygamous marriages, adoptions, and legitimations. In the case of marriage, the rule at common law has always been that marriage is monogamous.[3] However, the courts in the Straits Settlements have decided that since it was lawful for a Chinese domiciled in China to take a secondary wife, at least before May, 1931,[4] then the Chinese as a whole are polygamous.[5]

In respect of a husband's rights over his wife's property, the common law gave certain specific rights.[6] But the courts in the Straits Settlements held that a marriage contracted between Chinese according to Chinese rites conferred no marital rights on the husband with respect to his wife's property.[7] So far as legitimacy was concerned this was determined by birth in lawful wedlock (common law) or by virtue of statute. But in the Straits Settlements the status of legitimacy was held to depend upon the law of China. Legitimation likewise depended upon the domicile of the father: in the case of a father possessing a Chinese domicile, legitimation by subsequent monogamous or polygamous marriage was possible.[8] Somewhat inconsistently, the courts have rejected legitimation by subsequent recognition.[9]

The application of private international law principles in the Straits Settlements

---

1 Summarized in R. St. J. Braddell, *The Law of the Straits Settlements: A Commentary* 2 vols (2nd ed., Singapore, 1931). See vol. I, 62–94. Attention is directed especially to the following judicial decisions: *R.* v. *Willans,* 3 Ky. 16; *Choa Choon Neoh* v. *Spottiswoode,* 1 Ky. 216; *Ong Cheng Neo* v. *Yeap Cheah Neo and ors.* 1 Ky. 326. *In the goods of Khoo Chow Sen,* 2 Ky. Ecc. Rs. 22; *Tan Kiong* v. *Ou Phaik* (1900) 5 S.S.L.R. 77.

2 The earliest example of this basis is a statement by Maxwell C. J. in *Chulas* v. *Kolson* (1877) Leicester's Reports, 462 where the Chief Justice said: "their own laws or usages must be applied to them on the same principles and with the same limitations as foreign law is applied by our courts to foreigners and foreign transactions."

3 *Hyde* v. *Hyde,* L.R. 1, P. & D. 130. The judge in this case, however, expressely limited the application of this principle to societies where polygamy is not recognized.

4 The Chinese Civil Code seems to have made some attempt to prohibit polygamy. *cf.* Book IV, Art., 985, ". . . a person who has a spouse may not marry again." The Code did not, however, place any restriction on the formalities required to celebrate a marriage except that there should be some ceremony, that the marriage should be open to the public, and that there be two or more witnesses. Art., 982. *cf.* J. V. Mills, "Marriage in England, Singapore, and China," 31 *Journal of Comparative Legislation and International Law* Series 3, Part II, 25–36 at p. 28. On the problems which Art., 985 raised for many Chinese *cf.* H. McAleavy, "Some Aspects of Marriage and Divorce in Communist China" in J.N.D. Anderson (ed.) *Family Law in Asia and Africa* (London 1968) pp. 73–89 at pp. 73–74. In *China Shiu Sui Ping* v. *Chan Din Tsang* [1958] H.K.L.R. 283, the Hong Kong court recognized a Chinese customary marriage which took place in China after May 1931. This marriage was recognized for divorce purposes as being "a Christian marriage or its civil equivalent," Hong Kong Divorce Ordinance 1952, s. 2.

5 *Khoo Hooi Leong* v. *Khoo Chong Yeok* [1930] A.C. 346 at 352. *Cheang Thye Pin* v. *Tan Ah Loy* [1920] A.C. 369. *Khoo Hooi Leong* v. *Khoo Hean Kwee* [1921] A.C. 529.

6 See C. H. Withers Payne. *The Law of Administration of and Succession to Estates in the Straits Settlements* (1932) 25 ff.

7 *Lim Chooi Hoon* v. *Chok Yoon Guan* (1893) 1 S.S.L.R. 72.

8 *Re Choo Eng Choon* (1911) 12 S.S.L.R. 120 at 224 ff.

9 *Khoo Hooi Leong* v. *Khoo Chong Yeok* [1930] A.C. 346.

was plagued by difficulties. By the very nature of the conflict, where one of the systems of law was unwritten or if written was subject to local modification, difficulties of proof were common. This difficulty was made greater by admitted local variations in Chinese law. Further, English conflict rules pre-supposed a relatively settled domicile and also the existence of a technical legal system not unduly affected by such matters as race or religion. Neither of these assumptions was fully justified in the Straits Settlements. This has led to some internal inconsistencies such as the recognition of legitimation by subsequent marriage but not by subsequent recognition.[10]

Finally the courts in the Straits Settlements have recognized Chinese law and custom on the ground of "natural justice." In the present context this appears to cover such matters as the interpretation of common law in dependent territories, the application or non-application of common law distinctions outside England, and the assumptions made by judges.[11] In Penang and Malacca this position remains unchanged, but in Singapore Chinese law now has no effect because of the provisions of the Women's Charter (Ordinance 18 of 1961, amended by Ordinance 9 of 1967).

The Federated and Unfederated Malay States. Generally, the law applicable in any Malay State at the time when it became subject to British protection remained in force notwithstanding the treaty. It was subject only to legislative amendment. There was local legislation in the Federated Malay States but not in the Unfederated States. The legislation was piecemeal and left many gaps which the judges attempted to fill as well as they could. The outstanding example of this is the Selangor case of *Re Yap Kwan Seng's Will*[12] where the judge had to consider whether the rule against perpetuities applied in that state. In the course of the judgment it was said[13] that the general law of England was never adopted in this state though English principles and models were utilized. The judge recognized the rule against perpetuities on the grounds of public policy and of comity with the laws of the Straits Settlements.[14]

Johore, an Unfederated Malay State, had adopted part of English law on the grounds of comity with the Federated States and the Straits Settlements. In addition the court found that an interpretation of the terms of Johore legislation demanded the use of common law principles.[15]

This brings us to the systems of legislation in the two classes of Malay States. In each of the Federated States there was legislation known variously as Orders in Council and Enactments.[16] The state legislation was published in a revised edition in 1935 and showed the law in force as of 31 December 1934.

In the case of the Unfederated States, each of them was governed by the laws of their respective State Councils. The legislation from these States has been irregular,

---

[10] For a summary of the whole topic of private international law principles in the Straits Settlements see J. V. Mills, "Marriage in England, Singapore, and China," 31 *Journal of Comparative Legislation and International Law* (1949) Series 3, Part II, 25–36.

[11] Examples of this can be found in *Carolis de Silva* v. *Tin Kim* (1904) 9 S.S.L.R. 8. *Cheng Ee Mun* v. *Look Chun Heng* [1962] M.L.J. cxxxvi (comment) and 411 (report).

[12] (1924) 4 F.M.S.L.R. 313.

[13] (1924) 4 F.M.S.L.R. 316–18.

[14] The courts have also applied rules of equity in the Federated Malay States. *Motor Emporium* v. *Arumugam* [1933] M.L.J. 276 at 278 (Selangor).

[15] *Goh Eng Seong* v. *Tay Keng Seow* [1935] M.L.J. 50.

[16] Negri Sembilan from 1883, Pahang from 1889, Perak and Selangor from 1877.

and only from Johore and Kedah are there revised editions of the laws. Authority on the hierarchy of precedent is sparse but in cases concerning Chinese law and custom the courts seem to have assumed a uniform body of Chinese custom and have given effect to Straits Settlements and Federated Malay States decisions.[17]

In only one of the states of Malaya, Perak, has there been any legislation in Chinese law. This is found in Perak Order in Council No. 23 of 1893 as amended by Order in Council No. 26 of 1895. This purported to lay down the substance of Chinese law in the State of Perak as to marriage, adoption, inheritance, and intestacy. This order has been considered in three cases. In *Yap Tham Thai alias Yap Fook Siong* v. *Low Hup Neo*[18] the court held that the estate of an intestate Chinese dying domiciled in Selangor should be distributed according to the principles set out in the Perak Order in Council as modified by local custom. In *Teh Suan* v. *Ang Thuan and anor.*[19] the court approved the order as stating the Chinese law of infancy. In *Tan Sim Neoh* v. *Soh Tien Hock*[20] the court approved the adoption of a son despite provisions of the order which provided to the contrary.

We can conclude that the legal basis of Chinese law in these states has been largely an *ad hoc* recognition by the courts with only minor legislative assistance. This is in strong contrast to the position in the Straits Settlements. Chinese law remains a valid system of personal law in these states today and it is almost completely case law.

Sabah, Sarawak and Brunei. The position in these states presents some contrast to legal bases in both the Straits Settlements and in the Malay States. In *Kho Leng Guan* v. *Kho Eng Guan*[21] the court stated the sources of law in Sarawak as:

(a) Orders or written laws enacted by or with the authority of the *Raja*.
(b) English law in so far as it is not modified by (a) and in so far as it is applicable to Sarawak.
(c) Certain law and custom of races indigenous to Sarawak including the Chinese. The court also said that whether or not Chinese law is to be admitted is a question which must be determined according to the rules of English law.

These general principles have been defined, expressly in respect of Chinese, in *Chan Bee Neo and ors.* v. *Ee Siok Choo.*[22] The court held that it would apply Chinese custom:

(a) When the custom is expressly regulated by a Sarawak Ordinance; or
(b) When the custom is expressly regulated by rules made under an Ordinance; or

---

[17] See the cases cited in the most recent decision on Chinese custom. *In Re Ding Do Ca decd.* [1966] M.L.J. 6. It was held, however, that the courts of the Federated Malay States had no jurisdiction to deal with issues affecting conjugal rights among the Chinese. *Choi Wai Ying* v. *Cheong Weng Chan and ors.* [1933] M.L.J. 301. See also *Lim Chye Peow* v. *Wee Boon Tek* (1871) 1 Ky. 236, but see *contra R.* v. *Loon: re Khu Lak Neoh* (1864) W.O.C. 39.

[18] (1922) 1 F.M.S.L.R. 383; (1925) 6 F.M.S.L.R. 13.

[19] (1922) 2 F.M.S.L.R. 43.

[20] (1922) 1 F.M.S.L.R. 336.

[21] [1928–41] S.C.R. 60.

[22] [1947] S.C.R. 1.

(c) Where the custom is recognized expressly or impliedly in a Sarawak Ordinance.[23]

The actual effect of these two decisions is illustrated in *Li Khoi Chin* v. *Su Ah Poh*[24] where it was held that the validity of a Chinese marriage in Sarawak is dependent upon registration. In a later case, *Chiew Boon Tong* v. *Goh Ah Pei and anor.*,[25] the court in Sarawak held that a marriage is not valid unless registered under the provisions of the Chinese Marriage Ordinance (cap. 74).

This brings us to a situation where there is direct legislative authority in the provisions of Chinese law. This is also the situation in Brunei.[26] So far as Chinese law is concerned there are, however, two reported cases which show elements of conflict. In *Liu Kui Tze* v. *Lee Shak Lian*[27] the High Court of Sarawak, North Borneo (as it then was), and Brunei had jurisdiction in divorce with respect to Chinese customary marriages on the following grounds:

(a) That the present court is the direct successor to the "Chinese Court" first set up by Order IX of 1911.
(b) That this jurisdiction has not been disturbed by any later order or enactment.
(c) That the practice of the former Resident's Courts has always been to take jurisdiction in respect of these marriages.

However, in *Lim Siew Yun* v. *Soong Ah Kaw*[28] the court in Brunei held that it had no jurisdiction on Chinese divorce on the ground that there was no legislation conferring such jurisdiction. The present position in these states thus remains somewhat obscure.

Hong Kong. The legal basis of Chinese law and custom in Hong Kong is set out in the Committee's Report[29] on pages 4–5 and pages 82–121. This can be summarized in the following propositions. First, that in view of the Supreme Court Ordinances (beginning with No. 15 of 1844 and ending with the Ordinance of 1873) the effect was to introduce English law as it was in 1843 as the general law of the Colony. The main question for determination is the construction of section 5 of the Ordinance of 1873 which provides that English law shall be the law of the colony except insofar as it is inapplicable to local circumstances or to the customs of its inhabitants or is modified by local legislation.[30] In Appendix I, (pp. 82–121) which is concerned with this question, the Committee considered Straits Settlements cases in opposition to Hong Kong cases. The Committee concluded (though not unanimously) that English law was the general law of the Colony.

The committee recommended, however, that it should not be applied if it would

---

[23] This was followed and applied in *Wong Teck Giak and anor.* v. *Ting Ni Moi* [1950] S.C.R. 1 and 39 (appeal).

[24] [1950] S.C.R. 17.

[25] [1956] S.C.R. 58.

[26] This state is not part of the Federation of Malaysia but has a special relationship to it.

[27] [1953] S.C.R. 85.

[28] [1960–63] S.C.R. 105.

[29] *Chinese Law and Custom in Hong Kong*. Report of a Committee appointed by the Governor in October 1948. (Hong Kong: Government Printer, February, 1953.)

[30] This is very similar to the provisions of the Straits Settlements Charters.

cause injustice or oppression (pp. 114–15) or if Chinese law *prima facie* applied (pp. 115–17). On the other hand Chinese law should not apply if it would lead to the application of some doctrine fundamentally opposed to the conceptions of English law (pp. 117–19). The committee recognized that both laws should be modified by local legislation and cited the judgments in *Ho Tsz Tsun* v. *Ho Au Shi & ors.*[31] and *Chan Shun Cho* v. *Chak Hok Ping*[32] as examples of this.

The various territories considered so far show some similarities and some differences in the attitudes of the courts to Chinese Law. The rest of this paper will be given over to description of the peculiar problems faced in each territory and problems common to all; and specifically the ways in which the courts have dealt with Chinese law and custom especially where they vary in their solutions.

The Extent and Scope of Chinese Custom

Before commencing with the substance of this section we should note the variable content of Chinese custom. The judicial decisions reported show that the courts, while using the words "Chinese custom" as a general term, have in fact been adjudicating upon somewhat localized rules as to marriage, divorce, adoption, etc. Indeed, this point emerges clearly if one compares, for example, the various Orders in Council (Perak Orders 23/1893 and 26/1895) and Reports on Chinese custom (Straits Settlements 1926 and Hong Kong 1953). This, of course, must seem perfectly obvious but the courts have sometimes been misled into regarding "expert evidence" or that body of laws known as the *Ta Tsing Lu Li* as stating a body of regulation common to all Chinese.[33] Bearing this caution in mind we may consider the specific fields in which Chinese law and the common law have interacted.

The Money-Loan Association "Hwei."[34] A *hwei* is a group of individuals who join together for the purpose of contributing money to a common pool over a fixed period of time. The contributions are made at meetings at which bidding for the contributions paid at that meeting takes place. The person who offers the highest rate of interest is the successful bidder. A simple example will illustrate this. Suppose a *hwei* is composed of ten persons who meet once a month and whose monthly subscription is $100.00. In the first month the "head" collects $900.00 and he keeps this sum as a loan to himself free of interest. In the second month the successful bidder will receive eight subscriptions plus the head's $100.00 repayment and so on down until all have placed a bid.[35]

---

31 (1915) 10 H.K.L.R. 69.

32 (1925) 20 H.K.L.R. 1.

33 See for example: *Nonia Cheah Yew* v. *Othmansaw Merican and anor.* (1861) 1 Ky. 160; *R.* v. *Sim Boon Lip* (1902–03) 7 S.S.L.R. 4; *Wong Pun Ying* v. *Wong Tin Hong* [1963] H.K.L.R. 37. The Straits Settlements Chinese Marriage Committee (Singapore Government Printer, 1926), however, took evidence from the Straits and Chinese born Hokkien, Cantonese, Teochew, Hakka and Hailam communities.

34 The spelling of this term (and *sim-boo-kian* on p. 732 below) is that used in the law reports and is continued here for ease of recognition when dealing with legal documents. Sometimes *Hwei* is also referred to, incorrectly, as *tontine*.

35 There is a Tamil version of this in Malaysia known as *kuthu:* see C. Gamba, "Poverty and some Socio-Economic Effects of Hoarding, Saving and Borrowing in Malaya." 3 *Malayan Economic Review* (1958) 33–56 at 39–41.

The question which has confronted the courts in all the territories above is, what is the nature of the legal relationships which arise when a member defaults on payment of principal or interest? The courts have been unanimous in holding that a *hwei* is not a gambling association, neither is it a money-lending association. But they have been far from unanimous in deciding whether or not the members are related in law, and if they are related, then what the nature of this relationship is. A typical example of the confusion which has arisen is found in *Fan Ngoi Lam and ors.* v. *Asia Cafe and anor.*[36] Here the court found that *hwei* consisted of a verbal agreement to be bound by the rules of the association, but the rules did not constitute an agreement or set of agreements between the head and each member. Later in the judgment the court said that "the nature [of the association] is one of mutual trust." And a little later the judge managed to say that it is "a mutual contract." There are two choices here: either it is an association based on some principle of equity or it is a contractual entity at common law. There is support for both choices.

Equity: The only support for this proposition, apart from Fan's case above, is to be found in two Hong Kong decisions. In *Chan Ka Lam and ors.* v. *Cheung Chung Kong and anor,*[37] the court held that the head is a trustee in respect of monies paid to him by the members. In *Un Yan Sing and ors.* v. *Fong Lun San*[38] the court said that the head was an implied trustee for the members and the court expressly founded its jurisdiction in equity and not in common law.

Common Law: There is greater support for the basis of the *hwei* being founded in contract but the nature of the contract and the extent of contractual relations is still a matter of dispute. The cases are divided between two alternatives. First, it has been held in seven cases that the contract is between the head and each member separately. From this it follows that the head is liable to each member for payment of subscription and for the repayment of loans. The receipt given by the member who obtains a loan is in the nature of a promissory note and, on proof of default, a member may sue the head for this sum.[39]

The second alternative is that each member contracts with all other members. The contract is to abide by the rules of the association and to observe all the liabilities necessary for its operation.[40] The case of *Loi Teck Uh* v. *Chieng Lee Tieh*[41] provides an interesting link between the two contractual situations. The court held:

(a) That the head contracts with each and every member to pay back each member's contribution and to guarantee repayment by each successful tenderer.

---

36 (1929–30) 24 H.K.L.R. 1.

37 (1915) 10 H.K.L.R. 157.

38 (1913) 8 H.K.L.R. 89.

39 *Chow Cham* v. *Yuet Seem* (1910) 5 H.K.L.R. 233; *Soo Hood Beng* v. *Khoo Chye Neo* (1896) 4 S.S.L.R. 115 (manager is agent for members); *Lau Chuo Kiew* v. *Hü Chee Soon* [1966] M.L.J. 126; *Lee Pee Eng* v. *Ho Sin Leow* [1958] S.C.R. 18 (an agreement to repay money tendered for and received is an enforceable agreement); *Luk Dai Chung* v. *Ngu Ee Nguok* [1966] M.L.J. 119 (head may be liable to the members for the debt of a member); *Ngu Ee Nguok* v. *Lee Ai Choon* [1965] M.L.J. 32 (default by a member must be proved and the onus of proof is upon the person asserting); *Tan Siew Hee & ors.* v. *Hü Sii Ung* [1964] M.L.J. 385 (the receipt given by a successful tenderer, which is in the nature of a promissory note, raises the presumption of [oral] contract for which there must be consideration and evidence is admissible to show want of consideration).

40 *Chan Iu Sang* v. *Tam Wai Sang* (1927) 22 H.K.L.R. 129.

41 [1960–63] S.C.R. 325.

(b) The members contract with the head to lend money and to take part in the *hwei*.
(c) The members contract with each other through the head who is agent to tender and to make such payments as may be required.

The I.O.U. which is signed is a written acknowledgement of debt, though it is only *prima facie* proof of this and may be rebutted by other evidence.

The basis of *hwei* seems, then, to be founded in contract and not in equity since the members contract at least with the head to observe certain rules and conditions.[42]

Polygamous Marriages—Validity and Form.[43] Chinese polygamous marriages are valid in (east and west) Malaysia and in Hong Kong though no longer in Singapore.[44] In West Malaysia and Singapore (prior to 1961 or 1967) recognition of these marriages demanded the satisfaction of three tests: (a) long continued cohabitation; (b) intention to form a permanent union, and (c) repute of marriage. These requirements, however, have not always been demanded and the Federated Malay States and Straits Settlements cases show variations in the courts's approaches to polygamy.

A summary of the relevant cases illustrates this. In *Cheang Thye Phin* v. *Tan Ah Loy*[45] the court held that it would presume a secondary marriage from evidence of cohabitation and repute. It also said that a ceremony was not essential for such a marriage. In *Chu Geok Keow* v. *Chong Meng Sze*[46] the court said that mutual consent was necessary and that ceremony, contract, and repute are evidentiary only. In *Re Khoo Thean Tek's Settlements*[47] the court said the element of "permanence" is necessary to constitute a valid secondary marriage and that *factum* and intention must be present upon which long habit and repute may be founded.

The courts have also, in some cases, stated that a presumption as to marriage exists in respect of secondary wives. In *Ong Cheng Neo* v. *Yeap Cheah Neo*[48] the court laid the onus of proof on the person disputing the existence of a marriage. In *Woon Kai Chiang* v. *Yeo Pak Yee*[49] the court held that where a Chinese male cohabits with a woman and subsequently marries (i.e. goes through a form of mar-

---

[42] See also the statement of Lord Herschell in *Clarke* v. *Dunraven* [1897] A.C. 59 at 63 . . . "undertaking to be bound by . . . rules to the knowledge of each, is sufficient, I think, where these rules indicate a liability on the part of one to the other, to create a contractual obligation to discharge that liability. That being so, the parties must be taken to have contracted that a breach of any of these rules would render the party guilty of that breach liable. . . ."

[43] Such marriages cannot be contracted in Singapore possibly since 1961 but certainly from 1967—Women's Charter (Ordinance 18 of 1961 as amended by 9 of 1967). However, the problem of polygamy linked with considerations of domicile may still give rise to problems in Singapore Courts.

[44] I agree with David Buxbaum (25 *Journal of Asian Studies* (1965–66), p. 639, footnote 78) that secondary relationships do probably continue in Singapore despite the Women's Charter.

[45] (1921) 14 S.S.L.R. 79.

[46] [1961] M.L.J. 10.

[47] [1928] S.S.L.R. 178; [1929] S.S.L.R. 50 (appeal). See also: *Lee Choon Guan decd.; Lew Ah Lui* v. *Choa Eng Wan* [1935] M.L.J. 78; *Lee Seang Neo and ors.* v. *Low Hin Tuan and ors.* (1925) 5 F.M.S.L.R. 154; *In the Estate of Lee Siew Kow decd.* [1952] M.L.J. 184; *Ngai Lau Shia* v. *Low Chee Neo* (1921) 14 S.S.L.R. 35; *Seow Beng Hay* v. *Seow Soon Quee* [1933] M.L.J. 111 (a man may marry a *t'sip*—secondary wife—before a *t'sai*—first wife). *Soh Eddie* v. *Tjhin Feong Fah* [1951] M.L.J. 124; *Tan As Bee* v. *Foo Koon Thye and anor.* [1947] M.L.J. 169; *Re Yeo Seng Whatt decd.* [1949] M.L.J. 60 and 241; *Re Yeow Kian Kee decd. Er Gek Cheng* v. *Ho Ying Seng* [1949] M.L.J. 171.

[48] (1877) Leicester's Reports 314.

[49] [1926] S.S.L.R. 27.

riage) another woman, a presumption in favor of a former marriage arises. This may give rise to a further presumption that the woman is at least a secondary wife.

In *Nonia Cheah Yew* v. *Othmansaw Merican and anor.*,[50] the court held the material factors in proving a Chinese marriage were that the woman should be given away by her nearest male relative and that there should be some publicity among friends of the couple. This emphasis upon form does not appear so much in later cases. However, a Chinese marriage ceremony has been held to confer the status of (at least secondary) wife for purposes of statutory interpretation.[51]

The courts have distinguished between a valid polygamous marriage and bigamy and the principle was early laid down that the distinction must depend upon the relevant provisions of Chinese law.[52]

In Sabah and Sarawak the position on Chinese marriages is slightly different in that these marriages are regulated by statute[53] and their validity is therefore to be judged by the requirements of the ordinance the most important of which is registration with a Registrar of Chinese marriages.[54] In the case of an unregistered Chinese marriage only the court can determine whether it is valid.[55]

In Hong Kong the position of the law in respect of secondary marriages seems broadly similar to that in Malaya and Singapore. Thus, in *Ng Ying Ho and anor.* v. *Tam Suen Yu*[56] the evidence required to show that a woman was a *t'sip* included being received into the husband's family, and formally introduced to them, worshipping at the ancestral tablets, and serving tea to the principal wife.

The courts in each of the three territories mentioned above have had to face their own peculiar problems in respect of Chinese marriages. In Singapore, Malaysia, and Hong Kong, apart from the general question of polygamy, the problem of inter-racial marriages has arisen. There is only one reported case from Hong Kong, *In Re the Estate of Kishan Das.*[57] The court was asked to decide upon the validity of a marriage between a Hindu man and a Chinese woman celebrated according to Hindu rites. It was held that since there was no evidence of the woman having become a Hindu, the marriage was invalid. The court specifically said that the lack of such evidence rebuts the presumption of marriage. In this decision there seems to have been an undue reliance upon the form of marriage which also tends to determine capacity.

In the Straits Settlements and Malay States cases this has been avoided. In *Carolis de Silva* v. *Tin Kim*,[58] the court determined the validity of a marriage between a Singalese man and a Chinese widow on the grounds of cohabitation and repute. Perfection of form was held not to be essential to validity. Similarly in *In re Tay Geok Teat decd.*,[59] the court determined the validity of a marriage between a Chinese man and a Japanese woman on grounds of cohabitation and repute.

However, the recognition of inter-racial marriage has not been without difficul-

---

[50] (1877) Leicester's Reports 167.

[51] *Soong Voon Sen* v. *Ang Kiong Hee* [1933] M.L.J. 262.

[52] *R.* v. *Yeah Boon Leng* (1890) 4 Ky. 630: see also *R.* v. *Sim Boon Lip* (1864) W.O.C. 39 and *R.* v. *Teo Kim Choon* [1947] S.L.R. 58.

[53] The Chinese Marriage Ordinance, 1933 (Cap. 74 revised laws 1946—see especially section 4).

[54] *Chien Boon Tong* v. *Goh Ah Pei and anor.* [1956] S.C.R. 58.

[55] *Chien Boon Tong* v. *Goh Ah Pei and anor.* [1956] S.C.R. 58.

[56] [1963] H.K.L.R. 923: see also *Au Hung Fat* v. *Lam Lai Ha* [1959] H.K.L.R. 527.

[57] (1932–33) 26 H.K.L.R. 42.

[58] (1904) 9 S.S.L.R. 8.

[59] [1934] M.L.J. 83.

ties: these have resolved around the notion of *consensus*[60] as being the fundamental element of common law marriages. The outstanding example of this situation is the decision in *Re Abraham Penhas decd.*[61] The case decided the validity of a marriage between a Jewish man and a Chinese woman celebrated in Singapore by Jewish and Chinese rites on the basis that it was a common law marriage. The Privy Council held that as there was consensus to enter into a marriage, the marriage was valid. Consensus was taken as a sole criterion but in respect of marriages between two Chinese the courts have found that the elements of intent, cohabitation, and repute are necessary to establish validity.

There are thus two sets of requirements: where one party only is Chinese then the common law marriage doctrine of *consensus* applies. An essential element to this is that the marriage is monogamous. On earlier authority, if both parties are Chinese then three requirements are necessary.

However, in *Yeow Kian Kee decd: Er Gek Cheng* v. *Ho Ying Seng*[62] a Chinese *secondary* marriage was found to exist solely on the basis of consensus. How is this to be reconciled with *Penhas*? If *Penhas* is accepted then the doctrine of consensus should apply to Chinese secondary marriages. But this is not possible. On the other hand, if *Penhas* is rejected then it is not possible to have a valid common law marriage except where one of the parties is racially non-Chinese. This is quite unacceptable.

These two decisions should be read in the light of *Yee Yeng Nam* v. *Lee Fah Kooi.*[63] This decision makes clear that in Malaysia it is possible for Chinese to contract marriages which may be either monogamous or polygamous at inception. It seems from the tenor of the decision that the type of marriage actually existing between the parties is a matter of fact to be proved to the Court's satisfaction. In this case the marriage was held to be monogamous because the parties were married under the Straits Settlements Christian Marriage Ordinance 1940, which, though it does not provide that a marriage under its provisions is monogamous, enables persons married under it to enter into a monogamous marriage.

The courts in the former North Borneo Territories have not had to face this problem but have had their own particular problem. This has resolved around the custom known as *sim-boo-kian*. This describes the situation where a girl is "purchased" for a sum of money with the intention of bringing her up as a prospective bride for the son of the family. The purchase price is known as *brian.*[64] A breach of the agreement by taking the girl away, for example, is liable to result in the payment of damages and/or the return of *brian*. This form of marriage was recognized in *Yek Hing Po* v. *Tou Nih Hiong*[65] but in *Pang Chin* v. *Pang Chon*

---

60 On consensus generally see *R.* v. *Willis* (1843–44) Cl. & F. 534.

61 [1950] M.L.J. 104; [1953] A.C. 304 *cf.* Maurice Freedman, "The Penhas Case: Mixed and Unmixed Marriage in Singapore," 16 *Modern Law Review*, (1953) 366–68.

62 [1949] M.L.J. 171.

63 [1956] M.L.J. 257.

64 This term is not Chinese and it does not appear in any of the standard Malay or Indonesian dictionaries. It appears to be *Dyak* and is used to mean bride price: see 4 *Sarawak Museum Journal* (1935) No. 15, Part IV, 395.

65 [1953] S.C.R. 59: see also *Chia Ah Kiaw* v. *Tan Ka Yong* [1928–41] S.C.R. 115.

Pee[66] the court refused to recognize the custom of "buying and selling children" on the somewhat humorous ground that this was not a valid contract of sale at common law. The court has, however, upheld a marriage where a girl was given to a family so that she might become the wife of a son of the family.[67]

Divorce. This question has provided little difficulty in any of the three territories. There is only one reported case from Hong Kong and from the views of the committee[68] divorce appears to be laid down in the *Ch'ing* law. The outstanding feature of this law is that it provides for divorce by mutual consent. In *Lee Wah Fui* v. *Lan*[69] the court held that a contract of mutual divorce was sufficient to dissolve a marriage celebrated in Hong Kong according to customary rites.

In Malaya and (prior to 1961) in Singapore the law regarding Chinese customary divorce is well settled. A secondary wife may be divorced if she has shown disobedience to her husband or to the principal wife; if she has been guilty of immoral conduct. In addition, a husband must notify his relatives and clansmen of the divorce.[70] On the general principle of divorce the courts have held that Chinese may only divorce according to custom so long as they marry under custom. If they marry under the provisions of any ordinance, then the grounds of divorce must be as determined by the ordinance.[71] The courts will not allow a woman to divorce her husband unilaterally.[72]

Customary divorce in former North Borneo is recognized by the courts on the general principle that the court has jurisdiction because the present High Court is the direct successor to the "Chinese Court" (Order IX, 1911), that this jurisdiction has not been disturbed by any later order or enactment and because the practice has always been to grant divorces in respect of Chinese marriages.[73] The jurisdiction has been extended to cover decrees of judicial separation.[74] The courts have insisted that the practice of mutual divorce, which they recognize, has no effect without a declaration by the court.[75]

Unlike the courts in Malaya and the former Straits Settlements the courts in Sarawak, Sabah, and Brunei have not laid down general principles on grounds for divorce. They have instead preferred to accept evidence on a case by case basis as to the custom of different dialect groups. In one case the court even accepted, on the basis of expert evidence, that there was no custom governing *Hakka* divorce as the practice was to leave this matter to the courts.[76] This is probably incorrect, the weight of authority being against such a conclusion.

---

66 [1952] S.C.R. 18.

67 *Loh Chai Ing* v. *Lau Ing Ai* [1959] S.C.R. 13. This was a *Foochow* marriage and is known as a *T'ung Yang-Hsi* marriage. *cf. sim-boo-kan* above.

68 *Chinese Law and Custom in Hong Kong*—report of a committee, (Government Printer 1953). See pp. 26–28, 46–49.

69 [1964] 2 All. E.R. 248: Buxbaum, 25 *Journal of Asian Studies* (1965–66) 641 note 86.

70 *Re Lee Gee Chong decd.* [1965] M.L.J. 102. *In the estate of Sim Siew Guan decd.* [1932] M.L.J. 95: see also *Woon Ngee Yew & ors.* v. *Ng Yoon Thai & ors.* [1941] M.L.J. 32.

71 *Re Soo Hai San and Wong Sue Foong* [1961] M.L.J. 221.

72 *Cheng Ee Mun* v. *Look Chun Heng and anor.* [1962] M.L.J. 411.

73 *Liu Kui Tze* v. *Lee Shak Lian* [1953] S.C.R. 85.

74 *Chien Mau Ong* v. *Wong Suok* [1956] S.C.R. 97: compare *Lim Siew Yun* v. *Soong Ah Kaw* [1960–63] S.C.R. 105.

75 *Wong Chu Ming* v. *Kho Lieng Hiong* [1952] S.C.R. 1.

76 *Yong Mong Yung* v. *Chai Shong* [1964] M.L.J. 424.

The courts have accepted the following grounds for divorce:

Foochow:

(a) desertion;[77]
(b) failure to maintain;[78]
(c) that the parties are completely out of sympathy and find it impossible to live together.[79] The court refused to recognize lack of intelligence as a ground for divorce.[80]

Hakka:

(a) if both parties agree to a mutual divorce;[81]
(b) failure to maintain;[82]
(c) if the wife has left and there is no possibility of reconciliation.[83] In an earlier case the court refused to recognize this ground.[84]

Henghua:[85]

(a) ill treatment by the husband;
(b) failure to maintain for at least a year.

Adoption and the Rights of Adopted Children to Succeed to Property. The Hong Kong courts have consistently recognized adoption on the basis of *T'sing* law.[86] The primary reason for adoption has been held to be to prevent the extinction of a family and an adoption for such a purpose is valid.[87] As proof of an adoption the court has accepted as evidence that formalities of adoption have been performed and that records of the adoption exist in the form of records in family books, at temples and inscribed on tablets.[88] The custom of adoption will be given effect to so long as it does not conflict directly with any ordinance. The Infants' Custody Ordinance (cap. 13), for example, has been held not to be inconsistent with customary adoptions in Hong Kong.[89]

So far as Hong Kong is concerned, the committee appears to have assumed that an adopted child stands in all respects as a legitimate natural born child in the matter of succession. This has not been the case in Malaya and Singapore regarding either testate or intestate property. Most of the reported cases have re-

---

77 *Lee Yung Kiang* v. *Ling Yun Tie* [1965] M.L.J. 87. See also *Tang Sui Ing* v. *Goh Tien Liong* [1964] M.L.J. 406.

78 *Loh Chai Ing* v. *Lau Ing Ai* [1959] S.C.R. 13. See also *Tang Sui Ing* v. *Goh Tien Liong* [1964] M.L.J. 406.

79 *Tang Sui Ing* v. *Goh Tien Liong* [1964] M.L.J. 406.

80 *Loh Chai Ing.* v. *Lau Ing Ai* [1959] S.C.R. 13.

81 *Kong Nyat Moi* v. *Leong Sing Chiang* [1965] M.L.J. 73.

82 *Lo Siew Ying* v. *Chong Fay* [1959] S.C.R. 1.

83 *Lo Siew Ying* v. *Chong Fay* [1959] S.C.R. 1.

84 *Thia Whee Kiang* v. *Kueh Eng Seng* [1955] S.C.R. 75.

85 *Siaw Moi Jea* v. *Lu Ing Hui* [1959] S.C.R. 16.

86 *Chinese Law and Custom in Hong Kong*—report pp. 49–53. The committee cited an extract from a report made in 1883 which contained "forms" for the transfer of a son and deed of sale of a son into adoption and a letter of instructions referring to an adopted son, see pp. 194–99. See also *In the goods of Chan Tse Shi* (1954) 38 H.K.L.R. 9; *Wong Yu Shi and ors.* v. *Wong Yin Kuen* [1957] H.K.L.R. 420; *Chan Yue (alias)* v. *Henry G. Leong Estates Ltd.* (1953) 37 H.K.L.R. 66.

87 *In the state of Ngai I: Ngai Chung Shi and anor.* v. *Ngai Yee Mui* (1927) 22 H.K.L.R. 105.

88 *Cheang Thye Gan* v. *Lim Ah Chen and ors.* (1921) 16 H.K.L.R. 19.

89 *Lui Yuk Ping* v. *Chow To* [1962] H.K.L.R. 515.

quired the court to make a decision as to whether the term "children" in a will means adopted children. The weight of authority is to the effect that it does if this can be gathered from the terms of the will itself.[90]

So far as intestate property is concerned, the position is less clear. In *Re Chu Siang Long*[91] the court held that the adopted child of a Chinese was entitled to the joint administration of an estate in preference to a nephew. This decision was expressly based on the provision of the charters which directed that respect be given to local custom. However, this decision was overruled in *Khoo Tiang Bee et Uxor* v. *Tang Beng Gwat*[92] on the grounds that the law as to Chinese adoptions is uncertain, and that it would add one more to the many conflicts of laws in the Straits Settlements where the uniformity of the laws of inheritance must be preserved as far as possible. Some support for the first ground is given in *In the goods of Goh Siew Swee decd.*[93] where the court refused to accept books on Chinese law as evidence.

It is probably settled law now that adopted children will not succeed to an intestate estate in Malaya. This is because the Distribution Ordinance 1958 restricts the status of adoption to persons formally adopted under the Adoption Ordinance of 1952.[94] A similar situation exists in Singapore under the provisions of the Women's Charter.

In Sarawak, Sabah, and Brunei there is no direct authority on adoption, but it is likely that the courts will demand that to be valid it must be regulated or recoginzed (expressly or implicitly) by some ordinance. Thus in *Wong Teck Giak and anor.* v. *Ting Ni Moi*[95] the court decided the question of custody of a child on these criteria. In *Li Khoi Chin (aliases)* v. *Su Ah Poh*[96] the court said that the law of Sarawak would recognize an adoption made outside Sarawak where the persons concerned were domiciled in the country of adoption.

Legitimacy and Legitimation. This topic is almost entirely confined to Malaya. There are no Hong Kong decisions reported, and the topic is not now relevant in Singapore. There is, however, one case from Sarawak[97] on intestate succession and legitimation by subsequent recognition. The court held that this form of legitimation would be recognized on the basis of Chinese custom.[98] The courts in the Straits

---

[90] Cases to the effect that "children" means adopted children: *In re Kho Khye Chear decd.* [1938] M.L.J. 224; *In re Lim Yew Teok decd.* [1937] S.S.L.R. 243; *Quaik Kee Hock* v. *Wee Geok Neo* [1886] 4 Ky. 128; *Re Tan Hong decd.* [1962] M.L.J. 355; *Re Teo Soo Piah decd.* [1950] M.L.J. 176; *Re Yeo Soo Theam decd.* 1937 S.S.L.R. 276; *Cheok Chin Huat* v. *Cheok Chin Soon* [1937] S.S.L.R. 103; *Re Tan Cheng Siong decd.* [1937] S.S.L.R. 293; *Tan Phee Teck* v. *Tan Tiang Hee* [1952] M.L.J. 240.

[91] (1877) Leicester's Reports 460.

[92] (1877) 1 Ky. 413. This case was cited with approval by the Privy Council in *Re Choo Eng Choon decd.* [1930] A.C. 346 at 355.

[93] (1911) 12 S.S.L.R. 18.

[94] See *Re Loh Toh Met: Kong Lai Fong* v. *Loh Heng Peng* [1961] M.L.J. 234. Similarly, the adoption of a person into the family of a man already deceased at the time of adoption is no longer valid—see *Tan Sim Neoh* v. *Soh Tien Hock* (1922) 1 F.M.S.L.R. 336.

[95] [1950] S.C.R. 1 and 39 (appeal).

[96] [1950] S.C.R. 17.

[97] *In the estate of Chan Chin Hee decd.* [1948] S.C.R. 6.

[98] The court approved the following grounds: (a) If the parents of the father wish to recognize the child. (b) If other elders of the family wish to recognize the child provided the father consents. (c) A person's name carved on a tombstone is evidence, not necessarily conclusive, of his legitimation.

Settlements and Federated Malay States have consistently refused to give effect to this form of legitimation.[99]

However, legitimation by subsequent marriage was and (in Malaya) is recognized.[100] The reason for this is that this is an issue which must be decided with regard to the validity of the union between the parents and the obligations arising out of that union as set out by Chinese law and custom.

It is difficult to see why this principle should not be extended to legitimation by recognition. The position on this subject may very well vary as between the states of West Malaysia and East Malaysia and this is unfortunate.

The topic of wills falls into two main categories: (a) construction; and (b) trusts for charitable uses and the rule against perpetuities.

Construction: There is very little material from Hong Kong on the topic of wills generally. The matter was formerly governed by the Chinese Wills Validation Ordinance 1856 and the Wills Act 1861 (U.K.). The committee proposed that Chinese, whatever their domicile, might dispose of their property by will and that oral wills should not be permitted.[101] Reference may also be made to *Fu Chuen Sang and anor.* v. *Cheung Ching Tak and ors.*[102] where it was held that a "wish" for a wife to adopt a son did not create a precatory trust. It should be noted that this case was decided solely on English authorities.

There are only two reported cases from Sarawak[103] in which it was held that the validity and construction of a Chinese will are to be governed by English law. If the will attempts to dispose of property according to Chinese custom then it will be given effect to if the custom is regulated or recognized by a Sarawak ordinance or by rules made under any Sarawak ordinance.

In both the Straits Settlements and the Federated Malay States the validity of wills made by Chinese was tested by reference to English principles of construction (this is apart from questions of charitable uses). In *Lee Eng Nam* v. *H. T. Jones*[104] it was held that a Chinese widow could make a will because there was nothing either in the common law or in the Perak Order in Council to show lack of testimentary capacity.

In *Re Lee Kim Chye decd.*[105] the court held that when a Chinese marries a secondary wife after making a will such marriage revokes the will.

Trusts for charitable uses—perpetuities: Trusts for charitable uses fall into two classes: a trust for the purchase of land to be used as a burial place for a person or family; and trusts for the performance of ancestor worship.[106] In the only two cases reported from Hong Kong the court held that bequests for "worshipping

---

99 *Khoo Hooi Leong* v. *Khoo Choong Yok* [1930] S.S.L.R. 127. *In re Khoo Tek's Settlements* [1929] S.S.L.R. 50.

100 *In the estate of Choo Eng Choon decd.* (1911) 12 S.S.L.R. 120 at 224.

101 *Chinese Law and Custom in Hong Kong*—report pp. 63–64.

102 [1961] H.K.L.R. 219.

103 *Chan Bee Neo and ors.* v. *Ee Siok Choo* [1947] S.C.R. 1. *Re Tay Lim Tiang decd.* [1955] S.C.R. 17.

104 (1923) 3 F.M.S.L.R. 42.

105 [1936] M.L.J. 49.

106 Variously referred to in the reports as *sin chew, chin shong.*

expenses" and "Ancestor's Sacrificial Fund" were invalid as offending the rule against perpetuities though they were not superstitious uses.[107]

After some hesitation the courts in Malaya and Singapore have held that a trust for the purchase of burial ground is a valid charitable trust.[108] This is so even though the use of the property was for members of a certain *seh* only.[109] The justification for this appears to be that a *seh* is a public charity since it is set up to provide burial and worship facilities for its members.[110] Similarly, trusts made for the establishment and upkeep of temples and worshipping places have been considered valid.[111]

Trusts for the purposes of ancestor worship have two aspects. First, the courts have had to consider whether or not they are valid or are superstitious uses. Once again, after some hesitation, they have been held to be valid trusts. In *Re Khoo Cheng Teow decd.*[112] the court held that such a gift is not superstitious but is more in the nature of a gift, for example, to say Masses and may be approved on the same grounds. In an earlier case, *Choa Cheow Neo* v. *Spottiswoode*[113] a gift for the purpose of *sin-chew* was held invalid on the ground that it was not charitable, being of benefit to the testator only. However, in *Lim Chooi Chuan* v. *Lim Chew Chee*[114] a trust providing for the carrying out of *sin-chew* by the members of one *seh* was held charitable in that it benefitted one part of the public.

The second aspect is the question of perpetuities. A trust for *sin-chew* is valid only if drawn so as not to infringe this rule.[115] In addition it must be certain. Thus, for example, a *sin-chew* trust for the benefit of a "Chinese family" has been held bad for uncertainty.[116] Similarly, a direction to spend income on "yearly ceremonies according to Chinese custom" was held uncertain.[117] Where a trust for *sin-chew* is impressed on real property outside the jurisdiction the court will judge the validity of the direction according to the law of the place where the property is situated. Thus, where the real property was in China and the trust valid at Chinese law, the courts recognized it.[118]

As with all other facets of Chinese custom so far considered any custom must be proved or provable to the satisfaction of the court.[119]

Administration and Succession.[120] Apart from adopted persons the main problem

---

107 *In Re Chan Quan Ee* (1920) 15 H.K.L.R. 74; *Lan Leung Shi* v. *Lau Po Tsun* (1911) 6 H.K.L.R. 149.

108 *Lee Poh Lian Neo and ors.* v. *The Chinese Bankers Trust Co. Ltd.* [1941–42] S.S.L.R. 28.

109 *Cheang Tew Muey and ors.* v. *Cheang Cheow Lean Neo & ors.* [1930] S.S.L.R. 58.

110 *Yeoh Him & ors.* v. *Yeoh Cheng Kong and ors.* (1889) 4 Ky. 500: see *contra. Re Yap Kuan Seng. decd.* (1924) 4 F.M.S.L.R. 313.

111 *Tan Chin Ngoh* v. *Tan Chin Teat and ors.* [1946] S.L.R. 14; *Re Low Kim Pong's Settlement Trusts* [1938] S.S.L.R. 144.

112 [1932] S.S.L.R. 226: see also *Ong Geok Neo* v. *Chee Hoon Bong and ors.* (1893) 1 S.S.L.R. 53; *Phan Kin Thin* v. *Phan Kuow Yung* [1940] M.L.J. 35.

113 (1869) 1 Ky. 216.

114 [1948–49] M.L.J. Supp. 66.

115 *Re Tan Kim Seng decd.* (1911) 12 S.S.L.R. 1. *Re the trusts of Wan Eng Kiat* [1931] S.S.L.R. 57.

116 *Re the trusts of Wan Eng Kiat* [1931] S.S.L.R. 57.

117 *Re Chen Ah Sang decd.* [1949] M.L.J. 14.

118 *Ng Eng Kiat* v. *Goh Lai Mui & ors.* [1940] S.S.L.R. 78.

119 *Choy Mien Hew* v. *Choy Weng Tung and anor.* [1932] S.S.L.R. 126. See also *Li Chik Hung* v. *Li Pui Choi* (1911) 6 H.K.L.R. 12 where the law as to "ancestral property" had to be proved on the ground that there is no such form of property in English law.

120 Not including the rights of adopted persons—see above "adoption".

current in this topic has arisen in respect of the rights of secondary wives to administer and succeed, especially with respect to intestate property.

The Hong Kong courts have long settled the law in the colony that in succession to property the operative law is *T'sing* law or local Chinese custom. However, the law as to the mechanics of administration is English law. Thus, for example, the grants of letters of administration is governed by English law but the manner of distribution is government by *T'sing* law.[121] The substance of Chinese law must of course be proved to the satisfaction of the court.[122] On administration, the Hong Kong courts have held that a concubine[123] and a widow may administer. The widow may, however, administer only so long as she remains a member of her late husband's family. The fact that she re-marries does not affect this so long as (the court held) she introduces her second husband into the house of her late husband.[124]

On the right of a widow to succeed, the court has held that she has no absolute right but, subject to her right of maintenance, on behalf of the male succession.[125] If the male line becomes extinct the property will descend to the surviving female relatives of the last deceased male member: this right is not confined to daughters or spinsters.[126]

The courts in former North Borneo have made no pronouncements specifically on administration and succession apart from the general principle that any proved or accepted Chinese custom will prevail over English law.[127] Presumably this is subject to the overriding authority of Sarawak statutes and rules.[128]

The courts in Malaya and Singapore have consistently held that the distribution of a Chinese intestate estate is governed exclusively by the Statute of Distributions. In *Lee Joo Neo* v. *Lee Eng Swee*[129] the court gave two reasons for this. First, that immovable property is governed by the *lex loci rei sitae* and Chinese law cannot be incorporated within the Statute of Distributions. Second, that movable property is governed by the law of the domicile which does not allow Chinese law to be incorporated in the Statute. This has been recently approved in *Re Chia Eng Say decd.*[130] where the Court said it would not consider any Chinese customs with respect to the Statute.[131]

---

121 *Wong Pan Ying* v. *Wong Ting Hong* [1963] H.K.L.R. 37: see also *Chan Yeung* v. *Chan Shew Shi* (1925) 20 H.K.L.R. 35; *Ho Cheng Shi* v. *Ho Sau Lam* (1920) 15 H.K.L.R. 35; *Chan Shun Cho* v. *Chak Hok Ping* (1925) 20 H.K.L.R. 1; *Ho Tsz Tsun* v. *Ho Au Shi and ors.* (1915) 10 H.K.L.R. 69.

122 *Li Chik Hung* v. *Li Pui Choi* (1911) 6 H.K.L.R. 12.

123 *Ho Sau Lam* v. *Ho Cheng Shi* (1916) 11 H.K.L.R. 92.

124 *In Re the Estate of Ngai I.* (1927) 22 H.K.L.R. 105.

125 *Tang Choy Hong* v. *Tang Shing Mo & ors.* (1949) 33 H.K.L.R. 58.

126 *In Re the estate of Ngai I.* (1927) 22 H.K.L.R. 105.

127 *Re Tay Lim Tiang decd.* [1955] S.C.R. 17.

128 *Kho Leng Guan* v. *Kho Eng Guan* [1928–41] S.C.R. 60.

129 (1887) 4 Ky. 325.

130 [1951] M.L.J. 130.

131 Attention is here drawn to the case of *Yap Tham Thai (alias)* v. *Low Hup Neo* (1922) 1 F.M.S.L.R. 383; (1925) 6 F.M.S.L.R. 13. Here it was held that succession to the estate of an intestate Chinese domiciled in Selangor should be distributed according to the broad principles of Chinese family law as set out in the Perak Order in Council (No. 23 of 1893) as modified by certain rules of local custom. In coming to this conclusion the court based itself upon the following grounds: (a) There is no Chinese personal law similar to that of Muslims or Hindus; (b) There is a common law of Selangor applicable in this case; (c) The intestate must be regarded as of "British nationality."

This case was, however, a decision from the Federated Malay States into which English law was never introduced in its entirety. The judge, therefore, seems to have assumed that the Statute did not

As far as secondary wives are concerned the result of applying the Statute has been that the courts will order joint administration of intestate property.[132] In the Straits Settlements, the court has ordered equal shares of intestate property to be given. The reason for this is that since English law provides no rule for determining the proportions, the court cannot order any proportion other than an equal share. Though in China the second wife may have no right to share, this was held immaterial in the Straits Settlements because a first wife would not find it any easier to establish her right to letters of administration than would the second.[133]

The courts have also had to deal with the situation of succession to the estate of deceased secondary wife. The court presumed intestacy from the rarity of wills among Chinese women of her class[134] and then went on to hold that, in the absence of proof to the contrary, such a woman could not have a successor. Her estate was therefore declared *bona vacantia*.[135] In effect this decision overruled the decision in *Yap Kan Keow and anor.* v. *Low Hup Neo and anor.*[136] which itself arose out of and is part of the decision in *Yap Tham Thai (alias)* v. *Low Hup Neo*.[137] The question remains unsettled except that now the new Distribution Ordinance, No. 1 of 1958, may help to solve the problem.

This completes our summary of judicial decisions in the three territories. Each of these territories has had its own method of dealing with substantive provisions of Chinese law which are largely dependent upon their differing legal bases. The bulk of Chinese law has been dealt with, however, in a remarkably similar fashion in each of the territories.

At the present time each territory in which Chinese law is still a valid system of personal law (i.e. Malaya, Sabah, Sarawak, Brunei, and Hong Kong) is facing new problems which are themselves partial results of the past treatment of Chinese law. The only exceptions to this generalization are the states of Sabah, Sarawak, and Brunei where because of the commonsense approach of the courts in refusing to lay down principles at substantive Chinese law,[138] the continued validity and flexibility of this law remains unimpaired.

Current Problems

Hong Kong. The report of the committee on Chinese law and custom in Hong Kong drew attention to various problems facing the judiciary in 1953. The most important of these appears to be the problem of domicile as determining the jurisdiction of Hong Kong courts. This is especially serious in view of the judg-

---

apply in the Federated Malay States and that he was subject to local legislation *viz.* the Perak Order in Council. Distribution of an intestate estate is now governed by Ordinance No. 1/1958 replacing cap. 71/1930—revised laws of the Federated Malay States, 1935.

[132] *In the goods of Ing Ah Mit* (1888) 4 Ky. 380.

[133] *In the goods of Lao Leong An* (1893) 1 S.S.L.R. 1.

[134] *Lee Siang Neo and ors.* v. *Low Hin Tuan and ors.* (1925) 5 F.M.S.L.R. 154.

[135] *Official Administrator F.M.S. for Chua Swee Sim Neo decd.* v. *State of Selangor and ors.* [1939] M.L.J. 175.

[136] (1925) 6 F.M.S.L.R. 13.

[137] See note 131 above.

[138] Preferring instead to rely upon expert evidence on a case by case basis and refusing to be bound by too rigid a scheme of precedent.

ment in *Lau Leung Shi* v. *Lau Po Tsun*[139] where it was held that as long as a Chinese continued to worship at his ancestral temples, he could not get a domicile of choice in the colony. The committee recommended,[140] quite rightly, that this artificial test on change of status should not continue. The suggested solution was to raise a presumption in favor of change of domicile on the following grounds:

(a) If a Chinese has lived in Hong Kong for seven years after attaining the age of twenty-one; and before the date at which he claims a new domicile.
(b) If he married in Hong Kong and lived there for five years after the date of marriage and before the date at which he claims a new domicile.
(c) If he has acquired British nationality.
(d) If he was born in Hong Kong and has resided there continuously.

These have now been given statutory effect in the Divorce (Amendment) Ordinance (44/1956). The committee also recommended the passing of a bill entitled the Chinese Law and Custom (Miscellaneous Provisions) Ordinance containing the same provisions and determining also what matters should be settled by common law on questions of domicile, capacity, and change of status.[141] There are as yet no reported cases on this topic and the effects of this legislation and of the committee's recommendations remain to be seen.

Malaysia (not including Sabah, Sarawak and Brunei). Because of the judicial history of the Federated and Unfederated Malay States an entirely different set of problems arises in Malaya. These revolve around the Chinese Christian who has entered into a series of polygamous marriages. We may illustrate this with two examples.

The first of these is *Re Loh Toh Met: Kong Lai Fong* v. *Loh Heng Peng*.[142] In this case the Court had to decide what law governed the validity of various marriages entered into by a Christian Chinese now deceased. The deceased died possessed of three wives and eleven children (of whom four were ostensibly adopted). He had been brought up a Roman Catholic though he was sporadic in his religious observances. On this evidence the trial judge held that the deceased was a person professing the Christian religion under the Christian Marriage Ordinance.[143] From this the judge concluded that the deceased had been obliged to marry under the Ordinance and in that all his marriages were entered into by Chinese ceremony, none of them was valid.

On appeal, however, the Court held that the deceased was not in fact a Christian and that being a man of "Chinese race" the provisions of his customary law should apply to him. The introduction of "Christian" into this decision is unfortunate and, because of the provisions of the Ordinance, unnecessary.[144] It is the law that a Chinese even if professing the Christian religion can enter into a polygamous marriage by Chinese customary rites. Christianity by itself is not qualification for a state of monogamy. Similarly, the introduction of "race" is also unfortunate. I

---

139 (1911) 6 H.K.L.R. 149.

140 Report of the Committee *op cit.* pp. 66–67 and Appendices 18 and 19.

141 *Ibid.* pp. 306–09 (Appendix 21).

142 [1961] M.L.J. 234.

143 Cap. 82 revised laws of the Straits Settlements 1936.

144 See a note on this case by David C. Buxbaum in (1963) 5 *Malaya Law Review* 383–87.

should guess that anthropologists would not generally classify the Chinese as a race. If the Court makes this a criteria in any decision then it runs the risk in the future of having to determine whether a person of mixed ancestry is a member of the "Chinese race." The Court instead must concentrate upon establishing the personal law of any litigant.

One further point arises from this decision. The four adopted children of the deceased failed in their claim for a share in the estate. This was because the Distribution Ordinance 1958, of Malaya, restricts the status of adoption to those persons formally adopted under the Adoption Ordinance of 1952. The Courts have consistently refused to recognize adoptions at customary law among the Chinese in Malaya and this has caused not inconsiderable hardship. The Chinese themselves feel a sense of injustice at this state of affairs.[145]

The second example of this situation is *Re Ding Do Ca.*[146] The issue in this case was whether or not a Chinese who had married under the Christian Marriage Enactment[147] could subsequently contract a marriage under Chinese custom while the first marriage was still subsisting. The Court held that he could as there was nothing in the Enactment which corresponded to s. 4 of the Civil Marriage Ordinance[148] which would prohibit such a union (*Thomson L. P.*). In effect the judge refused to equate Christianity with monogamy, but instead equated "Chinese" with polygamy.

It is submitted that both equations are wrong and subject to the difficulties of proof outlined in respect of *Loh Toh Met.* The solution appears to force a return to a factual ascertainment of personal law leaving aside as irrelevant race or Christianity. In the case of a Chinese Muslim the position is different. He is subject to Islamic law: the faith includes a legal system. A Chinese Christian, however, is not subject to "Christian Law": there is no such thing. He is governed by his personal law insofar as this remains effective under statute.

To summarize: Chinese law continues to be a viable system of personal law in (east and west) Malaysia and in Hong Kong, though no longer in Singapore. Judicial pronouncements have been comparatively more common in Malaysia than in Hong Kong and this is probably a reflection of the wider scope and effect of statute in Hong Kong. The cases from this area also show a proportionately greater interest in matters of business transactions and organizations conducted according to customary rules.

The future of Chinese custom in these areas is assured though limited mainly to matters of family law. Even here, however, there is increasing statutory interference which seems directed at trying to bring the substantive provisions of custom in line with the rest of the law. Singapore has gone the furtherest in this endeavor and has completely banned the recognition of Chinese family law, most notably in its refusal to countenance polygamous marriages. How effective this has been on the lower stratum of Singapore society is unknown but it would not be surprising if many of these unions were still being entered into. But even in

---

[145] See Maurice Freedman, "Colonial Law and Chinese Society," *Journal of the Royal Anthropological Institute* (1950) lxxx 97 at 112.

[146] [1966] M.L.J. 220.

[147] Christian Marriage Ordinance 1956 (Malaya). This is a substantial re-enactment of cap. 109 revised laws of the Federated Malay States, 1935.

[148] Ordinance No. 44 of 1952.

Singapore some vestiges of Chinese custom come to the surface now and again. Thus, the traditional "peacemaker" is still active in minor matrimonial affairs and in the Chinese business community (report in the *Straits Times,* 25 May 1966). This is a subject which needs detailed exploration.

In the lower courts in Malaysia the magistrates have recognized the cutting off of a white cockeral's head as a form of oath (report in the *Straits Times,* 25 February 1968, 17 March 1968). These examples, isolated though they are, emphasize that much research must be done at grassroots level.

KEY TO ABBREVIATIONS

A.C.	Appeal Cases. United Kingdom, 1866-current.
Cl. & F.	Clark & Finnelly. House of Lords Cases. 12 vols. 1831–1846.
F.M.S.L.R.	Federated Malay States Law Reports. By J. R. Innes and McLean. Cases decided from 1922–31, 7 vols. New Series by H. C. Willan 1932–47. No report 1942–45.
H.K.L.R.	Hong Kong Law Reports. Hong Kong, 1906-current.
Ky.	Kyshe's Law Reports. By J. W. N. Kyshe. 4 vols. Vol. 1—Civil cases with a historical-judicial preface 1786–1885. Vol. 2—Criminal, Admiralty, Bankruptcy, Ecclesiastical and *Habeas Corpus* cases. Vol. 3—Magistrates Appeals. Vol. 4—Cases 1885, 1890; Rules and Orders of Court 1885–1890.
Leicester	Leicester's Reports: by S. Leicester (also known as Straits Law Reports—Leicester). Cases decided in the Supreme Court of the Straits Settlements, 1 vol. 1877.
L.R.P. & D.	Law Reports. Probate and Divorce Cases. 3 vols. 1865–1875.
M.L.J.	Malayan Law Journal. Cases decided in Malaysia, Singapore and (from 1963–64) Sarawak, North Borneo and Brunei. By B. A. Mallal. 1932–current.
M.L.J. Supp.	Malayan Law Journal Supplement. By B. A. Mallal. Contains cases unreported and some cases noted in [1949] M.L.J.: published in 1957. [1949] Supplement published in 1951.
S.C.R.	Supreme Court Reports. Cases decided in Sarawak, 1928–41, 1946–51. From 1952 includes reports from North Borneo and Brunei. Ceased publication with the volume for 1960–63.
S.L.R.	Singapore Law Reports. Cases decided from 1946–49, 1953–56. 8 vols.
S.S.L.R	Straits Settlements Law Reports. Old Series, 1893–1907. New Series, 1926–1941/42. Published under the direction of the Singapore Bar Committee.
W.O.C.	Woods Oriental Cases. A selection of the cases decided in the Supreme Court of the Straits Settlements. By R. C. Woods, Jr. Penang: 1869 (reprinted Sweet & Maxwell, London, 1911).

INTERNATIONAL BUSINESS/GOVERNMENT INTERACTIONS

International Business/Government Interactions

17

Perspectives on Government-Business Interaction in Japan

Eugene J. Kaplan

Some general observations as to the *nature of the government's powers* vis-à-vis industry in Japan are important to an understanding of the limitations of government-business interaction in that country. Take the authority given to what some observers refer to as the "ubiquitous" MITI, for example. Despite its very intensive involvement in the industrial development process, MITI is only one of several government agencies with a say in the workings of "Japan Incorporated." The Ministry of Finance, which regulates the flow of funds within and outside the economy, probably has even more influence over the course of the Japanese economy, although it exercises its powers somewhat less visibly. Some experts claim that this direction over the channeling of funds is the essence of "Japan, Incorporated."

In any case, as far as MITI is concerned, that agency can, depending on the circumstances:

- Directly control inflows of certain imports and foreign capital;
- allocate direct financial assistance and indirect fiscal incentives (only with the Finance Ministry's concurrence);
- organize and finance special industry programs in technology development and production rationalization (under legislative charter and with the cooperation of its client producers).

These MITI functions are sanctioned by a varying mix of formal authority and informal consensus between that Ministry and its clients. MITI can and does find instances where it cannot direct industry to carry out its objectives. This is certainly the case with respect to formal combinations of producers—a much sought for objective in all three of the industries case studied. The government cannot effectively interpose its judgments on the corporate structure. It can encourage but not dictate mergers or formal combinations. MITI has therefore sought, generally with little success, to stimulate consolidation through its exercise of a variety of levers over industry. The case studies provides specific examples of the kinds of situations where MITI has been able to use its authority effectively and where it has not.

The *priority assigned* to the development or restructuring of an industry also determines whether and to what extent government-business interaction will take place. While pervasive, government-business inter-

Reprinted from *Japan: The Government-Business Relationship* (U.S Department of Commerce, February, 1972), pp. 56-72.

action does not take place in all sectors of the Japanese economy, or to the same degree in those where it does happen. As the case studies corroborate, interaction between government and business has been greatest in those industries and sectors which have been assigned the highest priority in Japan's economic development. Moreover, government-business interaction has intensified at the really crucial stages of the development of a new growth industry, or the restructuring of one already well under way.

This is certainly the case with respect to the computer and motor vehicle industries. The government, indeed the whole of the Japanese establishment, was late in recognizing the computer's critical importance. MITI had several alternative concerns of major priority during the late 1950's. Foreign exchange crises placed critical importance on developing export industries such as consumer electronics and import substitute industries like chemicals and petrochemicals. The automobile industry was just achieving design automony and was approaching the take-off stage. Steel was in its critical Second Rationalization period, requiring funds for massive expansions of capacity. These were among the higher policy priorities than computers. However, once computers moved into the high priority category, MITI increasingly took the initiative in its relationship with the industry and became highly aggressive both within the government's bureaucracy and among the computer manufacturers in guiding the development effort. Nor did the Japanese government take any interest in the early beginnings of the auto industry in that country until about 1930. But once they did, as the motor vehicle case study shows, the pace of government-business interaction accelerated rapidly.

In contrast to all these very busy areas are a growing number of instances where such government-business interaction as may take place has become fairly routine in nature. These cases even include several major and also a few high priority Japanese industries. It isn't that these firms and industries do not have any contact with the government, formal or informal. Most of them do, in fact, check periodically with the authorities. They do so if only to keep the government advised of their plans and operations. That would be very much in accord with the general Japanese practice of keeping in close touch and on good terms with the authorities. Yet, when things go well, even in high priority industries, the contacts between business and government can be fewer and a great deal less involved. That is also the case with industries and enterprises which may be just too small or insignificant to warrant the time or attention of the bureaucrats who monitor Japan's economic progress and development. The interests of these smaller firms and enterprises may be subsumed in some larger business grouping or association to which they no doubt belong. A group or association like the Central Federation of Small and Medium-Sized Enterprise Association is probably in close touch with the government agencies concerned. But generally speaking, government-business interaction occurs mainly where the government has a special reason for wanting to influence the development or structure of an industry.

Shortfalls of Government-Business Interaction

The interaction between business and government in Japan can be terribly effective in some cases, virtually impotent in others.

MITI's efforts until now to help develop the Japanese computer industry have been largely crowned with success. On the other hand, the history of the government's efforts since the late 1950's to restructure the auto parts and assembly sectors of the motor vehicle industry has been a chronicle of failure. It takes two parties to interact and government-business interaction doesn't always develop. Nor does the interaction that takes place necessarily accomplish what the government would like it to do. Some of the most outstanding examples of the failure of government-business interaction have resulted from government efforts to merge and consolidate firms in order to increase the international competitiveness of the industry concerned. Take the case of the attempts made to rationalize the Japanese motor vehicle industry. This objective was considered an imperative by MITI; a prerequisite before American and other foreign auto makers could be permitted to establish operations in Japan. Mergers, although not specifically programmed, were encouraged. Specific parts manufacturers were approved for government loans by the government-industry Auto Parts Committee under criteria heavily influenced by MITI. The criteria are revealing: other things being equal, large firms were favored over small firms, specialized favored over diversified, and exporting favored over non-exporting. Given the constraints of the affiliate system, MITI wanted to develop a small group of large, specialized parts firms capable of competing with American suppliers.

Even more importantly, MITI hoped to bring about a consolidation of the automobile industry into fewer and larger groups of auto producers through bureaucratic inducement. The objective was to emerge with something like a Big Two or Three with the minority share of the market producers affiliated through merger and cooperative production arrangements around Toyota and Nissan.

MITI's ambition for rationalization of the motor vehicle industry, however, exceeded the willingness and even the ability of the business interests concerned to bring it about along the lines contemplated. At one time, MITI reportedly suggested that the number of primary parts manufacturers could be reduced to 45. There presently remain over 300. The difficulties MITI encountered in its efforts to consolidate the parts sector of the auto industry were mild, however, compared to what the auto case study terms MITI's "profound" frustration in its efforts to consolidate the automobile producers.

Such efforts go back quite a way. In 1955 MITI suggested that auto producers cooperatively develop a prototype Peoples Car, then permit MITI to select one design and subsidize its production by a single privileged manufacturer. The auto manufacturers quietly but strongly objected to a subsidy for a single company and the plan never reached the Diet. This was perhaps the manufacturers' first resistance to MITI policy. Then again, in 1961 when MITI proposed to the Industrial Structure Advisory Council that passenger car production be organized into groups based on the car's basic design type, industry consensus was lacking. Toyota and Nissan offered no opposition, but the remainder of industry objected. After a series of unsuccessful discussions, MITI dropped its proposal. One after the other, four of the six separate auto producer affiliation agreements negotiated in the late 1960's fell apart. Attempts to link Isuzu Motors with another Japanese motor vehicle producer were particularly unsuccessful. The 1966 contemplated Fuji-Isuzu, the 1967 Mitsubishi-Fuji-Isuzu, the 1967 Mitsubishi-Isuzu, and the 1968 Nissan-Isuzu agreements were never consummated. Instead, Mitsubishi chose a joint venture with Chrysler as its minority partner. Isuzu likewise linked up with an American producer, General Motors. A third Japanese motor vehicle manufacturer with a relatively small share of the market, Toyo Kogyo, is reportedly negotiating a joint venture agreement with Ford. This was not quite what MITI had in mind.

It is apparent from this record that numbers of firms in the motor vehicle assembly and parts industry, if not interested in the course urged upon that industry by MITI, certainly chose to ignore such guidance. Interaction has failed in a number of other cases where business interests proceeded their own way against official wishes. The steel case study describes, for example, the decision of Sumitomo Metals to increase its capacity and market share at a time when MITI and the other producers in the industry agreed that new investments should be made only to replace existing capacity. This was the recommendation of a special committee of the Japan Iron and Steel Federation created in 1965 to develop an investment schedule for the industry for the next five years. The committee's view was that these restraints were called for in view of the impact of the recession of 1964-65 on the demand for steel. MITI backed this majority view which, of course, also represented its position under the existing system of industry consensus under the Ministry's watchful eye. Production cartels in several product areas were in effect at the time, and the general industry pattern was to avoid price instability by moderating production levels.

Sumitomo, one of three firms then modernizing its facilities, continued its installation which technically was a replacement but which in fact meant a substantial improvement in its productivity. In addition, the firm continued to increase production while the larger producers moved more cautiously. Sumitomo has long had the most aggressive investment policy of any company in the industry. Its posture has long been to remain as independent as possible from MITI direction. Unlike other steel companies, Sumitomo assiduously avoided until fairly recently even hiring any retired MITI bureaucrats. MITI's reaction to such defiance has been a pragmatic one, and this drama is still being played out.

There are instances other than those described in the case studies which illustrate the shortfalls of government-business itneraction. The prolonged attempts of the U.S. and Japanese governments to work out an agreement on voluntary control of Japanese exports of wool and synthetic textiles to this country have been attributed, in part by some observers of the Japanese economic scene, to a failure of government-business interaction. The government has never been involved with the Japanese textile industry on the same scale as with the three industries case studied or any of the other high priority growth industries of the postwar era. Even when government was assisting the modernization of the textile industry during the 1960's, MITI's role in those programs hardly compared with its far more extensive involvement in the development of the computer industry.

Why Government-Business Interaction Works—When It Works

Why then is there such a difference in the extent to which interaction takes place and is effective? Why does it succeed in some instances and fail in others? The following examples drawn from the case studies shed light on the answers to those questions.

The case studies show that government-business interaction in Japan works best when there is consensus—within industry, within the government, and between the two groups. Another major set of circumstances which determine what gets done is the strength and attitude of the client relationship between the government and the industry concerned. The computer industry, of the three industries case studied, is a notable example of the Japanese consensus of a dependent, in fact infant, industry, a powerful bureaucracy, and an urgent national priority.

Consensus between government and business in Japan can be facilitated by financial incentives which lubricate the consensual process, by MITI's role as a catalyst and initiator in developing consensus, and by the presence of retired bureaucrats in the industry concerned. Consensus, of course, also comes most easily, and is reached most frequently, when the fundamental interests of business and the government are congruent.

The influence of financial incentives—loans, tax concessions and even subsidies—upon the consensual process has already been covered in some detail in the preceding discussion. One additional example of this influence can be cited here. It has to do with the Nissan-Prince merger in the motor vehicle industry. It will be recalled from the previous chapter how the MITI Minister's father helped arrange with his friend, the Chairman of Prince Motors, a crucial private meeting. At this meeting the Minister and MITI Vice-Minister emphasized the advantages which Prince as well as Nissan would derive from the merger. This evidently was one of the ways in which administrative guidance on this matter was given to Prince's top management. In addition, the chief executive of the Japan Development Bank entered the discussions and promised financial assistance to the merger. There were, of course, other reasons, perhaps more important, as to why this merger was consummated. It served many purposes well. Not the least of these was avoiding bankruptcy for Prince which was then in a weakened financial position. Nissan also badly needed the additional passenger car capacity which Prince's modern and under-utilized plant provided. The essential stimulus to this merger was financial rather than bureaucratic in more ways than one. The initiative for such a move came from Prince's creditors, not shareholders. So the prospect of a Japan Development Bank loan of about $15 million profferred at such an appropriate time to the merged company certainly must have influenced the outcome. It helped the Nissan and Prince management, as well as their creditor banks, appreciate the wisdom of a merger which MITI greatly desired.

The episode also illustrates MITI's role as a catalyst and initiator of consensus. The presence of retired bureaucrats in the top management ranks of the steel industry help MITI fill this role. As previously mentioned, retired MITI-men may leave the government as vice-ministers and wind up on the board of directors of a steel company. These ex-career civil servants may lack business experience but they do provide a valuable channel of communication to the authorities. Consensus in the steel industry, at least between the government and the industry giants Yawata and Fuji (before their merger into Nippon Steel) has also been facilitated by the background and experience of other senior executives in these firms. These two producers have been managed by people who grew up in the steel industry while it was under government control. They view the industry as associated with the interests of the government and the nation. As the steel case study so well puts it,

> The influence of the steel industry's traditional relationship with the bureaucracy and in fact with the broader economic policy-making community in and out of government, should not be overlooked. Their mutual recognition of Japan's dependence on steel is well-founded. Early in 1970, steelmaker's preliminary capital budgets for the next five years indicated that a full 10% of Japan's total capital investment for the period would be in steel capacity. The industry has been easily the most critical element in Japan's remarkable post-war economic phenomenon. Its impact on the international competitiveness of Japanese ships, autos, bearings, and machinery has been profound. It is at once one of Japan's biggest importers and exporters. It dominates domestic funds flow accounts much like the

U.S. government dominates domestic capital markets. Recognition of its critical position has been strong. If the thesis that Japan's leaders of business and government share common perceptions of Japan's national interest has any validity, it must apply to Japan's traditional steelmakers.

As all three case studies show, consensus is easiest to come by when the interests of business and government run parallel. Consensus is not totally out of the question when interests diverge, however. When the stakes involved are not critical or the costs to business of meeting the government's goals are not prohibitively high, consensus can also be achieved. In the early stages of the computer industry's development, for instance, both government and industry were concerned with expanding the industry's capacity and widening its product range. There also was a strong mutuality of interest in identifying and solving the bottlenecks, technological and other, as they surfaced. The interests of government and business began to diverge however, when the government concluded that some consolidation of the industry was called for. According to the president of the industry's trade association, consolidation is likely to be "naturally" evolved eventually. In the Japanese way, "naturally" means no liquidations or unfriendly acquisitions heavily influenced by MITI. It also signifies that the pattern of consolidation will be settled only after lengthy discussions with the bureaucracy, bankers, and other business interests involved.

Rationalization has also been the sticking point of government-business interaction in the motor vehicle industry. Apart from the Nissan-Prince merger, only two of the six other separate auto producer affiliation arrangements negotiated were consummated. Both these cases involved Toyota, which saw its way clear to conclude such arrangements because they would enable it to offer a larger product line. The Hino Motor Company's trucks and Daihatsu's mini cars complemented rather than competed with Toyota's.

While the degree of interaction varies by industry and according to the stage of development of that industry, it also depends on who the players are. Some industries, in fact different firms and corporate executives within the same industry, lend themselves more readily than others to the interaction process. An industry, or enterprise, may have grown and prospered, may also have established itself, without the government's help. That is entirely possible in Japan. As long as it can maintain its independence, such an industry or firm is better placed to follow a course of its own choosing than an industry dependent on the government for future as well past support and assistance. The government's ability to influence an industry's course of action often depends on the client relationship of that industry to the government. Financial constraints and, in some cases, poor performance have been known to temper the resistance of a particular firm to the government's wishes.

It also follows that the response of many Japanese businessmen to the government's guidance is conditioned by their concern about the consequences of non-compliance. There can be a cost to alienating MITI or other government agencies. The industrialist or his company which does not comply is not necessarily likely to suffer any immediate reprisal. Retaliation is not usually the Japanese way. Nor is the government likely to take any sort of action to assert itself in a way that might slow down the rate of Japan's economic progress. Non-conformists probably will be tolerated as long as they produce the results sought for the Japanese nation. The business establishment itself might bring pressure to bear on the mavericks to conform for a variety of reasons. But such pressure does not necessarily assure the compliance or conformity sought.

The risk, such as it is, to which non-conforming firms and corporate executives expose themselves is that the government's support and assistance may be slow in coming should that need arise in the future. The impact of the government's displeasure might register even outside the ministries. As the steel industry study notes, the lending policies of private sector banks might be influenced unfavorably by press accounts of any plans by mavericks to defy MITI and the Industrial Structure Council. That unhappy prospect can persuade some crisis-minded Japanese businessmen to follow administrative guidance. They are all the more inclined to do so since they recognize that, on the other hand, the government feels obligated to help and support those firms which have cooperated and done its bidding.

How this client relationship and concern over maintaining the government's goodwill facilitates government-business interaction can be seen in the computer case study. The Japanese component of the computer industry benefited greatly from certain aids and incentives provided by the government. Direct financial assistance, tax concessions, joint technology development, and access to the patents and know-how of MITI's Agency for Industrial Science and Technology stimulated and assisted the industry's growth. In addition, MITI encouraged compliance with its guidance through discretionary allocation of product type and quantity within a cartel, through selective approval of competitive imports, and through government procurement of computers. Boston Consulting Group's analysts point out that no computer manufacturer has elected to act independently and hence jeopardize his long-run position. The potential rewards in a market growing in excess of 30 percent annually are large.

When the Japanese steel industry was at its weakest in the immediate postwar period, the steel case study notes, the government's power vis-a-vis its industry clients quieted any differences of opinion as to which firm would be allowed to add a certain type of capacity at a given point of time. Until the late 1950's, the government maintained a great deal of control over the industry by virtue of its authority to set quotas and allocate raw materials. These weapons were little used, at least not visibly, under conditions of high market growth then prevailing. The industry's problems became more complex as MITI began to give up its powers. Firms found it harder to agree on capacity and production allocation as MITI's powers of persuasion diminished.

MITI, of course, is still far from being a paper tiger. Even a maverick in a relatively strong position, like Sumitomo, has to consider the consequences of continuing to buck the current, if its opposition or lack of cooperation is absolutely unyielding. MITI, the steel case study notes, attempted to discipline the company in 1966 by limiting its allocation of imported coking coal to what MITI considered appropriate levels. The demand for steel recovered sharply and by 1967 Sumitomo's additional capacity was needed to meet domestic requirements. So Sumitomo never really felt the effect of this action. Nevertheless, Sumitomo has to weigh the consequences against whatever gains it may accrue by going its own way. That Sumitomo may be giving some thought to this prospect is indicated from recent reports that that firm has now hired, in an executive capacity, its first retired MITI official.

Some Reasons Why Interaction Fails

It follows that if consensus among the parties concerned helps government-business interaction achieve its objectives, the lack of consensus would lead to failure. Their inability to achieve intra-governmental consensus has also forced MITI to abandon or delay putting certain of its industrial development proposals into effect. Also cited previously, were instances when other government agencies, particularly the Ministry of Finance, successfully opposed action or programs advocated by MITI. The veto power of the Ministry of Finance, over inducements to industry based on government funding or tax concessions, is very formidable.

There is another richly illustrative example of where MITI's best laid plans went awry for lack of consensus within the government as well as with industry. It has been described in the auto case study and in somewhat greater detail in other sources.[26] The setting is 1962, a time when most major currencies had recently become convertible, and import restrictions were being eased in other major world markets besides the United States. MITI, concentrating on improving the international competitiveness of Japanese industry, was concerned with the structure of a number of industries, autos, petrochemicals, and tires among them. MITI believed the necessary structural changes could be brought about if it was given comprehensive authority from the Diet to undertake, in cooperation with industry and the City Banks, major programs for producer specialization, establishing appropriate investment levels, and promoting mergers and groupings. A Development Bill for Specific Industries was drafted to that end by MITI. The bill further called for:

- designating strategic industries that needed special attention to help them increase their international competitiveness;

- exempting such industries for five years from the provisions of the Anti-Monopoly Act;
- extending various forms of incentives such as special tax privileges and long term, low interest loans.

Preoccupied with the need for Japanese industry to compete on world markets, the ruling LDP party's leadership strongly favored enactment of the proposed law. The Prime Minister observed that, "The Japanese automobile manufacturers will not become competitive with General Motors and Ford under the current situation." Their endorsement, however, was not enough to carry along the Ministry of Finance. The Finance Ministry was in sympathy with the objectives of the measure but concerned lest it give MITI the deciding voice in industrial policy. Because of the existing rivalry between the two ministries, the Ministry of Finance did not wish to surrender to MITI any of its independence or freedom nor that of financial institutions under its guidance. The Finance Ministry's price for withdrawing its opposition to the Bill was to have it rewritten to relieve the Ministry and its affiliated financial institutions from any obligation to abide by the final decision of the MITI-industry-bank group as to which firms and industries should receive financial assistance.

The Bill was opposed by the Japanese Socialist Party and the Fair Trade Commission. Both were for strengthening antitrust in Japan rather than weakening it. A coalition of representatives of small and medium size businesses, farmers, and unions also joined in opposition to the proposed measure. Even the auto producers, who would have benefited under the Bill's provisions, did not favor it, for reasons which reveal much about the attitude of business toward government in Japan. According to the auto case study, some producers complained that the proposed law would extend the industry's intimacy with government beyond desirable limits; these producers did not want to jeopardize their autonomy. Moreover, there was no financial urgency, at that time, for any of the secondary producers to consolidate with each other or the Big Two (Toyota and Nissan) in order to stay in business or to finance the required growth.

In the end, the opposition proved too much. MITI made three abortive attempts to get the Bill enacted by the Diet, after strongly promoting it and lobbying on its behalf. These attempts failed for lack of consensus, among other reasons. MITI finally decided to shelve the Bill permanently.

There have been other occasions when MITI has underestimated the degree of opposition to its proposals. The fight over the Yawata-Fuji steel merger turned out to be bitter and prolonged. The Fair Trade Commission, encouraged by the opposition of many if not most prominent academic economists and other influential segments of Japanese public opinion, challenged the merger. Neither MITI nor most business and LDP leaders had attached much weight to the independence of the FTC and the strongly held belief of its chairman in antitrust policies.

The Japanese Fair Trade Commission is a quasi-judicial body independent of the Diet except for the budget and the appointment of its commissioners. Modeled somewhat after the U.S. Federal Trade Commission, its responsibility is to hear and decide violations of Japan's Anti-Monopoly Act. Though hardly a powerful agency, the Fair Trade Commission is called the fourth branch of government when it comes to the antitrust field. The merger illustrated the limits of MITI's influence on both the FTC and the firms involved. While MITI played the role of adviser during the merger crisis, Yawata and Fuji did not follow its advice.

Lack of consensus in certain instances necessitated a change of plans, even in the development of the computer industry to which the highest priority had been attached. The establishment of the Japan Electronic Computer Corporation (JECC), which made it possible for the thinly financed Japanese corporations in that industry to establish a system of computer rentals, is one such case. As originally conceived by MITI, the JECC was to be jointly owned by the Japanese component of the industry and the government. The manufacturers opposed it because they were fearful of additional MITI leverage over their operations. The Ministry of Finance was reluctant to allocate funds for the government's equity share in the JECC. A compromise, therefore, had to be designed from which JECC emerged as wholly industry-owned, but with its operations heavily financed by loans from the Japan Development Bank.

The motor vehicle case study also raises some question as to whether consensus was ever really reached in joint government-industry planning for rationalization of the auto parts industry. It is not publically clear, according to the Boston Consulting Group's analysts, whether such plans fully took into account the independent views of the industry. These views were supposedly put forth by the auto producers and primary parts manufacturers who sat on the Auto Parts Committee and the newly appointed advisory Auto Parts Policy Research Committee. These were the consensus-making, plans-formulating bodies intended to harmonize differing points of view. MITI at that time advocated the creation of large "unit system" or sub-assembly producers. This proposal was not well received by the industry. Lack of movement in the desired direction since then does reflect a lack of interest, certainly of consensus, on the part of the motor vehicle industry in MITI's proposals. The fact was that the auto producers were not interested in MITI's plans for restructuring the auto parts sector because they were working on this problem in their own way. The auto makers considered that they were already reorganizing their parts affiliates, and reallocating production among themselves, more efficiently than would be done under the MITI proposals.

Most interesting, perhaps, of the various limitations on government-business interaction revealed by the case studies are the rigidities built into the Japanese economic system. Take, for example, the need for merging companies to obtain agreement from each of the company or "enterprise" unions involved, since each has a stake in the outcome and is concerned about losing its identity. Or the need to first disengage and then acceptably reestablish relations with the several, usually different, major commercial banks of the firms involved in the merger. The ability of Nissan and Prince to overcome these two types of obstacles characteristic to Japanese mergers helped consummate that one.

Japanese companies are generally also unwilling and unable, because of their commitment to the lifetime employment system, to dismiss personnel made redundant by a merger or other type of affiliation. Moreover, there often is the rather delicate matter of management succession in any new combination.

Technical assistance and licensing agreements, as the computer case study shows, can also constitute an obstacle to effective government-business interaction when merger or consolidation is involved. In the Japanese computer industry each producer maintains a separate technical and licensing arrangement with a different American computer manufacturer. This would have to be taken into account in any realignment of the industry. A merger might well jeopardize the continued access of the new firm to the patents and know-how previously available to those producers party to the merger.

When the goal is consolidation or rationalization, Japanese corporate structure can also be an obstacle. Most manufacturers in the computer industry, for example, are part of multiple business corporations whose computer business is vertically related to others and not large horizontally. Along the same lines, the motor vehicle case study points out how the traditional financial and managerial relations of the assembler and parts supplier have proven to be a block to consolidation. This indeed was the case in the Prince-Nissan merger, an otherwise seemingly successful one.

Mergers are not especially attractive to Japanese firms for other reasons. There really are only two conditions which would influence a competitor to withdraw from a high growth industry; the prospect of more profitable investment elsewhere in the short run, and inability to finance the growth. The financially able and willing firm, however, will continue to invest and compete. So it was in the automobile industry that consolidation failed because of lack of financial pressure on so many of the producers, either in the form of lower profitability or higher absolute funding requirements.

A producer's opposition to consolidation can have emotional and traditional roots as well. As has been noted before, Japanese are group oriented and attached to the groups with which they are affiliated. The prospect of self-imposed production rationalization arrangements with, or formal absorptions into companies in other industrial groups can be distasteful. The status of one's company determines the range of one's potential in Japan. Because group consciousness is so intense among the Japanese, employees of Prince, the smaller company, felt looked down upon by the employees of Nissan, one of the leading car manufacturers. Engineers and executives of Prince, one student of the subject reported,[1] felt humiliated to be associated with Nissan employees. Thus economically reasonable actions like the rationalization of sectors of industry in Japan may often be made impracticable, or at least delayed, by social obstacles of this nature despite the government's efforts to persuade or influence the private sector to move in that direction.

SUMMING UP

When all the Exceptions and Nuances of the Government-Business Relationship Have Been Taken Into Account, "Japan, Incorporated" is an Economic Fact of Life.

The huge success of the Japanese economy rests on the initiative and entrepreneurial skill and drive of its businessmen. Their efforts have been fostered, encouraged, and enhanced at certain critical times and in key areas by the interaction of government and business, primarily big business. This concerting of the talents and operations of businessmen and bureaucrats has facilitated the channeling of resources from the mature to the growth sectors of the Japanese economy. Government and business have interacted often, in many ways, and in many areas to help maximize Japan's economic growth.

There is a Special Style and Scope to Interaction Between Government and Business in Japan Which Makes It Distinctive.

Some elements of government-business interaction in Japan are evident among the other private-enterprise economies of the West. There is some semblance in the industrial-military complex in the United States of the kind of government-business relationship that exists in Japan. The emphasis placed on setting priorities for the Japanese economy found its precedent in the French system of indicative planning. In a number of Western European countries, governments and highly organized business communities maintain close relations. What makes government-business interaction in Japan different from what takes place in other countries is the extent and scale of such interaction. A qualitative difference, a style peculiar to the Japanese, derives from Japan's history and culture with its

[1] Chie Nakane, *Japanese Society* (Berkeley: University of California Press, 1970), p. 109.

emphasis on the consensual approach, a tradition of government leadership in industrial development, and a generally shared desire to advance the interests of the Japanese nation. This style is what enables "Japan, Incorporated" to merge and reconcile varying interests in so many cases.

But "Japan, Incorporated" is not the Colossus nor the Conspiracy Between Government and Business That Its Most Severe Critics Make It Out to Be.

It must be viewed in perspective. "Japan, Incorporated" is not a monolithic system in which government leads and business follows blindly. It is rather more of a participatory partnership. The partners work best together when there is consensus within the government, among the industry and business interests involved, and between the two groups. Such consensus is reached most easily and frequently when the fundamental interests of business and government are congruent. When they are not, business can and frequently does follow an independent course.

The Government Depends More on Inducements than Controls to Persuade Business to Follow a Desired Course.

The government's direct control powers have been steadily waning. Even when these powers were at their peak, the government usually preferred friendlier types of persuasion. Indeed, in contrast to the limited range and often muffled use of controls and other forms of direct administrative guidance, the array and effectiveness of aids and incentives used by the government is dazzling. Financing, tax concessions, subsidies, technical assistance, and other inducements are often used in innovative and skillful ways. The carrots are larger than the sticks.

Interaction Between Government and Business is Pervasive in the Japanese Economy but not All-Encompassing.

The managers of "Japan, Incorporated" focus their attention mainly on the growth sectors of the Japanese economy. A major objective of the conglomerate to which "Japan, Incorporated" is likened is the coordination of its various component operations so as to yield the maximum return for the Japanese nation. The conglomerate's managers plan on continually shifting resources from mature to dynamic industries in order to advance the rate of economic growth. The degree and success of government-business interaction not only varies from industry to industry but in time within the same industry.

On Balance Government-Business Interaction has been an Important Factor in Japan's Economic Growth.

Though limited in scope and not always successful in attaining the objectives sought, interaction between government and business has contributed substantially to Japan's striking economic progress. This interaction has facilitated the development and expansion of most, if not all, of the high priority and growth industries of postwar Japan. These are the industries, like electronics, automobiles and steel, which have pushed Japan to the head of the international growth league. They are also among the industries which have made the greatest impact on the American public and the U.S. economy. "Japan, Incorporated" may thus appear to be more formidable and wide-ranging than it actually is. But its accomplishments are very significant indeed.

The prospects are the Government-Business Relationship will change only slowly.

The government's direct controls over business, unless renewed, will continue to be liberalized. Moreover, the government may well be less occupied in the future with industrial development, and more with the other complex and troublesome issues that confront other more consumer-oriented economies. Changes in the fabric of Japanese society, however, which will tend to weaken the very strong cultural influences that facilitate and encourage business and government interaction in that country are less predictable. Consensus more than directives, shared objectives as much as authority, effective communications more than controls, inducements rather than commands, will continue to make government-business interaction an important feature of the Japanese economic system for some time to come.

18

International Business Negotiations:

CHARACTERISTICS AND PLANNING IMPLICATIONS

A. Kapoor

This section offers a general introduction to the subject of international business negotiations, especially those involving host governments of developing countries. The following areas are considered: the nature of negotiations and reasons for its growing importance; major mistakes committed by the American international company (IC) in negotiating, especially with host governments of developing countries; changes in the relative negotiation strength of the IC and the host country over the duration of an investment; and an approach to planning for international business negotiations.

The growing change and uncertainty characterizing Asia (and other parts of the world) requires particular attention to planning for negotiations by and between the IC and the host governments of developing countries.

BACKGROUND

NATURE OF NEGOTIATION

In general, negotiation occurs within a context which might be viewed as being composed of five concentric circles[1] (Figure 1).

First, negotiation is characterized by four Cs which represent common interests (something to negotiate for), conflicting interests (something to negotiate about), compromise (give and take on points), and criteria or objectives (determining the objective and the criteria for its achievement).

Second, the political, economic, social, and cultural systems constitute the environment of a country and directly influence the approach to negotiation adopted in that country.

Third, the term perspective includes the ability to understand environmental factors in more than one country which might appear to be unrelated to the negotiation situation but in fact have a significant influence on it.

Fourth, over time the negotiation strength of the IC changes vis-a-vis the host country, requiring reassessment of the four Cs and other dimensions of the negotiation contract.

Fifth, international business negotiations involve more than one country and therefore are influenced by more than one context of negotiation outlined in Figure 1.

FIGURE 1: The Context of Negotiation

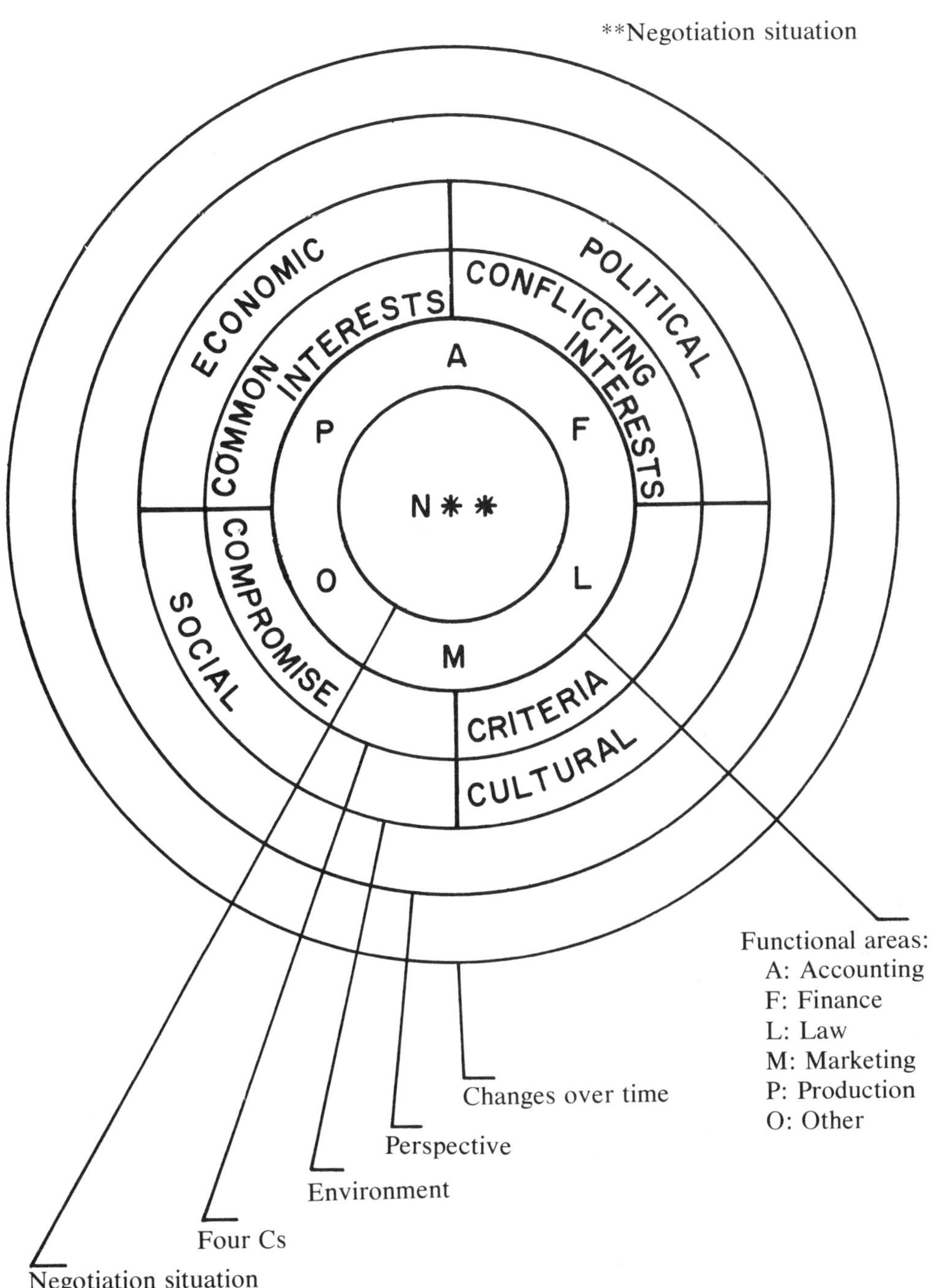

Negotiation is an art which is developed through the study of the social, cultural, political, and economic systems of the host country, combined with a practical application of the knowledge thus acquired. Successful negotiations do not depend primarily on an expertise in technical, financial, accounting, and legal analysis. In brief, *negotiation is the use of common sense under pressure to achieve objectives.*

REASONS FOR GROWING IMPORTANCE[2]

Four major developments over the past decade have contributed significantly to the growing importance of international business negotiations, especially between the IC and host governments of developing countries.

First, for political and economic reasons, governments of many developing countries are playing a growing role as regulators and participants in the economic affairs of their countries, which results in greater interaction between the IC and host governments.

Second, the intense competition from non-U.S.-based ICs both in terms of selling and direct investments means that the developing countries can now satisfy their requirements from a larger range of alternatives. This will continue to improve their negotiation position vis-à-vis any IC.

Third, a growing range of key decision makers in the IC and host developing countries are gaining an increasing commonalty in terms of international outlook, an understanding of technology, and a realistic assessment of the need of the IC and the developing countries for each other. This commonalty is promoting a greater sense of equality, resulting in growing emphasis on negotiations in reducing their differences.

Fourth, the existing change and uncertainty is causing review and renegotiation (if not dismantling) by countries of traditional economic and political relations with other countries. Economic considerations are being given greater recognition by governments, which results in growing involvement and interaction of the IC with governments.

MAJOR MISTAKES IN NEGOTIATION

Developing a list of "do's" and "don'ts" in negotiation is always fraught with dangers of simplification and oversight. However, the following list illustrates types of mistakes committed by the IC especially in negotiations with host governments in developing countries and should be viewed with reference to the context of negotiation outlined in Figure 1. The mistakes are organized into four broad and interrelated categories of empathy, role of governments, decision-making characteristics, and organizing for negotiation:

Empathy.

1. *Failure to place yourself in the other person's shoes:* It is not sufficient merely to know the position and approach of your opponent to a negotiation; even more important is to understand the reasons which prompt him to adopt the particular stance.

2. *Insufficient understanding of different ways of thinking:* Reaching the same conclusions is important, but in negotiations it is even more im-

portant to know the thought processes by which individuals from different cultures reach the same conclusions.

3. *Insufficient attention to saving face of the opponent:* "Winning" in a negotiation situation should not result in a loss of face for the opponent, especially in countries where personal honor is a sensitive issue.

4. *Insufficient knowledge of host country:* Often the negotiator does not have sufficient knowledge of the history, culture, and political characteristics of a country in which he is negotiating.

Role of Government.

5. *Insufficient recognition of the nature and characteristics of the role of government in centrally-planned economies:* The desire for rapid development, distrust of private enterprise, lack of indigenous entrepreneurial talent—these and other considerations have prompted host governments to play a major role in planning for the economic development of their countries.

6. *Insufficient recognition of the relatively low status assigned to businessmen:* Not only are government officials in planned economies powerful, but they often look down upon the businessman who is viewed as being concerned only with questions of profits and not the broader national aspirations of the society.

7. *Insufficient recognition of the role of host government in negotiations:* Negotiations in developing countries are generally tripartite in nature, involving the foreign company, the local company, and the host government.

8. *Insufficient recognition of the perception of host countries of the role of ICs' home government in negotiations:* Regardless of what the reality of the situation is, the host government believes that the foreign company uses the muscle of its home government in negotiations with the host government.

Decision-making Characteristics.

9. *Insufficient recognition of the economic and political criteria in decision making:* Host government officials place particular stress on political considerations in evaluating investment proposals in keeping with the general orientation of the type of organization to which they belong.

10. *Insufficient recognition of the difference between approval at one level and implementation of such approval at other levels of the government:* Gaining approval of the central government for an investment does not mean that other levels of the government will automatically implement the approval.

11. *Insufficient understanding of the role of personal relations and personalities in decision making by the host government:* Host government officials possess considerable discretion in interpretation of policies and regulations relating to foreign investments.

12. *Insufficient allocation of time for negotiations:* It simply takes longer in certain countries to present a proposal to gain a reaction and to offer a response because of distance, mutual suspicion, different ways of thinking, and the internal decision-making structure of the government and the IC.

Organizing.

13. *Insufficient attention to planning for changing negotiation strength:* The negotiation strength of the IC and the host country changes over the duration of a project.

14. *Interference by headquarters:* Headquarters personnel sometimes interfere directly in negotiations, causing serious damage to the credibility of the country-level managers and the field negotiations.

15. *Insufficient planning for internal communication and decisions:* Several parts of an organization have an interest in an ongoing negotiation and their views and preferences have to be recognized in negotiating for a particular package of terms of investment.

16. *Insufficient recognition of the role of the negotiator in accommodating the conflicting interests of his group with those of the opposing groups:* The negotiator plays a crucial role as interpreter, intermediary, and counselor both to his own group and to the opposing group on what can be achieved in a particular negotiation.

17. *Insufficient recognition of the loci of decision-making authority:* Decisions are seldom made by any one branch of government but are shared across agencies and ministries because of the particular characteristics of government organizations.

18. *Insufficient recognition of the strength of competitors:* The tendency to underestimate the competitive strength and negotiation skills of non-American companies is a source of weakness in the American company's planning for negotiation.

19. *Insufficient attention to training executives in the art of negotiation:* Executives are seldom trained or encouraged to develop negotiating skills.

JAPANESE NEGOTIATION CHARACTERISTICS

An understanding of negotiation characteristics of Japanese companies especially in developing countries is essential for U.S.-based ICs in order to compete more effectively with the Japanese. (The list below is for purposes of illustration.)

1. *Planning:* Japanese appear to engage in far more detailed planning than do American companies before entering into negotiations.

2. *Government relations:* In keeping with Japanese tradition, Japanese companies place far greater stress on cultivating effective relations with key officials of the host government.

3. *Decision making:* In general, Japanese executives overseas have limited authority which requires constant interaction with the corporate level. Because of the group and consensus orientation of decision making, Japanese companies send more executives to a negotiation than do American companies.

4. *Intermediaries:* Large trading companies often undertake international business development for many other Japanese companies. At times the identity of the "client" company is not known to the host country until later stages of negotiation.

5. *Multinational precedents:* Unlike American companies, at present the geographic scope and volume of Japanese foreign direct investments are limited. Therefore, Japanese companies are far less constrained by multinational precedents, thus permitting them frequently greater flexibility in accepting different terms of investment in different countries.

6. *Investment terms:* Unlike American companies, Japanese companies initially accept limited equity and control in the hope of gradual escalation.

7. *Corporate provincialism:* In comparison with their American counterparts, the most senior levels of Japanese management are typically marked by a fundamental lack of understanding of non-Japanese ways of thinking and feeling.

8. *Superiority/inferiority complex:* Japanese tend to suffer from an inferiority complex in dealing with the developed countries, and display a superiority complex in dealing with the developing countries.

9. *Language:* Unlike American companies, Japanese are faced with a fundamental problem because of their ignorance of English and other languages of international business transaction. This characteristic accounts for the many policy and operational problems in negotiations faced by the Japanese.

10. *Informal process:* Unlike American companies, Japanese place far greater stress on informal processes of negotiation. The formal application is often used only at the concluding stages of negotiation.

CHANGES IN NEGOTIATION STRENGTH[3]

Unfortunately, the IC seldom plans for changes in its negotiation strength over time vis-à-vis the host country. This section illustrates four general ways in which the IC acquires and loses negotiation strength in an investment.

1. Through *operational capabilities* by increasing alternatives, by intelligence, and by publicity.

2. Through a package of economic and political *contributions and losses* resulting from IC activities in the host country.

3. Through *association* with one or more of several groups including local partner and governments (host, home, and others).

4. Through *action* by control over the duration of negotiation and by purposeful rotation of executives and development of executive skills for negotiation.

OPERATIONAL CAPABILITIES[4]

Increasing Alternatives. Negotiation strength of a party is influenced by the range of alternatives available to it, including alternative sources of supply of desired resources/markets on acceptable terms.

In the past two decades, alternative sources of supply for the host country have steadily increased, adding to the negotiating strength of the host country vis-à-vis the IC. Japanese and American companies are increasingly competing with each other for investments in Southeast Asia, an advantage to the host countries. The South American countries are beginning to favor investments made by Japanese and European companies in order to reduce their dependence on U.S. companies. Conversely, Thailand and Indonesia are encouraging American investment to reduce the predominance of Japanese investors. The American IC needs to place greater emphasis on understanding the nature and motivations of various sources of international competition for markets/resources of developing countries in planning for negotiation with host countries.

Over the duration of a project the alternatives available to the host country are likely to decrease less rapidly than those for the IC in the host country. Before investing in a country both the IC and the host country often possess a significant range of choices. However, once agreement is reached and implementation commences, the element of choice is reduced to a greater extent for the IC than for the host country. For example, in the fertilizer industry, the host country might seek more than one foreign investment. The terms it negotiates with new investors could be used to seek changes in the terms allowed to the earlier investors who have greatly reduced negotiation strength because of their fixed investments in the host country. The IC, therefore, needs to plan for changes in its negotiation strength over the duration of a project.

Information. Information refers to facts relating to a particular industry, project, or other aspects of a relatively objective nature. The ICs' comparative advantage of information on an industry vis-à-vis the host country changes over the duration of a project. The clear advantage at the entry stage is reduced appreciably in the eyes of the host country by the time a project reaches the operational stage. The host country, with the additional information it now has, often finds certain terms of the project no longer satisfactory. This assessment might result in re-negotiation of original terms or a desire to hasten the stage of greater indigenous control of the project.

The IC is faced with an important policy question: Would negotiations be more effective and agreements more lasting if the IC provided more information on its activities and objectives to the host government? Should host governments specify the types of information they seek from ICs for more effective assessment and negotiation with ICs? In any event, host governments will continue to press the IC for information, and in one way or another they will get it. Information which is extracted from the IC is likely to be less credible in the eyes of the host government than information which is voluntarily furnished by the IC.

Publicity. The IC is the subject of growing controversy and publicity, especially in developing countries. But why is publicity used in negotiations, and how does its role change over the duration of a project?

Publicity is used by a party to improve its position in negotiations. In many developing countries, the press is controlled or strongly influenced by the government or large indigenous business organizations. Therefore, the IC exposed to publicity in a foreign country is generally at a disadvantage.

Moreover, the intelligentsia (such as editors and correspondents) usually maintain a critical attitude toward the IC.

Some of the reasons for using publicity for negotiation are: to secure a specific response from an opponent; to encourage public discussion, especially where political implications are involved; to justify a particular decision in the eyes of the public; and to reduce alternative courses of action by adopting a particular public stance.

Publicity will have a growing effect on the negotiation strength of the IC. The growing concern, criticism, and interest in the IC in the developing countries; the growing body of information being developed on the contributions of the IC to the U.S.A.; and the limited and often biased but influential body of information on the effects of the IC on the host country—these and other developments will require explicit recognition by the IC of the role of publicity in planning for negotiation.

The amount of publicity appears to be related to some stages of a project more than to others. In large foreign investment projects, the entry stage is characterized by a great deal of publicity. A new and foreign element is being introduced into the local context with implications which excite extensive reporting and comments. Publicity tends to decrease appreciably during implementation unless there are major difficulties or controversies. However, at the inauguration of a project publicity increases because of the involvement of leading local political and government figures in the inauguration ceremonies. In general the amount of publicity declines during operations. It then picks up again during the decline stage as the IC is exposed to growing criticism. Thereafter, there is a great deal of publicity during negotiation for divestment and expropriation.

The role of publicity in negotiation must be seen within the broader context of the role of information in negotiation. As suggested earlier, greater equality of information between the IC and the host government could contribute to more lasting agreements between them. The IC needs to view publicity also as a means of informing opinion-forming groups in host countries of the nature, characteristics, and contributions of the IC which have become subjects of growing interest and controversy. Therefore, publicity should be explicitly recognized and systematically included in the IC's planning for negotiation with a host government.

CONTRIBUTION PACKAGE

The IC and the host country not only disagree on the adequacy of the IC's economic contributions but also on the relative weight assigned by each party over time to the economic versus political effects of IC activities. The differences between the IC and the host country generally increase over the duration of a project and need to be recognized in planning for negotiation with host governments.

Major Economic Arguments. The IC typically uses economic arguments to influence the host government, such as the effect on the foreign investment climate, the economic benefit to the host country (including the effect on the domestic investment climate), and the use of bilateral bargains.

The nature of the foreign investment climate in a country is produced by many factors, such as taxes, customs, foreign investment procedures, delays in decision making, violation of contract terms, and effective settlement of terms of withdrawal. The IC often tries to persuade a host country that it will be of benefit to the country to create or maintain a favorable investment climate. This is easier to accomplish when the host country feels that foreign investments are very desirable. For example, the potential effects on the foreign investment climate is a strong argument with the current Filipino government but carries less weight with the Indian government.

Another determinant is the relative attractiveness of a country for foreign investors. Iran, Brazil, and Japan are some of the countries attractive to most foreign investors. "Attractiveness" increases the host government's choice and reduces the need for heeding the requirements of any single source of investment. For example, Thailand might attach particular weight to the arguments of U.S. companies since the Thais wish to reduce the predominant role of Japanese investors.

In addition to the foreign investment climate argument, the IC stresses potential economic benefits or losses to influence the host government. Foreign investments have a multiplier effect on the host-country economy, resulting in benefits which are often even greater than those of the original investment, by offering constructive competition, improving working conditions, contributing to the development of local resources and of local managerial and entrepreneurial skills.

The economic benefit/loss argument has varying degrees of impact in the process of negotiation between the IC and the host government. In the developing countries, the argument does not change the existing attitudes on the part of the host country regarding policies toward economic development and the role of the public and private sectors, including the role of foreign investors. Policies of host governments in these areas are based on considerations which extend considerably beyond mere economic factors. However, specific policies of the host government on operational elements (import policies, foreign technicians, etc.) might be influenced, especially if it is attempting to attract foreign investments.

The IC and the host government use bilateral bargaining largely based on economic considerations to influence each other. Such bargains require two-way trade-offs—each party giving and getting. Bilateral bargaining stresses that the IC and the host country recognize that each has something to offer or deny to the other, thereby creating a mutuality of interests. This argument will gain in importance in the ICs' efforts to influence host governments and must be effectively integrated in planning for negotiation.

Economic/Political Weighting. From the very initial stages of project development, the IC places far greater weight than host-country government officials on the economic aspects of a project than on the political ones.

Because of the political implications of their decision, an important consideration for host-government negotiators becomes how to achieve the necessary economic benefits without exposing themselves to political attack (including charges by the indigenous business community). Of course, it is often impossible to do so. However, to the extent to which it is possible, officials will attempt to achieve at least the appearance of national control even though the real situation might be quite different. At times, the appearance is as important as the reality.

The relative economic and political weighting changes over the duration of a project. At the entry stage the host country seeks the IC's economic resources which it lacks; the emphasis is on economic contributions. However, the political considerations remain important especially in a large project. As the project reaches and proceeds beyond the stage of operations, in the eyes of the host government the value of the economic contributions of the IC is significantly decreased and political considerations gain in importance. By the time of forced divestment or expropriation, the host government stresses the political considerations more than the economic ones. The IC, however, continues to stress almost exclusively the economic aspects with the result that at and beyond the divestment stage the IC and the host government differ sharply over their respective emphases on the economic and political aspects.

The IC should place far greater emphasis in planning for negotiations on non-economic considerations which are important to the host government in evaluating projects. Additionally, the IC should also develop information on the non-economic contributions made by it to the host society for use in negotiations with the host government.

THROUGH ASSOCIATION[5]

An association with an individual or organization of an explicit (acknowledged and/or publicized) or an implicit (unacknowledged or suspected) nature influences negotiation strength of a party. How effectively the association can be used for negotiation purposes depends largely on what the adversary believes that group's strength to be. Therefore, the implicit and explicit perception and reality dimensions must be considered in discussing changes in negotiation strength through association.

Local Affiliations. The IC's negotiation strength is influenced by its affiliations with powerful local groups and individuals such as prestigious and influential law firms, employing a member of a powerful family, inviting influential individuals to serve on the board of directors of a company, and/or gaining support of other American companies operating in the host country.

In general, the local partner is a source of power for the IC at the time of entry because of special relationships in the host country. However, the local partner is also a liability for the IC, especially when he falls from favor of the host government because of certain consequent actions. A rapid change of political leaders, as occurred recently in Thailand, often places indigenous businessmen in an uncertain relationship with the new leaders.

Economic policies of such countries as India against the concentration of economic power in a few private business enterprises also reduces the effectiveness of local partners.

Over the duration of a project the influential local partner can become a strong adversary of the IC. For example, a large American company started to implement a joint venture in Iran. The local partner then started to create problems for the IC by making representations against the IC to senior host-government officials.

If possible the IC generally attempts to carefully limit the use of the local partner in its dealings with the host government. The IC recognizes that the local partner can both help and hurt it in relations with the host government.

Carefully selected and timed fresh inputs (technology, exports, etc.) by the IC to the joint venture are a means of retaining its negotiation strength vis-à-vis the local partner. Otherwise, the local partner is likely to become a hindrance to the IC in the joint venture. This needs to be recognized and systematically incorporated in planning for negotiation.

Governments: Host and Home. The IC partially controls its negotiation strength through association with the home and host governments. The relative value of these sources of negotiation strength changes over time and according to the type of project.

Host Governments. For four main reasons governments of many developing countries are playing a growing role as regulators and participants in business enterprises: an ideological preference for a greater role in public sector enterprises; suspicion and distrust of the private sector; availability of large capital investments only from the public sector; and a willingness of ICs, particularly from Japan and Europe, to associate with governments.

Especially in developing countries, association with the host government can be a source of negotiation strength for the IC as it is the major locus of power on questions of foreign investment. For the same reason, the host government is also a source of weakness in the IC's negotiations with the government. This is especially true in industries which are reserved for the public sector, which means that the IC can participate in that industry only through association with the host government.

Because of the dual nature of the host government in the venture—as a business partner and as a sovereign—the chances of conflict with the IC are greater than in the case of a venture between two private parties. Most developing countries are strongly inclined toward greater indigenous control over economic enterprise as a matter of ideology, local expertise, or domestic political realities. Pressure for greater local control over a period of time typically finds expression first in state enterprises with foreign associations.

The IC must recognize the growing role of governments in developing countries as partners in business enterprises, the need to develop executive skills in this area, and the recognition of such features in planning for negotiation with host governments.

U.S. Government. Developing countries believe that the American IC has access to and uses the strength (through trade, investment, and military policies) of the U.S. Government in negotiation. In some cases, with significant policy implications, such association might exist. But for the vast majority of foreign investments by U.S.-based ICs, does the U.S. Government engage in trade-off negotiations with foreign governments to promote and protect the economic interests of the ICs?

U.S. embassies, especially in developing countries, suggest that an implicit effect of trade-off does exist. In time, a country has usually received varying amounts of aid and other assistance which could be interpreted as "IOUs" from the U.S. to the host country. At some stage the U.S. Government might wish to collect on some of the "IOUs." The collection does not take the form of explicitly saying that "we gave you so much aid, now you need to give preference to an American company," or "you need to modify legislation which is detrimental to American companies." The implicit nature of the "IOUs" tends to be reflected largely in the form of ease of access to government officials, in faster access to policy pronouncements, in preference for an American project over a non-American one (all other things being equal), in the benefits of understanding and shared experiences which accrue as a result of joint programs conducted over a period of time. These characteristics, however, are determined by the nature of individuals involved rather than official aid policies.

There are several reasons why trade-offs are rarely used by the U.S. Government on behalf of the ICs. (1) The objectives of the U.S. Government go far beyond the economic and commercial to include regional and international political and security considerations. (2) Moreover, meaningful long-term relations with foreign countries, especially the developing ones with strong nationalism, require that they be treated as equals, especially by the larger powers. (3) Inability to control the IC further discourages the U.S. Government in engaging in trade-off negotiations with foreign governments for the IC. (4) The U.S. Government historically has had a policy of maintaining a distance from the IC.

In the vast majority of cases, the IC does not seek U.S. Government influence, strongly preferring to have the host government view it as an independent entity. This approach has been adopted by the IC because it has not found the U.S. Government particularly helpful in dealing with host governments, because of their different and at times conflicting objectives and because of the different orientation and ways of thinking of government officials and business objectives.

Despite these factors, in the eyes of the host government there exists a firm, irrevocable belief that the ICs possess sufficient influence on the U.S. Government to have it engage in trade-off negotiations with a host government to promote and protect the interests of the IC. An explicit expression might not occur and is not important; the IC's awareness of the perception of the host government offers it an important source of negotiation strength.

In addition, the IC benefits by any indirect expression of such influence. For example, one or more members of Congress might make public statements suggesting review of U.S. aid and assistance policies for a particular country.

The host government's perception of the close liaison between the IC and the U.S. Government is quite different from the reality. The implication of this reality/perception gap is that the policies of governments (both host and home) and the ICs are affected—not necessarily in conformity with their interests. It would probably be better for all if the reality were more fully understood.

NEGOTIATION STRENGTH THROUGH ACTION

Certain actions, such as controlling the duration of negotiation and executive rotation and development of negotiation skills, influence the negotiation strength of a party.

Duration of Negotiation. The duration of a negotiation strongly influences both the range and level of detailed coverage of issues. Therefore, being able to specify a limited duration for negotiations and gain acceptance of it by other parties means that the superior position of one party is being accepted by the others at a given moment of negotiation.

"Deadlines" for negotiation strength are used differently depending on the specific characteristics of a project. At the entry stage of negotiation, the IC might possess greater discretion whether or not to specify deadlines. However, during and after the stage of implementation until divestment, the IC tends to lose some of its power vis-à-vis the host government and consequently its power to specify time deadlines. At the divestment or expropriation stages, the IC has made the decision to withdraw (or has been forced to withdraw). However, negotiations for compensation and other matters often occur after the fact, especially in the case of forced withdrawal. In such negotiations, the strength of the IC is greatly reduced and it is generally up to the former host country to specify time deadlines.

Executive Rotation and Skills. In general, the IC changes executives more in keeping with normal rotation policies than with reference to the particular requirements (including negotiations) of a project. For example, especially in the case of the first investment in a country, once agreement is reached and the necessary documents signed, the IC's negotiators leave and a new team of executives is assigned for implementation of the project. Often such a policy is detrimental to the IC's negotiation position. The continued involvement of at least one of the principal negotiators from the principal negotiators from the IC beyond the stage of entry into implementation is useful. Both corporate executives and host-government officials are rotated between countries and departments. Therefore, agreements reached between one group of executives and officials might require at least review if not renegotiation, especially where negotiators from either side are changed. The major importance of "understandings" as against formal agreements in effective dealings between the negotiators further endorses the need for retaining involvement with the project of at least one of the original negotiators.

The nature of demands on the chief operating officer of a project vary with the duration of a project. At the entry stage, skills in negotiation are essential, requiring individuals who are more generalists than specialists. During implementation, individuals with more specific skills (engineering, procurement, construction) are involved when operations require administration and effective government relations. Divestment and expropriation stages often require skills not dissimilar to those needed for entry but are used to obtain a different set of objectives.

The American IC has devoted limited attention to the general subject of developing executive skills which include, especially, the art of negotiation with host governments. However, the growing importance of negotiation in international business transactions (discussed earlier) means that the executive of the U.S.-based IC must possess far greater skill in the art of negotiations. Such skills are required not only at the country but also at the regional and headquarters levels.

INVESTMENT LIFE CYCLE

The absolute necessity for planning for changes in negotiation strength has been stressed. This section presents in outline form an approach to planning for negotiation by use of the investment life cycle (ILC) (Figure 2).

The ILC refers to a project in a country and not to the IC's range of projects in a country. It focuses on contributions made by the IC to the host country and stresses that the values assigned to the contributions are largely based on subjective factors.[6] The ILC states that, over time with respect to a project in a country, the negotiation strength of the IC will decrease vis-à-vis the host country. The changes in strength can be generally anticipated and planned for in order to benefit from the standpoint of negotiation strength.

Additional characteristics of the ILC are:

- The value assigned to contributions changes over time.
- The pace of change in values differs between the IC and the host country.
- The values assigned are composed of both economic and non-economic considerations.
- The changes in values assigned result in changing negotiation strength.
- The changes in negotiation strength require changes in attitude of executives in dealing with host governments.

Assuming that the basic idea of changing negotiation strength is recognized by the IC and the host government, six important uses of the ILC can be recognized.

First, the ILC facilitates planning for negotiation on a project by recognizing the reasons and the implications for changing negotiation strength (which are generally in favor of the host country). Acceptance of this characteristic by the IC would ease recognition of the fact that the contractual

FIGURE 2
Investment Life Cycle and Negotiation Strength

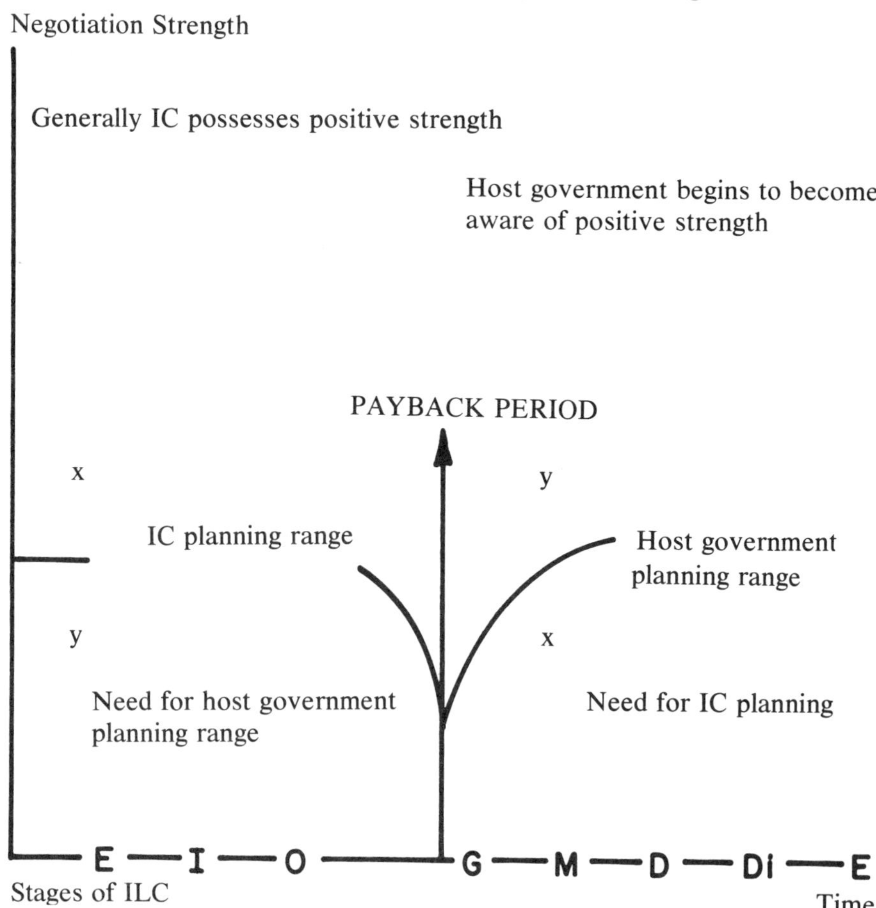

E: Entry; I: Implementation; O: Operations; G: Growth; D: Decline; Di: Divestment; E: Expropriation; Other stages can be added.

x: Negotiation strength of company
y: Negotiation strength of host country

Negotiation strength: perception of value of resource contributions which changes over time and is influenced by a variety of considerations

Resource Contributions:

IC—Technology, management, organization, capital (particularly foreign exchange), access to international markets

Host country—Capital, access to country resources, goodwill

and ownership rights of the IC will be honored by the host government only as long as it feels that in balance the country is gaining. The ILC is also useful for the host government as it demonstrates that the government is not more powerful than the IC at all times, and is especially weak during the early stages of a project.

Second, the ILC encourages the IC and the host country to emphasize their relative contributions to each other's objectives over time.

Third, the ILC encourages decision makers and planners to evaluate resource contributions as they influence negotiations, directly or indirectly.

Fourth, the ILC can be used by the IC at the country, regional, and headquarters levels and provides a common measure for internal planning for a project in a particular country.

Fifth, the ILC assists in simplification of a highly complex, subjective and changing range of variables over time which affect the process and outcome of negotiations.

Sixth, the ILC stresses the need for visualizing and planning for the project over its life cycle and not only until the payback period.

There are several areas which are not covered by the ILC. Additional research, however, is likely to offer a greater degree of specification in most if not all of these areas.

- It cannot specify the exact shape of the negotiation strength curve except to state that over time in a specific project the strength of the IC is likely to decline while that of the host country is likely to increase.
- It cannot specify the pace of movement of the negotiation strength curve through different stages of the ILC except that the pace appears to be accelerating.
- It cannot specify the length or duration of a stage of the ILC except to observe that increasingly each stage is being reduced in time.
- It is based primarily on the judgment (subjective expectations) of decision makers in the IC and the host country.
- It is not predictive in the specific sense of saying what will happen, when, why, and how. The ILC is predictive in the far more general sense of highlighting the broad changes in negotiation strength over time.

The basic theme of the ILC is the attitude and approach of an individual and an organization to develop a wider and longer perspective, to recognize the changing power relationships, and to anticipate, plan, and effectively implement specific actions which are expressed through negotiation.

NOTES

1. For additional characteristics see the concluding chapter of A. Kapoor, *International Business Negotiations: A Study in India* (Princeton, N.J.: The Darwin Press, 1970).

2. See John Fayerweather (ed.), *International Business-Government Affairs: An Era of Accommodation* (Cambridge, Mass.: Ballinger Publishers, 1974).

3. For comments on changing relationships between the IC and the host country over time, see H. B. Thorelli, "The Multinational Corporation as a Change Agent," *Southern Journal of Business*, July, 1966; Richard D. Robinson, *International Business Policy* (New York: Holt, Rinehart and Winston, 1964); Peter P. Gabriel, "Investment in the LDC," *Columbia Journal of World Business*, Summer, 1966.

4. For detailed comments on this and related areas see Jack Behrman, J. Boddewyn and A. Kapoor, *International Business-Government Communications: U.S. Structure, Actors, and Issues* (Lexington, Mass.: D. C. Heath and Company, 1975).

5. For additional comments see A. Kapoor and J. Boddewyn, *International Business-Government Relations: U.S. Corporate Experience in Asia and Western Europe* (New York: American Management Association, 1973).

6. The changing relationship over time between the IC and the host country has been noted by other scholars including Thorelli, Robinson, and Gabriel. There are two relatively new dimensions highlighted by the investment life cycle outlined here. First, it adopts a more focused approach to identifying some broad stages in the life of a project. Second, it interprets the stages for their bearing on negotiation strength of the IC and the host country.

19

How to Negotiate in Japan

Howard F. Van Zandt

Trade between the United States and Japan can best be described in superlatives. Except for Canada, no other nation sells so much to, or buys so much from, the United States as Japan does. This trade is growing at a rapid rate, too. Exports and imports in 1970, estimated at $10 billion, will be approximately 80 percent above what they were just four years ago.

Although it would seem that all is cherry-blossom pink in our commercial relations, examination of the trade reveals problems. In the first half of the 1960s, the United States recorded a modest export surplus annually with Japan. In the last half, however, a reversal took place, and the excess of imports from Japan in 1969 rose to $1.4 billion—the biggest deficit ever in trade between two nations. If present trends were to continue, by the middle 1970s the deficit would rise to the impossible level of $4 billion to $5 billion annually. It is clear that we are going to have to sell more to the Japanese or buy less.

There is another problem in our commercial relations: Japan's restrictions against foreign equity investments. No foreign company may establish a subsidiary or enter into a joint venture in Japan—except in liberalized businesses—without first obtaining government sanction. If granted at all, approval will normally be only on the basis of the foreign company's taking a minority position. (In only 11 percent of existing joint ventures is there foreign control.) Prior to September 1970, there were 204 liberalized types of business, but they were in areas of so little interest that only 17 applications for investment had been made in the previous three years.

The Japanese are taking measures which will give some relief both in trade and in foreign equity investments. The government is lowering tariffs more rapidly than required under the 1967 Kennedy Round tariff-cutting agreement. By the end of 1971 the government will have reduced by two thirds the number of products that are now virtually barred from entrance into the country. Under new rules announced in September 1970, automatic approval will be given to establishment of joint ventures having up to 50 percent foreign ownership in several hundred categories of businesses formerly restricted. The year 1971 will witness more liberalization.

Thanks to these changes in government policies, opportunities for Americans to serve the Japanese market will soon be freer of restrictions than at any time since the 1920s. Spurred by the need to redress the trade imbalance,

---

Howard F. Van Zandt, "How to Negotiate in Japan," *Harvard Business Review* (November-December, 1970)

some companies will want to export products from the United States—an increasingly attractive possibility in view of Japan's foreign exchange surpluses—and others will decide to establish manufacturing joint ventures in Japan.

Whatever route is taken, the success or failure of U.S. businessmen will be determined by a myriad of negotiations with Japanese businessmen and government officials. Although Americans can fairly quickly learn how to sell, invest, and operate in European countries, this is not the case in Japan with its unique East Asian type of culture. In order to deal constructively with the Japanese, considerable sophistication will be required. Thus, it will be desirable to study such things as their sensitivities, preferences, behavioral patterns, and psychology.

FEATURES OF BEHAVIOR

Let us begin by looking at distinctive behavioral characteristics of the Japanese that influence their negotiations with U.S. executives. In my experience, 13 such characteristics need to be singled out for attention:

1. EMOTIONAL SENSITIVITY

The Japanese possess a greater emotional sensitivity than do we Americans. For example, a friend recently came to my office, bringing a small potted Chinese bamboo. He explained that in his garden was a large bamboo which had had a baby. He carefully nourished the little one until it was big enough to put in a pot and bring to me. He advised me on its care. Whenever I look at it, I think of the fine man who gave it to me, and of the thousands of acts of kindness I have received at the hands of Japanese. The sons of Nippon appreciate it when foreigners show emotional sensitivity, too.

2. HIDING OF EMOTIONS

Professor Chie Nakane of Tokyo University, after years of studying Europeans, Indians, and Americans, reports that Japanese are as emotional as Italians, but that Japanese emotion is directed toward or against others, whereas the emotions of an Italian may only reflect his feelings at the time and have no relationship to others. What is more, the Japanese go out of their way to conceal their sentiments.

Although personal feelings play a significant role in Japanese behavior, a stranger from overseas may never realize it. The proverb, *No aru taka wa tsume wo kakusu* ("An able hawk hides his talons"), illustrates the point.

One evening at a party in Tokyo, the host, the president of a large Japanese company, remarked to me in his language that an executive from Lucerne, with whom he had been chatting cordially in English, did not like Japanese people. My host added, "I will not do business with a man who does not like us." The visitor from Lucerne had concealed his dislike during his stay —or thought he had—but the president saw behind the mask. Even though the deal proposed by the Swiss would have been mutually profitable, the Japanese executive refused to proceed.

Unless hungry indeed, Japanese are unwilling to do business with someone they think may prove to be arrogant or unpleasant.

3. POWER PLAYS

Japanese dislike the bold use of power and try to avoid situations where this takes place. Many foreigners wondered in the 1960s why the government, which had a huge majority in the Diet, did not vigorously punish the rioters who had caused disruption of so many universities. Instead, the Prime Ministers took a low posture and waited for public opinion to turn against the radicals. When at last the police were called in, the rioters were suppressed without brutality and without splitting the country politically.

The Japanese do not like naked displays of power in business either and have developed a remarkable ability to conciliate. They go to court only about one fiftieth as often as do Americans, since in making a decision a judge will perforce display public power nakedly, so someone must lose face. Foreigners should, if at all possible, avoid going to court to settle differences in Japan.

4. AMAERU AND PATERNALISM

Notable among the many Japanese characteristics of behavior that differ from those common in the Occident is one which is called *amaeru*. It may be defined as a longing to be looked after and protected. The greatest single cause of difficulty for foreign managers in Japan is personnel relations, and a lack of understanding of *amaeru* is at the root of much of the trouble.

This trait is one of the forces that have led to the lifetime employment system so widely followed. When a young man joins a good-sized company, government agency, or university faculty, he expects to remain until he reaches retirement age. He develops a feeling of dependence on his employer, and realizes that his fate and that of the organization are interrelated.

The impatience of the lifetime employment system should be kept in mind by Americans when negotiating. Japanese employees are completely loyal to the organizations for which they work, whether foreign or native, and will go to great lengths to defeat competitors. Also, if the deal an American is proposing will require recruitment of many new employees, the Japanese will want to be reasonably sure that those to be hired will be given steady employment. Many a scheme fails to materialize because such assurance is lacking.

5. GROUP SPIRIT

The Japanese prefer to work as members of groups rather than individually. This characteristic is often cited as one of the most important in explaining Japan's economic success. When negotiating, one should remember that it is not sufficient to convince just one person; the whole group must be won over. The instinct for group rather than individual action is carried over into politics. Few nations have spawned such a small number of dictators as Japan has.

The preference for group rather than individual action may be attributed in part to the Buddhist teaching called *shujo no on*, or feeling of obligation to the world and all living things for one's success. A man who has this belief attributes his good fortune to the assistance and joint efforts of others, rather than to his own wisdom, intelligence, or hard work.

The proverb *Deru kugi utareru* ("The nail that sticks up is hit") reflects the preference for group action. In the lifetime employment system, it is desirable that no one makes a conspicuous mistake. If decisions are made by a group, there is no danger of a single person having to be struck down like a nail when a decision proves to have been wrong.

6. 'RINGI' PROCESS

Well over 90 percent of all large Japanese companies, and many small ones, follow a decision-making system known as *ringi*. Government agencies also follow it. The system is based on the principle that decisions will be made by groups, in accordance with a free consensus. Usually it is formalized by a sort of buck slip, or *ringisho*, which carries pertinent facts and a recommendation prepared by someone at the middle-management level. The proposal is passed upward and horizontally to all who are concerned. Each man who sees the *ringisho* is expected to study the proposal and affix his seal to it. Ultimately it reaches the president of the company, and when his vermilion seal is stamped, the policy is officially adopted. The fact that many men—perhaps 20 or more—will have sealed the proposal has the effect of taking the responsibility away from any one individual.

If a person's reaction to a proposal is negative, his best chance to stop or change it will come in the many conferences that may be called to consider the proposal. However, once a consensus has been reached in conference, it is awkward to block the decision, for a unilateral disapproval offends the Japanese group spirit. Some men, however, do so by pigeonholing the *ringisho*. Others show their objection by affixing their seals upside down. In some organizations, a man may pass the buck by stamping his seal sidewise, which, by custom, means that he has seen the proposal but not passed judgment on it.

Since the *ringisho* is originated fairly well down in an organization—usually by the section specifically assigned responsibility for the subject—it might seem that top management would lose its authority. But, in actual fact, a proposal may be conceived by the president, his directors, or his department heads. The task of drawing it up and documenting it, however, is usually referred to someone at a less lofty level.

In some companies, *ringisho* are brought before the executive committee meetings attended by the president, vice presidents, and inside directors and are freely discussed. This helps resolve differences of opinion.

In comparing American and Japanese decision-making processes, one may soon learn that whereas in the United States a considerable proportion of management ideas are conceived in the executive suite and imposed from the top down, in Japan the reverse is true. More often than not, proposals start from somewhere down the line.

7. SPECIAL INTERESTS

Besides the normal influences, decision making in Japan is sometimes swayed by cliquism and sectionalism just as in many other countries. Before World War II, for example, the military clique was the most powerful single force in establishing governmental policy. In the past few years, business and agricultural interests have exercised considerable influence in the government.

In Japan, as in other Oriental countries, "face" is a factor. Sometimes an organization will decide on a certain course, not because of economic or political reasons, but in order to save face for some important person.

8. DELAYS IN DECISIONS

Unfamiliarity with decision-making practices are at the root of many misunderstandings between Japanese and Occidentals. To illustrate:

In one case I recall, a Pennsylvania company insisted that certain action be taken by a Tokyo company because it was covered by a contract. The Japanese agreed to study the matter. When, two months later, nothing apparently had happened, the Philadelphia officers were sure the president of the Tokyo company did not intend to carry out the agreement. Actually, this was not the case at all. The management had referred the matter to low levels, where a *ringisho* had been drawn up with a proposal to proceed as the Americans desired. The proposition was so complicated, and involved so many different levels and departments of the organization as well as government agencies, however, that to move it and arrange to the necessary conferences on the way required over 60 days. During the whole time that Philadelphia was steaming, the local representative knew precisely each day where the *ringisho* was, and saw to it that it was acted on as speedily as was possible.

It has been my experience—sitting in the middle, as it were, of correspondence between Japan and North America, Europe, and Australia—that the Japanese run into long delays when government approvals are required. When governments are not involved, however, the time required for decision making is not much different from ours.

9. THREE-CORNER TALKS

Foreigners soon discover that at least three parties are involved when an agreement is being negotiated, viz., the Japanese company, the foreign company, and the Japanese government. It is complicated enough for two companies to reach a decision between themselves; it is several times more difficult when a political body must also be satisfied.

The participation of the government may at times be a convenience to the Japanese company. If the foreign company's terms are severe, the government will doubtless demand that they be softened. If the Japanese company wishes to delay its decision, the government will be blamed. If at last the Japanese concern decides against the joint venture, the government may play a face-saving role and deny the application.

Sometimes a fourth party, the Japanese company's bank, will also become a party to the negotiations. Should it oppose the proposition, however, this will usually be kept from the foreigners lest they think that the Japanese company's credit is poor.

10. BUREAUCRATIC PROBLEM

Cabinet ministers and members of the permanent bureaucracy are all subject to pressures from trade associations, Diet members, university professors, private businessmen, and countless domestic lobbying groups, each arguing in its own interest. Except for advice from the Foreign Ministry, foreign embassies and governments, international trade associations, and a handful of internationally-minded businessmen, government officials are not subject to much urging that they give a balanced view to international as well as domestic considerations.

The slowness with which the government has removed restrictions on imports and foreign-equity investments is a reflection of this imbalance of pressures. The government recognizes the problem, however, and is trying to broaden thinking by sending junior officers of ministries besides Foreign Affairs to overseas posts for assignments of up to three years.

11. AVOIDANCE OF 'NO'

The next trait of the Japanese is another one that most Occidentals find hard to understand.

As Professor Chie Nakane of Tokyo University states: "Expression of *no* is virtually never used outside of completely reciprocal relationships, and from superior to inferior. You rarely receive a *no* from a Japanese; even when he means *no* he would use *yes* in the verbal form."

Foreigners long resident in Japan learn to recognize clues which mean *no*. For example, if, when pressed for an answer, a Japanese draws breath through his teeth and says "sah" (it has no meaning), or says, "It is very difficult," the chances are strong he means *no*.

Short-time visitors, when dealing with Japanese who forget that foreigners don't know the clues, are often misled. Typically, the stranger from overseas, after presenting his ideas and assuming that agreement has been reached, will enplane for home, satisfied with himself and the Japanese. The local representative of the U.S. company then has to find out if agreement was really reached—or if the Japanese merely gave that impression in accordance with the ancient Oriental custom of telling high-level people what they *want* to hear rather than the real facts.

For instance, I recall well a case where a visitor obtained a commitment from a Japanese concern to take some action. But, after the visitor had boarded his plane for Honolulu, the president of the Japanese company told me: "I know of course that we cannot carry out our promise, but I didn't want to hurt his feelings and spoil his trip. Now you must cable him and explain it can't be done!"

The practice of telling people what they want to hear, rather than the facts, causes trouble, even with resident foreigners. The best way I have found to avoid being misled is to conceal, if I can, what answer I want to receive. Even when soliciting opinions from my Japanese subordinates, I make it a policy to try not to give a clue to what answer is desired.

12. VALUE OF FRIENDSHIP

Friends are often called on in Japan to give help. The more good friends a man has, the more secure he feels. There are degrees of friendship, however. Professor Chie Nakane makes the following observation:

> The relative strength of the human bond tends to increase in proportion to the length and intensity of actual contact. The reason the newcomer in any Japanese group is placed at the very bottom of the hierarchy is that he has the shortest period of contact. This is a primary condition of the seniority system, which dominates Japan. Therefore, the placement of an individual in a social group is governed by the length of the individual's contact with the group. In other words, the actual contact itself becomes the individual's private social capital. . . .[2]

One of the principal handicaps under which foreign companies operate is that only rarely do they have on their staffs Westerners who have the private social capital—old friendships—to which Professor Nakane referred. The longer the contact, the greater is its value. The average resident Occidental stays about two years. If, during this time, there is frequent contact with certain Japanese businessmen or government officials, there would be opportunity to make meaningful friendships. Unfortunately, too few Westerners find these opportunities, and most complain that they have no close Japanese friends.

13. NO ARGUMENTS, PLEASE

Among the characteristics that confound visitors when negotiating is the Japanese reluctance to enter into arguments. When challenged, a Japanese usually will not retort, argue, or even discuss a point when he feels he is right. He just remains quiet. A Japanese authority has compared children's quarrels in Japan and Europe and reports that a prompt retort is not expected in Japan but is in Europe.[3] In both areas the characteristic develops early.

When negotiating, Occidentals should remember this innate trait and should not consider the Japanese as stubborn or close-minded because of it.

ART OF NEGOTIATING

Negotiating in Japan, whether for the purpose of concluding a joint venture agreement, selling a product, or some other task, usually involves a predictable series of steps and actions. What are these steps? How should the U.S. businessman try to take them?

PLANNING THE TALKS

Once a U.S. company has decided to go to Tokyo, it should prepare its representatives for a long stay and arm them with exhaustive explanations of what is to be offered. Plans should also be made to undertake thorough investigations of local circumstances in Japan. On the average it takes about six times longer, and is three times harder, to reach an agreement on the other side of the Pacific than in the United States. There are many reasons for this, including the need to use interpreters and the fact that neither Americans nor Japanese know much about each other's thinking processes.

Since interpreters will be required from the first day on, it will be wise to learn some basic rules for using them before commencing negotiations, I recommend the following:

1. Brief the interpreter in advance about the subject and give him a copy of the presentation to study and discuss.

2. Speak loudly, clearly, and slowly. (Some Americans try to talk with a cigar in the mouth—an egregious mistake.)

3. Avoid little known words, such as "arcane," "heuristic," or "buncombe."

4. Maintain a pleasant attitude.

5. Explain each major idea in two or three different ways, as the point may be lost if discussed only once.

6. Do not talk more than a minute or two without giving the interpreter a chance to speak.

7. While talking, allow the interpreter time to make notes of what is being said.

8. Assume that all numbers over 10,000 may be mistranslated. Repeat them carefully and write them down for all to see. The Japanese system of counting large sums is so different from those of the West that errors frequently occur. Also, the number billion should be avoided, as it means 1,000,000,000,000 in Europe, and 1,000,000,000 in the United States.

9. Do not lose confidence if the interpreter uses a dictionary. No one is likely to have a vocabulary of 40,000 words in each of two languages, and a dictionary is often essential.

10. Permit the interpreter to spend as much time as needed in clarifying points whose meanings are obscure.

11. Do not interrupt the interpreter as he translates. Interrupting causes many misunderstandings, usually leaves the visitor from overseas only half informed, and gives the Japanese side a feeling that the foreigner is too impatient to be competent.

12. Do not jump to conclusions, as Japanese ways of doing things are often different from what foreigners expect.

13. Avoid long sentences, double negatives, or the use of negative wordings of a sentence when a positive form could be used.

14. Don't use slang terms, as, for example, "If you will let me have half a 'G' at six bits a piece, it'll be gung ho with me." Rather, state simply, "I want 500 at 75 cents each."

15. Avoid superfluous words. Your point may be lost if wrapped up in generalities.

16. Try to be as expressive as possible by using movements of hands, eyes, lips, shoulders, and head to supplement words.

17. During meetings, write out the main points discussed; in this way both parties can double check their understanding.

18. After meetings, confirm in writing what has been agreed to.

19. Don't expect an interpreter to work for over an hour or two without a rest period. His work is exhausting and a nervous strain.

20. Consider using two men if interpreting is to last a whole day or into the evening, so that when one tires the other can take over.

21. Don't be suspicious if a speaker talks for five minutes and the interpreter covers it in half a minute. The speaker may have been wordy.

22. Be understanding if it develops that the interpreter has made a mistake. It is almost impossible to avoid making some errors, because Japanese and European languages are so dissimilar.

23. Be sure the Japanese are given all the time they want to tell their side of the story. If they hesitate, ask the interpreter for advice on what next to say or do.

GOOD PERSONAL RELATIONS

The Japanese go to great lengths in establishing the right emotional basis for business. In their eyes, emotion is often more important than cold facts in decision making.

For instance, an employee of a Japanese trading company who was assigned to Latin America was told, before leaving Tokyo, "Don't engage in business for one year—just get acquainted with people." He did exactly that, learning to play the guitar and to sing native folk songs. He also learned the local language. Later, in a critical stage in a negotiation, he impressed officials of the host country during a period of relaxation by playing the guitar and singing folk songs. He was so much appreciated for his personal warmth that in time he was decorated by the Latin American government. His company got many orders, too.

Occidentals who do business with Japanese may not have time to learn how to strum a *samisen* or sing *jouri* dramatic ballads, but in some way they should try to find out-of-office ways of relating to local people.

Entertainment affords opportunities to get acquainted away from the strain of the conference table and is much used by Japanese businessmen in promoting goodwill. A term commonly used to describe the process is *Naniwabushi*, which means to get on such good personal terms with someone that he will agree to do you a favor when called on. A person gets on these good terms in various ways, one of which is entertainment. Advertising agencies and movie makers spend about 1.8 percent of sales proceeds on entertainment. The construction and real estate businesses spend about 1 percent. Popular types of entertainment are golf, geisha parties, and invitations to see sumo matches, kabuki, and other forms of amusement.

Gift giving is also customary and is a factor in negotiating. The gifts may be expensive, including such articles as mink coats, but in most cases they are worth not over 10,000 yen ($27.78). Many government officials receive cases of soft drinks in the summer and salted salmon in the winter. There is no bribery in giving such gifts, as the value of any one is insignificant. Sometimes more soft drinks or fish are received than can be consumed at home, so disposers are called, who buy the surplus at discounts of 30 percent to 40 percent, and then sell it in turn to housewives at 10 percent to 20 percent below the market price.

Americans who visit Japan on business are advised to bring U.S.-made souvenirs to give to their customers. The cost should normally be not over $25 to $30 per item.

MAKING A PRESENTATION

Normally the first person a Westerner will meet in a Japanese organization will be of high status, perhaps the director in charge of the foreign affairs division. Executives of this department, although they open the door to the U.S. company, usually do not possess the power to influence decisions. Therefore, they will arrange meetings with concerned internal departments, such as manufacturing, marketing, finance, purchasing, engineering, and research and development.

If the proposition proves interesting to the appropriate internal departments, meetings will be scheduled two or three times a week for a month or more, depending on the complexity of the subject. In one important case in which I was involved, I attended meetings three or four hours a day, six days each week, for nearly two months! The results of this lengthy presentation justified the effort.

There are several reasons why so much time must be spent in conferences.

1. The Japanese desire thorough explanations of every point. In describing and explaining new products and ideas, it will be found that the employment of visual aids is of especial value, for the eyes can supplement what is being said by the interpreter. Samples, models, photographs, maps, sketches, diagrams, catalogs, pamphlets, books, leaflets, blueprints and so on are indispensable.

At the end of meetings, it may be desirable to give the conferees copies of printed matter and photographs to take back to their offices for further study. Where a formal presentation is made, it is also helpful to use slide films with synchronized recordings, 35mm slides with recordings, or talking motion pictures. The sound should, of course, be in Japanese. It is often beneficial to lend the audio-visual material to the Japanese so that they may then repeat the showings before other groups within their own organization and, if appropriate, to the government officials concerned. If a presentation has aroused enthusiasm, the borrowers will in effect assist in the selling by showing the material.

2. The Japanese use meetings in order to size up their visitors. They study not only what the Occidentals say, but also the character of the strange people from beyond the seas. Since the Japanese spend so much effort in

studying the personalities of those around them and comparing notes with one another, they seem to have developed considerable skill in judging people. It should be kept in mind that they rarely do business singly; they usually go in twos and threes in accordance with the group concept.

STYLE OF APPROACH

One thing that they particularly look for is sincerity. Some Japanese, to show their honesty and sincerity, will go so far as to mention a few of the good qualities of competing products during their presentations. A study of reactions of Japanese university students to persuasive communications revealed that two-sided, rather than one-sided, arguments were most effective with those who were, at the outset, opposed to the position being advocated.[4]

One test of sincerity is whether a man shows something in print to support his presentation. The Japanese feel that when a man is willing to put his case in print, where all may challenge what he has said, it is likely that he will be accurate so as not to lose face. Also, because their own spoken language is overfull of homonyms, oral statements are often misunderstood. When something is written in Japanese-Chinese characters or in English, the homonym misunderstandings disappear.

Occidentals coming to Japan should bring with them published material describing their company and its products. If some of this material has appeared in a respected technical or trade publication of general circulation, its credibility increases.

When dealing with visitors or resident foreigners, a Japanese will often request copies of cables and correspondence they have received from home offices in response to questions that have been asked during negotiations. The requests test the sincerity of the foreigners as well as reflect the high respect given by Japanese to written material. Also, the requests imply that the Japanese feel that the visitors or residents are working as middlemen who seek to solve problems and bring to fruition a mutually beneficial transaction, rather than as adversaries. It is desirable to establish such rapport.

Since the Japanese prefer a low-pressure sales approach and value sincerity so highly, Westerners are advised to build up their case a step at a time, using modest language rather than making extravagant claims. This strategy gives the Japanese opportunities to ask questions that would be missed if the visitors told their whole story in one lengthy, uninterrupted outflow of eloquence. The Japanese like to feel that the parties to a negotiation work together to establish the facts both pro and con.

In making a presentation, it should be remembered that Japanese and Americans have different objectives in doing business. The former continually stress growth, steady jobs for their own employees, full employment in the nation as a whole, and superiority over competitors. Profit, as a motive, falls behind these needs. But U.S. executives are motivated only by profit—or, at least, that is the way Japanese businessmen see it. When negotiating in

Japan, Americans do well to appeal first to the four popular local objectives, and only then discuss profit.

OVERCOMING OPPOSITION

At some time during the negotiations, a crisis usually arises. It is liable to last for several weeks, and, during this period, the Japanese side may not wish to continue conferences. Westerners should keep channels open with the Japanese company during this time, even if there are no formal meetings.

One step that may be taken is to make discreet inquiries of men at lower levels who are known to be friendly, asking who is opposing the deal and why. The inside friends, with their company's best interest foremost, may even go so far as to suggest what approach is likely to be most effective. If the Japanese company president or some other high officer is in favor of the proposition, he may arrange for a private luncheon at which the chief opponents of the plan will explain their views to the perplexed visitors.

A Japanese businessman, when confronted with opposition, often follows a practice of what is called "selling one's face." He will drop in on his customer or the government official—whoever is blocking him—for a casual talk from time to time without making an appointment. He will just say, "I was passing by and dropped in to say hello." I know of men who have made 15 or 20 calls of this kind before they were able to get things moving forward.

It is not uncommon, during the crisis stage, to enlist the aid of a common friend and ask him to find out what is holding up the negotiations and to do what he can to get things moving again. If the go-between is someone who is a member of a club or other group to which an opponent belongs, or is an alumnus from the same university or high school, he is likely to have considerable influence. The old school tie has great worth in Japan.

DRAWING UP THE CONTRACT

After the crisis has passed, conferences have been resumed, and it becomes apparent that the Japanese, in general, are willing to go ahead with the proposition, a "Heads of Agreement" should be drawn up and initialed by both parties.

Often Occidentals make the mistake of presenting a detailed, one-sided, lengthy legal contract at this stage. This frightens the Japanese and immediately identifies the foreign negotiators as adversaries. Of course, a written contract should be made. But it should be developed jointly in the course of negotiations and be little more than a statement of the points that have been agreed to and understood.

Westerners usually want the contract to indicate commitments, conditions, and restrictions in precise language which will not be liable to later misintepretation. On the other hand, the Japanese feel that the written agreement should be a declaration of intention and deal in specifics only where it describes the technology of services which the foreign company is expected to provide. Each may find it necessary to make some concessions to the other's viewpoint in this respect.

CLOSING DISCUSSIONS

When the contract is being drawn up, there will come a time when agreement must be reached on unclosed points which have, until then, been put aside. It is at this stage that—because of the American desire to "get on with it" and the Japanese custom of being silent for what is too long a time by U.S. standards—tactical errors are liable to occur.

Americans often don't know how to cope with silence. They can't understand what is going on. Briefly, this is what is happening:

When a pause or impasse in the discussion develops, the Japanese remain quiet, not feeling a compulsion to say anything. Many Japanese can even refrain from answering when a question is asked them, responding to it by drawing air through their teeth and then sitting back as though pondering what to say. When a couple of minutes have passed, and no comment is forthcoming, Americans become uneasy and feel that they must make some sort of statement. It is at this point that they often voluntarily give in on a disputed point or say something they should not say, just to get the conversation going again.

There will, at all stages of the negotiations, but particularly near the end, be occasions when it is desirable to reach a compromise. The Japanese, though good conciliators, like to do it in such a way that neither side appears to have made a forced concession. Therefore, they object to frank, clearly defined compromises or to agreements to split the difference when the problem concerns something like price, delivery, or quantity. Instead, they like to develop a formula based on whatever facts and ideas can be bent to conform to the objective.

It is also common, near the end of the negotiations, for the Japanese to insist on a large amount of data to justify the action that is being taken. Some of this will be needed for internal company use, but a considerable amount will be required to satisfy the government. If the Westerners refuse to supply the information requested, thinking it unnecessary, the Japanese may find it impossible to go through with the deal.

One of the reasons for demanding so much supporting data—all in visual form—is that, should the venture fail, no one can then be rebuked; that is, no one will be blamed for recommending that his company proceed on a project if all the known evidence justified it.

When, at last, all the data have been assembled and the agreement has been put in form for signing, the time for final executive decision making comes. The *ringisho* decision document referred to earlier will be drawn up and the papers forwarded upward to the executive committee.

If the agreement has been worked out fairly by the conferees, differences have been settled in a satisfactory manner, and proper government informal sanction has been obtained, it is almost certain that the contract will be approved and signed by the Japanese. If, however, they obtained the impression during negotiations that the Westerners might later be arrogant or unreasonable, or be unwilling to give sufficient technical and other support to the project, they may be influenced by these facts not to sign.

Hopefully, the hour will finally arrive when no more facts are required—just calm, concentrated effort at reaching a decision. There will be long periods of silence interrupted by light discussion, some of it irrelevant to the project. Finally, after the last cup of tea has been consumed, a consensus will emerge. The Japanese word for the inward understanding that all seem to reach simultaneously is *kan*, which may be defined as emotional attunement. Whatever it is called, a decision will be made, and, if all goes well, a new Japanese-American relation will commence.

CONCLUSION

As this short exposition indicates, negotiating with the Japanese involves complications unknown in the Americas and Europe. The culture is an old one, and, since the Japanese politico-economic system is so successful, there is little likelihood it will be rapidly changed.

The nation is in sound fiscal condition, as nations go, despite the high-debt ratio of its corporations. The national debt is small; individual indebtedness is inconsiderable; the economy is well balanced, not dependent on any one product, and therefore not as subject to boom or bust as it was in the early part of the twentieth century, when silk was so important. In addition, the stated objectives of Japanese business—to achieve growth, to improve the livelihood of the public, and to benefit the nation generally—appeal to the idealism of most young people. What is more, there are many economists in Japan who believe that within 15 years the per capita annual income will rise to $10,000. This would mean that the average family would have over $20,000 after taxes, to spend each year. Should Japan's income rise as forecast, it would be by far the richest market in the world.

Accordingly, there should be no hesitation on the part of U.S. businessmen to learn the art of doing business with the gentlemen of Japan. The complications may be great—but the magnitude of the opportunity is extraordinary.

NOTES

1. "Analysis of Japanese Social Structure," in *Lectures on Characteristics of Japanese Management,* International Management Program for Foreign Executives in Japan, International Management Association of Japan, 1st Session, July 30 to August 1, 1964, Hakone, Japan.

2. "An Analysis of Japanese Social Structure," *Management Japan*, October-December 1967, p. 34.

3. Kanji Hatano, "Children's Quarrels," as quoted by Muchitaro Tada, "A Content Analysis of 'Yakuza' Fiction," *Japanese Popular Culture*, edited and transcribed by Hidetoshi Kato (Tokyo, Charles Tuttle, 1959), pp. 182-183.

4. Eliott McGinnies, "Some Reactions of Japanese University Students to Persuasive Communications," *The Journal of Conflict Resolution*, December 1964, p. 486.

ADDENDUM: YANKEE TRADERS IN THE MIKADO'S EMPIRE

Here is some advice that might well be given before dispatching a company representative to Japan:

A FEW 'DON'TS'

Don't lose your temper in front of the Japanese. Their proverb, *Tanki wa sonki* ("A short tempter means a lost spirit"), illustrates how they feel.

Don't regard human problems coldly, for this violates their emotional sensitivity.

Go out of your way to avoid being egotistical, unrelenting, harsh, or abrasive, for these four disagreeable characteristics have been attributed to Americans in popular fiction, and Japanese who are unfamiliar with Americans are looking for such behavior.

Do not engage in flattery or sugarcoat your compliments, for the Japanese consider people who talk this way as lacking in sincerity. There are plenty of nice things you can say and still be factual.

Do not try to high-pressure the Japanese into buying something or taking action. If pressed too hard, they may dig in their heels and take twice as long to make a decision. There are much more effective ways to influence them.

Don't use the table-pounding technique. The Japanese almost invariably respond negatively to such power tantrums—particularly in the case of Americans, for they react to their Occupation-era memories by firmly opposing American power plays, thus demonstrating their independence.

Don't tell them how to run their country. They think they are doing pretty well—and have evidence to back them up. Some Japanese feel that foreigners who give unsolicited advice are either ignorant of local circumstances or arrogant, even though the visitors may just be trying to be helpful.

A FEW 'DOS'

Be as courteous as you can, for the Japanese are on the whole an especially polite people and appreciate this behavior in others. (In public opinion polls in Japan, the British and French are regarded as the most polite. Americans are usually rated near the bottom.)

If you should become exasperated, remain cool and keep a smile on your face if you can. If you cannot do so, try to show no emotion. Do not allow your temper to goad you into saying something insulting or, worse, taking offensive action. The Japanese believe in their proverb, *Nama byoho wa okizu no moto* ("Crude tactics cause great injuries").

Go out of your way to be goodnatured, practical, sociable, frank, responsible, and efficient, for these are desirable traits which Japanese expect to find in Americans. Don't disappoint them.

Speak a little Japanese if you can. They will appreciate the effort.

Avoid criticizing the United States, its institutions, and its leadership, for an American company cannot be considered separately from the whole. If foreigners are led to think that the country is falling apart, they will have doubts about its companies, too.

Learn as much as your time will permit about Japanese history, for without some understanding of the past it will be difficult to understand the present.

Recognize that the Japanese have reason to be proud of their culture and business accomplishments. They will appreciate Westerners who want to learn all they can about the country.

20

Conflict on Contracts and Why Things are What They are in China

Victor H. Li

China-U.S. trade is again a reality after a hiatus of more than 20 years and the American entrepreneur should proceed with the proper mixture of enthusiasm and caution. He should be enthusiastic because China does represent new opportunities for U.S. technical goods—and possibly for licensing agreements. He should be cautious because there may be a few surprises in store for him in the way the Chinese do business and because the market place may not be as large as he thinks.

There will be few new wrinkles in the technical aspects of trade in discussions with Chinese negotiators. The American can discuss f.o.b., c.i.f., revolving L/Cs, turnkey projects, demurrage, etc. and be reasonably confident his Chinese counterpart will know what he is saying and will apply the same meanings. The same holds true for Chinese banks and the People's Insurance Company, which generally follow Western-style documentation and contract language in the international business field.

However, there are more subtle differences—and things to watch for—in dealing with the Chinese than is evident in business relationships with the state trading countries of Eastern Europe. These arise partly because the Chinese are who they are, with their own culture and with a 150-year history of grievances against the West, plus the fact they are sensitive about their current status as a great world power, but still with a developing economy.

Taking these broader generalizations and narrowing them down to specifics, the American businessman should know:

- The Chinese preference for gradually building relationships rather than plunging headlong into new ventures.
- The subtle differences between Chinese and American contracts, particularly in reference to the arbitration and force majeure clauses.
- How the Chinese behave in contract disagreements.
- The difference between contracts for Chinese imports and exports.
- The political considerations he may face in dealing with the Chinese.

Taking the last first, Americans may encounter politics in their personal dealings with Chinese bureaucrats. This could range from lectures on Chairman Mao's thoughts to harangues against U.S. Government policy in Southeast Asia, or the U.S. trade embargo. (It is unlikely there will be a demand that Americans publicly denounce their Government's foreign policies as

Reprinted by permission of *Worldwide P & I Planning* (January/February, 1972).

has been the case with some Japanese business delegations in the past few years.)

There is no doubt the Chinese are extremely touchy in all their economic dealings with foreigners, who for 150 years—starting with the British opium wars—have been sources of irritation and suffering for them. The American embargo was merely the latest of a whole series of sore spots—Western demand for trading privileges, foreign concessions, extraterritorial rights, a seizure of Chinese territory which led to several wars.*

It is unrealistic to think they will forget these matters in their current dealings with foreigners. This is particularly true for Americans. Through its vigorous enforcement of the embargo, the United States has waged economic warfare against China for over two decades. And, despite all the trips President Nixon or his advisors may make to Peking, many grave and lasting differences still separate the two countries. American businessmen, therefore, should expect to receive their share of harangues.

But this political problem should not be exaggerated. Except for the Japanese, foreign businessmen have not generally found political pressures excessive or intolerable. These include businessmen from West Germany, a former World War II adversary, and Australia (which not only has troops in Vietnam, but political alliances throughout Southeast Asia as well, which are aimed at countering China's influence).

The major exception to relative moderation in pushing political considerations into dealings with foreign businessmen has been Japan—an important factor to American firms who may think of approaching the China market through their Japanese subsidiary or one of the larger trading firms. However, the China-Japan situation is fairly unique. Besides proximity, there is a considerable overlap of political and economic interests in Asia plus a substantial number of Japanese aggressively urging that their country radically change its China policy. In such a situation, Peking has a special interest in influencing the formulation of Japanese policy toward China.

For example, recent Japanese business delegations to China have sometimes publicly criticized their government's policies and the revival of Japanese militarism. Also, a good deal of current Japanese exports to China is through companies designated as "friendly firms" by a pro-Peking Japanese trade organization. And in 1971, Peking took a strong stand on Taiwan, saying China would not do business with Japanese firms having substantial interests in Taiwan or South Korea—either trade or investment. (It is much too early to tell if there will be black-listing of U.S. companies with Taiwan or Korean investments.)

* There are also historical reasons why Japan has not pressed for long-term credits from some of its Western trading partners. (It will be interesting to see if this will also apply to the United States.) To some Chinese officials, these credits recall the early twentieth century when, in effect, China was partially pawned to Western powers for loans and credits. Thus, direct investment—or any measure which would give the foreigner control over the economy—will be discouraged.

THE DRIVE FOR KNOW-HOW

In addition to political problems, doing business with China may involve peculiarities stemming from the present conditions of its economy. The Chinese buy foreign goods not only for the items themselves, but also for the manufacturing know-how involved.

Therefore, as part of the sales contract, the Chinese negotiator assigned to the American seller of technical equipment will ask for vast quantities of documentation on production know-how. *The American will balk at this suggestion, though in the past, the Chinese have obtained this know-how as part of the sales price. But, in my opinion, when faced with a firm refusal, they would now be willing to accept royalty arrangements.*

Recently, the Chinese have bought only some sections of a processing machinery line, substituting for the rest less complex and less expensive units which require more labor. This type of substitution may affect the performance of the entire machine system or complex. *Therefore, I feel strongly that the sales contract should carefully spell out assurances covering the extent of product performance.*

There are many reasons for China's drive toward self-sufficiency. It will reduce their dependence on foreign powers. The American embargo, the 1960 withdrawal of Soviet technicians, or even a lack of spare parts from abroad for machines already sold to China could, they feel, exercise considerable influence over the development of the Chinese economy and consequently over the political options available to Chinese leadership.

The halting of purchases of turnkey projects since the Cultural Revolution of 1966 may be an indication of this attitude. Rather than depending on foreigners to set up plants in China, the Chinese now prefer to send their own technicians abroad to learn the manufacturing and assembling process. These technicians then take delivery abroad, and will try to assemble the plant in China by themselves—a technique that has not always lived up to the plan behind it.

HOW TO BEHAVE

In doing business with China, the American businessman should also realize at this point in time, that it is hard to separate trade from existing political relations. If he performs poorly in China or if the Chinese think he performs poorly, this may lead to more misunderstandings which may further exacerbate existing antagonisms.

The following examples admittedly are somewhat exaggerated but they do indicate how ill feelings arising from trade relations could impair development and improvement of political relationships. (After all, U.S.-China trade at this point in time is very much a symbolic item.)

Suppose a U.S. businessman walked through the Canton Trade Fair ordering 4,000 of this, 8,000 of that, etc. When he finished "splurging," the Chinese most likely would politely thank him for his interest, but would not sell him anything.

The Chinese might view the American as the typical "ugly" capitalist who thinks money creates access to all things. They would particularly resent his lack of sensitivity to the Chinese preference for gradually building relationships with trading partners rather than plunging into large, one-shot deals with any stranger who comes along offering handsome sums of money.

On his part, the American businessman might not know that many items at Canton are for display only and that Chinese production and export capacity are limited, and to a large extent already allocated to existing trade partners. If he insisted on pressing unduly for goods, this would force into the open the fact that the Chinese are exaggerating their economic ability. This would be an unnecessary puncturing of an otherwise pleasant and harmless façade.

Moreover, the American might go back to the States with some serious misgivings. The Chinese refusal to sell what they were displaying for sale might seem to indicate a high degree of unreasonableness or even irrationality. Alternatively, he might feel the Chinese had refused to sell because they always move in mysterious and inscrutable ways, unfathomable to the Western mind. This could mean the Chinese are unpredictable and impossible to deal with not only in trade, but in the political area as well.

A U.S. pharmaceutical company might want to donate to the Chinese Government a large supply of drugs out of humanitarian desire to relieve suffering. The Chinese might be highly annoyed by the implication Big Brother must dispense charity to those who cannot care for themselves. More significantly, they might also consider this offer a manifestation of Western imperialism—different in form, perhaps, from what the West practiced in China for a century prior to the Communist takeover, but no different in underlying content, attitude, or potential damage to the future development of a strong and independent China.

TALK RATHER THAN ARBITRATE

While the above two examples are hypothetical ones that could lead to misunderstandings and strained personal relationships, in actuality the Chinese will go to great lengths to avoid any kind of formal arbitration over the disagreements, problems, and tensions which inevitably arise in international business. All Chinese contracts have a clause requiring disagreements be settled through "friendly negotiations" first, before arbitration. The Chinese usually insist on arbitration before a Peking tribunal, although they have occasionally agreed to arbitration in major European cities.

The most important thing to know about this arbitration clause is that it is almost never invoked. As far as I know, the Peking tribunals have decided only one or perhaps two cases, although there were a number of cases where proceedings were begun and then settled "out of court." There also have been very few arbitrations conducted outside of China, except in maritime matters where arbitration is a commonly-accepted international practice.

When a dispute arises, the Chinese expect the two parties to negotiate a mutually acceptable adjustment without resort to arbitration. Indeed, they regard any attempt to begin arbitration proceedings, even before the Peking tribunals, as a violation of the promise to negotiate in a friendly manner.

The Chinese take the position that all difficulties can be fairly resolved amicably. This feeling stems from both a Confucian and a Marxist belief that the nature of man is basically good and therefore two reasonable men should be able to settle their differences rationally. Marxism holds that society can be made to operate in a rational manner, and, for it to be rational, then its major component (man) also must be rational. Confucianism says straight out that man's nature is basically good and therefore a man would also perceive and choose what is rational and reasonable.

The Chinese, by definition, are reasonable men. But how can they ensure that the foreign trader also will be reasonable? One method is to build relations with any particular trader slowly and gradually, first giving him a little bit of business and then increasing the amount as he proves himself able and reasonable. (In addition, if he wishes to continue doing business with China, he had better maintain his reasonableness!)

This process can be described in another manner. Where a foreign trader and the Chinese have considerable dealings, their relationship extends both in scope and time beyond the contents of any single contact or dispute. In almost all instances, the primary consideration for both parties is preservation of the overall relationship, even where this requires giving up "rights" in a particular contract. This does not mean that contract provisions are unimportant. On the contrary, they play a major roll in determining what is a reasonable solution in each case. However, one cannot be too rigid trying to claim one's rights. Thus, sometimes one gives and sometimes one gets. And in the long run, the two balance out. Looked at in this manner, the non-Chinese use of the arbitration clause is much less unsettling.

* * *

No company anywhere runs to court or arbitration every time a problem arises. The point to be noted, however, is that the Chinese take this method seriously. *The essence of the Chinese method of doing business is the conscious effort to develop and maintain broad on-going relationships with their trading partners, and to operate as much as possible within the confines of such relationships. This helps explain why the Chinese prefer not to lead into large transactions where they have not had extensive prior dealings. It also accounts for their wariness of one-shot transactions where there is no larger relationship to moderate tensions and demands that arise from carrying out that single transaction.*

Of course, these considerations operate in both directions. Having found someone with whom they can work, the Chinese have a decided interest in maintaining and enhancing the relationship. And they have shown considerable loyalty and favor to those foreign firms or individuals who have demonstrated helpfulness and friendship over long periods of time. For those American companies who will be newcomers to China trade, this means they will be at a disadvantage vis-à-vis firms which are "old friends" of China, such as Hong Kong's Jardine Mathiwson or West Germany's Jebsons, but that once they join the latter category, they too will receive favored treatment.

In addition to the way they feel about arbitration, there are other items to watch for. Chinese *force majeure* clauses often are quite vague; for example, saying no more than "The seller shall not be responsible for delays due to *force majeure*." This term usually encompasses war, flood, fire, and natural calamity, as in the West. But it sometimes also covers riot, failure of refrigeration, and damage by pest, and generally does not cover strike-caused delays. Similar drafting and interpretation problems may arise out of an occasional Chinese penchant for vague terms. Many contracts include clauses calling for "best material and finest workmanship," and for both sides to exert "greatest efforts" to implement the contract. What exactly these terms entail is a little hard to say.

Another area where problems may arise involves letters of credit. Foreign buyers are required to give irrevocable L/Cs confirmed by a prime bank. However, L/Cs issued by Chinese banks usually are not confirmed, the theory being Chinese banks are completely reliable. In addition, drafts drawn by Chinese sellers under a letter of credit are made *without* recourse. I am not sure what can be done about these problems; perhaps all that is possible at this time is to warn the U.S. businessman that they do exist, but so far, Chinese traders and banks have proven highly reliable.

THE STANDARD CONTRACTS

Except for purchase of turnkey projects and similar major transactions, the Chinese use standard contracts in their foreign trade. Consequently, many contract terms are, in practice, not negotiable. Of course, all this is a question of bargaining power, but U.S. businessmen should not overestimate their strength in this area. Since foreign trade is a state monopoly, the Chinese side wields considerable bargaining leverage. Also, Chinese negotiators are bureaucrats more than businessmen, and may be more rigid in adhering to fixed forms.

Chinese exports to industrialized countries consist largely of minerals and agricultural products. Consequently, export contracts are simple since there is no need for elaborate product descriptions. Sales are c.i.f., with a Chinese chartering company handling the shipping, and the People's Insurance Company handling the insurance (usually at 110 percent of the cost). A letter of credit is opened some days before loading on board, and payment is on presentation of the usual documents. In addition, the Chinese Commodity Inspection Bureau inspects the exports. Findings are final, although there are several levels of administrative appeal within the Bureau. (Incidentally, this agency has a good international reputation for the way it does its work.)

Chinese imports are conducted in a similar manner, although since complex machinery often is involved, the entire transaction is more complicated. Purchases are f.o.b. and payment, letter of credit. The Commodity Inspection Bureau again handles inspection and decisions are final. On technical machinery, the Bureau may ask the foreign seller to provide the means and the standards for conducting the tests. On imported goods, Americans should be warned that the Bureau is sometimes over-zealous in its inspection. Instead of sampling a shipment, inspectors have been known to open up all crates and packages for a personal look at each item. There often is a penalty clause for a delivery delay, usually at one half of one percent per week, with a right to cancel the entire contract after a certain number of weeks.

There are a number of differences in import and export contract terms, all of which favor the Chinese side. The most important: There is usually no penalty clause for delay in delivery by Chinese sellers. This is quite fortunate from the Chinese viewpoint since they often are late in making delivery! In addition, foreign buyers have to open letters of credit considerably earlier than Chinese buyers, and foreign exporters have to give immediate notice of completion of loading; their Chinese counterparts usually get more time.

The statement has been repeated so often that it almost has become an old saw: The Chinese are hard bargainers, but once an agreement is reached, they are meticulous in carrying out their obligations. (This reputation is justified with one major exception, delay in delivery of Chinese exports.) Indeed, they take contract terms so literally, they sometimes make trouble for themselves. One German manufacturer sent better-performing machinery than was called for in the contract and at the same price. Instead of thanks, he received a claim for deviating from contract terms. This case may be exceptional; nevertheless, the Chinese expect strict compliance by both sides.

* * *

Having to work within the context of a central plan and to deal only with middlemen will present some special problems to the American businessman. To begin with, it will be difficult for him to distribute his descriptive literature to the potential, ultimate users of his product. Usually, he will be able to do little more than send literature to the appropriate trading corporation or to the China Committee for the Promotion of Foreign Trade, and hope that they will pass on the brochures to the correct people. If the ultimate user does not receive the literature or is not convinced by it, then he will not place a purchase request with the central planners. Moreover, in negotiating on contract terms, the American businessman will probably not know the quantity called for in the import plan, nor the flexibility on price allowed the Chinese negotiators.

Related problems exist for export planning. Since much of Chinese exports are agricultural, the amount available for sale depends on uncertain variables such as the weather and vagaries of local production and transportation. In addition, some exports are residual items, left over after domestic needs have been fulfilled. Thus, the foreign businessman has difficulty determining what and how much is available for sale, how anxious the Chinese are to sell particular products, and an accurate delivery date.

While most Chinese middlemen negotiators are expert traders and familiar with some of the technical aspects of the goods they deal in, they frequently are not familiar with how Chinese goods are produced or how foreign goods will be used. This problem was especially serious during the Cultural Revolution when political personnel with no technical expertise joined the negotiation teams.

The use of these middlemen slows down the course of negotiations considerably. Very often, when technical problems or questions come up, Chinese negotiators must retire to consult ultimate producers and users and their technical experts. This process tends to make negotiations less flexible, since trading corporations often act under instructions from principals they represent, and are reluctant or unable to depart very far from these instructions.

ADDENDA

TWO VIEWS—PROSPECTS FOR U.S.-CHINA TRADE IN 1980

Professor Robert Dernberger of the University of Michigan has made a series of four projections of U.S.-China trade volume for 1980. His projections are based on carefully stated assumptions about the state of the Chinese economy, trade policies, and political relations between the two countries. These assumptions cover the following spectrum of possibilities:

	(In millions of Dollars)			
	Most Pessimistic	Relatively Pessimistic	Least Pessimistic	Optimistic
U.S. exports to China	-0-	$25	$325	$650
U.S. imports from China	-0-	$25	$200	$250

My own estimate—at best, only an educated guess—is that Chinese exports to the United States in 1980 will be in the range of some tens of millions. Chinese exports to industrialized countries consist mainly of textiles and foodstuffs; neither will find an easy U.S. market.

American exports to China is a more complex problem. The United States may be in a poor competitive position vis-à-vis countries such as Japan and West Germany on moderately complex technology. Radar landing systems or other "strategic defense" advanced technology may continue to be barred from U.S. export. This still leaves a substantial intermediate area where large sales might be made—older generations of jet planes and computers, vehicle assembly operations, refining and cracking plants, etc. But China's demand for Western products may decline in the future, as its leadership, for political reasons, decides to produce goods that might be purchased more cheaply abroad—thus ridding itself of dependency on the West.

By 1980, my estimate is that, assuming a reasonable improvement in political relations, U.S. exports to China will be in the $100-$200 million range. This is nothing to sneer at; it might include some spectacular individual transactions, with a significant impact on some sectors of our economy.

THE FRENETIC PACE OF A CANTON TRADE FAIR

Twice a year, in the Spring and Fall, the month-long Canton Fair attracts several thousand foreign businessmen. For example, at the 1971 Autumn fair, Chinese authorities invited some 5,000 foreign businessmen to Canton, half of whom were Japanese. About a third of China's annual export contracts are concluded at each Fair. For the remaining third, Canton is still important, as many of the initial contracts and intermediate negotiations are carried on there.

Although only a few Chinese import contracts are negotiated at Canton, the Fair is an opportunity for Western sellers to meet with the appropriate potential buyers. These contacts can be followed up directly later on.

While it is difficult to generalize, many businessmen ascribe a certain Kafkaesque quality to a Canton fair. (Mild culture shock is perhaps a better description.) The Westerner feels isolated in a strange place. His living quarters, while certainly adequate, still may lack the amenities. There is no place to go for relaxation or for a change of scenery. Nor is there any let-up in the pressures. He is constantly going from one exhibit to another and from one negotiation to another. And in the evening, he may be invited to attend a lengthy Chinese opera or "revolutionary" entertainment several hours long.

This atmosphere seems to affect the Western businessman. Some describe being in such a fog that after a couple of weeks they sign contracts which they otherwise might not have. In part, this comes from an urge "to sign a contract, any contract." After all, that is why one visits the Fair. Besides, everyone else is signing away, and one does not want to be left out.

More concretely, the bringing together of many businessmen dealing in similar goods makes for keen competition. The Chinese are in an excellent position to ask one foreigner for a price quotation, then ask another to beat that price, then return to the first businessman, etc. The foreigner may also have communications difficulties with his own headquarters. While international telephone and telegraph are available, some visitors have expressed a reluctance to use them.

Finally, there is the time element. The long Canton stay not only is discomforting and expensive, but the Westerner may not be able to be away from the office a month. Consequently, he is anxious to complete a transaction and leave. But the Chinese are in no hurry. They can move slowly and casually, while the foreigner fidgets and gets more anxious.

I am not suggesting the Chinese deliberately create such an atmosphere in order to facilitate sales. Indeed, there seems to be a greater demand for Chinese goods than what can be produced. Nevertheless, such an atmosphere does exist, and Americans going to the Fair should be prepared.

21

Graft: Almost a Way of Life

Far Eastern Economic Review

Like the gods and goddesses who abound in Asia, each with many faces, many hands, and many names, corruption in Asia has diverse aspects and numerous ingenious ways of extorting an illegal "buck." It is an old institution, variously called bakhsheesh, *"tea money" and* salaam. *Then, as today, the official who stood between the people and the ruler had to be appeased. Currency controls, travel restrictions and the "barbed-wire" entanglements of restrictions that are used by Asian governments in the name of economic planning have further stimulated its growth as do scarcities of resources and consumer commodities. Its cruellest form is the exploitation of the poor who want food and medical care.* REVIEW *correspondents report.*

PAKISTAN

How to buy a Sherman tank

Lahore: To underscore the futility of several highly-publicised moves to stamp out corruption, in the late 1960s a reporter asked President Ayub Khan's Cabinet secretary, Agha Abdul Hameed, what purpose the latest anti-corruption plan would serve. The secretary replied, with matching cynicism: "I shall be surprised to learn of a human society free of corruption. It is just a question of form and relative degree."

With their pronounced trait of paying lip-service to the ideals of Islam while merrily practising the opposite, leaders of public opinion in Pakistan vociferously condemned the secretary's remarks. In the process, they frequently recalled a saying of the Prophet of Islam: "Accursed are both, the one who takes and the one who gives a bribe." Corruption is now all pervading, and so much a part of life that it no longer shocks anyone.

In the early 1950s, two punitive laws were passed against corrupt politicians, and special anti-corruption police and courts were established. But the laws against the politicians were used for "fixing" political rivals. Inevitably, the anti-corruption department itself became a nest of corruption, justifying its existence only by the prosecution of cases of petty bribery.

The leaders of the 1958 coup added a new dimension both to corruption and the fight against it. Charging almost all the top politicians with corruption, they disqualified them from holding any elected office. They also purged the top

---

Reprinted, by permission, from *Far Eastern Economic Review* (September 6, 1974).

layer of bureaucracy of most of the former British Indian civil service officers. But despite this, the ruling élite, with Ayub Khan at the apex, broke all records of corruption. The choicest lands were grabbed by military officers.

There was plenty of money to go round, for the Western world, impressed by the "political stability" under Ayub and his "sound economic planning," poured in millions of dollars in loans and grants. With industrial development, imports substitution and encouragement to new entrepreneurs as keystones of the official economic policy, unheard of opportunities of patronage were created. An unrealistic exchange rate – Rs 4.50 compared with its open market value of Rs 14 to US$1 – added fuel to the fire, and by 1967 a position was reached when practically all that was required to launch a major industrial project was official patronage alone, even without requisite capital and experience.

Corruption is now so well entrenched that the dismissal of 303 top officials by former president Yahya Khan and over 1,300 by Premier Zulfikar Ali Bhutto at the inauguration of their terms has not made the slightest dent in the attitude of the bureaucracy. This is primarily because the dismissed officials have been allowed to retain their ill-gotten gains. For instance, a federal secretary dismissed by Yahya Khan had received gifts at his daughter's wedding which included eighteen cars, 57 refrigerators and 97 sets of jewellery. He was never asked to return any of the gifts. Similarly, bureaucrats who "won" huge sums from businessmen at card tables were never made to account for their winnings.

Bhutto has received thousands of complaints about corruption involving a wide range of officials from the police to Revenue Department clerks.

Policemen are long past the stage of confining themselves to tackling crime. Irrespective of enhanced salaries and other service benefits, the force now gets its cut from burglars, hold-up men and protection racketeers. Exceptionally remunerative police stations are auctioned off by high police officials to the highest bidding subordinates, who make good their promises through regular stipends from brothels, gambling dens, narcotics pedlars and smugglers. Some police stations make as much as Rs 10,000 (US$1,010) to Rs 15,000 a month, shared all along the line.

Apart from police stations, some railway stations are also auctioned off to the highest bidding station master and goods clerk. Railway stations in thriving market towns make as much as Rs 300,000 a year. Harassed businessmen, particularly those dealing in perishable goods, never obtain a wagon until the obliging booking clerk's helpful suggestion of propitiating "the swines at the other end of the line" is accepted. Ticketless travel is now so institutionalised that railway staff and police have their regular daily quota of half-fare passengers.

On one of the branch lines in Tharparkar district of Sindh Province not a single ticket has been sold on the daily passenger train for the past three years. Even on the trunk line, tickets are rarely available at the counter, but can be bought from other sources. It is also widely known that iron scrap dealers in Lahore have for years been dependent on supplies from the local railway workshop complex. Understandably, locomotives have been reported stolen.

Another agency where corruption is allegedly rife is the Public Works Department, which is claimed to have "built" expensive non-existent bridges and roads. Shoddy workmanship in many of the department's projects is explained by the 30%-45% cut the contractors have to give to its officials.

The most remunerative and pivotal official agency is believed to be the Revenue Department, which keeps records of ownerships, assesses land and water tax and collects rice and wheat under the policy of "voluntary sale to the Government" at the support price – always lower than the prevalent market rate. In the department, the notations of the Rs 150-per-month *patwari* (land recorders) are indecipherable, except by another *patwari*, and in most cases these alone decide the title of a property. His stranglehold over the records is so complete that even financial commissioners in need of proving their title to family properties have been known to buy his favours.

The most heinous aspect of corruption in recent times is its penetration of the higher ranks of the judiciary. Some lower courts have been prone to corruption for a long time because magistrates, in addition to their judicial duties, have certain executive functions which enable them to collect bribes through their clerks on every copy of documents sought by the public, and every transaction which has to be officially registered. District and high court judges had been largely honest, until recently. But this integrity of the superior courts proved their undoing, as Ayub Khan, repeatedly annoyed by the courts' verdicts obstructing some of his orders, inducted new judges who proved less troublesome. Inevitably, many of these judges found their salary of Rs 3,500 per month, in addition to free accommodation, much too low for their valuable services. Now it is no longer a secret that money paid through certain lawyers can buy favourable verdicts from some courts. Mercifully, the Supreme Court, staffed by judges of the old school, is still free from any breath of scandal.

The evil of corruption also extends to the Income Tax Department, which can halve one's tax for a consideration, and does so aggressively. A special police party sent to ensnare the personal secretary of an income tax official in the federal capital in June was locked up in a room by the tax collectors and had to be freed by an armed contingent using tear gas. The Excise Department obtains its monthly stipends from factories, which show lower returns to dodge excise duty and income tax and also to cheat shareholders. The Labour Department obtains its share from employers by ignoring labour laws.

Power generation and distribution are State monopolies, and no power connection, either for domestic or industrial use, can be acquired without paying Rs 50-Rs 2,000 in bribes. Given a mutually satisfactory settlement, power can be supplied at about one-quarter of its real price. In Lahore – Pakistan's second biggest town – 30%-35% of electricity is lost on the distribution network due to what are officially described as "unauthorised connections." Farmers who do not keep officials in good humour find their tube-wells idle.

The Irrigation Department often shuts off canals for "urgently needed repairs" at times when the land most needs water. But the repairs can be put off if the farmers pool together to pay for the sluice gates to be raised.

Furtherance of party interests has become another source of irregularities. For instance, during the National Awami Party (NAP) rule in the Frontier Province, arms licences were issued to anyone going through party channels. "Please issue" was written so automatically by the ministers that it was jotted on one application by a rustic Pathan asking to buy a Sherman tank. The Pakistan People's Party (PPP) gained some notoriety by allocating ration depots to its supporters.

Although corruption has spread to almost every walk of life in Pakistan, it is now generally accepted that it has diminished at senior levels. However, two top politicians in Baluchistan were given permits to export rice, netting each Rs 5 million.

At the federal level, one minister has been accused of inducting as many as eighteen of his close relatives into Government jobs. Legislators in Parliament have also raised the issue of the claim that large payments were made for inclusion in the Pakistan-Mecca caravans of pilgrims. The legislators themselves are not free from corruption. Their votes on important issues are often influenced by official favours – jobs for relatives, admissions of sons and daughters to medical, engineering and other professional colleges, permits for cars, which are in short supply in the country, transfers of troublesome officials from their constituencies and grants of bank loans on easy terms.

Banks have seldom granted loans on commercial considerations alone. Irrespective of the soundness of securities, borrowers still have to pay up to 5% to bank officials. The banks maintain lavish guest-houses, and even brothels, for obliging officials at holiday resorts and almost all the principal towns. Jobs are offered to relatives of patronising Government bureaucrats – who are themselves advanced interest-free loans.

Admission to kindergartens in major towns is still impossible except with the support of a minor politician or an official. Similarly, admissions to hospitals are impossible unless there is the right sponsorship.

Public response to corruption verges on apathy. No political party or any other organisation has taken up the issue. Leaders of pressure groups – student organisations for one – are easily appeased. The situation endorses a famous American economist's view: "Perhaps some degree of exploitation is inescapable in the process of economic development of a country, but it is only in Pakistan that exploitation is practised as a national policy."

SINGAPORE

The 'Mr Clean' of Asia

By Peter Jordan

Singapore: For many years Singapore has had the reputation of being the least corrupt of all Asian states and, indeed, with the Nixon scandal and the recent examples of skulduggery in high offices in Britain, it could probably be said to be one of the least corrupt nations in the world.

The biggest problem Singapore now faces is the Government's reluctance to admit that any corruption exists. The Prime Minister, Lee Kuan Yew, is reported to have made it clear to the local press that the governmental machinery is quite capable of cleansing itself and should the press expose such matters it would be at its own peril.

Comparatively recently, an official left Government service and later it was announced that he had returned all his honours and decorations to the State. Whether he also returned the other benefits that were popularly believed to be the cause of his downfall was not disclosed to the public. It is such lacunae that disturb those Singaporeans who really care about the social structure of their country. The result at a lower level is that Singaporeans are never quite certain what is being withheld from them and what is above-board.

Since many of Singapore's rich are highly conspicuous consumers, there is sometimes a feeling expressed by those who are only salary- or wage-earners that so much wealth could not have been accumulated without some "oiling" of the machine – something to which the average Singaporean has no access. He feels oppressed and harassed. Not by the all-powerful figure of his Prime Minister, but by the arrogant power displayed by the petty official, against whose judgement there is no recourse, unless he has connections to take the matter higher, or is literate and brave enough to write to the "letters to the editor" column of a newspaper.

In the 1972 election, the almost 30% protest vote (including spoilt ballots) probably derived more from dissatisfaction over the corruption among the lower-level officials than from any major disagreement over the People's Action Party policies. Without either "tea money" or an active press, there is no means for the average citizen to smooth his way through the vast governmental bureaucracy.

For the foreign investor, there is no need to oil the machine, except by strictly legal means, such as buying his citizenship through the stipulated size of his investment, or, at a lower level, agreeing to build a swimming pool for the house he wants to lease for two or three years. Of course, this is not corruption, but merely the favouring of the rich over the not-so-well-off.

BANGLADESH

The playground for opportunists

Dacca: All the stories of illicit dealings in Dacca might – like the clever but sinister plots of a macabre novel – be amusing, if their meaning were not so tragic and their cost in human misery were not so great. The stories are told again and again in Dacca, Chittagong, Khulna and thousands of Bangladesh's villages. Every person has seen and remembered some share of the new folklore of post-independence corruption.

The folklore is genuinely new while the scale of its topic is unprecedented. Although the bribe, the kickback and the payoff all existed as *bakhsheesh* (gratuity) in the past, they never in the living memory of Bengal reached the plunderous magnitude which has been practised in the past two and a half years.

Bangladesh, as the erstwhile East Pakistan, was a quiet and distant place – a province. Travellers normally journeyed from Southeast to South Asia via Bangkok, Rangoon and Calcutta, skipping Dacca. There were few international flights into the city and after 1965 there were no flights through Calcutta, currently the main transit point for Bangladesh.

In July 1970, more than six months before the Pakistani crackdown, this correspondent met in Dacca a young French student travelling "on the cheap" in Asia. He angrily complained that Dacca was the only "currency controlled" city between Saigon and Beirut where, despite a hard search, he could not find anyone willing to change dollars on the blackmarket. Annoyed, he opined that the relation of eastern Bengalis to the wily but profitable ways of the world market was simply *"trés innocénts."*

Whether or not this supposed innocence ever existed, it was certainly lost after independence, as nearly US$2,000 million worth of relief commodities, aid, contracts and international business poured from the overseas cornucopia. Civil war and independence had suddenly catapulted Bangladesh from a backwater region on the periphery of the world market into a nation with increasingly strategic importance for the region.

In response to the extraordinary despair wrought by the civil war, international relief agencies and friendly governments donated generously to Bangladesh in order to stave off hunger and to assist in reconstruction. Much honest and dedicated work was done by Bangalees and foreigners, but beginning as early as the days of refugee relief in India, it became clear that relief operations were also becoming the playground of opportunist and profit-minded groups. The representatives from OXFAM and other international relief agencies, who, from their base in Calcutta, became distressed about missing shipments and the low level of actual supplies reaching the camps, were told not to probe too deeply – if they valued their personal safety.

After independence, operations began in earnest in Bangladesh. But the newly-formed Bangladesh Red Cross began acquiring a reputation as more of a political, rather than humanitarian, organisation. Representatives of the Swiss-based International Committee of the Red Cross (ICRC) in Dacca opposed for months its accreditation as a national Red Cross society. Besides alleged abuse of funds and commodity grants, ICRC officials were disturbed by the fact that the Red Cross was, and continues to be, headed by Gazi Gulam Mustafa who is also the Chairman of Dacca City's Awami League. Previously, the post of Red Cross chairman was considered non-political and honorary – usually occupied by a justice of the High Court.

During 1972, international relief agencies became increasingly disturbed about large quantities of goods appearing on the blackmarket which had been funnelled through the Bangladesh Red Cross. Tony Hagen, the first director of the United Nations Relief Operation in Bangladesh, recently observed that roughly one out of seven tins of baby food and one out of thirteen blankets donated ever reached the poor.

Corrupt practices in relief were by no means the exclusive realm of enterprising Bangalees. There are a few known instances of foreigners having enriched themselves. A former official of a relief organisation's transport section, which at one time controlled the import and shipment of millions of dollars worth of goods, is said to have recently purchased a hotel in Sardinia from his Bangladesh "earnings."

The overall social effect of heightened corruption has been to seriously set back the course of economic recovery. From the distribution of more than 15,000 import licences to Awami League compatriots in 1972 to the emergence of "phantom" textile mills receiving scarce yarn quotas, output following the circuitous routes of the blackmarket has not led to a consistent expansion of production. Most illicit fortunes were made through merchant activities of trading illegally-procured commodities rather than from the actual production of goods. The money so earned has in most cases not been reinvested in productive activities, but has gone to the purchase of real estate, precious metals, automobiles and into foreign accounts.

The debate within the Government in recent months over new investment policies has revolved around the issue of how to mobilise "black money" for productive investment. The recent denationalisation of various industrial sectors, and the raising of the investment ceiling from Ta 2.5 million (US$192,500) to Ta 30 million, have been widely interpreted here as a concession to "black money" interests with a view to drawing their fortunes away from the arena of the illicit merchant trade and into the business of "honest" production.

Over the past six months the Government itself has made a great deal of noise about its attack on the corrupt interests within the State sector and in the private "hoarder's" trade. Legislation was recently added to the Special Powers Act which will formally legitimise the establishment of special tribunals to handle "corrupt elements."

In late April, Prime Minister Sheikh Mujibur Rahman declared a "limited emergency" and called out the armed forces to check border smuggling of jute and rice to India, and also to deal firmly with "anti-social" market elements within Bangladesh. In the first two weeks of the army's operation, there was widespread belief that real results would be achieved and the country was cautiously optimistic. But within a month the new psychological edge had been lost. The army had picked up two Awami League Members of Parliament in whose homes they found arms caches and stocks of smuggled goods. In Comilla, a high Awami League party worker was roughed up by the army.

The Awami League Working Committee was promptly called into national session by nervous district committees. The result was that new controls were imposed on the army's operation. Although one of the Members of Parliament involved was temporarily suspended from the League, the cases have been effectively dropped. The army operation, thereafter, quickly lost its vigour.

In early July, the Government's "anti-corruption" campaign hotted up again. Six Cabinet ministers and three State ministers were compelled to resign. In the midst of a new propaganda drive against corrupt elements, it was publicly presumed that the dismissals were linked to an attempt to clean up the Administration. Nevertheless, no such direct link was ever publicly made by the Government. In the month and a half that has followed, nearly 200 lower-level officials in administration and nationalised industries have been dismissed from their posts under Presidential Order No. 9. The Order does not require that any private or public explanation be given for a dismissal.

The most serious consequence of mushrooming corruption has been that it has destroyed the spirit of self-sacrifice and struggle which emerged at the time of the independence fight. Many critics of aid to the current Government consider the nearly $2,000 million in relief and rehabilitation assistance donated after 1971 to have been a prime source for the criminalisation of the country's politics and for the internal defeat of those favouring a more self-reliant approach.

INDIA

A common goal: Get-rich-quick

New Delhi: Introducing a motion in Parliament on July 23, expressing lack of confidence in the Government, the leader of the Communist Party of India-Marxist (CPI-M) described Prime Minister Indira Gandhi as the protector of black money and the fountain-head of corruption. Two weeks later, a Member of Parliament belonging to Mrs Gandhi's Congress demanded that the party's presidential candidate, Fakhruddin Ali Ahmed, should have the courage to declare his personal assets before he assumed office. There were allegations that he had amassed wealth and could hardly be the head of a state striving to establish a socialist society.

The prevailing feeling is that corruption in Indian public life is all pervasive. Not only the President and the Prime Minister but lesser dignitaries, businessmen, bureaucrats, contractors, journalists, vice-chancellors, teachers, doctors and nurses all come under suspicion. Jyotirmoy Bosu, CPI-M member of the Lok Sabha (House of the People), alleged that the Congress party had received a donation of Rs 10 million (US$1.03 million) as *quid pro quo* for raising the prices of automobiles. Similar charges were levelled against the Congress when concessions were made to the sugar barons of Uttar Pradesh on the eve of the elections there in February.

Jayaprakash Narayan, who is leading a crusade against corruption in Bihar, told the Prime Minister that her protégé, Mrs Nandini Satpathy, had spent Rs 3 million on her election campaign in Orissa. He wanted to know how she had obtained such a large sum. Mrs Gandhi blandly replied: "We don't have any money."

Asia's 'Mr Fixit.'

Elections undoubtedly involve corruption, with black money and clandestine expenses for campaigns. According to the law, no Parliamentary candidate can spend more than Rs 35,000; in the case of state assembly elections, maximum individual expenses cannot exceed Rs 13,500. These figures are for the larger states and come down to as low as Rs 6,000 and Rs 2,500 respectively depending on the size and population of the state. There is no ceiling on what political parties may spend on their campaigns, but each candidate has to send a return on his individual expenses.

The Congress and other political parties used to accept donations from big business houses; this was statutorily banned, but now it is being suggested that companies should again be allowed to contribute funds to political parties. Big business makes donations in order to propitiate the powers that be – and as the Congress has been continuously in power in the Centre and in most of the states, it has received the largest bounties. In return, licences are issued, tax evasion is condoned and other benefits extended to the donors. With galloping inflation (the value of the rupee is now about 30% of what it was in 1949), no election can be won without incurring expenses far in excess of the prescribed ceilings.

Many observers feel that the banning of company donations to political parties has driven the process of business houses' financing election campaigns underground, and that the problem is now more acute. As it is, contributions are not always in money but often take such forms as supplying jeeps and cars, printing posters, giving advertisements in party papers and other publications and deputising company staff for campaign purposes. Simultaneously, there are charges that many candidates, especially those belonging to the ruling party, rig polls and intimidate voters.

Elections are also responsible for the reckless spending of public money. Hundreds of foundation stones were laid in Uttar Pradesh by the Prime Minister for projects of questionable utility as a sop to the voters. When elections are over and if no party has secured a comfortable majority, there is vigorous horse-trading and open purchase of members of legislative assemblies (MLAs). There was a time when MLAs were offered Rs 25,000-Rs 50,000 to cross the floor, and some of the clever ones crossed more than once.

Foreign money is also believed to play a key role in elections. There are various ways to arrange clandestine transfers of funds. The rupee holdings under PL-480 American aid were for a long time said to be a source of patronage of the rightist elements. As India has rupee trade with the Soviet Union and East European countries, they too have large funds in India to support leftists. The report of an inquiry into the role of foreign cash is top secret.

When a businessman has to grease the palms of officials to get anything done, he becomes unscrupulous with the consumer. A textile mill may pay excise duty on only part of the cloth it makes; the excise inspector is bribed. Where a brewery is licensed to make only 50,000 litres of beer, it may produce 100,000 litres – another excise official is bribed. Prohibition, enforced in many states until a few years ago, not only corrupted and enriched police forces, but also created a new rich class of bootleggers.

Patriotism and national good are now being forgotten as get-rich-quick becomes the motto, with no one wanting to be left behind. The blanket ban on the import of many articles and the high price of gold have led to smuggling on an enormous scale. Smugglers can now dictate terms to the Government, because they also contribute to political funds. From the coast of Gujarat up to Cochin, the writ of the smuggler runs supreme.

Large-scale smuggling and black money on which taxes have not been paid have led to what Finance Minister Y. B. Chavan has described as a parallel economy. Most of these undeclared funds are held in cash, gold or property. When an urban property is bought or sold, the transaction has two phases: Part of the amount is paid in "white" and the balance in "black" money. The white is a bank transaction, the other is in cash. A tax-dodger will invest his undeclared money in an urban property, converting maybe half of it into white money. To check this racket, the income tax authorities have decided that they will have the option to buy properties if they think they are undervalued. But valuation officials and income tax officers are not always honest.

As the value of the rupee steadily

declines, more and more people are buying gold and property, or send their money abroad – a common practice with importers and exporters.

Exporters under-invoice goods and by arrangement with their customers abroad, operating through codes, build up reserves in foreign accounts; similarly, importers have their bills bloated, the difference going into clandestine transactions.

The planned economy obliges India to operate a "Control Raj." Anybody wanting an official sanction – to set up a factory or change a brand name, to secure an import licence or to move rice from one district to another – has to oil the proper joints in the administrative machinery. There is "speed" money; there is "hush" money. In 1973, fifty-four firms allegedly misused 206 licences, valued at about Rs 30 million, according to Central Bureau of Investigation (CBI) sources.

Many foreign entrepreneurs in India appear to accept "greasing palms" as a way of business. The large resources at their disposal give them an edge over Indian firms. They may offer lavish trips abroad, or send an official's children to their home country on some sort of fellowship or for employment. Recently, the Chairman of the Monopolies and Restrictive Trade Practices Commission, J. L. Nain, expressed surprise at the Government's decision to offer the licence for a detergent plant in West Bengal to a foreign firm, when the Commission itself had recommended the case of an Indian house. This happened soon before the elections in Mrs Gandhi's home state, Uttar Pradesh.

Local investors, although sometimes out-smarted by their overseas competitors, are no less artful. Before elections in Uttar Pradesh, many leading companies which had been trying to obtain licences to expand were given the necessary authority. "Elections," as one businessman said, "are the best things that can happen to us."

Adulteration of food and drugs is another form of corruption. Last year, 245 people died from adulteration in West Bengal alone, according to police statistics. Granulated mud was sold in the Punjab as fertiliser. Turmeric powder may be half cow-dung; wheat and rice will have iron filings and pebbles; even life-saving drugs may be death-dealing poisons. Recently, a score of people died in Lucknow because of sub-standard glucose used in a hospital.

CHINA

Old traditions die hard

Those of prejudiced opinions, given to generalisations about corruption being endemic in Asia, usually have to admit to two exceptions – China and Singapore – which allegedly "prove the rule." It is generally granted that Mao Tse-tung has largely wiped out corruption in China.

One visitor to Canton was forced to take a long tricycle-rickshaw ride right across the city late at night. The fare – paid in advance – was the equivalent of a few cents. Embarrassed by this outmoded and humiliating form of transport, the passenger offered the rickshaw man – in a place where neither could be observed – a "tip" amounting to several times the fare. It was proudly refused.

The incident – almost impossible to imagine in any other Asian city – can only be explained in terms of a combination of the fear of being caught and a resurgence of national pride. Observers stress one factor or another according to their own political prejudice. But against such an example, one must set the experience of other visitors to China who have found tips accepted and even had property stolen.

The recent anti-Lin, anti-Confucius socialist education campaign has revealed that corruption and dishonesty still create problems in China and that the visitor's experience – in this field, as in so many others – hardly reflects Chinese realities.

Overseas Chinese visitors are better able to spot the surviving areas of decadence than foreign devils. They report that, although gambling is forbidden, card games, mostly poker, are still played, and if money is not put in the pot, then cigarettes are used instead of coins or chips.

Publicity campaigns to fight crime were launched last year at commune level in various parts of the country. Posters denounced theft, blackmarket activities and other "anti-revolutionary conduct." In Kwangtung Province, plans to escape to capitalist Hongkong were listed among the crimes.

The blackmarket in China appears to centre around illegal purchases of clothing, forging food ration coupons, fiddles with the allocation of work points and under-the-counter deals in building materials. At a higher level, other forms of corruption included extortion, profiteering (apparently rampant in the resale of cement bags) and false returns of harvest statistics. These are regularly denounced, and those convicted given wide publicity in surrounding communes, often being subjected to the humiliation of a parade in public before they are taken away to serve their sentence.

More commonplace crimes still occur, including robbery with violence. According to posters put up in Canton last year, two men had been sentenced to death before a firing squad and a woman sentenced to five years corrective labour, having been convicted of keeping a disorderly house – an unexpected aberration in puritanical China. Of course, one of the men was predictably described as an "agent of Taiwan," while the other had allegedly raped an eight-year-old girl. According to the poster, the woman had been in the habit of luring young men to her home, plying them with drink and offering them young women.

Such isolated stories would appear to be exceptional in the world's most disciplined society, where the huge majority live in village communities and can indulge in little anti-social activity without their neighbours knowing. Nevertheless, it would be surprising indeed if, after a century of foreign exploitation, wars and corrupt government, the People's Republic had eliminated crime and corruption in a mere two and a half decades.

For untold centuries the average Chinese has automatically assumed that public officials have to be bribed, not only for special favours but for the normal execution of their duties. Similarly the officials, from the mandarin downwards, have regarded their offices as a means of enriching themselves and of furthering the interests of their families. It is at such ingrained attitudes of mind that the latest anti-Confucius campaign is aimed.

Early on in the campaign, a student set the tone by accusing his father of having pulled strings to get him his university place. The student's accusations were sympathetically reported by the *People's Daily*. At village or production brigade level, parents who want their children to be given easy jobs or to be recommended for further education are in the habit of giving "sweeteners" (piglets, chickens or other produce from their private plots) to the official responsible.

At a higher level, the problem was summed up by an article last year in the theoretical monthly journal *Red Flag*, entitled "Check corruption; Never be contaminated." Directed at Party members and cadres, it warned against the ever-present danger of bourgeois thinking, and warned the cadres against the landlords and the bourgeoisie who "hide themselves in dark corners and never stop for a single day to spread a corruptive and decadent style of life and ideology." It implied that such people were still using "sugar-coated bullets" to subvert officials with flattery, bribes and even pretty girls.

The article revealed that corruption was not confined to the remnants of the rich and ruling classes. It listed, among the corrupt influences infecting China today, the abuse of power by officials seeking personal prestige and self-enhancement and individuals or individual groups promoting their own interests at the expense of others.

The article maintained that such "sinister trends" as "going through the back door instead of the front door" constituted a limited problem and would inevitably be resisted by the people and the cadres. Nevertheless, it must be taken seriously and vigilantly guarded against. The Party must "conscientiously" accept the supervision of the masses: "We must never have the notion of privilege in our minds and never exploit our positions for our own interest."

Since the article was published, posters in the anti-Confucius campaign appearing in Chinese cities, towns and factories have revealed that the problem is less limited than *Red Flag* implied. Numerous complaints have been aired alleging abuse of power by officials. The heart of the problem lies in the fact that power and prestige are the main rewards within an egalitarian society. Cadres would be less than human if they did not savour the perks of office – the chauffeured car, the tailored uniform, the banquet for foreign friends. And they would be less than Chinese if some, at least, did not abuse that power by enhancing their own positions and those of their relations. The roots that the current anti-Confucius campaign is trying to pull up go very deep.

HONGKONG

The emergence of a new order

Hongkong: The ambitious task which the Government undertook six months ago in its latest bid to stamp out corruption seems to have gained a strong foothold in the community, despite its long acceptance of bribery as an integral part of life. The new anti-corruption drive followed the dramatic flight from Hongkong to Britain last summer of former police chief superintendent Peter Godber while he was under investigation for amassing an alleged fortune of HK$4.3 million (US$849,800).

The creation of the powerful Independent Commission Against Corruption (ICAC) in February was apparently the result of the Hongkong Government's belated realisation that there was a threat of an erosion of public confidence if it failed to come to terms with the problem. The ICAC started off with an impressive series of arrests and subsequent prosecutions, which appears to have had a favourable impact on the people. According to preliminary figures, a total of 3,355 complaints have been received by the ICAC.

The present strength of the ICAC is about 550, and it is expected to grow larger pending approval of more funds from the Government (the budget for the current year is about HK$15 million). It has three main sections: the operations wing, which is responsible for investigation and prosecution; the prevention section, which is primarily engaged in plugging loopholes in the law; and the community relations wing, which deals with publicity.

It has been a time-honoured belief among Hongkong residents since early colonial days that money and expensive gifts are the best means to procure favour and to secure immunity from official interference. This is particularly true of the refugees who came from China during the early 1950s, many of whom were already sophisticated in the art of bribery.

The malaise also strained the honesty of many expatriate civil servants who realised that a few extra dollars could be made by turning a blind eye to the illegal activities that were rife in a society in which they were considered foreigners. It has been estimated that payments to officials for toleration of illicit activities in 1972 amounted to US$68.83 million, representing 26% of their official emoluments for that year (REVIEW, Nov. 12, 1973). It was also believed that corruption in the Government, as far as large payments were concerned, was probably confined to only a small number of civil servants.

At the street level, "syndicated" corruption is rampant, mainly involving narcotics, gambling and prostitution rackets. Corruption here is said to be controlled by the police at divisional level. The Godber escape and the formation of the ICAC were followed by a wave of resignations from the police force and other Government departments which have daily contact with the public. The Commissioner of Police, Brian Slevin, recently had to tell his Chinese detective sergeants that honest men should not be afraid of the graft-hunters. The officers had sent him a petition seeking protection against ICAC victimisation.

Corruption is slowly being rejected by the younger generation in the colony. Anti-corruption rallies have been organised and public forums held by students to encourage official and community efforts to tackle the problem.

It is not only civil servants who have been tainted by corruption. It is common knowledge that buyers for big companies expect kickbacks. Cargo space can be purchased from shipping agents, and factory owners can operate with sub-standard safety measures if they are prepared to pay "tea money." Newspapers, mainly Chinese language, are also alleged to be infested with corruption.

Corruption here is as old as Hongkong itself and has been the subject of numerous official inquiries. The current drive to eliminate it by the ICAC, with its considerable powers, should prove to be more successful than its predecessors.

THAILAND

Accusing the foreign touch

Bangkok: Thai Premier Sanya Dharmasakti confiscated more than US$25 million worth of property left behind by Thailand's former military rulers who were forced into exile last October. Although much of the property was no doubt acquired legally (and if they can prove legal title before the end of this month they will be able to reclaim it), a proportion was obtained by means which in the West would be considered corrupt.

It is said the Police Department presented Field Marshal Prapas Charusathiara with a Singha beer carton stuffed with Baht 100 (US$5) notes on his 60th birthday. Narong Kittikachorn reputedly wielded major influence in the rice trade, traditionally Thailand's largest export commodity. He is also alleged to have been involved in drug trafficking. And according to rumours, the military leaders allegedly received substantial gifts in return for approving such major investment projects as the second Bangkok airport, the Kra Canal, and a petrochemical complex. One survey of the exiled trio's property found that they owned shares in, or were directors of, more than 100 local companies, including banks, mining, transportation, oil, cement, hotel, and automobile concerns: all businesses which loom large in the national economy and which in various ways depend on Government cooperation and support.

The corruption of the former military regime was certainly a major factor behind its collapse. The people's anger and frustration were expressed last October when the headquarters of the Board of Investigation was destroyed. It is alleged that the Board, the regime's anti-corruption body, which was controlled by Narong, was often used by him to cover up his own dealings.

But if the integrity and honesty of the present Prime Minister are not in doubt, it is equally clear that corruption generally has not diminished under the new civilian Government. Recently, the Chairman of the National Audit Council estimated that the country was losing Baht 100 million a year because of corruption. Another official claims that Government departments mis-spent more than Baht 1,000 million of the national budget last year. However, if corruption is defined in its Western sense (and the Thais use the English term only because there is no popular equivalent), this is an underestimate.

At one level, military dictators, their ministers and generals have not hesitated to use their enormous power and influence for personal profit. At the other end of the ladder, a vast and unwieldly bureaucracy of poorly-paid civil servants have learned to supplement their income by selling their own modest services for "tea money."

Opponents of a leading Thai personality alleged he received a percentage cut of Thailand's first oil deal with China last year. This has been denied. Diplomats from neighbouring countries believe the large-scale smuggling of Thai rice, timber, and other goods can only be possible with the complicity of Thai police and senior officials. Similarly, there is obviously official complicity at some levels, mainly in the provinces, in drug trafficking.

The governors of two provinces are currently under investigation for corrupt dealings in the sale of rice from public warehouses. The head of the State-owned Thai Maritime Navigation Company was recently dismissed for alleged corruption and mismanagement. Scandals in the Royal Irrigation Department and the Royal Mint have made headlines in recent years, but for the most part corrupt practices do not attract publicity.

The Immigration Department is a notorious case, with brokers handling large bribes and payoffs from would-be immigrants to officials. An international news agency in Bangkok, anxious to receive prompt and efficient service for its many telephone and telex lines, periodically entertains post office officials and hands over "tea money." A foreign embassy hosting a reception asks the police to close off a road and at the end of the evening distributes money to grateful policemen.

The Thai police force, with its tremendous power and unlimited opportunities for graft, has its own reputation. There is a Thai saying: A soldier's wife counts bottles of whisky, a policeman's wife counts piles of money.

Some observers here believe that the present state of affairs is a symptom of the general corruption of Thai society as a result of its domination by foreign interests. Others point out that corruption in Thailand operates as an unspoken and unwritten means of redistributing income. It is understood that few civil servants can live on their official income, particularly with current rates of inflation, and so senior officials tolerate their unofficial sources of supplementary income. But no one doubts that more people suffer from corruption than benefit from it, and an increasing number of students and intellectuals find it repugnant.

A leading Thai columnist, Sumalee Viravaidya, recently wrote: "Until we recognise that integrity must be rewarded and cheating punished from an early age, until we revise our value system, until the privileged in our society learn to obey laws and accept the consequences of breaking rules and regulations without resorting to pulling rank, we will never cure this grave sickness in our society . . ."

TAIWAN

The 'red envelope' system

Taipei: With perhaps one or two exceptions, corruption does not exist at the highest political levels in Nationalist China. The Chinese communists have many appellations for President Chiang Kai-shek. "Thief" is not among them. Premier Chiang Ching-kuo, the elder son of Chiang Kai-shek, has become the *bête noire* of the dishonest civil servant.

Taiwan has its full share of endemic Asian corruption, but some might say that the leadership has no reason to be corrupt, that its nests are already feathered. That is so with respect to ordinary creature comforts but it does not extend to conspicuous consumption. Leaders of both the Government and the Kuomintang live well but modestly. The shock of losing the mainland had its effect. The Generalissimo came to Taiwan pledged to cleanse the party.

Any exceptions to the rule of Taiwan honesty in high places involve land transactions. Values have doubled again and again in recent years. Officials who were in a position to know where housing or roads or other major projects would go were in a position to profit immensely. One or more may have done so. But the crime is hard to pinpoint and charges have not been filed.

Taiwan has three unitary systems of government – those of the national level (which supposedly represents all China), the provincial level and Taipei. Legislators, councillors and the like do not have much opportunity for grafting. They must be content with their allowances, their prestige and a bit of favouritism now and then. Votes need not be bought. Power is solidly in the hands of the Kuomintang.

The Control Yuan, sometimes called the watchdog of the Sun Yat-sen five powers system of government, does keep an eye out for political corruption. Its impeachments do not have the force of law, however, and are valuable principally for the publicity content. The Bureau of Investigation of the Justice

Ministry is staffed by young college graduates and has been the most active agency in combating corruption in the bureaucracy, and tax matters. Attrition has recently been high among customs' officers. One high-ranking official is under sentence of death as the result of a smuggling case at the northern port of Keelung.

At bureaucratic levels which deal with the public, the "red envelope" system is nearly universal for those who want quick processing of a licence application or some other paper. Many of the charges are institutionalised. If you want the power turned on at your new house quickly, there will be a charge. Grafting is involved in granting drivers' licences, in car inspections and so on. This is petty stuff, for the most part, and is to be found throughout Asia. The angry citizen who does not want to bribe a bureaucrat may be able to escape the levy, provided he is prepared to accept a delay.

Police shakedowns are principally concerned with Taiwan's wide-open prostitution and other forms of vice. The householder is left alone. So is the automobile driver, although the motorcyclist may find himself subject to occasional exactions. Vice and especially sex peddling is currently under attack.

"Yellow oxen" buy up all the tickets to the more popular movies. The "service charge" is around 20%. Tickets for express trains also disappear into the pockets of scalpers and require the payment of a premium. All efforts to end these practices have failed.

At the last joint examination for college entrance, cheating that involved electronic devices was detected. Ringers have been caught taking the tests. The actual conduct of the examination is so tied up in red tape and secrecy that internal corruption would be difficult, if not impossible. Medical services involved additional payments to see the doctor of the patient's choice. Doctors are carrying on a feud with income-tax collectors.

Contractors complain that a red envelope must be provided at every step of a building's progress – from approval of the plans to connection of utilities. Land transfers are slow without a little oil to speed the machinery.

Bogus medicines have become a major problem – accentuated by Taiwan's excellent printing and packaging. About the only way to judge their authenticity is by the cut-rate prices. Adulterated foodstuffs constitute a new problem. Some cafes are said to be serving hamburgers made from imported dog food.

Business and industry have their share of corruption. The biggest of all involves taxes. The uniform invoice system, which is supposed to provide a guideline to transactions, is more honoured in the breach than the observance. Big business may sin less often, but that could be because the need is not so great. The more powerful have their own way of doing things. They can obtain credit at bank rates; the small business has to go to the blackmarket and pay up to 3% a month for loans. Double or treble bookkeeping is common. Enforcement is possible but difficult when nearly everyone has some degree of guilt. The same is true of payment (or non-payment) or individual income taxes.

Many of those who have supplied Taiwan's more than $1,200 million worth of foreign and Overseas Chinese investment do not know the full story of doing business in Taiwan. Necessary payments are made by employees who are local nationals. Those who are supplying the capital may also turn their backs and look the other way. At the stratospheric level, where David Rockefeller is discussing operations of the Chase Manhattan Bank with Cabinet ministers, there will not be the slightest hint of such goings-on.

Complaints of rural corruption receded when the Government decided to sell fertiliser for cash as well as in kind. Supplies are sufficient, in most cases, and credit is available. The last big agricultural scandal involved the banana trade with Japan and cost P. Y. Hsu his job as head of the Central Bank and Chairman of the Foreign Exchange and Trade Commission.

The military is a law unto itself with regard to corruption. If offenders are to be punished, the veil of secrecy is pulled down on the military court proceedings. Nothing is announced. With the three services getting about 40% of the national budget, temptations are obviously present. Scrutiny is close, however, and it is probable that the army, navy, marine corps and air force take care of their own but see that no one is unduly enriched.

JAPAN

A lack of moral guidelines

Tokyo: Japan's gigantic and powerful bureaucratic structure, including police and other anti-crime agencies, and the avaricious business community are, generally, "clean" and honest. Government and corporate officials are as a whole not susceptible to corruption. Where monetary and other kinds of bribery may serve in many other countries as a lubricant, either for facilitating business transactions or silencing corrupt practices, they are largely inoperative in Japan. The police have proudly reported that Japan is one country where such practices are least rewarding and profitable.

However, honesty and cleanliness in no way govern the politicians and businessmen of Japan. The mere fact that most lower-echelon Government and corporate officials are almost stoically ethical does not mean that bribery does not pay off in this country. Covered by a thin layer of puritanism is a gigantic corrupt sanctuary where a massive traffic of money and self-centred personal relationships, motivated by mercenary interests and a hunger for power, transcends public interest.

Even though offering a bribe is punishable by imprisonment, either offered or accepted by public servants, there is a fundamental absence of integrity or propriety in the minds of political and business officials. It is, perhaps, the absence of such moral guidelines (there is no psychological difference between "crime" and "sin" in Japanese) that has produced serious scandals involving politicians and businessmen which, however, have remained unprosecuted by law or condemned by public opinion.

There are many cases in which the ethical integrity of political and economic leaders could be questioned. The most recent was the election scandal involving a young member of the House of Councillors (elected on July 7).

Thirty-two-year-old Etiaro Itoyama, elected by more than 250,000 voters, is alleged to have spent more than ¥2,000 million (US$6.5 million) through a vast election machine in which his billionaire father and very rich father-in-law allegedly played a leading role and in which an uncle, Ryoichi Sasakawa, a doyen of the Japanese underground structure, is believed to have played a more decisive, but invisible, role.

While more than 100 people, including Itoyama's father-in-law, have been either questioned or detained on suspicion of violating election laws, Sasakawa has not surfaced at investigations.

The Itoyama incident is not an isolated case but one of many brought to light in corrupt election campaigns. Behind the arrest of at least 1,000 campaigners (mostly for ruling Liberal Democratic Party candidates) in connection with the July election are loose and lax laws governing elections and political funds.

For example, a successful candidate cannot be removed from elected office unless his chief campaign manager is found guilty of election law violations. In addition to the extreme difficulty of proving the guilt of the defendant, it usually takes years to try the man. Indeed, justice delayed is not justice denied but profits the suspected villain who, even if he is convicted, is usually parolled or pardoned under appropriate excuses such as "in commemoration of Okinawa coming back to Japan's sovereign power," or "on the auspicious occasion of the Imperial birthday."

Equally basic but more expenditious is the political fund control law which provides more loopholes than restrictions on traffic of political funds and which is considered as the source of all political evils. In the semi-annual reports which political associations (1,958 registered as of 1973) have to submit to the Ministry of Local Autonomy, for instance, sources of donations must be indentified but those of membership fees need not be accounted for. Monetary sources reported to the Ministry are said to be less than 20% of total donations.

Another example is the ¥19,600 million raised in 1973 and reported as such to the Ministry by the National Association, the fund-raising arm of the Liberal Democratic Party, which is believed to be no more than one-third of the total which the Association collected from its members (9,800 corporate and organisational members and 76,000 individual members) in that year.

LAOS

A flourishing malaise

By A Correspondent

Vientiane: Corruption has long been endemic in Laos. At all levels of society, in all walks of life (save perhaps the Buddhist monkhood) kickbacks, payoffs, bribes and what are euphemistically described as *ngern kah sah* (tea money) payments have become part of the natural order of things. National Assembly deputies have bought their way into Parliament, army officers have padded out their meagre salaries by inventing phantom battalions, customs men have grown fat by levying their own private duties on incoming goods and regional bureaucrats and military warlords have, for a suitable rake-off, allowed Thai timber interests to illegally cut down almost every stick of valuable timber in their domain.

But if this sounds like an unduly bleak picture, it should at once be pointed out that this sort of corruption is almost certainly confined to those areas of the Mekong Valley that have traditionally been under the control of the Vientiane side. Corrupt practices are anathema to the Pathet Lao and now that the Laotian leftists have steadily expanded the area under their control, these not-so-arcane arts are now practised in that 20% of the country that is yet to experience the reforming zeal of the Lao Patriotic Front.

The presence of the Pathet Lao in the new coalition Government does not seem to have had a sobering effect on the corrupt ministers, policemen, generals and officials of the Vientiane side, however. Although they may feel that a gloomy shadow now looms above them, there is little evidence to suggest that these traditional corruptors have begun cutting back on their private business deals. Indeed, the presence of the Pathet Lao in Vientiane and the prospect of an eventual Pathet Lao takeover in Laos only seem to have encouraged a number of people to speed up their activities.

For example, in recent months corrupt generals along the Mekong Valley have intensified the illegal logging that is robbing Laos of precious teak, mahogany and rosewood forests. The aim appears to be simple: cash in on record world timber prices and salt away as much money as possible while the going is good.

In what was perhaps the most incredible chapter in the history of Lao wartime corruption, certain powerful right-wing interests actually sold arms and ammunition to the North Vietnamese and the Pathet Lao at a time when Laos was locked in a bitter life and death struggle with the communist forces.

An area-by-area analysis of corruption in Laos reveals a depressingly prevalent incidence of illegal activities, many of them linked closely with the clannish right-wing families which have dominated Laotian public life for centuries. In politics, for example, the pathways to power in Laos are strewn with assorted official functionaries who found to their obvious delight that helping an aspiring politician into office can be an immensely rewarding activity. Although the blatant election rigging of the late 1950s had already become a thing of the past, there was no lack of skulduggery when the recently-dissolved National Assembly was elected early in 1972. As always, money – and not just personal popularity – was often a deciding influence.

Even some of the more prominent National Assembly deputies found they had to grease a few palms in order to retain their seats in that election; one deputy who was trying for one of the three available seats came in an unsuccessful fifth and was only returned to power after an exchange of money and the intervention of some powerfully-placed friends in the Government. In Laos in 1972, the dispensation of money and favours was still an enormous help for anyone standing for public office. Once in power, though, there were all sorts of rewards for the patriotic Assemblyman and when the rightist-dominated body was shut down recently, many deputies did not bemoan the loss of their legislative functions so much as the loss of the side benefits that traditionally go with the job.

In the Cabinet, too, corruption has long been widespread and, until the return of the Pathet Lao, it would probably have been a fairly safe bet to say that those who were involved in assorted shady practices probably outnumbered those who were not.

In the military field, the tales of official corruption are legion. One Western military attaché says that, in his experience, the average Royal Lao Army colonel in Vientiane would own about five houses. The average general would own a lot more. In Laos, most senior generals are paid no more than US$70 per month and yet generals own bowling alleys, cinemas, office blocks and luxury air-conditioned houses.

Padded pay packets for "phantom" units are one well-tried method of raking off army funds, and in Laos there are plenty of instances of this, experts say. Although senior American military men claim that no more than 5% of the soldiers in the Forces Armees Royale (FAR) are "phantoms" (3,000 men out of 60,000), the Pathet Lao has put the figure at 10% and many Western sources say this is quite possible. One military attache, on a visit last year to an FAR unit near Paksane in Central Laos, found an FAR battalion of only eleven men. A normal battalion is around 350-400 men. The same attaché says he has also seen 30-man battalions. When he asked the commander of a 30-man battalion where the rest of his men were, the commander "could not say."

The so-called "Mafia system" in the FAR the selling of American-supplied arms and ammunition to the enemy – ensured that the North Vietnamese and Pathet Lao forces in Southern Laos "got all they wanted" in the way of war supplies from the FAR, said the attaché. Powerful rightist groups operated freely in war goods, often bypassing any middlemen and dealing directly with the NVA and the Pathet Lao. "The adjective I would use for all this is 'massive' corruption," said the attaché. "It was unbelievable, simply unbelievable."

In the former CIA-Meo stronghold of Long Cheng, sources say, it is not uncommon for the average army major to have three batmen and a jeep. Quite often, the sources say, two batmen will be assigned to help the major's wife in the home while the third will be told to drive the jeep around the valley, picking-up and dropping-off people so the major can supplement his army income as a part-time taxi operator. The jeep (and the fuel it uses) is provided by American aid.

One of the most celebrated stories about corruption since the time in 1970, when a new Laotian ambassador to France was found with 68 kilos of heroin in his luggage, concerned a group of army officers who were linked with the theft of around $100,000 worth of drugs from an American installation in Vientiane. The drugs, including generous amounts of lomotil, were obviously destined for resale on the blackmarket.

Things may change dramatically in the coming years, but right now, corruption is alive and flourishing in Laos.

PART III:
Internationalization of Japanese Companies

22

Japanese Multinational Firms

Yoshi Tsurumi

IN THE MID-1960S, it became apparent that Japanese firms had added another dimension to their international activities, namely, direct investments abroad. This private "capital export" increased markedly after 1968. By the end of 1971 this cumulative direct investment abroad of equity, portfolio and loan combined approached $6 billion—not counting the profits being ploughed back into the retained earnings of overseas subsidiaries of Japanese firms.

This article offers theories of Japan-based multinational firms which attempt to explain not only the profiles of Japanese direct investments abroad but also the changing directions and patterns of such profiles. It is hoped that these theories will enable one to predict the timing, nature and scope of direct investments abroad by Japanese firms. They should provide policy guides not only for Japanese firms but also for firms and countries which are affected by Japanese exports and direct investments abroad.

I. Burenstam-Linder and Vernon Hypotheses of International Trade and Japanese Investments Abroad

Hypotheses developed by Burenstam-Linder and Vernon help explain the changing patterns of composites of Japanese exports especially for the post-war period up to mid-1960s.[1] Both Burenstam-Linder and Vernon postulated that a country exports goods for which substantial domestic markets exist. In particular, Vernon's hypothesis has it that products

[1] Burenstam-Linder, S., *An Essay on Trade and Transformation*, Uppsala, Almqvist and Wiksells, 1961. Vernon, R., "International Investment and International Trade in the Product Cycle", *Quarterly Journal of Economics*, May 1966. For the collection of the works by so-called neo-technologists, see Wells, L. T. (ed.), *Product Life Cycle and International Trade*, Division of Research, Harvard Business School, Boston, 1972.

Reprinted, by permission, from *Journal of World Trade Law* (January/February, 1973). This paper is based on the interim findings of the Harvard research projects of Japan-based multinational firms. The projects are financed by the Ford Foundation and are coordinated by Professor Raymond Vernon.

developed for the American markets will be transferred first to Europe and Japan and later to developing nations as the technological levels of the follower-nations are improved, mainly through the followers' emulation of American technologies. A follower-nation like Japan will absorb new technologies from the United States in order to supply domestic markets with new products. Later, Japan will begin to export these products. Of late, however, a number of exceptions to the Japanese exports predicted by the Linder-Vernon propositions has appeared. A number of firms is actively and increasingly exporting manufactures that are not yet in demand at home. Does this mean that Japanese firms are expanding their business horizons? Are they likely to go one step further from exports to direct investments abroad?

II. From Export-Supremacy Preoccupation to Export-Induced Direct Investments

In the case of Japan, direct investments abroad will continue to reveal export-led patterns far more strongly than will American and European direct investments. This is because Japan is generally less technologically advanced than the United States and Europe, and is distinctly more technologically advanced than her Asian neighbors and other developing nations.[2] The recent technological innovations of Japanese firms have been directed to the improvement of production processes rather than to the outright development of new products. This makes it difficult for them to command distinct advantages in manufacturing activities in the developed nations. In addition, the vast and growing domestic market provides Japanese firms with an inherent advantage for exploiting an economy of manufacturing scale. Under these circumstances, it is natural that Japanese firms should prefer to continue with their active exports from the familiar supply bases of Japan unless their export markets are threatened by protectionist policies of the importing countries or by Japan's loss of international competitiveness in the goods of high labor content.

Therefore, in order to analyse export-induced direct investments abroad by Japanese firms, the changing patterns of Japan's export of manufactures must be reviewed briefly. Although the chronological demarcation is somewhat arbitrary, the early 1960s ended an era in which low value-added goods and low technology-content goods dominated Japan's exports. This was also the time when Japanese manufacturing industries had finally absorbed the basics of both manufacturing skills and domestic market cultivation. It is well known by now that Japan achieved this industrial and trading strength under careful government

[2] In the light of the evidence that the United States is in the main at the origin of international flows of technological innovations, the direct investments of multinational firms are explained by direct technology transfer to the countries technologically inferior to the investors (downstream investments), see Vernon, R., *Sovereignty at Bay* (New York: Basic Books, 1971).

control aimed at rationing foreign exchange among strategic firms and at keeping foreign direct investments out of Japan.

When economic growth became a household word in Japan after the early 1960s, Japan was clearly in the different stage of industrial growth. The economy showed a substantially greater annual growth rate. The export composites of Japan began increasingly to reflect the changing industrial structure of the Japanese economy.

Every year, greater value-added goods and higher technology-content goods relative to pre-1960 exportables comprised an increasing portion of total exports of Japan.[3] At the same time, the United States came to absorb an ever-increasing portion of Japan's exports of manufactured goods. Toward the end of the 1960s, around one-third of Japan's exports went to the United States.

This occurred partly because Japanese manufactures of greater value-added and higher technology-content became competitive in the United States both in terms of quality and price, and partly because American markets of consumer goods became so finely segmented that they demanded the kind of finished goods Japan was best able to supply, e.g. portable television sets, compact cars, smaller refrigerators, smaller washing machines for apartment dwellings, electric and electronics appliances, motor-cycles, and portable typewriters. Japanese adaptive research and development (R & D) activities that readjusted essentially American products to Japanese market conditions thus began to pay off handsomely.

Even such industrial goods as steel and iron products, heavy electrical equipment, metal-working machinery, and precision instruments were increasingly exported to the North American markets. In these manufactures, Japanese producers are aided not only by their R & D accomplishments oriented to improved production processes but also by the economies of scale that they gained from a large market in Japan.

The strategy of riding an international product cycle

Toward the end of the 1960s, Japanese manufacturers had built up technological capabilities and manufacturing experience to the point of developing new products that Japanese markets were not yet ready to accept in quantity. Rather than waiting for Japanese markets to demand these new products, Japanese manufacturer-innovators exported such new products to the United States, which was ready to purchase them in ever-increasing quantities. A few years later when Japanese markets began to demand these new products, Japanese manufacturer-innovators

3 Yoshi Tsurumi, "R & D Factors and Exports of Manufactures of Japan", in Wells, L. T. (ed.), *Product Life Cycle and International Trade*, Division of Research, Harvard Business School, Boston, 1972.

were not only able to continue with their exports to the United States, they were also able to supply Japanese markets with products streamlined during earlier export-oriented production. Thus, as innovative exporters expanded the horizons of their domestic markets, they became able to export goods without substantial domestic market demands for these goods. And this aberration is not limited to large firms. There are many small-to-medium firms that are thriving on exports of consumer appliances that are in great demand in the United States but not yet in demand in Japan. A case in point is a firm in Tokyo that manufactures exclusively for export to the United States varieties of scuba diving equipments. After over six years of success with these exports, this firm is now cultivating a primary demand for scuba diving goods in Japan. In a few years, this firm hopes to build up scuba diving sport among the pleasure-seeking youth of Japan. And these exports are different from more conventional "export-oriented" enclaves one can find in developing nations in that far-sighted Japanese exporters eventually were able to cultivate Japanese mass markets for their new products.

However, the strategy of exploiting time lags in market demands along an international product cycle—from the United States, then to Japan, and finally even to developing nations—is but an extension of the earlier strategy of "import substitution". Conceptually, this strategy works as follows:

Stage 1: Import substitution

Japanese manufacturers adapt "foreign born" products to Japanese markets in order to replace imports with their own home-made products. Governmental restrictions on imports provide insulated home markets for Japanese manufacturers.

Stage 2: Scanning advanced markets for new products

Instead of waiting for foreigners to bring new products to Japan, Japanese manufacturers scan advanced markets, notably, the United States, for products to be adapted to Japan. Mainly through adaptive R & D efforts on the basis of licensed technologies, Japanese manufacturers are ready to supply Japanese markets with new products when the markets come to demand them. At this stage, in addition to adaptive R & D skills and manufacturing expertise, firms need to develop efficient ways to monitor advanced markets. Their own look-out posts called branch offices, must be supplemented by frequent "intelligence tours" in such markets by executives and engineers. For small firms that are individually too weak financially to maintain look-out posts, the industry association, the government commercial attachés and trading firms can perform vital "monitoring" services.

Stage 3: Supplying advanced markets with new products before Japanese markets

Once Japanese manufacturers establish distributional networks in the advanced markets, notably, the United States, for "standard and mature" products, they are in a position to add "new" products to the established distribution channels even before Japanese markets are ready to demand such new products. For example, the sewing machine industries of Japan produced and exported zig-zag automatic models to the United States about four years before Japanese consumers began to trade their straight-stitching models in for zig-zag automatic models. The manufacturers of television sets of Japan produced and exported color television sets to North America almost five years before Japanese consumers began to replace their monochrome television sets with color sets.[4]

Stage 4: Riding an international product cycle from start to end

From stage 1 to stage 3, Japanese manufacturers improve their technological skill. Starting with mere imitative and adaptative R & D efforts at stages 1 and 2, Japanese manufacturers improve their technological capabilities to the point of conducting renovative and innovative R & D efforts. Success of the stage 3 strategy depends partly on the manufacturers' ability to produce products without relying on technologies purchased from the United States and partly on manufacturers' marketing skills abroad.

As Japanese manufacturers' technological skills are improved further, they can exploit markets along an international product cycle from the U.S. market to developing nations. For example, Sony's video-corder (compact combination of video-taping equipment and transistorized tape-recorder) was first introduced in the United States. Currently, the automobile firms of Japan are incorporating new design features and partial improvements first in the cars to be exported to North America. In both cases the prerequisites to success are the fact that manufacturers have long established their own brand names and distribution channels in the United States as well as the fact that the final consumers of their products are essentially those of their older vintage products.

When a country like Japan develops new products and maintains technological leads, its exportation of new products survives international competition for a considerable period of time. In such an instance, Japan not only gains a technological lead over other nations, including the United States, but also is able to compete favorably with other nations in

4 Macintosh and Tsurumi, "Multinational Strategies for Survival", in *Proceedings of the Winnipeg Meetings of the Canadian Association of Schools of Business*, 6–9 June 1970.

terms of production costs, even when such products later become standard products in the world trade market. Even when Japan's technological lead fades away, her substantially large home market and low wage level can provide Japanese innovators with the benefits of both large-scale production and wage cost advantages. Even after developing nations begin to compete with Japan in world markets, Japanese industries can call on their subcontractors in Japan to produce exportables rather inexpensively. Although the wage gap between large firms and medium-to-small firms is being closed, there still exists a material difference in total wage and related costs between the two.

No doubt, the strategy of riding an international product cycle from stage 1 to stage 4 will be observed among the manufacturers of industrial goods of Japan. In the case of industrial goods, however, because of a shorter emulation lag between Japan and the United States, the time lag between manufacturers' exports to the United States and their subsequent introduction of improved products to Japan will be materially shorter than in the case of consumer goods. On the other hand, Japanese exports of industrial goods to developing nations will last longer than their exports of consumer goods; industrial exports will continue even after consumer goods come to be manufactured in these nations.

The observations thus far lead one to conclude that Japanese firms would prefer to export from Japan. While the worldwide marketing network of Japanese trading firms reduces the risks of foreign exchange handlings and overseas market developments, few firms would venture abroad, unless forced to do so, beyond setting up marketing bases and raw material supply bases.

III. Japanese Trading Firms as Initiators of Japanese Direct Investments Abroad

There is no denying that Japanese trading firms have played positive roles in (1) importing necessary raw materials and capital equipment to Japan; (2) exporting in turn whatever Japan could export at any given time; and (3) scanning foreign countries for new technologies to be introduced into Japan. When individual manufacturing firms in Japan are too small and too weak financially to cultivate overseas markets, trading firms can amass their resources to bring Japanese manufacturers in contact with foreign markets. Ever since Japan adopted the import substitution path to industrial growth in the late nineteenth century, trading firms have been instrumental in assisting manufacturing firms to gain raw material supplies abroad as well as in shipping Japan's exportables to foreign markets.

There are about 5,000 trading firms in Japan, but the leading ten firms carry out approximately 80 per cent of sales volume handled by all the trading firms. The combined sales turnovers of the largest ten trading firms equal roughly to 30 per cent of the present GNP of Japan. A typical "large" trading firm employs around 10,000 people and has about eighty overseas offices and stores, fifty domestic branches in order to gross annually $10 billion worth of goods and services. Over one-half of its annual turnover comes from its domestic distribution and marketing activities. And on the basis of its strong domestic distribution activities, the trading firm has developed a massive international trade business. It provides finance, market information as well as distribution channels at home and abroad for Japanese manufacturers.

As long as Japanese exports were "low value-added", "low technology-content", and "standard" products, trading firms' contacts with foreign brokers, jobbers and distributors of such standard products amply served Japan's needs. These standard products rarely required customer service after sales. There was no need for extensive customer education about the usage of products. However, beginning about 1960, as Japanese exportables came to be increasingly dominated by "high technology-intensive" and "high value-added" products of diverse nature, after-sale customer service and even pre-sale engineering became vital.[5] And Japanese trading firms were ill-prepared to provide such technical expertise.

Increasing need for customer service networks abroad required exporting firms to establish their own marketing bases far beyond mere contacts with brokers and jobbers who dealt in standard products. At this juncture, leading trading firms were confronted with a choice. If they did not take the initiative in setting up customer service networks with or for Japanese manufacturers, they would have been reduced to handling low technology-content products. By combining the financial and marketing strength of trading firms with the technical expertise of manufacturing firms, however, trading firms not only assured themselves of a sustained voice in expanding technology-intensive exports, they also helped Japanese manufacturing firms improve their access to overseas markets.

At the same time, the growing manufacturing industries of Japan required lasting and expanding sources of adequate supplies of raw materials. As a result, Japanese trading firms either independently or in conjunction with manufacturing firms developed industrial raw materials abroad, mainly for importation to Japan. By 1971, the functions of the trading firms of Japan had changed considerably.

Once involved in manufacturing and sales activities abroad, the leading ten trading firms quickly realized that it was to their advantage to continue taking the initiative in Japanese direct investments abroad.

5 For example, Mitsui Bussan, the second largest trading firm of Japan owns Canadian Motors Inc. in order to sell and service Toyota automobile lines exclusively in Canada. Only recently, in late 1971, Toyota bought its way into the minority position of the CMI. Mitsui's initial move of buying the CMI from a Canadian entrepreneur was necessary for maintaining its car exports to Canada.

Once established locally, the trading firms began to scan Japanese manufacturing sectors for product-related technologies to be transferred directly abroad in order to commence—often with local partners—manufacturing operations oriented to the local economy. When this happens, the investing trading firms skip the exporting stage of the products that are to be manufactured with the transferred technologies. A case in point is C. Itoh Trading Company that brought a plastic bag technology from an engineering firm in Tokyo to its joint venture with the largest instant coffee company in Brazil.[6] This joint venture was recently created to replace jute bags with plastic bags in the packaging of Brazilian agricultural products.

More conventionally, when the export markets of Japan are threatened by the importing governments' forced import substitutions especially in the developing areas, the trading firms are quick to persuade their Japanese suppliers to set up manufacturing bases inside the countries adopting such import substitution policies. The manufacturers in Japan that are unfamiliar with marketing and financial risks associated with direct investments abroad are initially willing to buy the trading firms' services in exchange for the latter's equity participation in the overseas ventures.

All told, the multinational strategies of the leading trading firms of Japan will continue to influence the timing and nature of Japanese direct investments abroad. Early in 1972, there was a distinct sign that the leading trading firms of Japan had decided to promote actively trade among other countries as well as their own manufacturing activities abroad (manufacturing activities epitomized by the previous case of C. Itoh in Brazil).

IV. Emergent Patterns of Japanese Direct Investments Abroad

The cumulative profiles of Japanese direct investments abroad during 1951–69 are summarized in Table 1. For this table, only those investments that were used to acquire equity of locally incorporated firms are compiled. And these incorporated firms include sales firms established by investors. For example, Table 1 reveals that about 30 per cent of all the investments were carried out by "commercial" firms in North America. For the investment by area, North America topped all the areas by receiving about 42 per cent of all the equity-based direct investments of Japan during 1951–69. One can expect these observations in the light of the export-induced patterns of Japanese investments abroad. North America had come to receive over 50 per cent of Japanese exports toward the end of the 1960s. And both trading firms and manufacturers had been actively opening up marketing bases in North America, notably in the United States.

[6] *Nikkei* (The Economic Journal of Japan), 23 February 1972, p. 7.

TABLE 1

JAPANESE DIRECT INVESTMENTS ABROAD (EQUITY BASE ONLY)
(1951–69 Cumulative, $ million at Yen 360 to $1)

Investor	Area							Per cent
	North Amer.	Central, L. Amer.	Asia	Europe	Middle East	Africa	Oceania	
Manufacturing:								
Foods	1·4	3·1	15·9	4·7	—	0·6	2·4	2·7
Textile	3·0	40·4	55·1	0·9	—	11·0	0·8	10·8
Lumber and pulp	35·0	—	2·6	—	—	—	0·4	3·6
Chemicals	1·9	5·4	12·7	1·2	—	1·4	0·7	2·3
Iron, steel, non-ferrous metals	0·9	56·7	28·4	—	—	2·2	4·0	9·0
Machinery	2·6	31·3	7·9	1·5	—	—	0·4	4·2
Electric and electronic equipments	0·3	11·4	28·2	0·6	1·4	0·7	2·6	4·4
Transportation	15·0	60·8	3·9	3·2	1·0	—	0·7	8·3
Others*a*	1·2	3·6	23·9	1·6	0·4	—	0·4	3·0
Resources:								
Agriculture, forestry	2·9	1·7	5·5	0·4	—	—	1·8	1·2
Fishery	1·2	4·6	2·9	0·1	0·1	0·8	1·0	1·0
Mining	39·2	3·4	23·2	—	—	0·8	10·2	7·5
Commercial:								
Construction	4·6	0·4	1·6	—	—	—	—	0·6
Commercial*b*	252·2	13·6	9·9	22·6	0·5	0·1	7·5	29·8
Banking, insurance	47·2	13·8	4·7	8·9	0·9	0·2	1·1	7·5
Others*c*	21·2	9·5	7·5	3·3	—	—	0·6	4·1
Per cent	41·7	25·2	22·7	4·7	0·4	2·0	3·3	100·0

a Others include ceramics, leather goods and rubber products.
b Direct investments by trading firms.
c Others are dominated by investment banking and securities firms.
Source: Tokei Geppo (Statistics Monthly), no. 4, vol. 31 (April 1971), Toyo Keizai, Tokyo, pp. 4–5.

However, if one decomposes Table 1 by singling out only those direct investments that have also manufacturing bases and compares this static profile of Japanese direct investments with that of the United States, say, as of March 1972, one will obtain a comparison like that shown in Table 2. The question one must ask, then, is how this comparative profile of Japanese investments abroad is going to change if it is to change at all.

Small-to-Medium Sized Manufacturing Firms as Forerunners of Japanese Direct Investments Abroad

Students of Japan's post-war economic growth have heard that Japanese small-to-medium sized firms with less than $167,000 of paid-in capital

TABLE 2

JAPAN—U.S. COMPARISONS OF DIRECT INVESTMENT PROFILE, MARCH 1972

	Japan-based	U.S.-based
Size of parent firms	(1) 40 per cent of investments by small-to-medium sized firms. (2) Large R & D intensive firms go abroad often with their small sub-contractors.	(1) Large R & D intensive firms dominate the overseas investments. (2) Small-to-medium sized firms may have sub-contracting relations with foreign manufacturers.
Where invested	Three-quarters of investments in developing nations. Overwhelmingly in Asia.	Two-thirds in developed nations.
Organization of subsidiaries	Joint venture dominant. Many minority interest.	Fully-owned or majority controlled.
Partner, if any, of subsidiaries	(1) Many with Japanese trading firms and local partners. (2) With other Japanese firms in the same "industrial group" in Japan.	On its own or local partner.
Parent's control over subsidiary	Loose.	Close.
Parent-subsidiary relations	Disjoint. Local market oriented.	Globally integrated.

and with less than a few hundred employees have produced sub-contracting work for large-sized firms as well as such high labor-content products as handicrafts, ceramics, electrical and electronics parts, toys and apparel for export. They existed because their labor supply was relatively abundant and their wage level was materially lower than that of the large-sized firms. Because the labor market for small-to-medium sized firms was separate from that of larger firms, the high wage level of growing large firms was not, in the past, transmitted to small-to-medium firms so long as there existed a general surplus of labor.[7]

However, heightened economic growth after the mid-1960s has caused a severe "labor shortage" and has resulted in narrowing the wage level gap. Under these circumstances, one expects to see some alert small-to-medium size entrepreneurs venturing out of Japan for plant investment in high labor-content products. Besides, the product-related technologies possessed by these small-to-medium sized firms of Japan are of the kind that is immediately transferrable to the neighboring

[7] Y. Tsurumi, *The Industrial Relations System in Japan*, Harvard Business School, Boston, ICH11 G1, 1966.

countries. In fact, Japanese investments in Okinawa (before its reversion to Japan), Hong Kong, Taiwan and recently in Korea can be characterized as such moves to take advantage of abundant labor and low wage rates in assembling exports of high labor-content. Small-to-medium sized firms that felt the squeeze from rising labor costs in Japan went into these neighboring Asian nations even before large firms of Japan moved in for the same reasons.

Table 3 reveals this trend. Of 397 cases of direct investments (equity based) by small-to-medium firms in Japan, 73 per cent—288 cases—was undertaken by them on their own accord. The rest consists of team efforts with larger Japanese firms. Okinawa (87 per cent), Taiwan (76 per cent), and Korea (91 per cent) received overwhelmingly independent attention from Japanese small-to-medium sized firms. This was also true of Hong Kong until the end of the 1960s. The arrow indicates the peak period of direct investments by small-to-medium firms of Japan thus far. It reveals investors' preferences for cultural proximity as well as for a lack of hostility towards the Japanese on the part of host governments.

It is only recently that such countries in South-east Asia as the Philippines, Thailand, Singapore, Malaysia and Indonesia began to receive an increasing amount of Japanese direct investments.[8] Thus far, two distinct characteristics have emerged for Japanese investments in manufacturing bases in South-east Asia. First, these investments are overwhelmingly Japanese reactions to threats to their export markets. The import-substitution policies of the host governments confronted Japanese exporters with a choice of either opening up a manufacturing base or losing the market. Small-to-medium sized firms of Japan whose consumer goods were in demand in South-east Asia were invited to participate in Japanese trading firms' direct investments or to participate in a project in which large Japanese manufacturers of machinery, automobile and appliances needed parts suppliers on the scene. Thus, a second characteristic of Japanese direct investments in South-east Asia has emerged: Japanese investing firms not only joined local partners but also other Japanese firms. Since these initial investments are oriented to the local markets, little effort has been made either to integrate them with similar ventures in other areas or to integrate them with their parent businesses in Japan.

Generally speaking, parts manufacturers' investments are first initiated by a desire to service the overseas subsidiaries of their familiar contractors in Japan. However, as the local market grows—especially in Singapore—a number of Japanese electronics and electric parts manufacturers go there, on their own, to supply parts to subsidiaries of such

[8] For example, early account of Japanese investments in Singapore is covered by Hughes and Seng (ed.), *Foreign Investment and Industrialization in Singapore*, Australian National University Press, Canberra, 1969.

TABLE 3

ANNUAL DIRECT INVESTMENTS (EQUITY) BY SMALL-TO-MEDIUM FIRMS OF JAPAN: BY AREA
NUMBER OF INVESTMENT PROJECT

Fiscal Year	S.E. Asia	Hong Kong	Taiwan	Korea	Okinawa	S.W. Asia	West Asia	Oceania	Europe	Africa	North America	Latin America	Total
1951					1								1
1952					1								1
1953			1										1
1954													0
1955						1							1
1956					1							3	4
1957													0
1958	2	1				3							6
1959	3				2	1					1		7
1960		1	1		6	1		1				2	12
1961	1	3	1		1	1				2			9
1962	2				↓ 1	5						1	9
1963	5	1	3		3	1			1	2	3		19
1964	5	4			3	1				1		1	15
1965	4	2	2							3	1	3	15
1966	3	3	20			1	1						28
1967	5	↓ 1	32		2			2				1	42
1968	4		44	2		1		1	1	1		1	55
1969	12	6	↓ 42	10	6			1		2	3	3	83
1970	↓ 18	3	19	↓ 41	2		1				2		89
Sub-Total A	64	25	165	53	29	16	2	5	2	11	10	15	397
B	(32)	(16)	(124)	(48)	(25)	(10)	(2)	(5)	(2)	(4)	(10)	(12)	(288)
B/A	0·50	0·64	0·76	0·90	0·87	0·63	1·00	1·00	1·00	0·37	1·00	0·80	0·73

N.B.: *B* denotes the number of projects that the small-to-medium firms undertook of their own accord. Investments in West Asia, Oceania, Europe, North America and Latin America consist overwhelmingly of sales firms. Firms that have a share capital of less than £50,000 ($167,000) are defined as small-to-medium.

Source: Yokobori, K., "Chusho Kigyo no Kaigai Toshi" (Overseas Investments of Small to Medium Firms), *Chusho Kiogy to Kumiai*, no. 322, December 1971, Tokyo, p. 3.

established American and European firms as G.E. and Philips.[9] In the future, this kind of independent investment by intermediate suppliers of industrial goods will no doubt increase in number.

In terms of investment area, it can be predicted that Japanese activities in Africa and the Middle East will be similar to the pattern of Japanese direct investments in South-east Asia, mainly reacting to the forced import substitution policies of the host governments. And Japanese trading firms will bring in Japanese manufacturers for direct investments in these areas.

Future Patterns of Japanese Direct Investments

Investments by industry (Table 1) reveal that all the industries are represented in the overseas ventures. However, one can see that foods and chemicals are under-represented relative to their respective position in the Japanese domestic industrial structure. Further investigation should reveal that processed foods, pharmaceuticals, cosmetics and toiletary goods are domestically strong but extremely weak abroad.

For these consumer goods, there exist formidable entry barriers in terms of distribution channels, brand name and consumer acceptance, and sales promotional activities abroad. Besides, leading American and European firms have long held their market positions even in Asia, as well as in the developed nations. Accordingly, Japanese pharmaceutical, cosmetics, processed foods and toiletary goods are conspicuously absent from both Japan's exports and its direct investments abroad. And this tendency will persist for a long time. Although one or two firms in the above-mentioned "soft consumer goods" may succeed in generating some exports after considerable investment of manpower and time in market development, in the main, these firms will be forced to stay in Japan. Some of these firms will be interested in selling their market "know-how" in Japan to American and European firms desiring to invest in Japan. Accordingly, the joint ventures between Japanese firms and foreign firms or even outright take-overs of Japanese firms by foreign firms will be seen in Japan.

Traditionally, the trading firms of Japan have avoided handling such "soft" consumer goods as pharmaceuticals, processed foods, cosmetics and toiletry goods, both at home and abroad. Not only have European or American versions of these products been long considered superior to those produced by Japanese firms, but also they have required intensive as well as extensive marketing activities oriented to consumers. And, trading firms have found that marketing "soft" goods was time consuming and unprofitable. Thus, the trading firms which have provided marketing guidance and skill for other industries' exports or overseas direct invest-

9 *Nikkei*, 16 February 1972.

ments have little to offer to the producers of pharmaceuticals, cosmetics, toiletry goods and processed foods (with the exception of canned goods) of Japan.

For manufacturing industries other than these consumer goods, the future direct investment patterns can be hypothesized as follows for (1) technology intensive oligopolies, (2) production scale-dominated oligopolies and (3) innovative and entrepreneurial small-to-medium sized firms.

Technology-intensive oligopolies like electric and electronic appliances, and machinery, and scale-dominated oligopolies like steel, automobiles, synthetic fibre and chemicals prefer to continue exporting to countries of both technological superiority and of technological inferiority.[10] Therefore, in areas like North America and Europe where their export markets are threatened little by the host countries' import-substitution programs, oligopolies have little incentive to open manufacturing facilities. Subsidiaries with marketing functions will dominate the direct investments of such industries in North America and Europe.

However, four distinct exceptions to the above-mentioned pattern will become increasingly apparent: (a) technology-intensive oligopolies opening plants on a limited scale in North America and Europe for assembling the newest products of all their product lines; (b) scale-dominated oligopolies like steel obtaining a minority equity participation in the existing U.S. or European oligopolies of the same industry; (c) scale-dominated oligopolies like synthetic fibres (whose customers in North America and Europe are weak financially) backing Japanese weaving firms to open a limited manufacturing operation; and (d) scale-dominated oligopolies like automobiles opening assembly plants on completely knocked-down basis or helping their parts suppliers set up manufacturing plants in North America.

This will happen increasingly as long as the United States turns more and more towards discrimination against imports. Besides, industrial commodities like iron and steel may be conceivably heading toward the eventual fate of other similar commodities, as, for instance, oil. The oligopolistic desire to sustain stable market situations for international "majors" is likely to precipitate even interlocking corporate ownership on an international scale. The time may well come when a leading steel maker of Japan obtains a minority ownership of a financially or technologically weak American steel firm. Or an American firm will request a Japanese firm to hold mutually a minority ownership.

On the other hand, among entrepreneurial small-to-medium sized firms in Japan there may be the investors who will not only spread their manufacturing operations to countries relatively technologically inferior

[10] For clarification of this concept, the author has benefited much from discussions he had with Professor Raymond Vernon of Harvard Business School.

to Japan, but also will attempt to infiltrate even the United States.[11] On the surface, these infiltrators will resemble technology-intensive oligopolies. They will nevertheless be "leaders" in their own fields back home and will possess product-related technologies not possessed by their American counterparts. But their major motivation to set up a manufacturing base outside Japan will be (1) to reduce the transportation costs of their exports and (2) to avoid a high tariff as well as (3) to learn American techniques of marketing and management by monitoring the U.S. market closely. Unlike large Japanese firms that have or can purchase a share in the foreign investments of the leading trading firms, these entrepreneurial small to medium sized firms will liken their ventures in the United States to local athletes competing in the Olympics. If they fare well in the United States, they will be able to reap prestige and confidence. For this purpose, their commitment to the ventures in the United States will be no less total than athletes' commitment to the Olympics. Even profit motives may well take a second seat to the continued excitement of running a manufacturing plant in the United States.

A case in point is the Japan Miniature Bearings Company that obtained in July 1971 entire facilities and employees of a Los Angeles plant of the Swedish ball-bearings manufacturer, SKF. Until then, the JMBC exported miniature ball bearings to the United States from Japan and it had 30 per cent of the miniature ball bearings market of the United States—a market that was estimated to be worth around $400,000 a year. The JMBC had developed a unique "mass producing" method and machine to manufacture miniature ball bearings and had been a giant in Japan even in the "mini" market of miniature ball bearings. The JMBC was motivated to set up a plant in the United States mainly by the U.S. Defense Department's order to eliminate "imported" miniature ball bearings from defence contracts. And the JMBC's investment in the United States was no less motivated by the firm's desire to use its Los Angeles plant as the prestigious training place for its promising Japanese managers-to-be.

All told, however, entrepreneurial infiltrators into "mini" markets in the United States by Japanese small-to-medium sized firms will probably be limited to industrial products. Unlike consumer goods that require sophisticated marketing skill for success, industrial goods can promote themselves basically on the basis of product quality, price and delivery terms. What is needed is seasoned manufacturing skill that is easier to transfer from Japan to the United States. For example, jet coasters and other amusement park equipment are akin to industrial goods as far as the marketing of the machine is concerned. And these machines

[11] For European direct investments in the United States, see Faith, N., *The Infiltrators*, Hamish Hamilton, London, 1971. This book deals with the factors motivating European firms to infiltrate back into the United States which is in the main technologically more advanced than Europe.

are assembled by small-to-medium firms in Japan as well as in the United States. Savings on transportation costs, tariffs and manufacturers' insurance available only to the U.S. "made" equipment may well dictate Japanese manufacturers to set up assembly plants in the United States. When this happens, the Japanese investors will have in mind the calculated design to promote themselves in Japan as the aggressive firms that have successfully invaded the American market. Mecca, a producer of equipment for amusement parks, has investments in the United States which are motivated by their perceived promotional advantage in Japan.

In terms of investing areas, it is likely that Japanese investments in Mexico and Panama will rise. These investments will be mainly oriented to servicing the great market to the north, the United States. Even when a large and technology-intensive firm of Japan opens up an assembly plant for new products in the United States, its plant location may well be determined by the balance between logistical convenience to the final market and convenient procurement of parts from Mexican contractors.

Another factor that may well influence the timing and the scope of Japanese direct investments abroad is the possibility that the further growth tempo of the Japanese economy outstrips the future logistical ability of the Japanese manufacturing industries in procuring vast amounts of raw materials abroad for processing them at home and then later exporting an increasing portion of finished and semi-finished goods abroad again. When this happens, a growing number of firms, especially those in the sector of processing raw materials, will move plants abroad. Some of them will even become motivated to move their plants to more sparcely populated areas than Japan in order to escape from stricter anti-pollution regulations at home.

V. Conclusion

Until very recently, the Japanese government either forbade outright or severely discouraged direct investments abroad by Japanese firms. This myopic policy was deemed necessary because the yen was internationally inconvertible and weak, and Japan needed to ration scarce foreign exchange for the importation of food, raw materials and industrial goods. This inward oriented industrial policy succeeded in developing diverse industries that have gained world-wide export competitiveness. All these culminated in the "Nixon Shock" of August 1971, when the yen and Japanese protective industrial policies came under fire from all quarters of the world, notably from the United States.

Now, with uncomfortably large dollar reserves, the Japanese government sees manufacturing bases abroad for Japanese firms as necessary for continued exports of high value-added goods as well as exports of such abstract products as manufacturing know-how, management skills and informational services. Thus, the first financial constraint upon Japanese direct investments abroad is rapidly being eased.

Be this as it may, Japanese firms doing business abroad will have to learn fast. Unlike mere exporting activities, manufacturing operations abroad require an investing firm to restructure not only its parent-subsidiary relations and communication style but also its entire staffing and promotional considerations. If there is one potential advantage that a multinational firm holds over a local firm, it would be the multinational firm's ability to create an organization encompassing more than two national boundaries, an organization throughout which not only capital but more importantly, market and manufacturing information flows more readily. In order to reap this advantage, Japanese multinational firms may well have to revise their conventional corporate structure and decision-making practices. Their resistance to these changes may well produce the next constraint upon the growth opportunities of Japanese direct investments abroad.

Furthermore, it is obvious now that the Japan-U.S. economic relations have taken on more characteristics of rivalry than of complimentarity. Competitive relationships between Japanese firms and American firms not only in Asia, Latin America, Africa, but also in North America and Europe will be bound to increase. Meanwhile, the Japanese government and business community will be grudgingly letting American and European direct investments enter Japan. Thus, the outcome of the competitive relations among Japanese, European and American firms that have grown multinational or are going to become multinational, will be dependent upon each investing firm's managerial capability as well as R & D abilities, rather than upon any government's specific measures to foster its own country-based multinational firms. R & D abilities provide firms with opportunities to monopolize new products; whereas, managerial capability enables innovative firms to diffuse their new products world-wide all along the product life cycle of the products from origin to end.

And this competition among Japanese, American and European firms is not limited to the rivalry among large firms. Small-to-medium firms of the United States and Europe will also face the infiltrating attempts of Japanese small-to-medium firms.

23

The Strategic Framework for Japanese Investments in the United States

Yoshi Tsurumi

By the first quarter of 1973, Japanese direct investment abroad totalled $6 billion,[1] with natural resources accounting for approximately half of this investment. Sales subsidiaries, set up to maintain export supremacy for Japanese manufacturing bases, continued to account for the major share of Japanese participation in the European and North American markets.

Manufacturing still represented only a small portion of total Japanese investment abroad. At the beginning of 1973 overseas manufacturing production averaged about 1.5 percent of the country's total manufacturing production. Approximately half of Japan's manufacturing subsidiaries were located in Asia, with the remainder located in Latin America. Most of these subsidiaries have been set up by smaller and medium-sized firms in an effort to protect their export markets.

Recently, however, Japanese direct investment abroad, particularly in manufacturing facilities, has been expanding at an exponential rate. Faced with diverse external pressures and with the ever-changing realities of Japan's position in international trade, Japanese manufacturing firms have begun to exploit new opportunities that the past strategy of export supremacy failed to provide. As a consequence, they have been rearranging their internal organization in order to implement new foreign activities in the 1970s.

This has led to a new pattern of Japanese direct investment in the developing countries, where most manufacturing facilities are located. Investments are being integrated and coordinated more closely than ever before by headquarters in Japan. Moreover, the major markets for the products being manufactured in these markets have become the industrial countries, primarily the United States, Europe, and recently Japan itself.

While most Japanese manufacturing investments will continue to take place in the developing nations, some Japanese manufacturers now possess the financial and technological capabilities which permit greater involvement in the manufacturing industries of the industrial countries, including the United States. Such involvement, however, will also require other skills if Japanese companies are to minimize the disadvantages of producing in high labor cost countries as two case studies of recent Japanese investments in the U.S. market illustrate.

Reprinted, by permission, from *Columbia Journal of World Business* (Winter, 1973).

OFFSHORE PRODUCTION

In the past four years, Japanese electrical and electronic equipment manufacturers and assemblers of household appliances have been moving the intensive labor portion of their production lines to Hong Kong, Korea, Malaysia, Taiwan, Indonesia, and Singapore. Such moves have been in response to labor shortages, which caused significant wage increases in the Japanese domestic market, and to the demands for lower prices in the domestic and foreign markets for these products.

Similar pressures have also been felt by manufacturers of industrial goods with a small value added content. These pressures, coupled with the 17 percent revaluation of the yen in 1971 and the subsequent yen float in 1973, have made standard products of high labor content uncompetitive in the Japanese and foreign marekts. This has forced many manufacturers to move to off-shore production bases.

In addition, manufacturers who initially invested in developing nations in order to protect their markets have been pressured by host governments to export from these markets. Even without local governmental pressure, manufacturers have found that their scattered Asian investments were operating inefficiently and that products from these small-scale operations were not competitive in world markets. In order to overcome this problem, Japanese companies that have cultivated export markets in the United States and Europe have been integrating their intermediate production operation in Asia and Latin America. Finished products from these areas are being exported to Europe and the United States.

STAGE 1: INVESTMENT IN DEVELOPING COUNTRIES

The investment strategies of Stage 1, which involves investment in the developing countries, can be explained in terms of the international product cycle.[2] In essence, manufacturers based in Japan have absorbed technologies developed initially by other countries such as the United States and exported these products back to these countries. However, adaptation in product designs and manufacturing processes have been made to accommodate Japanese production and markets.

As Japanese product technologies are absorbed by its Asian neighbors and as the acute labor shortage forces manufacturers to concentrate on products yielding greater value added per available man-hour, Japanese manufacturers have sought off-shore bases in the developing countries. The key to success in these markets is that production techniques can be transferred without the need for much local manufacturing experience.[3] Also, the lack of indigenous competition eases Japanese entry into these markets. As a result, Japanese direct investments in manufacturing industries abroad will continue to be directed mainly to markets in developing nations.

STAGE 2: INVESTMENTS IN ADVANCED COUNTRIES

Unlike the direct investments of Stage 1, the successful operations in the United States and Europe will require new strategies and will be more closely tied to marketing skills. In these markets substantial product and brand acceptance is necessary. Moreover, success will depend on adequate distribution channels, and control over pricing and promotion. Japanese manufacturers seldom have an advantage in production costs over their counterparts in the advanced countries, particularly in the United States. Therefore, marketing is the only area in which producers in the United States can hope to reap special premiums by exploiting economies of scale. In order to minimize the disadvantages of manufacturing in a high labor-cost country, products introduced in the United States must be relatively new and specialized.

Moreover, the successful exploitation of the synergistic effects of combined Japanese and U.S. management techniques may require the construction of facilities in the United States. Two successful examples of such Japanese investments in the United States are the Sony Corporation, which has undertaken an expansion of the assembly production of color television sets and has subsequently started the production of TV picture tubes, and the Nippon Miniature Bearing Company, Ltd. (NMB), which has expanded and diversified its product lines of miniature ball bearings and other precision industrial parts.

THE SONY CASE

Beginning with the successful transistorizing of portable radios about 20 years ago, Sony has introduced innovations in video-recorder sets and color televisions. In order to establish itself in the major markets of the world, Sony has chosen from the outset to market under its own brand name and through its own distribution channels. Its strategy of building up its own marketing facilities abroad has enabled it to add new products to existing marketing channels in the United States and Europe even when the Japanese market was not ready for them. By the time the Japanese are ready for such products, Sony will have accumulated sufficient experience to outproduce imitators in Japan or elsewhere.

In order to finance its worldwide strategy, Sony has avoided the limitations of Japanese financial markets by establishing a position in the financial markets of the United States and Europe. It is keenly aware of the handicaps of conventional Japanese corporate methods of employee training and decision making which hinder development of an eclectic mental attitude vital to international activities. The present head of Sony, Mr. Akio Morita, once experimented with living in New York instead of directing U.S. operations from Japan. Japanese managers and engineers were instructed to speak the language of the host country themselves and to avoid grouping together on as well as off the job.[4] Sony's innovations in human resource development are not limited to foreign operations. In Japan, Sony is noted for its variety of personnel administration practices, all of which are designed to cultivate and to reward individual initiative and expertise without jeopardizing group loyalty.

Increases in sales of color television sets in Japan and abroad, especially in the United States, had for some time forced the firm to operate at or beyond its production capacity in Japan. In 1971 the market in Japan was showing signs of approaching the saturation point, with over 60 percent of urban households owning at least one color set. The United States, on the other hand, with twice the population and a greater income per household showed strong potential for further growth, with only 40 percent of its urban households owning color sets.

After evaluating market trends, possible transportation savings and lower costs for components such as cabinets and semi-conductors, Sony decided to expand its operations by direct investment in the United States. Both Sony's innovative products and marketing drives commanded a $30 to $50 premium over comparable products in the United States. And because sets have only one electronic gun as opposed to three guns, the firm was able to save high assembly labor costs in the United States. In 1972, Sony began construction of a color television plant outside San Diego, California. Manufacturing capacity will be expanded so that in the near future over half of Sony sets sold in the United States will come from its California plant. Upon succeeding in the assembly operations, Sony has transferred from Japan the capacity to manufacture color picture tubes so that the integration of manufacturing operations will provide additional advantages. Additionally, the success of its United States operation may lead Sony to contemplate a venture in Europe as sales increase there.

THE NMB CASE

In 1971, NMB purchased a run-down plant in Chatsworth, California, from SKF, a Swedish-based multinational. NMB, like Sony, is a relatively young firm and is headed by a strong entrepreneur-president, Mr. Takami Takahashi.

By developing a process for producing commercial grade miniature ball bearings at internationally competitive costs, NMB has made inroads in the U.S. market. Because this market was limited in Japan by a lack of developed industries for precision instruments, NMB vigorously cultivated the U.S. market. With judicious use of volume discounts and sales-through-consignment, NMB carved out around 40 percent of the U.S. market for commercial ball bearings. Meanwhile, their sales activities were enhanced by a program of inviting important United States users of miniature ball bearings to their plant in Karuizawa, Japan. NMB's position in the United States was firmly established after winning the confidence of these customers.

Like other industrial goods, the ball bearing market divided into one consisting of standard products of commercial grade, and one of specialized products of high skill content. Price competition is a factor in the former market, while entry into the latter demands effective services and a close interaction between sales engineers and the manufacturing plant.

NMB had neither production skill nor experience in managing sales engineers. As it had in the past, NMB could have hired foreign engineers to bring specialized production know-how to its Karuizawa plant. Instead, NMB chose to close the learning gap in sales and engineering by opening a manufacturing plant in the United States. The close interaction between market and plant which is essential for any effective penetration of a market for specialized products ruled out the servicing of this area from Japan.

In Spring, 1971, the U.S. Department of Defense prohibited the use of imported ball bearings in defense-related products. This ruling precipitated NMB's search for a plant site in the United States. Learning of SKF's intention to sell its miniature ball bearings plant in Chatsworth, it immediately made a cash offer. The deal was concluded in a matter of hours because the search for a plant site had provided NMB with sufficient information to evaluate the asking price. NMB invited all employees of the SKF subsidiary to remain, with full credit given to accumulated seniority. This offer was natural to NMB, a firm bred in Japanese corporate culture, which respects an employee's seniority and guards his well being. At that time, NMB did not realize that this typically Japanese treatment of employees later helped to set an in-plant atmosphere which improved the plant's operations. NMB's personnel policy and the prospect of expanded operations even attracted back a number of able workers and plant managers who had left the SKF subsidiary.

As a result of the Japanese seamen's strike which paralyzed the shipment of machinery from Japan, the NMB team in the United States discovered the synergistic effect of mixing Japanese and United States methods of production. While the strike was on, the NMB plant in California had to make do with SKF machinery and, more significantly, its machinists, engineers, and workers. By the end of the seamen's strike, NMB management had discovered that the engineering experience and manufacturing skill embodied in the machine-man interactions at the California plant were far more appropriate to U.S. operations than those of its Japanese plant. U.S. methods were designed to maximize the utilization of scarce man-hours and the skill of the machinists and technicians permitted multifunctional machines to operate at much higher speeds and with greater precision than their Japanese counterparts.

On the other hand, Japanese methods of smoothing the flow of manual handling and finishing goods permitted a longer production run for standard operations. Furthermore, engineers in the NMB plant in California adapted the Japanese method of breaking up multifunctional operations into a chain of simple, specialized operations, and successfully designed a machining operation for bearing rings which permitted a drastic reduction of the rejection rate from 30 percent to less than 5 percent. Later, automatic sorter-testers for finished products, which NMB had developed for mass production methods in its Karuizawa plant, were installed in the Chatsworth plant, and in less than ten months, the entire production capacity of the plant increased beyond any peak for the old SKF plant. This achievement was remarkable, especially in view of the fact that, at the time of NMB's takeover, plant capacity was down to less than one-tenth of the previous peak during the SKF period.

The Karuizawa plant adopted the United States production processes and realized an immediate reduction of 80 man-years (40 men per shift per year) in the finishing processes for bearings. Presently, the Karuizawa plant is reassessing its entire operational methods so that the U.S. experiences can be adapted. In these days of labor shortage and high man-power cost, the Japanese plant manager at Karuizawa now realizes the advantage of having a closer tie with the U.S. manufacturing operations.

The advantages of the synergy between Japanese and U.S. methods were not limited to the production of miniature ball bearings. NMB diversified operations with spherical ball bearings, rod-ends, micrometers, and precision instruments. The location of the NMB plant in California brought the firm into closer contact with the engineering and marketing bases for these new products in the United States. This location also enabled the firm to tap the managerial talent of the United States in such fields as cost and inventory control, merger and acquisition, and management of sales engineers. By hiring able management know-how, the NMB system as a whole was able to share directly in the surplus managerial capacity of NMB in United States operations. Management energy was used to expand operations in the United States through productive diversification. Further new plant construction, as well as the acquisition of existing firms, is now being planned.

NMB's success in the United States gave new confidence to its management and, in the spring of 1973, NMB began operations in Singapore, where the manufacturing operations of standard products of commercial grade will be transferred from Japan. In developing nations which suffer a more severe shortage of manufacturing skills and experience, the manufacturing processes which NMB (Japan) had developed to fit the realities of its own plant in Japan appear to be more relevant than current U.S. methods. By pooling Japanese and U.S. experience, NMB can now execute its production objectives among three manufacturing bases: the United States, Japan, and Singapore.

The new strategic vista of the NMB system is now looking toward the corporate financing fields. By placing shares of NMB (America) on the United States over-the-counter market, NMB has acquired an additional source of capital. NMB (Singapore) will enable the firm to tap the Singapore Asia-dollar market and to pool the earnings of the NMB system as a whole during the initial period of exemption from corporate income taxes granted under the Singapore Development Plan.

BENEFITS FROM THE UNITED STATES

The preceding examples of Sony and NMB illustrate the advantage of the international cycle of product and technology upward into the United States. The specific gains derive from market penetration and from the wealth of managerial, engineering, and financial resources of the United States. For example, Sony is now more closely in touch with specific pulses and stimuli of the United States and it responds with innovative R & D activities oriented to the characteristics of a high income and mass-market society.

The possibility for improved marketing and R & D activities would appeal to other Japanese firms, which are finding it increasingly difficult to obtain licensing agreements from U.S. firms. The segment of the U.S. market which can be penetrated by Japanese and other Asian exports is being exhausted. New competitors in Asia, either United States-owned or indigenous, are already cutting into the Japanese share of United States markets for mature and standard products. One distinct solution to this difficulty is for Japan to open manufacturing bases in the United States after having cultivated independent marketing abilities. Acquisition of existing firms or joint ventures with United States entrepreneurs may well provide Japanese late-comers with the two necessary success conditions of having both a marketing and a manufacturing base in the United States. The recent move by the Fuji Communication Company, which concluded a joint venture with a medium-sized United States computer and electronics firm, can be explained by Fuji's desire to acquire ready technological and marketing bases in the United States.

During the 1970s, small- to medium-sized Japanese firms will find it increasingly necessary to seek engineering and managerial skills in the United States. Scientists and engineers are already in short supply in Japan and their training and experience are narrower than those of their U.S. counterparts. Moreover, man-year costs for one skilled worker in Japan are not lower than those of the United States. It takes about ten years to train a skilled worker in Japan. Labor costs of skilled workers with ten years seniority and of scientists and engineers are comparable to their counterparts in the United States. Besides, Japanese firms determine wages on the basis of seniority and age, which pushes up the man-power costs as employees get older. Therefore, if Japanese firms desire additional sources of managerial and engineering skills at reasonable costs, they will have to look to the United States, where these talents are relatively abundant.

The costs of plant site development and building in the United States are aproximately one-half to one-third of those in Japan. Suitable plant sites are nearly impossible to locate in crowded Japan and, when taken into consideration with the strategy of riding the international cycle of product and technology into the United States, many Japanese manufacturers will contemplate obtaining manufacturing and marketing bases in that country.

BENEFITS TO THE UNITED STATES

Apart from the employment opportunities that Japanese investments may create for the economy as a whole, more specific benefits will accrue to United States firms involved in Japanese direct investments. In particular, small- to medium-sized firms in the United States, whose strategic plans have been limited to the domestic market, will acquire the global views of internationally-minded Japanese firms. Immediate access to the Japanese market, which is one of the largest and fastest growing in the world, will provide additional benefits. Moreover, entry will be provided to other overseas markets, which Japanese firms have already cultivated. The synergistic effect of combining Japanese and United States management styles can only appear when each will strive to learn from the other, as was demonstrated from the experience of NMB (America) and NMB (Japan). When this is done, management and employees in the United States will find it personally beneficial to work for the Japanese-controlled firm.

CONCLUSION

The strategy of riding the international cycle of product technology has been the central force behind large United States firms going multinational. However, small- to medium-sized firms in the United States, lacking product innovations, have been rather provincial and have chosen to stay in the shrinking market for specialized products in a limited regional market. In theory, the kind of strategy implemented by NMB could have been reversed by an alert United States manufacturer. Japanese efforts to restrict United States direct investments in Japan might be a factor preventing them from linking with Japan. However, this does not explain the apparent reluctance displayed by small- to medium-sized United States firms when they are approached by Japanese manufacturers. This reluctance appears to be very much an initial problem for leading Japanese firms seeking to invest directly in the United States.

Conceivably, a few more examples like Sony, NMB, and Fuji, may well inject new competitive spirit into not only the large, but also the small- to medium-sized firms in the United States. Certainly, many Japanese firms are awakening to the opportunities of overseas investing. Nevertheless, even increased investments by Japanese firms in the United States will not change the asymmetry that now exists between United States direct investments in Japan, and the Japanese presence in the United States. Any attempt by Japanese manufacturers to invest directly in the United States should serve to change the anti-foreign investment attitude prevailing in Japan. All told, Japanese direct investments in the United States should not only be a psychological therapy for both sides, but also a challenging institutional innovation for any management seeking to maximize the synergistic effects of combining United States and Japanese ways.

NOTES

1. Estimated by the author on the basis of data gathered for the Multinational Enterprise Project of Harvard Business School, coordinated by Professor Raymond Vernon and financed by the Ford Foundation.

2. For the application of this theory to overseas investment patterns of U.S. manufacturing industries, see: Raymond Vernon, *Sovereignty at Bay*, Chapter 3, Basic Books, New York, 1971.

3. For an analysis of the international transfer of process-related technologies, see: "Transfer of Process-related Technologies Abroad: A Case of Direct Investment of Japanese Firms," mimeograph presented at the study seminar of the Multinational Enterprise Project, Harvard Business School, January 4-5, 1973.

4. This approach differs from the Matsushita (Panasonic) approach to doing business in a foreign culture. Matsushita exports "Matsushitism" by activities such as singing the corporate anthem and chanting the "Seven Spirits of Matsushita" in native languages.

24

Made in America (Under Japanese Management)

Richard Tanner Johnson and William G. Ouchi

On the assembly line of a U.S. company in Atlanta, Georgia, 35 American women put together transistor panels in a prescribed set of steps. In Tokyo, at another plant of this company, 35 Japanese assemblers use the same technology and the same procedure to manufacture the same part. The only real difference between the two lines is their productivity: The Japanese workers turn out 15 percent more panels than do their American counterparts 7,000 miles away.

In Sony Corporation's plant at San Diego, California, some 200 Americans make 17- and 19-inch television sets on an assembly line that is identical with Sony's typical assembly line in Japna. In this case, however, the similarity does not end there: The American workers produce as much for Sony in San Diego as the Japanese assemblers do for Sony in Tokyo.

What is more, our interviews with 20 other Japanese companies operating in the United States suggest that, in many instances, they are outperforming American companies in the same industries. (The Addendum gives some details on three of the companies studied.)

What contributes to the Japanese success, even when the workers are not Japanese? What can Westerners learn from these successes that they can apply to their own organizations? We can offer no quick and easy answers to these questions. At any rate, there is no formula that could be applied in the United States to solve all productivity problems. In fact, some of the techniques described here as Japanese are part of the standard operating procedure of Occidental companies. Other aspects of Japanese management are inseparable from the Japanese culture itself and cannot be used in America. Yet, with these disclaimers made, there is still truth in the observation that nowhere on this planet can we find a successful industrialized society whose managerial approach is as different from ours as is that of the Japanese. By examining these differences, this article tries to provide a fuller understanding of the strengths and shortcomings of our own approach.

But as the contrasting illustrations from Atlanta and San Diego indicate, the Japanese approach has some features that are exportable. In this article we try to identify the factors underlying the success of some Japanese companies in the United States, and we show how American employees have received Japanese methods.

Richard Tanner Johnson and William G. Ouchi, "Made in America (under Japanese Management)," *Harvard Business Review* (September-October, 1974).

I
EXPORTED MANAGERIAL STYLE

In our study we observed five important aspects of this managerial approach: (1) emphasis on a flow of information and initiative from the bottom up; (2) making top management the facilitator of decision making rather than the issuer of edicts; (3) using middle management as the impetus for, and shaper of, solutions to problems; (4) stressing consensus as the way of making decisions; and (5) paying close attention to the personal well-being of employees.

1. 'BOTTOM-UP' PROCESS

The Japanese manager is not bound by Western traditions of authority and hierarchy. He believes that change and initiative within an organization should come from those closest to the problem. So he elicits change from below. He relies on his sales force and distributors to innovate in the marketplace and on his hourly workers, foremen, and middle managers to improve the production process.

In the Western world, authority is equated with hierarchical position. As a person rises in the organization, he has more to say about directing its course. He makes the key decisions and sets policy; on his judgment the welfare of the organization depends. The Japanese executive, on the other hand, is not burdened with having to be a "decision maker" in this Western sense. Nor is he, in the image of Andrew Carnegie or Alfred Sloan, expected to stake out bold new frontiers for his company and guide it with firmness and resolve. The Japanese top manager is a much less isolated figure. While the Japanese meticulously define the status of the leader, his role in the decision-making process is little differentiated from that of others in the organization. Rather, he sees his task as improving on the initiative of others and creating an atmosphere in which subordinates are motivated to seek better solutions. So the responsibility for the corporation's success rests not just with him but with all employees.

As a consequence, the Japanese executive encourages a flow of initiative and information from lower levels up. When hired by a Japanese subsidiary in the United States, the American manager often undergoes an Alice-in-Wonderland experience. He finds himself in a topsy-turvy world in which many of the conventions of Western-style management are reversed. The bottom-up style of decision making can be very frustrating for an American accustomed to the issuance of orders from above. In one interview, an American manager in a Japanese-owned company said:

> Our Japanese executives seem to be waiting to rubber-stamp our initiatives, while the American executives are waiting for the Japanese top management to establish objectives, to say what we're trying to accomplish so we know what to initiate. I think we fall between the chairs. We've never received any objectives! Are they to increase sales? Make a profit? I've asked, but we get no answers!

Most of the Japanese companies studied have an open-door policy; any employee has access to any manager, regardless of the chain of command. Such access is facilitated by the fact that the higher managers spend little time in their offices and much time in the large open areas filled with desks. A typical Japanese company in Tokyo has few private offices. Those that exist are for the convenience of high-level executives and for occasions when privacy is necessary.

The contrast with American places of work tells something about the differing attitudes toward employees in the two cultures. Many of the Japanese interviewed expressed the belief that the private office contributes significantly to the communications problems that seem to plague their American counterparts. Said the Japanese controller of Sony in the United States: "Private offices are a status symbol in this country. I worry about those walls. Americans spend a lot of time in their offices and call people in. But there is a possible problem—it creates distance between managers and their subordinates and colleagues."

This distance inhibits the free flow of information and initiatives from below and can create situations in which a manager feels threatened by a subordinate's suggestion or criticism. In Japan, it is not considered an affront when a junior manager questions the opinion of his superior. As one American manager put it, "Americans will disagree with their boss rarely but violently; the Japanese disagree often but politely."

2. SENIOR MANAGER THE FACILITATOR

To conclude that the Japanese executive is passive would be a mistake; he plays a key role in shaping decisions. When a subordinate brings in a proposal, the manager does not simply accept or reject it. Instead, he tactfully asks questions, makes suggestions, provides encouragement, and, if necessary, sends the person back for more answers. This sequence may recur, and if it does, the proposal generally improves each time. If the two ultimately decide that the proposal has merit, the manager refers it to others higher in the organization. They repeat the same questioning process.

Many U.S. managers feel that they will lose their subordinates' respect if they fail to set objectives and issue orders. They are puzzled by the complex web of relationships in Japanese organizations. For their part, Japanese managers feel that their system is more effective and more rewarding for all involved. One of them in the United States told us:

> In Japan, knowing the company is very important so that you understand what the company wants you to do even if they don't tell you what to do. The emphasis is on using your own mind and on figuring out in each situation what is best for the company. That is expected of you. But in the United States the American managers want objectives. That makes the situation seem simpler, but it means that you miss opportunities.
>
> All the Japanese here have had problems managing the Americans. The Japanese expect subordinates to think, but the American attitude is "You tell me what to do and I'll do it—but it's your responsibility." Some Americans in Japan say a Japanese company is like the army, but I think the American system is more like the army."

3. MIDDLE MANAGER THE MOLDER

Almost without exception, the Japanese managers we interviewed had endeavored to apply the "bottom-up" style of management in the United States. But they learned that this approach presupposes certain behavior on the part of the senior manager's subordinates. In the Japanese system, junior managers are not functional specialists who carry out their boss's directives; rather, they are both initiators, who perceive problems and formulate tentative solutions, and coordinators, who, in liaison with others in other functional areas, help shape a composite plan before presenting it to their superiors. When a Japanese national filled a middle manager's slot in the companies surveyed, the system usually worked smoothly. When an American was placed in such a position, however, he encountered difficulties more frequently. Many of the Japanese we talked to offered reasons for these difficulties. Here is a typical explanation:

> American managers rarely coordinate well. They lack human skills and seem much less familiar with other parts of the organization. A good Japanese-style middle manager knows everybody, and so he can get good information. That helps very much. When such a man makes a recommendation, all the coordination is already done. This process takes time; maybe a big decision takes half a day or more. And he spends a lot of time on the phone, talking. He does not spend a lot of time on substance; his subordinates do that. But when he presents his proposal to the department head, all the functional areas are on board, and implementation is immediate once the decision to move is made.

To be sure, the concerns expressed by the Japanese are shared by many Western-style managers in U.S. companies. Even so, the Japanese in general place much more emphasis than do Americans on coordination skills. Japanese managers expect their subordinates to communicate outside the chain of command with other functional areas. Virtually every American we interviewed cited the stress on lateral communication as one of the major differences between Japanese and U.S. organizations.

Earlier we mentioned the large, desk-filled open areas in Japanese plants. A look at one of these provides a glimpse of the middle manager in action. Customarily he sits at a desk that adjoins a long working table. Around the table his subordinates—assistants, researchers, and secretaries—work side by side like college freshmen at the library during exam week. He does little during the day which his subordinates are not aware of. There are many such groups in the large room. Since each manager is just a turn of his swivel chair from another, he can easily turn to the next and discuss a problem that has arisen. Subordinates cannot help hearing what is going on—a further advantage. Moreover, since the department head is nearby, he too is kept in constant touch. Thus, all are well aware of not only the issues facing the organization but also others' problems and perspectives.

In interviews, Japanese managers assigned to U.S. subsidiaries often expressed polite surprise at how weak in communications skills American managers are. They quoted Americans as complaining "I've spent my whole damn day on the telephone" and "I didn't get anything done because people kept interrupting me." What the American views as petty distractions from his job, the Japanese views as central to his job.

To a substantial degree, the Japanese have exported the open work setting to the United States. This arrangement offers several benefits other than the strictly motivational ones. First, it fosters consistency in behavior. The middle manager, for example, would find it difficult to treat subordinates differently from superiors. Second, it puts a premium on performance, since everyone is witness to everyone else's work. Finally, of course, it greatly assists evaluation of performance at all levels.

4. DECISION BY CONSENSUS

This communication process is the key to the slow difficult way the Japanese have of working toward a decision. It is not really "participative management," the policy of having superiors and subordinates cooperate that has been adopted by many U.S. companies. Instead, it is an attempt to reach a consensus based on close coordination of the activities of each functional area affected by an issue.

For the Westerner, a decision process based on consensus conveys a host of Parkinsonian horrors—interminable meetings, endless squabbling, and ultimate indecision. Such is often the case in the Western system, where individualism is prized, where value is given to making decisions quickly, where a slow process of choice is often equated with inefficiency, and where interpersonal skills are not always well developed. For the Jaapanese, the consensus process has a very different connotation. Since management elicits initiative from below, arrival at a consensus does not require a chain of command in which each superior strives to leave his stamp on a proposal. Moreover, their meetings do not degenerate into adversary proceedings in which participants either strive for supremacy or accept less meaningful generalization as their only common ground.

Contrary to what many Westerners think, the Japanese system does not demand that all participants "sign off." Those who affix their seals to the document containing the decision are indicating their consent, which is not the same as their approval. Each participant is indicating satisfaction that his point of view has been fairly heard, and while he may not wholly agree that the decision is the best one, he is willing to go along with and, even more, to support it. In this manner, the Japanese sidestep the nearly impossible task of attaining unanimity. The Japanese vice president of a major Japanese bank put the idea of consensus this way: "Many people review a decision, so it is very difficult for a manager to be arbitrary. We try our best to persuade others, but if others disagree, we think, 'Maybe my idea is wrong after all.' "

From the Japanese point of view, a group decision is important because in most cases there are many alternative solutions, any one of which might work. The group decision creates commitment of all parties to the chosen solution. The findings of behavioral science suggest that often the quality of commitment to a decision rather than the quality of some dimension of the decision itself is the most critical factor in the fate of a project.

This decision process is not without costs. On occasion, the Japanese are so concerned with their desire for smooth relationships that important issues fail to get a full airing. Managers who disagree with a proposal will sometimes remain silent rather than upset the relationships they have so carefully cultivated. Furthermore, the process unquestionably consumes a great deal of time. Consider the reaction of an experienced American banker who joined a large Japanese bank as its senior vice president for loans:

> When I walked in here, I couldn't see how they ever got off the ground—so damn methodically slow, I thought they must never get anything done. I was openly critical. But then I found they were already making money, and our little bank back in Salinas took years before it did. We've had rather careful scrutiny of every loan made—and we haven't lost a nickel since I've been here. The reason? In passing every decision through five people, you're bound to pick up the key issues. There's little chance of all five loan officers missing the forest for the trees.

5. CONCERN FOR THE EMPLOYEE

When one thinks of how the Japanese treat their employees, the word *paternalism* may come to mind. It is well known that the Japanese organization traditionally offers its workers housing, extensive on-site recreation facilities, and lifetime employment. The Japanese operating in the United States have not come to that point yet; nevertheless, on both sides of the Pacific, concern for the whole employee—not for just his work performance—is a characteristic of the Japanese company. This concern, the Japanese are convinced, is essential to attaining productivity and high standards. It is, however, more than a matter of policy; it is a philosophy, as we can see in the remarks of the Japanese chairman of a ball-bearing manufacturer in the Midwest:

> U.S. firms rate employees solely on productivity and believe personal matters should be left at home. The Japanese believe we have to take the whole person into account and constantly ask ourselves, "Is he happy?" A good foreman should be able to tell by an employee's face if he's happy or if he's had a fight with his wife, and so forth. I do not think this attitude is found in American firms. Perhaps that is why you have good relations among people within a particular work group but problems in vertical relations.
>
> My impression is that American companies lack spiritual quality. We're trying to instill that here. I go into the plant and talk to people. The president should know every worker by name. Of course, in the very large companies this is impossible, but at least two levels of management above the foreman should know the employee by name. To have spiritual and mental communication with the workers, you have to know their names. For example, an employee's wife had her seventh baby yesterday. I must be familiar enough with this situation to ask him, "Is your baby due today or tommorow?" People have to know they count.

A seasoned American at a Japanese electronics plant echoes this statement and reflects what many in other companies surveyed said: "The Japanese are concerned with the employee *and* the product. Americans just care about the product. The Japanese appear very much to want the employee to be comfortable. I never get the impression that the higher-up Japanese managers don't have the time to talk. They usually seem concerned, whereas American bosses convey a 'you have to work, that's all there is to it' attitude."

II

CASE OF THE MISSING ADS

When several Americans came to work as department heads at one of the largest Japanese automotive firms in the United States, they had all been reading extensively on Japanese methods. Most of them had come from a major American automotive company, and all had had long experience in the industry. Inevitably, under the pressure of business in this fast-growing organization, they turned instinctively to their accustomed Western management techniques. They looked to the Japanese nationals at the top levels of the organziation to give them direction, objectives, and priorities. But nothing was forthcoming; the Japanese were waiting patiently for initiatives from them.

After a time, upon the Americans' initiative, an organization chart was drawn up in an effort to settle where the authority and responsibility for decisions rested. It was a thoroughly American document, showing in neat boxes the various departments—parts, service, sales, marketing, planning, and so on—and the vertical relationships, with the Japanese president at the top and the lowest sub-department on the bottom. The Japanese, who rarely draw up organization charts (and who, if they do, invariably make them read horizontally, like a flow chart), tolerated the American version as a "when in Rome" accommodation. But the chart did not solve the problems; the organization was not functioning well, and the decisions were not being made.

For example, there was the simple problem of timing the availability of advertising media for the introduction of new models each year. In the U.S. market, this occurs in October; in Japan, new models are introduced in January. From the parent company in Japan, the advertising materials consistently arrived two to three months late for the introduction of new models. Year after year, the U.S. distributors complained about the delay. The American heads of the sales and advertising departments took the problem up the chain of command and requested their Japanese president to contact Japan and straighten the matter out. He did contact Japan—but the problem remained.

By chance, other developments in the organization provided an opportunity for overcoming the difficulty. Beginning in the early 1970s, top management in Japan began to assign a Japanese "coordinator" to each American department head. The coordinators, usually promising young executives in training for international assignments, were to become acquainted with U.S. business practices. It was not too long before they began observing with dismay that the American managers tended to concentrate on their functional roles and to expect coordination between functions to occur at the senior management levels—as is the practice in many U.S. companies. To the Japanese, it appeared, as one put it, "as if the various departments were separate companies, all competing against each other."

As inveterate communicators, some coordinators began to pick up problems that cropped up in one department and share them with their counterparts in other departments. In this roundabout way, the Americans learned what their colleagues were doing. Coordination between departments improved.

Soon the Japanese coordinators became aware of the difficulties typified by the late arrival of the advertising materials. True to their training in U.S. companies, the Americans were sending a report on every problem up the chain of command. Japanese top management in the United States would listen to each complaint, then send the American manager back for "more information." Translated, this meant "Come back with a proposal." Not comprehending, the Americans became increasingly impatient and frustrated. Occasionally, as in the case of the ads, the problems became so serious that the Americans insisted they be reported to Japan. The Japanese president obliged them, but the parent company remained unresponsive. The reason was simple: Since Japanese organizations are unaccustomed to dealing with problems from the top down, the Tokyo organization did not know how to handle a letter from the president of the Japanese subsidiary in the United States to the president of the parent company in Japan.

Once the coordinators understood the nature of the difficulty, remedying the advertising materials lag and similar problems was easy. A coordinator would simply pick up the telephone and call somebody at his managerial level in Tokyo. In a few days an answer would come back—and in this manner the matter of the ads was resolved.

The coordinators took some time—and the American department heads a somewhat longer time—to realize that the neat boxes in the organization chart were not interacting. By U.S. standards, the Americans were doing a good job. But without American superiors to make decisions and weave the organization together, they found that their effectiveness was diminished. To bridge the gap in managerial styles, the coordinators created a shadow organization. In this manner they not only solved the coordination problem but also involved the parent organization.

III

MILLIONS OF JOHN WAYNES?

Most of the companies we studied had avoided crises in managerial styles —like the one just described—by placing Japanese in the key slots and relegating Americans to less vital positions. However, many Japanese managers expressed a desire to Americanize further by promoting U.S. managers into Japanese-held positions. But there are risks in trying to straddle two cultures; perhaps an organization should try to remain predominantly American or predominantly Japanese. Without a fortuitous circumstance, such as the arrival of the coordinators at the U.S. auto plant, an organization that has attempted to compromise between the two styles may find itself functioning ineffectively.

Even so, the success of many Japanese operations in the United States —especially in terms of productivity—causes some businessmen to wonder whether they can borrow with profit from the Japanese style. In these days of growing worker disenchantment over assembly-line jobs and with frustration reaching into the managerial ranks, expressions of satisfaction from Americans working for Japanese companies cannot be dismissed lightly. A statement by one of Sony's American managers makes the point: "You get the feeling around here that they care about people, whereas in my previous work experience, with U.S. companies, they cared only about output and meeting the profit projections."

That the Japanese approach does not fit neatly into standard Western categories bothers some Americans. It is not truly permissive, given its emphasis on loyalty and performance and the social penalties for deviant behavior. Some might term it "humanistic"; yet Japanese managers express strong commitment to productivity and quality as goals. "Paternal" fails as a one-word description, in view of the Japanese emphasis on initiative from below.

For those who want to understand the Japanese approach—even more so for those who want to employ Japanese techniques in U.S. companies —it is essential to recognize the widely differing assumptions on which behavior in the two cultures is based. These differences are especially pronounced in the Japanese and American attitudes toward individuality and self-sufficiency. The American emphasis on these qualities contributes to competition and rivalry in organizational life. The American is buffeted by two streams of thought. One the one hand, the frontier spirit has instilled in our culture a belief in an individual's capacity to rise according to his abilities. Americans are exhorted to be like Horatio Alger—competitive and ambitious. On the other hand, by Constitution and by custom, ours is a culture dedicated to equality. But in a large American organization, the consequence of equality can be impersonalization; in the effort to treat all men equally, all men are often treated the same. As one Japanese executive observed, "You Americans treat each other like IBM cards—the only dfference is where the punch holes are."

Thus, the American's two belief systems forever bind him in tension. The contradictions of our culture lead either to rivalry and disruptive behavior, as individuals strive to "get ahead" by pursuing their interests aggressively, or to an inconclusive middle ground, where the pressure to "go along" makes it easy to avoid taking initiatives or hazarding risks.

The Japanese is faced with no such dichotomy. His assumptions about individuality enhance rather than detract from meaningful cooperative action. Moreover, a Japanese might be the first to point out that cooperative endeavor is what complex organizational life is all about.

He sees himself far less as an individual than he does as a part of his family or work group. His achievements as an independent entity are not as important to him as his role in furthering the well-being of people associated with him. In his work setting the company considers him as a whole person more than an American company would, for the Japanese are interested in how he fits in with the group in every way, not in just how he fits in as a producer.

It is possible that Japanese methods are more suitable for crowded organizational life than the Western approach. Obviously, the American system of management, with its emphasis on ingenuity and entrepreneurial genius, has many strengths. But it rests on the underpinnings of a frontier society that exalted individualism and had more than enough opportunity to go around. In just 50 years, we have changed from a society in which most people lived on farms to a nation in which most people live in cities. Many Americans work in large, complex organizations, in close contact with other people. Under these circumstances, perhaps some of our deep-seated American values are inappropriate for these times. The West could accommodate ten thousand John Waynes spread over the vast landscape. But millions of John Waynes employed under ten thousand corporate roofs may not, in the long run, prove workable.

As American society continues to mature and develop, its structure will inevitably change. It is possible that a basic alteration in the relationship between company and employee, from chairman of the board down to janitor, may occur. By studying how the Japanese manage a network of complex relationships, we can learn a great deal about how to live and work as a collectivity.

ADDENDUM

THREE SUCCESS STORIES

The Japanese companies whose experiences are described in this article have been generally successful in their U.S. ventures. Here are three examples, chosen because they reflect different approaches to capturing market shares in the United States.

In comparing two companies that assemble products in both the United States and Japan, we noted that Sony has achieved higher productivity. With the typical Japanese approach to personnel relations, the company treated its employees as "whole persons" rather than as so many productive units. Not only is productivity at Sony high, but also absenteeism and turnover are low: The averages at Sony's San Diego operation range from 25 percent to 50 percent below those at other electronics companies in that area. (All but a few of the Japanese companies in this study, incidentally, reported lower than average rates of absenteeism and turnover.)

In contrast to Sony, a Japanese producer of miniature ball bearings has handled its work force in a rather traditional American fashion. As a consequence, absenteeism and turnover at its operations have equaled or slightly exceeded the averages for like companies in its geographical area. It has single-mindedly pursued a constantly increasing share of the market. Underpricing its U.S. competitors and outperforming them in product quality and volume, the company has greatly increased its market share. It purchased its factory from a large manufacturer whom it had virtually driven out of the miniature ball-bearing field. At the time of the study, the American work force, most of which the company had inherited from its former rival, was operating on a three-shift basis to keep up with burgeoning demand.

In California, a Japanese bank has grown twice as fast as most small banks in the state. Its growth is only partly due to captive business from Japanese companies establishing subsidiaries on the West Coast. Americans working for this bank repeatedly refer to the aggressiveness and esprit de corps that the Japanese staff instills in fellow managers and workers. Management has kept operating costs low by maintaining staff levels at a minimum. Committed to avoiding layoffs during slow periods, the Japanese are motivated to avoid overhiring. So they carry on extensive cross-training. This gives the bank the flexibility to put anybody from the loan officer level on down into a teller's window to handle peak traffic rather than avoid having to hire extra tellers to solve the peak-load problem. This practice enriches the hourly employee's work by providing him with a variety of different tasks he can perform. It also puts considerable group pressure on absentees and eventually reduces absenteeism.

25

Japanese-American Economic War?

SOME FURTHER REFLECTIONS

Martin Bronfenbrenner

> I cannot think of any major industry in America that is not subject to great invasion or attack by the Japanese. The Japanese system is the most effective monopoly that has ever been developed in the economic history of the world. The Japanese will do whatever they need to do to take over whatever part of the richest markets in the world that they want to take. They zero in on a segment of our market and take it over. Then they will move into the next segment and the next.
>
> — Ely M. Callaway and Donald F. McCullough, US textile executives

> The real target of our international trade and monetary moves was Japan — not the Europeans. US patience was worn thin with the one-sided, lopsided, inequitable, unfair economic and monetary treatment we have received from the Japanese. The day of bowing and scraping to them is over. From now on the Japanese will have to give more than they get or suffer the consequences.
>
> — Pierre Rinfret, Wall Street economic and financial consultant

Such statements are important. They date from 1971, and do not reflect the majority sentiment of American business, labor, or agriculture — yet. They are not reflected in the official statements of American governmental bodies or commissions — yet. One can also find in Tokyo or Osaka anti-American equivalents to these anti-Japanisms. Their main thrust is that the US wants Japan to suffer from its own loose fiscal and monetary policies, particularly those connected with the Vietnam War.[1] They too do not represent Japanese business, labor, agriculture, or government circles — yet.

As a professional economist, an amateur Japanologist in America, and an amateur Americanist in Japan, I have tried to push the "yet" as far as possible into the future. For such efforts one is called pro-Japanese in America and pro-American in Japan: blessed are the peacemakers!

Reprinted, by permission, from the *Quarterly Review of Economics and Business* (Autumn, 1973).

I.

"A Japanese-American Economic War?" was the subject of my Koizumi Lecture at Keio University in December 1970, when the Nixon and dollar shocks were looming up on the horizon. Before that lecture was published,[2] the shocks had come, skirmishing had broken out, and belligerent statements like those quoted at the beginning were rising in number and vehemence.

This lecture isolated, and discussed separately, five groups of issues exacerbating Japanese-American economic relations and also proposed somewhat vague and general solutions. These solutions were in some cases close to the Japanese position and in others close to the American one. They were in all cases in the direction of greater freedom of international trade and capital movements. I still believe them to constitute a "package" preferable on balance to what has actually come about, preferable particularly from the viewpoints of consumers in both countries. But of course, the package is far from Pareto optimality. (The Japanese rice farmer and orange grower would have been hurt; likewise the Japanese computer industry and its employees; likewise the American steel and textile industries and their employees.) The issues and my proposed solutions were, in capsule form:

(1) "Voluntary" Japanese quotas on Japanese exports to the US, imposed under US pressure. This was the most pressing immediate issue in late 1970. (Proposal: Enact no more quotas; scrap the existing ones.)

(2) Tariff and nontariff barriers imposed by Japan against US exports. (Proposal: Concentrate on eliminating nontariff protection, particularly the extralegal *gyōsei-shido* "administrative guidance" of Japanese customers.)

(3) Alleged Japanese "dumping" in the US market. (Proposal: Drop the great majority of the charges, which are based on novel and self-serving redefinitions of "dumping."[3])

(4) Foreign, and particularly American, entrepreneurial direct investment in Japan. (Proposal: Rapid and complete liberalization, accompanied again by scrapping extralegal "administrative guidance.")

(5) Yen revaluation, still a "submerged" or "background" issue in 1970. (Proposal: A "clean" float of the yen, with minimal intervention by the Bank of Japan.)

While reaffirming (almost) all the contents of my 1970 lecture and 1971 publication, I now wish to go a little further. It appears that underlying the five issues given, are two others meriting exploration. The first such issue is a theoretical one, relating to the standard economic problem of the gains from international trade. The second issue is less economic than psychological; it relates to "ways of doing business" in the two countries, particularly ways of conducting negotiations.

II.

Conventional trade theory assumes full employment in each trading country, and identifies the gains from trade as cheaper imports when all countries specialize partly or completely along lines dictated by comparative advantage. The theory also takes the structure of international comparative advantage as given in the short run, and as changing over time only exogenously. That is to say, changes in comparative advantage are assumed independent of the commercial policies of the trading countries.[4]

Following the Keynesian revolution of the 1930s, trade theorists dropped the assumption of full employment in each trading country. This required them to consider a second set of gains from trade, which could not be added to the first set but often conflicted with it. This second set of gains, in a country with less than full employment, comes from exports. They consist precisely of increased employment, output, and growth. The technical process bringing them about is summarized under the head of "export multiplier."[5]

More recently there has begun yet another revolution in trade theory, which is still far from complete. We may call it a Hicks-Arrow revolution, although neither of these Nobel laureates is primarily an international economist. The Hicks component in this incipient revolution, called "induced technical change," dates from 1932 and takes explicit account of the fact that a firm or country can alter the rate and direction of technical progress by changing the amount and allocation of its research and development (R&D) expenditures. The Arrow component, called "learning by doing," dates from 1962 and modernizes the traditional "infant-industry" argument for protection. The claim is that with public or private investment in any particular branch of industry, a country can bring about the augmentation of both labor and capital inputs to that industry, even without overt technical change, relying upon a learning process akin to the anthropologists' "acculturation."

What the Hicks-Arrow revolution means in trade theory is recognition that a country, or at least a large country, can within wide limits shift its pattern of comparative advantage by changing the volume of its internal investment (particularly but not exclusively R&D) and rechannelling it among different industries. Comparative advantage, in other words, is itself subject to conscious change, either piecemeal by private firms or large-scale and deliberate by public authorities.

The usual twist a country wishes for its comparative-advantage structure is a concentration upon high-wage, high-labor-share industries and industries with high-income elasticities of world demand.

The shift to high-wage and high-labor-share industries, if successful, mollifies class conflicts between labor and capital by providing large increments of prestigious, highly skilled, and highly paid employment, and shifting the functional income distribution in favor of labor without imposing losses on capital. The shift to high-world-income–elasticity industries reduces the likelihood of the country's facing dangerous balance-of-payments problems, although it cannot guarantee any country a favorable balance.[6] In the Japanese case, a set of industries has been found which satisfies both these criteria simultaneously, and Japan has indeed become a surplus country at least temporarily. In addition, the shift has had the expected effect of raising growth rates as conventionally measured, primarily because of labor and capital augmentation.

Conversely, an advanced country feels abused when changes in the international pattern of comparative advantages force it to retain or resume the position of exporting raw materials and handicrafts while importing the products of prestigious modern industry. Were the bilateral Japanese-American trade imbalance to be filled exclusively by increased exports of American farm products and other raw materials to Japan, Americans would continue to resent Japan's "treating us like an underdeveloped country." In the case of lumber, this sentiment has combined with resentment of inflated lumber prices (resulting in considerable part from increased Japanese demand for American products) to include calls for export reduction in the face of the unfavorable American payments position.

The United States enjoyed a shift in its pattern of comparative advantage in its sleep, so to speak. The shift was an autonomous by-product of the settlement of the country, the exploitation of is resources, the immigration of European labor — and two world wars. The Japanese, on the other hand, have been guiding their pattern of comparative advantage with increasing success almost since the Meiji Restoration of 1868 by an increasingly self-confident and detailed system of consultative or indicative planning.[7] Since the early 1950s, the Japanese gains through their comparative-advantage twist have come largely at the expense of the United States, which had "arrived" one or two generations earlier. The bilateral Japanese-US balance, which had historically been in favor of the US, shifted in favor of Japan in the mid-1960s. By the early 1970s, the annual balance in Japan's favor exceeded $4 billion (including capital movements), the largest bilateral imbalance, to the best of my knowledge, between any two countries in the recorded history of international trade! As this shift accentuated the worldwide shift from dollar surplus to dollar glut, and as Japan was (after Canada) the major US trading partner, it was natural if unreasonable for American resentment to focus upon the bilateral Japanese-American balance.

The Japanese comparative-advantage twist many Americans consider somehow immoral because of the guidance and planning involved. They would prefer to see international comparative advantages remain as they were in the late 1940s, or if they were to change at all, to do so slowly and naturally, without either prodding or acceleration by a foreign government. It is easy for Americans to forget what American (and German) economic advances had done to British and French international economic positions in the period 1880–1950, because the US government had refrained from active twisting, and the Anglo-French problems could be ascribed to "natural forces" exclusively.

Applying trade theory as revolutionized by Hicks and Arrow, we can see that the US and Japan desire to achieve and maintain comparative advantage in the world economy over much the same set of distributionally desirable, trade-balance-desirable, and growth-desirable modern industries. Such competition is probably inevitable, but it need not degenerate into economic warfare. To avoid such degeneration, rules of the competitive game should be established, but not too rigidly to allow change when necessary. Rules should be worked out and adapted to changing conditions not only by the unwritten law of market practice but by conference, compromise, and agreement among the various competitors (not only bilaterally by Japan and the United States or trilaterally by addition of the EEC).

III.

This brings us face to face with the second underlying problem of Japanese-American economic relations, namely, the disparity between the methods of reaching and interpreting agreements in the two countries. A mere economist without expertise in sociology, psychology, or organization theory should not rush in where angels fear to tread, unless it be to encourage the angels to overcome their fears and rush in to correct his mistakes.

Very crudely indeed, then: the American negotiation system tends to be hierarchical and legalistic. In many cases, it is also dominated by some "terrible-tempered Mr. Bang."[8] A few top men, backed by assistants and attorneys, meet for a few hours or days, reach some sort of agreement, and reduce it to writing in a formal document binding over a definite time period. Things are often done the way "the terrible-tempered Mr. Bang" wants them done, not because he is right but because he outshouts and outthreatens the opposition, and Mr. Bang's lawyers embody Mr. Bang's temper tantrums into enforceable contracts, no matter how many technicians "know" that Mr. Bang's ideas will not work. If subordinates' interests on either side are injured by the agreement, they can quit. If they sabotage the agreement, they can be fired. If they are never told about it, do not understand it, or cannot believe it is meant seriously — or if the agreement is based on technical misunderstanding — it often breaks down in practice. In this case, the whole process may be repeated, without waiting for the original agreement to expire.[9]

The Japanese "economic miracle" has inspired extraordinary international respect for the alternative (black magical?) Japanese negotiation method, featuring the so-called *ringi* system.[10] Here each negotiator's "position paper" (*ringi-sho*) has already made the rounds of his backers and subordinates. Each has had the opportunity to comment on it in advance, and to suggest revisions so far as his own interests or operations are concerned. Also, before agreements are finalized, these backers and subordinates have another opportunity to raise questions and objections. If the questions cannot be answered or the objections cannot be met, the draft comes back for modification again and again, until everything is clear and everyone reconciled. Every effort is made to avoid injury to any interest group. And if indeed someone must be hurt, those who are helped are expected to make some sort of side agreements with the aggrieved parties, compensating them here and now or promising to do so later on. And should agreement for any reason be unworkable as reached, or should it cause unexpected loss to some participant, nobody sues anyone else or insists upon specific performance. Instead, modification is the order of the day. The "terrible-tempered Mr. Bang" has his Japanese counterparts,[11] but the *ringi* process permits them to cool down and restore themselves to rationality.

But the *ringi* process takes time, and time may be of the essence. In which case, the Japanese system gets involved in red tape and paralysis at unforeseen moments of crisis. The Japanese-American impasses of 1970–71 and 1972–73 have both been cases in point.

Japanese dislike, and with reason, references to "Japan, Inc."[12] so far as the term implies that government and business bureaucracies — in J. K. Galbraith's term, "technostructures" — dominate the economy and ride roughshod over the rest of the population. Actually, the Japanese conservative Establishment seems to harbor at least seven overlapping and participating interest groups. For Japan to make any significant voluntary policy change in response to outside complaints about Japanese export surpluses and closed internal markets, something will have to be done for each of them, to be sure that none is disappointed in its legitimate expectations.

IV.

Who are these seven groups? What are their main concerns, and why is each important? The following list represents an attempt to answer these questions.

(1) The export interests, primarily big business and particularly the trading companies (*shōsha*). These are main sources of campaign funds for the Government party (Liberal Democrats, *Jiyūtō*). They want to minimize yen upvaluation and dislike the uncertainties of floating exchange rates.

(2) The import-competing interests, of which the most important is organized agriculture, the rural mass base of the Government party. They do not want trade liberalization or yen upvaluation, both of which mean cheaper imports.

(3) Medium and small business interests, who form the increasingly shaky urban mass base of the Government party. Many of these are in either export- or import-competing branches of the economy, covered under (1) and (2). In addition, and usually more important, small business fears the competition of foreign firms on the Japanese market to a greater extent than big business does,

and with good reason.[13] Small business is indeed the main opponent of capital liberalization.

(4) The labor interests, whose antigovernment militance the Establishment would like to blunt. Japanese workers are attached to lifetime employment (*shūshin-koyō*) and the security it provides. They do not want to see their employers subject to foreign competition which might drive them out of business, force them to personnel cuts, or reduce their capacity to increase wages. On this point, the interests of organized labor harmonize with those of small business.

(5) The capital-export interests, mainly in mining, lumbering, petroleum, and the initial levels of resource processing generally. Like the exporters in (1), these are major sources of Government party financing. These firms, predominantly large, are willing to reduce the Japanese balance of payments in the short run by investing large sums abroad, particularly in developing countries. On the other hand, they require protection against the risks of nationalization, and they have had difficulty finding acceptable foreign partners.[14] It follows that these interests are hesitant, do not want to be rushed, and demand additional government support.

(6) Civil service interests, especially in two ministries,[15] oppose any forms of liberalization which threaten their own discretion, status, and power. These are the people who operate Japanese administrative guidance on a day-to-day basis; they are the administrative guides. Intellectually gifted, products of elite law schools (and sometimes self-taught in economics), occasionally arrogant, these people are attracted to the civil service despite low salaries by the power it gives its members while they are young and forceful. Moreover, a Japanese civil servant faces retirement at 55 and must consider the possibility of a post-retirement advisory capacity with some firm for whom he has done favors during his tenure. Liberalization, obviously, lessens the civil servant's opportunity both to exercise discretionary power and to do special favors for potential future employers.

(7) The taxpayer interests, whose importance to any party's mass base need no spelling out. The Japanese taxpayer has come to expect lower rates and/or higher exemptions almost every year, especially in his income taxes. It would be bad politics to disappoint the taxpayers merely to compensate persons whose interests have been hurt in securing agreements with the United States.

V.

It is a fiendishly difficult problem in game theory to devise a Pareto-optimal package of provisions, arrangements, and side payments which can simultaneously avoid injury to any of these seven interest groups and not cheat a little on one's concessions to the American side. It should surprise nobody that the Japanese have found no quick solution and have asked continually for more and more time. The Americans have, however, come to interpret such requests for time as evidences of Oriental deviousness and insincerity, rather than as faith in the Marshallian long run.

The problem may conceivably be soluble if we allow side payments to otherwise injured parties (special subsidies, perhaps, or tax reliefs, or low-interest loans), if we take account of third-country trade, and so on. Or the problem, like the squaring of the circle, the reduction of π to a rational number, or putting 100 percent of the people in the top 10 percent of the income distribution, may have no solution at all. We do not know. The only point is that no quick and easy solution has been found so far, or is likely to be found in the immediate future.

In which case, if indeed some Japanese interests must suffer to assuage the aggrieved Americans, it would seem good Japanese political strategy for the Japanese government to avoid injuring that interest themselves and to refuse assent to any agreement which injures it. If the injury comes unilaterally from the American side, the Japanese government can shift all blame to the unreasonable foreigners who refuse to understand Japan's position. What these unreasonable foreigners do, the Japanese government may not be able to undo. But it may instead avenge what it cannot undo, and from successive reciprocal vengeances springs economic warfare.

VI.

If this analysis is approximately right, the lowest-political-risk strategy for the Japanese side in the present confrontation is to continue stalling for time and leave the offensive to the Americans. A possible form of the American offensive move, as of the 23 March Nixon speech already mentioned, appears to be a punitive surcharge upon dutiable imports from countries which the Americans judge to be undervaluing their currencies, or "frustrating" the effects of their upvaluations upon their bilateral balances with the US. Such legislation, if enacted, would be aimed primarily at Japan.

Should the US enact discriminatory legislation against Japan, or turn generally protective along the lines of the Burke-Hartke Bill, Japan will probably react. We may assume that the reaction will injure American exporters to Japan, American competitors with Japanese exports primarily in third countries, and American-affiliated companies already operating in Japan.[16] This reaction may arouse further American legislation, and so back and forth in a pattern of hostilities which may either escalate or die away, depending on whether the successive reactions increase or decrease in intensity.

Pending enactment of discriminatory legislation, however, the Tanaka cabinet has adopted a conciliatory stance. At the moment (May 1973) the prospect for amicable settlement appears at least temporarily brighter than it did earlier in the year. The February 1973 dollar devaluation (from ¥308 to ¥265 to the dollar) coincided with an accelerated rate of Japanese domestic inflation. Japan has experienced two unfavorable monthly trade balances, and the Economic Planning Agency has estimated a decline in the bilateral Japanese-US balance from $4.2 billion in 1972 to $2.7 billion in 1973. Premier Tanaka has also proposed a "fifth round of capital liberalization" designed to mollify the Americans while retaining protection for agriculture and postponement of capital liberalization for 22 industries (including food processing, retail trade, computers, and photo film, which had been focuses of American attention).[17] It is not yet possible to estimate the extent to which this conciliatory music "hath charms to soothe the savage breast," but my biased sample of savage breasts (members of the US Chamber of Commerce in Japan) suggests little basis for long-term optimism, primarily because the institutions of "administrative guidance" remain unaffected.

VII.

These remarks are not intended as alarmist. In fact, I am the reverse of an alarmist. In suggesting a floating yen in 1970, I anticipated a possible 5 or 10 percent upvaluation resulting, not the 25 or 30 percent that has occurred. Similarly, in using the dirty word "economic warfare," I have in mind only brush-fire skirmishes and guerilla sniping. Between Japan and America, there is only infinitesimal chance of resort to the full economic-warfare arsenal — competitive devaluations, embargoes, preclusions, multiple currencies, blocked accounts, currency blocs, and so on. But even so, the situation of the representative consumer and citizen in each skirmishing country will suffer under brush-fire economic guerilla action as compared with peacetime normality, unless of course he enjoys for its own sake the atmosphere of mutual suspicion, recrimination, and general unpleasantness. Should brush-fire economic warfare develop, a corner may therefore be turned and relations be normalized, but the vague game-theoretic considerations of Sections IV–VI make it difficult to see where that corner is located, let alone how it can be turned tomorrow or the day after.

NOTES

1. For example, International Trade and Industry Minister Yasuhiro Nakasone is quoted in the *Mainichi Daily News* (24 March 1973) as strongly rejecting President Nixon's criticisms (in a Washington address the previous day) of Japanese trade policies, and as saying that "the United States is letting dollars flow out to the world at the sacrifice of other countries."

2. Two versions were published, in the Autumn 1971 issues of this journal and of *Keio Economic Papers*. The American version had had one more revision than the Japanese, but both were based on the situation immediately prior to the Nixon New Economic Policy of August 1971.

3. "Dumping" is increasingly being redefined to cover all cases where imports force American firms to cut either production or domestic prices. The effective popular rubric speaks of "disruption" of the procedures of "orderly marketing."

4. This is an elementary textbook summary, omitting most of the graduate seminar level qualifications and complications.

5. But in an "overheated" economy with "too much money chasing too few goods," multiplier analysis demonstrates instead an additional gain from imports, in providing more goods and reducing the inflation rate.

6. I owe a debt of thanks to the anonymous referee of this journal at this point; the original draft of this article did not preclude the contrary interpretation that any country could obtain a permanent favorable balance by shifting comparative advantage in the same direction that Japan did.

7. The best elementary introduction to the Japanese planning system is to be found in a US Department of Commerce "guide for the American businessman" [2].

8. The original "terrible-tempered Mr. Bang" was a comic strip character of the 1920s and 1930s. Among famous American players of the role have been John L. Lewis (in labor negotiations) and John Connally (in financial negotiations). In international politics, the names of Adolf Hitler and Joseph Stalin also come to mind.

9. An example meaningful both to Japan and the United States is provided by the Smithsonian currency arrangements of December 1971, which were intended to end international financial crises but which collapsed 14 months later.

10. Compare [2, pp. 32–34, and also Note 20, p. 74], with further references cited.

11. Sometimes named *Muriyari* and *Ōbō*.

12. See [2, pp. 14–16 and 70 f]. For a view by an American scholar (Gerald Curtis, Columbia University political scientist) supporting the Japanese view, see [1].

13. The good reason is that the Japanese Government will not allow large firms to fail, but feels no compunction to prop up the smaller ones. In addition, the large firms have preferential access to bank credit, often from banks with whom they have *keiretsu* (conglomerate-type) affiliations, but small firms do not. The "horrible example" always cited in this connection is Coca-Cola, which has allegedly driven "hundreds" of small Japanese beverage companies into bankruptcy.

14. In countries where nationalistic or anti-Japanese sentiment is rising, the Japanese dislike the blatancy of the wholly owned Japanese branch plant or subsidiary company. In this respect, they are profiting by American mistakes.

15. These are the Ministries of Agriculture and Forestry (*Nōrinshō*) and International Trade and Industry (*Tsūsanshō*).

16. In the interview already cited (Note 1), Japanese International Trade and Industry Minister Nakasone threatened that "Japan would delay further liberalization of imports if the US adopted discriminatory trade policies toward Japan."

17. For details, see [3] and for interpretation, [4]. For the specific problems of one key industry, computers, there is a chapter in [2, pp. 78–101].

REFERENCES

1. Gerald Curtis, "Trying to Destroy 'Japan, Inc.' Myth," *Asahi Evening News*, 8 February 1973.

2. Eugene J. Kaplan, *Japan: The Government-Business Relationship* (Washington: US Government Printing Office, 1972).

3. *Mainichi Daily News*, 26 April 1973.

4. ———, 30 April 1973.

26

Japan's Role in Southeast Asia

Noritake Kobayashi

JAPANESE INVESTMENTS IN SOUTHEAST ASIA TOWARD 1980

GENERAL OBSERVATIONS ON THE PRESENT SITUATION

As of the end of 1972, the aggregate total of Japanese overseas investments amounted to (U.S.) $6.26 billion with the number of investments reaching 6,276. They consisted of equity investments in the amount of $3.17 billion (4,492 in number of investments), loans $2.33 billion (976 cases), real estate acquisition and similar investments $466 million (323 cases), and branch establishments $290 million (485). Geographically, investments in Europe totalled $1.59 billion (representing 665 cases of investments) accounting for 25.5 percent of the entire dollar volume, North America $1.38 billion (1,695 cases) for 22.1 percent, Asia $1.27 billion (2,658 cases) for 20.4 percent, Latin America $853 million (777) for 13.6 percent, Middle East $599 million (40) for 9.6 percent, Oceania $419 million (284) for 6.7 percent, and Africa $135 million (157) for 2.2 percent (See Appendix 1).

Only $4.48 billion were invested abroad by the Japanese for 20 years between fiscal 1951 and fiscal 1971. Therefore, for the 9-month period in 1972 they registered a marked growth of $1.78 billion representing as high a rate of growth as almost 140 percent.

Japanese investments in Asia have also recorded a tremendous increase in recent years and amounted to $1.27 billion by the end of 1972. Two years ago, at the close of fiscal 1970, the accumulated total of such investments was no more than $780 million, thus again giving a 163 percent growth in 21 months (See Appendix 2).

These Asian investments consisted of equity investments in the amount of $632 million (representing 2,015 cases of investments), extension of loans $600 million (337 cases), establishment of branches $26 million (258), and others $15 million (48).

One point which may be worthy of note is the fact that the number of investments in this area is far greater than those in any other areas, representing 42.4 percent of the total number. In terms of dollar volume, however, they represent only 20.4 percent, implying that investment per project is smaller than those elsewhere.

Reprinted, by permission, from the Institute of Southeast Asian Studies (Current Issues Seminar Series No. 3, 1973).

ANALYSIS OF INVESTMENTS IN SOUTHEAST ASIA

Let us here focus our attention more closely on Japanese investment activities in Southeast Asian countries.

Fields of Investments. By the end of 1970, textiles have received the largest dollar volume of investments: $41 million from Japan. They were followed by steel and metals with the investment of $36 million, machineries $29 million, other miscellaneous industries $26 million, chemicals $25 million, mining $24 million, electrical $21 million, and agricultural and forestry $20 million. Generally speaking, investments in manufacturing activities were concentrated in Thailand and those in natural resource developments in the Philippines and Indonesia.

Objective of Investments. According to "Japanese Private Investments Abroad," that is, the published results of a field survey undertaken in 1971 by the Export and Import Bank of Japan, three chief motives for Japanese businesses to invest in Southeast Asia were:

1. expansion of sales in host-country markets, representing 36 percent of the answers to the question of motives;
2. establishment of local manufacturing facilities in defence of overseas markets that were hitherto covered by finished product exports from Japan in the face of tightening of import regulations by host-country governments, 31 percent, and;
3. seizing new market opportunities in host countries in meeting challenges from other Japanese competitors who were also anxious to enter into such markets, 16 percent.

A more comprehensive explanation of reasons why Japanese businesses sought opportunities in Asia was given by the Ministry of International Trade and Industry (MITI) survey undertaken at the end of March, 1971, and published in November, 1972. MITI divided "motives" for overseas into two categories, one is market-oriented and the other management-oriented.

As for the market-oriented motives, 40.8 percent of those who answered the MITI questionnaire had endorsed the results of the Export and Import study introduced previously, that is, they made their investments in defense of their former export markets by going into local production. Another 13.9 percent made their investments to expand their sales in host-country markets. A particularly interesting new development found from the MITI survey was that an increasing number of those who were interviewed answered that their prime objectives were to sell locally-produced products not only for and in host-country markets but also to export them to third-country or even to Japanese markets (18.4 percent and 11.2 percent respectively).

In the older Export and Import Bank survey only 7.5 percent each of those who made investments in Southeast Asia aimed at exports of the locally-manufactured products to third country or Japanese markets (See Appendix 3b).

According to the MITI study 37 percent of those who answered the questionnaire emphasizing the importance of utilization of manpower available in host countries led other management-oriented motives for investments in Southeast Asian markets. It was followed by 19.2 percent relying on various incentives given by host-country governments for induction of necessary foreign capital and technology. A total of 18.2 percent emphasized an advantage of producing goods near their markets.

In the previous Export and Import Bank survey only 11 percent highlighted the importance of availability of manpower in Southeast Asia (See Appendix 4b).

Since the MITI survey does not distinguish Southeast Asia from the rest of Asia in connection with its explanation of motives, it is difficult to compare its results with those of the Export and Import Bank. However, it is apparent from the tenor of the two reports that the Japanese are becoming more aware of the advantages of utilizing local manpower in Southeast Asia and conforming to the requirements of host-country governments to export locally-produced goods to third-country markets. These advantages and requirements have hitherto been limited largely to East Asia, including Hong Kong, Korea, and Taiwan.

Environmental Problems. The biggest complaint that the Japanese have in entering into the Southeast Asian market is the complicated and inefficient administrative procedure of host-country governments. Some 29 percent of the companies which were interviewed for the Export and Import Bank survey emphasized this point. Many complained of difficulties in importing raw materials, parts, and components due to the shortage of foreign exchanges in host countries, particularly in the Philippines and Indonesia (28 percent). Shortage of labor meeting quality requirements and general economic recession were another important source of complaints (19 percent in both cases). A number of Japanese businesses complained of political instability and severe control imposed on foreign capitals by host-country governments (19 percent in both cases). In connection with the latter, the Export and Import Bank report made a particular reference to localization programs then progressing in Thailand, Malaysia, Singapore, and Indonesia, stressing the need for majority ownership of joint-venture equity by host-country nationals, employment of local people in proportion to racial construction of host-country society, and increase of export percentage of locally-manufactured goods. Other difficulties confronted by Japanese businesses included obstacles in securing funds necessary to run local operations (14 percent), progressing inflation, unsatisfactory distribution and marketing facilities (10 percent and 8 percent), poor electric power and transportation facilities, and high taxes (7 percent respectively). (See Appendix 7.)

The development of export-processing zones in Singapore (Jurong Town Corporation) and the Philippines (Mariveles) is considered generally to offer good incentives for Japanese business. However, prices of locally-processed goods are still high because of the scale of base markets. Also, progress of industrialization programs in neighboring countries is creating difficulties in exporting such products to such third-country markets.

Scale of Investments. In accordance with the previously cited MITI report, the majority of overseas operations are run by companies incorporated in host countries which have equity capital of more than 100 million yen but less than 1 billion yen. They were followed by a group of companies with equity of more than 10 million but less than 30 million yen and then by those with more than 50 million yen but less than 100 million yen equity. As a result of the survey, MITI reports that 59.4 percent of local companies representing Japanese direct investments had equity capital less than 100 million yen and that the scale of such investments has been much smaller than those which were made by either American or European-based multinational enterprises.

As to the percentage of Japanese shareholding in these companies incorporated abroad, Japanese investors have a 100 percent control over 46 percent of such companies. (In case of manufacturing companies, this percentage drops to 19 percent.) The Japanese held majority positions in 32 percent (in case of manufacturing outfits 46 percent) and only minority positions in 22 percent (35 percent).

In reference to companies operating in Southeast Asia, the Export and Import Bank reported that 70 companies were capitalized on a scale of more than \$300,000 but less than \$1 million, 50 companies with capital more than \$100,000 but less than \$300,000, 38 companies with capital more than \$1 million but less than \$5 million, and 20 companies with capital less than \$100,000 (cf. Appendix 5a).

In 16 out of 229 companies operating in Southeast Asia, the Japanese maintained a 100 percent control. The Japanese owned 24 companies on a 50/50 equity-sharing basis with local partners. The Japanese held minority position in 22 companies (cf. Appendices 5b and 5c).

A total of 957 operating units of Japanese companies surveyed by MITI reported that the number of employees per unit was 172. In case of manufacturing units this average increased to 309 persons per unit of operations.

Partners of Joint Ventures. In Southeast Asia one third of 87 companies surveyed by the Export and Import Bank answered that they had chosen overseas Chinese as their joint-venture partners. Ten companies made partnerships with central-government agencies in host countries. Local private partners other than overseas Chinese were chosen as partners by 49 companies

Profitability of Investments. At the end of 1970, it was disclosed by the MITI report that 60.7 percent of businesses established abroad had profits from the operations of the accounting year then coming to an end. Some 23.9 percent suffered deficits. Another 15.4 percent remained at breakeven. If we take into consideration losses of such businesses already accrued and accumulated prior to the accounting year 1970, particularly in the formative stage of the businesses, the number of business establishments which enjoy profits free from encumbrances would reduce to 50.2 percent. Another 32.3 percent still had accumulated losses from preceding accounting years. Only 23.9 percent paid dividends from their operations in 1970.

Among companies operating in Southeast Asia in March, 1970, 74 percent had profits from their latest accounting year, 4 percent remained at breakeven, and 22 percent suffered deficits. Taking into account accumulated profits and losses in previous years, 62 percent had profits, 2 percent were at breakeven, and 36 percent had losses. Some 42 percent paid dividends (See Appendix 6b).

Out of 14 companies engaging in natural resource development projects in Southeast Asia, only 4 companies were left with accumulated profits and the remaining 10 suffered accumulated losses in March, 1970.

Resource development investments may not always be expected to run profitable businesses in host countries because their primary interests are in assuring continuous flows of imports of products locally developed to Japan. However, only 5 out of 28 companies in this field accomplished their target of imports scheduled originally; 6 companies kept their schedule and 17 companies fell behind the schedule.

Future Plan of Investors. For the future, 81 percent of the overseas establishments reported to the Export and Import Bank that they would anticipate an improvement in their businesses, 15 percent expected that their businesses would level off, and 4 percent predicted lack of improvement.

Among 424 companies which predicted a better future, 284 companies had plans for production facility investments, 164 for introduction of new products, and 27 for finding new opportunities in export markets (See Appendix 8).

In the Southeast Asian countries, out of 199 establishments under survey, 156 had an optimistic prospect. Only 9 companies returned negative answers, the rest forecasting levelling off of their businesses.

FUTURE PROSPECTS: MAGNITUDE OF FUTURE INVESTMENTS

Toward 1980, the Committee to examine Industrial Structure, a special study group organized under the Ministry of International Trade and Industry, predicted that the aggregate total of Japanese overseas investments will reach, by 1975, the level of $11.5 billion and by 1980, $26 billion, the amount exceeding those of the present American investments in Canada. The rate of growth of investments was also predicted to be phenomenally high, that is, the annual rate of investment increase in 1975 will be about 27 percent, representing an annual flow of $2 billion, and in 1980, 22 percent representing $3.5 billion.

Forecasts of Directions of Investments. Four general directions of investments are foreseen by the Industrial Structure Committee.

In the first place, $15 billion representing 57 percent of the aggregate total of 1980 investments will be placed in natural resource development projects. The rate of growth in this field is expected to surpass the average rate by 6 percent reaching to the high level of 28 percent.

Secondly, about $9 billion representing 35 percent of the total volume will be invested in Southeast Asia. In connection with these investments, a bigger emphasis will be placed on the utilization of efficient but still comparatively cheap manpower available in the area.

Thirdly, Japanese investments in the Untied States and Europe are expected to increase greatly in the 1970s.

Due to the minus gap now expanding between Japan and these two areas in the balance of trade and payments, Americans and Europeans are becoming increasingly impatient to allow big flows of goods in terms of exports from Japan to continue. If the Japanese do not wish to lose the big and valuable markets in the economically advanced countries, what can they do? An obvious alternative will be to replace the exports with local production, thus broadening reciprocal effects of international division of labor to recover an appropriate balance in trade and payments.

Lastly, it is hoped in Japan that during the 1970s, reallocation of industries from Japan to developing countries will progress as it is generally considered to be a good solution to her domestic environmental problems which are now worsening.

When Japan has realized the high level of industrialization which it long wished to achieve, the country began to suffer from all sorts of environmental problems—for example, air and water pollution, and over-concentration of people in metropolitan areas creating serious city problems. Many people in Japan at present wish to discard the pollution-creating industries for cleaner air and water and for a more pleasant life in the cities. In the meantime, we are aware that in the world and particularly in developing Asia, there are many countries which have enough space for industries and which are anxious to have in their own countries the types of industries some of us wish to abandon. We also know very well that if it had been properly and better planned from the beginning, we could have prevented the so-called pollutive effects of the industries about which we complain.

With good prior planning and proper care, therefore, some of the Japanese industries may be shared by our neighbors in Asia by removing their operation site from crowded Japan to more spacious lands in Asia. The Industry Structure Committee predicts that such reallocation of industries will progress in the 1970s parallel to Japanese efforts to step up their investments in natural resource development projects.

Need for Conflict Resolution. However can our intention to invest abroad be justifiable and honorable? The tremendously big volume and high rate of increase will have effects surprising the people and governments in host countries. Impacts of such investments may be so fast and enormous that, we are afraid, they may create unnecessary doubt about the motives of investors and suspicion about their real intent. We have already been denounced and criticized in Thailand and elsewhere as being an economic exploiter and imperialist. We are concerned that these negative reactions may increase and become so serious that we will not be able to continue our overseas activities, if we do not administer our foreign investments properly before it is too late. In other words, we are interested in finding ways to avoid conflicts and if such conflicts unfortunately accrue, to solve them to the satisfaction of all the parties concerned.

Government Guidelines for Future Investments in Southeast Asia. The basic attitude and policy adopted by the Ministry of International Trade and Industry regarding our investments in the 1970s in Southeast Asia on the suggestion of the Industry Structure Committee may be summarized as follows:

1. Japanese private investors must be prepared for an effort to harmonize the effects of their investments with the local interests of host countries primarily for economic take-off and development.
2. Japanese investments should be planned and implemented as a subsystem in a grand design of economic coordination with developing countries sponsored by the Japanese government.

As more concrete measures for the implementation of the above-cited policy, MITI has drawn up the following seven guidelines for investments in developing countries including those which are in Southeast Asia.

1. Overseas investments should be harmonized with local requirements for economic development and other policies of host-country governments. Particularly in natural resource development projects, investors are encouraged to undertake processing of the resources in host countries before they are taken out of Japan.
2. It is preferred that Japanese direct investments take the form of establishment of joint ventures with local partners. Increased local participation in the equities of such joint ventures is welcomed.
3. Japanese investors should cooperate with people in host countries in developing managerial talents from among such people. Promotion of local employees to management positions of overseas establishments is encouraged.
4. To enlarge "fall-out" effects, investors are encouraged to develop industries surrounding the target field of direct investments and also to contribute to the local technology development efforts by extending necessary technical assistance.
5. Investors should reinvest profits locally acquired in order to develop a firmer base in host-country societies.
6. Investors should give due cognizance and respect to the labor and trade customs of host countries lest their aggressive behavior should cause any confusion and chaos in the economy and social system of host countries. At the same time, excessive competition in host-country markets should be avoided.
7. Investors should not concentrate their investments in any particular field of industries lest their behavior produce unnecessary concern in host countries to the effect that Japanese investors may dominate and take over such a field and/or local economy in toto.

MITI AND JETRO FIELD SURVEY

REACTIONS OF HOST-COUNTRY GOVERNMENTS TO INCREASE JAPANESE INVESTMENTS

Some of the problems of foreign business activities as visualized by host-country governments in Southeast Asia are given below.

General. For seventeen days in February, 1973, I had an opportunity to visit six countries in Southeast Asia heading a mission organized under the auspices of the Japanese Government, more specifically MITI and JETRO. The purposes of the mission were (1) to study management of operating units belonging to American- or European-based multinational enterprises doing business in Southeast Asia, (2) to compare the management of such multinational enterprises with those of Japanese businesses operating in the same area, (3) to meet and discuss with government officials of host countries about their evaluation of foreign (that is, both Japanese and others) business activities and the impact on their countries, and then (4) to find a way for Japanese businesses to become more multinational.

As I am still working together with other members of the mission to write our report, I am not in a position to make a public statement about the results of the study; yet I think that some of the remarks made by host-country government officials were very much relevant to today's speech in which I am trying to find an appropriate role for Japanese businesses to play in the 1970s in Southeast Asia.

Impact of Foreign Corporate Activities on National Economies of Host Countries. To our question, what do you think is the impact of foreign corporate activities on your national economy, the patterns of answers received from government officials were somewhat uniform, recognizing the "very important" impact of such activities on their countries' exports and imports and also on long-run balance of payments. As many of the countries obviously suffer from a shortage of internal resources both in terms of capital and necessary commodities and depend heavily on a foreign supply of such resources, all offícals we met, with an exception of a Filipino, thought that foreign corporate activities had a "very important" impact on the national incomes of their countries.

Advantages of having Foreign Businesses in Host-Country Society. Be it of as much importance as it may, what did government officials of host countries think about advantages of having foreign businesses in their countries? In connection with this question, the answers we received can be classified into two different groups.

The first of the two groups represented by officials from Thailand, Malaysia, and Indonesia emphasized the merits of having foreign businesses in their countries in terms of creation of employment opportunities and receipt of capital necessary for the economic development of their national economies. The second group's answer was more indirect but I thought they saw the heart of the matter more clearly. Officials from Singapore and the

Philippines valued more the "innovative managerial know-how" that was brought into their countries accompanying direct investments of multinational enterprises than the simple accumulation of capital and/or the creation of new job opportunities in their domestic markets. They seem to feel that money and jobs are equipped with managerial talents, and personalities who can organize and use these resources more efficiently will carry the ball over the others. In other words, they gave preference to the transfer of "intangible assets/resources" which they believed would have more value and permeating "fall-out effects" for their long-run economic development than those of "tangible assets" represented by capital and commodities.

Of course, it is unfair to compare the two groups on the same level because there are a great deal of differences between them in terms of varied stages of economic development. However, I must say that it was a very interesting contrast.

Disadvantages of having Foreign Business in Host-Country Society. On the reverse side, what did officials of countries we visited think about disadvantages of having foreign businesses in their countries?

Differing from Japanese experiences, many of the countries in Southeast Asia have maintained a very liberal policy, taking freely foreign economic resources into their own countries. However, in more recent years, they have tried to be more selective in admitting such resources into their countries. This means that they admit them only when these resources can contribute to the economic development of host countries. In this connection, complaints I received are three-fold.

In the first place, businesses of advanced countries are so big and powerful that when they enter into host-country markets, they tend to dominate a particular field of industry, thus denying in fact local efforts to develop the identical field of industry by themselves.

Secondly, officials we met often complained that foreign capital is apprehensive of the importance of efficiency so much so that they tend to neglect the training of local people and take the field of business (that is, domestic trading) away from them. On this point, severe criticisms were directed to the practice of Japanese trading companies.

Thirdly, in government offices of many countries, I heard complaints that foreign businesses are uncooperative in terms of following the policies of host-country governments to encourage exports of locally-manufactured products rather than the sale of them in domestic markets.

Overall Requirements of Host-Country Governments to be met by Foreign Business. From the above observations of the general attitude of host-country government officials, the general requirements to be met by foreign businesses operating in the area can be stated in a summarized form as follows:

1. Foreign businesses entering and operating in Southeast Asia should create local employment opportunities.
2. They should contribute to local capital formation.

3. They should transfer innovative managerial know-how and assist host-country people in developing local managerial talents and personnel, and
4. They should cooperate with efforts of host-country governments to enlarge exports of locally-produced goods to third-country markets, thus earning more foreign exchange deemed to be necessary for domestic economic growth.

On the negative side:

1. They must not enter into some fields of business which are reserved by host-country governments for work and efforts of local people, and
2. They must not be too aggressive to dominate particular fields of industry, resulting in the practical exclusion of local people from such fields.

DIFFERENCES BETWEEN JAPANESE AND AMERICAN OR EUROPEAN-BASED BUSINESSES IN DOING BUSINESS IN SOUTHEAST ASIA

Local Evaluation of Differences. In my interview with host-country government officials, I had a questionnaire prepared asking "what do you think are the differences between Japanese businesses operating in your country and those of American or European origins? Please compare their differences on (1) ownership policy, (2) control policy, (3) management development policy, (4) transfer of local customs, (6) marketing, (7) production, (8) procurement of materials and parts, (9) research and development, (10) financing, (11) public relations and advertising, (12) employment policy, (13) efforts to adapt to the host-country requirements, and (14) efforts to prevent pollution. Provided you find differences, which of the two practices of businesses of different origins do you think are more favorable to you or, in reverse, less favorable to you? Please signify your answer with a plus sign for favorable and a minus sign for less favorable."

It is obvious that the types of answers we can draw from the above-explained questions are rather relative in their implications. For example, assume we received a plus answer to the eighth point. What does it mean? It means that our practice is better than those of American- or European-based multinational enterprises. But there is no way to be sure whether people in host countries approve of Japanese practices 100 percent or not. However, suppose we received a minus to the eighth point. We can be apprehensive of the fact that there is no guarantee that American and European practices are approved by local people 100 percent, but Japanese practices are disliked more. So, there is room to improve our practices at least up to the level of the so-called multinational enterprises. Of course, when we undertook this mental exercise, at the back of our mind there was an assumption that as far as international business is concerned, many American- or European-based companies have had more experience in making adjustments to local requirements of host countries than their Japanese counterparts; thus we need to close the gap.

The results we gathered from the questionnaire were rather disastrous and disheartening.

In the first place, we found that in the eyes of host-country government officials, Japanese practices of management development policy (point 3), transfer of resource policy (point 4), and employment policy (point 12) have serious disadvantages because of (i) poor communication problems existing between Japanese managers (including head office staff and local expatriate managers) and local employees of host countries and (ii) neglect of efforts by Japanese to develop managerial talents from among local people.

Secondly, host-country government officials seem to feel that there is plenty of room for Japanese to improve their understanding of local customs (point 5) and efforts to adapt to host-country requirements (point 13). In this regard, we were criticized to the effect that (i) Japanese tend to be more hesitant and so ambiguous in expressing their views that they often confuse host-country governments and even open up room for an under-the-table talk. It was also emphasized that (ii) in the absence of necessary communication, Japanese advice to host-country people, though it was well meant originally, is often taken as imposition of Japanese "preconceived ideas."

Thirdly, Japanese marketing activities (point 6) are widely criticized as being too aggressive. The Japanese are so conscious of efficiency and impatient for local people to grow up, that they tend to take away jobs from people in host countries. Trading companies are so speculative in their practices that they often interfere with the stability of prices of necessities in host societies. The Japanese are only engaging in local production as a substitute to exports and therefore are unwilling to cooperate with a host-country government's export drive. These were included in the criticisms against Japanese marketing practices.

Lastly, largely on account of linguistic difficulties from which many Japanese suffer, some criticisms were heard about control policy (point 2), production (point 7), and finance practices of Japanese businesses (point 10), but they were not as serious as those we heard concerning already explained features of Japanese management.

Reason for Differences. The Japanese are comparatively new in conducting businesses abroad, including business in Southeast Asia, whereas some of the American- or European-based multinational enterprises we visited had more than 100 years of business experience in the area.

Management resources including know-how and capital to transact global business possessed by many Japanese businesses are smaller and thinner than those which are possessed by American- and European-based multinational enterprises.

Being a newcomer in the field with smaller stock of resources to command, the Japanese businesses tend to become more hasty and short-sighted in conducting business abroad. As a result, their behavior or relationship with the host society has often been visualized by people in Southeast Asia as more ruthless than those of their American or European counterparts.

Japanese is not a popular language in the area, whereas almost everyone understands and speaks English as a result of its colonial history.

On top of that, the Japanese are insular and love to live among themselves in a well-structured, closed society. Therefore, many of my countrymen lack real will and ability to mix with people cross-culturally.

I believe that these are some of the important reasons why many Japanese practices have remained different from those of the West or of the East and are often criticized by both today.

CONCLUSION: RESTATEMENT OF THE PROBLEM

PROBLEMS OF THE JAPANESE TO BECOME MORE MULTI-NATIONAL IN ORDER TO PLAY THEIR ROLE IN SOUTHEAST ASIA

In spite of the existence of unpopular features attributed to the Japanese way of conducting business abroad, the MITI-JETRO sponsored study also revealed that all of the host-country government officials, without exception, looked toward the future for expanded cooperation from Japan. Some asked for Japanese assistance in their much desired regional developments. Others sought for cooperation from Japan in undertaking feasibility studies of new projects which they believed would contribute to their country's economic development and take-off. Still many others asked for practical cooperation in the supply of money and in personal development both on technical and managerial levels. There seems to be much we can do for Southeast Asia. It is also worthy to remember that there is a strong urge and program for Japanese businesses to go abroad. A meeting of minds between the two may not be so difficult as one may think. However, the trouble is that all the people in the recipient countries hope to have our cooperation and assistance in the way and manner they wish, and they may not always be identical to those which we are ready to offer.

If Japanese businesses wish to survive and grow in Southeast Asia where we can see the rise of nationalism on every horizon, we must learn how to harmonize differences of opinions and interests between the offerer and the offeree. The act of adjusting oneself to host-country requirements is one that has been sought after for the past fifteen-odd years by the so-called multinational enterprises with some success and at the same time with a lot of disheartening failures.

To live through this age of discontinuity requiring new adjustments, Japanese businesses as well as American- or European-based multinational enterprises should learn how to build a bridge over the credibility gap now developing in Southeast Asia. It is hard for everyone concerned. But as it is difficult, the price paid to those succeeding in overcoming such hardships will no doubt be well worthwhile.

Practical Approaches for Japanese Businesses to solve Problems. So much for philosophizing about the problem. If we return to the more practical aspects of the problem, what are the steps Japanese businesses should follow if they wish to be accepted as really multinationals and to play expected roles in Southeast Asia?

Let us go back to overall requirements of host-country governments as explained earlier.

The MITI and the Export and Import Bank surveys told us that we have already made considerable progress in making our contribution to the creation of local employment and to the formation of local capital markets.

Though people in the host-country government complained that we are not cooperating with the host country's export drive, our surveys previously discussed revealed the fact that we are making good progress in this direction. The comparative slowness of the shift of emphasis by Japanese businesses from domestic sales to export sales is mainly due to the recent and somewhat sudden shift of host-government policies, the pace of which many Japanese corporations have found a bit too fast to catch up in such a short space of time.

As already explained, lack of experience and stock often force the Japanese businesses to go into hasty and short-sighted excessive competition in the markets they entered. This is something we must remember and correct. However, there is a consensus among many learned Japanese that time will solve this problem. Otherwise, it will be very difficult for many Japanese businesses already operating in Southeast Asia to survive through the shift in emphasis of host-country government policies from import substitution to exports.

Regarding the criticism against our great trading companies speculating in commodity transactions, thus confusing the local economy, I can only say that by nature they are speculative and they are being so for their own survival. As a private enterprise, they may find it difficult to live in any other style of life. However, in this connection an encouraging sign was observed in the suggestion made by the Industry Structure Committe to MITI that was lately adopted by MITI as its official guideline, that is to say, "Japanese investments should be planned and implemented as a subsystem in a grand design of economic coordination with developing countries sponsored by the Japanese Government." If and when these guidelines are implemented and a workable relationship between the government and the trading companies in the so-called grand design of economic coordination makes good progress, I believe the present situation, which I must admit is somewhat acute and difficult on the stability of the host-country economy, will be much softened and relaxed.

And last, but not least in importance, is our failure in the past to transfer appropriate managerial know-how to countries that wished to receive it from Japan. Also important is the slowness of our businesses in admitting locally-hired employees to key positions in host-country operations or in corporate headquarters. Because of the large linguistic handicap and the resulting difficulty in communicating with each other ending up in the broadening of the "credibility gap" between Japanese and local people, it would, I am afraid, take more time to solve this problem than any others.

On my last trip to Southeast Asia, I recalled one of the Japanese expatriate managers remark as follows: "When all the telex communications between overseas establishments and headquarters are transacted in Japanese, and when all the customers we deal with in host country societies are Japanese, with or without certain exceptions, how can we promote and utilize the service of local people who may not understand the fine nuances of our language?"

In my opinion, at least at the present stage of international business (that is, mostly consisting of exports or export-extended local production), what I heard from my Japanese colleague on my last tour may well be justifiable. However, as I explained, we are entering into the age during which overseas direct investment will increase at an annual rate twice as fast as for exports, heading up to $26 billion toward 1980. If the future life and death of Japanese business is dependent on the accomplishment of this target, again in my opinion, no one can survive if they remain as insular as they have in the past. Let us recall some learned professor's words, "business is a human engagement." For the expanded global operations, we need a staff of managers also recruited and trained on a global scale. As I made repeated references before, it is a difficult task. Moreover, I do not know when in future this type of shift of emphasis in managerial talent recruitment and development policy begins to bear its practical significance. However, one thing is clear: Those who are ready in time can no doubt overcome the difficulty and continue to grow in the now expanding age of globalism. "For making timely shift when opportunity is ripe, let us start management recruitment and development today. Because tomorrow may be too late."

APPENDIX 1: JAPANESE OVERSEAS INVESTMENT AS OF 31 DECEMBER 1972

	Direct Investments		Loans		Other types of Investments		Establishment of branches		Total (B)	
	No. of investments (x) *1	Vol. of investments (y) *2	No.	Vol.	No.	Vol.	No.	Vol.	No. (w) *5	Vol. (z) *6
Asia	2,015 (44.9) *3	632 (20.0) *4	337 (34.5)	600 (25.7)	48 (14.9)	15 (3.2)	258 (53.2)	26 (9.0)	2,658 (42.4)	1,273 (20.4)
Latin America	440 (9.8)	502 (15.9)	285 (29.2)	342 (14.7)	38 (11.8)	6 (1.3)	14 (2.9)	2 (0.7)	777 (12.4)	853 (13.6)
Near East	32 (0.7)	11 (0.3)	- -	- -	2 (0.6)	370 (79.4)	6 (1.2)	218 (75.4)	40 (0.6)	599 (9.6)
North America	1,181 (26.3)	856 (27.0)	201 (20.6)	433 (18.6)	191 (59.1)	71 (15.2)	122 (25.2)	23 (8.0)	1,695 (27.0)	1,384 (22.1)
Europe	493 (11.0)	1,003 (31.7)	71 (7.3)	570 (24.4)	30 (9.3)	3 (0.6)	71 (14.6)	17 (5.9)	665 (10.6)	1,592 (25.5)
Africa	117 (2.6)	52 (1.6)	28 (2.9)	81 (3.5)	3 (0.9)	0 (0)	9 (1.9)	1 (0.3)	157 (2.5)	135 (2.2)
Oceania	214 (4.8)	109 (3.4)	54 (5.5)	307 (13.2)	11 (3.4)	1 (0.2)	5 (1.0)	3 (1.0)	284 (4.5)	419 (6.7)
Total (A)	4,492	3,166	976	2,334	323	466	485	289	6,276 (C)	6,255 (C)
$\frac{A}{C}$	(71.6)	(50.6)	(15.6)	(37.3)	(5.1)	(7.5)	(7.7)	(4.6)	(100.0)	(100.0)

*1 Represents number of investments *2 million US$ *3 $\frac{x_{\%}}{A}$ *4 $\frac{y_{\%}}{A}$ *5 $\frac{w_{\%}}{C}$ *6 $\frac{z_{\%}}{C}$

Source: Ministry of Finance

APPENDIX 2a: JAPANESE PRIVATE INVESTMENTS ABROAD (INDUSTRIAL CLASSIFICATION)
(in thousand US$)

Fiscal year / Industries	'51-57		'58		'59		'60		'61		'62		'63	
	No.	Acct.	No.	Acct.	No.	Acct.	No.	Acct.	No.	Acct.	No.	Acct.	No.	Acct.
Food Stuffs	5	712	1	83	10	4,339	12	1,562	13	2,988	4	2,619	10	6,706
Textiles	11	10,698	3	1,873	5	3,422	9	10,980	7	6,317	9	2,803	16	7,655
Pulp & Wooden	3	15,556	1	22,693	0	10,598	1	1,397	0	300	0	300	2	9,037
Chemical	4	157	1	95	3	122	8	736	2	298	7	927	16	3,330
Iron & Metal	2	1,878	0	2,133	3	3,787	3	2,571	4	27,157	3	616	11	2,897
Machinery	6	6,423	1	991	4	2,220	4	1,176	3	642	3	1,045	8	10,241
Electric Appliances	1	24	4	117	3	189	3	495	8	1,308	9	2,235	5	294
Transport Machinery			4	13,288	1	15	1	2,405	3	3,052	5	8,838	2	3,810
Others	10	1,311	8	1,154	5	654	7	6,555	2	2,119	7	1,368	14	3,141
Sub-Total	42	36,759	23	42,427	34	25,346	48	27,877	42	44,181	47	20,756	84	47,111
Agriculture-Forestry	7	1,319	0	250	0	538	3	1,149	0	300	6	1,633	3	1,919
Fisheries	12	1,463	2	234	5	429	7	2,130	6	1,082	5	961	2	484
Mining	25	17,176	5	13,148	4	11,510	10	44,630	5	104,086	12	34,366	3	25,534
Sub-Total	44	19,958	7	13,632	9	12,477	20	47,908	11	105,468	23	36,961	8	27,937
Construction	-	-	-	-	-	-	-	-	1	12	3	938	4	4,497
Commerce	231	13,120	25	4,216	51	10,930	59	11,716	45	5,142	66	14,148	88	13,505
Finance-Insurance	10	4,289	4	1,843	5	1,769	2	2,654	3	3,458	6	4,517	8	6,651
Others	40	4,428	19	2,520	24	2,535	22	2,570	31	6,546	34	22,106	31	26,275
Sub-Total	281	21,837	48	8,579	80	15,234	83	16,940	80	15,158	109	41,709	131	50,929
TOTAL	367	78,554	78	64,640	123	53,062	151	92,729	133	164,811	179	99,425	223	125,977

APPENDIX 2a (continued)

'64		'65		'66		'67		'68		'69		'70		Cumulative total	
No.	Acct.	No.	Acct.	No.	Acct.	No.	Acct.	No.	Acct.	No.	Acct.	No.	Acct.	No.	Acct.
2	3,568	10	3,583	5	1,618	12	6,877	7	6,233	14	4,167	30	15,785	135	60,841
19	13,504	16	5,549	15	11,270	20	16,664	31	15,120	52	34,040	46	49,898	259	189,798
2	10,347	1	3,937	5	36,419	4	2,360	5	17,280	6	3,315	14	78,815	44	212,354
5	631	20	4,178	12	9,104	16	3,345	17	4,956	24	6,286	40	25,467	175	59,632
8	15,494	5	·4,432	6	6,013	9	19,724	9	3,878	23	38,241	13	9,110	99	137,926
6	1,142	3	3,185	6	3,074	19	6,954	19	5,141	19	9,373	37	15,629	138	67,236
7	1,862	14	2,744	20	5,102	21	6,096	29	6,579	39	21,960	43	21,885	206	70,890
7	5,858	3	20,571	5	14,106	5	11,996	1	4,311	2	11,430	4	2,850	43	102,530
8	3,529	9	1,378	23	2,978	19	3,484	53	5,175	50	6,892	77	21,754	292	61,492
64	55,935	81	49,557	97	89,684	125	77,500	171	68,668	229	135,705	304	241,193	1,391	962,699
2	670	6	7,216	2	4,834	8	5,665	16	10,625	23	12,009	18	9,566	94	57,693
3	659	4	1,317	10	1,050	10	2,518	6	1,533	8	4,904	16	8,453	96	27,218
4	20,916	12	33,664	17	72,147	14	58,625	15	158,681	31	297,301	38	234,955	195	1,126,743
9	22,245	22	42,197	29	78,032	32	66,809	37	170,840	62	314,216	72	252,974	385	1,211,654
3	3,797	1	8,228	2	6,269	2	1,330	1	725	5	7,004	10	5,003	32	37,805
79	11,206	68	23,050	88	19,559	115	48,018	124	119,358	200	54,995	253	54,141	1,492	403,105
7	14,513	6	29,596	9	20,865	3	46,045	13	49,769	9	43,821	30	92,099	115	321,889
31	12,591	31	4,112	28	12,598	29	35,166	38	147,813	63	111,840	99	258,038	520	659,137
120	42,107	106	64,986	127	59,292	149	130,561	176	317,663	277	217,659	392	419,281	2,159	1,421,935
193	120,291	209	156,739	253	227,008	306	274,867	384	557,174	568	667,579	768	913,449	3,935	3,596,306

APPENDIX 2b: JAPANESE PRIVATE INVESTMENTS ABROAD (REGIONAL CLASSIFICATION)

(in thousand US$)

Fiscal year / Regions	'51-'57 No.	Acct.	'58 No.	Acct.	'59 No.	Acct.	'60 No.	Acct.	'61 No.	Acct.	'62 No.	Acct.	'63 No.	Acct.
North America	101	26,681	9	27,503	34	20,354	36	13,236	27	13,822	39	16,370	50	51,227
Latin America	77	26,034	35	23,204	31	12,802	31	22,383	28	39,218	33	29,016	41	21,192
Asia	132	23,771	23	2,879	45	9,277	64	18,855	48	28,384	75	24,047	83	26,284
Middle East	6	242	3	10,818	1	9,125	1	36,015	3	77,889	1	23,896	1	14,671
Europe	40	1,310	5	159	6	925	11	1,005	20	5,171	19	3,340	33	4,335
Africa	-	-	-	-	1	95	2	434	5	287	3	392	9	5,997
Oceania	11	515	3	77	5	484	6	801	2	39	9	2,364	6	1,671
Total	367	78,552	78	64,640	123	53,062	150	92,729	133	164,811	179	99,425	223	125,977

(in thousand US$)

'64 No.	Acct.	'65 No.	Acct.	'66 No.	Acct.	'67 No.	Acct.	'68 No.	Acct.	'69 No.	Acct.	'70 No.	Acct.	Cumulative total No.	Acct.
34	27,360	53	44,119	70	108,610	65	56,867	82	184,992	139	129,283	173	191,552	912	911,976
47	44,213	48	58,932	32	54,414	34	40,671	39	39,950	53	100,523	56	46,121	585	558,673
79	30,358	74	35,346	108	28,912	165	97,075	197	79,716	286	199,119	367	175,725	1,746	779,745
0	11,539	0	11,420	4	24,836	2	19,866	2	28,137	3	37,868	6	27,790	33	334,113
20	3,862	18	4,656	17	2,066	21	30,814	39	151,148	42	93,506	107	335,537	398	638,434
10	2,004	10	1,799	8	4,099	5	2,327	6	42,663	16	18,473	23	13,877	98	92,447
3	954	6	466	14	4,072	14	27,248	19	30,570	29	88,808	36	122,848	163	280,918
193	120,291	209	156,739	253	227,008	306	274,867	384	557,174	568	667,579	768	913,449	3935	3596,306

Source: Appendices 2-8 were taken from the Export-Import Bank of Japan, *Japanese Private Investment Abroad* (October 1972), pp. 6-7, 11-12, 24, 26, 29, 30, 33, 37 and 38.

APPENDIX 3a: MAJOR MOTIVES OF JAPANESE BUSINESS TO INVEST ABROAD (INDUSTRIAL CLASSIFICATION)

(No. of Investee Firms)

	Foodstuffs	Textiles	Chemical	Ceramic	Iron & Metal	Machinery	Electric appliances	Other Manufacturing Industries	Total
Defending local markets in host countries on account of difficulties in exporting goods from Japan		6	4		8	7	13	2	43 (18%)
Participation in new markets of host countries	3	7	1		9	3	4	11	38 (16%)
Sales of products in expanding markets of host countries	3	9	11	1	9	13	16	15	77 (33%)
Exporting finished goods to third countries		18		2	1	2	8	13	44 (19%)
Exporting finished goods to Japan	4	5	2		1	2	3	11	28 (12%)
Other		1	2					1	4 (2%)
Total	10	49	20	3	28	27	44	55	234 (100%)

APPENDIX 3b: MAJOR MOTIVES OF JAPANESE BUSINESS TO INVEST ABROAD (REGIONAL CLASSIFICATION)

(No. of Investee Firms)

	East Asia	Southeast Asia	West Asia	Latin America	Africa	Sub-total	North America	Europe	Oceania	Sub-total	Total
Defending local markets in host countries on account of difficulties in exporting goods from Japan	14	21		3	2	40		1	2	3	43
Participation in new markets of host countries	19	11		4	2	36		1	1	2	38
Sales of products in expanding markets of host countries	29	24	2	4	3	62	9	3	3	15	77
Exporting finished goods to third countries	38	5		1		44					44
Exporting finished goods to Japan	15	5			2	22	1		5	6	28
Other	2	1				3			1	1	4
Total	117	67	2	12	9	207	10	5	12	27	234

Note: This table covered only overseas projects conducted by manufacturing industries in fiscal 1968 and fiscal 1969.

APPENDIX 4: ADVANTAGES VISUALIZED BY JAPANESE BUSINESSES IN MAKING THEIR INVESTMENTS ABROAD (INDUSTRIAL CLASSIFICATION)

(No. of Investee Firms)

	Food-stuffs	Textiles	Chemical	Ceramic	Iron & Metal	Machi-nery	Electric Machinery	Other	Total	The last research
Governmental protective policy for industries in host countries	1	17	6		20	12	19	4	79 (34%)	191 (47%)
Abundant supply of human resources		24	2	2	4	7	19	29	87 (38%)	80 (20%)
Abundant supply of raw materials and energy resources	3	1	2		1	1		8	16 (7%)	30 (7%)
An advantage in producing close to the consumer markets	3	3	10	1	2	2	3	10	34 (15%)	70 (17%)
Trade of products with other countries		3			2	1	3		9 (4%)	15 (4%)
Other	1		1			2		1	5 (2%)	20 (5%)
Total	8	48	21	3	29	25	44	52	230 (100%)	406 (100%)

APPENDIX 4b: ADVANTAGES VISUALIZED BY JAPANESE BUSINESSES IN MAKING THEIR INVESTMENTS ABROAD (REGIONAL CLASSIFICATION)

(No. of Investee Firms)

	East Asia	Southeast Asia	West Asia	Latin America	Africa	Sub-total	North America	Europe	Oceania	Sub-total	Total
Governmental protective policy for industries in host countries	22	40		8	4	74	1	1	3	5	79
Abundant supply of human resources	76	7	1	1	1	86		1		1	87
Abundant supply of raw materials and energy resources	2	6			2	10	1		5	6	16
An advantage in producing close to the consumer markets	10	10	1	1	2	24	6	1	3	10	34
Trade of products with other countries	6	1		1		8		1		1	6
Other				1		1	2	1	1	4	5
Total	116	64	2	12	9	203	10	5	12	27	230

APPENDIX 5: SCALE OF JAPANESE OVERSEAS INVESTMENTS (SCALE OF INVESTMENTS PER PROJECT)

(No. of Investee Firms)

Capital	Manufacturing industries		Agriculture-forestries, fisheries & mining		Construction and Service industries		Total	
Less than $100,000	148	24%	30	24%	6	23%	184	24%
More than $100,000 less than $300,000	167	27%	26	21%	7	27%	200	26%
More than $300,000 less than $1,000,000	169	28%	29	24%	8	31%	206	27%
More than $1,000,000 less than $5,000,000	106	17%	26	21%	5	19%	137	18%
More than $5,000,000 less than $10,000,000	11	2%	4	3%			15	2%
More than $10,000,000	12	2%	9	7%			21	3%
Total	613	100%	124	100%	26	100%	763	100%

APPENDIX 5b: SCALE OF OVERSEAS OPERATING UNITS BY NUMBER OF EMPLOYEES

(No. of Investee Firms)

Industries / Employees	Manufacturing industries		Agriculture-forestry, fishery & mining		Construction and Service Industries		Total	
Less than 50	157	28%	38	44%	13	59%	208	32%
51 - 100	82	15%	12	14%	3	14%	97	15%
101 - 500	237	43%	24	27%	6	27%	267	40%
More than 501	76	14%	13	15%			89	13%
Total	552	100%	87	100%	22	100%	661	100%

APPENDIX 5c: PERCENTAGE OF JAPANESE OWNERSHIP IN OVERSEAS OPERATING ESTABLISHMENTS

The percentage of capital participation by Japanese Investor Firms	- 24%	25-49%	50%	51-74%	75-99%	100%
Total	111	205	125	93	97	134
Manufacturing industries	79	176	116	82	74	86
Agriculture-forestry, fisheries & mining	31	24	8	7	20	36
Construction & service industries	1	5	1	4	3	12

Note: The figures indicate the number of investee firms.

APPENDIX 6a: PROFIT AND LOSS STATEMENT OF JAPANESE BUSINESS OPERATING ABROAD (INDUSTRIAL CLASSIFICATION)

(No. of Investee Firms)

	Profit during the recent period						Accumulated Profit						Dividend				Total Number of Answers
	Surplus		Break-even		Defi-cit		Surplus		Break-even		Defi-cit		With di-vidends		No divi-dends		
	No.	%	No.	%	No.	%	No.	%	No.	%	No.	%	No.	%	No.	%	
Agriculture & Forestry	5	31	1	6	10	63	4	25		12		75	2	12	14	88	16
Fisheries	10	50	1	5	9	45	9	45		11		55	3	15	17	85	20
Mining	13	65	1	5	6	30	9	45	1	10	5	50	5	25	15	75	20
Sub-total	28	50	3	5	25	45	22	39	1	33	2	59	10	18	46	82	56
Foodstuffs	29	67	2	5	12	28	20	46	2	21	5	49	14	33	29	67	43
Textiles	62	75	5	6	16	19	51	63	3	29	4	35	42	51	41	49	83
Chemical	25	61	5	12	11	27	23	56	1	17	2	42	14	34	27	66	41
Ceramic	11	92			1	8	9	75		3		25	7	58	5	42	12
Iron & Metal	31	62	5	10	14	28	25	50	2	23	4	46	16	32	34	68	50
Machinery	29	54	5	3	20	37	23	42	2	29	4	54	11	20	43	80	54
Electric Machinery	37	58	1	1	26	41	34	53	3	27	5	42	23	36	41	64	64
Other	31	46	3	4	34	50	28	41	3	37	4	54	15	22	53	78	68
Sub-total	255	62	26	6	134	32	213	51	16	186	4	45	142	34	273	66	415
Construction & Service	8	67			4	33	3	25			9	75	3	25	9	75	12
Total	291	60	29	6	163	34	238	49	17	4	228	47	155	32	328	68	483

APPENDIX 6b: PROFIT AND LOSS STATEMENT OF JAPANESE BUSINESS OPERATING ABROAD (REGIONAL CLASSIFICATION)

(No. of Investee Firms)

	Profit during the recent period						Accumulated Profits						Dividend				Total Number of Answers
	Surplus		Break-even		Deficit		Surplus		Break-even		Deficit		With dividends		No dividends		
	No.	%	No.	%	No.	%	No.	%	No.	%	No.	%	No.	%	No.	%	
East Asia	98	56	13	7	64	37	82	47	7	4	86	49	55	31	120	69	175
Southeast Asia	99	74	6	4	29	22	83	62	3	2	48	36	56	42	78	58	134
West Asia					1	100					1	100			1	100	1
Latin America	42	58	4	6	26	36	31	43	3	4	38	53	18	25	54	75	72
Africa	16	64	4	16	5	20	15	60	3	12	7	28	13	52	12	48	25
Sub-total	255	63	27	6	125	31	211	52	16	4	180	44	142	35	265	65	407
North America	20	50	2	5	18	45	14	35	1	2	25	63	5	12	35	88	40
Europe	6	46			7	54	5	38			8	62	3	23	10	77	13
Oceania	10	43			13	57	8	35			15	65	5	22	18	78	23
Sub-total	36	47	2	3	38	50	27	36	1	1	48	63	13	17	63	83	76
Total	291	60	29	6	163	34	238	49	17	4	228	47	155	32	328	68	483

APPENDIX 6c: DIFFERENCES BETWEEN THE SCHEDULED AND THE ACTUAL IMPORTS OF JAPANESE BUSINESSES IN THE FIELD OF NATURAL RESOURCE DEVELOPMENT

(No. of Investee Firms)

	Agriculture-forestry	Fishery	Mining	Total
Imports beyond schedule	1	2	13	16 (22%)
Imports as scheduled	7	4	8	19 (26%)
Sub-total	8	6	21	35 (48%)
Imports below schedule	16	12	11	39 (52%)
Total	24	18	32	74 (100%)

APPENDIX 7: ENVIRONMENT DIFFICULTIES ENCOUNTERED BY JAPANESE BUSINESSES OPERATING ABROAD

Region	Total		East Asia		South-east Asia		West Asia		Latin America		Africa		Sub-total		North America		Europe		Oceania		Sub-total	
No. of Answers	694		244		205		3		99		37		588		53		19		34		106	
	No.	%	No.	%	No.	%	No.	%	No.	%	No.	%	No.	%	No.	%	No.	%	No.	%	No.	%
No. of firms which have had some difficulties abroad	413	60	145	59	125	61	2	67	79	80	22	59	373	63	20	38	8	42	12	35	40	38
Particulars of difficulties	413	100	145	100	125	100	2	100	79	100	22	100	373	100	20	100	8	100	12	100	40	100
Unstable political situation	50	12	4	3	19	15			18	23	7	32	48	13			2	25			2	5
Inflationary pressure	62	15	8	6	12	10			38	48			58	16	4	20					4	10
Economic depression	50	12	9	6	24	19			8	10	2	9	43	12	5	25	2	25			7	18
Restricted import of maintenance parts because of foreign currency deficit in host countries	62	15	11	8	35	28			9	11	6	27	61	16					1	8	1	3
Low productivity of labour	75	18	15	10	24	19			15	19	4	18	'58	16	11	55	1	13	5	42	17	43

Region	Total		East Asia		South-east Asia		West Asia		Latin America		Africa		Sub-total		North America		Europe		Oceania		Sub-total	
No. of Answers	694		244		205		3		99		37		588		53		19		34		106	
	No.	%	No.	%	No.	%	No.	%	No.	%	No.	%	No.	%	No.	%	No.	%	No.	%	No.	%
Severe treatment for foreign capital	73	18	30	21	19	15			19	24	3	14	71	19					2	17	2	5
Complicated administrative procedure	132	32	62	43	36	29			21	27	7	32	126	34			4	50	2	17	6	15
High Tax	39	9	12	8	9	7	1	50	15	19	1	5	38	10					1	8	1	3
Financial difficulties	90	22	42	29	18	14			18	23	1	5	79	21	5	25	1	13	5	42	11	28
Shortage in transportation and electric power	20	5	6	4	9	7			2	3	1	5	18	5			1	13	1	8	2	5
Incomplete marketing route	38	9	18	12	10	8	1	50	2	3	6	27	37	10	1	5					1	3
Different commercial practices	22	5	10	7	3	2			6	8			19	5	2	10			1	8	3	8

APPENDIX 8: FUTURE PLANS OF JAPANESE BUSINESSES OPERATING ABROAD

	Manufacturing industries	Agriculture-forestry, fishery & mining	Construction and Service industries	Total
No. of answers	564	97	23	684 (100%)
Not to have new plan	213	37	10	260 (38%)
To have new plan	351	60	13	424 (62%)
Expanded improved equipment	230	42	12	284
The production and sale of new products	164		2	166
Expanded export	27			27
Examining second plan		8		8
Reduce or abandon business	7	6		13
Others	18	5		23

Note: Duplicated answer was permitted.

27

Japan's Mid-East Economic Diplomacy

Terutomo Ozawa

Suddenly the Mideast has emerged as one of the world's richest markets. It is estimated that the oil-producing nations in that region will amass a cash surplus of about $60 billion by the end of 1974—despite their considerable efforts to spend their oil revenues to modernize their own economies and despite the sizeable sums contributed to regional development funds designed to assist their non-oil-producing neighbors. The rich Arab nations are, for the moment at least, being inundated by wealth undreamed of, and are, happily for the world's businessmen, at a loss as to how to dispose of it wisely. There is no shortage of advice, both solicited and unsolicited. Bankers, consultants, and industrialists from all over the world, as well as officials of various governments and agents of international organizations such as the United Nations, are making pilgrimages to the Middle East, offering consultations and blandishments, jockeying for business and favors. As might well be expected, among the most active and eager of the nationals seeking to capitalize on opportunities in the Mideast are the Japanese.

Since Japan is dependent on the Mideast for about 85 percent of her oil supply, her stake in the Mideast is extraordinary. The recent quadruple rise in the price of crude oil since the beginning of 1974 has made the Mideast Japan's biggest import partner; the Mideast now outstrips Southeast Asia and the United States, previously Japan's first and second suppliers. Moreover, the rich Mideast is rapidly becoming one of Japan's most important customers for exports in practically all manufacturers, ranging from petrochemical plants and ships to motorcycles and desk-top calculators. This development is a reprieve for market-pressed Japan. Partly because of her recent important liberalization and increased capital outflows and more importantly because of soaring prices of oil and other imported raw materials, Japan's foreign reserves have quickly diminished. Now Japan has returned to her well-trod route of export promotion. Yet she can no longer expect to expand her exports to the United States, Europe, and neighboring Asian countries as rapidly as in the past without creating political frictions. In these markets, equally troubled by oil-pinched trade difficulties, protectionistic feelings are on the upsurge. The Middle East is, at the moment, perhaps the only market to which Japan can direct her export drive without incurring the wrath of local interests.

Indeed, the appearance of "made-in-Japan" products, together with that of Japanese businessmen, is becoming conspicuous throughout the

---

Reprinted with permission from the Fall, 1974, issue of the *Columbia Journal of World Business*.

region. Even in the remote corners of the Arabian desert, goat keepers are now seen riding Honda motocycles instead of camels. Toyotas and Datsuns are making their debut on shining new highways as quickly as they are constructed. As recently as last October, Americans were the biggest single suppliers to the Arab world. Although Japan was greatly dependent on oil from Saudi Arabia, Iran, Kuwait, and Abu Dhabai, she scarcely had economic relations with the Arabs in fields other than oil, which was, after all, imported mainly through the international oil majors. In a very short span of time, however, Japan has made an astonishingly swift and successful advance into the Mideast market, taking advantage of the rapidly changing political and economic climates of the region. This essay discusses how Japan, initially badly shaken by the oil embargo, has come out as a substantial gainer in the Mideast market.

FROM INITIAL PANIC TO OPPORTUNISM

When the Arab oil embargo was announced in October, 1973, the Japanese reacted emotionally to the prospect of a sudden grinding to a halt of their gigantic industrial wheel. In the ensuing month the Economic Planning Agency made some gloomy predictions; it said, for example, that if the 10 percent cutback of oil shipments should continue until September, 1974, the real growth rate of GNP for fiscal 1974 would be a mere 1.7 percent. Further, the real growth rate would become negative by as much as 5.5 percent in the event of a continuation of the oil cutback throughout 1974. Abruptly, the outlook for the Japanese economy became clouded; it was possible that the worst recession in Japan's postwar history might occur. Expected reductions in industrial output and higher fuel costs would also mean aggravation of supply shortages and inflation, which had already reached serious levels. Many Japanese consumers turned to the hoarding of daily necessities such as sugar, soap, light bulbs, and toilet paper, creating hysterical scenes at supermarkets. A local bank had a run on deposits because of a groundless rumor. The panic-prone mentality of the Japanese clearly reflected their deep-seated feeling of insecurity and the fragility of their confidence in their resource-scarce economy.

However, as in similar situations in the past, the emotional frustration and anxiety of the Japanese was soon replaced by realistic and aggressive self-defensive actions. Business leaders, in particular, quickly saw the need to take a pro-Arab stance and to seek openly an assured supply of oil. They urged the government to send a special envoy to the Mideast. Japan maintained a politically neutral policy on the Arab-Israeli conflict.

True, even before the outbreak of the October War the tentacles of Japanese industry were reaching purposefully toward the Mideast oil-producing nations. The Japan-Iran Investment Council, designed to assist Iran's economic development, had already been formed—and a plan had also been underway to set up a similar organization for Saudi Arabia. But the oil embargo provided a decisive impetus to these movements. The Japan-Saudi Arabia Cooperative Association formally came into existence on October 12, 1973, with Ataru Kobayashi, chairman of Arabian Oil Co., as its head. Similar organizations to extend economic cooperation on a bilateral basis with each of other Mideast oil-producing countries rapidly came under consideration.

These moves of Japanese industry dovetailed with the so-called multipolar resources diplomacy pushed by the government. Because of her increased dependence on overseas energy resources, Japan was eagerly seeking ways to ensure energy supplies by diversifying supply sources. Japan tended to reduce in proportion, if not in absolute terms, its lopsided reliance on the United States, particularly its U.S. oil interests, and to seek out independent energy sources in other areas such as the Mideast, Latin America, and the U.S.S.R.

The prime official architect and promoter of this policy was the Ministry of International Trade and Industry (MITI). In October, 1973, following up on the momentum gathered by industry and the urgency created by the Arab oil crisis, the MITI quickly moved to establish a comprehensive semi-governmental organization, called the Middle East Cooperative Center, designed to coordinate and support the activities of privately-established cooperative organizations and to channel governmental funds for economic assistance to the Mideast. In the following month MITI also announced a policy to increase gradually Japan's import of crude oil directly from oil-producing nations. Currently, Japan is purchasing the bulk of her oil through international oil majors. In 1972, for example, a mere 2 percent of the total crude imported was obtained directly from oil-producing countries. The MITI's new policy aims at raising the ratio to a level of as much as 40 percent by the end of the decade.

As a first step toward achieving this goal the MITI worked out a plan to expand the role of the Japan Petroleum Development Corporation (JPDC), a government-created institution whose function was, under the original setup, confined to a supportive role in assisting industry to explore oil and natural gas resources abroad. This institution extended or guaranteed exploration loans, leased drilling equipment, offered technical assistance and served as an information center. The MITI now intends to revise the existing laws to assign much more active capacities to the JPDC, enabling it directly to acquire concessions, to participate in investments in oil-producing countries, and to stockpile crude oil.

Understandably, Japan's rush for direct bilateral agreements disturbed not only the Western oil majors but also their governments, particularly that of the United States, which advocated a solid front of the oil-consuming industrial countries against the price-hike demands of the oil-producing countries. Their startled reaction was clearly reflected in Western reporters' descriptions of Japan's move as "a blatant surrender" or "an unabashed effort." Yet Japan, reassured in part by the recalcitrant attitude displayed by France toward U.S. leadership, pushed her oil diplomacy vigorously during the oil cutbacks.

The Tanaka Administration dispatched special envoys, one after another, to the Mideast. The first on the road was Vice Prime Minister Takeo Miki, who visited eight Arab nations, including Saudi Arabia, Kuwait, and Egypt in December, 1973. A month later, his visit was followed in quick succession by those of Minister of the MITI Yasuhiro Nakasone, former Foreign Minister Zentaro Kosaka, and Speaker of the House of Representatives Shigesaburo Maeo. Their missions were not exactly defined; they were sent for the purpose of "explaining Japan's position on the Mideast." Their real intent was, no doubt, to curry favor of the oil-producing nations for an assurance of oil supplies. In exchange, Japan offered generous financial and technical assistance for the economic development of the region. In fact, the administration was extremely eager to seek favor—so much that the amount of aid and loans offered by these envoys added up to about $3 billion (including $1 billion each to Iran and Iraq, and $280 million to Egypt), an amount five times as large as the total amount of official Japanese aid (approximately $600 million) appropriated in 1972.[1] Indeed, this phase of diplomacy momentarily left both the Ministry of Finance and the Ministry of Foreign Affairs worried about the consequences.

All in all, Japan's diplomatic efforts proved quite effective. Her willingness to extend economic cooperation was soon matched by the eagerness of Mideast countries to request Japan's cooperation for industrialization, and the visits made by Japan's government officials were promptly reciprocated by officials of the Arab world—partly as a calculated gesture to show the West that there were alternative sources of technical expertise needed by the Arabs for industrialization, but mostly in an earnest search for industrial and technical assistance.

During the visit of MITI's chief, Iraq promised to provide Japan with 160 million tons of crude oil, liquified petroleum gas, and petroleum products over the next ten years in return for Japan's economic and technical cooperation, including a $1 billion loan at 5.25 percent per annum.

No sooner had the new year of 1974 arrived than the oil cutbacks to Japan were removed and Japan was placed on the Arabs' list of "friendly nations." The Japanese were further gratified to learn that the Arabs, after all, had not curtailed oil shipments to Japan as much as originally planned and that Japan's oil reserves had not dwindled as much as feared.

Then in February, 1974, came a visit to Japan by Saudi Arabian Oil Minister Sheik Ahmed Zaki Yamani; he reached an agreement on Japan's economic and technological cooperation with Saudi Arabia. He reportedly stated that "Japan is in the No. 1 position both to help us and to be the recipient of Saudi Arabian oil on a long term basis."[2] In the same month, Japan also received from Algeria a mission headed by Industry and Energy Minister Belaid Abdessalam. The Algerians solicited Japan's cooperation for their second four-year industrialization program. This contact resulted in numerous business relations between the two countries as will be discussed below. Egypt also secured Japan's commitment to a loan of $240 million for repair work on the Suez Canal and other projects when Egyptian Vice Prime Minister Mohammed Hatem visited Tokyo.

INDETERMINATE POLICY AND LUCK

In contrast to its determined Mideast foreign policy, domestic economic measures introduced by the Japanese were hesitant. Although the government did announce a program of emergency measures to cope with the oil crisis in November, 1973, it was rather half-hearted in implementing the program. Besides, the program itself remained very broadly stated and ambiguous as to specific strategies. It was designed:

- to launch a nationwide oil economy drive;
- to reduce consumption of oil and electric power by 10 percent in 12 energy-consuming industries (i.e., steel, automobile, shipbuilding, petrochemicals, electric machinery, auto tire, synthetic fiber, aluminum refining, nonferrous metal smelting, cement, sheet glass, and paper);
- to legislate emergency laws that would empower the government to restrict the use of fuel and to prevent speculation;
- to strengthen measures for reducing aggregate demand and holding down prices; and
- to take steps actively to find new sources of energy.

Lack of any action was observed with amazement by a Western reporter:

> Private and government economists warn that Japan's fuel supplies are dwindling quickly and that serious shortages could crop up as early as next month. But the streets and highways, even on Sundays, seem more clogged than ever with pleasure drivers. . . No industrialized nation, at least on paper, is more vulnerable to a prolonged oil squeeze than Japan. . . .Yet, despite this vulnerability, no country's population or government seems to have done less to prepare for the crisis that a prolonged oil shortage will bring. . . .But while the British make plans for a three-day workweek and Sunday driving bans spring up through the rest of Europe, the Japanese sit and wait.[3]

The "sit-and-wait" attitude was probably tolerated because of Japan's stepped-up oil diplomacy, which seemed to promise that Japan's energy clouds would have some silver linings. In any event, whether this lack of policy action was an intended gamble on the part of the Tanaka Administration, or whether it was merely a result of the administration's incompetence in planning and implementation, the stake involved was enormous. According to an estimate made by the MITI, Japan's stockpile of crude oil and oil products, standing at a 57-day supply at the end of October, 1973, would fall to the precarious level of a 32-day supply by the end of March, 1974, were it not for restrictions on oil consumption.

Both policy makers and outside observers watched in suspense as the indeterminate attitude of the administration turned out—by sheer luck—to be perhaps the best short-term strategy. In sharp contrast to the British economy which resorted to the Draconian measure of a mandatory three-day work-week and produced "the bleakest Christmas since the war" with serious implications for the longer-run state of its economy, the Japanese economy came out of the storm largely unscathed—readier than ever to expand output for the shortage-prone world market.

With the lifting of the oil embargo, the usual mood of optimism returned and permeated the Japanese economy. Committed to its recent program of import liberalization, the Japanese economy turned to exports as a way of meeting the high bill of imported oil which had shot up from $7 billion in 1973 to an estimated $15 billion for 1974. Although the government denied any new measures to stimulate exports, Japan's exports in January, 1974, measured on a letter-of-credit basis, reached $1.73 billion—an increase of 40.5 percent over the previous year's figures. Half of the increase was said to be attributable to inflation, but another major cause was the unloading of a wide variety of petroleum-based products, such as chemical fertilizer, plastics, and synthetic fibers—the goods Japanese manufacturers and trading companies had stockpiled during the oil cutbacks. Exports continued to climb and recorded in May the highest monthly figure in history—$5 billion or 60.5 percent over those a year ago.[4]

The buoyed-up mood of industry and the brightened prospect for Japanese exports soon led to new business plans to invest in heavy and chemical sectors again, despite the recently announced decision of the MITI to curb investments. The steel industry, for example, intends to increase its investment spending as much as 40 percent in 1974-75. Both the petrochemical and the aluminum smelting sectors are reportedly planning to double their investments, and the oil refining investment will increase as much as 90 percent.[5] Although the tight money policy designed to prevent runaway inflation depressed the growth rate of the Japanese economy for the first half of 1974, the optimism of the business sector is most likely to lead the economy to a quick recovery once the monetary rein is slackened.

TRADING COMPANIES AS VANGUARDS

The government's favor-seeking diplomacy under the pressure of the oil crisis has ended up successfully, paving the way for industry to advance. Japan's omnipresent general trading companies are the spearheads. Practically all of Japan's industrial projects in the Mideast are either intermediated by, or participated in, by trading companies in one way or another. A long time before the sudden recent emergence of the Mideast as the world's economic focal point, Japanese traders were laying out their marketing networks and cultivating local businesses. Only a year ago they were the only resident Japanese in the desert kingdoms and sheikdoms. This fact is clearly illustrated by the following episode:

On a hot day in July, 1973, a Japan Air Lines jumbo jet lifted off from Amsterdam's Schipol Airport and was very soon hijacked by a band of Palestinian guerillas.

Changing its course to the southeast it put down at Dubai in the United Arab Emirates. In Dubai, at the time, there was only one resident Japanese. He was not a diplomat, nor an accredited correspondent of any newspaper—he was a representative of Japan's leading trading organization, the Mitsubishi Corporation. Eventually, the jumbo jet left Dubai and, landing at Benghazi, in Libya, the passengers were freed and the plane was blown up. Not surprisingly, there were two representatives of the Marubeni Corporation in Benghazi and they, together with the five members of that company's Tripoli office and representatives there of Mitsui & Co. and of Sumitomo Shoji Kaisha, were very active in caring for the passengers of the plane and in conveying messages to Tokyo.[6]

The trading companies have been commission brokers for both domestic and foreign trade throughout Japan's industrial history. Their demise was rumored once in the face of the increasing takeover in the postwar period of global marketing and purchasing functions by Japanese manufacturers themselves. But the trading companies have rejuvenated themselves as indispensable providers of world-wide information and as active participants, both financially and managerially, in Japan's new emerged multinationalism. They have an unparalleled network for gathering information on political and economic conditions in practically every important corner of the earth —their ability is often said to be on a par with that of the CIA. Although there are more than six thousand trading companies in Japan, most significant are the top ten companies, whose combined total sales are equivalent to nearly 30 percent of Japan's GNP.[7]

Exhibit 1 shows major projects secured or being negotiated by Japanese industry as of the end of June, 1974, each involving big trading companies directly or indirectly. These contracts may not yet be significant in scale, but they certainly mark a strategically important beginning by providing footholds for the further advance of Japanese industry.

Particularly worth noting is Japan's new advance in Algeria, made in response to the latter's call for assistance in economic development. To carry out various projects for Algeria's second four-year economic plan, five major Japanese trading companies (Mitsubishi Corporation, Mitsui & Co., Marubeni Corporation, C. Itoh & Co., and Sumitomo Shoji Kaisha) signed an agreement with SONATRAC, Algeria's state-owned oil-gas corporation, which represented the Algerian side. Twenty other giant Japanese corporations[8] are expected to participate in the assistance program. This is the first time that an assistance program for economic development, normally concluded as an intergovernmental agreement, has been entrusted to a group of trading companies. This unprecedented arrangement may mark a new approach to developing countries by Japanese business. No doubt, Japan's major trading companies have a unique organizational capacity to provide concerted and comprehensive industrial and technical assistance to developing countries since each represents its own *keiretsu* group—an oligopolistic conglomerate of heterogeneous, yet mutually complementary, firms which came to replace, or to reinforce, its former *zaibatsu* group.

Thus, the above agreement is most likely to assure well-coordinated economic cooperation from Japanese industry.

In April, 1974, SONATRAC also signed a contract with Toyo Engineering Corporation and C. Itoh & Co. to establish, on a turnkey basis, a huge plant maintenance and repair complex for Algeria'a pipe-line making, oil refining, petrochemical, natural-gas liquefying, and mining industries. The Japanese group is expected to "set up a staff of 3,000 technicians at the center for taking over all of the maintenance work hitherto handled by European and U.S. firms and also to train machinery processing and repairing experts."[9]

The ability of Japanese trading companies to organize overseas production is not limited to their closely affiliated compatriot firms alone, however. They are becoming increasingly active in pulling together industrial firms of major countries in a truly multinational setup. This trend is clearly evidenced by the overseas activities of C. Itoh & Co. which recently organized an iron mill venture in Egypt. The $200 million mill, to be constructed near Alexandria, is a joint venture among the Egyptian government (50 percent ownership), C. Itoh & Co., Korf-Stahl AG of West Germany, and Compahia Vale do Rio Doce of Brazil. Korf-Stahl will supply technology to directly reduce iron ore to sponge iron; the Brazilian partner will provide iron ore; and Egypt will provide natural gas to fuel the plant.[10] C. Itoh also succeeded in setting up a multinational petrochemical company, called Saudi Hydrocarbon, in Saudi Arabia with the participation of Ashland Oil of the United States, Sunkyong-Teijin and Chon Engineering, both of South Korea, National Chemical of Saudi Arabia, and Teijin of Japan. This venture is expected to start its operation in 1976, producing petrochemical derivatives initially, but later developing into an integrated petrochemical complex with an ethylene plant as its center.[11]

Thus, Japan's trading companies have emerged as eager and efficient organizers to arrange projects on a multinational basis whenever such opportunities exist. With an expanded role to play, these companies are making all-out efforts to strengthen their Mideast operations by reorganizing their corporate structures, by placing able staffs in the region, and even by enrolling some of their employees at Arab universities to produce regional experts.

In addition to individual financial aid promised to each oil-producing country, the Japanese government has offered to help Arab nations establish a Pan-Arab telecommunications network, a project planned by the Arab Telecommunications Union formed by 14 Arab nations in Cairo. The project is estimated to cost approximately $330 million, and the Japanese government has indicated its willingness to extend a loan of $70 million. Initially, several Japanese companies, notably Nippon Electric Co. which had already set up highly rated microwave facilities in Mideast countries such as Iran, Egypt, and Libya, maneuvered separately to win orders. But Nippon Electric has recently formed a multinational consortium with Hughes Aircraft of the United States and Thomson-CSF of France to tender a comprehensive bid

EXHIBIT 1: MAJOR JAPANESE PROJECTS IN THE MIDDLE EAST (at the end of June, 1974)

Country	A. Under Construction		B. Under Negotiation	
	Project	Contractor	Project	Bidder
Abu Dhabi	LNG station	Chiyoda Chemical & Engineering		
	LNG tank	Ishikawajima-Harima		
	Cement plant	Ishikawajima-Harima		
Algeria	2 cement plants	Kawasaki, H. I.	Oil Refinery	Chiyoda Chemical & Engineering
	Ethylene plant	Toyo Engineering		Japan Gasoline Toyo Engineering
	Repair center	Nippon Steel Toyo Engineering		
	Telecommunications networks	Fujitsu		
	Consulting for economic development planning	The Long-Term Credit Bank of Japan		
Iran	Cement plant	Kawasaki, H. I.	Cement	Kawasaki, H. I.
	Cement plant	Ishikawajima-Harima		
	Vinyl chloride plasticizer plant	Mitsubishi, H. I.	Textiles	Mitsubishi Corp.
	Galvanized steel sheet plant	Kawasaki Steel		
	Plant manufacturing & engineering firm	Chiyoda Chemical & engineering		
Iraq	Fertilizer plant	Mitsubishi, H. I.	2 fertilizer plants	Mitsubishi, H. I.
			LPG plant	
			Oil refinery	Mitsubishi, H. I. Sumitomo Shoji
Kuwait	Seawater desalination	Ishikawajima-Harima	Power generation	Ishikawajima-Harima Tokyo Shibaura
			Prawn fishing & processing	Nissho-Iwaii
Libya			Seawater desalination	Hitachi Sasakura Engineering
Ras Al Khaimah	Cement plant	Ishikawajima-Harima		
Saudi Arabia	2 oil refineries	Chiyoda Chemical & Engineering	Lubricator plant	Chiyoda Chemical & Engineering
	2 cement plants	Ishikawajima-Harima	Truck plant	Nissan Motor Co.
	Steelworks	Nippon Steel Nippon Kakan K.K. (in joint venture with U.S. and European steel firms)		
	Steel pipe plant	Sumitomo Metal Industries Sumitomo Shoji		
	Agricultural development planning	Pacific Consultants K.K.		
Sudan			Fertilizer plant	Toyo Engineering
Syria			Oil refinery	(a group of Japanese firms)
Qatar	Steelworks	Kobe Steel		

SOURCE: Compiled from reports published in *Nihon Keizai Shimbun*.

for the project. Hughes will be in charge of designing, developing, and producing a telecommunications satellite and its system, and the other two companies for constructing ground facilities.[12]

Shipbuilding is another area in which the Japanese economy has benefited from the newly acquired economic power of the Arab world. Largely because of its long-standing business ties with Kuwait Oil Tankers Co., Sasebo Heavy Industries Co. has recently secured an order for a 260,000 dwt tanker, the seventh supertanker to be constructed for Kuwait by the company—all paid for in cash. Kuwait also placed an order with Mitsubishi Heavy Industries Co. for another still-larger 394,000 dwt crude carrier. These companies and other Japanese shipyards are expected to receive more orders from those Arab countries which are eager to develop their own merchant fleets to transport oil.[13]

Japan's export of consumer products is also likely to rise at a phenomenal pace, since its export drive is now firmly directed to the Mideast. For example, since Bahrein and Jordan have just started television broadcasting, and since Kuwait, Dubai, and Saudi Arabia will soon follow suit, the region is no doubt a prime target for Japanese color manufacturers, whose sales at home and in overseas markets have recently become sluggish.

DEBACLE IN A SHOW-CASE PROJECT

Japan's oil diplomacy and industrial advance in the Mideast has not been without snags. Its vigor was somewhat weakened in March, 1974, when the Iranian government turned down Japan's offer to help construct an oil refinery and petrochemical complex with a financial assistance of $1 billion. Iran's rejection was due perhaps to a combination of economic and political reasons. Iran, in addition to shipping to Japan, wanted some part of the refineries' naptha output to be used as feedstock for "downstream" petrochemical projects. Such an expanded plan would cost Japan another $1 billion, for which the Japanese government was reluctant to make a commitment. Iran also appeared to be annoyed by Japan's rapprochement with Iraq, with which it has had border skirmishes. Toyota's proposal to build an automobile assembly plant also hit a snag. The company had planned to produce 50,000 vehicles a year while the host country demanded a plant capacity of 500,000 vehicles.[14]

Japan's debacle in the Iranian petroleum project, which had been intended to be a show-case of economic cooperation on a bilateral basis, provided Japan with an opportunity to review its precipitate Mideast diplomacy, formulated under the pressure of the oil crisis. Indeed, Japan's impetuous rush for bilateral deals was severely assailed by the United States. With oil in abundant supply again, Japan recovered from its initial fluster, and began to mend its relations with Western countries. In April, 1974, the Japanese government formally announced its intention to move from the bilateral approach to a multilateral policy, with an emphasis on cooperation with other industrial countries, particularly the United States. The announcement of this policy change proved timely—or perhaps was so designed, since the Arab world, having initially directed its oil weapon against the United States, quickly made a 180 degree turn to become pro-American when the peace agreements with Israel were skillfully mediated by the United States. Then President Nixon's triumphant Mideast visit climaxed this drastic shift in the political atmosphere of the region. Egypt in particular is now bent on inviting capital and technology from the capitalist countries to accelerate its industrialization. How real and meaningful the announced policy turnabout of the Japanese government is remains to be seen. However, in the light of recent disarray in the diplomatic front of the Western powers themselves, France signed a massive bilateral deal in July, 1974, with Iran for the sale of $5 billion worth of nuclear reactors and other high-technology items; and U.S. Treasury Secretary William Simon visited the Middle East in the same month offering development aid on a bilateral basis.

ARENA FOR NEW GLOBAL COOPERATION

The emergence of the Mideast as an affluent economic region is definitely a boon to the Japanese economy, constantly in search of new markets for its export of manufacturers as well as for capital and technology. In fact, the increased bill for oil imports is an easily surmountable problem for Japan over the long haul, if not in the short-run, and it is but a small price to pay in light of the potential benefits Japan can expect from its successful advance in the Mideast.

Yet political developments in the Arab world, still delicately balanced by the power plays of the United States and the Soviet Union, are only dormant. As the vital supplier of crude oil to the industrialized world, the Mideast is a convergent point of the most intensive diplomacies of the individual countries. Economic nationalism is another factor to be reckoned with. In the face of these political complexities, Japanese industry is cognizant of the political risks involved in doing business on their own. What is more, the projects demanded by the Mideast countries are often so huge that the multinational approaches in financial and industrial arrangements are increasingly called for.

Similar views of the prospects of business development in the Mideast and a need for cooperation are probably shared by many firms of other industrialized countries. Relatively unrestricted movement of capital and labor into the Arab world, particularly from neighboring countries into Saudi Arabia and Abu Dhabi, has already taken place. A *de facto* economic integration thus appears to be in the making. The Mideast may turn out to be an unexpected arena in which the current world-wide business trend toward multinationalism can reach a higher level of global industrial cooperation.

NOTES

1. "Tanaka's Oil Diplomacy is Proving Expensive," *The Japan Economic Journal*, February 12, 1974.

2. *Time*, February 11, 1974.

3. "Full Steam Ahead. Japan. Most Vulnerable of All to Energy Crisis Seems Least Concerned," *The Wall Street Journal*, December 20, 1973.

4. *The New York Times*, February 5, 1974, and June 12, 1974.

5. "Japan's For Investing Again," *The Economist*, May 4, 1974.

6. Jun Takeda, "Japanese Trading Companies," *Japan Quarterly*, Vol. XX, No. 4 (Oct.-Dec., 1973), p. 407.

7. For a discussion of the ten firms' recent activities in the international arena, see, for example, Alexander K. Young, "Internationalization of the Japanese General Trading Commission," *Columbia Journal of World Buisness*, Spring, 1974.

8. "Big Traders Promise to Assist Algerian Projects," *The Japan Economic Journal*, February 12, 1974.

9. "Massive Repair Complex is Planned in Algeria," *The Japan Economic Journal*, April 23, 1974.

10. "Egypt, 3 Firms Plan A Major Iron Mill Near Alexanderia," *The Wall Street Journal*, June 14, 1974.

11. "International Petrochemical Firm is Set up in Saudi Arabia," *The Japan Economic Journal*, July 30, 1974.

12. "Nippon Electric is Actively Pushing Sales of Facilities to Arab Nations," *The Japan Economic Journal*, February 19, 1974, and "NEC, Hughes, Thomson Join to Win Arab Order," the same *Journal*, July 23, 1974.

13. "Arab Countries Move to Buy Large Tankers," *The Japan Economic Journal*, January 29, 1974.

14. "Iran Attracts and Frustrates International Firms," *Business International*, May 3, 1974, p. 142.

15. "Toshiba Defeats USSR to Grab Kuwait Power Order," *The Japan Economic Journal*, July 9, 1974.

PART IV:
Selected Topics and Future Evolution

THE PACIFIC BASIN

The Pacific Basin

28

Business Rediscovers the Pacific Basin

Business Week

An expanding web of trade and investment links. The Japanese lead the way

Mainline Corp., one of Australia's biggest construction companies, plans to develop a "second home" subdivision in California's Squaw Valley.

Consolidated Navigation Corp., of Hong Kong, Associated Maritime Industries, Inc., and GATX Oswego Corp., of the U. S., and Camerna Navigation Corp., of Liberia, will join with local investors in Taiwan next month to build a giant shipyard at Kaohsiung capable of turning out 350,000-ton oil tankers.

Marcona Corp., a San Francisco mining and shipping company, got a $66-million loan last year from two Japanese trading companies to build a plant in Peru that will ship iron ore pellets to Japan.

First National City Bank of New York and Tokyo's Fuji Bank have set up Asia Pacific Capital Corp., with dual headquarters in Singapore and Hong Kong, to finance investments in many countries.

What all these ventures have in common is their geographical location around the rim of the Pacific Ocean and their pooling of resources and business knowhow drawn from a number of countries in the region. Lacing the Pacific, a web of investment links as well as a rapidly rising volume of merchandise trade (table) is gradually creating a community of interests among businessmen in the diverse nations that make up the vast region. "The Pacific Basin is the fastest growing economic area in the world," says Kenneth H. J. Clarke, president of the Canadian Marketing Div. of International Nickel Co. of Canada, and president of the Pacific Basin Economic Council (PBEC), a San Francisco-based organization of business executives from the U. S., Japan, Canada, Australia, and New Zealand. The council, which aims to promote regional business ties, invited observers from Southeast Asia, Latin America, Korea, and Taiwan to take part in its annual conference last month in Sydney, Australia. The group is considering opening membership to representatives of China and the Soviet Union as well.

Businessmen in the Western states are moving aggressively to exploit the opportunities in the Pacific. Already, about 50% of the foreign trade of the five Pacific states—California, Washington, Oregon, Alaska, and Hawaii—is with Asia, and another 15% with Canada. California now does more trade in automobiles from Japan than from Detroit, notes R. L. Davidson, Tokyo-based vice-president of First National City Bank of New York. State-sponsored trade missions from the West Coast regularly tour the Pacific in quest of expanded markets, while representatives of the Japan External Trade Organization (JETRO) stump the Western states prodding businessmen and ranchers to sell more to Japan and thus help to narrow the trade gap between the two countries. Japan's recent liberalization of import restrictions will spur an even greater flow of goods from the U. S.

A big stake. As long ago as 1903, speaking in San Francisco, President Theodore Roosevelt somewhat prematurely labeled the Pacific the "region of destiny." Today, the 33 countries around its rim, ranging from primitive to highly industrialized, are anything but a coherent economic community. Except for the PBEC, a private group, there is still no regional organization to promote economic development of the area as a whole.

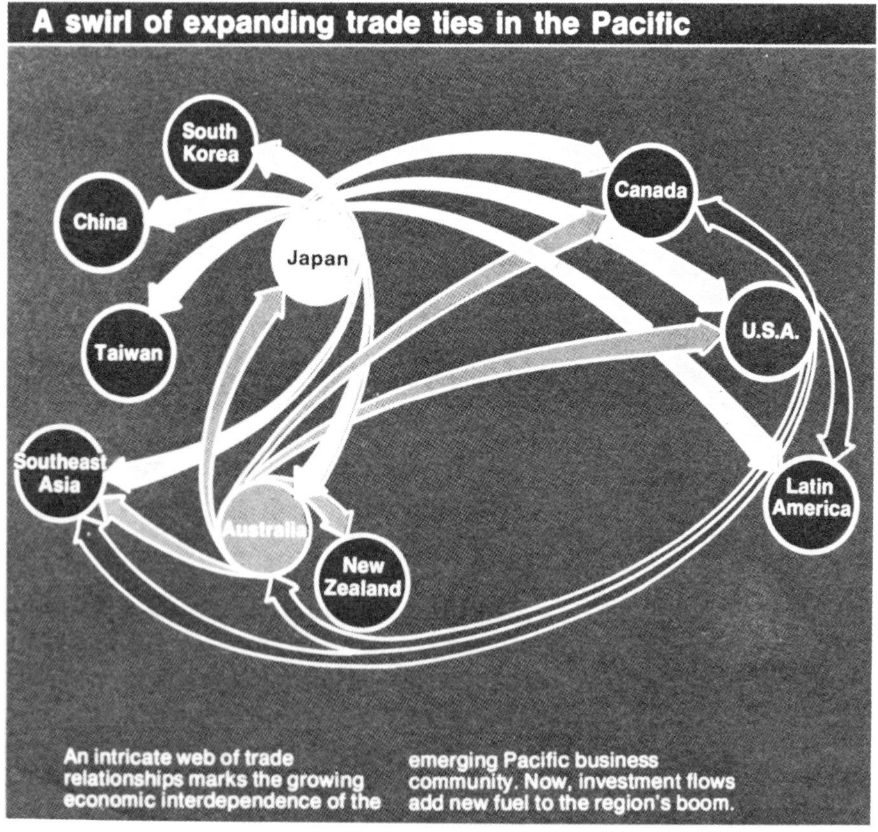

An intricate web of trade relationships marks the growing economic interdependence of the emerging Pacific business community. Now, investment flows add new fuel to the region's boom.

Robert P. Van Nutt

Exporter	Importer	Billions of dollars
U.S.	Japan	$4.9
	Other Asia	3.6
	Australia & New Zealand	1.0
Canada	Japan	.8
	Australia & New Zealand	.2
	China	.2
Latin America	Japan	1.6
	U.S. West Coast	.9
Southeast Asia	Japan	4.2
	U.S.	3.5
Taiwan	U.S.	1.3
	Japan	.4
Australia	Japan	1.6
	U.S.	.8
	Southeast Asia	.5
	New Zealand	.3
Japan	U.S.	9.1
	Southeast Asia	6.3
	Latin America	2.2
	Canada	1.1
	Taiwan	1.1
	South Korea	1.0
	Australia & New Zealand	.9
	China	.6

Despite this, U. S. businessmen—particularly in the Far West and Hawaii—and their counterparts in other Pacific countries are enthusiastic about the future. The area is "primed for very rapid growth in trade and investment in the '70s and '80s," says Dr. Shelley M. Mark, an economist and director of Hawaii's Planning and Economic Development Dept. "We think all the economic factors are in place."

The main thrust behind this development, of course, comes from the U. S., the world's biggest trading nation, and Japan, the fastest growing industrial power. Two-way trade between the two countries has been growing at an annual rate of 20% in recent years, and last year it climbed to nearly $14-billion. The U. S. also has a $14-billion investment stake in the Pacific area, including investments in Latin countries that border on the Pacific. Japan is expected to pour an estimated $25-billion into overseas investments in the next decade, much of it in the Pacific region.

Mark: 'The area is primed for very rapid growth in the 1970s and 1980s'

Australia and New Zealand are also looking more and more to trade with their Pacific neighbors, now that Britain has joined the European Common Market. Australian Prime Minister E. Gough Whitlam told the PBEC conference that his country, with its vast natural resources, is now in a "seller's market" for raw materials that are in increasing demand throughout the world. He said that Australia's relations with the U. S. and Japan would increasingly turn on the question of using and sharing resources.

Economic growth. Meantime, the small countries along the Western fringe of the Pacific, from Korea to Taiwan and Singapore, are growing at spectacular rates and contributing to the economic upsurge in the area. And, observes Hawaii's Dr. Mark, "Mainland China adds a brand-new dimension, unimagined at this point, which will be of very great importance in the future." Among delegates at the PBEC conference in Sydney was John L. Gillis, senior vice-president of Monsanto Co., en route home from a trip to China. There, he arranged to import gum resin into the U. S. and discussed sales of equipment for China's expanding chemical industry. China is "very keen on Pacific Basin trade," he says.

The Chinese are wary of becoming too dependent on trade and technical ties with any one country. But at the spring trade fair in Canton last month, it seemed clear that the Chinese have decided that they do not have time to develop their own technology in many fields and are eager to buy equipment and knowhow from abroad. They invited representatives from such U. S. oil equipment makers as Hughes Tool, Hydril, and Baker Oil Tools to the fair.

To pay for imports of such goods, the Chinese will have to step up their exports, and oil from reported large offshore pools is a prospective hard-currency earner. The likeliest customers for Chinese oil are the big Pacific powers—Japan and the U. S. China is also a major potential supplier of labor-intensive manufactured goods such as textiles, inexpensive watches, cameras, and radios. Developing nations around the Pacific are natural markets for such products.

Businessmen are also factoring into their calculations the potential for trade with Soviet Asia.

Anatole Myshkov, Russian deputy consul general in San Francisco, told a recent conference on Pacific trade in Seattle that Russia is interested in importing electrical power generating equipment, lumbering machinery, and agricultural equipment from the Pacific Northwest. Because of the 6,000-mile breadth of the Soviet Union, he said, it is "cheaper, simpler, and more convenient" for the Russians to import products into their Far Eastern provinces from the U. S. West Coast than from Eastern Europe.

Investments. To finance trade and investment, U. S. banks are expanding throughout the Pacific. Last year, Bank of America opened its 32nd and 33rd branches in the region. Warren Gross, representative in Tokyo of Seattle-First National Bank, hopes that his bank's bid for a branch in Japan will be helped by Washington state's recent adoption of an alien bank act, opening the way for Japanese banks to set up in Seattle. And U. S. East Coast banks, as well as foreign banks, are setting up subsidiaries on the West Coast to get a share in the boom. The latest was New York's Chemical Bank, which opened a subsidiary in San Francisco last month to finance trade by West Coast companies with Asia, South America, and other Pacific areas. Says Chandler L. Mahnken, president of the subsidiary: "We are expanding our Far East business tremendously. This is a stepping stone to business in the Pacific Basin. You have to be on the scene."

The newest development, though, is the flow of investments across the Pacific in several directions. U. S. companies, of course, have been investing throughout the region for many years, in everything from iron mines in Australia to transistor plants in Southeast Asia. Marcona's project in Peru is an example of a growing trend to joint ventures with investors from Japan and other countries. The Japanese government's recent decision to ease restrictions on foreign ownership in most industries is expected to spur new U. S. investments in Japan.

Meantime, businessmen in other Pacific countries are exploiting investment opportunities throughout the region. Australia's Mainline Corp., in addition to Squaw Valley, plans a beachfront condominium development in Hawaii and is looking at ventures in Washington state, according to Chairman Ian D. McLachlin. John Lysaght (Australia), Ltd., an affiliate of steel producer Broken Hill Proprietary Co., has 10 steel products plants scattered across the Pacific.

Stepping stone. The biggest investment push, though, is by Japanese companies looking for raw materials and, increasingly, foreign supplies of manufactured products. Chiyoda Chemical Engineering & Construction Co. has purchased 20 acres of waterfront in Seattle for a factory to produce pollution control equipment. Near Everett, Wash., Japanese and local businessmen have set up a company to make concrete pilings for sale in the Pacific Northwest. Last April, Seattle's Weyerhaeuser Co. announced an agreement with Jujo Paper Co. and Mitsui & Co. to manufacture newsprint in the U. S. for export to Japan. "Japan will move toward offshore sourcing of manufactured goods," predicts President George J. Weyerhauser.

Investments are beginning to flow across the Pacific in many directions

Japanese companies also are moving into manufacturing in the U. S. for the domestic market, with plants such as Sony Corp.'s San Diego television factory. Kaiser Resources, a subsidiary of Kaiser Steel Corp., ships coal to Japanese steel companies from a huge strip mine in British Columbia and is trying to sell an interest in the venture to the Japanese. Hawaii, already a mecca for Japanese tourism and business conferences, will serve as a stepping stone for some Japanese companies moving into the U. S. market, predicts Chinn Ho, a prominent Hawaiian developer. Ho, who is chairman of Capital Investment of Hawaii, Inc., has just sold a hotel and two golf courses to Dai Ichi Kano Kaihatsu Co., of Tokyo. As another example of the stepping stone process, Honolulu's Hawaii Corp. recently announced that it has taken an option on 30 acres near Macon, Ga., for a joint venture with two Japanese partners to build a textile printing plant.

Perhaps the most convincing sign of transpacific business interest, though, is a summer course that the University of Washington is offering to Japanese businessmen. It invites them to pay $2,500 for a one-month course in "How to invest in the U. S."

29

U.S.-Japanese Investments in the Pacific Basin:

THE INTENSIFYING BATTLE

A. Kapoor

INTRODUCTION

This paper discusses the following selected questions relating to the Pacific Basin: How can it be defined? Why is it of growing importance? Why is it likely to be a business battleground between Japanese and U.S. companies? What are likely to be the characteristics of the battleground? What are the policy implications for the U.S.-based international company (hereafter referred to as IC).

The key observations presented here are:

1. Latin American and Asian countries will engage in a growing exchange of information and experiences. One important area of such exchange will be on the ways and means of controlling the IC.

2. U.S. and Japanese companies will engage in head-on competition both in selling and in terms of direct investment in Latin America and Asia.

3. The IC will need to develop a wide perspective on the Pacific Basin in its organizational structure—among its personnel and in its long-range planning.

4. As a purely Pacific power, the Japanese appear to be better positioned for a Pacific Basin perspective than is the case for U.S. companies.

5. The "honeymoon" period of Japanese investments in Latin America will end in the coming decade or sooner.

6. The Japanese government is likely to orchestrate closely the international activities of Japanese companies. Therefore, U.S. companies and the U.S. government will have to decide what role, if any, should be played by the U.S. government in countering the challenge mounted by Japan Inc.

7. By the mid-1980s, if not sooner, host Latin American and Asian countries will have acquired sufficient experience (in terms of duration and volume of both U.S. and Japanese investments) to develop meaningful comparisons. The IC will have to formulate policies on how to use such comparative information within the overall framework of sharing information with governments.

Reprinted by permission. Working Papers Series, Graduate School of Business Administration, College of Business and Public Administration, New York University (November, 1974).

WHAT IS THE PACIFIC BASIN?

The Pacific Basin is defined to include all the countries surrounding the Pacific Ocean.[1] The Soviet Union and the People's Republic of China are also Pacific Basin countries. However, in this paper, the focus is on the United States, Japan, and the Asian and Latin American countries touching the Pacific Ocean.*

REASONS FOR GROWING IMPORTANCE

The pattern of growing trade flows within the Pacific Basin can be seen in the Diagram and Table in the preceding article from *Business Week*. This information illustrates the extent and pattern of trade flows within the Pacific Basin. It is not a complete description; only part of the trade flow patterns are recognized. However, it can be readily observed that the Pacific Basin has a sizeable volume of trade and investment flows.

The Pacific Basin offers attractive opportunities for new investments by U.S. and Japanese companies. In regard to U.S. companies, many Latin American countries reflect growing hostility and restrictions on investments resulting in U.S. direct investments in the region, from 20 percent ($8.9 billion) of total outstanding book value in 1964 to 18 percent ($16.6 billion) in 1973. (The figures are approximate to indicate trends.) In general, Africa is still highly fragmented, characterized by small markets with limited purchasing power. It is a relatively unknown area to many U.S. companies. The Middle East offers high potential for greater investments over the coming decade, but for the time being, U.S. companies have limited investments because of political and economic uncertainties in the region, the small size of several local markets, and limited experience of U.S. companies in doing business in the region. Therefore, of the developing areas, Asia provides a growth region for direct investments, which have increased from 4 percent ($1.7 billion) of total outstanding book value in 1964 to over 6 percent ($5.6 billion) in 1973, and the growth of investments will continue over the coming decade.

Japanese companies have been particularly active on the Asian side of the Pacific Basin with foreign direct investments increasing from under $400 million in 1964 to $1.03 billion (23 percent of total outstanding) in 1972 and are expected to reach $9 billion by 1980. However, growing anti-Japanese feelings in Asia, coupled with the desire for diversification, is encouraging the Japanese to invest in other developing countries.

---

*In strict adherence to the definition of Pacific Basin used here, Brazil is not a part of the Pacific Basin. However, for our purposes references are made to Brazil which now has almost equal amounts of U.S. and Japanese direct investments. Therefore, Brazil permits observations on the pattern of U.S. and Japanese competition, reaction of the host government, and the indigenous business community. Other countries are watching the Brazilian scene to note policy implications for themselves.

The greatest growth has occurred in Latin America (with particular emphasis on Brazil) for several reasons: The presence of Brazilians and to a lesser extent of Peruvians of Japanese descent has facilitated the inflow of Japanese investments. Latin America also possesses vast quantities of raw materials and potential for food production—both of which are of critical importance to the Japanese. The region also provides sizeable markets for exports of Japanese products, a critical consideration for Japan because of its high dependence on exports for foreign exchange earnings. The large dollar holdings of the Japanese, especially in the recent past, offers better purchasing power in the dollar trading area (which includes Latin America) than in non-dollar areas, which serves as an additional inducement to invest in Latin America. The Japanese have very limited knowledge of Africa and the Middle East. Though raw material related investments in these regions will definitely grow, the major priority region for Japanese investments (in addition to Asia) in the coming decade will be Latin America.

In brief, the Japanese will extend beyond their traditional area of investment (Asia) into the traditional area of investment of U.S. companies (South America). Conversely, U.S. and Japanese companies will compete with each other both in Asia and in South America.

From the standpoint of the host Asian and South American countries of the Pacific Basin, the competition among Japanese and U.S. companies presents important policy implications. For one, the host countries will be in a better bargaining position with foreign investors as they will have a wider range of alternatives to choose from.[2] In addition, over the coming decade the developing countries on the Asian and South American sides of the Pacific Basin will develop greater exchange of information relating to the IC. The Latins possess greater experience with the U.S. company, while the Asians know more about the Japanese.

SELECTED CHARACTERISTICS OF THE BATTLEGROUND[3]

GENERAL INVESTMENT ENVIRONMENT

In general terms three characteristics can be identified—importance of raw material supplies, economic associations, and role of governments. The subsequent section deals with selected specific characteristics of the battleground.

As a matter of policy, nation states will place strong emphasis on securing a guaranteed supply of essential raw materials over a period of time. Because of its critical dependence on imports of raw materials, Japan will make important moves to secure its sources. Japanese companies will be closely orchestrated and supported by the Japanese government. The U.S., on its side, though richly endowed with natural resources will compete to maintain its access to outside raw materials.

Therefore, one major area of competition between U.S. and Japanese companies will be for raw materials. The competition coupled with the desire of host governments, particularly in South America, to reduce their dependence on the "gringo" will result in exerting strong competitive pressure on U.S. companies to modify terms of operations to be more in keeping with the preferences of host governments.

It is likely that in the coming decade or sooner Japan will attempt to structure some form of economic association with Brazil and the Andean Common Market countries to gain preferred access to their raw materials and end markets. The South American countries, for their part, might be tempted because of the desire to diversify their economic partners to reduce dependence on trade with the U.S.

Some form of long-term economic association between Japan and one or more of the Association of Southeast Asian (ASEAN) countries will occur within the 1970s. Besides their desire for raw materials, the Japanese also must export, and the Asian region is of major significance in this respect.

The Asian countries recognize their economic dependence on Japan. In addition, they feel that, as an Asian country, Japan has longer lasting interests in the region than is true of Europe and the U.S.

The shifting economic alignments between the developed and developing countries of the Pacific Basin have several implications for the IC. It must learn to anticipate the changes and position the organization in order to benefit from them. For example, Japan will have to offer preferential access to imports from the developing countries of Southeast Asia. U.S. companies in Southeast Asia will then be able to benefit from such an economic alignment provided their operations in Southeast Asia are structured to cater to the Japanese market, as opposed to catering solely or largely to the needs of the local market.

The role of the Japanese government is likely to grow in importance and scope. In addition to entering into economic alignments with other countries in the Pacific Basin, the Japanese government will closely orchestrate the activities of Japanese companies operating in the region to ensure that they follow through to achieve obejctives set by the government. The extreme dependence of Japan on foreign raw materials and end markets—coupled with emerging anxieties over the motives of Japanese companies (profits or national service)—are prompting the Japanese government to play a major role in their control. There is also a growing feeling within the Japanese government that it should take the initiative in reorganzing Japanese companies in order to make them more competitive outside of Japan.

If the Japanese government plays such a role on behalf of Japanese companies, it will constitute a powerful challenge for U.S. companies operating in the region. It will raise fundamental policy questions regarding the role of the U.S. government in protecting its interests and those it shares with the U.S.-based ICs operating overseas. Therefore, an important characteristic of the Pacific Basin battleground will be what patterns of collaboration, if any, are forged by U.S. companies and the U.S. government in response to actions taken by the Japanese.

SPECIFIC INVESTMENT CHARACTERISTICS

Table 1 compares some of the direct investment characteristics of Japanese and U.S. companies. In terms of amount of foreign direct investment, size of parent company, place of investment, local ownership arrangement, extent of control over subsidiary, knowledge about the investor on the part of the host country, and the role of the home government, the Japanese and U.S. investors differ. In general, the terms accepted by the Japanese for initial entry into a country are more in keeping with the preferences of the host South American and Asian countries than is the case with U.S. companies.

An important difference between U.S. and Japanese executives is in the geographic scope of their international exposure. In general, Japanese executives responsible for the international operations of their companies are more conscious of the Pacific Basin than is true of U.S. executives. Two reasons account for this difference. First, Japan is a purely Pacific power. It is oriented heavily to that area. Second, a significant number of Japanese executives with international responsibilities have had direct field experience in Asia. Before, during, and after the Second World War, Asia remained a region of major economic and political significance for Japan. Executives with experience in Asia have been delegated the long-term responsibility of developing business in other parts of the world, including Latin America. Japanese foreign trade and investment activities have grown too fast to develop a sufficient number of Japanese executives for inter-

TABLE 1

JAPAN-U.S. DIRECT INVESTMENT PROFILE: A COMPARISON

Characteristic	*Japan-based*	*U.S.-based*
1. Amount of foreign direct investment (1972)	Approximately $10 billion in terms of book value	Approximately $100 billion in terms of book value
2. Size of parent firms	40 percent of investments by small- to medium-sized firms	Large R & D intensive firms dominate the overseas investments
3. Where invested	3/4 of investments in developing nations. Overwhelmingly in Asia	2/3 in developed nations
4. Organization of subsidiaries	Joint venture dominant. Many minority interests	Fully-owned or majority controlled
5. Partner, if any, of subsidiaries	Many with Japanese trading firms and local partners With other Japanese firms in the same "industrial group" in Japan Host government often a partner	On its own or local partner
6. Parent's control over subsidiary	Loose	Close
7. Parent-subsidiary relations	Disjoint. Local market oriented	Globally integrated
8. Involvement of home government	High	Minimal

Source: Additions made to table developed by Professor Yoshihiro Tsurumi

national operations. In addition, the unique characteristics of Japanese management along with the almost exclusive use of the Japanese language does not permit the use of non-Japanese personnel. Therefore, as Japanese companies have advanced internationally, they have had a relatively limited cadre of executives to call upon for business development and management purposes. U.S. companies, in contrast, have expanded overseas over a much longer duration of time, have developed a large cadre of internationally-oriented executives, used executives of various nationalities, and encouraged executives to specialize in particular regions.

CHANGES OVER TIME

The investment characteristics of the Japanese are likely to change over the coming decade, making their pattern relatively more similar to that of U.S. investments. Conversely, investment characteristics of U.S. companies, in regard to such aspects as ownership requirements, will begin to resemble those of Japanese investments. In addition, by the end of the coming decade, both Latin and Asian countries will have had enough experience with both U.S. and Japanese investments to permit meaningful comparison of their relative costs and contributions from the viewpoint of the host governments. Therefore, the long-range planning by the IC should recognize not only the existing set of characteristics of Japanese investments, but also the reasons and the directions of change in them over the coming decade. A few characteristics of investment and the likely pattern of change are highlighted here for purposes of illustration.

First, especially in Latin America, the image of the Japanese will change from being one of welcome alternatives to the "gringo" to that of being permanent guests competing with local companies, remitting scarce foreign exchange, and experiencing growing conflicts with the host government. The host countries will develop greater knowledge of the strengths and limitations of Japanese companies. And as with most foreign investments in developing countries, the high and often unrealistic initial expectations of the host countries will be far in excess of what the Japanese will be able to deliver.

However, it is unlikely that the host Latin countries will permit the type of free-wheeling and relatively unchecked investments permitted by Thailand and Indonesia during the initial stages of their respective programs of attracting foreign investments. Unlike the Latin countries, these Southeast Asian countries had very limited experience with foreign investors and did not impose specific requirements and regulations on them.

Second, the large Japanese companies, especially, will undertake a growing range of foreign direct investments in various parts of the world. Particularly in strategic decision areas, these operations will move in the direction of greater centralized control and coordination by corporate headquarters. Three conditions are likely to promote such a move by the large Japanese companies: (1) The greater efficiency of centrally coordinated (and at times integrated) U.S.- and Europe-based ICs will make it competitively necessary for the Japanese to move in a similar direction. (2) The sheer growth in size and complexity of international operations will require greater central coordination, especially in strategic decision areas. (3) With the desire of strengthening the position of Japanese companies in competing with foreign ICs *outside* of Japan, the Japanese government will strongly encourage greater rationalization (including greater coordination, control, and integration) of Japanese ICs.

These developments in the international operations of Japanese ICs are likely to develop rapidly, with a specific set of objectives (such as guaranteed supply of raw materials), and under the strong direction of the Japanese government. In many respects, the emergence of the Japanese ICs will be unlike the U.S. experience, requiring a different approach in formulating policies and programs of action for an effective response.

Third, the involvement of the Japanese government in the activities of Japanese companies will create a somewhat different reaction in the host developing regions of South America and Asia in the Pacific Basin. In comparison to the Latin American countries, the Asians have only recently emerged from political colonialism. Therefore, at present there is perhaps a greater tolerance of foreign influence. The economic dependence on Japan also makes the Asian countries more tolerant of Japanese influence.

The South American scenario, however, is different. These countries became politically independent over a century ago, and during the past several decades have been highly sensitive to what they consider to be economic colonialism of the U.S. In addition, South America has limited economic dependence on Japan. For these reasons, the South American countries are likely to react far more negatively to the use of the muscle of the Japanese government on the part of Japanese companies in dealing with host governments.

U.S.-based ICs will also undergo changes over the coming decade. Greater delegation of responsibility at the country level, more organizational flexibility to respond faster to changing requirements, greater ability to function effectively as a minority partner with shared management control, greater ability to interact effectively with host governments—these will be some of the positive changes in the U.S.-based IC. It will also possess an important measure—namely, the option to compare its performance in the Pacific Basin countries with that of Japanese and other foreign investors.

POLICY IMPLICATIONS FOR THE IC

The changing nature of the Pacific Basin poses several policy implications for the U.S.-based IC, and a few are highlighted here for purposes of illustration. They fall into two broad but interrelated categories—changes within and external to the IC.

Three areas of internal review and change can be identified. First, IC management, particularly at the regional and country levels, will need to develop a Pacific Basin-wide perspective in order to effectively formulate and undertake policies and programs of action. At present, the orientation of the IC executive is too strongly limited to the traditional geographic lines of Latin America and the Far East.

Second, the IC needs to develop a plan for flow of communication between the Asian and the South American regions to exchange ideas and information and for Pacific Basin-wide planning. At present, there is a limited interaction—typically on an ad hoc and informal basis, if at all—between the South American and Asian regions.

Third, the IC needs to develop executives who are skilled to operate in several parts of the Pacific Basin. The countries around the Pacific Ocean represent an awesome human mosaic and it is not sufficient for the executive to possess only an Asian, a South American, or a Communist country business background. What is needed is the development of a "Pacificocrat" who is trained and oriented to conduct business on a Pacific Basin-wide basis. The "Pacificocrat" will be a far more multinational individual than an "Asiocrat" or "Eurocrat," who is limited to the Asian and European countries.

Three areas of review and planning external to the IC need to be recognized. First, in the coming decade, U.S. and Japanese companies will have sufficiently long histories of operations and volume of investments in the Latin and Asian countries of the Pacific Basin to permit meaningful comparisons by the host governments and the companies. What does the IC plan to do with information offered by such comparisons? It will need to view this question within the broader framework of the sharing of information by the IC with governments (particularly the host governments) for more meaningful and lasting dialogues between the IC and governments.

Second, it is likely that there will be an adverse reaction to Japanese investments in one or more Latin American countries. One consequence can be the formulation of more strict investment regulations by the host countries. Even when the restrictive regulations are intended for a particular source of investment (such as the Japanese in Thailand under the Alien Decrees), they are applied to all sources of foreign investment. What should be the policy of the U.S.-based IC (because of its own interests) to prevent the development of an adverse reaction? In the event an adverse reaction does develop, what should be its policy?

Third, what should be the policy and programs of action of the U.S.-based IC to counter the challenge in the Pacific Basin, not only from Japan but also by the U.S.S.R. and the People's Republic of China? It will need to formulate and promote its ideas on the desired role of the U.S. government in IC activities.[4]

NOTES

1. The Pacific Basin has been defined often to refer largely to the Asian side of the Pacific Ocean; see Harold B. Malmgren (ed.), *Pacific Basin Development: The American Interests* (Lexington, Mass.: D.C. Heath and Company, 1972), and Donald R. Sherk, *The United States and the Pacific Trade Basin*, Federal Reserve Bank of San Francisco, undated.

2. For additional comments, see Chapter 6 of A. Kapoor, *Planning for International Business Negotiations* (Cambridge, Mass.: Ballinger Publishers, 1975).

3. See A. Kapoor, ''Japan, Southeast Asia and Latin America: The Emerging Crossflows,'' speech delivered at the Council of the Americas, New York, 1973.

4. See Jack N. Behrman, J. Boddewyn, and A. Kapoor, *International Business-Government Communications: U.S. Strategies, Actors, and Issues* (Lexington, Mass.: D. C. Heath and Company, 1975).

30

Natural Resource Dependency and Japanese Foreign Policy

Saburo Okita

THE current oil crisis has once again demonstrated to Japan her high dependency upon supplies of natural resources from abroad. When these supplies of foreign resources are obtained smoothly, the Japanese economy progresses favorably; however, once imports are interrupted, the impact on the Japanese economy is immediate and severe. According to the statistics, oil accounted for 74.9 percent of Japanese primary energy supply in fiscal 1972 (ending March 31) of which 99.7 percent was imported, and only the remaining 0.3 percent produced domestically. Of this imported oil, 80 percent came from the Middle East—43 percent from Arab oil-exporting countries and 37 percent from Iran alone.

In November 1973 it was announced that the oil supply from the Arab nations to Japan was to be reduced by 25 percent from the supply level in September 1973. As a result, projections were made that even if the oil supply from other areas remained unchanged, the total volume of oil imports would be reduced by about ten percent in 1974 and that the growth rate of GNP in 1974 would be negative. The real growth rate of the Japanese economy in the past ten years has averaged ten percent per year, and even in "recession" years, real growth has been four or five percent. Negative growth, a real recession, has never been experienced since the end of World War II. Naturally the immediate reaction to this projection was that Japan would be very seriously affected indeed.

Summarizing the energy picture in fiscal 1972, we note that three-fourths of Japan's primary energy was supplied by oil, and the rest by coal (16.6 percent), hydroelectric power (6.3 percent), natural gas (0.8 percent), atomic energy (0.7 percent), and other sources (0.8 percent). Since two-thirds of the coal is imported, the degree of dependence on imported energy was 86 percent, and the domestic supply of energy was only 14 percent.

The experience of other countries shows that the level of economic activity has a close interrelation with the supply level of energy. With most of the energy supply dependent upon im-

---

ported oil, a slowdown in all economic activities in Japan is an inevitable result of restricted oil supply.

In the United States, the share of oil in primary energy consumption is about 46 percent, of which 32 percent was imported in 1972. Arab nations supplied only 12 percent of this imported oil. Thus, only about two percent of the total primary energy requirement was supplied by oil from Arab countries. Clearly, the relative importance of Arab oil to the U.S. economy is marginal. From the viewpoint of self-sufficiency in resources, it is very apparent that there is a big difference in the basic conditions of Japan and the United States. In the United States a policy of self-sufficiency like "Project Independence" could be contemplated, whereas in Japan attaining self-sufficiency in energy would mean a drastic reduction in the level of economic activity as well as in the standard of living.

Japan's energy supply before World War II depended mainly on domestic coal and hydroelectric power. In 1935, primary energy supply came 62 percent from coal, 19 percent from hydropower, nine percent from oil and ten percent from other sources such as charcoal and firewood. Oil imports came mainly from the United States and the Dutch East Indies in those days. Oil was a key resource for the military, and a large portion of oil imports was earmarked for military use. The total volume of imported oil in 1935 was 4.2 million kiloliters (26 million barrels), of which crude oil was 1.3 million kiloliters and oil products 2.9 million kiloliters. In 1973, by contrast, imported oil amounted to 306 million kiloliters (about two billion barrels), of which crude oil was 286 million kiloliters and fuel oil products 20 million kiloliters. The ratio of the domestic to foreign supply of energy was still relatively high until the mid-1950s, but the high rate of economic growth sustained since that time has caused the volume of energy demanded in Japan to far outgrow the supply capability of domestic resources. This has produced the present extremely high rate of import dependence.

II

Until recently Japan was relatively self-sufficient in food. However, dependence upon imported food has increased recently as the quality of the Japanese diet has been upgraded. Consumption of livestock products especially has increased with the rising level of personal incomes. Backed by domestic price-support policies the production of rice, which is the staple food in Japan, has attained self-sufficiency (and even surpluses a few years ago). Other food crops are, however, in short supply. The ratio of self-sufficiency in wheat for domestic consumption was 5.3 percent in 1972, whereas it had been 40.6 percent in 1955. As for soybeans, which are also indispensable to the Japanese diet, the degree of self-sufficiency has been reduced to 3.6 percent in 1972 from 4.1 percent in 1955. Incidentally, the memory of the so-called "soybean shock" caused by the U.S. government embargo on soybean exports last summer is still fresh. Fortunately, this embargo was lifted after only a short duration and since then shipments have been uninterrupted. This experience, however, once again reminded people in Japan of their heavy dependency on imported foodstuffs.

The Japanese diet in recent years has improved remarkably, as the following table illustrates:

PER CAPITA FOOD INTAKE PER DAY

	Fiscal Year				
	1955	*1960*	*1965*	*1970*	*1972*
Calories	2,217	2,290	2,408	2,471	2,516
Protein (grams)	65.7	69.5	73.7	76.9	78.2
(animal protein)	(16.9)	(21.2)	(26.8)	(31.8)	(33.5)
Fat (grams)	22.2	29.1	40.2	51.9	56.5

As a result of this improvement, life expectancy has increased to the level of the Scandinavian countries and infant mortality has been reduced to the lowest level in the world.[1] Diseases due to malnutrition, like tuberculosis, have nearly disappeared.

Diet upgrading was partly supported by the growing consumption of livestock products in Japan. For example, per capita consumption of milk and milk products and meat—beef, pork and chicken—per year has risen dramatically.

YEARLY PER CAPITA CONSUMPTION OF DAIRY AND MEAT PRODUCTS—(In Kilograms)

	Fiscal Year				
	1955	*1960*	*1965*	*1970*	*1972*
Milk & Products	12.1	22.3	37.4	50.1	51.8
Meat	3.2	5.0	8.8	13.1	15.4
Beef	1.1	1.1	1.4	2.0	2.4
Pork	0.7	1.1	2.7	4.7	5.6
Chicken	0.3	0.8	1.9	3.8	4.7

[1] The average life expectancy in Japan was 70.5 years for males and 75.9 years for females in 1972. These life-spans are about 25 years longer than those in the 1930s.

On the other hand, feed grains needed for the production of these livestock products, such as maize and sorghum, depended upon imports. In 1973, the import volume of feeding maize was 5.8 million metric tons which was about 20 times that of 1955, and of sorghum 3.3 million metric tons which was over 100 times that of 1955. According to the Ministry of Agriculture and Forestry in Japan, the rate of self-sufficiency measured by original calories (that is, converting calories of livestock products into calories of animal feed needed for the production of livestock) was 53 percent in 1972.

Total import volumes of major agricultural commodities, wheat, soybeans, maize and sorghum, amounted to 18.1 million metric tons in 1973, well above the total domestic production of rice (12.1 million metric tons) in the same year. Imports of these major agricultural commodities are heavily dependent on the supplies from the United States, the U.S. share being 67 percent for wheat, 88 percent for soybeans, 92 percent for maize and 75 percent for sorghum. In total, in 1973 Japan depended for 81 percent of these items on supplies from the United States (against 70 percent in 1972).

As Lyle P. Schertz has stated in his article "World Food: Prices and the Poor" (*Foreign Affairs,* April 1974): "While population growth has obviously been a significant factor in increasing world food demand, an even more striking feature of the demand situation has been the sharp recent increase in cereal consumption per capita in developed countries where population has not been growing rapidly." This is because diet upgrading in developed countries goes along with growing consumption of livestock products, which in turn requires increases in the supply of feed grains. Japan is a typical example of this process. In addition, the present level of livestock consumption in Japan, in spite of remarkable improvements in the past, is still substantially lower than that of the United States. An average individual in Japan consumes a sixth of the volume of meat and one-fifth the volume of milk and milk products as compared with a person in the United States. Japan still has much room for increased food consumption in the future.

After experiencing the "soybean shock" and observing the worldwide food shortages over the past two years, some opinion makers believe that Japan should raise her ratio of self-sufficiency in food. According to international comparisons made in a recent government report on agriculture, the ratio of self-sufficiency in cereals was over 100 percent in the case of the United States, Canada and France and 70 to 80 percent in the case of Italy and West Germany. The United Kingdom, known for its high dependency on food imports, has succeeded in raising its degree of self-sufficiency from 55 percent to 65 percent over the past ten years. Compared with these figures Japan's record of 53 percent is the lowest among major industrial countries. It is, however, extremely difficult to increase self-sufficiency in view of the mountainous topography. Only 16 percent of the total land area is cultivable. According to an estimate recently made by the Ministry of Agriculture and Forestry, twice the currently available cultivated land area is needed to become self-sufficient in food and maintain the present level of nutrition. A more realistic target is to prevent further declines in the self-sufficiency ratio for food.

In addition to major agricultural commodities, dependency upon imported but supplemental foods is also increasing rapidly. The import value of shrimp, lobster and prawn, which the Japanese greatly favor, amounted to more than $320 million in 1972. Imports accounted for 85 percent of total consumption in Japan. Supplying countries included Indonesia, Thailand, Mexico and some African countries.

Similar trends can be observed in timber resources in Japan. Through the 1950s self-sufficiency in timber resources was nearly 100 percent; in 1972, 58 percent of total timber consumption was imported. Rapidly increasing consumption and fluctuations of demand growth following the business cycle in Japan have frequently caused economic problems in timber-exporting countries.[2]

III

Japan's iron and steel industry has expanded briskly since World War II. Japanese crude steel output in 1973 totaled 119 million metric tons, nearly equal to the level of production in the United States and U.S.S.R. (136 million and 131 million metric tons, respectively). Again, internal supply capabilities for raw materials for steel production are extremely limited. Most raw materials used by the iron and steel industry, especially

[2] In 1972 the major sources of timber supplies included: the United States (36.7 percent), Indonesia (15.3 percent), the U.S.S.R. (13.1 percent), Malaysia (12.2 percent), the Philippines (9.7 percent) and Canada (4.2 percent).

iron ore (92 percent), and coking and bituminous coal (59 percent), depend upon imports. In the prewar period, iron ore was imported from neighboring countries in Asia such as Korea and China, and during the early postwar years iron ore was imported mainly from Malaysia and India.

Now the main supplier of iron ore to Japan is Australia, which accounted for 43.3 percent in 1972. India with 16.1 percent and Brazil with 8.4 percent follow, and supply sources are now global, not regional. Japan's 1972 imports of iron ore amounted to 111 million tons and accounted for 42 percent of the total world trade in iron ore. Coal for the iron and steel industry comes mainly from the United States and Australia. The iron and steel industry of today is a typical example of a processing industry founded on ready access and completely dependent upon imported raw materials.

Bauxite, which is the principal raw material for aluminum, is not produced in Japan at all, and its supply thus depends entirely on imports from abroad. Japanese aluminum output in 1972 totaled 1,009 thousand metric tons, one-fourth of the total output of the United States. Bauxite imports in 1972 came from Australia (60.2 percent), Indonesia, (21.5 percent), and Malaysia (16.4 percent).

Japan was once a copper-exporting country; this is no longer true. Owing to the high rate of economic growth, copper consumption has increased and 72.8 percent of newly produced copper in 1972 depended upon imported ore. Including imported copper ingots, about 84 percent of total copper consumption is import dependent. Major ore supplying countries are Canada (37.5 percent), the Philippines (32.9 percent), and Australia (7.5 percent). Supplies from Africa and Latin America are expected to increase in the future.

IV

In sum, to support the economic activities and the living standards of the people of Japan, various kinds of natural resources must be imported in large quantities and from countries all over the world. Moreover, the rate of dependence on imports of these resources has already reached a remarkably high level and is likely to increase still more in the future. When the world-resources trade is a buyer's market, and one can buy resources on favorable terms, then the kind of structure characteristic of the Japanese economy has been considered advantageous. Moreover, the development of marine transportation, especially of large tankers and ore carriers, has greatly reduced the cost of long-distance transportation. Thus it has been possible to produce and profit by importing raw materials and processing them in factories in the industrial centers located on the seacoast of Japan.

Now the world economy must face changes such as the strengthened bargaining power of the resource-exporting countries, the intensification of so-called "resource nationalism," and limits in world resource supplies. Under these circumstances, what are the proper economic policies for Japan to pursue?

First, the diversification of resource supply is necessary. Regarding oil resources, it is desirable that the present high dependence on Middle East oil should be reduced. Japan will have to promote coöperation with oil-producing countries and regions such as Siberia in the U.S.S.R., Alaska in the United States, and Indonesia. It is nearly impossible, however, to reduce substantially the dependence on the Middle East because of the distribution of existing oil reserves and development potential.

With regard to coöperative development of resources in Siberia, a complementary relationship between Japan and the U.S.S.R. does exist. A few years ago in Moscow, when the author had a chance to talk with Professor Nicolai Neclassof, Chairman of the Council for Research of Production Power, he said that though a large quantity of various natural resources had been found in Siberia, this region, especially its eastern part, did not have projects to utilize these resources. When he visited Japan, however, he found that here was a country, east of Siberia, which needed resources in large quantities. He noted that the development of the huge resources in Siberia to meet Japan's growing resource requirements was a mutually beneficial relationship for both parties. In view of the importance to the Japanese economy of imported resources, the development of resources in Siberia such as oil, coal, natural gas and timber is considered an attractive proposal. The supply volume of these resources, however, is expected to be relatively modest compared to Japan's total requirements for these raw materials.[3] Basically, Japan will

[3] For example, the supply of 25 million tons of oil annually from Siberia—now proposed by Soviet negotiators—would account for only five percent of Japan's total oil consumption in 1985.

continue to remain dependent for her resources on global-wide supplies.

Secondly, Japan may coöperate with resource-exporting countries to establish processing industries in these countries and gradually convert her imports of raw materials into imports of processed goods. For example, Japan's aluminum industry is importing bauxite and consuming a large amount of electric power generated by burning imported oil in order to produce aluminum. Instead, Japan may import aluminum while coöperating in the establishment of aluminum industries in energy-rich countries. A similar formula may be applicable for other industries such as petrochemicals, iron and steel, nonferrous metals and the pulp and paper industries.

The development of processing industries in resource-rich countries implies that these countries will export processed goods in addition to raw materials, so that if Japan increases imports of these goods, responding to their need for markets for their new products, benefits will accrue to both parties. Moreover, in constructing these industries, there is opportunity for coöperation in supplying technology and capital goods from Japan. Negotiations are occurring concerning: the construction of such industries as oil refineries, petrochemicals, fertilizers, aluminum, steel, etc.—based on energy resources—with Middle East countries; power development and the construction of aluminum industries in areas rich in hydroelectric power resources like Sumatra in Indonesia, Papua-New Guinea and New Zealand; and the building of pulp and paper industries in forest-resource-rich countries such as Indonesia, Brazil and the U.S.S.R.

The third policy direction is to modify the industrial structure into one which consumes less energy. A report on "Trade and Industrial Policy in the 1970s," published in 1971 by the Council for Industrial Structure (under the Ministry of International Trade and Industry), has already recommended policies for developing energy-saving and knowledge-intensive industries in the future. As there is a high standard of education and technology in Japan, it should be possible to reduce the component of imported raw materials per unit cost of the products by way of promoting growth in the technology-intensive industries. Science and technology development which can substitute for the shortage of resources is indispensable for the future of Japan. As for energy, it is necessary to promote research in atomic energy, solar heat, subterranean heat and others. Regarding food, we need development of the technology to produce single-cell protein using oil or methanol, and to use this at least for livestock feed. It is also necessary to develop industries which do not consume large amounts of energy and raw materials and to produce goods with higher value-added by promoting further development of such industries as electronics, precision machinery and fine chemicals.

The fourth policy direction is to encourage a resource-saving way of life among the people of Japan. If greater importance is placed on the further development of mass transportation, savings of both energy and raw materials are possible by avoiding an excessive reliance on motor cars. In the diet of the Japanese, it may be desirable to discourage the increasing consumption of livestock products in excess of nutritional requirements to maintain health standards. To improve the quality of life, it may be desirable to emphasize a pattern of life which does not require the consumption of a large quantity of material. Policies to encourage the recycling of material, the reduction of waste, supplying durable products, etc. are also necessary for Japan.

Finally, the possibility of slowing down the rate of economic growth should be considered. It may be unreasonable to expect a rapidly increasing supply of energy in the future, particularly in imported oil and oil products which expanded at a rate of 16.4 percent per year during the period from 1968 to 1973, which supported the ten percent annual growth rate of GNP during the same period. Although the elasticity of the growth rate of imported oil to that of GNP is gradually being reduced, it is realistic to assume that the two will be closely linked for several years even if policies for economizing on consumption are implemented. Expansion of energy sources other than oil is difficult.

For example, atomic energy now accounts for only 0.7 percent of the total energy supply in 1972. According to a government plan, however, the electric power capacity of atomic energy will amount to more than 30 million kilowatts (KW) in 1980, and 60 million KW in 1985. About ten percent of total energy demand is expected to be supplied by atomic energy in 1985. It will take a long period of time and require a huge amount of investment until substitute energy resources come to play a significant part in the total energy supply. Even if the technical feasibility of other energy sources such as solar energy and subterranean heat is discovered, 20 or 30 years may be needed until these newly developed energy sources will have significance in the total energy supply.

Thus the major supply source of Japan's energy will continue to be oil for many years to come. Based upon the above premises, if foreign oil supplies to Japan grow at a rate of six or seven percent per year, economic growth will be nearly the same. This implies that it is not likely that Japan will maintain her ten percent rate of economic growth for the future. In a sense this is even desirable, as a slower rate of growth will enable Japan to avoid the frictions caused by rapidly expanding her share in world markets, to solve domestic environmental problems, and to provide time for the people to adapt themselves to the rapidly changing social and economic conditions.

V

With respect to the international aspects, what are the proper diplomatic policies for Japan to pursue? In Japanese *kendo* (fencing) terminology there is a posture called *happo-yabure* implying "defenseless on all sides." As described earlier in this article, Japan's dependence on imports of raw materials, energy and food is so complete that policies attempting self-sufficiency in any of the key items appear unrealistic. Diversifying sources of supply, economizing on the use of raw materials and energy, stepping up efforts for increased production from indigenous resources, and building up emergency stocks of energy and food—all these are feasible and should be pursued with seriousness. But the basic character of the heavy dependence for key items on overseas resources will not change.

One of the policy directions stemming from this fundamental condition is the pursuit of a diplomatic policy of being friendly with everybody, or at least not making serious enemies anywhere. Mr. Takeo Miki, Deputy Prime Minister, visited New York and Washington shortly after his visit to the Middle East last December. Recently Mr. Shigeo Nagano, Chairman of the Japan Chamber of Commerce and one of the dynamic business leaders, visited the United States to attend a U.S.-Europe-Japan business consultation meeting and shortly after returning home went to Peking to talk with government leaders there. After a two-day stay in Japan he then flew to Moscow to discuss Siberian development with Soviet leaders. Such journeys may be interpreted as lacking principle, but under the circumstances Japan is now facing, particularly regarding the supply of essential commodities from abroad, a policy of "friends with everyone" may be justified as the basic principle of Japan's diplomacy in the present and future decades.

In this same context, a view often expressed by foreign observers—that Japan will eventually build up military strength to match the size of her Gross National Product—may be considered a fallacy. In order to make *happo-yabure* an effective diplomatic policy, Japan must avoid becoming a danger to any other country in the world. If Japan started to build up military strength then at least some other countries would interpret this as a dangerous sign and in turn fortify themselves militarily vis-à-vis Japan. This might touch off repercussions which would be inconsistent with the basic vulnerability of Japan's resource base. Just before the outbreak of the Pacific War in 1941, Japan had petroleum stockpiles for military purposes of three million kiloliters or 19 million barrels; in 1973 Japan this would have met consumption needs for just three days!

As the postwar Japanese economy has outgrown the domestic raw material and energy base, so it has also outgrown the Asian base of supply. For major commodities, the supplies from East Asia (including China) and Southeast Asia as a percentage of total imports into Japan in 1972 were: petroleum, 15.2; coal, 0.3; bauxite, 37.9; iron ore, 3.3; copper ore, 33.3; natural rubber, 97.1; maize, 20.4; soybeans, 7.7. The old concept of the "Greater East Asian Co-Prosperity Sphere" is no longer valid for this reason alone. The history of the 1930s, when Japan embarked upon military adventures disregarding rational economic calculations, is not likely to recur.

There are a few additional fundamental considerations. First, détente among the major powers and an absence of serious confrontations among countries of the world will enable Japan to avoid facing very serious and embarrassing choices. Second, in order to enable Japan to maintain exports of manufactured goods for earning the necessary foreign exchange to finance imports, a market-oriented, open and outward-looking economic system is preferred to a strait-jacketed, planned economy. Third, world trade and monetary systems which allow for free flows of commodities are essential for Japan's economic survival. These factors will necessitate that Japan follow a policy of internationalism rather than nationalism.

NATURAL RESOURCES

31

Natural Resource Industries and the Multinational Firm:

THE NEW INTERNATIONAL ENVIRONMENT

Zuhayr Mikdashi

INTRODUCTION

The form by which multinational firms (MNCs) develop natural resource industries, especially in developing countries (LDCs), is undergoing radical change. Gone are the days of wholly subsidiaries and inviolable long-term concessions, as recent actions by OPEC countries dramatically illustrate. But government involvement is not the exclusive province of LDC producers of primary commodity. Advanced countries among the natural resource exporters have a history of government involvement in, and control over, natural resource industries. The consuming (importing) nations as well have attempted to influence, either directly or through the MNCs in the extractive industries, the terms upon which they received such commodities.

The very nature of the natural resource-based industries makes them a prime target for governmental action and international conflicts of interest. Their frequently large size and the economies of scale in exploitation, require large scale, frequently multinational firms to carry out efficiently the exploitation. The low price elasticities of demand and supply, in the short run, make it possible to shift large slices of the net benefits from resource production from one country to another by manipulating supply or demand.

This paper describes the actions over the recent past of natural resource exporters and importers in attempting to meet their national objectives. It analyzes the broad types of actions toward asserting national control over resources through contract renegotiation, joint ventures, phase-outs (which we shall call "naturalizing foreign investment"), and the recourse to interruption of natural resource flows in foreign trade and actions in defense of such interruptions. First, however, the potential for conflicts of interest and shifting alliances will be briefly examined for the three groups of principal actors in international development of natural resources: the host (exporting) countries; the importing countries; and the MNCs which are mainly responsible for the development of production and trade. The paper will conclude with an assessment of the prospects for future policy actions in the extractive industries.

Reprinted by permission of the author. This study (January, 1975) is a part of the N.U.U. Project on the Multinational Firm in the U.S. and World Economy. It is adapted from a larger study *Resource Industries: A Multinational Prospective*. The editorial assistance and substantive comments of Professor Robert G. Hawkins are appreciated.

OBJECTIVES AND CONFLICTS AMONG THE PARTIES

EXPORTING COUNTRIES

The ultimate aims of the resource-exporting countries are, of course, economic development, rising income per capita, and economic and political security. The role of natural resources is to contribute to those goals in an optimal way. Unfortunately, there are substantial uncertainties surrounding natural resources which make policy planning extremely difficult. One is the price of the resource—which may be influenced by new discoveries, the development of substitutes, the pace of demand growth in the world market, as well as the policies of other suppliers. Another uncertainty is the actual amount and quality of the natural resources.

Constrained by the uncertainty, exporting governments, developed or developing, are generally guided by the goal of optimizing their long-run national benefits from the exploitation of their resources. These benefits are economic, social, and political; some are readily measurable, while others are not. But the uncertainty leads nations to actions which reduce their dependence on, and susceptibility to, primary commodity markets. One method is the industrialization of their raw materials as a means of diversifying their economic structure and of stabilizing their income at rising levels, and as a means of increasing employment opportunities and skills. This is a view held by both developing[1] and developed primary exporting countries.[2] Besides industrialization, diversification of their economic structures and of their trading partners is also a common objective. This reduces the economic instability and political insecurity which results from dependence on a few commodities, a few partner countries and/or companies, and the vicissitudes of the primary commodities markets.

In addition, governments sometimes attempt to raise the contribution of their natural resources to domestic objectives by exploiting the short- or intermediate-run inelasticity of demand for their commodities and push up the price. Such concern for higher revenues in the near short run may be acute for some governments, although the danger exists that such action may accelerate the substitution process for their commodities. But this pricing policy may be rational for the exporting country, given their needs and priorities for socioeconomic development, but not at all optimal from the view point of the international firms involved in the exploitation of the resources.[3] A contrary situation sometimes arises when future prices (in real terms and presently valued) are likely to be higher (e.g., with oil in the recent past). Assuming that there is no immediate need for funds, optimal policy would call for a deferral of production.[4]

A dominant strategy for several exporting countries in the 1970s involves the effective assertion of sovereignty and the exercise of national control over key sectors.[5] Such actions are clearly intended to reduce the uncertainty associated with primary production, but also to increase the power of the local government over the price and rate of exploitation of its resources.

Such action may, however, bear a cost to the economy. For example, "many Latin Americans and their governments prefer to restrict foreign capital in order to gain control over their own affairs, even if such a course signifies a sacrifice of some national economic growth."[6] This view is shared by a number of other countries, developed or developing, whose leaders may trade off economic activity or material prosperity for reducing dependence on foreign elements, and raising their level of self-reliance.[7]

This strategy of achieving national control over their natural resources is common among less developed countries. But several developed countries (DCs) have also voiced concern over the dominant role of foreign companies. Host country leaders do not want foreign capital (hitherto largely U.S.) to increase its share of ownership and control in the national economy beyond "tolerable levels." Among developed countries with natural resources, Canada and Australia have taken active steps to encourage domestic enterprise and capital to buy back—at least partially—foreign investments or to preserve domestic enterprises for national ownership and control in certain key sectors of the economy.[8] And the British, Norwegian, and Dutch governments have acted to promote national operators—including state-owned—in the development of oil and gas in the North Sea.[9] Even resource-importing developed countries restrict foreign capital, reserving certain activities for domestic enterprises, including Japan, the United States, and European countries.[10]

Thus, the exporting countries seek higher prices, more certainty, and greater control over their national resources—including the advanced countries who are net importers. The strategies include industrialization, diversification, and control over supply. This does not imply that exporting countries do not seek and need the capital, technology, marketing systems and management capabilities of the MNCs in the development of the resource potential. Even a country such as Egypt with an official "socialist" political system seeks a "healthy partnership" with foreign investors.[11]

IMPORTING COUNTRIES

Importing countries, of course, require natural resources to further their economic growth and income objectives, and sometimes even for their strategic and national defense objectives. More directly, they seek low prices of primary imports, and a steady and secure source of supply. Yet, they must also operate in a state of uncertainty over future price, the actions of their suppliers, and the possible development of substitutes locally.

This uncertainty has led to governmental actions to reduce the uncertainty. These involved reduced dependence on foreign supply—by developing local sources of supply and substitutes and by conservation in use; by purposely diversifying the foreign sources of supply; and by imposing economic sanctions against foreign suppliers which disrupt the supply or manipulate prices of imported resource products.

United States. The United States, the world's largest consumer of natural resources, has yet to develop a central, comprehensive policy with respect to minerals and natural resources, aside from securing "adequate, dependable, and hopefully low-cost supplies."[12] Some attempts have been made recently, in that direction, however. The most notable effort is Public Law 91-631 (1970) which states that the policy of the federal government at the domestic level is:

> . . .to foster and encourage private enterprise in (1) the development of economically sound and stable domestic mining, minerals, metal and mineral reclamation industries, (2) the orderly and economic development of domestic mineral resources reserves, and reclamation of metals and minerals to help assure satisfaction of industrial security and environmental needs, (3) mining, mineral and metallurgical research, including the use and recycling of scrap to promote the wise and efficient use of our natural and reclaimable mineral resources, and (4) the study and development of methods for the disposal, control, and reclamation of mineral waste products, and the reclamation of mined land, so as to lessen any adverse impact of mineral extraction and processing upon the physical environment that may result from mining or mineral activities.

At the international level, the U.S. law is vaguely general in advocating "measures necessary to maintain an adequate flow of minerals for America's future growth." Subsequent statements reveal a sharper focus, especially a heightened awareness of the country's dependence on imports of certain key materials. The growth in potential world demand is such that the United States, along with other major industrial countries, have become concerned, for strategic as well as for economic reasons, about assuring the regular availability of raw materials over the longer term at competitive prices.[13]

Japan. Japan, while third in the consumption of minerals after the United States and the Soviet Union, is the world's largest mineral importer. It has non-existent or limited domestic supplies in nearly all the major minerals, such as oil, coal, uranium, iron ore, or copper. This explains the Japanese government's anxious concern for a systematic minerals policy and for security of supplies.[14]

Japan's mineral policy objectives are basically four: low prices, stable prices, security of supplies, and reduction in the level of dependence on overseas supplies, even if such reduction must be at the expense of the growth in the gross national product.[15] The Japanese strategies for achieving security of supplies are essentially two: (a) geographical diversification of sources of imports, and (b) the acquisition of direct mineral producing rights by Japanese enterprises, thereby reducing their reliance on the hitherto dominant method of importing from non-Japanese intermediaries. The strategy of direct mineral rights, in effect, calls for vertical integration of the mineral-using industries upstream, namely from the fabricating end to the raw materials source.

The instruments the Japanese government has used in support of its minerals policy are fiscal, financial, and administrative. Tax incentives are offered for investments by Japanese enterprises in mining ventures. Moreover, the state-owned Metallic Mineral Exploration Agency (created in

1963), and the Japan Petroleum Development Corporation (1967), subsidize the domestic exploration and development of minerals, and finance Japanese overseas mining ventures and their import of mineral products. These financing activities are carried out in cooperation with Japanese governmental agencies such as the Export-Import Bank, the Overseas Economic Cooperation Fund, the Japan Overseas Development Corporation, and the Bank of Japan (BOJ). Assistance is limited to exclusively Japanese firms for their development of minerals for the Japanese market.[16]

The Japanese government can, furthermore, resort to moral suasion or issue "administrative guidance" through the Ministry of International Trade and Industry (MITI) to influence Japanese-based enterprises. This was the case in creating Kyodo Sekiyu, a domestic oil refining-marketing venture, through the guided merger of five small companies. The new company became eligible for cheap credit through the Japan Development Bank.[17] On March 5, 1973, MITI established guidelines for the direct purchase of crude oil from oil-exporting countries.[18] The major objective of MITI is to obtain information, seek coordination of company actions, and avoid excessive competition. These guidelines are apparently generally heeded by Japanese oil firms. For example, Australia's Minister for Minerals and Energy noted that the Japanese mineral industry, closely monitored by the Japanese government, used "traditional divisive tactics" to obtain better terms from competing Australian export groups.[19]

Continuous exchanges, discussion, and close cooperation are of long standing between government departments and private industry in Japan. Industrial groups such as the Petroleum Association (Sekiyu Renmei)[20] participate in the discussion of industrial policy issues, and assist in the formulation of industrial policy.[21] In many ways the Japanese government is much more involved in corporate decisions than the U.S. government.[22] The execution of Japanese policy in securing natural resources from abroad is a dramatic case in point.

France. France, like Japan, offers assistance to national firms searching for minerals overseas with a view to satisfying the domestic French market. Through the state-owned agency Bureau de Recherches Géologiques et Minières (B.R.G.M.), the French government assists financially the exploratory efforts of French firms in LDCs seeking critical materials for the French market. Prior to 1972, French official assistance was largely limited to petroleum; since then all minerals are eligible for such aid. Furthermore, the French government decided in 1972 to offer French enterprises a total of 300 million francs over a five-year period for carrying out overseas mineral prospecting.[23] It considered nationally desirable the vertical integration of French enterprises upstream to raw material sources overseas for a total of at least one-quarter to one-third of the country's requirements.

Efforts for Self-Sufficiency. Many importing countries, such as the United States, have offered extensive help for domestic exploration in an effort to increase self-sufficiency. Through the Office of Minerals Exploration

(OME) and the Defense Minerals Exploration Administration (DMEA), U.S. private enterprises are eligible for governmental aid when exploring for strategic and critical minerals and metals.[24] Other countries have offered financial support to ventures exploring for minerals in their territories—regardless of company nationality. For example, tax concessions, subsidies, or technical assistance provided by the Australian Commonwealth government to petroleum exploration ventures amounted to about A$419 million in early 1973, excluding assistance from state governments in Australia.[25]

It is difficult to assess and compare the various incentives or protections offered by countries to their natural resource ventures. The nature, conditions, and ranges of measures of aid or protection vary widely. Moreover, the period and tax treatment of industrial aids to natural resource development vary considerably. A comparative study of West European aid regimes showed that Italy, Eire, and Great Britain generally outpace other European countries in their respective global aid programs to their enterprises.[26]

As greater awareness has occurred of the limitations of availability of natural resources beyond national frontiers, some industrial powers have become increasingly sensitive to security of foreign supplies and for the need to develop new production capacity, both at home and abroad. This may sometimes carry the need for higher import prices, especially if the MNCs of the price-supporting country can contribute positively to offset the home country's balance of payments costs through repatriated profits or otherwise. Another reason for an importing country supporting a price increase in imports may well be to protect domestic producers, encourage local exploration, and spur improved conservation practices. Import restrictions or domestic subsidies could also accomplish the same objective of reducing imports, and are actively being proposed in some oil-importing countries. The spurring of domestic search might pay off ultimately in the development of domestic production at competitive costs, eliminating or reducing the dependence of that country on imports. A third reason may be that the mineral-importing country expects trade offs, or compensations from the beneficial mineral-exporting country or countries. Such compensation could pertain to economic or non-economic areas, such as occurred when Japanese policy toward Israel changed in the 1973-74 petroleum crisis.

Governments of industrial powers, such as the United States, Britain, France, Belgium, the Netherlands, and Japan, have at times offered support to their enterprises, both political and economic, against attempts by mineral-exporting countries to alter the terms of business contracts entered into with foreign enterprises. Industrial countries could use political and military actions as well as economic ones. With respect to the latter, the United States has, *inter alia*, enacted legislation (including the so-called Hickenlooper and Gonzalez Amendments) to withhold aid provided through bilateral or multilateral channels[27] from countries which fail to offer "prompt, adequate, and fair compensation" for American property nationalized by aid recipients.

MULTINATIONAL CORPORATIONS

The objectives of MNCs can generally be summarized in the optimization of profits (or rate of return on equity, or stockholder wealth) in the long-run, given the risk and uncertainty in their operating environments.[28] Yet the strategies by which MNCs pursue the profit optimization goal varies greatly from company to company, depending among other things upon the firm's perception of risks of particular ventures, the structure of the industry, and the history and experience of the firm.

Yet, there are characteristics of the multinational company in resource industries which color its relationship with host countries. One is the tendency toward, and attainment of, large size, which is associated with efficiency, profitability, and market power. Another is the MNC's superior access to market and technical knowledge. Another is the flexibility of the MNC in pricing, taxation, and sourcing. Obviously, each of these characteristics affects the position of the firm relative to the host government and home government in the distribution of the gains from natural resource exploration. However, the more obvious and dramatic examples appear in relation to the LDC host country.

Size, Diversification, and Integration. To strive for size, diversification, and vertical integration is common among resource enterprises, be they based in the Western or in the Eastern hemisphere. This was clearly put by the chief executive of an Australian enterprise: "We believe your company derives considerable strength from the diversified and integrated nature of its operations. Integration provides maximum access to research, development, and financing resources. Diversification protects share holders from sole dependence on the short-term success of a particular product or activity."[29] Another example is found in the 1971 merger of two major French firms, Pechiney and Ugine Kuhlmann. The former firm was largely in minerals/metals, and the latter in chemicals/metals. The objective was not "systematic gigantism" (although the merger gave the new company quasi-monopoly power in France in such commodities as aluminum) but diversification and the ability to exploit a larger number of options available to the enterprise, to rationalize management, to attain economies of scale, and to support more research and development.[30] And it is common knowledge that the major international oil companies have pursued an active program of diversification of both sources of crude and product, are vertically integrated, and have a major advantage of size with respect to research and exploration.

Flexibility. The flexibility of the large MNC in the natural resource industries may take many forms. These include the shifting of sources of supply as market conditions change, having access to several sources of finance, and of technology. But the very frequently cited advantage is the MNC's flexibility in setting transfer prices.

One presumed advantage which the MNC can use in its endeavor to maximize long-term returns is to set transfer prices among its affiliates, to the extent this is possible, with a view to reducing their global tax burden.[31]

This can be done, within limits, by splitting their vertically integrated profits so as to declare lower taxable profits in high-tax countries, and higher taxable profits in low-tax countries.[32] But there is some doubt as to the extent to which this is a factor in MNC strategy in resource industries.

In exercising their discretion in setting inter-affiliate transfer prices, MNCs in resource industries may be more frequently prompted to show the least returns on those functions which are readily accessible to actual and potential competitors, in order to discourage their entry and/or their predatory competition. By comparison, they will show highest returns on those functions most accessible, for reasons of technology, size, or other barriers, to competitors.[33] Many of the international enterprises are conscious of the need to be able to justify their transfer prices by market criteria, since in every country in which an affiliate operates, it is increasingly subject to the surveillance of the tax authorities. The flexibility which an MNC may use to reduce tax burdens or reduce its risk and uncertainty at the expense of the host and/or home governments has thus probably decreased in the recent past.

Knowledge and Bargaining Strategy. It has historically been argued that large MNCs had substantial superiority in negotiating the terms of entry and operation with developing countries rich in natural resources.[34] The source of the MNCs' advantage surely included their size and resources; their capacity to exploit economies of scale, advanced technology, and know-how; their superior organizational and managerial ability; and their extensive market outlets. But much of this advantage can be summarized as superior knowledge about markets, and historically these factors have favored the international companies in bilateral negotiations with mineral-exporting LDCs.

Even the government of a developed country like Australia has admitted to the strong bargaining power of foreign mineral companies and the capture of economic rents from Australia.[35] And some claim that the power of the giant international enterprises transcends national boundaries, and comes close to forming independent supra-national entities. An illustration of such power perhaps may be found in the international prorationing of petroleum implemented by international oil companies following the reduction in Arab oil exports to selected destinations in late 1973. In fact, the international oligopoly partially thwarted Arab action, by diverting non-Arab oil supplies from countries not affected by Arab cutbacks, in favor of the affected countries. This redistribution of world oil supplies was made in accordance with what the international companies deemed as "equitable."[36] Available evidence tends to support the view that the supra-nationality characteristic of international firms has not always been exaggerated. Moreover, it is reasonable that executives of MNCs have enjoyed and exercised some measure of discretionary power—subject to the constraints of the home and host country, their industrially advanced parent countries perhaps wielding the greater influence. This was suggested in an official Canadian report on

MNCs which said that "the investment decisions of foreign-controlled corporations tend to reflect the laws and industrial priorities of foreign governments and economies."[37]

But others contend that the "supra-national" power of international business is a myth in a world of nationalistic nation-states in which home governments frequently fail to unite with and support the actions of their MNCs abroad.[38] And some LDC government negotiators have recently come close to matching the competence and skill of the negotiators of the international companies they confront, and have gained considerable expertise concerning the markets in which their countries are involved. Moreover, international companies are induced to show restraint in their bargaining lest they create resentment and retribution, perhaps ending in future nationalization. The vigor of international competition among MNCs has greatly increased in the last decade, and offers alternative partners for a host government, thereby increasing its bargaining power and providing a possible substitute for a host country's lack of information. This assumes, however, that the host government concerned has the ability to take advantage of that competition—which is not always the case. But the pendulum of bargaining power may be swinging toward the host-country resource owners.

COMMON AND CONFLICTING INTERESTS

The MNC in the extractive industries sometimes finds itself as a buffer between the interests of the host exporting country and the home importing country. But on certain issues, it will have common interest with the home country; on other issues it will share a common interest with the host country. Thus, the extent to which MNCs heed or influence governmental objectives varies from one country to another and from issue to issue.

Home governments have clearly responded to the wishes of their firms on several occasions. The official reason frequently cited is the national interest. For example, in January, March, and October, 1971, the U.S. Department of Justice considered that U.S. anti-trust law did not apply to the actions of U.S. and other Western petroleum companies to join forces to bargain collectively on production, tax, and price matters with OPEC. The rationale for permitting this collective company action was to permit an oil company bloc to face the OPEC governmental group in order to moderate oil price increases to Western consumers.[39]

There is, perhaps, a general tendency to establish symbiotic accommodations among major protagonists in international resource development. A symbiosis between the MNCs and governments of home industrial countries where the principal economic interests of the MNCs generally lie has occasionally been sought in the dealings of the two groups with host-country groupings, such as OPEC. The United States government led in 1974 the formation of such a framework comprising major Western energy consuming countries, viz., the United States, Canada, EEC, Norway, and Japan, and to include the interests of the major MNCs in the oil industry.

On other issues, resource-exporting countries and the international oligopolists have common interests. For example, higher product prices, restrictive entry of alternative sources or substitutes, maintaining business stability, and securing growth of sales may all find a commonality of interest between the MNCs and the host countries. One of the many advantages which international corporations can offer resource-exporting countries is that they can lobby in favor of relaxing trade barriers with their home-country authorities. The greater their interests in the host countries, the more intense is likely to be their lobbying. This was apparently the case with Anaconda, with the help of Kennecott, in successfully fighting the suspension of tariff concessions sought by a majority of U.S. domestic producers, and favored by the U.S. administration in the 1950s.[40]

The above review of objectives and interests of major parties to resource industries has stressed the dominant ones. It should be emphasized that the MNCs have resources which exporting countries need, that the importing countries have the markets which the exporters and MNCs require, and that the exporting countries need to convert their resources into the means of sustained economic development. There is, therefore, a major harmony of interest. But the specific interests of the parties conflict over how and on what terms the resources are exploited and the gains divided. These general conflicts get translated into specific positions frequently conflicting on given issues.

It would be unrealistic to leave the impression that objectives and interests within the groups of parties are uniform or necessarily consistent.

POLICY ACTIONS AND PROBLEMS IN THE NEW RESOURCE ENVIRONMENT

Within the context of actual and potential conflicts of interest between the parties in the development and international trade in natural resource products, and with the evolution of new market conditions, several general policy trends are already well advanced and are likely to continue. These trends are mainly, but not exclusively, the result of actions by governments of the resource-exporting MNC host countries. They include assertions of sovereignty concerning the form and terms with which host governments do business with MNCs in the resource field, with actions to interrupt and to defend against the interruption of the flow of natural resources in international trade.

"NATURALIZING" FOREIGN INVESTMENT

Perhaps the most widespread focus of host-country policies in natural resource industries has been to bring the ownership and/or control of capital investments and mineral rights more directly under the direction of the host government. This is a tendency encompassing both the advanced industrial countries as well as, and perhaps more emphatically, the LDCs. The means with which this policy objective has been attempted are quite varied, and involve a strengthening of the conditions and terms of new involvements with MNCs as well as changing the rules-of-the-game for existing affiliates of MNCs and concessionaires. We can conveniently group these diverse actions around (a) those involving a change in or renegotiation of the economic conditions and terms of doing business with existing foreign MNCs; (b) those which relate to requirements for joint ventures with a host-government agency; and (c) those designed to ultimately phase-out, or divest, the MNC of its equity ownership in local operations.

Changing the Terms and Conditions of Doing Business. In principle, the terms offered to a foreign MNC should not fall below a range which makes it worthwhile for the enterprise to locate in the country concerned. To estimate the optimal level, a government should ascertain the competitive economic advantage its territory has over the next best alternative location; and it should then set the terms so as to capture most (or all) of that advantage for itself.

Once an operation is underway, the outcome may be very different from that expected by either the host government or by the MNC. This may result from the failure in expectations in the commercial, technical, or geological sphere. It may involve error in the adverse direction, so that the project proves to be unprofitable for the MNC and unsuccessful for the host country; or it may have erred in the favorable direction, bringing in higher than expected profits and meeting the expectations of the host country.

In the latter case, there has been a strong tendency for host countries to demand, and of late to obtain, a renegotiation of terms or perhaps act unilaterally to change those terms, in effect using the fixed capital of the MNC as a "sunk-cost" hostage to validate its desired change. Such *ex post* changes in conditions can and have been justified on several grounds.[41]

The first justification, mentioned above, is that some developing countries with limited sophistication have been faced by skilled company negotiators who have exploited their superior knowledge by obtaining terms more favorable than required to induce the firm to enter. The most grotesque extremes can be seen in the many cases that could be described "in which the U.S. company representative bargained determinedly for relief from local taxes even though the savings would be almost exactly offset by the higher United States taxes that result from the loss of foreign tax credits."[42] And a leading international enterprise acknowledged that "competition among developing countries in providing incentives can become so great that overly generous incentives are offered."[43] These countries may forego tax revenue in their attempt to attract foreign investments. But these incentives may prove in fact meaningless if the home country denies such incentives by applying the full home tax rate to all income from foreign investments. This situation obviously calls for an *ex post* change in the financial terms of the investment with a view to enabling the host country to capture from the foreign affiliate the tax proceeds which are payable on that affiliate's profits in the host country, but are in fact paid abroad because of the host country's overly generous incentives.

A second justification for the host country's intervention to change the business terms of an enterprise is to eliminate discrimination against the local economy. Empirical investigations have shown that the majority of developing countries paid "higher than competitive prices" for their oil imports.[44] Developing countries seek to obtain terms (prices) similar to those which MNCs have offered to developed economies. Equal treatment for poor countries, as compared with the rich, should cover various commodities entering international trade, and should apply to price, quality, regularity of supplies; and when this does not occur, host countries will demand appropriate changes in contract terms.

A third reason for changing the economic terms under which foreign MNCs operate may be the existence of windfall profits for the MNC. There is ample precedent for such renegotiations in industrial countries. A number of countries have enacted legislation to permit the renegotiation of certain terms of contracts between government and private business. Renegotiation can be set at specified intervals, or be linked to certain changes in circumstances. For example, the U.S. Renegotiation Act of 1951, as amended, aims at profit limitation on contracts (and their subcontracts) entered into by Federal governmental agencies, notably those concerned with defense, aviation, atomic energy, procurement, and maritime transport. The Act empowers its Board, by agreement with private companies or by order, to recoup excessive profits as defined by the Act from contractors and related parties (such as banks, insurance companies, lessor companies, manufacturers' agents, and brokers). The Board determinations of excessive profits and voluntary refunds and price reductions exceeded $2.5 billion by mid-1973.[45]

U.S. government decisions on normal return and excessive profits are not confined to procurement contracts; they also pertain to the public utilities field. Moreover, the U.S. authorities have stretched their regulation of normal return to companies operating beyond their national boundaries. Thus, the U.S. Federal Power Commission recommended that return on equity investment by a U.S. company (El Paso) from the export of Algerian natural gas to the United States be limited to 16 percent of equity investment in this project.[46]

The renegotiation of the terms of long-term contracts provides a measure of flexibility for adapting to changing circumstances, and reduces the chances of confrontation, deadlock, and default. Renegotiation may sometimes help the firm by lightening its fiscal burden and easing its other terms should mineral discoveries prove disappointing. Renegotiation may also provide the host country with the opportunity of sharing in windfall gains, or from tax credits in the firm's home country. The desirability of renegotiation has been underscored by Kindleberger: "Renegotiations of contracts with long life when the underlying conditions change is familiar in the Anglo-Saxon tradition."[47]

Some LDCs have attempted to emulate the U.S. experience. They have, on several occasions, asked for the renegotiation of contracts for the exploitation of their natural resources. Several host governments, as owners and lessors of these resources, have claimed the right to recoup excess profits of the MNC. Others have asked for equity and management participation in mineral ventures. Of course, there are many computational problems in ascertaining what are "normal" and what are "excessive" profits. The present techniques of financial accounting are quite imperfect in measuring the economic concept for a business enterprise in a given period of time, and are far from uniform world-wide.[48]

One of the major problems in determining the existence of "wind-fall" profits is to ascertain the actual size of a venture's profits attributable to a host country. This problem is most common in the case of an oligopolistic MNC characterized by vertical integration, such as in the petroleum industry. Raw materials or intermediate products need not always be valued at market prices, as noted above. Accordingly, profits generated by a given function or activity in a host country in a vertically integrated firm have to be imputed.

Different approaches have been followed by tax authorities in assessing business profits for vertically integrated MNCs. Notable approaches include (a) prorating the consolidated profits of the international firm in accordance with the geographical location of invested capital (for example, a refinery or pipeline transport);[49] (b) attributing a "normal" or "reasonable" return on the firm's investments in the processing, manufacturing, or servicing functions, and leaving the residual as profits on exploration and extraction of minerals; (c) attributing a "normal" or "reasonable" return on invested capital in the exploration for, and production of, minerals; (d) valuing sales receipts—and consequently profits—on the basis of whatever evidence exists on arm's length prices in the open market; and (e) negotiating "acceptable" taxable profit margins by the interested parties (the parent country, the host country, and the international firm), and agreeing on methods for changing them.

The latter approach provides a greater opportunity for adjusting the definition as information becomes available. With the availability of more information, and the increased expertise of their officials, LDCs were able to raise their returns from their primary exports. According to the Government of Jamaica, "due to the bauxite industry's control over information, the terms of the contracts agreed upon in several instances proved later to be unfavorable to the Government, causing substantial loss of revenue."[50]

From the host country's point of view, whether economic rents are reaped by taxes, royalties, or governmental participation is a matter of legal formality; its capture for the local economy is the only thing of economic consequence. In selecting one method of payment versus another, an international enterprise, by comparison, is concerned with selecting the one which will reduce its global tax payments. The enterprise, for example, will be affected by the tax treatment in its own country of its payments to host countries.

Joint Ventures. A second definite policy trend is to resort to joint ventures as the only acceptable medium by which foreign MNCs are permitted to participate in certain sectors. Countries at an early stage of development, being careful not to jump too quickly into the race to gain control over their foreign-owned and -operated enterprises, see joint ventures as a possible intermediate step. "We are a small country of limited means . . . Other countries can afford to go faster by taking big leaps ahead. For us, it would be more prudent to move slowly but safely. First of all, we have to constitute the cadres necessary for the exploitation of our resources and the development of our country."[51]

Through joint ventures, host governments hope to influence their foreign partners more effectively for the host-country's interest than they would be able to influence a 100 percent foreign-owned concessionaire. Such influence might show up in inducing the joint venture to carry out other business activities ranking high in national priorities. For the president of Zambia (Kenneth Kaunda), joint ventures between foreign companies and the national group (called ZIMCO) are more conducive to the development of the host country than is total national ownership.[52]

A number of foreign concessionaires have offered host governments participation in their ventures at a future date after the start of operations and sometimes after reaping the attractive profits they sought. One example is the iron concession granted by Peru to Marcona Mining Company in 1952. The Peruvian state-owned steel company, Corporacion Peruana del Santa, holds an option to acquire 50 percent ownership in 1982 (namely, thirty years after the original award date) without cash investment.[53]

Saudi Arabia was a leading exponent of participation in 1973. Its Minister of Petroleum and Mineral Resources defended participation on the grounds that it satisfied the host country in gaining majority control over its natural resources, and in providing it with an organic commitment on the part of the international companies which remain interested in giving the joint venture access to the fruits of continuous research and development, and access to markets.[54] By 1974, however, the success of OPEC's price-raising strategy had changed this government's position to one in which total local ownership was the goal.

MNCs have recently accepted, albeit reluctantly, the process of host-country participation as inevitable in resource industries. Some host governments have already obtained majority ownership, but foreign partners generally retain assurances that they will share effectively in decision making in the major business areas of budgeting and planning, production and control, pricing and marketing, organizing and staffing, etc. On such assurances, MNCs have sometimes accelerated and encouraged the "naturalization" process.

Host governments have generally been able to enter into partnership with MNCs only when they could offer comparatively attractive terms for domestic inputs (i.e., large deposits or low cost of exploitation), fiscal incentives, assured domestic and/or export markets, or when they could play on the competitive rivalry of several MNCs. The resistance of MNCs to any threat to its centralized control, or to its full ownership of ventures in host countries, has been broken only when strategic inputs—which could be technology, raw materials, capital, managerial know-how, or others—or market outlets are available outside the oligopolists,[55] or when the exporting countries have become tightly organized. In support of majority ownership by the host country in joint ventures, one empirical investigation dealing with Canada concludes that "the alleged redistribution of oligopoly profits from foreigners to Canadians may be an illusion"[56] if minority ownership of foreign enterprises were promoted.

To increase national ownership of key industries, several developed countries have offered financial aid to private nationals. The Australian government, for example, established on June 10, 1970, an Australian Industry Development Corporation to assist financially Australians who are interested in acquiring ownership of, and eventually control over, industries and resources hitherto dominated by foreign interests. LDCs, as compared with Canada or Australia, are far less equipped to protect their interests with minority ownership, or through private joint-venture partners. There are many examples of "straw men" domestic partners, private or state owned, that do not play an active role in the enterprise labelled "joint."

There is not always a confluence of interests between the host government and local private joint-venture partners with foreign MNCs. Whereas private local partners are interested in maximizing their private gain in the joint venture, whether that gain is derived from market imperfections or otherwise, host governments are generally not solely or primarily concerned with immediate profits. They are more directly greatly interested in transferring to the domestic economy managerial and technological skills, and access to foreign markets. The international enterprise is naturally reluctant —unless forced to—to acquiesce to such transfers in fear of losing its competitive advantages.[57] For the LDC resource exporters the joint venture with the host government as local partner is, and will likely continue to be, the preferred arrangement.

Service Contracts and Divestment. A third process of "naturalization" of foreign firms involves the elimination of the equity participation of the MNC, and the substitution of negotiated contracts for the continued supply of its services. In their search for self-reliance and development, host countries have sought to assume the principal role in the management of their resources. But this does not preclude the need to use expatriate skills for certain functions such as international marketing, financial and technical management, until local capabilities are developed. Some countries have favored the service contract approach or limited tenure of foreign ventures as opposed to "joint-venture" participation. Under one type of popular service contract arrangement, the foreign firm would assume the managerial-technical responsibility and underwrite over a pre-arranged period the financial-operational risks of building and/or operating a domestic venture pending the development of national capabilities. In return, the venturing foreign firm would receive a "fee." The fee could be a payment in kind or in money; it can be fixed or graduated in relation to size of discoveries of natural resources, the size of production, profits, foreign exchange savings, ventured resources, or according to other measures of input or performance.

Service contracts are extremely flexible devices which meet the needs of host countries for filling gaps in managerial know-how, technology and other inputs. They can be adapted to widely diverse circumstances, and may satisfy a host country's objective of greater control over its natural resources consistent with maximum national economic gain.[58] They are also likely to survive under changed political conditions or revolutionary upheavals in host countries more easily than traditional types of direct investments and control by the MNC. The higher staying power of a service contract is a result of the fact that the ownership-managerial control rest with the host country while the terms of a contract can be renegotiated far more easily than a joint venture. Also, a service contract normally has a definite duration so that the prospect for foreign involvement is for a limited period.

For existing foreign direct investments, few MNCs have offered voluntarily, as a matter of policy, purchase options or the phasing out of their ownership and control of affiliates in LDCs in favor of national interests. But with the growth of economic nationalism, foreign-owned ventures may have to accept a gradual divestment (also known as faae out or attenuation) of their ventures in host countries, starting at a reasonably early date, say within 15 years from the beginning of commercial operations. The expatriate companies would then cease being direct owners in host countries to become suppliers of know-how and buyers of materials from their erstwhile operations, then owned by host national companies. Optimal divestment calls for devising a framework for the orderly, gradual, and appropriate timing of transfer of ownership and management from expatriate firms to host-country interests—in order to permit proper learning of the business over a period of partnership with the international firm.

Scholars and policy makers have advocated the transfer of ownership and control of foreign ventures to local interests as a means of speeding up their economic development.[59] Foreign firms could be induced to pass on new technology on a royalty basis or service contract basis. But it is also possible that total local ownership to the outright exclusion of foreign interests can reduce the availability of foreign capital and know-how, and slow down development. In some technology-intensive industries, MNCs may simply ignore a potential host country which requires "fade out" or forbids foreign equity ownership. But with many natural resources approaching worldwide scarcity, this does not appear to be the case for the extractive sector. There is surely an optimal mix for a country of what is politically desirable in terms of foreign ownership and what is economically achievable in national development with various levels of foreign participation. In a number of cases, foreign firms continue to contribute to host economies through an unending broadening and deepening of their involvement. Accordingly, "a program of divestiture that cuts off this process could be hurtful to the governments that were demanding it."[60]

For developmental purposes, foreign investment could therefore be girded to serve "as a rotating fund that temporarily, over periods of varying lengths, depending on the kind of investment, offsets the shortage of technical and financial resources on the part of local enterprise." According to this view, "the foreign investor should be prepared at all times to transfer majority interest in the firm to local investors and be ready to seek other investment opportunities in those activities where technological contributions continue to be of fundamental importance."[61] The host country may take the initiative in pointing to those activities or sectors of the economy where a transient role for foreign enterprise is welcome.

In order to smooth the transfer of foreign interests in developing countries, while not hurting the prospects of availability and flow of foreign capital and know-how to developing countries, there may therefore be a need to set up a novel international financial institution, with regional or national affiliates. This might be called the International Divestment-Investment Corporation (IDIC). This corporation would be entrusted with the functions of supervising the progressive liquidation of foreign investments and the transfer of their ownership and management to national interests. It should also act as a bridging financier and/or a trustee for a period of transition, if expatriate firms are ready and willing to make the transfer of assets, while national interests may not have adequate financial resources to pay for the transfer at that time, or may not have the managerial capacity and technical know-how to administer these assets. IDIC could furthermore be entrusted with the function of guarantor of debtor obligations, and could be called on to act as a neutral arbiter in settling disputes or disagreements with respect to valuation of assets to be transferred. Finally, IDIC could act as an investment catalyst channeling divested resources into new productive ventures of various developing countries.

The above-mentioned functions of financial intermediary would require IDIC to have resources of its own. Whether these resources should be raised from the international money and capital markets, or whether they should be raised from existing international financial institutions deserves a special investigation. Such an investigation would also have to assess the basis of contributions to be made by divesting-investing firms, host countries, and parent countries. On this point, Raul Prebisch commented, "It may perhaps be difficult to understand how an advanced country could contribute financial resources in order to enable Latin American (and other LDCs) private initiative to obtain control of undertakings which would otherwise remain in the hands of the developed country's private enterprise. But this would be too shortsighted a view . . . The continuing process of technological improvement will leave foreign enterprise ample scope for action, since as soon as domestic initiative has acquired a controlling interest in certain enterprises, new opportunities for association on a basis of reciprocal benefits will supervene."[62] To some business enterprises, the previously mentioned "new opportunities" could very well fail to materialize in one country—though not necessarily in a region or in the developing world at large.

Already, the Commonwealth Development Corporation (CDC)—specifically set up in 1948 by the British Treasury with a view to contributing to the development of LDCs (until 1969 confined to the Commonwealth) through equity capital, soft-term loans, and managerial know-how—has agreed to arrange for a gradual transfer to local ownership and management of the productive enterprises it has helped set up. This transfer is done selectively.[63] Other countries have also specialized investment institutions aimed at floating developmental projects with divestment features in favor of host countries—notably West Germany (German Development Co.), and Denmark (Danish Industrialization Fund for Developing Countries).[64] A broadly similar function is performed by the International Finance Corporation (IFC), a member of the World Bank group, although the IFC is committed to assisting solely private enterprises—to the explicit exclusion of government-owned and/or controlled institutions—while no such limitation is found with, for example, CDC.

In support of divestment of foreign private investors in favor of local interests, an executive of IFC commented that "absentee landlordism in industry has had its day." He noted that in IFC's experience, it was not difficult to find local partners, and to live with them in peace and harmony.[65]

Divestment could come after a period during which the foreign investor regained the original capital and adequate profits—given the risks attendant to his investment. The appropriate period would thus be longer for a company exploring for a mineral in a virgin territory, as compared with exploration in an already proven territory. Flexibility should obtain in the sale of investments, and the host government and its nationals should be eligible to exercise the purchase option over reasonably long periods, to allow for their ability to pay for, and/or manage, the venture. Equally, the expatriate company should be given the opportunity of running the venture for a longer period alone, or in partnership with local interests, if the two parties find it in their mutual interest to do so.[66]

It is probable that leading creditor-investor developed countries and their MNCs would be reluctant to support an institution such as IDIC.[67] Given such political difficulties, it may be more practical for each host country to set explicitly the legal framework for foreign enterprises—with divestment, re-investment, or other guidelines pre-agreed on in individual contracts, and adapted to meet the particular needs of a country and the MNCs concerned. There have been a number of cases in which MNCs have accepted on a voluntary basis the conversion of their investments into joint ventures with domestic enterprises, both state-owned or privately-owned. There are also cases where the international enterprise has voluntarily divested or sold one affiliate to develop other activities.

A notable example occurred in Mexico. Mineral deposits in that country are owned by the state, and mining concessions were given, until 1961, for perpetuity—assuming normal conditions. The Mexican government introduced in 1961 tax laws reducing to 25 years the life of mining concessions, with renewals subject to majority (51 percent and above) equity interest by Mexican nationals. To induce such "Mexicanization," the government granted a 50 percent reduction in production and export taxes. Several international enterprises have found the Mexican offer enticing. Anaconda, traditionally the largest producer of Mexican copper, took advantage of the Mexicanization law in 1971. Its principal obstacle in the process of divestment was a "shortage of liquid investment capital in Mexico available to purchase a majority interest."[68] The largest group of Mexican investors with available resources turned out to be governmental agencies.

In another case, the International Telephone and Telegraph Company (U.S.) sold, in 1969, its telephone system operation in Peru to the government for $17.9 million and agreed to use $8.2 million from the proceeds to expand locally in the hotel business and to set up a joint venture with the government for the construction of a telephone equipment factory.[69]

Probably the most elaborate agreement for divestment-investment has been that between a Canadian holding company, viz., Brazilian Light and Power Company, Ltd., and the federal government of Brazil. The company, which is controlled by North American and West European capital, agreed to sell in 1966 its telephone assets for $93.3 million. It concurrently agreed to reinvest $65 million in Brazilian ventures, and to observe important guidelines, mainly: (a) the enterprises invested in should contribute to Brazil's development; (b) investment should be used to add to productive capacity, not to buy out existing owners; and (c) investment should be as a minority shareholder only. The Brazilian precedent could well offer a pattern worthy of emulation by other developing countries.[70]

The policy of requiring foreign private enterprises to divest gradually major portions of their ownership and control in favor of local interests (including employees) has been incorporated in the Andean Pact.[71] The latter group includes Columbia, Equador, Bolivia, Peru, Chile, and Venezuela. The Pact requires an obligatory divestment on the part of all wholly-owned foreign enterprises of a minimum of 15 percent of the capital within a period not exceeding three years from the date of enforcement of the Cartagena Agreement, or the date of initial production of the enterprise. Divestment is gradated to 51 percent in favor of nationals, with slower schedules (over twenty years) for Bolivia and Ecuador as compared with Chile, Colombia, and Peru (over fifteen years). In *quid pro quo* for gradual divestment, the divesting firms benefit from the duty-free movement of goods within the five countries.

Some MNCs have responded individually or collectively to the wish of several developing countries to promote and strengthen their national small business enterprises—using the divestment approach. The leading example of collective cooperation is the Atlantic Community Development Group for Latin America (ADELA), an investment company supported by 235 international corporations and banks, mostly from the United States, Canada, Western Europe, and Japan. ADELA's function is to engage in joint ventures with private or public enterprises in Latin America, as a minority shareholder. Its purpose is to start new industries which it gradually relinquishes once the proejcts are well established. As put by its president, "ADELA is not simply an 'investment.' More than a mere provider of capital, it stimulates private initiative and provides development services and financing to economically viable new projects and for the growth of existing enterprises. *It shares the high initial risk inherent in new ventures in developing countries and divests when enterprises mature.*"[72]

ADELA's remarkable contribution lies in the initiative and capability it has in identifying, studying, structuring, promoting, and implementing projects with maximum economic impact. These are defined as labor-intensive projects (construction, tourism, agribusiness excluding natural resources) and/or those producing and exporting non-traditional goods.[73] Late in 1973, ADELA's cumulative loans and investments exceeded $1 billion, serving some 400 small enterprises in over twenty Latin American countries.[74]

The concept of ADELA is extremely popular with developing countries, and many policy makers and scholars find that its advantages could be substantial if it were not restricted to small enterprises, to the exclusion of medium- or large-sized national enterprises in developing countries.

With adequate incentives, a divestment-investment mechanism applying to foreign enterprises could yield the host country concerned valuable benefits in the transfer of technology and know-how, in the development of managerial ability, in innovating methods and processes of production, and in creating successive and successful ventures, hopefully leading to a self-sustained momentum of progressive development. The orderly transfer of management and ownership to national interests need not, furthermore, lead to a divorce between the international firm and its erstwhile affiliate. The new domestic venture can and may well be advised to maintain business relations with its former parent, especially to arrange for managerial and technical cooperation, and the use of trade marks to take advantage of the MNC's continually evolving technology. It is also in the interest of the divested domestic venture to arrange to maintain normal trading relations with the former international parent and its clients. This strategy is especially beneficial in the case where the domestic venture is producing specialized items which fit specifically the production system of the international enterprise. It is also useful when the domestic venture does not have ready access to international markets, or to the requisite technology. This co-operation builds economic interdependence of buyers and sellers.

Divestment can also be profitable for the MNC. Divestment will often enable the erstwhile mother company to maintain service contracts for technical know-how, marketing arrangements, and other matters. It may also improve the divesting firm's return on equity—especially if host countries offer tax incentives which are not nullified by home countries. A 2 percent annual divestment rate would result in a 50-year-life company, and a 3.6525 percent in a 27-year-life company. It has been demonstrated that in countries with a 50 percent income tax rate, reductions of the tax rate to 45 percent for a 2 percent annual divestment, and to 40 percent for a 3.65 percent annual divestment are more profitable to stockholders of the divesting firms than conventional corporate ventures with a perpetual life.[75] Divesting with profit has the advantage of attracting foreign investments and providing a mechanism to convert established foreign ventures into national ones. Divestment of MNCs from their ventures in LDC mineral exporters may very well prove to be in the interest of the importing countries if it promotes harmony and amity between producer and consumer. One Western economist even surmised that if international companies pulled out completely from oil-exporting countries, the latter—especially the ones with large reserves—would then be tempted to compete prices down. He accordingly recommended, in the interest of the developed industrial countries and their consumers, that the international companies divest voluntarily their producing ventures in host countries.[76]

Under other circumstances, divestment may harm the interests of MNCs and their home countries. If divestment cuts them off from cheap sources of resources, or increases the uncertainty in sourcing of primary commodities, this would be the case. For the firm, the rate of return may be lower as well. A U.S. presidential commission came out bluntly against programs aimed at facilitating the sale and transfer of ownership of U.S. foreign affiliates to host countries.[77] There is some evidence that major U.S. MNCs have had significant influence on the U.S. government to resist divestiture or nationalization of their ventures abroad even when the U.S. public interest was not necessarily or unequivocally adversely affected.[78] Divestment or nationalization has to be done with at least the tacit approval or neutrality of major industrial countries—lest these countries use their potent trade, aid, and other instruments against LDCs. For example, if "prompt, adequate, and effective" compensation acceptable to nationalized U.S. interests had not been paid, the U.S. President can cut bilateral aid (so-called Hickenlooper Amendment of the Foreign Assistance Act), and instruct U.S. executive directors in the World Bank Group, the Asian Bank, and the Inter-American Development Bank to vote against any loan for the benefit of the country concerned.[79]

Several LDCs believe, however, that compensation to international firms for take-overs should be negligible, or even negative. They have argued that these firms' "excessive profits" in the past and their inadequate payments of tax to host countries is ample justification.[80]

The programmed fade-out of foreign investors, with the substitution of service contracts, is thus of great appeal to LDCs, especially for resource industries. More LDCs are likely to resort to such requirements in the future. This form of naturalization may have mutual benefits for both the MNC and the host country, but only if the terms are tailored appropriately. To date, the experience has been mixed. As noted, for broader use and success of this device, specialized institutions to develop the funding and expertise to ease the transition may be required.

INTERRUPTIONS OF RESOURCE FLOWS

Purposeful interruptions of resource flows to accomplish certain objectives are not new. Governments, trade unions, and companies have utilized blockades, embargoes, boycotts, strikes, and the like for centuries to accomplish their own ends. The power and disruptiveness of such action was dramatically illustrated in the interruption of crude petroleum flows by producing countries in late 1973 and early 1974. This had a major effect on international trade. Whether it portends a new trend in the form and policy tools in international business remains to be seen. But it was not an isolated event. This section briefly reviews interruptive actions by various groups of countries in the past, and assesses various efforts by groups of countries to neutralize or minimize the unfavorable effects of such actions.

Basis minerals and several other commodities are, of course, vital to modern economics. This has led to a wide international concern for "security of supply" and for "security of demand." The term security may convey different meanings to different parties: (a) It may mean the continued and regular physical availability of commodities regardless of the attached economic or non-economic terms, or (b) it may mean such physical availability at economically and politically acceptable terms (prices) to the parties concerned.

For the United States, for example, national security with respect to oil has four major objectives, all having to do with security of *supply*, as defined by the director of the U.S. Office of Emergency Preparedness (George A. Lincoln):

1. Maintain a satisfactory level of domestic reserves of crude oil, supplemented from secure sources of foreign supply;
2. Maintain spare capacity to produce and deliver crude oil when international factors disrupt supplies from other sources;
3. Maintain refinery capacity in the United States adequate to meet both defense and essential civilian needs in periods of disruption of normal world oil trade; and
4. Provide a petroleum industry in the United States with the capacity to meet the nation's defense and essential civilian needs at all times.[81]

In the United States, restrictions on oil imports were in force from 1958 to 1973 to protect the domestic petroleum industry and thus preclude undue dependence on the vicissitudes of foreign policy—admittedly at a cost to U.S. consumers.[82]

Observers are generally familiar with aspects of supply security,[83] and the oil crisis of 1973-74 has reinforced that familiarity. But the concept of demand security has recently begun to receive attention, at least by academicians and analysts.[84] "Demand interruption" refers to the decision of one or more of the industrially developed countries and their international enterprises to interrupt, curtail, or boycott directly or indirectly the demand for the regular exports of one country or a group of countries. As on the supply side, such interruptions may be prompted by mixed politico-economic motives, such as a change in the political regimes of certain countries or the nationalization of foreign assets. The LDCs faced by demand interruption may not have the resource flexibility and the administrative ability to change their pattern of exports in the short or intermediate run. In addition, the absence of a diversified economic base precludes them from making up for a loss of exports in one commodity by increased exports in other commodities. These countries, faced with demand interruption, could have their socioeconomic programs and their internal stability impaired.

One example of demand interruption was that connected with the nationalization of the Iranian oil industry in 1951. For over three years, Iran was faced with a total boycott of oil exports instituted by major international companies which supported the Anglo-Iranian Oil Company (later British Petroleum Company) in challenging the legitimacy of Iran's nationalization. Moreover, Anglo-Iranian and the British government threatened companies which might break the boycott with confiscation of Iranian oil on the high seas and with legal action. Also, the World Bank and the IMG initially denied financial assistance to Iran, and the industry boycott was maintained until the October, 1954, settlement—on the grounds that compensation originally offered by the Iranian government to British Petroleum was inadequate. The impact of the suspension of oil flows on the Iranian economy, dependent for some 80 percent of export earnings on oil, was shattering.

Another example of demand interruption was the French decision in mid-1971 to boycott Algerian oil which had been traditionally selling in France (about two-thrids of total exports). In this action, the French were prompted by their dislike of Algeria's move to nationalize partially (up to 51 percent) hitherto French-controlled companies in Algeria, and by their disapproval of compensation terms offered originally by Algeria in June, 1971. Moreover, the French government was reported to have made representations (a) to the United States government to cause a ban on prospective Algerian gas imports into the United States; (b) to the World Bank and other financial institutions to block any loans to Algeria until France received for its nationalized interests terms it deemed satisfactory; and (c) to other trading partners of Algeria, notably West European countries, Japan, and the U.S.S.R.[85] The dispute between Algeria and France was resolved by the end of 1971.

Supply interruptions, such as the reductions and embargoes on oil exports in 1973-74, which have their sources in LDCs have been widely publicized.

Yet, there have been several cases of supply interruptions or curtailment initiated by individual developed countries (for example, the U.S.A.) or a group of countries (for example, the EEC).

Among Western countries, the United States is well-known for its articulate official policy of denying so-called strategic exports to given countries on grounds of political difference or opposition. The definition of strategic commodities has sometimes been so widely interpreted as to include consumer goods. The Trading with the Enemy Act was enforced against the Soviet Union and its allies in 1947, against China in 1949, against Cuba in 1960, and against Chile in 1970. With the help of various forms of pressures, the U.S. government has exerted pressure on non-socialist nations to participate in its embargoes. For example, the neutral Swedish government was forced to discriminate in its trade with Communist nations in the 1950s thanks to the U.S. threat to deny Sweden essential raw materials. Also in the 1960s, the U.S. succeeded in preventing the Swedish steel industry from procuring nickel from Cuba, thanks to threats to stop large Swedish exports of special steel to the United States.[86] Cuba was even denied for 13 years oil not only from the United States but also from other sources, thanks to the influence the U.S. wields over the international oil oligopoly. The U.S. would not lift its economic embargo vis-à-vis Cuba unless "Cuba pursued a more restrained international course."[87]

As noted, Arab oil exporting countries have also resorted to the boycott approach, with a view to furthering their political goals. They instituted late in 1973 and until early 1974 a reduction of oil supplies to certain destinations, notably to the United States. Their reason was political-strategic: to affect policies by U.S. and other industrial countries toward Israel and the Middle East.[88] Earlier, some 900,000 barrels per day of oil supplies were denied to Western Europe following Israel's bombardment of oil terminals in Syria during the October, 1973, Middle East hostilities.

Since the U.S. government is considered a champion of free trade and private enterprise, its 1973 action on soybean exports is most revealing. On June 27, 1973, the U.S. Commerce Department imposed abruptly an embargo on the export of soybeans, cottonseeds, and their byproducts. The embargo was replaced a few days later by a system of export licenses which forbade new orders and limited exports of soybeans to 50 percent and of soybean oil-cake and meal to 40 percent of the amounts of the then outstanding export contracts. The U.S. action caused the outright violation of contracts freely entered into between its firms and other countries. The significance of the U.S. action was all the more important in view of the fact that the United States produced some 90 percent of world soybean output, and the fact that for Japan and several West European countries soybeans are a major source (90 percent) of protein and animal feed. The *London Economist* commented: "But dare Japan and Europe continue to rest their agriculture and food supply on a product (or a producer country, this author adds) that may overnight be declared to be unavailable."[89]

The U.S. government action was prompted by the desire to curb rising costs of U.S. livestock producers who rely on soybeans for animal feed.[90] But a leader of the American Soybean Association argued that the decision could mean "less meat for the (American) dinner table and bring us to a rationing situation."[91] Whatever the merits of the export restriction case at the domestic level—that the U.S. government as a leader of private enterprise can feel free to renege, *ex post*, on firm contracts entered into between its enterprises and other nations—reflects sadly on the rules of open international trade. The French President commented that it would be unimaginable for Europe to remain dependent on outsiders (the U.S.A.) for its food products.[92] Notwithstanding the lifting of restrictions on October 1, 1973, Europeans and Japanese have lost confidence in the United States as a reliable and cheap supplier.[93] The U.S. Agriculture Secretary commented, "The export controls we had on soybeans this year were disastrous in many respects."[94]

Also prompted by their own regional interest, the EEC had asked member countries for the authorization to cut down exports of grain through export levies. Such restriction of trade in an essential commodity does not take into consideration the need of consumers for that commodity outside the EEC.[95]

To lighten the burden of supply (or demand) interruptions, short or prolonged, one could visualize permanent multilateral mechanisms calling for set rules and standard mobilization of aid on a voluntary basis, as and when interruptions occur. A second approach, largely the existing situation, would have the consuming countries devise one or more remedies on their independent initiatives. A third approach could consist of having a standing committee which would convene at short notice to consider the problem at hand. The first approach has the merit of permanency; it also provides participants with prior knowledge of what to expect in the event of interruptions happening, and accordingly reduces uncertainty. The second approach leaves matters completely unstructured. The third approach is a compromise: It provides for the firm opportunity of discussing matters—wth no commitment regarding the nature or size of relief to the suffering country.

In their search for greater security in basic commodities, several countries have adopted individual measures—such as building stockpiles or reserves of strategic and critical materials as the United States has done. Alternatively, the promotion of vertically integrated "national companies" with access to raw materials from various sources has appealed to some governments (Japan). Others, as shown below, have attempted to achieve inter-country cooperation and mutual assistance programs. An international office which offers logistics—to begin with—may prove generally acceptable and workable—especially if among the beneficiaries are the least developed countries.

Developed Market Economics. In the past two decades, the Western developed countries have taken prior steps individually and collectively to meet possible emergencies in supply interruptions. For example, after the nationalization of the Suez Canal "in July, 1956, but two months prior to its closure, planning measures for such an (interruption) eventually were undertaken by American companies through a Middle East Emergency Committee, set up by the (U.S.) Foreign Petroleum Supply Committee. A similar organization was set up by the Organization for European Economic Co-operation (OEEC) . . . Essentially the same mechanism was reactivated (in 1967) by OECD"—including the developed countries of North America, Western Europe, Oceania, and Japan.[96]

More specifically, the intergovernmental OECD Oil Committee collects and analyzes data on current and prospective conditions of demand and supply for petroleum and gas. It advises, plans, and administers the scheduling, apportioning, and storage of oil supplies for the benefit of member countries in periods of emergencies. Begun at the time of the Suez crisis in 1956, all OECD European members except Finland have participated in the monitor of a stockpiling program, and in apportioning domestic and imported oil supplies in periods of emergency, but not including stocks accumulated before the crisis. Of total supplies to be shared out, 90 percent would go to an emergency stockpile to be allocated to countries facing special problems.[97]

The OECD governments have authorized company representatives to organize themselves into an international Industry Advisory Body, and to meet on an ad hoc basis in the event that oil supplies are threatened. Periodic meetings are held between the Oil Committee and leading executives of oil companies in member countries to discuss the problems of the industry.

Besides the OECD Oil Committee, Western countries coordinate their domestic and international emergency preparedness planning within their defense organizations. The leading example is that of the North Atlantic Treaty Organization (NATO). The focus is not only on military emergency planning, but also on the civilian one. NATO's Petroleum Planning Committee meets periodically, usually in Brussels.[98]

It has been suggested that "the most realistic way to keep supply interruption from being employed as an instrument of policy is to render such interruption useless. If this could be accomplished, the threat to use oil as a weapon would be an empty one, and its actual use, if attempted, futile."[99] The objective of assuring supplies, according to Western analysts, can best be achieved—assuming no military intervention or political coercion—by building inventories or keeping some domestic reserves unproduced in order to buy time for developing additional or alternative sources to reduce dependence on foreign supplies and to counter emergencies. OECD European countries agreed that a necessary minimum stockpile of crude oil and products in 1973 was equivalent to 50 days of current consumption. The minimum is in process of being raised to 90 days.[100]

The net benefits, if any, derived from reducing dependence on international trade for key commodities are both economical and political. On the economic side, the importing country seeking a higher degree of self-sufficiency could avoid the exploitation of its consumers (e.g., through higher prices) by foreign producers organized into a cartel. On the political side, the importing country could reduce the leverage for political pressure exercised by major foreign suppliers.

LDC-Importing Countries. The LDCs, by comparison with DCs, do not yet have multinational mechanisms designed to protect them against unforeseen interruptions in the trade or supply of basic commodities. It is suggested that a Commodity Insurance Fund(CIF) be set up for the purpose of assisting these countries during periods of interruptions, financially or in kind through compensatory supplies from alternative—admittedly more costly—sources. The Fund could also involve the creation of an international stockpile agency to be financed by international organizations (e.g., the IMF) and by assessments levied on participating member countries (probably based on their per capita income, population, and imports of raw materials concerned). The CIF could conceivably be supported by the richer countries, including oil-exporting countries, as part of their aid programs.

For several countries, sudden interruption of trade flows—especially certain commodities—is similar in its effect to a natural disaster. The World Community has already recognized that hardships arising from the latter have to be alleviated. In fact, as of early 1972, the Secretary General of the United Nations had a Disaster Relief Co-ordinator reporting to him. His function is *inter alia* to "mobilize, direct, and co-ordinate the relief activities of the various organizations of the United Nations system in response to a request for disaster assistance from a stricken state." Besides, he has to coordinate UN assistance with assistance given by inter-governmental and non-governmental organizations. He has also to promote the study, prevention, and control of disasters, and provide advice to governments on pre-disaster planning.[101] The assistance which is offered in natural catastrophes could conceivably be extended to other catastrophes, if the majority of UN members agree to it. To obtain such an agreement is difficult.

LDC-Exporting Countries. Primary exporting countries have taken public cognizance of the impact of demand interruptions on their economies. The OPEC Conference, in fact, instructed "the Secretary General to convene a Working Party of experts from Member Countries at Headquarters in order to prepare a study on the establishment of a fund to assist any Member Country affected by actions taken against it by oil companies."[102] The matter was still under study in 1973. There are, nevertheless, examples of one or more OPEC member countries assisting another member country. For example, Libya provided Algeria with a $100 million advance, after Algeria was faced in mid-1971 with a boycott from the oil companies following its partial nationalization of French concessionaires. The Algerians managed to overcome their financial difficulties, and to settle with the French companies, without having to make use of Libyan credit.[103] Iraq received credits from Kuwait and Libya following the boycott it faced in 1972 after its nationalization measures.

Primary commodity exporting countries seek the most realistic way to keep demand interruptions from being employed, and to render such interruptions useless. The most practical approach in the short run is to have adequate international financial reserves, as some have. In the longer run, they should aim at a balanced diversification of their economic resources, at a reduced dependence on primary exports, and at a joint insurance mechanism. With respect to the latter suggestion, Algeria, Iraq, and Libya agreed on May 23, 1970, to create a joint cooperative fund to aid any of the contracting states which "may suffer harm as a result of a confrontation with the exploiting oil companies."[104] The fund had, as of 1973, not yet been set up.

CIPEC countries have also attempted to face up to the boycott of their exports, and more generally, to "economic aggression." The latter term was defined as "any act which impedes or hinders the exercise of the sovereign right of countries to dispose freely of their national resources in order to further their development." CIPEC countries agreed that members should not take advantage of the situation created by the aggression, such as replacing the markets of the victimized country. They also agreed to study methods of raising funds to assist that country, and to coordinate in this matter with other organizations of LDCs exporting raw material—notably OPEC.[105]

To summarize, supply (and demand) interruptions in primary commodities are not new, and have been employed by advanced countries as exporters and importers, and more recently by LDCs as exporters (suppliers). The ultimate means of neutralizing the effects of such interruptions is local self-sufficiency, but this is not possible for all countries and ignores the static economic gains from international trade.

Efforts at international cooperation to relieve the harm of trade interruptions are perhaps most advanced among the industrial countries, but serious attempts are now being made among LDCs. Such efforts are likely to become more intensive in the future.

SUMMARY AND A PROPOSAL

This paper has attempted to show that the interests of the major actors of the exploitation and international trade in natural resources may sometimes conflict, and have led not infrequently to open confrontation. Host exporting countries, seeking the translation of their natural resources into the means of development, favor high prices and steady and certain markets for their exports and find their objectives opposed by the consuming importing countries, which desire low prices and certain sources of supply—also for purposes of economic development and rising national incomes. The MNCs, which historically have been the repository of the technological, marketing, managerial, and financial expertise in the industries, seek to maximize their shareholder's wealth, and in so doing seek to widen the spread between the ultimate (total) cost of production and final sales price (excluding taxes). In so doing, it will sometimes find common interest with the home country, sometimes with the host country, and frequently with neither.

The outcome of this mixture of conflicting and harmonious interests is changing considerably, as the balance between supply and demand in would-be markets changes, as the sophistication of the governments of supplier countries has changed, and as the competitiveness among MNC owners of technology and expertise has intensified. One result is the increased willingness by both advanced countries and LDCs to use the interruption of supply (or demand) of primary commodities to achieve economic or political objectives. Although such interruptions have a long heritage, their *effectiveness* in situations of scarcity—e.g., the OPEC supply interruption in oil; the U.S. soybean interruption—are surely greater than before. Efforts at self-sufficiency and multilateral schemes to reduce the vulnerability of countries to trade flows interruptions are not far advanced except in specific instances, but the search for solutions will surely continue.

Another result is the increasing assertion of producing host countries of national control over natural resources. This, again, has a long heritage —especially in the advanced countries—but has accelerated in the recent past in LDCs. Three forms of this assertion of national control are identifiable —and frequently exist simultaneously within the policy mix of LDCs: renegotiation and change in contract terms as conditions (including bargaining power and information) change; the requirement that MNCs accept joint-venture partners in certain activities; and the use of contractual phase-out periods from foreign firms—after which service contracts may be substituted as a means of acquiring the needed services available from the MNC.

It was emphasized that these policy tendencies need not necessarily be contrary to the interests of the MNC, or of the importing home country. But in any event, the popularity of all these means of increasing host-government control is high and rising, and will surely persist in most LDCs over the years ahead. The obvious conclusion is that foreign *equity* involvement in natural-resource industries will become increasingly rare and contractual terms for natural-resource exploitation ever more flexible.

If negotiated terms, whether on technical, managerial, marketing, or other contracts, or on the terms of joint ventures are to become more common, the need for reliable information for each party is even more pressing so that contract terms may be set in a fair and economically efficient way. Indeed, much of the existing skepticism over the MNC equity involvement in LDC resource-exporting countries stems from the belief that host countries were taken advantage of by MNCs in negotiating the terms of entry, most frequently because of a great inequality between the market information and negotiating expertise of the MNC and the host country.

AN "INFORMATION EXCHANGE": A PROPOSAL

Technical, marketing, and logistical information in natural-resource industries is important, but unfortunately scattered, difficult to collect, and constantly changing. Since up-to-date information reduces the possibilities of misunderstanding and disappointments between contractors, and since the use of negotiated contracts (in one form or another) will increase in international involvement in natural-resource exploitation, a relatively modest effort to institutionalize the flow of key information to all parties may improve significantly the atmosphere and success of such negotiations. This would be particularly important for information not readily accessible to LDCs—especially the small and poor countries which are not members of OPEC, CIPEC, ITC, or similar groupings.[106]

An institution, perhaps called the Resource Advisory Service (RAS), might serve such a function. RAS could conceivably be run on a cost basis, with fees payable eventually by beneficiary countries out of profits derived from the information supplied. Payment for services could well turn out to be much less expensive than alternative courses of action—notably sole reliance on profit-making firms which could exploit their position of knowledge.

RAS's function could consist of centralizing the collection, storage, and dissemination of information to member countries and their agencies, to MNCs, and to home importing governments. The scope of the information should, in principle, be worldwide and cover notably (a) trade and freight figures; (b) costs of various inputs; (c) information on markets, credit, and technological opportunities; (d) fiscal charges, trade barriers, or incentives current in countries concerned; and (e) a roster of firms, institutions, and experts dealing with various aspects of the resource in question.

RAS would offer many interrelated advantages. It could preclude exploitation of ignorance; bring competitive forces to work; reduce uncertainty and facilitate decision making; permit more efficient and effective use of opportunities and negotiators; reduce losses from miscalculations or premature commitments; reduce the scope for bigotry, venality, misunderstanding, or even conflict; publicize the relevant experiences of other nations; and permit a wider and quicker access to technical knowledge, managerial know-how, credit opportunities, tax information, etc. Impartiality and speed in responding to requests from member countries and their enterprises would obviously be essential to a successful operation of RAS.

If it should be overly ambitious for the proposed RAS to collect and act as a central repository and disseminator of information in the natural-resources field, a smaller initial step would have RAS act as an intermediary advising on the various *sources* for such information. Should individual countries —most likely LDCs—be unable to secure out-of-the-way information through their own means, RAS may then undertake to provide it, and advise on its authenticity and accuracy.

Moreover, it will be more manageable for RAS to start its activities with one or few commodities (probably those where information is comparatively not readily accessible to LDCs) and/or one subject matter of developmental significance, say taxation.[107] Once proven workable and successful, its activities could be enlarged to encompass progressively the whole field of natural resources. The idea of such a scheme has already been favorably discussed by the United Nations Committee on Natural Resources, and other UN forums.[108] It would involve the cooperation of interested national, regional, and international organizations.

Availability of managerial and technical information in itself is not sufficient for the transfer of know-how. For such a transfer to be successful, there is need for person-to-person contacts to adapt information and skills to the particular needs of the individual countries concerned. In addition, feedbacks have to be arranged on a permanent and a regular basis in order to control, evaluate, and improve the relevance of the information made available. To go beyond information availability into advising on its efficient use, there is need for effective links between the RAS and the beneficiary countries. Those links can be established through experts who are prepared to assist in drafting legislation, in designing the relevant supervisory departments and agencies, in helping to formulate plans and forecasts of demand and supply, in pointing out up-to-date competitive terms of contracts and new market opportunities.

Resource advisers should not be expected to assume decision making prerogatives in their dealings with member states or MNCs. Their function should be limited to elucidating alternatives or options, and to analyzing and sizing elements of costs and benefits for various courses of action. They should also contribute to building the self-reliance of policy and decision makers in LDCs, and their capacity to make effective use of information in protecting and promoting national interests

NOTES

1. See, "Industrialization: Key to Future OPEC Policy?," *Middle East Economic Survey (MEES), Supplement*, Beirut, March 23, 1973, pp. 1-4.

2. "Suggestions from responsible authorities in the United States that Canada should reduce its secondary manufacturing industry and concentrate on the exploitation and processing of natural resources are as insensitive as they are uninformed. We have the fastest growing labor force in the world. Extractive and processing industries could not begin to absorb the labor force we have today, let alone provide the new jobs we need now and in the future." From a speech by Mitchell Sharp delivered in New York on September 21, 1971, quoted in *The Washington Post*, October 24, 1971, p. C6.

3. As revealed in a study of the copper industry: The private producers feel that high prices and rapid exploitation are not the proper long-term policy, and at the discount rates appropriate for producers this is an entirely possible assertion. But an underdeveloped nation, with very large needs for foreign exchange and capital

for investment and critical shortages of both, is unlikely to agree that this is the optimal policy. It is not necessarily irrational for an underdeveloped country to prefer very large returns per year for a shorter period to somewhat smaller returns for a longer period.

Source: Charles River Associates, *Economic Analysis of the Copper Industry*, prepared for the General Servcies Administration, Cambridge, Massachusetts, March, 1970, p. 174.

4. The Saudi Arabian Minister of Petroleum and Mineral Resources expressed it thus: Most of the oil-producing countries with large (monetary) reserves are likely to reach a stage of financial saturation where it will be impossible to increase internal expenditure without running a grave risk of inflation. These producing countries realize that the appreciation in the price of a barrel of oil in the ground is greater than the increase in the rate of interest on the unused portion of their revenue.

Source: "Yamani on Participation," *MEES, Supplement*, September 22, 1972, p. 4.

5. See, notably, the proceedings of the United Nations' Sixth Special Session of the General Assembly on "Raw Materials and Development," New York, April, 1974.

6. Joseph Grunwald, *Foreign Private Investment: The Challenge of Latin American Nationalism* (Washington: The Brookings Institution Reprint No. 204, 1971), 228n. See also, speech delivered by Salvador Allende, late president of the Republic of Chile, before the General Assembly of the United Nations, December 4, 1972—printed by Embassy of Chile, Washington, D.C., 39 pp.

7. See, notably, "Declaration on the Establishment of a New International Economic Order," by the Group of 77 Developing Countries at the United Nations General Assembly's Sixth Special Session on the Problems of Raw Materials and Development, New York, April 12, 1974.

8. For Canada, see, for example: "Canada: Mineral Policy Objectives," *Mineral Trade Notes*, U.S. Bureau of Mines, Washington, October, 1973, p. 18; "United States and Canada: Good Neighbors, but—," Interview with Pierre Elliott Trudeau, Prime Minister of Canada," *U.S. News & World Report*, Washington, D.C., July 3, 1972, pp. 32-35; "Exclusive Interview by Charles Lynch with Prime Minister Trudeau," in *The Ottawa Citizen*, Ottawa, October 29, 1971, p. 7; and "Trudeau: Canada Moving to Wean Itself from U.S.," *The Washington Post*, November 2, 1971, p. A23. See also, Canada, Department of Energy, Mines and Resources, Mineral Resources Branch, *An Approach to Mineral Policy Formulation*, by W. Keith Buck and R. B. Elver (Ottawa, 1970), p. 2; John Fayerweather, "Canadian Attitudes and Policy on Foreign Investment," Michigan State University, *Business Topics*, Winter 1973, pp. 7-20; and "C.D.C. Wins Right to Buy Shares in Texasgulf Bid," *The New York Times*, September 6, 1973, p. 51.

For Australia, see: annual reports of the state-owned *The Australian Industry Development Corporation*, based in Canberra; and Committee for Economic Development of Australia, The Minerals Industry in *Australia*, Melbourne, October, 1972, pp. 25-27.

9. See "When are the British like the Arabs? When it comes to developing a major natural resource," *Forbes*, New York, June 15, 1973, p. 88.

10. See, for example, Yusakee Furuhashi, "New Policy Toward Foreign Investment? Issues in the Japanese Capital Liberalization," *Michigan State University Business Topics*, Spring 1972, pp. 33-38. U.S. Department of State, Bureau of Intelligence and Research, *The Multinational Corporation and National Sovereignty*, Research Study No. 1 (Washington, D.C., January 22, 1971), p. iii; also, "Increasing Investment in U.S. by Foreigners Irks Many in Congress," *The Wall Street Journal*, New York, January 22, 1974, p. 1.

11. With the passage of time, the exchange of ideas, the successes or the failures of joint enterprises, it has become clear to foreign investors that there are certain fields of activities that should be left to local capital and initiative, that they should bring with them a positive contribution to the economy of the country (not only in the form of a participation in capital) but also in technological advancement, and that they should give the local citizens adequate opportunities to assume responsibility on a gradual basis. It has also become clear to developing countries that if they want the cooperation of foreign capital they must start by indicating the fields in which they would welcome such cooperation and then when foreign capital is invested in agreed ventures and activities they must give it a fair chance to make adequate profits; they must give the necessary guarantees for its safety, for the transfer of its profits; and they must not construe every movement as an attack on their sovereignty.

Source: Abel Mon'em Kaissouni, Chairman, The Arab International Bank. Speech delivered at a meeting of the American-Arab Association for Commerce and Industry, New York, November 3, 1971; see also, American-Arab Association for Commerce and Industry, "Egypt Seeks New Investments," *Bulletin of the American-Arab Association* (New York, November, 1971), pp. 1-2.

12. Hollis M. Dole, Assistant Secretary—Mineral Resources, U.S. Department of Interior, "Mineral Policy—The Art of the Possible," in *Mining Congress Journal*, June, 1972, Vol. 58, No. 6.

13. See, President Nixon's Energy Message, submitted to Congress on April 18, 1973—reproduced in *Petroleum Intelligence Weekly (PIW)*, Special Supplement II, April 23, 1973; and U.S. Congress, *Potential Shortages of Ores, Metals, Minerals*, Defense Production, 92nd Congress, 1st session, September 22 and 23, 1971, Vol. 2 (Washington: Government Printing Office).

14. See, "White Paper on 'Prospect of Natural Resources Problems in Japan,' " *Economic Reports*, Japan External Trade Organization, Vol. XXI, No. 1, Tokyo, 1972, pp. 35-60.

15. OECD, *The Industrial Policy of Japan*. Paris, 1972, p. 58; also, Hideo Suzuki, Mining Policy Section, Ministry of International Trade and Industry (MITI), "National Minerals Policy," *Mining Magazine* (London), November, 1971, Vol. 125, No. 5, pp. 455-56; "Rising GNP Must be Reduced to Overcome 'Energy Crisis,' " *The Japan Times*, September 26, 1973, p. 10.

16. *The Industrial Policy of Japan, ibid.*, pp. 59 and 134-35; and Suzuki, *op. cit.*, p. 457.

17. Royal Dutch/Shell, *The Japanese Oil Industry*, Shell Briefing Service (London, August, 1971), p. 3.

18. The Institute of Energy Economics, *Energy in Japan*, Quarterly Report No. 22, Tokyo, September, 1973, p. 3.

19. Speech by R. F. X. Connor to the N.S.W. Division of the Securities Institute of Australia, Sydney, August 10, 1973, p. 13.

20. Royal Dutch/Shell, *The Japanese Oil Industry,* Shell Briefing Service (London, August, 1971), p. 3.

21. See, Y. Djimi, Vice Minister of MITI, "Basic Philosophy and Objectives of Japanese Industrial Policy," June 24, 1970, in *The Industrial Policy of Japan, op. cit.*, pp. 11-31.

22. See, for example, Howard F. Van Zandt, "Learning to do Business with 'Japan, Inc.,' " *Harvard Business Review*, July-August, 1972, pp. 83-92.

23. *Le Monde*, May 12, 1972, p. 19; "French Plan for Metals Stockpile," *The Financial Times*, May 12, 1972, p. 29; "France—Our Very Own," *The Econo-*

mist, May 6, 1972, p. 98; "Matieres Premieres—Un conseil interministeriel met au poin un plan d'approvisionnement de la France," *Le Monde*, May 12, 1972, p. 19; and "La France consolide sa politique d'approvisionnement en matières premières à usage industriel," *Les Echos*, Paris, April 19, 1972, p. 16.

24. U.S. Congress, *Twenty-first Annual Report of the Activities of the Joint Committee on Defense Production*, 92nd Congress, 2nd Session, House Report No. 92-843 (Washington: Government Printing Office, February 21, 1972), p. 282.

25. Statement by the Minister for Minerals and Energy, Canberra, June 4, 1973.

26. Secretariat General du Gouvernement, La Documentation Française, "Les Aides à l'Expansion Industrielle Regionale dans les Pays du Marche Commun," *Notes et Études Documentaires,* September 11, 1972, p. 14.

27. Notably the Inter-American Development Bank, the Asian Development Bank, and the International Development Association.

28. This objective has been reiterated by executives of several MNCs involved in natural-resource industries:

"Growth for growth's sake is self-defeating. . . Pounds of metal shipped and profits earned are no longer synonymous. For Alcoa, we have said, to be first in aluminum is not necessarily to be first in pounds (of weight), but it most assuredly is to be first in profitability."

Source: W. H. K. George, "The Aluminum Industry: Strategy for Profit," address to the Organization of European Aluminum Smelters, London, September 10, 1971, p. 5—typescript.

"We are not much attracted by growing industries as such. Growth is one factor, but many rapidly growing industries have miserable rates of return. We are primarily interested in those industries in which Noranda can obtain a good rate of return over the long term through some competitive advantage."

Source: Alfred Powis, "The Scope and Diversification of the Noranda Group of Companies," *Western Miner*, Toronto, January, 1971, p. 22.

29. The Broken Hill Proprietary Co., Ltd., Chairman's Address at Annual General Meeting, September 8, 1971, Melbourne, p. 8.

30. Pechiney's chairman Pierre Jouven at the Annual General Meeting, held on June 7, 1971, in Paris. Similar views were expressed by the chairman of Ugine Kuhlmann, Pierre Grezel, at the Annual General Meeting, held on June 22, 1971, in Paris.

31. See Zuhayr Mikdashi, *The Community of Oil Exporting Countries: A Study on Governmental Cooperation* (London: Allen and Unwin, and Ithaca: Cornell University Press, 1972), p. 42.

32. Statement of Emilio G. Collado, Executive Vice President, Exxon Corporation, before the Group of Eminent Persons to Study the *Impact of Multinational Corporations on Development and on International Relations*, United Nations, New York, September 11, 1973, p. 21.

33. Raymond Vernon, *Sovereignty at Bay: The Multinational Spread of U.S. Enterprise* (New York: Basic Books, 1971), p. 138.

34. "In negotiations between companies and (LDC) governments, there is a great disparity in technical ability. The company representatives earn perhaps ten or even twenty times as much as those in the official side; they can devote much more time to advance study; they are cosmopolitan and sophisticated enough to exploit differences in temperament and attitude among their opponents, using flattery and mild ridicule; above all, they can draw on the experts of their whole organization (in law, accounting, engineering, etc.). The atmosphere is that of bargaining between two nations, of which the foreign company is much the stronger."

Source: Dydley Seers, "Big Companies and Small Countries: A Practical Proposal," *Kyklos*, Basel, Vol. XVI, Fasc. 4, 1963, p. 602.

35. Commonwealth Treasure, *Overseas Investment in Australia*, Canberra, Australian Government Publishing Service, May, 1972, p. 92.

36. See statement of a Shell official (Geoffrey Chandler) reproduced in *The Guardian Weekly with Le Monde*, London, December 15, 1973; "Oil Companies Warn France of 10 to 15 percent Cuts Next Month," *International Herald Tribune*, Paris, November 23, 1973, p. 2; and "France Tells Oil Groups They Face Marketing Nationalization if Cutbacks are too Drastic," *The Times*, London, November 22, 1973.

37. Government of Canada, *Foreign Direct Investment in Canada*, Ottawa, 1972, p. 5.

38. See, for example, witnesses, statements, and submissions in: U.S. Congress, *A Foreign Economic Policy for the 1970's*, Part 4, *The Multinational Corporation and International Investment*, Hearings before the Subcommittee on Foreign Economic Policy of the Joint Economic Committee, 91st Congress, 2nd Session, July 27, 28, 29, and 30, 1970 (Washington: Government Printing Office); also U.S. Senate, Subcommittee on Multinational Corporations, *The International Telephone and Telegraph Company and Chile*, Hearings, 83rd Congress, 1st Session, Washington, 1973.

39. *The Wall Street Journal*, January 28, 1971, p. 4; also March 8, 1971, p. 21; and *MEES* (Beirut), October 29, 1971, p. 1-2.

40. James L. McCarthy, "The American Copper Industry, 1947-1955," *Yale Economic*, Spring 1964, No. 4, pp. 92-93.

41. See, Z. Mikdashi, *The Community of Oil Exporting Countries*, *op. cit.*, p. 194.

42. Louis T. Wells, "The Multinational Business Enterprise: What Kind of International Organization?," *International Organization*, Vol. XXV, No. 3, 1971, p. 460.

43. Statement of Emilio G. Collado, Executive Vice President, Exxon Corporation, before the Group of Eminent Persons to study the *Impact of Multinational Corporations on Development and on International Relations*, United Nations, New York, September 11, 1973, p. 20.

44. United Nations Economic and Social Council, *Report of the Secretary-General to the Committee on Natural Resources*, January 3, 1972, p. 2 (E/C.7/20/Add. 2). See also Michael Tanzer, *Investment Requirements and Financing of Petroleum Refineries in Developing Countries*, United Nations Inter-regional Seminar on Petroleum Refining in Developing Countries, New Delhi, January 2, 1973, pp. 15 and 16 (ESA/RT/AC.5/14); and P. H. Frankel and W. L. Newton, *Delivered Cost of Crude Oil to Petroleum Refineries in Developing Countries*, United Nations Inter-regional Seminar on Petroleum Refining in Developing Countries, New Delhi, January 9, 1973, pp. 10 and 11 (ESA/RT/AC.5/4).

45. The Renegotiation Board, *Sixteenth Annual Report, 1971* (Washington: December 31, 1971), pp. 1-2; *Ibid.*, *Seventeenth Annual Report, 1972* (Washington: December 31, 1972), p. 12; and *Eighteenth Annual Report, 1973*, (Washington: December 31, 1973), p. 13.

46. Federal Power Commission, *Initial Brief of Commission Staff* (on Algerian Gas Imports by El Paso), Washington, August 16, 1971, p. 25; and Federal Power Commission, Opinion No. 622, Washington, June 28, 1972, p. 13.

47. C. P. Kindleberger, *American Business Abroad* (New Haven: Yale University Press, 1969), p. 151.

48. For details, see Z. Mikdashi, *A Financial Analysis of Middle Eastern Oil Concessions: 1901-65*, Praeger Publishers, New York, 1966, pp. 244-45, and Appendix II; also *ibid.*, *The Community of Oil Exporting Countries*, *op. cit.*, pp, 138-42.

49. See, for example, Z. Mikdashi, "Towards Maximizing Oil Revenues, with Special Reference to Transit Countries of the Middle East," *Middle East Economic Papers 1961*, American University of Beirut, pp. 64-68, and Z. Mikdashi, "Some Economic Aspects of Pipeline Transport in the Arab World," Third Arab Petroleum Congress, Alexandria, October, 1961, pp. 1-26.

50. The Government, in reply to a questionnaire from the UN Secretary-General, stated that: "Agreements with the bauxite and alumina companies were renegotiated in 1957, and again in 1962-63 (and again in 1970-74) when it was apparent that the older valuations placed on the mineral were inadequate. In every instance the effects of renegotiations were unequivocally favorable. Neither reinvestment nor capital inflow declined, but in fact has continued to increase apace. Foreign investors pay mineral royalties, and income tax on profits earned in the operative basis of assessment is on national profits which are negotiated between the companies involved and the Government."

Source: United Nations General Assembly, *The Exercise of Permanent Sovereignty Over Natural Resources and the Use of Foreign Capital and Technology for Their Exploitation*, Report of the Secretary-General, September 14, 1970, New York, pp. 107-108 (ref. A/80581).

51. "Interview with Mr. Mana Said Otaiba," Minister of Petroleum and Industry of the United Arab Emirates, *Arab Oil and Gas*, December 16, 1971, p. 10.

52. "In order that this growth may continue unfettered ZIMCO is going to need money and technical expertise and this is where our philosophy of permanent partnership as against transient partnership is in our opinion particularly suitable to our situation. We need to augment our domestic sources of investment with foreign sources of investment. We need to augment our domestic skills with the sophisticated technical know-how of other countries. We need partners in progress."

Source: Zambia Industrial and Mining Corporation Limited, *Chairman's Statement, 1971*.

53. To a well-informed researcher, the concessionaire Marcona had exploited to advantage the fact that it had among its shareholders the politically influential Prado Family.

Source: Charles W. Robinson, president of Marcona Mining Company, Competition in the Sale of Iron Ore in World Markets," XI Convención de Ingenieros de Minas del Peru, December, 1969, p. 2 (typescript).

54. The Saudi Arabian Minister explained: "Nationalization in the oil industry is a step which entails undesirable consequences for the nationalizing state for a number of reasons. Nationalization does not guarantee the state concerned the means to market its crude, particularly if the quantities involved are substantial. . . The real problem is how can any state, Arab or otherwise, continue the search for new oil resources once it embarks on nationalization. The question is not one of finance but a question of the technology which is required for drilling operations. . . Thus, because of the complexity of oil drilling and marketing operations, nationalization would be a catastrophe. If I nationalize the oil resources of my country, the oil companies will withhold investments for oil exploration and there will be difficulties. There is, however, an alternative method of control, while at the same time maintaining the continued outlets for our output, and this alternative is participation. On the other hand, if we nationalize our crude and try to sell it on the international market, the prices will crash resulting in a drastic drop in our revenue. Thus, what is said about nationalization is just a way of inflaming the demagogic sentiments of the public and is against the national interests of the Arab nation."

Source: *MEES Supplement*, January 5, 1973, p. 3.

55. See also Louis T. Wells, "The Multinational Business Enterprise: What King of International Organization?," *International Organization,* Vol. XXV, No. 3,

1971, p. 458. See also L. G. Franke, "Do Joint Ventures Still Make Sense in Europe," *Worldwide P & I Planning*, Stamford, Conn., January-February, 1972, pp. 22 and 25-30.

56. That author argues that "the ultimate impact of promoting minority ownership may be to erode the political basis of other, more effective policies seeking to control foreign investment behavior."

Source: Thomas Horst, *On the Benefits of Domestic Minority Ownership of Foreign Controlled Firms*, Harvard Institute of Economic Research, No. 176, pp. 2-3.

57. See, for example, Lawrence G. Franko, *Joint International Business Ventures in Developing Countries: Mystique and Reality,* Centre d'Études Industrielles, Geneva, May, 1973, pp. 15-17.

58. See Meier, *Leading Issues in Economic Development, op. cit.,* pp. 306-308; and Peter P. Gabriel, "MNCs in the Third World: Is Conflict Unavoidable," *Harvard Business Review*; July-August, 1972, pp. 98-99.

59. See, for example, A. O. Hirschman, *How to Divest in Latin America, and Why,* Essays in International Finance, Princeton University, November, 1969; Paul Streeten, "Obstacles to Private Foreign Investment in the LDCs," *Columbia Journal of World Business*, New York, May-June, 1970, pp. 37-39; Grunwald, *op. cit.,* p. 241; and Alejandro, *op. cit.,* p. 340.

60. See, for example, Raymond Vernon, "Problems and Policies Regarding Multinational Enterprises," *United States International Economic Policy in an Interdependent World, op. cit.,* p. 999; also, Vernon, *Sovereignty at Bay, op. cit.,* p. 269.

61. Inter-American Development Bank, *Multinational Investment, Public and Private, in the Development & Integration of Latin America, op. cit.,* p. 15.

62. Raul Probisch, *Change and Development, Latin America's Great Task,* report submitted to the Inter-American Development Bank, Washington, D.C., July, 1970, p. 159.

63. The General Manager of CDC (Sir William Rendell) commented: "We tend to be 'ad hocers' on this, formulas that give options for purchasing X percent of the shares of such-and-such a company at such-and-such a price over a given period of years. In our experience it never really works out. But the answer is that it is our policy to dispose of our projects when we can get a reasonable price for them and when we can afford to do so, and particularly—I have stressed this—to local investors, not just to sell them to somebody in London who may wish to make an African investment—if there are such people. That is part of our policy."

Source: Peter Ady (ed.), *Private Foreign Investment and the Developing World, op cit.,* pp. 235-36.

64. John K. Freeman, "Channeling Funds for Development," *Columbia Journal of World Business*, Spring 1973, pp. 66-71.

65. William S. Gaud, Executive Vice President of IFC, "Private Foreign Investment in the '70s," Speech at the Annual Meeting of the Association Internationale pour la Promotion et la Protection des Investissements Privés en Territoires Étrangers, Munich, October 31, 1972, p. 9.

66. See also, R. Vernon, *Problems and Policies Regarding Multinational Enterprises, op. cit.,* p. 1000.

67. See, Inter-American Development Bank, *The IBD's First Decade and Perspectives for the Future,* Round Table (Punta del Este, Uruguay, April, 1970), pp. 38, 157, 233, 234, and 235.

68. The Anaconda Company, *Annual Report,* 1971, p. 9.

69. Friedmann and Beguin, *op. cit.,* pp. 397-99.

70. *Ibid.*, pp. 294-95.

71. See, "Common Treatment of Foreign Capital, Trademarks, Patents, Licensing Agreements and Royalties in the Andean Common Market," in *Journal of Common Market Studies*, June, 1972, pp. 229-359.

72. ADELA, *The ADELA Group*, Switzerland, 1972—italics supplied.

73. *Ibid.*

74. Collado, *op. cit.*, pp. 10-11.

75. Shann Turnbull, "Multinationals, Fading out with a Profit," *Development Forum*, Vol. 2, No. 5, Geneva, June, 1974, p. 3; also, Shann, Turnbull, "Eliminating Foreign Ownership," *Growth 26*, Committee for Economic Development of Australia, Sydney, December, 1973, pp. 1-13.

76. M. A. Adelman, "Is the Oil Shortage Real? Oil Companies as OPEC Tax-Collectors," *Foreign Policy*, New York, No. 9, Winter 1972-73, pp. 87-88.

77. In some countries, an important new deterrent to investment from abroad is developing—the "fade-out" arrangement, which requires that established as well as new foreign investors sell their ownership interests to local owners, either government or private, over a period of years. We believe the United States should actively discourage host countries from instituting fade-out requirements and from prescribing the form and extent of local equity participation.

Source: *United States International Economic Policy in an Interdependent World, op. cit.*, p. 251.

78. See, for example, the excellent study of a U.S. diplomat and economist, Richard J. Bloomfield, "Who Makes American Foreign Policy? Some Latin American Case Studies," Harvard University Center for International Affairs, March, 1972 (typescript); Mason Gaffney, "Benefits of Military Spending," paper presented at 10th Annual Conference, Committee on Taxation, Resources, and Economic Development, Madison, Wisconsin, October 25, 1971 (typescript); also, "U.S. Reportedly Withheld Ecuador Aid on I.T.T. Plea," *The New York Times*, August 10, 1973, pp. 37 and 40.

79. Ref. public laws 92-245, 92-246. and 92-247 of the 92nd Congress, March 10, 1972.

80. UNCTAD Secretariat, *Private Foreign Investment in Its Relationship to Development, op. cit.*, p. 18.

81. U.S. Senate, Committee on Interior and Insular Affairs, Hearings on *National Goals Symposium*, Part 2, 92nd Congress, 1st session (Washington, October 20, 1971). pp. 489-90.

82. Estimates of the cost of the U.S. imports program vary considerably. Evidence submitted to a Congressional Joint Economic subcommittee suggest, however, that net cost for the U.S. public has increased by "a rock-bottom minimum of $7.4 billion more in the six-year period ended in 1970 than in the previous half-dozen years."

Source: *The Washington Post*, January 9, 1972, p. A5.

83. See, for example, Sam H. Schurr and Paul T. Homan, *Middle Eastern Oil and the Western World* (New York: American Elsevier Publishing Co., 1971), pp. 14-16; and Resources for the Future, *Energy Research Needs*, A Staff Report prepared for the National Science Foundation, October, 1971 (National Technical Information Service PB 207-516).

84. See M. Tanzer, "The Naked Politics of Oil: Oil Boycotts" (Chapter 24) in *The Political Economy of International Oil and the Underdevleoped Countries* (Boston: Beacon Press, 1969), pp. 319-48.

85. *MEES*, June 18, 1971, p. 5; "Boumediene Analyzes Franco-Algerian Oil

Crisis," *MEES Supplement*, June 18, 1971; also *Petroleum Press Service* (London), June, 1971, pp. 204-05; *Washington Post*, July 28, 1971, p. A11; *Oil and Gas Journal* (Tulsa, Oklahoma), June 21, 1971, p. 80; and Sonatrach, "Algeria-Petroleum," in *Petroleum Times*, June 4, 1971.

86. Gunnar Adler-Karlson, "The Teacher of the Oil Arabs," *Dagens Nyheter*, Stockholm, November, 1973—reproduced by *OPEC Weekly Bulletin Review of the Press*, November 30, 1973, Vol. 4, No. 48, pp. 2-4.

87. U.S. Foreign Secretary Henry Kissinger at a press conference on January 10, 1974, in Washington, D.C.

88. See, for example, Fuad Itayim, "Arab Oil—The Political Dimension," *Journal of Palestine Studies*, Beirut, Vol. III, No. 2, Winter 1974, pp. 84-97.

89. "American Trade—Carrying a Bean," *The Economist*, July 7, 1973, p. 28; see also "Le Soja Nous Tient," *Journal de Geneve*, July 19, 1973, p. 1.

90. "The High Cost of Soybean Diplomacy," *Business Week*, July 7, 1973, p. 28.

91. "Threat in U.S. to Soybeans," *Herald Tribune*, Paris, July 10, 1973, p. 9.

92. "M. Pompidou: il est inimaginable que l'Europe depende de l'étranger pour les productions alimentaires," *Le Monde*, July 14, 1973, p. 28.

93. *The New York Times*, September 4, 1973, pp. 49 and 51.

94. *U.S. News & World Report*, September 24, 1973, p. 24.

95. See "La Commission europeéene voudrait freiner les exportations de deréales en les taxant," *Le Monde*, July 13, 1973, pp. 1 and 28.

96. S. Schurr and P. Homan, *Middle Eastern Oil and the Western World, op. cit.*, p. 14, footnote 12.

97. PIW, August 13, 1973, p. 4; and Organization for Economic Cooperation and Development, "Oil Supplies—1970," *The OECD Observer* (Paris), October, 1971, No. 54, p. 29; see also "Energy Policy in the European Community," *The OECD Observer*, June, 1972, pp. 36-39.

98. *21st Annual Report of the Activities of the Joint Committee on Defense Production, op. cit.*, p. 271,

99. S. Schurr and P. Homan, *Middle Eastern Oil and the Western World, op. cit.*, p. 15. See also, R. L. Gordon, "Without Rudder, Compass, Chart—The Problem of Energy Policy Guidelines," *Quarterly of the Colorado School of Mines*, Vol. 64, No. 4, October, 1969, p. 41.

100. "Getting Together," *Petroleum Press Service*, June, 1973, p. 203; and OECD, *Oil, the Present Situation and Future Prospects*, Paris, 1973, p. 83.

101. ECOSOC Resolution (E/L.1438), reproduced in UN Information Service, *Round-up of the 51st Session of the Economic and Social Council* (Geneva, July 30, 1971), pp. 31-32.

102. See, OPEC Communique in *MEES Supplement*, March 10, 1972, p. 5.

103. "Boumediene Acknowledges Libyan Support During Franco-Algerian Crisis," *MEES*, March 3, 1972, p. 4.

104. *MEES*, May 29, 1970, pp. 2-3.

105. Santiago Extraordinary Conference of Ministers, Resolution on "Measures of Defence and Solidarity," in: CIPEC, *The Copper Market*, 4th quarter, Paris, 72, Appendix 1.

106. See, for example, O. C. Herfindahl, *Natural Resource Information for Economic Development* (Baltimore: Johns Hopkins Press, 1969); and "Information as a key to Progress," *The OECD Observer*, Paris, April, 1972, pp. 6-8.

107. Dudley Seers recommended the creation of a similar international agency which would advise governments on tax and conservation matters: "Big Companies

and Small Countries: A Practical Proposal,'' *op. cit.,* pp. 605-6. See also, United Nations, *Science and Technology*, Report on the United Nations Conference on the Application of Science and Technology for the Benefit of the Less Developed Areas, Vol. II, *Natural Resources* (New York, 1963), pp. 195-96 and 200.

108. See, United Nations Economic and Social Council (ECOSOC), Committee on Natural Resources, *Report on the First Session*, February 22-March 10, 1971 (New York, 1971—E/4969; E/C.7/13), pp. 22-23; and *Report on the Third Session*, 6-17 February,1973, New York, 1971 (E/5247; E/C.7/43), pp. 12 and 40. Also ECOSOC Resolution 1761 B (LIV), and UNECOSOC, *The Impact of Multinational Corporations on the Development Process and on International Relations,* Report of the Group of Eminent Persons, New York, May 24, 1974, pp. 36 and 80 (E/5500/Add.1—Part I).

32

How Can the World Afford OPEC Oil?

*Khodadad Farmanfarmaian, Armin Gutowski, Saburo Okita, Robert V. Roosa, and Carroll L. Wilson**

ALMOST exactly a year ago, the members of the Organization of Petroleum Exporting Countries (OPEC) raised the price of their oil sharply. With subsequent adjustments, the average price of Middle East oil stood in late 1974 at about $10 per barrel, roughly four times the mid-1973 price.

Accordingly, over the five years 1975 through 1979, the oil-importing countries of the world will pay these OPEC countries a total of at least $600 billion (in 1974 dollars) subject to four conditions:

(1) that the importing countries individually can find the needed means of payment;

(2) that their average annual economic growth continues close to the estimated global rate of about four percent for the next five years, or about two percent per capita;

(3) that there are no major changes in the structure or stability of international political relations;

(4) that the price of Middle East oil remains near the $10 level.

Whether or not any of these conditions can be fulfilled is, to say the least, problematical. The first raises the specter of the possible inability of existing international institutions and payments

* The group responsible for this article, listed alphabetically, comprises five individuals, acting in their private capacities. The ideas expressed were developed in a series of meetings through the fall, and the text has been reviewed by each of the five authors. While not necessarily endorsing the text in every detail, all the members of the group fully subscribe to its central points and proposals. Many individuals from other OPEC and OECD countries who were consulted cannot be given individual acknowledgement here. The authors are indebted to Keith Josephson for extraordinary help in the task of intercontinental coordination.

mechanisms to cope with a financial problem of staggering proportions. It is to that problem that we will address our more detailed suggestions further on in this article. The importance of the second speaks for itself; prolonged stagnation of the world economy would surely have most serious human and political consequences. The third, if it were not fulfilled, raises even more nightmarish possibilities, on which one need not dwell here. Among them, the first three assumptions may seem to many to be on the optimistic side. In contrast, some would argue that the fourth assumption ignores the possibility of some drop in the oil price, say to $8 per barrel (in 1974 dollars) or even, a few think, to $6 per barrel. Without judging the likelihood of such changes, let us only note that they would change the volume of the required payments from something over $600 billion to around $500 billion (at $8 per barrel) or to roughly $400 billion (at $6 per barrel)—even if there were no increases in the volumes bought at these lower prices. Or, in the opposite direction, if the price were again to be raised in real average terms, the amount of payments could actually be greater.

The point is, that on any remotely realistic price assumption the scale and abruptness of the contemplated payments to the OPEC countries—ranging from $100 billion to $135 billion each year over the remainder of this decade at the assumed $10 price—present a huge transfer problem. Indeed, in 1973 the sum of all merchandise exports by all non-OPEC member countries of the International Monetary Fund was less than $500 billion. How can the enormous camel of oil transfer payments pass through the eye of that needle?

II

Certainly conservation of energy and conversion to alternative fuels cannot contribute importantly to the answer over the next five years. At most, the gain from conservation can be expected to slow the growth in uses of energy, so that after the initial reductions of 1974, the rate of use of OPEC oil over the remainder of the decade will probably grow slowly, averaging close to the 1973 volume. Nor is there much scope for early reduction of the dependence on OPEC oil through conversion to alternatives—not even in the United States, with its vast reserves of coal and its potentialities both for more oil and for producing oil from shale. Lead times are simply too long, and needed environmental constraints too complex, for major adaptation before the 1980s.

Nor can increased trade with the OPEC countries provide more than a fraction of the answer. The oil-producing countries cannot absorb such an inundation of goods and services, nor can the rest of the world physically divert one-quarter of all the goods that move in trade out of present channels and into the OPEC countries. The oil-importing countries will just as certainly, however, be competing with each other to earn as much as they can to help meet their oil deficits, and the question will be, as they reach desperately for each other's markets, whether they will also erect more menacing barriers against each other's exports. At best, the most they can earn from each other and through added sales of consumer and capital goods to the OPEC countries would appear to be only one-quarter to one-third of the total transfer that has to be made, if the four opening assumptions hold over these next five years.

The remaining $400 to $450 billion will have to be settled through transfers of claims rather than through the current movement of goods. The OPEC countries will become investors in either the productive real assets of the oil-importing countries, or in intangibles representing future claims on the producing assets and real income of the importing countries. Such massive shifts of debt and ownership to the OPEC countries may be theoretically conceivable for the oil-importing countries as a group, if their aggregate wealth were brought to bear on the problem on a totally unified basis. In practice, if they act individually, it is simply not conceivable that most of the importing countries can find matching inflows of funds, from OPEC countries at least, that would enable them to meet their oil deficit needs for very long.

This conclusion has been concealed, at least from the public, through most of the past year. Indeed, 1974 will surely prove to have been the easy year, not only because the payments themselves had not reached full magnitude until late in the year, but also because many old or new facilities could be called into initial use for channeling these growing payments flows, and because most oil-importing countries still had relatively large reserves of funds or borrowing power to draw upon—capabilities which are being rapidly exhausted in many countries.

Now a denouement, or a succession of denouements, is rapidly approaching. A looming problem is the ability of the major banks to continue to accept such a large volume of funds in the form of short-term deposits. In all likelihood, unless further approaches to cooperative action are made within the next few months, some oil-importing countries will have run out of goods to sell, or markets to reach, or capacity to borrow to cover their deficits, and a number may become unable to meet the servicing on the enlarged debts. Whether that would result in currency devaluations, in defaults by banking and business firms in those countries, in national debt moratoria, or in political revolution and debt repudiation, the entire structure of world payments, and of trade and financial relationships, would certainly be fractured.

Thus there is the immediate danger of progressive collapse triggered by defaults both by individual industrialized countries and by developing countries lacking natural resources. Yet, paradoxically, there is a great opportunity also, which lies beneath the surface of this immense "recycling" problem. In essence, the world today is starved for capital. Greater investment, not only in OPEC countries but everywhere, is an essential (though not in itself a sufficient) condition for the enlargement of output and lowering of real costs that offer the most effective counterforce to persistent worldwide inflation. In this situation, consumer payments for high-priced oil in the importing countries represent a diversion from other forms of consumption, in effect a form of forced saving, with the proceeds of these payments becoming, at least in part, investible funds in the hands of the OPEC countries. If the OPEC countries in turn had the proper outlets and were ready to employ their investible funds, they could make a crucial contribution to the capital formation that the world so urgently needs.

To date, the funds flowing to OPEC have not been truly effective in this investing function. To be sure, much has been done through creative private and governmental efforts to attract OPEC investors directly, or in roundabout ways, into useful investments in countries that need those proceeds to help pay for more oil. And much more can be done through diversified, disparate efforts. Yet it is surely too much to expect that the impending massive quantities of investible funds, becoming available at an unprecedentedly rapid rate, can all be distributed by an invisible hand into productive uses that will happen to occur in, or spill over into, the countries that need more wherewithal for making their oil payments. Thus the ultimate solution—a situation in which oil-importing countries, *both individually and as a group,* have developed the additional capacity to produce, export, and thus pay for their oil through the normal operation of the international economy—remains distant.

III

The astonishing fact, in the face of the largest single mutation in payments patterns that the modern world economy has ever experienced, short of war, is that so little dialogue about the problems ahead has yet occurred among the countries principally concerned—in the spirit of responsible nations consulting together over a staggering common problem. The questions of oil price, of goods availabilities and of potentials for lending, investing, or outright aid are all inexorably interrelated. Yet they are all being addressed separately, and even then not in a mutual exploratory appraisal by representatives of all three major interests—the oil-producing countries, the more developed oil-importing countries, and the oil-importing less-developed countries (LDCs).

The OPEC countries meet each other often, usually to take decisions with respect to reduced output or higher prices. The larger consuming countries have, each in its own way, worked out bilateral deals with individual producing countries, aimed at temporary improvisations to cover a few months' needs. A loose confederation has been formed among 11 or 12 of the consuming countries for the purpose of sharing absolute shortages in the event of another embargo against one or more of the group by the OPEC countries, and as this article went to press this was officially converted into an International Energy Agency of 16 nations, all members of the Organization for Economic Cooperation and Development (OECD). The International Monetary Fund has established a special "Witteveen facility" for borrowing modest sums from some OPEC members to be reloaned to Fund members suffering acute oil deficits. But apart from an "Interim Committee" within the IMF structure, there has been no joining of representatives of all sides of the problem, in a comprehensive exploratory review of the practical possibilities, and limitations, on all sides.

To be sure, several OPEC countries (notably Iran, Kuwait,

and Saudi Arabia) have themselves already extended beyond their own contributions to the IMF facility by beginning direct assistance to some of the needier developing countries. However, the need for such funds is well beyond the contributions made thus far. The forces of private initiative have been well represented, too, in quite another form of "recycling," as droves of salesmen with attractive investment opportunities to offer have swarmed through the OPEC countries.

Impressed by the variety and relative adequacy of the improvisations occurring in 1974, the United States has, however—until the Kissinger address of November 14 and the Simon address of November 18—avoided generalized consultations to deal with any major part of the transfer problem, apparently believing through most of 1974 that a hands-off approach of laissez-faire would suffice.[1]

Even as it shifted in mid-November to propose heroic but vague new plans for $25 billion annual recycling arrangements among the consuming countries, however, the United States seems to expect consuming countries to shrink their consumption of oil quite naturally as they proceed further in adapting to the increase of the oil price. It also apparently expects that the producing countries will be unable to agree on shares of a shrinking market and will consequently begin competing among themselves at declining oil prices—that the "cartel" will break apart. On the ground that extensive planned arrangements, even on a contingency basis, would merely delay the force of market pressures toward lower oil prices, the United States was, until November, extremely cool toward any proposed multilateral efforts to "recycle" the oil funds—that is, organized methods for routing some part of the OPEC oil receipts (through trade, investment, loans or aid) back to the countries which urgently need more funds to use for financing continued deficits and development. And even now, the United States proposes to organize the developed countries first, as a prerequisite to other contacts and negotiations involving either the developing countries or the oil-producing countries.

We believe that if this approach ever had merit, its usefulness is now at an end, for three interrelated reasons:

[1] Since the proposals by Secretaries Kissinger and Simon were made as this article was in the press, it was not possible for the authors to review together their reactions. Accordingly, all references to these proposals on this and the following pages are the responsibility of Mr. Roosa.

First, as already noted, the danger that one or more importing nations will simply not be able to pay for oil is immediate, within a matter of months. To be sure, following the lifting of the embargoes early in 1974, supplies have been adequate and payments strains moderate—a lull made possible by the various bilateral improvisations, by IMF or particular relief efforts, by some initial shrinkage in oil consumption, and by inadvertent OPEC financing arising from transitional delays in the actual transfer of funds through the major oil companies to the OPEC countries. The public alarm of a year ago has consequently waned. Yet several observers who have tried to work out projections of balance-of-payments and debt-carrying potentials cannot see how some important countries, even in 1975, can finance the scale of impending payments that each of them must somehow transfer across its own exchanges if oil is to flow, if the world economy is to have its prime energy supply, and if the four conditions stated at the outset of this article are to be fulfilled.

Second, brinkmanship is simply not a workable approach. It assumes an ignorance or susceptibility to pressure that does not exist among the OPEC countries; and most of all it postulates, or appears to postulate, an irreducible conflict of interest between oil producers and oil importers. Obviously, on the narrow question of price, their interests differ. From the standpoint of the consumers, it is argued that a reduction in the oil price would scale down the transfer problem; and that adaptation by the oil-importing countries would be relatively much less disruptive if the price were then to rise subsequently in modest increments from an adjusted lower level. But it is also argued, especially by producer countries, that continuing increases in the prices of their major imports, not entirely attributable to the increase in energy costs, should be taken into consideration in any discussion of the stabilization of future oil prices. Whatever chance there is for resolving the price question must surely depend, however, upon the development of much closer understanding, and the articulation of mutual interests, among the oil producers and the oil consumers. And the first step toward any such understanding must just as surely lie in beginning to discuss, together, the problems of transferring payments and the opportunities for constructive investment in the setting as it actually exists at the end of 1974. In the end, all the countries will have to act in a reasonably concerted manner if solutions are to emerge.

Third—and the most fundamental thesis of this article—progress toward effective solutions almost certainly requires major new methods and institutions. These cannot be created overnight. Yet they must be in place and in operation before the crisis becomes more serious. Even after giving effect to all other approaches or arrangements already under way for the transfer of capital and claims, as a supplement to the flow of goods and services to OPEC countries, a staggering $60 billion or more annually will remain unaccounted for.

IV

In the effort to reach a basic understanding, two central points must be fully accepted on both sides. The first has already been noted—that the oil-consuming countries must recognize that a reduction of the representative Persian Gulf FOB price from $10 down to $8, or even $6, per barrel, would still not reduce their transfer burden to the OPEC countries to readily manageable proportions. In annual gross payments, before any offset for sales of goods to the OPEC countries, or for any aid they may extend, the ranges would drop either to about $90 to $105 billion at the $8 price or to about $75 to $95 billion at $6. Taking account of other changes as well, that would only cut the "unexplained" annual residual to the $40 to $60 billion range.

The second point calls for oil producers to recognize what is at least the menacing possibility that, over time, the full impact of continuing the present prices of oil deliveries would be in effect to take, in gross payments from the consuming countries as a group, the greater part of any real growth in their per capita gross national product over the remainder of the seventies. Arithmetically, for example, the transfers from the industrialized OECD countries, by far the greatest consumers of oil, must amount to a continuing charge of three percent of the present total gross national product of this group of countries (roughly $3 trillion currently).

Static arithmetic is not, however, the real measure of the problem. On the one hand, the producing countries may well note that only a fraction of the required payments will be in the form of real resources. On the other hand, as seen from the consuming countries, the picture contains the threat of a freeze on growth that could be even more serious than the arithmetic would suggest. The diversion of a significant proportion of the income stream out of immediate consumption is bound to have a cumulative deflationary potential. And, as already noted, this deflationary potential could very well be compounded by the efforts of each nation to eliminate or at least reduce its oil-induced current account deficit. The resulting restrictions on trade could lead to a cumulative contraction of both domestic and international economic activity in which the damage would become very great.

From these points of analysis there emerges a central conclusion already touched on: that the resources diverted from consumption must be quickly channeled into real investment expenditures. Only those capital inflows to the OPEC countries which are attracted to productive investment elsewhere address themselves to the dual requirements of sustaining economic activity in the consuming countries and generating the ultimate means of payment. And only the availability of this kind of financing can reduce the pressure on individual countries to follow restrictive and combative current-account policies which would be detrimental not only to other consuming countries but to the world economy as a whole.

Thus, to both producer and consumer countries, each for their own reasons, the case for finding productive new investment for one-half to two-thirds of the proceeds of OPEC oil sales would seem to be compelling. Even if the oil price were to fall back as far as $6 per barrel, and if oil continued to flow on the present scale and with comparable distribution, no more than half of the indicated transfer to the OPEC countries as a group over the next five years could, in all probability, be met by sales of consumer or producer goods to them, or offset by direct OPEC grants-in-aid. The rest would have to be settled in claims of some sort, either simple interest-earning IOUs, or actual investments.

In the short term, there is no escape from the necessity of substantial borrowing to pay for current consumption. This is what in fact is happening, most notably in the case of Italy, and, over the next two years at least, the process of borrowing must continue and at a significantly increased rate. The problem here, as we shall see in more detail later, is to provide adequate means so that the less fortunate industrialized countries in particular will be able in practice to borrow effectively and thus keep themselves afloat.

But in the longer run, borrowing cannot do the job. Unless the borrower is able to achieve offsetting gains in production and rising current account earnings, he is bound in time—and despite any method of guarantees by others that may be devised—to lose standing as a borrower. The lender will have a deteriorating credit on his hands. The interests of both sides really require—whatever the probable price of oil may be—that the bulk of any oil payments that exceed the domestic import requirements of the OPEC countries be put back into the oil-consuming countries in the form of investment. Only in that way can the additional productive capacity of the oil-consuming countries be increased in order to generate the real current account surplus needed to service the continuing payments to the OPEC group.

That is, of course, much easier said than done. The individual OPEC countries differ widely among themselves in capacity to absorb consumer and capital goods, over the coming five years, and they differ correspondingly in the amounts left over for aid or investment elsewhere. The oil-importing countries differ, if possible, even more widely in their potentials for using new investment; and those potentials may have only slight relationship to the shortfall in particular countries' ability to pay for oil. As yet, no approach has been made to forming an overview, indicating where the more significant opportunities and gaps are, after taking account of everything else that energetic separate efforts may have done. And, of course, should there ever be agreement on the usefulness of an overview, and on how to go about making it, the questions of implementation—through multinational action or continued individual reactions—would still need exploration.

Nor can preoccupation with an overriding oil-payments problem be allowed to disguise the persistence, underneath, of all the same questions of balance in the payments flows among nations that have occupied the IMF and its Committees of Ten and of Twenty for several years. The "adjustment process" may have acquired new dimensions, but it is still there, with the issues of relative burdens of adjustment among countries still to be resolved. It is puzzling that the United States, which had taken a very positive role in earlier work on the adjustment process, should have stepped aside at the present critical stage when active, informal discussion among oil exporting and importing countries—to survey and appraise, well in advance of any negotiation—would have seemed an imperative prerequisite to finding viable solutions.

V

If and when an overall appraisal is attempted, it will (1) have to start with an outline of the *shortcomings* of financing arrangements thus far attempted, in terms of the more lasting needs and interests of both the OPEC and the oil-consuming countries, and indeed of sustainable order in world affairs. It will also (2) have to consider the various ways in which an *informational overview* could be organized, carried on and made meaningfully available to the countries and international organizations involved. And it will (3) want to explore *new methods* for bringing about results that can help assure the continued functioning of the international payments system and promote the further balanced growth of the world economy.

Without presuming to imagine the full scope of possibilities that could emerge—if leading representatives of the OPEC and the less developed and the more developed oil-importing countries were to fuse their experience in intensive informal and preparatory discussions of present shortcomings, of the scope of an overview, and of the usefulness of various financing methods—it is possible to suggest illustratively some of the considerations that might belong on the agenda.

Perhaps the most conspicuous shortcoming, late in 1974, is the heavy overburden already placed on the commercial banking systems of Europe, North America and Japan—to help finance and to transfer payments from importing countries to the major oil companies; to service the companies' transfers to the OPEC countries; to hold the balances acquired by the OPEC countries; and to redistribute the counterpart of those balances as creditworthy loans, the proceeds of which might hopefully flow onward to start the cycle over again. This process already has meant not only a ballooning of banking balance sheets, to the point of jeopardizing sound ratios of deposits and credits to capital, but it has also increasingly led to the dangerous extension of loan maturities beyond the maturity of deposits as well as a clogging up of the banking systems with purely "balance-of-payments" loans, often to governments or their agencies, at the expense of failing to serve traditional domestic credit needs.

Increasingly, as the oil payments reach cumulatively larger totals, individual banks and banking systems will become exposed to transfers among currencies in magnitudes far beyond established capabilities, and beyond prudent limits as to individual accounts or currencies. Even more critical than the breaching of operating norms is the increased sensitivity to the risks of fluctuation in foreign exchange rates, and vulnerability to deposit shifts that may impair functional liquidity—risking technical insolvency. To be sure, the central banks of most leading countries are working together to check any domino effects, should failures occur. And in time, sizeable OPEC balances will no doubt move on into other financial or investment instruments, whose markets do have a resilience and absorptive capacity that have not yet been fully used. But even in the broadest markets for equities, or bonds, or real property, the impact of amounts as sizeable as those in OPEC hands—or even rumors of OPEC interest—can have disruptive effects on the orderly pricing procedures through which values are determined.

In OPEC eyes, it would already appear, there are at least three serious shortcomings ahead, as the scale of receipts continues at the late 1974 pace: (1) limited liquidity, if the movements of these funds are not to disrupt banking systems and money markets which the OPEC countries themselves also need; (2) risks of loss through wide fluctuations in exchange rates, unless the OPEC countries, at the expense of some loss in their own flexibility, act to help assure the exchange-rate stability of the currencies they need and use; and (3) the erosion brought about by inflation in the prices of assets which they purchase, or in the value of the money in which they receive the earnings of the investment they acquire—unless they find some hedge against inflation that is more reliable than merely limiting their future production or spacing out the sale of their oil at inflationary prices.

The oil-consuming countries face the other side of these three risks, for they depend upon the same international banking facilities and financial markets, and are equally buffeted by inflation. But the overriding concern for many is how, during the months ahead, to earn or borrow enough hard currency to pay for their minimum oil requirements. Import quotas, export subsidies, exchange-rate depreciation, IMF drawings, crisis borrowing, or a moratorium on external debts are all among the possibilities. For some further time these extremes may be averted by the organizing of ad hoc rescue parties, either by particular OPEC countries, or by some more developed countries, or both. But unless prospects are opened for the deficit countries to earn their own way out eventually, or at least to earn the servicing on whatever debt can be obtained from somewhere, the further risk of debt repudiation and political overturn is grave.

Such, then, are the obvious shortcomings of the present institutional structure. Some of them, but by no means all of the critical ones, have been encompassed in the financial outline presented by Secretary Simon on November 18. His "financial safety net" approach for the guarantee of market borrowing, or for direct government loans, though extremely useful as a temporary expedient, should be designed to evolve into arrangements for sustained productive investment. The need of each oil-importing country over time is to develop a viable balance of payments, not to go on accepting improvised relief at the cost of future interest and amortization burdens. And there are, in any event, many unanswered and difficult questions of allocation, and of risk-sharing, in the Kissinger-Simon proposals which may take some time to sort out.

The next question concerns how a systematic overview of the interrelated problems of all oil-importing countries could be conducted. Since the problem on the surface concerns the approach of each individual country toward balance-of-payments equilibrium, one obvious candidate for the job is the International Monetary Fund. The hazard, for the OPEC countries which understandably feel underrepresented, and for many oil-importing countries which feel unappreciated, is that the IMF will be inclined to overdo its role. Instead of reporting on what is happening, the IMF will be tempted to tell countries on both sides what each country ought to do.

To get away from these difficulties, while at the same time taking advantage of the important resources of the IMF, a useful approach might well be to establish a special group, affiliated in some way with the IMF's "Interim Committee of Twenty," but structured to provide roughly equal representation of the OPEC countries, the oil-importing LDCs (less-developed countries) and the oil-importing industrialized countries. Such a group would be charged with monitoring the Fund's data gathering and alarm signaling efforts.

This group, or any other mutually agreeable arrangement that may be worked out for providing the continuous overview of payments patterns and strains, will presumably give close attention to the many roundabout ways in which deficit countries may, in the manner characteristic of a multilateral trading and payments system, gain a part of the OPEC reflow through sales or borrowing derived from OPEC purchases or investments elsewhere. But it will also have to be particularly alert to identify any sizeable gaps or lacunae which occur, or seem about to occur, after all practicable trade, investment and aid have been generated by existing markets and institutions, or by any new arrangements that may emerge either from the d'Estaing or Kissinger-Simon proposals of November. These gaps are likely to be of at least three kinds. It is surely not too early for a preliminary canvassing of views as to how each gap might possibly be filled.

VI

The first major gap, already all too evident, concerns the position of the less fortunate LDCs which lack oil or other natural resources and are thus by far the hardest hit of all consuming countries. For these countries, some needs will exist outside the usual bounds of lending by the World Bank or its affiliates, or by other regional development institutions. If their hopes for primary development are to survive the impact of increased oil prices, they will need funds to be committed on a long-term basis, with an indefinite postponement of servicing requirements and other highly concessional terms. Their ability ultimately to develop the current account surpluses that will be needed to service any loans depends, at least in part, on continuing modest inflows of oil, such oil derivatives as fertilizer, and other basic materials. Any aid they receive as loans must, consequently, be only slightly distinguishable from grants. No contributing country could expect more than nominal servicing, many years in the future, with the prospects for eventual repayment quite distant indeed—clearly not a "commercial proposition."

To be sure, some bilateral assistance programs by individual OPEC countries, as well as the aid efforts of several industrialized countries, are already temporarily reaching some needs of this extreme kind. But there would seem to be great advantage —both in the screening of these unusual recipient requirements and in the administering of loan programs—in a pooling of capabilities and resources by the leading OPEC and industrialized countries. Any arrangement for such purposes, while falling outside the scope of present IMF or IBRD activities, would necessarily depend heavily on coordination with the staffs of these organizations and of the United Nations Development Program. Whether any of the existing agencies should become more directly involved would also surely deserve consideration. In any case, whatever the arrangements, there would undoubtedly have to be special provision for representation more closely related to proportion of contribution. It might be expected that OPEC countries would contribute at least half of the comparatively modest sums that a supplemental emergency aid program of this kind would entail.

The gravity of the need in this area has already been recognized. The Witteveen facility of the IMF, thus far amounting to $3.4 billion, is in part directed at this need, although it is also available to hard-pressed industrial countries. Moreover, a more detailed proposal has been made by His Majesty the Shah of Iran in which equal numbers of OPEC, industrial, and developing countries were invited to establish a fund for the provision of aid to the developing countries. The financial contributions, which were to be made in equal amounts by the OPEC and industrial members, were to provide an annual aggregate addition to aid availabilities of approximately the same amount as the Witteveen facility. Each partner, of all three groups, would be represented by a governor, and the governors would select several executive directors, purely on their professional merits, to manage the fund, using the staff services of the World Bank. One of the objectives of such an organization would be to supplement existing aid programs without introducing any political biases.

Secretaries Kissinger and Simon have now endorsed a "separate trust fund" directed to this problem, with national contributions especially from oil-producing countries. Although lacking in full details, this is an important step toward the necessary new arrangements to meet this gap.

VII

The second great gap, suggesting the need for new facilities, concerns the industrialized countries for which oil imports are essential in sustaining overall productive capacity, but which cannot be expected to enlarge production and exports fast enough to pay fully for minimally needed oil imports at the new prices over the five years immediately ahead. Debt obligations of the governments of these countries would represent no risk of moratorium or repudiation, provided that they could place their debt with sufficiently long maturity to bridge a period of gradually enlarging export capabilities adapted to the changing markets of the world.

In such countries there are already substantial export earnings available to pay for imports, including a significant part of the oil imports; and there would undoubtedly be many individual firms capable of attracting outside financing in long term or equity form. But there would still be a missing critical margin which the various entities within the private sector could not be expected immediately to fill. Yet in the national interest there would be a justifiable public responsibility for filling that margin through government borrowing, in order to support the nation's overall economic performance. Instead of mere borrowing to pay for consumption, this would be borrowing to help maintain national viability, to obtain the added margin of oil needed for fuller use of a nation's potential. The results should appear, too, in balance-of-payments earnings on a scale sufficient to cover the servicing on such a debt of moderate maturity.

Virtually all of the industrialized countries, as well as most of those well along in the developing phase, could be expected to fall into this pattern of requirements at some time within the next five years. France, Italy, Japan and the United Kingdom, for example, have already arranged individually to borrow from OPEC and other countries, as well as from the commercial banking system. Some of these countries have also borrowed from international institutions. The United States, thus far apparently without governmental initiative, has already received several billion dollars as various OPEC countries purchased its government obligations in the public market. And indeed, OPEC purchases of government or other securities in the larger financial centers are likely to result, to some extent, in further passing along of loanable funds to still other oil-importing countries.

This is the process which the Kissinger-Simon $25 billion proposal for a "system of mutual support" would seek to help along by setting up "a common loan and guarantee facility" for the industrialized countries. And the two suggestions made earlier this fall, Helmut Schmidt's proposal of a multi-billion dollar international investment bank and Denis Healey's proposal of a $30 billion loan facility within the IMF, both address themselves to the same issue, from slightly different perspectives.

None of these proposals, however, engage the OPEC countries

in a responsible role, nor envisage that they would share in the risks which inevitably inhere in loans on such a vast scale to countries with widely varying economic prospects. A question well worth exploring, therefore, would be whether an additional facility, perhaps in the form of a mutual fund for OPEC investors, might add importantly to useful "recycling" machinery. An "OPEC Fund for Government Securities," attracting funds from any OPEC country wishing to utilize such a supplemental facility, might, for example, purchase only special direct issues of various governments. The terms of the instrument issued to OPEC investors in such a Fund would include orderly redemption features to prevent sudden withdrawal and resultant dislocation of the financial markets in the countries underwriting the issues.

The designing of such a Fund would have to recognize several limitations and several requirements. The terms of government issues offered to the Fund could not be so attractive as to compete unfairly with the variety of private activities, including the promotion of trade and the funding of loans or equity issues, that should be encouraged in order to evoke the maximum contribution by all other elements of each national economy, short of government financing. Nor should the availability of funds be such as to give undue preference to particular countries, or permit delays in needed domestic economic adjustment, or interfere with appropriate exchange rate changes.

Alongside limitations of this kind with respect to the borrowing countries, the OPEC countries would undoubtedly have several requirements. They will want a dominant voice in the administration of a Fund and may find difficulty in agreeing on the roles each of the OPEC countries should play. In order to minimize exposure to exchange rate variations among countries whose bonds are held, they may wish to have principal amounts, or interest payments, or both, indexed to some common market-basket of currencies such as the SDR, or possibly a basket of Middle Eastern currencies. They also presumably wish to hedge against inflation risks in the future by having some adjustment for sustained changes in the price levels of the world as a whole.

There will undoubtedly be other limitations and requirements —perhaps so many as to defeat a project of this kind. Yet even a sustained discussion of the various elements, and of their potentially conflicting interactions, could contribute importantly toward a mutuality of understanding among OPEC and oil-importing countries, as they participate together in attempting to evolve workable arrangements.

VIII

The third sector of activity in which additional facilities—beyond those already proposed by various governments—might help would be that of assisting the direct flow of OPEC funds into the capital formation that the world so clearly needs, through guiding new investment into private enterprises or joint ventures. Here there might be scope for an investment trust, or a family of trusts, which would place funds principally in new or outstanding issues of equity or debt, by going concerns of established capacity anywhere in the world. As a supplement to the bewildering array of individual deals already in progress, investment trusts could provide a particularly effective outlet for investing the funds of national governments, whose officials might welcome an opportunity to share a part of their responsibility for appraisal of investments with trust managers of the highest competence and integrity.

Once organized and staffed by selected experts or firms with broad and tested investment experience, an "OPEC Mutual Investment Trust" could concentrate its purchases of equities, for example, on new issues authorized by the existing stockholders of incorporated companies in the oil-importing countries. The issuing corporations, by making a special offering of their stock, would be inviting OPEC participation in their shareholdings in a proportion judged appropriate by existing shareholders and management. The proceeds would clearly be available for needed capital formation, while also enlarging the equity base on which additional borrowing could be arranged in the future. Similarly, private placements of debentures could be made by the Investment Trust, although presumably there would be a preference for convertibles in order to share more fully in growing earnings, and in the implied partial hedge against inflation that equities offer over longer periods of time. Particularly at presently depressed levels of equity prices, there is an almost unprecedented opportunity for capital appreciation, as an offset to the erosion of inflation, through the purchase of shares in the leading concerns of Western Europe, North America, Japan, Australia, and others. Diversification among firms and industries and countries should provide the greatest practicable assurance to the OPEC investors that their principal values can be maintained and earnings perpetually assured.

From the side of the oil-consuming countries, and the companies within them which might receive the OPEC trust investments, there is clearly an advantage in the trust form. It provides a buffer against the direct holding of voting stock by OPEC governments. The OPEC investors, in turn, can have the satisfaction of acquiring investments purely on their merit as sound earning assets, removing any possible implication of political motives or a desire to control the industry of another country. Moreover, the specialized management of these OPEC purchases and sales will shield the shares of companies in consumer countries from some of the sudden swings in price that could otherwise be set off accidentally by investors unable to devote full time to gauging factors affecting the timing and amount of transactions. A well-selected trust management should also assure OPEC investors the best possible combination of limited risk and moderate return available anywhere. The inescapable burden of owning capital is, of course, the taking of some risks—there is no "sure thing" for any investor, and no way of approximating risklessness for investors with funds as large as those of the OPEC countries—but diversification can balance risks and gains.

Purely as an indication of possibilities, a very tentative outline of some elements to be considered in designing a trust fund approach might be:

In the interests of the OPEC investors:

1. There might be several trusts for several different objectives, such as one for capital appreciation, another for income, and another a balanced fund; or there could be a separation as between real property and intangible property; or according to the country or group of countries in which investments are to be placed.
2. Depending on the nature of the assets, and the degree of liquidity required by provisions for redemptions, anticipated total return on average might range between six and eight percent.
3. As a guide to diversification, percentage limits within the total of a given trust fund might be set for holdings in a given country, or currency area, or individual company.

Companies might be rated, with minimum or maximum percentages for holdings of Class A, or AA, or AAA, for example; or limits could be placed on size of capitalization, say a $10 million minimum.

4. Individual trusts could be open end or closed end, but presumably shares of the trusts would not be listed on any public exchanges as they could only be traded among the relatively small number of OPEC countries. Since OPEC countries may wish to repatriate holdings as added investment opportunities become available domestically, trust shares should be redeemable according to terms related to the kinds of assets held by a particular trust.
5. Risks of nationalization of assets held by the trusts would be minimized by virtue of the fact that there would be a majority of shareholders or bondholders or partners from the private sector in non-OPEC countries. However, some consumer countries might consider giving guarantees against nationalization, and many would probably permit exemption from domicile taxation on dividends transmitted to the trusts.
6. Exposure to changing rates of foreign exchange would be minimized both through diversification and through specific guidelines set for the trust management.
7. Establishment of the trusts can be handled by a management company in which the nominal stock ownership would be held by each interested OPEC country and, if desired, by the leading investment institutions in key countries which the participating OPEC governments choose to provide advisory services and to assist in selecting the full-time staff of the management company. The company and trusts could be organized under the laws of Switzerland, or the United States, or elsewhere as desired. The Board of Directors of an "OPEC Investment Trusts Management Company" would presumably consist of at least one member from each participating OPEC country, with additional directors added according to a formula related to size of participation. Advisory firms might also have seats on the Board, or alternatively on an Advisory Board, authorized to consult directly with and review the performance of the active management. The Board should have authority to establish additional trusts for specified purposes under the laws of any country

designated in the bylaws, and to change any operating guidelines by a two-thirds vote.

8. The initial size of a trust might be set at $1 billion with share units of $1 million each. As all expenses of the management company, including custody and transfer of securities, should be a first charge on earnings, there need be no "load" on the actual subscription to any trust.

In the interests of the oil-consuming countries:

1. No trust should hold shares in any company which would bring the known total holding of such shares by OPEC governments or their agencies above, say, ten percent of the total outstanding, unless specific approval is obtained both from the management of the company and the government in which its head office is located.
2. The trusts should undertake to buy or sell shares (or debentures) in amounts above, say, one million dollars (or the equivalent in other currencies) only with the knowledge of the company. In this way the company may have first refusal of an opportunity to offer stock (or debentures) directly at the going market price or, if it wishes, to buy back such instruments at the going market price. This would help protect the trusts against creating an undue movement of the market price against their interests, and would assist the company in maintaining an orderly market for its obligations.
3. The trusts should undertake to give prior notice to the affected central banks whenever they contemplate transfers into or out of a particular currency in amounts of, say, five million dollars or more (or whatever benchmark each central bank wishes to set). In this way, undue disturbances to exchange rates could be avoided, as desired by the affected central banks, to the advantage of everyone, including the OPEC investors.
4. The directors should agree that voting shares in companies will be exercised by the management with a view solely to protecting the value of the investment, in a manner comparable to the normal exercise of such rights by leading trust companies in behalf of their clients, and not for any other purpose.

Should any measure of interest emerge for a trust fund approach among the OPEC and consumer countries, a more fully articulated prospectus would, of course, have to be developed to test its feasibility. On the basis of limited preliminary inquiries in the investment banking community, it would appear that an aggregate magnitude of $10 billion would not be out of the question in the first full year for trusts of this kind—at least in terms of the availability of acceptable investment outlets.

IX

The OPEC countries, whose principal product has been for so long underpriced and overused, must be able to convert their exhaustible oil into permanent capital and perpetual earnings, at home and abroad. They need, and undoubtedly want, both the enduring goodwill and the continuing economic prosperity of the oil-importing countries. They surely recognize their large stake in the economic prosperity of the world. They undoubtedly want capital markets of their own, and ready access to flourishing capital markets in other countries, to provide an assured base for the economic growth they rightly expect for their descendants.

The suggestions made here are meant only to illustrate the breadth and variety of the approaches and opportunities that should still be explored, before the world teeters any closer to the edge of an unnecessary stalemate—locked between rightful aspirations of the OPEC countries and limited capacity of the oil-importing countries to meet those aspirations rapidly. The urgent need is to begin a mutual exploratory process. Confrontation between oil-producing and oil-consuming countries has already produced a gulf of misunderstanding, both as to motives and as to potentialities, on both sides.

In the year that has been so largely lost, confusion and differences have multiplied while underlying economic tensions have, though subdued for a time, been inexorably moving toward crisis. There is barely enough time for a quiet sorting out of the interacting influences of trade, prices, aid, and investment. Informal exchanges, with the blessing and in time the participation of heads of states or governments, could still avert impending calamity during the remainder of this decade and begin construction of a viable system for the decades ahead.

33

The New Middle East, the Developing Countries, and the International Company

A. Kapoor

INTRODUCTION

The object of this section is to highlight a role which can be played by the international company (hereafter referred to as IC) in tranferrring resources from the oil-producing countries of the Middle East, especially those with revenues far in excess of their internal development needs, to other developing countries, particularly Asian ones. The major ideas presented here are:

1. The surplus oil-revenue countries in the Middle East (hereafter referred to as SORCs) will be placing increasing emphasis on investment (mainly direct instead of portfolio) in the developing non-Arab countries. Because the SORCs lack technical, organizational, and human resources, the primary form of investment will be financial participation in projects undertaken by well-established ICs.

2. A major strength of the IC is its ability to effectively transfer resources (capital, technology, organizational capabilities) from one country to another. In addition, investments by the IC in developing countries offer a relatively more secure and higher return on investment than those of local companies which will encourage the SORCs to collaborate with the IC in third-country investments.

3. Developing countries in Asia and elsewhere, affected by the energy crisis, are seeking investments (e.g., in petrochemicals) by SORCs. However, very few companies have developed specific programs of action or feasibility studies which can be presented to the SORCs for consideration. In addition, in the opinion of many SORCs, most developing countries do not have indigenous enterprises which offer investment security comparable to that provided by the IC.

4. An effective and long-term program for the transfer of resources by the IC from the SORCs to the developing countries of Asia (and elsewhere) can result in profits and goodwill for the IC in the investing and host countries.

5. However, in order to effectively develop and implement the type of approach outlined above, the most senior management levels of the IC will need to develop recognition of the long-range potential of the role of the IC as a vehicle for effective transfer and utilization of funds from the SORCs in other developing countries.

From a Seminar delivered at the Asia Society, 1974. Reprinted by permission.

6. Investments by the ICs in the SORCs represent only one part of their relationship. It is equally if not more important for the IC to view its investments in the SORCs as a means of developing trust and know-how in assisting the SORCs in investing outside of their local markets.

The balance of this paper offers selected investment characteristics of the SORCs, the existing attitude of the IC regarding investment in and with the SORCs, and general recommendations for the IC in transferring resources from the SORCs to developing countries with particular reference to Asia.

CHARACTERISTICS OF THE SORCs*

Estimates of SORC earnings through the mid-1980s range from $400 billion to over a trillion dollars. Local development is not likely to absorb more than 50 percent of the overall earnings of the Arabian Gulf countries; in all probability it will be less than that.** Therefore, the Arabian SORCs, especially, will have a large sum of money to expend in foreign countries—Arab and non-Arab, developed and developing.

The foreign expenditures by the SORCs will be in three general forms—loans, grants, and investments (portfolio and direct). A significant percentage of the foreign expenditures will be in the developed countries with particular focus on the U.S.A., followed by Western Europe and Japan a distant third. Portfolio investments will figure prominently in the developed countries because of sizeable, secure, well-established and well-regulated securities markets coupled with the presence of institutions and personnel who are qualified to undertake such investments for the SORCs. Additionally, this form of investment will offer some secrecy.

However, the investment context in the developing countries is different from that of the developed countries. First, the securities markets are small, undeveloped, and poorly regulated to generate investor confidence. Therefore, portfolio investments by the SORCs in the developing countries will be quite limited.

Second, as lenders and as donors, the SORCs will definitely seek security of loans and hope for effective utilization of donations. Involvement of well-established ICs in projects using SORC loan capital will offer greater confidence to the SORCs. This is likely to be particularly true for loans to other developing countries—both Arab and non-Arab.

Third, direct investments by the SORCs in developed countries will strongly favor well-established ICs for reasons of security and prestige. In addition, as in the case of Iran's 25 percent ownership of Krupp in West Germany, the SORCs will view such direct investments as a means of

---

* The SORCs are mainly the Arabian Gulf countries of Kuwait, Saudi Arabia, and the United Arab Emirates. Libya will also have surplus funds. Iran and Iraq, on the other hand, will be able to use all their earnings for local development purposes; however, they will also undertake foreign investments.

** The figures are not precise but broad "ball park" estimates which serve our purpose of highlighting broad trends.

gaining access to know-how and technology for their internal development needs.

However, local companies in developing countries do not instill confidence and trust in the SORCs. Therefore, in undertaking direct investments in the developing countries, the SORCs will seek the involvement of well-established ICs, especially those which are known and trusted by the key decision makers in the SORCs.

Fourth, institutions and individuals are available (although not entirely adequate for the task at hand) to assist in invesments by the SORCs in the developed countries. Conversely, there are hardly any institutions with the skills and orientation required to facilitate investments by the SORCs in the non-Arab developing countries. (This situation is definitely worse for Latin America than Asia because of South and Southeast Asia's historical linkages and physical proximity to the SORCs. Within the Arab world, financial and political institutions exist but not indigenous companies with the desired know-how and reputation in undertaking specific projects.)

Therefore, the IC is likely to serve as the major vehicle for investments by SORCs in the developing countries—both Arab and non-Arab. The quantities of SORC investments are likely to be sizeable in comparison with the present size of foreign direct investments, particularly in the Middle East, North Africa, and Asia.

The announced and proposed investments, loans, and grants by the Arab SORCs to other Arab countries are expected to amount to tens of billions of dollars by 1980, making the Arab SORCs the single largest foreign investors in the non-oil producing Arab countries.

If five percent of the foreign expenditures of the SORCs (conservatively estimated at $100 billion) by the mid-1980s are to the developing countries of Asia, it will make the SORCs among the top three foreign investors in the region along with Japanese and U.S. companies. Through normal leveraging, the SORC investment would result in activation of sizeable amounts of local capital and contributions by partners from third countries.

In brief, over the coming decade, the transfer of funds from the SORCs to Asia is likely to constitute a sizeable sum. The IC can play an important role in the transfer by facilitating and participating in the resultant projects in Asia. (The same observation applies to intra-regional investments in the Middle East, though the dollar volume will be much greater.)

The entire subject of SORC foreign investment is shrouded with mystery and any effort to identify major criteria for foreign investment is fraught with the dangers of oversimplification. However, for our purposes, four broad and interrelated reasons for making foreign investments can be identified: economic, political, religious, and humanitarian.

ECONOMIC

Security, along with reasonable assurances for an acceptable return on investment, appear to be the primary investment considerations of SORCs.

They seek to protect themselves financially. Once their oil reserves are depleted or viable alternative sources of energy are developed, the SORCs will have to provide for themselves from their accumulated investment base.

The developing countries of Asia provide attractive investment opportunities in petroleum-related and other industries. Of course, guarantees against loss of principal will be sought by the SORCs from the host government and/or from regional and international organizations. However, such guarantees, without the active involvement of the IC in a project, are not likely to be sufficient for the SORCs to undertake investments in the developing countries.

For economic reasons (and for secrecy) some SORC investments in Asia will be channelled through European and U.S.-based institutions. SORC capital, therefore, will then enter Asia as American or European capital—subject to the full protection of the home country. In the eyes of the SORCs, this arrangement would offer greater security. However, even under this form of "laundered" SORC capital, the SORCs are likely to seek involvement of the ICs in the projects.

POLITICAL

Inter-Arab relations are an important consideration in SORC foreign expenditures, particularly in the form of grants and loans to Arab governments. The smaller Arabian Gulf countries are uneasy over the military power of Iran. They might well seek closer economic, political, and military ties with India and Pakistan (and-or with other militarily strong countries) as a means of protection from Iran.

Iran is also seeking economic, political, and some form of military ties with South and Southeast Asian countries. The most obvious example is the recent visit and announcements of the Shah of Iran on some form of a "common market" arrangement with South and Southeast Asia.

From the standpoint of host Asian countries, sizeable SORC investments are sought not only for immediate benefits but also for a more fundamental and lasting reason: By investing in the Asian countries (or in any foreign country), the SORCs are offering a hostage to the host country. Therefore, the SORCs will be less inclined to act in a unilateral manner. The essential point is that the economic and political considerations merge into each other and neither one can be seen in isolation.

RELIGIOUS

Religion is an important force in the SORCs, though its intensity varies by country. Assistance to other Islamic nations is valued by the SORCs, and some specific actions (e.g., institutional development) have been taken along with financial contributions. In Asia several countries are officially Islamic states (Pakistan, Bangladesh, Malaysia, Indonesia) or have significant Islamic minorities (India, the Philippines).

In the coming decade, the SORCs are likely to make significantly greater expenditures in the Islamic countries of Asia. Investments will be one form of expenditure, and for reasons of security, the SORCs are likely to seek the collaboration of ICs. In fact, loans and grants by the SORCs will pave the way for more favorable treatment of their investment proposals by the host governments.

HUMANITARIAN

Severe poverty, especially in South Asia, is arousing humanitarian concern among the SORCs. In addition, it is beginning to be recognized that major political unrest in South Asia—a region with indigenously developed nuclear power—could have a seriously detrimental effect on the continued peaceful enjoyment by the SORCs of their new-found prosperity.

In brief, for economic reasons the SORCs are likely to seek collaboration with the ICs in undertaking investments in Asia. The loans and grants by the SORCs to Asian countries will facilitate SORC investments in these countries.

THE INTERNATIONAL COMPANY AND THE MIDDLE EAST

The role of the IC in collaborating with the SORCs in third-country investments has to be seen with reference to its attitude and current role on investing in the Middle East. By developing an understanding of the Middle East, the IC can then seek third-country collaborations with the SORCs.

At present, the majority of U.S.-based ICs, outside of the petroleum and defense-related industries, have a limited knowledge of the Middle East for several reasons: (1) the IC has had very limited and in many cases no interaction with the Middle East. (2) The sudden emergence of the Middle East as a place for selling and investment has caught most ICs by surprise, with the result that they are only beginning to develop their plans and strategies for the Middle East. (3) The uncertain political situation in the Middle East, coupled with attractive investment opportunities in other parts of the world, has inhibited rapid development of specific programs of action by the IC for the Middle East. (4) The IC has hardly any executives skilled in Middle Eastern business affairs and with a vested interest in promoting investments in the Middle East.

However, the cornucopia of wealth in the Middle East is attracting the attention of the U.S.-based IC. Sales to the Middle East will continue to reflect a sizeable increase even over the recent past. Direct investments will also reflect a notable increase, especially in the relatively large Middle Eastern countries, especially Iran, Saudi Arabia, Iraq, and Egypt. In short, the business involvement of U.S.-based ICs in the Middle East will increase significantly over the coming decade. During this time the IC will become better positioned to develop, promote, and implement specific projects in Asia (and in other parts of the world) in collaboration with the SORCs.

SPECIFIC EXAMPLES OF THIRD-COUNTRY PROJECTS

A few examples can be identified which are illustrative of the trend of SORC-IC collaborations for investments in Asia. Some projects are new, others are ongoing IC operations in which the SORCs have taken an equity interest, and several are at various stages of negotiation.

- Saudi Arabia has taken an equity interest in an ongoing oil refinery in South Korea which includes participation by an IC.
- Iran has invested in a major fertilizer and refinery complex in India in collaboration with the Standard Oil Company of Indiana.
- Several Southeast Asian countries are interested in seeking participation of the SORCs for petroleum-based projects such as fertilizers; and to strengthen their proposals they are seeking the involvement of well-established ICs. Some SORCs, on their side, are encouraging large petroleum-based ICs to collaborate with them in projects in Asia.
- Southeast Asian countries are seeking investments by the SORCs in major extractive projects involving the participation of ICs.
- SORCs are interested in investments in hotels in several Asian countries, especially in association with well-established ICs.
- A SORC is considering purchase of part of the equity of a major IC in South Asia provided that the IC retains at least 25 percent ownership of the project and enters into a ten-year management contract.
- An investment bank has been established in Southeast Asia by a SORC and a Japanese company for undertaking investments in Asia.

In the coming years, there will be several projects involving collaboration of the SORCs and one or more ICs. In large projects the local partner is likely to be the host government. The involvement of a SORC government in such projects is likely to assist the IC in dealing with the host governments.

GENERAL RECOMMENDATION FOR THE IC

Assuming that an IC finds merit in the approach outlined above and wishes to participate in it, it will need to recognize several dimensions, and the ones outlined below are for purposes of illustration.

First, the IC must develop a long-term perspective, as it will take time to develop the know-how involved in doing business in the Middle East, to gain the trust of key decision makers in the SORCs, to secure the understanding of the host countries, to generate an understanding within the IC, and to develop the personnel and organizational structure to undertake collaborations with the SORCs in third countries in the developing world.

Second, ongoing and proposed investments in the Middle East should be seen within the broader framework of developing programs and specific projects for collaborative undertakings with the SORCs in third countries. This approach can be an important bargaining point in favor of the IC in investing in a SORC.

Third, the IC will need to consider specific actions in order to effectively develop the idea of collaborative investments in third countries of Asia and other developing regions. A few specific areas of action are noted, as follows:

1. In many ICs the Middle Eastern region reports to European headquarters. Should this be changed in light of the special characteristics of the Middle East? Should there be greater involvement of other regional

headquarters to facilitate development of programs by the IC which reflect investment opportunities by the SORCs in various parts of the world? With reference to the potential of SORC investments in Asia, what should be the role of the IC's Asian organization in developing and presenting specific investment proposals to the SORCs? What should be the role of corporate headquarters? The essential point here is that investment flows by the SORCs, especially to other developing countries, are not facilitated by the existing organizational structures of the IC.

2. The IC is generally ignorant of the Middle East, especially at the most senior levels of management where basic policy decisions will be made on collaborative investments with the SORCs in third countries. However, there is also an additional problem which relates to the outlook of IC management toward the SORCs and all developing countries. Historically, the developing countries have invariably been the recipients of investments. But in the case of the SORCs, the region is both a recipient and a source of foreign investment. This requires readjustment of outlook of the IC in dealing with the SORCs because approaches which have been used in other developing countries do not include this unique feature of the SORCs.

3. A major limitation at the present time is that the IC lacks personnel qualified to do business in the Middle East. Efforts must be made to rectify this. In addition, the IC needs to train personnel who can facilitate the development of collaborative projects, especially among regions which have had limited investment flows in the past, such as the Middle East and Asia.

4. The IC should take the initiative in developing specific feasibility studies which it can market to the SORCs and to the host countries.

THE MULTINATIONAL ENTERPRISE AND LESS DEVELOPED COUNTRIES

The Multinational Enterprise and Less Developed Countries

34

The Impact of Multinational Corporations on the Development Process and on International Relations: SOME SPECIFIC ISSUES

United Nations Economic and Social Council

OWNERSHIP AND CONTROL

The capacity to make and enforce decisions is a fundamental issue for developing countries because multinational corporations can greatly affect the objectives of their national development plans through the control of strategic or key sectors of their economies, the control by the parent company of important decisions by the affiliate, and the impact of the affiliate on over-all monetary financial and trade policies.

In many host countries, there is widespread concern over foreign control of key sectors of the economy. It is most keenly felt in developing countries, where multinational corporations often dominate the mining and manufacturing sectors. Even in developed countries such concern is quite common, though to a lesser extent, particularly where there is strong indigenous competition or where the countries are themselves important foreign direct investors. There is no simple formula for allaying these anxieties. They are particularly acute when they reflect the search for a sense of national identity or the desire to reduce a country's dependence.

Each host country, therefore, has to decide, in the light of its own needs and aspirations, those areas of economic activity in which it will permit foreign direct investment and those which it wishes to reserve for indigenous companies.

The United Nations resolutions concerning permanent sovereignty of countries over their natural resources command special attention in this respect. We feel that recognition of a country's right to dispose of its natural resources must be accompanied by adequate international conditions to enable it to exercise that right effectively. Experience has shown that this is not always the case. If the help of multinational corporations is needed in exploiting natural resources, it may be preferable to enter into leasing or other types of contractual arrangements with them rather than allow them to own the resources or control the use of them. Public utilities and defence

---

This is Part II of the *Report of the Group of Eminent Persons to Study the Role of Multinational Corporations on Development and on International Relations* (June 9, 1974), for the fifty-seventh session of the Economic and Social Council, United Nations Organization.

industries are two other areas in which many countries at present do not allow foreign companies to hold any interests. The effect of a foreign presence in the advertising or communications industries should be carefully considered by countries that wish to maintain their cultural or sociological characteristics.

> *The Group recommends* that host countries should clearly define and announce the areas in which they are ready to accept foreign investment and also the conditions upon which such investment will be allowed in those sectors. In particular, developing countries should be encouraged to retain ownership of their natural resources or control the use of them.

Decisions taken by large corporations—domestic or foreign—in key industries may have a significant impact on the economy of a country and on its goals. To ensure that the decisions of the companies conform to national plans, Governments can exercise economic controls through legislative and administrative means. However, many decisions which affect the economy are taken within an enterprise. In general, indigenous enterprises are aware of the domestic conditions and national aspirations. Decisions taken by a local affiliate rather than by the parent company are usually more responsive to local conditions and national objectives.

There is a wide variation in the extent to which multinational corporations delegate authority to their affiliates. Many of them take centralized decisions on various matters concerning the production patterns and marketing policies of their affiliates in order to secure the maximum advantage from an appropriate division of labor and the most economic allocation of their resources. Sometimes these decisions work to the benefit of the affiliate. Inevitably, not every decision will satisfy each and every country in which the multinational corporations operate.

In some respects, the making of decisions outside the country in which they are to be implemented can introduce problems similar to those presented by dependence on international trade. In later sections, the various areas of tension that can arise from control by multinational corporations over their affiliates in the matter of decision making—for example, the fields of labor and exports—will be dealt with. Many countries take measures to insulate themselves against the worst fluctuations in international demand and supply. Similarly, countries may wish to protect themselves against action taken by the parent firms of foreign affiliates when it appears to be contrary to their own interests.

Sometimes, an attempt is made to achieve this objective by insisting that certain key positions in the affiliates of multinational corporations should be held by nationals and not by expatriates. While such a policy may help to train nationals for positions of responsibility, it does not solve the problem of control. A better method might be to reach an understanding with the multinational corporation about the nature of the decisions which are to be taken locally. At the initial stage of the negotiations, the multinational corporation could explain its general decision-making network and the manner in which the affiliate would be affected by it. Such information would permit the host country to determine whether its basic policies would be likely to be affected by foreign control. Thus, an evaluation could be made and the appropriate decisions taken. Experience shows that much frustration has come about because the host country did not at first perceive these issues properly.

On other occasions, countries seek control through local ownership. This is not always possible nor necessarily effective. Many multinational corporations prefer to retain full or substantial ownership of their affiliates because they believe that without it they will be unable to implement a global strategy of production and marketing that requires many important decisions to be taken centrally and with the group's over-all interest in view. In addition, they may wish to maintain control over the use of their technology and know-how. It should be noted, however, that control can also be exercised in many areas through a minority shareholding, if the majority of the shares are held by investors who have no common purpose and are not interested in exercising control, or if the majority of the shareholders are on such friendly terms with the multinational corporation that they do not wish to take a different view from it.

The search for ownership requires capital. This is not always readily available to developing countries and thus they need to decide where the resources can be used most profitably. Although we understand that, in certain key sectors, outright ownership is an important economic and political requirement for developing countries, the real issue is control. If control is obtained through other means, ownership merely influences the way in which the profits earned by an affiliate of a multinational corporation are divided between its parent company and domestic investors.

Ways of exercising control vary. As we have seen, serious conflicting interests are involved. Basically, host countries should define clearly the kind of policy the affiliates of multinational corporations should pursue wth respect to such essential matters as continuous access to technology, agreement on marketing procedures, repatriation of capital and profits, and so forth. If the country feels satisfied with the performance of an affiliate, the question of control diminishes in importance.

On occasion, host countries ask for a majority shareholding not only as a means of strengthening their influence over the policies of the affiliate beyond that exercised through general governmental powers, but also in order to secure a larger share of the profits of foreign direct investment. Here again, there may be alternative ways in which the Government and the multinational corporation can modify the distribution pattern—for example, through the reinvestment of profits over certain fixed periods, or the limitation of capital and profit remittances abroad. Also, national tax laws are important in this context.

On the other hand, if the only factor that keeps a home Government from seeking part or total ownership of an affiliate is lack of available capital, it is important that it should have access to adequate credit from international financial institutions. A country should not be prevented by lack of domestic capital from reaching the ownership pattern that it feels is necessary for its development plans. In that context, joint ventures and the reduction over time of foreign equity interests should be given favorable consideration as one of the options available to both parties.

> *The Group recommends* that where ownership is an important objective for host countries, consideration should be given to the establishment of joint ventures as well as to the reduction over time of the share of foreign equity interests.

We would like to make the observation that, in some developing countries at least, joint ventures between multinational corporations and domestic private enterprises may confer some benefits on a small elite group of nationals, but may make no material difference to the issue of control unless the national investors themselves are active and responsive to national priorities.

On occasion, arrangements with Governments may prove more attractive to multinational corporations since they carry a greater sense of security. It should be noted, however, that the conditions which gave rise in the beginning to a particular arrangement may not continue to exist over the long term. In the initial stages, for example, the host country may not be in a position to mobilize adequate capital, or it may be greatly dependent on the multinational corporation for technology and management. In time, all this may change.

If there is no possibility of the multinational corporation renegotiating or progressively reducing its equity interests, the relations between it and the host Government may begin to deteriorate. Since the costs and benefits of inward direct investment undergo major changes over time, host Governments and multinational corporations should, from the very beginning, provide for the possibility of renegotiations at later stages.

During the hearings, we were impressed by the account given of the work of the Atlantic Community Development Group for Latin America (ADELA). Formed by many corporations from a number of countries, none of which has a large share in the capital, its purpose is to engage in joint ventures with local private or public capital and to start new industries. It gradually relinquishes its investment once a project is well established and makes new investments with the resources thus released. Such an arrangement has favorable effects on the balance of payments of the host country: The capital, instead of being repatriated at the conclusion of the investment, is reinvested in the country. The technology and managerial skills which the investor provides are also switched to new fields as nationals take charge of the established industries. The formation of the Andean Group and the resulting enlargement of the market will provide an added stimulus for this sort of activity in that region.

Similar companies are beginning to operate in other continents. Such a scheme cannot be extended to the point at which it would replace other forms of private foreign investment, but we believe that some of its features can be usefully imitated: in particular, the multinational source of capital, the association with local, public, or private intersts, and the gradual switch from well-established projects to reinvestment in new ventures.

FINANCIAL FLOWS AND BALANCE OF PAYMENTS

Aside from technology, multinational corporations may supply financial capital to the countries in which they produce. This is usually welcomed, particularly by countries with a balance of payments deficit.[1]

In considering the effects of the inflow of financial capital on the balance of payments, there is a tendency to examine the problem from a very narrow point of view. Thus, attention is often confined to the cost of servicing the investment by remittances of dividends, fees, and royalties and the repatriation of capital over time. These figures have only limited relevance when the country has a choice between paying for capital goods out of its own export earnings and reserves or financing them against credits or grants, official or commercial, for the purpose. In practice this choice may not always be available. Other sources of finance may be under severe constraint, and the collaboration of the multinational corporation may be necessary for reasons of technology and know-how to establish the production facility.

The more basic issue with regard to balance of payments is whether the particular investment will mean a net contribution to the country's ability to meet foreign exchange rerquirements over time, after allowing for all the outgoings in servicing the investment as well as other consequential remittances, for example, through transfer-pricing devices.

In evaluating the effects of inward direct investment on the balance of payments, it must be borne in mind that developing countries have special international liquidity and cash-flow problems. While inward direct investment in the short term provides a measure of relief, the possibility that, in the long run, a problem it has failed to solve may be worsened is a constant cause of concern.

In our view, in order for correct decisions to be made, the problem should be considered not simply in terms of the impact of identifiable inflows and outflows attributable to the presence of multinational corporations, but in the wider perspective of the country's over-all development. The balance of payments is not an end in itself, and policies to deal with it must be part of an over-all economic policy. Except when imports are financed out of outright grants, any import must have an immediate negative effect in purely balance-of-payments terms. The form of financing, whether cash payment, or commercial or official credits, or against equity investment, affects the time over which the negative impact is felt as well as the magnitude of the impact. The more crucial question is that of ensuring that the totality of external finance available makes the maximum contribution toward the fulfillment of the country's primary goals, which may not be purely economic and may include concern over consumption patterns and income distribution.

In appraising foreign investment proposals by multinational corporations, host countries should thus assess their over-all contribution to development as well as their contribution to the country's ability to meet foreign exchange requirements, and compare them with possible alternatives.

Once a decision has been made to accept investment by multinational corporations on these wider considerations, a number of specific issues need attention. The question which often arises is whether multinational corporations should bring in the entire capital they need or whether they should have access to local sources. Apart from the fact that, in general, the larger the initial capital inflow, the greater the eventual outflow of interest and dividends, the structure of capital also influences the outcome. Interest on foreign loans is a fixed charge while dividends may be a flexible one. In so far as dividends may reflect higher risk of venture capital as compared with loan capital, they may be at a higher rate than interest. Borrowing from the local market may increase the return to foreign investment and lead to the remittance of profits which do not directly correspond to a previous inflow of foreign capital.

Other effects are no less important. There is, for example, the question of impact on the domestic capital market. If abundant domestic savings are available, the case for encouraging or even insisting that multinational corporations should tap them would be strong. On the other hand, this is not normally the case, and such a course would deprive indigenous industry of the capital it needs to fulfill national goals. Thus, it may be advisable to ask the multinational corporations to bring in all the capital they need.

Because of their concern with the balance-of-payments problem, developing countries sometimes restrict remission of dividends, royalties, and so on. Nevertheless, multinational corporations are often able to circumvent such restrictions through transfer pricing and other devices. Moreover, to build up a backlog of current-account dues awaiting repatriation can in the long run also generate balance-of-payments problems. What is important is to ensure that the contribution of multinational corporations to the capacity to earn foreign exchange is as high as possible, bearing in mind other development objectives. Further attention should be focused on such practices of the multinational corporations, such as restrictions on exports and transfer pricing, which may harm both their contribution to income and the balance of payments.

Developing countries have frequently expressed concern over the amount of local capital borrowing by multinational corporations, both as part of initial investment and for further expansion. They consider restrictions on remittance of dividends and other payments as one of the means at the disposal of Governments. For the reasons discussed above, however, host countries should consider carefully, even in periods of emergency, the negative effects of imposing any restrictions on such remittances.

Finally, it should be remembered that the system of trade and payments and the policies of national Governments may have a major influence on the behavior of multinational corporations as well as on policies of individual host Governments. Tariff and trade policies of developed countries affect the level of exports from developing countries. Instability in exchange rates may lead multinational corporations to move funds across national borders in a way which tends to accentuate this instability.

The effective implementation by developed countries of the United Nations scheme for generalized preferences on processed and manufactured goods from developing countries and the reduction of non-tariff barriers will ease the concern of developing countries about the impact of investments by multinational corporations on their balance of payments. We urge that current efforts and plans of the International Monetary Fund for monetary reform should take full account of the role of multinational corporations. In the long run, we would hope that the general agreement on multinational corporations will also amount to an international agreement on capital and investment, since most of the investment is by multinational corporations.

Meanwhile, the Group feels that, in assessing the impact of multinational corporations, host countries should attach greater importance to the kind of contribution these enterprises can make to their over-all development, and should take into account their impact on the balance of payments primarily for the purpose of making a choice, where such exists, between alternative methods of financing a project.

TECHNOLOGY

Technology is an essential input for production. It is bought and sold in the following forms: (a) embodied in physical assets as, for example, plants, machinery and equipment, and sometimes intermediate products; (b) as services of skilled and often highly specialized manpower; (c) as information, whether of a technical or of a commercial nature. From the viewpoint of the individual firm, technology, together with the cost of labor and materials and the size and structure of markets, is the main determinant of the type of products produced, and the way in which they are produced; and, in the case of a vertically or horizontally integrated multinational corporation, the country in which they are produced.

Knowledge may be proprietary or non-proprietary. It may be the exclusive property of a particular institution or it may be generally available. It may be disseminated through the learned journals and trade publications, by word of mouth, by imitation, or by example.

It is largely the ability of multinational corporations to generate and apply technology which accounts for their rapid growth in the past decades and their importance to economic growth.

The multinational corporations have become the most important sources of a certain type of technology. Their affiliates can draw upon the knowledge of the entire organization of which they are a part. This is one of their main advantages over indigenous firms, and one of their main attractions for host countries. In practice, however, the full transfer of knowledge may not take place—partly because it is not always suitable for use by the affiliate and partly because the parent company will not always wish to make it available.

By its very nature, the market for proprietary technology is highly imperfect. To begin with it is difficult to fix a precise price for technological information. Technological information is usually the most closely guarded aspect of modern production because imitation by others can eliminate profitable markets. Moreover, the buyer of technology needs to have information about what is available, at what cost and from what alternative sources, in order to decide what price he should pay. For all these reasons there is really neither a world market nor a world price for technology in the generally accepted sense.

In obtaining technology from multinational corporations, the enterprises of the developing countries are in a particularly weak bargaining position because of their lack of capital and necessary technical skills. More generally, the developing countries are in a vulnerable position because, unlike the developed countries, they do not participate in the two-way exchange of technology to any extent, so that the imperfections of an oligopolistic market are not even partially offset in their favor.

The developing countries are interested in obtaining wide, rapid, and easy access to adequate technology in order to accelerate their rate of economic and social advance. But this interest is not to be interpreted as being narrowly confined to continuing imports of technology from abroad. Equal importance attaches to the creation and strengthening of their own national technological capabilities so that they can continue their future development on a basis of self-reliance while participating, as equal partners with other countries, in the international advance and exchange of technologies.

Up to now, there has been no incentive for private enterprises to develop and disseminate production techniques which can be used by great masses of people without large and costly inputs of capital. Therefore, Governments of industrialized and developing countries should use public funds to develop such technology. Developing countries in particular should seek not only to acquire the capacity to select the most suitable technology for their purposes but also to develop the capacity to generate their own technology.

In addition, countries have to make a number of choices of great importance: choice of products, choice of technology, and choice of sources and ways of acquiring it. This highlights the need for an adequate mechanism for doing so—what we have called the technology of choice.

TECHNOLOGY OF CHOICE

In bargaining with a multinational corporation, a host Government may have several goals it wishes to achieve: import substitution and export promotion to relieve a balance-of-payments deficit; the creation of a substantial number of additional jobs in an area of unemployment; a general improvement in the level of living; or perhaps all of these together. How these different objectives interact, and the way in which they affect the total cost of a given project, is fundamental in deciding on a certain technology.

The first and most important technology, then, may well be the technology of informed choice. This exists in bits and pieces throughout the developed world. Its potential is gaining rapidly, but in its totality it is used by scarcely anyone—neither Government or multinational corporation.

This technology consists of the ability to gather more relevant data of more kinds than ever before, to treat a whole situation as the complex system which it truly is, to calculate the effects of the interactions of the components of the system, of the ultimate trade-offs between conflicting goals, and of the inclusion within such systems of social, economic, and cultural values.

While, in the last analysis, fallible human beings must make the choices, present-day technology as just described offers the opportunity to remove significant areas of ignorance and uncertainty, and to lessen the possibility of bad choices caused solely by lack of knowledge.

Since this technology of choice is far from mature, and is to be found in many places rather than in one place, an international institution such as the United Nations is well placed to aid developing nations in gaining access to it. The United Nations can certainly not be a leading source of such technology, but, through knowledge of the best practice in this field and of the growing and changing needs of developing nations, it can act as a conduit to channel the technology more rapidly and effectively than any one nation could do on its own. A limited example of how the United Nations might function in this field is found later in this report, under "Information Disclosure and Evaluation."

This technology of choice could be useful in tackling the variety of concerns about the technological effects of the presence of multinational corporations in developing countries. In this section, five such concerns in particular will be discussed: the choice of products; the choice of technology; the source of technology; the cost and conditions of acquiring technology; and alternative means of acquiring technology.

The Choice of Products. As a firm diversifies its markets, it tries, as far as possible, to supply those markets with what is is already producing. However, even when exporting, it may find that different national tastes and needs require modifications in the product sold to domestic consumers. When it engages in international production, there are added supply constraints, caused for example by differences in the availability and price of materials, and governmental import substitution policies. Even here, however, firms may well decide, on grounds of cost, to market and advertise an internationally standardized product rather than produce something specially adapted to the requirements of the local market.

The host country is concerned about the type of product supplied by an affiliate for two reasons. First, because of the resources which are needed to produce it, some products require labor-intensive methods and others more capital-intensive methods. Secondly, some products are more suitable to the needs of consumers, both industrial and household, than others. What is suitable may not always be easy to identify, particularly where consumption patterns are influenced by many pressures. Even if needs are correctly identified, there is no guarantee that firms will find it profitable to supply those needs. Often, the main constraint is the size of the market; sometimes it is technology. Firms are not always ready to engage in costly product innovation and development, unless they anticipate an adequate return on their expenditure.

Developing countries face a special problem in this respect. Products evolved for use in developed countries do not always answer their needs, and may even be undesirable. Their own research capacity may be limited or non-existent. In many instances, the smallness and fragmentation of the national market, at least in the initial stages, may create additional problems for developing the appropriate products.

> *The Group recommends* that before a multinational corporation is permitted to introduce a particular product into the domestic market, the host Government should carefully evaluate its suitability for meeting local needs.

The Choice of Technology. Once the decision on what to produce is taken, it becomes necessary to choose among alternative ways of doing it. Parent-firm technology introduced by multinational corporations is not always suitable to the needs of host countries. Often, developing countries insist on the most up-to-date technology, although it may not, in fact, be appropriate to their objectives. At the same time, it should be recognized that there may be instances in which a capital-intensive technology would actually yield the best results, for example, where there are important spin-off effects on local industry, or where multinational corporations produce in export industries or in industries in which no labor-intensive technology is available or could only be used with considerable increase in prices. In such cases, labor-intensive operations may have only a peripheral use, for example, in material handling and transportation.

In general, multinational corporations tend to reproduce technologies which they have already developed and which they are using in their home countries. These are apt to be capital intensive. In many developing countries, the cost of capital is kept artifically low through accelerated depreciation and investment allowances, low interest rates, and tax and duty exemptions for imported capital equipment. On the other hand, the market price of labor and social security provisions may overstate its true social cost.

The evaluation process is essential. It is here that local capacities must be strengthened. Unless a national infrastructure exists that is capable of choosing and weighing the total implications of the alternatives, the country cannot even begin to pose the problem. We feel strongly that international cooperation should be specifically directed to this end. We take note of the many worthwhile efforts that are under way in this field and would like to stress our firm opinion that they should be intensified.

> *The Group therefore recommends* that the machinery for screening and handling investment proposals by multinational corporations, recommended earlier, should also be responsible for evaluating the appropriateness of the technology, and that its capacity to do so should, where advisable, be strengthened by the provision of information and advisory services by international institutions.

The Source of Technology. A host country's undue dependence on the importation of technology may mean that it is in danger of never producing its own technology. Even developed countries, such as Australia or Canada, are faced with this problem.

No country in the world expects to be totally self-sufficient in technology; even the most advanced countries import as well as export it. But the fact is that basic research, which is the foundation of all technical advance, will for the foreseeable future be concentrated in those areas where the fundamental disciplines of knowledge are present in greatest profusion and where funds are available for conducting this increasingly expensive activity.

This appears to us to apply not only to universities and public institutes, but also, and especially, to the advanced research activities of private enterprises, national or multinational. Nevertheless, the capacity to invent and innovate is something which few countries can afford to do without. In seeking solutions to its own special problems, a country may use its own special resources, which may be abundant, but this necessarily calls for research, at the national level in the case of the larger developing nations, and at the regional level by the smaller one.

The skills used in engineering and manufacturing processes are a different matter, however. To the extent that these processes are at present best performed in a labor-intensive manner, the host country can establish both legal requirements and incentives to assure that an adequate and growing body of skilled workers is developed and remains within its borders. There are examples of successful legislation and incentives in this regard throughout the world today.

However, a word of caution is due here. As wages and volume of production rise, the necessary skills of engineering and manufacturing processes tend more and more to be built into the equipment and instrumentation itself, and less into the individual worker. A carefully planned and phased program to establish appropriate engineering skills within the country ought, therefore, to be a conscious aim of developing countries. The cost will be substantial, but it is well within the power of a host Government to regulate the scope and speed of such a program, and hence its cost.

Here again, by offering access to the best experience and best practice throughout the world, an appropriate advisory service within the United Nations can perform a valuable function.

> *The Group recommends* that host countries should require multinational corporations to make a reasonable contribution toward product and process innovation, of the kind most suited to national or regional needs, and should further encourage them to undertake such research through their affiliates. These affiliates should also be permitted to export their technology to other parts of the organization at appropriate prices.

The Cost and Conditions of Acquiring Technology. The transfer of technology takes place in a highly imperfect market in which the developing countries find themselves in a particularly weak position. The decisions which these countries make on the goods to be produced, on the type of technology with which to produce them, on the sources from which to obtain it, on the particular channels and mechanisms they employ for this purpose, and on the organizational forms through which this is done, have a major influence in determining the terms and conditions of the transfer, their current and future direct and indirect costs, and their impact on growth potential.

The sale of technology is a complicated transaction in which the charges are rarely, if ever, clearly stated. For subsidiaries of multinational corporations, most of the arrangements for the transfer of technology are implicit and do not usually form part of any written agreement. On the other hand, when joint ventures or individual enterprises of developing countries import a particular type of technology, it is usually done through an explicit contractual agreement, which may contain unfair or restrictive clauses and various limitations that work toward raising the costs of the transfer. For these reasons, the financial implications of the transfer process have always been most difficult to estimate.

Host countries, particularly developing countries, have been concerned about high expenditure for the acquisition of technology. For developing countries, one estimate (T/D106, p. 17) places the direct cost, consisting of payment for the right to use patents, licences, process know-how, and trade marks, and for technical services needed at all levels from the pre-investment phase to the full operation of the enterprise at about $1.5 billion in 1968, and further calculates the cost to be growing at a rate of about 20 percent a year. These countries are naturally anxious to acquire technology at the lowest possible cost. There is no formula by which the fair price of technology can be determined. Developing countries argue that the technology provided by multinational corporations has already been produced and that the corporations have already derived ample reward from its use in the developed countries for which it was primarily intended. Hence, the transfer to the developing countries does not entail any significant extra cost.

The multinational corporations, of course, do not see the problem in quite the same light and seek to obtain the best possible price for their technology. However, since a high proportion of the multinational corporations' transactions are on a package basis, the precise cost of the technology to the host country is frequently unclear. Furthermore, the multinational corporations point to the fact that the production of technology is costly and also highly uncertain. The return for successful innovation has to cover the cost of unsuccessful attempts as well.

Many questions have also been raised about the working of the patent system, with a view to reducing its restrictive character while still protecting the inventor. For developing countries, the high cost of technology is of special concern since the flow is virtually in one direction. When dealing with multinational corporations on a package basis, they rarely know the price paid for the technology unless it is clearly and separately specified in the form of royalties and technical fees. Proprietary rights may be used not only to inflate the cost of transfer but also to add a number of terms and conditions which can adversely affect the development interests of the recipient country. This has led certain countries or groups of countries, such as the Andean Group, to declare null and void agreements or contracts containing clauses which, among other things, permit the supplier to regulate or interfere directly or indirectly in the management of the purchasing company, establish the obligation to transfer to the supplier innovations or improvements developed by the purchasing company, establish the obligation to acquire various inputs from certain suppliers only, or limit the volume of production. Such restrictions explain an ever-growing preoccupation with the working of the patent systems and the decisions taken by United Nations bodies to work toward a revision of them.

One problem to which the revision should address itself arises out of the fact that multinational corporations take patents in every country to protect their innovations, although in some of those countries the process may not be used or the product may not be available. In that case, the patent is in fact sterilized and prevents any competing line of production. It should be considered whether a country which needs the product and can produce it competitively should not be granted the right to obtain a license from the multinational corporations.

It is against this background that the weak negotiating position of the developing countries vis-à-vis the multinational corporations needs to be strengthened by various types of action at the national and international levels.[2]

The main lines of the action center upon a revision of the international patent system, including both national patent laws of developing countries and the international patent conventions; the preparation of a truly international code of conduct in the field of the transfer of technology; and the establishment of institutions designed to help the developing countries in dealing with the complex tasks involved in the transfer process.

> *The Group draws attention* to the work of the Economic and Social Council and UNCTAD on technology (including decision 104—XIII—of the Trade and Development Board on exploring the possibility of establishing a code of conduct for the transfer of technology) and recommends that international organizations should engage in an effort to revise the patent system and to evolve an over-all regime under which

the cost of technology provided by multinational corporations to developing countries could be reduced.

The Group supports the establishment of a world patents (technology) bank to which any public institution may donate for use in developing countries patents which it owns or purchases for this purpose.

Alternative Means of Acquiring Technology. Many multinational corporations have already shown a willingness to supply technology to host countries without a direct investment stake. This is a welcome trend which may enable many developing countries to avail themselves of the services of multinational corporations, particularly in areas in which they wish to retain ownership and control. We would emphasize that such arrangements are not always of advantage to the host countries. Some of the benefits of the technology provided by the multinational corporations arise from their management and control over production. "Know-how" consists of the capacity to produce efficiently based on past experience and is much more than the technology which patents protect. The multinational corporations may often be providing both proprietary and non-proprietary technology, but, in many industries, technology becomes obsolete fairly rapidly and a constant supply of fresh technology based on continuing research is essential.

With this caveat, we believe that host countries, like any other buyer, should seek alternative ways of acquiring technology, and should also explore alternative sources of technology. These are many and varied. They include management and service contracts, turnkey operations, contractual joint ventures, co-production agreements, and other variations. In each of these contractual arrangements, ownership is left wholly or in controlling part in indigenous hands. The duration of the foreign firm's presence is limited, and explicit provision is made for the renegotiation of terms at specified intervals. We believe that multinational corporations should themselves be encouraged to form such relationships with institutions and Governments in host countries.

The possibility of acquiring technology from socialist countries on favorable conditions is widening. The experience of Japan, both as an importer and exporter of technology, is also very illuminating.

In the absence of any agreed norms for pricing new technologies, the best yardstick would be the market price for existing technologies. This means one must have knowledge about the price at which the technology for different types of products and processes is being bought and sold in the world. Unfortunately, lack of information on the subject makes such an approach very difficult. We would hope that the setting up of an information and research center on multinational corporations will help to remedy this deficiency.

Developing countries are also handicapped because they often do not know how to locate alternative courses of technology. Thus, there is a serious "information gap." Moreover, they are often unable to evaluate the alternatives or, by themselves, to use such technology effectively, which means that there is also a "capability gap." Here again, technical cooperation from appropriate international bodies would be of help. In the long run, however, only a sustained progam of indigenous education and training will suffice. In many cases, useful technical advice can also be obtained from independent consulting firms.

> *The Group recommends* that host countries should explore alternative ways of importing technology other than by foreign direct investment, and should acquire the capacity to determine which technology would best suit their needs. It also *recommends* that international agencies should help them in this task.

EMPLOYMENT AND LABOR

The International Development Strategy for the Second United Nations Development Decade in paragraph 7 of the preamble emphasizes that "the ultimate objective of development must be to bring about sustained improvement in the well-being of the individual and bestow benefits on all. If undue privileges, extremes of wealth and social injustices persist, then development fails in its initial purpose."

This premise has guided our deliberations on matters of special concern to labor interests. Improved levels of employment, wages, conditions of work, and distribution of income are indeed crucial in translating economic prosperity into the welfare of the individual. We recognize that the primary responsibility for achieving this rests with national Governments and the international economic system. However, labor unions, by the use of their bargaining strength, can contribute significantly to the improvement of wages and working conditions. It is therefore essential that host countries do nothing to reduce their strength, for example, by offering anti-union measures as part of the incentives to foreign investors. The impact of multinational corporations on the economies in which they operate must be viewed from these angles.

We have been greatly helped in our work by the report of the International Labor Organization, *Multinational Enterprise and Social Policy.*[3] In no uncertain terms, the report underlines the fact that for millions of workers, multinational corporations offer, on the one hand, opportunities for increased wages and better labor standards and, on the other, a threat to job security and to the effectiveness of collective bargaining.

EMPLOYMENT AND WAGES

While in recent years, most developed countries have been able to achieve and maintain high levels of employment and rising wages, for most developing countries large-scale unemployment remains a chronic concern.

In developing countries, the creation of productive employment is a formidable task and multinational corporations in that respect play only a marginal role. In most of those countries, the urgent need is to make agriculture more productive and, by raising the income of the farmers, to retain on the land more of the manpower which would otherwise flow to cities, adding to urban congestion and concealed unemployment. Aid from developed countries should be directed to that effect.

Differentials in the availability, cost, productivity, and skills of labor constitute critical factors which influence the investment decisions of multinational corporations, especially manufacturing enterprises.

Depending on the purpose and method of entry of the multinational corporations into the host country and type of technology used, the impact on the level of employment varies. Production based on labor-saving technology and concentrated in "enclaves," without backward or forward linkages—that is, without creating further activities, upstream or downstream, in the rest of the economy—may have little positive effect on employment; and where an investment takes the form of a take-over of an indigenous firm, and introduces more capital-intensive processes, the over-all impact may be negative.

When such production is export-oriented, as part of the world-wide location of sources of cheap inputs by horizontally or vertically integrated multinational corporations, the effect on employment may be positive, particularly if there are important spill-over and training effects. On the other hand, protectionist policies of industrial countries may nullify some of these favorable effects.

Unless full employment policies and adjustment assistance measures are successfully pursued in the developed countries, pressure for trade barriers against labor-intensive products from developing countries will persist, and employment policies in the latter countries will continue to be vulnerable. We were impressed with the fact that certain smaller developed countries have largely abandoned protectionist policies because they have managed to shift domestic production from low-skill to high-skill industries, while retaining those affected.

We do not wish to imply that developing countries should be condemned to be specialized permanently in low-skill industries, while developed countries should bestow on their labor the more advanced and more remunerative jobs. Some of the developing countries have already entered the field of sophisticated production. But this process takes time. At the earlier stages of development, it is a fact that only the simpler industries may be appropriate to the labor available. This division of labor should not be hampered by protectionist policies in the developed countries which would tend to retain less productive and less remunerative employment, rather than shifting gradually to the activities in which the workers can make their best contribution and obtain higher wages.

> *The Group recommends* that home countries do not hamper the process of transfer by multinational corporations of the production of labor-intensive and low-skill products to developing countries; and that they protect the domestic work force displaced by the transfer, through adjustment assistance measures such as retraining and re-employment in more productive and higher paying jobs, and not through restrictions on imports.

It has already been noted that one of the distinctive characteristics of many manufacturing multinational corporations is their flexibility in choosing where to establish their production units, particularly where these are intended to serve regional markets. Production may be increased or decreased, or new production shifted in response to world economic forces, new strategies of multinational corporations, or policies of individual Governments. In the long run, these shifts may operate to the benefit of the workers; much depends on what would have happened had the shift not taken place and on the ability of the domestic economy to redeploy resources efficiently. In the short run, however, they may cause serious structural difficulties, with the burden falling on the displaced workers and the Governments which have to finance their redeployment.

We recognize that individual home and host Governments are responsible for tackling the problem of unemployment. Because of their particular characteristics, however, multinational corporations have a special responsibility to Governments and unions to keep them informed of their production plans.

> *The Group recommends* that home and host countries develop plans concerning employment, and clearly inform the multinational corporations of the employment objectives.
>
> *The Group recommends* that home and host countries, through general budgetary support, the normal working of the social security system, or the establishment of social funds, provide for full compensation to the workers displaced by production decisions of multinational corporations. Recognizing that some developing countries do not possess adequate means for that purpose, the Group recommends that consideration should be given to the creation of an international social fund, including contributions by multinational corporations, which would supplement the resources available to such countries.

Some particular problems faced by host countries which arise from the entry of a multinational corporation from a high-wage economy into a low-wage economy will now be considered. They are all the more serious when the technology of the multinational corporation is the same in the host as in the home country and the other costs are no higher.

We do not wish to prescribe to the developing host countries how they should deal with the impact of the entry of firms with high productivity into an environment of general low productivity and low wages. But we believe that the over-all objective should be to avoid large inequalities in wages and earnings between the industrial workers and the poorer sections of the population, or among industrial workers themselves, thereby avoiding the undesirable creation of small "enclaves" of high-income groups.

However, a Government may choose to let the wages rise in the enterprises concerned in the hope that, through a demonstration effect or through the creation of other activities provoked by this increased purchasing power, the beneficial effects will spread throughout the population. On the other hand, a Government may wish to avoid disrupting the labor market and the ensuing inequalities, and thus it may prefer that multinational corporations should not pay wages higher than the local rates. In that case, a superior productivity could lead to very high profits. Through appropriate fiscal measures these profits may be siphoned off and the collected revenue or contributions allocated for development in general, or for the welfare of labor as a whole rather than simply for those who happen to be employed by a multinational corporation. Alternatively, where the production of multinational corporations is sold almost exclusively to the local market, price controls may be sufficient to prevent excessive profits and, through lower prices, to contribute to raising the real incomes of the population.

> *The Group recommends* that host countries take appropriate measures to obtain the maximum benefit from the entry of multinational corporations into their countries for as large a section of the lower income groups as possible.

Special problems arise concerning the employment of expatriates. Such personnel, mainly managers and technicians, expect not only to earn as much as they would at home but also something extra for serving overseas in what may be for them less congenial conditions. Here, we believe that multinational corporations should be persuaded to pay their expatriate staff, in local currencies, such salaries as would be commensurate with an appropriate standard of living in the host country, while the balance of their emoluments should be credited to their home account. Furthermore, the training of nationals should be intensified so that they will occupy as many as possible of the managerial and technicians' posts at salaries broadly in line with those paid in comparable posts within the country.

LABOR RELATIONS

Because of both the immobility of labor and the fragmentation of its organization across national boundaries, the greater transnational flexibility and the centralized decision making of many multinational corporations tilt the balance of bargaining power sharply in favor of the corporations. Decisions having repercussions on working conditions and the social rights of the employees are often made outside the country in which they are implemented, and the employees usually have no access to the decision makers.

Various forms and procedures have been introduced and followed in order to involve labor in the decision-making process of enterprises. They vary from country to country and labor unions among countries or even within a country do not have a common position on the most appropriate ones. The Commission of the European Committees addressed itself to this problem when it was considering the creation of European enterprises and the framework in which they should operate. In brief, a particular problem raised by multinational corporations for labor is the dual responsibilities of local and central headquarters.

> *The Group recommends* that the proposed commission on multinational corporations study the various forms and procedures that

could be evolved to ensure the participation of workers and their unions in the decision-making process of multinational corporations at the local and international level.[4]

The impact of national labor unions can be weakened or neutralized, and strikes may be circumvented by the threat of or by an actual shift of existing or new production to other countries, where unions are less effective or government policies prohibit or restrict free labor associations. Since labor organizations do not have means of international coordination comparable to those of multinational corporations, they find themselves in a weakened bargaining position.

The Group recommends that home and host countries permit free entry to unionists from other countries representing international or national organizations, engaged in legitimate investigations or other union missions, including entry at the invitation of the workers concerned or of their unions to assist them in their negotiations with multinational corporations.

The Commission of the European Communities, noting the anxiety created among workers as a result of the advantages possessed by the multinational enterprises, concluded that it ". . . considers the setting up of a trade union counterweight as essential for a balanced solution to this problem; however, it is not its task to organize this but certainly to encourage it."

Considering that labor problems involve employers and employees, often within the framework established by Governments, we believe that the parent company should delegate full powers to its affiliates in respect of wage bargaining.

In some instances, however, bargaining at a local level will not ensure the protection of labor's interests. First, if decisions concerning wages are taken centrally, labor organizations from the various countries affected should be free to bargain jointly at the headquarters of multinational corporations.

Secondly, as has already been described, many important decisions taken at the head offices of multinational corporations vitally affect the welfare of workers in other countries. Yet often, local unions are powerless to deal with the situation. For example, multinational corporations may use their capacity to shift existing production or to relocate new production when bargaining with local unions, or actually transfer it from one country to another. This makes it all the more imperative that multinational corporations give advance notice to the workers and their unions of any plans for investment, and of the closing down or the shifting of production facilities which might affect jobs, and that they enter into full prior consultations with them, as well as with the governmental authorities, to consider alternative employment opportunities, whether multinational or national, large or small.

Thirdly, in the case of strikes by workers in one country, multinational corporations may be able to deal with the problem by asking their other affiliates to increase their production. International solidarity of labor is one of the means by which such practices are counteracted. Labor unions have a tradition of the stronger and more experienced helping the weaker. We have noted that in a great many countries the right to strike is not subject to particular limitations as regards sympathy strikes in support of workers in another country. This does not mean that such strikes are more widespread or frequent. In some countries, however, there is a ban on such action either by legislation or judicial decision.

> *The Group recommends* that in the matter of sympathy strikes or other peaceful forms of concerted action, Governments should follow liberal rather than restrictive policies.

Such expression of labor solidarity may be contrary to the terms of wage settlements or too clostly for the workers, particularly in the developing countries. Then the only countervailing power to compensate for the special ability of multinational corporations to circumvent strikes in a particular country would be action by other Governments which may be prepared for the duration of the labor conflict to prohibit the export or import, by the parent or affiliates of a multinational corporation, of products and parts which could be a substitute for the interrupted production.

Again, although we have argued that, in the interests of national policy, wage negotiations should be conducted at a local union level, we believe that there are cases where matters should be dealt with on an international basis. Perhaps the most obvious of these is the protection of safety and health standards. In such cases we believe home and host Governments should facilitate transnational bargaining by the labor unions of all countries in which affiliates of a multinational corporation operate.

Moreover, home and host countries should enlist the cooperative efforts of the ILO and WHO to develop and monitor international occupational health and safety standards, which should be binding upon all multinational corporations, wherever they operate. Unitl ILO-WHO standards are developed, those organizations should review promptly existing national standards with a view to establishing fully adequate temporary international standards.

Finally, one of the difficulties labor faces in bargaining with multinational corporations is that it is inadequately informed about their activities or financial position. Reference has been made elsewhere to the need for an international standard accounting and reporting system of the activities of multinational corporations.

> *The Group recommends* that the international standards of disclosure, accounting, and reporting should include the data which are of special relevance for the purpose of collective bargaining.

LABOR STANDARDS

Many multinational corporations have good records in the field of labor standards. We believe that, through their affiliates, they have the opportunity to transmit those standards to countries where conditions are currently unsatisfactory. Reference was made earlier to the special case of many developing countries poorly endowed with natural resources which have to rely on labor-intensive technology and products for their development; we also recognize that countries are free to ratify or not to ratify international labor conventions. Nevertheless, we believe that the international community should bear major responsibility for eradicating racist policies, inhuman working conditions, and violations of the human rights of workers.

In this connection, we support the idea that home countries, both individually and collectively, should insist upon the adherence by the multinational corporations under their jurisdiction to certain internationally accepted basic principles and standards, as conditions of their investment abroad, and should impose certain sanctions on corporations that disregard them. Particularly important in this connection is the question of health and safety standards already mentioned. Many jobs carry certain hazards to the health and safety of workers. To guard against them, various measures have been adopted in the advanced countries. Developing countries, particularly if a line of production is being introduced there for the first time, may not even be aware of the hazards, much less of the measures taken in other countries to guard against them. Then, there are operations which result in a high element of fatigue which tells upon the health of the worker or his efficiency and output in the long run. The measures taken by developed countries to adjust working conditions in this respect should be made known to developing countries.

> *The Group recommends* that home countries should require multinational corporations to declare in all countries in which they operate, all measures of safeguards and special working conditions which they observe in their home countries to protect the health and safety of workers and to observe those measures in similar production processes in host countries with such changes and adaptations as the host Government may specify.

It is our strong belief that multinational corporations operating in developing countries, could act as spearheads in the drive for good labor practices. In some countries, for example, there is a flagrant disregard of labor's right of free association, scant respect for the labor code of the ILO, and even policies of racial discrimination. The multinational corporations could either take advantage of such degrading conditions to obtain an undue competitive edge, or they could contribute to an improvement of the situation and even a reversal of such practices.

> *The Group recommends* that, through appropriate means, home countries prevent multinational corporations from going into countries where workers' rights are not respected, unless the affiliate obtains permission to apply internationally agreed labor standards, such as free collective bargaining, equal treatment of workers, and humane labor standards.

The means at the disposal of home countries to that effect go from outright prohibition to the denial of tax credits for the taxes paid to host countries which violate human rights, to a ban on the entry into their own territory of the products produced in such countries, to the refusal of the benefit of investment insurance and guarantees.

In this connection, the Group wishes to recall that article 29 of the General Agreement on Tariffs and Trade requires the Contracting Parties to respect the principles of the Havana Charter pending its ratification. Such ratification may never take place. Thus, consideration should be given to the possibility of amending the GATT rules to include the text of article 7 of the Havana Charter,[5] which provides for respect for and the means of enforcement of fair labor standards.

The multinational corporations operating in developing countries can also act as spearheads in a drive for training in technical, managerial, and marketing skills. The Group recognizes that a number of multinational corporations have introduced training progams in developing countries, utilized local personnel in managerial positions and followed wage and labor standard policies which compare favorably with prevailing local conditions. The international community should encourage the adoption of more comprehensive efforts in this area.

CONSUMER PROTECTION

The aim of consumers is to obtain the best possible goods and services at the lowest possible prices. To a significant extent, these aspirations can be realized under competitive and efficient marketing conditions that are sensitive to local needs. However, as is pointed out in various parts of this report (see especially the next section), these conditions exist only in different degrees of imperfection. The constraints upon multinational corporations to be sensitive to consumer interests in all the countries in which they operate are likely to be inadequate.

Competition among multinational corporations and other large corporations often takes the form of sophisticated marketing techniques rather than real differences in price and quality. Thus, it is advisable for Governments to consider whether, and in what manner, advertising by multinational corporations as well as by national firms could be controlled to prevent the exploitation of consumers through false or misleading publicity. Multinational corporations in particular should be requested to explain the reasons for significant price differentials, whenever they occur, between identical products in comparable markets.

Producing the goods which respond to the real needs of individuals in the light of their social and economic conditions is a general problem. It is particularly important, however, in developing countries. Since products of multinational corporations are often geared to the consumption patterns of advanced countries, the needs of the majority of the population in poor countries may not be fulfilled. Consumers may be induced through intensive advertising to buy goods which otherwise they would not have felt they needed. Given the limited financial means of the great majority of the population of developing countries, such practices may lead to the diversion of scarce resources from basic needs to less basic ones. We believe that Governments have a right to discourage, or even prohibit in some cases, the importation or local manufacturing of certain products which they consider socially undesirable. For this purpose, host countries may consider it advisable to require prior authorization for the manufacture of products which are not otherwise imported or locally produced.

Since multinational corporations operate in different countries and sell across national borders, the issue of quality control and safety is also relevant in this context. In most developed countries, standards of quality and safety are prescribed for the sale of drugs, food, and machinery, and environmental controls have been put into effect. Developing countries do not always have adequate facilities for prescribing their own standards, which need not be identical with those required by home countries.

> *The Group recommends* that host countries should require the affiliates of multinational corporations to reveal to them any sales prohibitions and restrictions in manufacturing imposed by home or by other host countries with respect to the protection of the health and safety of consumers. They should then decide whether similar restrictions or warnings should be imposed on the sale and manufacture of those products in their countries; in such cases, such measures should apply to similar products regardless of their origin.

To complement the disclosure of restrictions aimed at protecting consumers, home countries could adopt appropriate methods for publicizing product bans, warnings, and environmental standards on a regular basis. This is particularly important because multinational corporations can manufacture in other countries products made with ingredients that have been prohibited in home countries as having been proved to be hazardous to health and life.

> *The Group recommends* that home countries should publicize prohibitions and restrictions on products, or ingredients of products, found to be hazardous to health, and should consider whether their export should also be prohibited or made conditional upon specific approval by the importing country.

National consumer organizations in developed countries play an important role in bringing to the attention of the public and the Government practices by multinational corporations and other firms which may mislead the consumer or expose him to serious hazards. We believe that national consumer organizations in both developed and developing countries should be encouraged and given the necessary facilities to work toward achieving their goals.

COMPETITION AND MARKET STRUCTURE

We recognize that the nature of multinational corporations dictates certain patterns of behavior which may restrain competition. While the allocation of markets may be rational from the viewpoint of an enterprise, when it is engaged in activities across national boundaries it is almost certain to clash with the interests of some countries. Mergers involving foreign firms may be beneficial to the enterprises involved, but the resulting changes in industrial structure may be contrary to the domestic or international public interest. In establishing affiliates in host countries, multinational corporations may find themselves competing with local firms. This increased competition may be beneficial, but it may also result in the take-over or elimination of local firms, which for various economic, political, and social reasons may be an undesirable development. The problem is complex: On the one hand, there is the variety yet lack of information about the business practices of multinational corporations and, on the other, the differences in principles and procedures followed by individual countries in dealing with these practices.

COMPETITION AND INTRACORPORATE PRACTICES

In our deliberation on this issue, we were greatly helped by the report of the *Ad Hoc* Group of Experts on Restrictive Business Practices (TD/B/C.2/119). We wish to emphasize the importance of this report, which is not limited to the case of multinational corporations but lists a broad series of conditions attached to the international use of patents, licences, know-how, and trade marks, as well as methods of pricing which may indirectly have the same effect; and it classifies such practices according to the degree of detrimental effect they may have on development. These undesirable practices relate chiefly to the prohibition of exports, tied sales, payments for technology which is of no use to the licensee, or royalties that extend beyond the life of a patient.

The *Ad Hoc* Group of Experts observed that the work of the World Intellectual Property Organization was chiefly directed toward ensuring the legal protection of patents and know-how, rather than limiting their abuse. They also noted that, although some developing countries were introducing screening procedures to control such abuse, others lacked the expertise necessary to do so. They advocated technical assistance for this purpose and called for an international agreement to ban the most undesirable restrictive practices and define those countervailing advantages which might justify an exception. They also established the principle that the same rules should apply to concealed practices resulting from the internal policies and directives of integrated multinational corporations.

While generally subscribing to the analysis and main conclusions of this report, we wish to make some additional observations.

A network of parent and affiliate companies differs in an essential respect from an independent company: The latter disregards the losses which its actions may provoke for its competitors; a multiplant company, seeking to maximize its over-all profit, has in interest in limiting the negative impact of one of its subsidiaries on another or on the parent company itself and will normally tend to suppress competition within its network.

The problem of allocation of markets arises typically in the case of corporations that produce similar and competing products in several countries. It should not be confused with various forms of specialization or with the establishment of branches to serve local markets. Thus, the problem seldom arises when a corporation chooses to produce different products in different countries, each being addressed to the world market, or produces various parts of the same product in different countries, to be assembled in one of them, in order to take advantage of the lowest possible costs. Avoiding the duplication of manpower, materials, and plant capacity is not the same as imposing restrictions. Nor, with few exceptions if any, should the allocation of markets be confused with the establishment of affiliates which make use of local resources to produce for local markets.

Market allocation within a multinational corporation, however, is more difficult to detect than where there are explicit agreements concerning, for example, the transfer of technology to independent licensees. On the other hand, the drawbacks of market allocation from the viewpoint of particular countries may be more difficult to disentangle from the advantages of large organizations, technology, and marketing that are associated with multinational corporations.

In this case most countries should be careful not to discourage the transfer of technology by rejecting a measure of control over its use which may be inseparably linked to its wider advantages. Such advantages usually accompany wholly-owned or majority-controlled affiliates rather than minority-owned ventures. In the latter case, export restrictions are tantamount to a cartel agreement.

The judgment of host Governments will be enhanced if, upon entry, multinational corporations detail clearly the conditions of their operations; that is, the extent and duration of, and the reasons for, possible export limitations or tied purchases. The bargaining power of individual host countries would be strengthened if there was some harmonization of policy between them to this effect.

The *Ad Hoc* Group of Experts on Restrictive Business Practices notes that the prohibition of cartels, even in the developed countries, is largely ineffective as far as exports and imports are concerned; indeed, cartels are sometimes officially encouraged in this field. Nevertheless, we wish to emphasize that an allocation of markets should be prohibited if it is achieved through cartel agreements between independent companies. This is recognized in the legislation of the United States as well as in the evolving European legislation. Such a principle should not be circumvented by linking together various plants and sustituting a multinational corporation for a cartel.

We believe that it is legitimate for host countries to insist that affiliates of multinational corporations should not, through restrictions on their exports, provoke a loss of potential foreign exchange earnings. One of the means at the disposal of host countries, which should be internationally accepted, is to relate profit available for remittance by an affiliate to its export performance.

We also believe that the restriction of export markets of an affiliate by a parent company should be considered *prima facie* contrary to the interest of the host countries, unless it can be shown that, in the absence of restrictions, the total benefit of the affiliate to the host country would be reduced.

Lastly, we believe that the question of market allocation can be effectively dealt with only by an international agreement containing some of the above provisions. Although some host countries have developed screening procedures to eliminate export restrictive practices, if the principles discussed above were to obtain an international consensus and preferably were incorporated in an agreement, the bargaining power of developing countries would undoubtedly be strengthened.

> *The Group recommends* that host countries should require multinational corporations to declare, upon their entry, their intentions concerning purchasing and export policies and to make clear the extent, duration, and justification of any possible restrictions.
>
> *The Group recommends* that host and home Governments, preferably through an international agreement, should prohibit the market allocation of exports by multinational corporations, unless it can be shown that such allocations are necessary to secure other benefits to the countries concerned.

Export restrictions and tied-purchase clauses commonly accompany licensing contracts for transferred technology. In many cases, the licenser would continue to export from the home country and would not sell the technology to the licensee if he were not protected from competition with him. Sometimes, export restrictions occur *de facto* when the licenser distributes exclusive license agreements in each country. Outright prohibition of such clauses might retard or make more expensive the commercialization of technology. On the other hand, in view of the critical role that export earnings play in the development process, host and especially developing countries cannot be prevented from taking advantage of their export capabilities.

International licensing agreements are normally registered in the countries where they are concluded. Notice of registered agreements should be given to other countries concerned and the United Nations information center.

We understand that several developing countries have already introduced policies for deciding whether the acceptance of restrictive clauses is compensated by a lower price for the technology acquired or by other advantages. Such policies are on the whole worth while.

The situation that faces host countries in respect of already existing contracts is different from that with new ones. It may be difficult to renegotiate the former. It is highly advisable, however, that for new contracts host countries should make provision for future review in case circumstances change substantially or after some agreed period. A renunciation of exports which might not appear to be a real sacrifice at the beginning of an operation could prove frustrating later.

In cases of regional integration, restrictive agreements may become serious obstacles to the free flow of goods and to industrial restructuring in the area. Although we believe that retroactive measures are generally ill-advised, we feel that, in the case of an agreement for close regional integration, even long-standing contracts should be renegotiated and export restrictions eliminated, whether or not renegotiation clauses were provided for in the initial contract. This should apply in cases of restrictions involving the sale of technology to licensees, as well as to market allocation among affiliates. The advantages of a broader market are compensation for the annulment of restrictive clauses.

> *The Group recommends* international recognition of the principle that restrictive clauses and market allocation by multinational corporations should be eliminated within regional groups of countries.

MARKET STRUCTURE

Governments of developed and developing countries are often concerned about the size of multinational corporations and their control over substantial sections of their markets. Because of their nature, multinational corporations can both combat competition and abuse their dominant positions more easily than national companies. On the other hand, multinational corporations are concerned lest they become the subject of conflicting anti-trust policies by different national jurisdictions.

Measures to control concentration, that is, to control the domination of any market by a small number of producers, were first introduced in the United States and are now common practice in various European countries and in Japan. In the absence of uniform national anti-trust laws or an international agreement and machinery, the spread of international production poses a serious dilemma. Either domestic concentrations are controlled only by the Government concerned and no action is taken on concentrations beyond the country's frontiers, or action by one Government has extra-territorial application and affects other countries.

Anti-trust provisions can even be abused by a country to prevent the joint association of subsidiaries of its multinational corporations in other countries which would make them more competitive, or the association of foreign companies which would increase their ability to compete in the domestic market of the country applying the legislation.

In the absence of international regulations, countries cannot altogether be denied the right to act as if they consider that a concentration would be detrimental to their own economies, even though other countries may be affected.

These various considerations lead toward a practical formula: A country taking action to stop a concentration which also affects other countries, whether merger, take-over, partial acquisition, or establishment of a joint affiliate by two or more companies, should do so only on a provisional basis, and should postpone the final decision until full consultations have been held with the other Governments concerned.

The difficulty remains, however, that the criteria and procedures of the Governments concerned may still diverge. Action to prevent undesirable transnational concentrations will be possible only if an international agreement is ultimately worked out on principles and procedures. The anti-trust policies and machinery of the European Communities, based on a supranational authority, the unratified Havana Charter, and the United Nations draft articles of a proposed agreement on restrictive business practices drawn up in 1953 by the *Ad Hoc* Committee on Restrictive Business Practices[6] and based on international agreement, are examples of the various ways in which Governments have attempted to deal with this difficult issue.

We believe that an international agreement is still the most effective approach. Certain basic principles applying to the activities of multinational corporations outside their home countries should be developed, with a view to obtaining broad acceptance.

One difficulty is that neither the United States procedure of forced divestment, without warning at the time the concentration was made, nor the European scheme of prior authorization for operations above a certain size, which by the delay it causes may disrupt the financial markets, may be generally acceptable. A possible formula, which would avoid some of the objectionable features of either the United States or European schemes, might contain the following points. First, mergers or acquisitions could take place only through outright purchases or take-over bids; secondly, any transnational association of firms above a certain size should be accompanied by a declaration of objectives of general interest, such as the rationalization of production or research and development, the increase of export capability, the improvement of working conditions, and so on. The association could proceed without delay, but if it was found to work against these declared objectives, which should conform to generally accepted criteria, forced divestment could take place.

> *The Group recommends* that preparatory work, through appropriate United Nations bodies, should be undertaken for the adoption of an international anti-trust agreement.
>
> *The Group recommends* that, until an international agreement on the issue is implemented, home countries should show restraint in applying their anti-trust policies if other Governments are affected, and that unilateral action should be taken only on a provisional basis pending full consultation with these Governments before the decision is final.

TRANSFER PRICING

One of the practices of multinational corporations which gives rise to particular concern among the countries in which they operate is the fixing of prices of goods and services traded between the corporation and its affiliates located in different countries. Intracorporate transfer pricing by a multiregional company within a country may matter little to a national Government, since all the benefits of the transaction are retained domestically. When engaged in by multinational corporations, however, it affects the distribution of the benefits of their activities between countries, and may stifle local competition.

Research has shown that, although intracorporate trade in goods within multinational corporations is concentrated within certain industries, such as motor vehicles and chemicals, more than one quarter of the value of all international trade in goods appears to be of an intragroup character. In addition, although much less well-documented, there is the provision of intracorporate services, for example, research and development, rentals of equipment, administration, and loans. The scope for price manipulation is therefore quite extensive.

We recognize all the difficulties inherent in the setting of the proper price in such intracompany transactions. The principle of "arm's length" prices can only be applied if there are outside transactions and a market. The principle of "cost plus," that is, the cost of production plus a margin for each supplier within the network of the corporation, allows an appraisal of the profitability of each branch, but is not always easy to apply. There is uncertainty about the best allocation of overhead costs, particularly of extensive and expensive research, and even more so when it is of a risky nature and is only successful in a few cases.

Apart from these intrinsic difficulties, transfer prices may be distorted either in pursuance of goals which are internal to the working of the multinational corporation concerned or as a response to "external" factors. Among "internal" motives the following may be listed: The varying degree of ownership in its subsidiaries may induce the parent company to make profits appear where its ownership is relatively large; there may be an incentive to reduce the apparent profits in a particular affiliate for purposes of wage bargaining; transfer pricing may be an indirect way of allocating markets, for instance, if the prices charged to an affiliate are such as to make its exports non-competitive.

The manipulation of prices may also respond to such "external" factors as the following: the diversity among countries in the rates of taxation or in the rules of assessment; the difference of taxation even in the same countries on the various forms of remuneration of capital, dividends, interests, and royalties, and the ensuing tendency to transform taxable income into non-taxable costs; the varying rules of exchange control by some host countries regarding the remittance of those various types of remuneration; the risk of changes in exchange rates; and finally, the risk of nationalization or expropriation.

The conditions under which multinational corporations will wish to take advantage of these situations will vary between countries and in the same country over time. For instance, the higher the rate of corporate taxation in a country, or the greater the risk that its currency will depreciate, the more inducement there is to lower the profits appearing in that country either by raising the prices charged to the affiliate or lowering those of its sales to other affiliates. Such manipulations amount to a transfer of income from country to country.

Individual countries may thus stand to gain or lose by the activities of price manipulation. In some cases, they may lose on one side and gain on the other; the higher the prices charged to an affiliate, the lower its taxable profits, but at the same time the higher the tariff duties it may be subject to.

The problem is an exceedingly difficult one for Governments to tackle; first, because there is a serious lack of data about its extent or effects, and secondly, because there are many ways in which a company can use this mechanism to switch income.

In the long run, a fair amount of research and fact-finding is necessary for the evolution of sound practices and policies. We note with satisfaction that transfer pricing has been engaging the attention of the United Nations Group of Experts on Tax Treaties, the International Fiscal Association, the Organization for Economic Cooperation and Development, and the Commission of the European Communities. We trust that, as a result of their efforts, it will be possible for the international community to agree upon a code which home and host countries alike will find practicable and advantageous to enforce.

Meanwhile, some action is clearly necessary. Some countries have begun to regulate transfer prices, chiefly in order to prevent tax evasion. Such legislation is particularly advanced in the United States Internal Revenue Code 482; in other countries, tax authorities are also developing their inquiries and the formulation of rules. The general principle is to refer to "arm's length" prices, that is, prices as they are or would be charged by an independent seller to an independent buyer. In case the nature of the product—the components of a machine, for instance, or new drugs—is such that there is no comparable independent transaction, the usual principle applied by tax authorities is a reference to the general practice of the company concerned.

> *The Group recommends* that home and host countries should enforce "arm's length" pricing wherever appropriate, and should elaborate rules on pricing practices for tax purposes.

We recognize the special difficulty which besets cooperation between countries in this field: Some countries may have legal and other objections to making the data derived from tax returns available to others, in particular when they derive special benefits from some transfer pricing practices. The proposals from the harmonization of taxation, discussed in the next section, aim in particular at eliminating some of the elements which induce distorted transfer prices.

> *The Group recommends* that home and host countries should introduce

provisions into bilateral tax treaties for the exchange of available information, and should consider the feasibility of an international agreement on the rules concerning transfer pricing for purposes of taxation.

Host countries should also review their exchange controls in order to reduce differences of treatment as regards remittances abroad for remunerations which are broadly equivalent, such as dividends and interest.

The basic solution for protecting the interests of the countries concerned as well as those of the various parties involved in the operation of a multinational corporation—affiliates, partners, customers, or workers—rests on the principle of disclosure, which we emphasize throughout this report and in particular in the last section, "Information Disclosure and Evaluation." The transfer prices at which a multinational corporation deals with or among its affiliates, as well as the prices in transactions with outside suppliers or customers, should either be publicized or made known to the interested parties upon request. This obligation would have a self-policing and self-restraining effect. Moreover, it would make possible the application of the principle of non-discrimination as expressed, for instance, in the United States by the Robinson-Patman Act:[7] A seller is prohibited from charging different prices to different buyers unless the difference can be justified by differences in the quantity or regularity of supply. Such a rule does not preclude different rates justified by markets, distances, or costs, or the sale of technology on concessionary terms for development purposes. The general rule, however, would go a long way toward eliminating undesirable practices, and in particular forestalling the unequal treatment by multinational corporations of their various affiliates as well as other interested parties.

TAXATION

Multinational corporations by their nature are subject to the tax laws of different countries. As these laws have been framed primarily to serve domestic needs and objectives, and also are subject to the play of political forces, they differ significantly from one country to another. The absence of coordination among Governments in tax policy matters has created a most unsatisfactory situation for home and host countries and multinational corporations alike, and, to a considerable extent, distorts the allocation of resources on a world-wide basis.

There is no standard rule to define the home country of a company; it may be based on the location of its head management, the country in which it is incorporated, or other criteria. Rates of corporate taxes vary widely, particularly among developing countries, as do the definitions of income and of deductible allowances. There are also wide differences in the treatment of income at the corporate and shareholder level: Some countries tax both, others apply a reduced rate at the corporate level on the profits distributed, or on the contrary, a reduced rate on the income received by the shareholders in consideration of the tax already paid at the corporate level.

The relief given on this account is neither uniform nor universal and may be limited to residents. Remittances to non-residents are commonly subject to a flat rate of withholding tax, which each country prescribes at its own discretion, except as agreed on in tax treaties.

For multinational corporations, however, the most serious divergencies stem from differences in the taxation of income from local sources and income from foreign sources. One extreme approach is based purely on the territorial principle: Income is taxed where it originates. Thus when it originates in the host country, the home country does not have any claim on it. Another extreme approach is the taxation of world-wide profits by home countries. Usually, however, this taxation takes place only at the time of repatriation; this deferment is an inducement to reinvest in the host countries if their rates are more favorable. On the other hand, the avoidance of dual taxation is not a matter of principle but is in many instances achieved either unilaterally through the relief granted by home countries or through the application of bilateral tax treaties; in the absence of such provisions, foreign investment is strongly discouraged.

Home countries that forgo the taxation of corporate profits earned abroad until they are repatriated stand to lose revenue on the profits channelled to tax havens where tax rates are low or nominal. Holding companies formed for the purpose of tax avoidance are proliferating. Host countries, especially developing countries, are encouraged to compete against each other in granting tax concessions to attract foreign capital, only to find that these concessions are sometimes nullified by home-government taxation of the higher income earned by multinational corporations.

Tax treaties are a common feature among developed countries, because there is normally a two-way flow of income between them, and each country is willing to give relief from double taxation to the residents of the other in exchange for the same advantage in return. Between developed and developing countries there are at present few such treaties, since income generally moves in only one direction. Thus, multinational corporations, which see their activities complicated by differences in the assessment of taxable income and in rates of tax, may be exposed to double taxation. They have, on the other hand, frequently found ways to minimize their burden at the expense of the revenues of either home or host countries (and occasionally both) through transfer pricing, including the allocation of overhead and other expenses between their affiliates, and by taking advantage of tax havens.

Clearly, the tax laws of nation-States, at least insofar as they affect companies originating or operating outside their territories, are in need of major changes. Ideally, we believe there should be an international standardization of tax arrangements which would be neutral in their impact on foreign investment, or have only such directional bias as may be agreed upon. To this end, we believe that a concerted international effort is urgently needed to explore alternative approaches and reach a consensus on broad general principles.

We note with satisfaction that the United Nations has sponsored meetings of a Group of Experts on Tax Treaties, and that substantial progress has been made in their five meetings at Geneva. Their aim is to develop guidelines to facilitate the establishment of a network of bilateral treaties between Governments of developing and developed countries for the avoidance of double taxation and the elimination of tax evasion, as well as assisting developing countries to increase their tax revenues. Guidelines have already been agreed upon by this Group of Experts (which consists largely of tax officials from developed and developing countries) as regards the tax treatment of interest, dividends, profits, royalties and fees, and other income and expenses. The work of the experts is expected to be helpful to all countries, and especially developing countries, in the negotiation of bilaterial tax treaties.

Concern was, however, expressed in our Group that such a network of bilateral treaties would entail a large number of treaties which might take a very long time to negotiate and implement. Moreover, they might differ, for instance, as to the amount of withholding tax on the remittance of earnings. Some of the present distortions in the activities of the multinational corporations, therefore, would not be removed. If, through the work of the Group of Experts on Tax Treaties, the provisions of these treaties could be standardized, with only a small number of clauses to be negotiated in particular cases, they would in fact amount to an international agreement on taxation, which we consider to be the final objective.

The Group recommends that the work of the Group of Experts on Tax Treaties should be speeded up, and that the bilateral treaties should be as uniform as possible so as to prepare the way for an international tax agreement.

The Group further recommends that developed countries should, without delay, embark on a policy of entering into such treaties with developing countries, bearing in mind the importance of increasing the flow of capital to and strengthening the revenues of the latter.

As this may not be achieved for some time, we consider it our duty to state the fundamental, and largely interrelated, objectives which should guide future action in this field: the avoidance of dual taxation; the avoidance of tax evasion, particularly through tax havens; the promotion of development, in the sense not only of growth but of reduction of inequalities.

In the light of such objectives, we have examined not only the existing practices—the territorial approach, and the taxation of repatriated income—but also alternative approaches which have been proposed or which might be applied by some countries.

An ambitious approach, which might appear ideal in theory, is that the world-wide profits of multinational corporations should eventually be allocated among the countries in which they operate according to an agreed *pro rata* formula. We noted that even in a federal union, such as the United States, no agreement could be reached among the states. The task of bringing about an agreement on these lines at an international level would be even more formidable, since the amounts of corporate taxes involved in central budgets are much more sizeable than in the local budgets of some states. Moreover, what would be allocated between countries would be the income, not the tax; thus competitive tax concessions between host countries could proliferate to a point which would be contrary to an equitable sharing of the tax burden between the corporations and the average citizens in a developing country. For reasons of practicability and equity, we cannot recommend such a system.

We have considered at length another scheme which is advocated by many economists and is contemplated in legislative proposals in the United States and in the European Communities. It calls for taxation by home countries of the global profits of their multinational corporations as if they were earned within their borders, while providing full relief for taxes paid to other countries. In other words, the principle of taxation of world profits would apply on an accrual basis and would not be deferred until such time as earnings abroad were remitted to the home countries. In this case dual taxation would be eliminated as a matter of principle; and thus it would not have to be dealt with on a case-by-case basis, through unilateral action or bilateral tax treaties. This proposal would tend to make taxation less important in decisions by multinational corporations to invest in one country rather than another. It would further tend to induce countries with low tax rates on corporate income to increase them to the level which is broadly common to the developed countries, and in this way increase the government revenues available for development and reduce inequalities. It would also tend to eliminate competitive tax concessions between countries for the purpose of attracting foreign investment. It might even go too far in this direction. While we have doubts about the advisability of special concessions to foreign corporations, we recognize that tax incentives may be necessary to encourage investment by national or foreign companies for growth or anti-cyclical purposes, to overcome the initial obstacles to investment, or to put over-all planning or regional policies into effect. Unless some additional provisions are introduced, the scheme would cancel out most of those incentives in the case of foreign corporations, and would also offset the inducements to the reinvestment of profits in the host developing countries.

We do not believe it advisable to prescribe a unique solution for such complex issues, but rather to insist on the objectives which have to be met and the supplementary provisions that would be required in each scheme for these objectives to be attained.

The strongest means to eliminate tax havens would be the taxation of world-wide profits on an accrual basis. The present widespread system of tax deferment should be amended so that earnings become subject to tax by home countries as soon as they are remitted abroad from the host countries; thus even if they are remitted to tax havens they will be taxed just as though they are repatriated into their home countries, unless there is proof that they are being reinvested, without delay, in another host country. Provision should be made to guard against the risk of corporations choosing tax havens as their headquarters in order to avoid home country tax on accrued or repatriated earnings. A powerful weapon in this regard would be to deny the right of establishment in other countries, particularly the main industrialized ones, to corporations operating from such a base; the consequent loss of markets would more than outweigh the attempted saving on taxes.

We have also considered the effects of standard tax practices on the form which the flow of capital assumes. Interest on capital brought from abroad is subject to withholding tax when remitted, while equity investment is subject to both withholding and profits tax. This entails a distorted inducement to resort to lending rather than equity. Host countries must insist on a proper debt-equity ratio for revenue purposes. This obligation, however, may be difficult to define and even more so to enforce, and may run contrary to what is required in terms of the most appropriate forms of inflow of capital. The distortion is not corrected when the territorial principle applies. The taxation of world-wide earnings by home countries, with a credit for taxes paid to the host countries, may tend to eliminate such distortion, since the less that is paid to the host countries the more is usually taxed by the home countries. In the standard pactice of today, however, this is only partly corrected, as the taxation of earnings from abroad by home countries takes place only when they are repatriated, if ever, and the elimination of dual taxation is not provided for on a general or complete basis. The taxation of world-wide earnings on an accrual basis, with full deduction of taxes paid to host countries, would in most instances provide a full solution.

As regards the impact on development, the present system of deferred taxation of world-wide profits until the time of remittance suffers from defects which should be corrected. It encourages competitive tax concessions in a way which increases the bargaining power of the multinational corporations as against the least powerful host countries—which may aggravate social inequalities. Host countries should agree to limit the extent of such tax concessions. The system, moreover, deprives some of the host countries of the benefits of the tax concessions which they allow: Home countries should agree to grant credit to the multinational corporations for the taxes legitimately spared. The system of taxation on an accrual basis with full tax credits would encourage an increase of corporate taxes in host countries. It should, however, avoid taxing away the concessions given by host countries for legitimate purposes of general or regional development, by granting credit for spared tax, or by granting of such tax concessions by the home country itself in favor of the developing host country. Whatever the scheme applied, developed home countries should refrain from granting excessive tax concessions in favor of their own development or their regional policies, such as can hardly be matched by poorer countries and may contribute further to steering foreign investment to developed rather than developing countries.

> *The Group recommends* that the various schemes which are or may be applied for taxation of multinational corporations should be supplemented by the provisions which it has suggested in each case to meet the various objectives which it has analyzed.

Given prompt and consistent action, reform of taxation in respect of multinational corporations could be a powerful tool in a concerted strategy for development.

INFORMATION DISCLOSURE AND EVALUATION

The pivotal importance of information disclosure and evaluation has been emphasized throughout this report. They are central to many issues discussed in the previous chapters and to the proposals for dealing with those issues, whether in connection with the promotion of labor welfare, the monitoring of volatile short-term capital movements, the choice of appropriate technology, the protection of consumer interests, the regulation of monopolistic practices, or the prevention of artificial transfer pricing and tax evasion. Progress in this area is thus essential for a wide range of policies and programs concerning multinational corporations, as well as for general development. The present chapter concentrates on a few concrete steps in this direction.

STANDARD ACCOUNTING AND REPORTING

Corporate accounting today is designed mainly for reporting to shareholders and for internal profit controls. The form varies from country to country, and reports of their various corporations are rarely comparable.

However, Governments need corporate reports which are comparable, regardless of national origin, and which will disclose, in usable form, the economic and social information they require for effective decision making. We believe that an international, comparable system of standardized accounting and reporting should be formulated.

Among the types of information which would be particularly useful to Governments and other interested bodies are: valuation and revaluation of assets and currencies in which they are denominated, inventories, research and development expenditure, start-up expenses, transfer prices, pension and other reserves, sources and timing of income, wages and other workers' benefits. The form in which the information is supplied would be designed primarily to suit the needs and uses of Governments and thus may not correspond to the usual custom and practice of corporations.

For the foreseeable future, we envisage that corporations will continue to report to their countries according to the various standards required of them. The international standard, together with a reconciliation, might then constitute additional data to be included in the annual reports of multinational corporations.

> *The Group recommends* that an expert group on international accounting standards should be convened, under the auspices of the commission on multinational corporations.

The composition of the expert group should include representatives of finance and planning ministries of developed and developing countries, chief executives of multinational corporations, labor officials, lawyers, economists, and professional accountants. The work of this group would need to be supported by the United Nations Secretariat, and more specifically by its information and research center on multinational corporations, as soon as this becomes operational. Its mandate should be to determine the kinds and the forms of information for which host and home Governments as well as other interested bodies have the most urgent need. On the basis of experience, the system can be refined and extended.

To implement the system, once devised, an attempt should be made to secure the voluntary agreement of a significant number of multinational corporations to add a column, based on international standards, to their present statements. They would set an example and provide an opportunity for experimenting with the international standards. Governments have an interest in obtaining such a form of reporting according to international standards from the corporations operating in their territory as it would facilitate comparisons. Moreover, in the case of corporations that operate transnationally, they are interested in obtaining an over-all picture of the operations with a proper breakdown between countries and with explanations of the method of consolidation.

Given the complexity of the subject, the expert group would require to hold a series of sessions, probably extending over a two-year period, in order to complete its task. Periodic reports should be submitted to the Economic and Social Council through the commission on multinational corporations proposed earlier. As experience is gained, further refinements and revisions of the system should be made by expert groups constituted on similar lines.

DISCLOSURE OF AGREEMENTS

Agreements concluded between Governments and multinational corporations contain information useful for many purposes. The importance of formulating appropriate terms and conditions in such agreements has been emphasized elsewhere.

Both national Governments and multinational corporations should overcome their concern about confidentiality. We believe that the public disclosure of the principal terms of agreements between Governments and corporations should be the rule rather than the exception. Such disclosures would assist enormously in increasing the confidence of both parties, in diminishing the present tendency toward too rapid obsolescence of agreements, and in reducing the variations which now exist between similar arrangements in different countries.

> *The Group recommends* that Governments should, as a rule, disclose the principal terms of agreements between them and multinational corporations; the information and research center on multinational

corporations should serve as the depository for information on such agreements. The center should also prepare digests and summaries of such information.

OTHER, NON-FINANCIAL REPORTING

In addition to standard accounting information, and terms and conditions of agreements, Governments and social groups have a natural interest in corporate performance in respect of such items as the number of nationals employed at various levels, the percentage of materials from local sources, the structure of multinational corporations and the nature of their affiliations with other corporations. The public disclosure and collection of such information is subject to the same considerations as the disclosure of agreements.

The Group recommends that the machinery for formulating and implementing Government policies toward multinational corporations, recommended earlier, should devise procedures for the collection of information about the performance of multinational corporations in specific areas.

SYSTEM FOR EVALUATION BY HOST GOVERNMENTS

Even if all the above recommendations are implemented, the kind and form of information available to developing countries is likely to be insufficient for an in-depth evaluation of the costs and benefits of alternative decisions. Such an evaluation would have to take into account social costs and benefits, which would include external as well as international economics, and indirect as well as non-economic effects. For example, an evaluation of investment proposals would have to be based on world prices, especially where the domestic price structure is distorted by high tariffs or monopolies; it would also have to be concerned with environmental effects.

Thus, a selective approach is also needed in many cases, so that the relevant information can be obtained in sufficient detail, when it is needed, without being overburdened with an unmanageable mass of extraneous information. This approach necessitates the setting up of a machinery in which particular projects may be evaluated (for example, costs and benefits of foreign investment) or specific problems investigated (for example, monopoly, transfer pricing, tax evasion).

Moreover, increased access to information is of little use to Governments unless they possess adequate systems and capacities to interpret and evaluate it. Such an evaluation is not limited to specific projects at the micro level, but must be related to the general framework at the macro level as well. Host countries, in particular, must place emphasis on developing the necessary expertise as well as machinery for evaluation. The United Nations should be prepared to assist host, especially developing, countries, upon request, in acquiring and improving this capacity.

NOTES

1. If the investment is made in the form of imported machinery and equipment and the multinational corporation inflates their prices, the financial inflow may be overstated.

2. The main lines of such action were set out in paragraphs (37) and (64) of the International Development Strategy for the Second United Nations Development Decade, and UNCTAD resolutions 39 (III) on the transfer of technology, and resolution 73 (III) on restrictive business practices.

3. Studies and Reports, New Series No. 79 (International Labor Office, Geneva, 1973).

4. Such participation, as well as other joint negotiations referred to below, can only be effective if the means of communication at the disposal of labor are comparable to those of multinational corporations. The latter should allow the representatives of the workers reasonable leaves of absence and travel expenses appropriate to that purpose.

5. In this connection may be noted a statement by the Subcommittee on Multinational Corporations of the United States Senate Committee on Foreign Relations, to the effect that if such indiscriminate support were to be sanctioned as normal, no country could welcome the presence of multinational corporations, and "over every dispute, or potential dispute, between a company and a host Government in connection with a corporate investment, there would hang the specter of intervention." (*International Telephone and Telegraph Corporation and Chile, 1970-1971*, report to the Committee on Foreign Relations of the United States Senate by the Sub-committee on Multinational Corporations, United States Government Printing Office, Washington, D. C., 21 June 1973, p. 18.)

6. *Official Records of the Economic and Social Council, Sixteenth Session Supplement No. 11,* annex II.

7. Public Law No. 692 in *United States Statutes at Large*, Vol. 49, Part I, p. 1526.

35

Multinationals and Developing Countries:

MYTHS AND REALITIES

Peter F. Drucker

FOUR assumptions are commonly made in the discussion of multinationals and the developing countries—by friends and enemies alike of the multinational company. These assumptions largely inform the policies both of the developing countries and of the multinational companies. Yet, all four assumptions are false, which explains in large measure both the acrimony of the debate and the sterility of so many development policies.

These four false but generally accepted assumptions are: (1) the developing countries are important to the multinational companies and a major source of sales, revenues, profits and growth for them, if not the mainstay of "corporate capitalism"; (2) foreign capital, whether supplied by governments or by businesses, can supply the resources, and especially the capital resources required for economic development; (3) the ability of the multinational company to integrate and allocate productive resources on a global basis and across national boundaries, and thus to substitute transnational for national economic considerations, subordinates the best national interests of the developing country to "global exploitation"; (4) the traditional nineteenth-century form of corporate organization, that is, the "parent company" with wholly owned "branches" abroad, is the form of organization for the twentieth-century multinational company.[1]

II

What are the realities?

In the first instance, extractive industries have to go wherever the petroleum, copper ore or bauxite is found, whether in a developing or in a developed country. But for the typical twentieth-century multinational, that is a manufacturing, distributing or financial company, developing countries are important neither as markets nor as producers of profits. Indeed it can be said

[1] The author acknowledges his indebtedness for advice and helpful criticism to Dr. Tore Browaldh, Chairman of Svenska Handelsbanken and recently a member of the U.S. Group of Eminent Persons studying multinationals, and to Dr. Ernst Keller, President of Adela Investment Co., S.A., Lima, Peru.

bluntly that the major manufacturing, distributive and financial companies of the developed world would barely notice it, were the sales in and the profits from the developing countries suddenly to disappear.

Confidential inside data in my possession on about 45 manufacturers, distributors and financial institutions among the world's leading multinationals, both North American and European,[2] show that the developed two-thirds of Brazil—from Bello Horizonte southward—is an important market for some of these companies, though even Brazil ranks among the first 12 sales territories, or among major revenue producers, for only two of them. But central and southern Brazil, while still "poor," are clearly no longer "underdeveloped." And otherwise not even India or Mexico—the two "developing" countries with the largest markets—ranks for any of the multinational companies in my sample ahead even of a single major sales district in the home country, be it the Hamburg-North Germany district, the English Midlands or Kansas City.

On the worldwide monthly or quarterly sales and profit chart, which most large companies use as their most common top-management tool, practically no developing country even appears in my sample of 45 major multinationals except as part of a "region," e.g., "Latin America," or under "Others."

The profitability of the businesses of these companies in the developing countries is uniformly lower by about two percentage points than that of the businesses in the developed countries, except for the pharmaceutical industry where the rate of return, whether on sales or on invested capital, is roughly the same for both. As a rule, it takes longer—by between 18 months to three years—to make a new operation break even in a developing country. And the growth rate—again excepting the pharmaceutical industry—is distinctly slower. Indeed, in these representative 45 businesses, 75 to 85 percent of all growth, whether in sales or in profits, in the last 25 years, occurred in the developed countries. In constant dollars the business of these 45 companies in the developed world doubled—or more than doubled—in the last 10 to 15 years. But their business in the developing countries grew by no more than one-third during that period if the figures are adjusted for inflation.

[2] I have no data on Japanese-based multinationals; but in developing countries the Japanese are still mainly engaged in extractive and raw-material-producing business.

Published data, while still scarce and inadequate, show the same facts. Only for the extractive industries have the developing countries—and then only a very few of them—been of any significance whether as a source of profits, as loci of growth, or as areas of investment.

The reason is, of course, that—contrary to the old, and again fashionable, theory of "capitalist imperialism"—sales, growth and profits are where the market and the purchasing power are.

To the developing country, however, the multinational is both highly important and highly visible.

A plant employing 750 people and selling eight million dollars worth of goods is in most developing countries a major employer—both of rank and file and of management—and a big business. For the multinational parent company, employing altogether 97,000 people and selling close to two billion dollars worth of goods a year, that plant is, however, at best marginal. Top management in Rotterdam, Munich, London or Chicago can spend practically no time on it.

Neglect and indifference rather than "exploitation" is the justified grievance of the developing countries in respect to the multinationals. Indeed, top management people in major multinationals who are personally interested in the developing countries find themselves constantly being criticized for neglecting the important areas and for devoting too much of their time and attention to "outside interests." Given the realities of the business, its markets, growth opportunities and profit opportunities, this is a valid criticism.

The discrepancy between the relative insignificance of the affiliate in a developing country and its importance and visibility for the host country poses, however, a major problem for the multinationals as well. Within the developing country the man in charge of a business with 750 employees and eight million dollars in sales has to be an important man. While his business is minute compared to the company's business in Germany, Great Britain or the United States, it is every whit as difficult—indeed it is likely to be a good deal more difficult, risky and demanding. And he has to treat as an equal with the government leaders, the bankers and the business leaders of his country—people whom the district sales manager in Hamburg, Rotterdam or Kansas City never even sees. Yet his sales and profits are less than those of the Hamburg, Rotterdam or Kansas City sales district. And his growth potential is, in most cases, even lower.

This clash between two realities—the personal qualifications and competence, the position, prestige and power needed by the affiliate's top management people to do their job in the developing country, and the reality of a "sales district" in absolute, quantitative terms—the traditional corporate structure of the multinationals cannot resolve.

III

The second major assumption underlying the discussion of multinationals and developing countries is the belief that resources from abroad, and especially capital from abroad, can "develop" a country.

But in the first place no country is "underdeveloped" because it lacks resources. "Underdevelopment" is inability to obtain full performance from resources; indeed we should really be talking of countries of higher and lower productivity rather than of "developed" or "underdeveloped" countries. In particular, very few countries—Tibet and New Guinea may be exceptions—lack *capital*. Developing countries have, almost by definition, more capital than they productively employ. What "developing" countries lack is the full ability to mobilize their resources, whether human resources, capital or the physical resources. What they need are "triggers," stimuli from abroad and from the more highly developed countries, that will energize the resources of the country and will have a "multiplier impact."

The two success stories of development in the last hundred years—Japan and Canada—show this clearly. In the beginning, Japan imported practically no capital except small sums for early infrastructure investments, such as the first few miles of railroad. She organized, however, quite early, what is probably to this day the most efficient system for gathering and putting to use every drop of capital in the country. And she imported—lavishly and without restraints—technology with a very high multiplier impact and has continued to do so to this day.

Canada, in the mid-1930s, was far less "developed" a country than most American republics are today. Then the liberal governments of the 1930s decided to build an effective system for collecting domestic capital and to put it into infrastructure investments with a very high "multiplier" effect—roads, health care, ports, education and effective national and provincial administrations. Foreign capital was deliberately channeled into manufacturing and mining. Domestic capital and entrepreneurs were actually discouraged in the extractive and manufacturing sectors. But they were strongly encouraged in all tertiary activities such as distribution, banking, insurance and in local supply and finishing work in manufacturing. As a result a comparatively small supply of foreign capital—between a tenth and a twentieth of Canada's total capital formation—led to very rapid development within less than two decades.

There is a second fallacy in the conventional assumption, namely that there is unlimited absorptive capacity for money and especially for money from abroad. But in most developing countries there are actually very few big investment opportunities. There may be big hydroelectric potential; but unless there are customers with purchasing power, or industrial users nearby, there is no economic basis for a power plant. Furthermore, there is no money without strings. To service foreign capital, even at a minimal interest rate, requires foreign exchange. At that, loans or equity investments as a rule constitute a smaller (and, above all, a clearly delimited) burden than grants and other political subsidies from abroad. The latter always create heavy obligations, both in terms of foreign and domestic policy, no matter where they come from.

A developing country will therefore get the most out of resources available abroad, especially capital, if it channels capital where it has the greatest "multiplier impact." Moreover, it should channel it where one dollar of imported capital will generate the largest number of domestic dollars in investment, both in the original investment itself and in impact-investment (e.g., the gas stations, motels and auto repair shops which an automobile plant calls into being), and where one job created by the original investment generates the most jobs directly and indirectly (again an automobile industry is a good example). Above all, the investment should be channeled where it will produce the largest number of local managers and entrepreneurs and generate the most managerial and entrepreneurial competence. For making resources fully effective depends on the supply and competence of the managerial and entrepreneurial resource.

According to all figures, government money has a much lower multiplier impact than private money. This is, of course, most apparent in the Communist-bloc countries; low, very low, productivity of capital is the major weakness of the Communist economies, whether that of Russia or of her European satellites. But it is true also of public (e.g., World Bank) money elsewhere: it generates little, if any, additional investment either from within or from without the recipient country. And "prestige" investments, such as a steel mill, tend to have a fairly low multiplier impact—both in jobs and in managerial vigor—as against, for instance, a department store which brings into existence any number of small local manufacturers and suppliers and creates a major managerial and entrepreneurial cluster around it.

For the multinational in manufacturing, distribution, or finance locating in a developing country, rapid economic development of the host country offers the best chance for growth and profitability. The multinational thus has a clear self-interest in the "multiplier" impact of its investment, products and technology. It would be well advised to look on the capital it provides as "pump priming" rather than as "fuel." The more dollars (or pesos or cruzeiros) of local capital each of its own dollars of investment generates, the greater will be the development impact of its investment, and its chance for success. For the developing country the same holds true: to maximize the development impact of each imported dollar.

The Canadian strategy was carried on too long; by the early 1950s, Canada had attained full development and should have shifted to a policy of moving its own domestic capital into "superstructure" investments. But though the Canadian strategy is certainly not applicable to many developing countries today—and though, like any strategy, it became obsolete by its very success—nevertheless it was highly successful, very cheap and resulted in rapid economic growth while at the same time ensuring a high degree of social development and social justice.

What every developing country needs is a strategy which looks upon the available foreign resources, especially of capital, as the "trigger" to set off maximum deployment of a country's own resources and to have the maximum "multiplier effect." Such a strategy sees in the multinational a means to energize domestic potential—and especially to create domestic entrepreneurial and managerial competence—rather than a substitute for domestic resources, domestic efforts and, even, domestic capital. To make the multinationals effective agents of development in the developing countries therefore requires, above all, a policy of encouraging the domestic private sector, the domestic entrepreneur and the domestic manager. If they are being discouraged the resources brought in from abroad will, inevitably, be wasted.

For by themselves multinationals cannot produce development; they can only turn the crank but not push the car. It is as futile and self-defeating to use capital from abroad as a means to frighten and cow the local business community—as the bright young men of the early days of the Alliance for Progress apparently wanted to do—as it is to mobilize the local business community against the "wicked imperialist multinational."

IV

The multinational, it is said, tends to allocate production according to global economics. This is perfectly correct, though so far very few companies actually have a global strategy. But far from being a threat to the developing country, this is potentially the developing country's one trump card in the world economy. Far from depriving the governments of the developing countries of decision-making power, the global strategy of the multinationals may be the only way these governments can obtain some effective control and bargaining leverage.

Short of attack by a foreign country the most serious threat to the economic sovereignty of developing countries, and especially of small ones, i.e., of most of them, is the shortage of foreign exchange. It is an absolute bar to freedom of decision. Realizing this, many developing countries, especially in the 1950s and early 1960s, chose a deliberate policy of "import substitution."

By now we have all learned that in the not-so-very-long run this creates equal or worse import-dependence and foreign-exchange problems. Now a variant of "import substitution" has become fashionable: a "domestic-content" policy which requires the foreign company to produce an increasing part of the final product in the country itself. This, predictably, will eventually have the same consequences as the now discredited "import substitution," namely, greater dependence on raw materials, equipment and supplies from abroad. And in all but the very few countries with already substantial markets (Brazil is perhaps the only one—but then Brazil is not, after all, "developing" any longer in respect to the central and southern two-thirds of the country) such a policy must, inevitably, make for a permanently high-cost industry unable to compete and to grow. The policy creates jobs in the very short run, to be sure; but it does so at the expense of the poor and of the country's potential to generate jobs in the future and to grow.

What developing countries need are *both*—foreign-exchange earnings and productive facilities large enough to provide economies of scale and with them substantial employment. This they can obtain only if they can integrate their emerging productive facilities—whether in manufactured goods or in such agricultural products as fruits and wine—with the largest and the fastest-growing economy around, i.e., the world market.

But exporting requires market knowledge, marketing facilities and marketing finance. It also requires political muscle to overcome strongly entrenched protectionist forces, and especially labor unions and farm blocs in the developed countries. Exporting is done most successfully, most easily and most cheaply if one has an assured "captive" market, at least for part of the production to be sold in the world market. This applies particularly to most of the developing countries, whose home market is too small to be an adequate base for an export-oriented industry.

The multinational's capacity to allocate production across national boundary lines and according to the logic of the world market should thus be a major ally of the developing countries. The more rationally and the more "globally" production is being allocated, the more they stand to gain. A multinational company, by definition, can equalize the cost of capital across national lines (to some considerable extent, at least). It can equalize to a large extent the managerial resource, that is, it can move executives, can train them, etc. The only resource it cannot freely move is labor. And that is precisely the resource in which the developing countries have the advantage.

This advantage is likely to increase. Unless there is a worldwide prolonged depression, labor in the developed countries is going to be increasingly scarce and expensive, if only because of low birthrates, while a large-scale movement of people from pre-industrial areas into developed countries, such as the mass-movement of American Blacks to the Northern cities or the mass-movement of "guest workers" to Western Europe, is politically or socially no longer possible.

But unless the multinationals are being used to integrate the productive resources of the developing countries into the productive network of the world economy—and especially into the production and marketing systems of the multinationals themselves—it is most unlikely that major export markets for the production of the developing countries will actually emerge very quickly.

Thus, the most advantageous strategy for the developing countries would seem to be to replace—or, at least to supplement—the policy of "domestic content" by a policy that uses the multinationals' integrating ability to develop large productive facilities with access to markets in the developed world. A good idea might be to encourage investment by multinationals with definite plans—and eventually firm commitments—to produce for export, especially within their own multinational system. As Taiwan and Singapore have demonstrated, it can make much more sense to become the most efficient large supplier worldwide of one model or one component than to be a high-cost small producer of the entire product or line. This would create more jobs and provide the final product at lower prices to the country's own consumers. And it should result in large foreign-exchange earnings.

I would suggest a second integration requirement. That developing countries want to limit the number of foreigners a company brings in is understandable. But the multinational can be expected to do that anyhow as much as possible—moving people around is expensive and presents all sorts of problems and troubles. Far more important would be a requirement by the developing country that the multinational integrate the managerial and professional people it employs in the country within its worldwide management development plans. Most especially it should assign an adequate number of the younger, abler people from its affiliate in the developing country for from three to five years of managerial and professional work in one of the developed countries. So far, to my knowledge, this is being done systematically only by some of the major American banks, by Alcan, and by Nestle. Yet it is people and their competence who propel development; and the most important competence needed is not technical, i.e., what one can learn in a course, but management of people, marketing and finance, and first-hand knowledge of developed countries.

In sum, from the point of view of the developing countries the best cross-national use of resources which the multinational is—or should be—capable of may well be the most positive element in the present world economy. A policy of self-sufficiency is not possible even for the best-endowed country today. Development, even of modest proportions, cannot be based on uneconomically small, permanently high-cost facilities, either in manufacturing or in farming. Nor is it likely to occur, let alone rapidly, under the restraint of a continental balance-of-payments crisis. The integration of the productive capacities and advantages of developing countries into the world economy is the only way out. And the multinational's capacity for productive integration across national boundaries would seem the most promising tool for this.

V

That 100-percent ownership on the part of the "parent company" is *the* one and only corporate structure for the multinational, while widely believed, has never been true. In so important a country as Japan it has always been the rather rare exception, with most non-Japanese companies operating through joint ventures. Sears, Roebuck is in partnership throughout Canada with a leading local retail chain, Simpson's. The Chase Manhattan Bank operates in many countries as a minority partner in and with local banks. Adela, the multinational venture-capital firm in Latin America, and by far the most successful of all development institutions in the world today, has confined itself from its start, ten years ago, to minority participation in its ventures, and so on.

But it is true that, historically, 100-percent ownership has been considered the preferred form, and anything else as likely to make unity of action, vision and strategy rather difficult. Indeed, restriction of the foreign investor to less than 100-percent control or to a minority participation, e.g., in the Andean Pact agreements or in Mexico's legislation regarding foreign investments, is clearly intended as restraint on the foreigner, if not as punitive action.

But increasingly the pendulum is likely to swing the other way. (Indeed, it may not be too far-fetched to anticipate that, a few years hence, "anti-foreign" sentiment may take the form of demanding 100-percent foreign-capital investment in the national company in the developing country, and moving toward outlawing partnerships or joint ventures with local capital as a drain on a country's slender capital resources.) The multinational will find it increasingly to its advantage to structure ownership in a variety of ways, and especially in ways that make it possible for it to gain access to both local capital and local talent.

Capital markets are rapidly becoming "polycentric." The multinationals will have to learn so to structure their businesses as to be able to tap any capital market—whether in the United States, Western Europe, Japan, Brazil, Beirut or wherever. This the monolithic "parent company" with wholly-owned branches is not easily capable of. When companies, for example the West Europeans, raise money abroad, they often prefer financial instruments such as convertible debentures, which their own home capital markets, or the United States, do not particularly like and cannot easily handle. There is also more and more evidence that the capital-raising capacity of a huge multinational, especially for medium-term working capital, can be substantially increased by making major segments of the system capable of financing themselves largely in their own capital markets and with their own investing public and financial institutions.

But capital is also likely to be in short supply for years to come, barring a major global depression. And this might well mean that the multinationals will only be willing and able to invest in small, less profitable and more slowly growing markets, i.e., in developing countries if these countries supply a major share of the needed capital rather than have the foreign investor put up all of it.

That this is already happening, the example of Japan shows. Lifting restrictions on foreign investment was expected to bring a massive rush of take-over bids and 100 percent foreign-owned ventures. Instead it is now increasingly the Western investor, American as well as European, who presses for joint ventures in Japan and expects the Japanese partner to supply the capital while he supplies technology and product knowledge.

Perhaps more important will be the need to structure for other than 100-percent ownership to obtain the needed managerial talent in the developing country. If the affiliate in the developing country is not a "branch" but a separate company with substantial outside capital investment, the role and position of its executives become manageable. They are then what they have to be, namely, truly "top management," even though in employment and sales their company may still be insignificant within the giant concern.

And if the multinational truly attempts to integrate production across national boundaries, a "top management" of considerable stature becomes even more necessary. For then, the managers of the affiliate in a developing country have to balance both a national business and a global strategy. They have to be "top management" in their own country and handle on the local level highly complex economic, financial, political and labor relations as well as play as full members on a worldwide "system management" team.[3] To do this as a "subordinate" is almost impossible. One has to be an "equal," with one's own truly autonomous command.

VI

Domestically, we long ago learned that "control" has been divorced from "ownership" and, indeed, is rapidly becoming quite independent of "ownership." There is no reason why the same development should not be taking place internationally—and for the same two reasons: (1) "ownership" does not have enough capital to finance the scope of modern large businesses; and (2) management, i.e., "control," has to have professional competence, authority and standing of its own. Domestically the divorce of "control" from "ownership" has not undermined "control." On the contrary, it has made managerial control and direction more powerful, more purposeful, more cohesive.

There is no inherent reason why moving away from "100-percent ownership" in developing countries should make impossible maintenance of common cohesion and central control. On the contrary, both because it extends the capital base of the multinational in a period of worldwide capital shortage and because it creates local partners, whether businessmen or government agencies, the divorce between control and direction may well strengthen cohesion, and may indeed even be a prerequisite to a true global strategy.[4]

At the same time such partnership may heighten the development impact of multinational investment by mobilizing domestic capital for productive investment and by speeding up the development of local entrepreneurs and managers.

[3] For a full discussion of this organization design, see my recent book *Management: Tasks; Responsibilities; Practices,* New York: Harper & Row, 1974, especially Chapter 47.

[4] On very different grounds, Professor Jack N. Behrman, former Assistant Secretary of Commerce in the Kennedy Administration and a man with encyclopedic knowledge of how the multinational economy works, reached similar conclusions. See his *Decision Criteria for Foreign Direct Investment in Latin America,* New York: Council of the Americas, 1974.

Admittedly, mixed ownership has serious problems; but they do not seem insurmountable, as the Japanese joint-venture proves. It also has advantages; and in a period of worldwide shortage of capital it is the multinational that would seem to be the main beneficiary. Indeed one could well argue that developing countries, if they want to attract foreign investment in such a period, may have to *offer* co-investment capital, and that provisions for the participation of local investment in ownership will come to be seen (and predictably to be criticized) as favoring the foreign investor rather than as limiting him.

VII

The multinational, while the most important and most visible innovation of the postwar period in the economic field, is primarily a symptom of a much greater change. It is a response to the emergence of a genuine world economy. This world economy is not an agglomeration of national economies as was the "international economy" of nineteenth-century international trade theory. It is fundamentally autonomous, has its own dynamics, its own demand patterns, its own institutions—and in the Special Drawing Rights (SDR) even its own money and credit system in embryonic form. For the first time in 400 years—since the end of the sixteenth century when the word "sovereignty" was first coined—the territorial political unit and the economic unit are no longer congruent.

This, understandably, appears as a threat to national governments. The threat is aggravated by the fact that no one so far has a workable theory of the world economy. As a result there is today no proven, effective, predictable economic policy: witness the impotence of governments in the face of worldwide inflation.

The multinationals are but a symptom. Suppressing them, predictably, can only aggravate the disease. But to fight the symptoms in lieu of a cure has aways been tempting. It is therefore entirely possible that the multinationals will be severely damaged and perhaps even destroyed within the next decade. If so, this will be done by the governments of the developed countries, and especially by the governments of the multinationals' *home* countries, the United States, Britain, Germany, France, Japan, Sweden, Holland and Switzerland—the countries where 95 percent of the world's multinationals are domiciled and which together account for at least three-quarters of the multinationals' business and profits. The developing nations can contribute emotionalism and rhetoric to the decisions, but very little else. They are simply not important enough to the multinationals (or to the world economy) to have a major impact.

But at the same time the emergence of a genuine world economy is the one real hope for most of the developing countries, especially for the great majority which by themselves are too small to be viable as "national economies" under present technologies, present research requirements, present capital requirements and present transportation and communications facilities. The next ten years are the years in which they will both most need the multinationals and have the greatest opportunity of benefiting from them. For these will be the years when the developing countries will have to find jobs and incomes for the largest number of new entrants into the labor force in their history while, at the same time, the developed countries will experience a sharp contraction of the number of new entrants into their labor force—a contraction that is already quite far advanced in Japan and in parts of Western Europe and will reach the United States by the late 1970s. And the jobs that the developing countries will need so desperately for the next ten years will to a very large extent require the presence of the multinationals—their investment, their technology, their managerial competence, and above all their marketing and export capabilities.

The best hope for developing countries, both to attain political and cultural nationhood and to obtain the employment opportunities and export earnings they need, is through the integrative power of the world economy. And their tool, if only they are willing to use it, is, above all, the multinational company—precisely because it represents a global economy and cuts across national boundaries.

The multinational, if it survives, will surely look different tomorrow, will have a different structure, and will be "transnational" rather than "multinational." But even the multinational of today is—or at least should be—a most effective means to constructive nationhood for the developing world.

36

The Multinational Company/Host-Country Venture:

A BETTER WAY

A. Bertram

CAN MULTINATIONAL COMPANIES SURVIVE IN THE DEVELOPING COUNTRIES?

So much has been written lately on the multinational company (MNC) that one might ask: Why another article? As an executive who has worked for an MNC all of his adult life in senior executive positions—presenting, interpreting, and defending the MNC to host governments and citizens of developing countries—I believe the lessons that I have learned will be helpful to other executives working in the same environment. Hopefully my revelations will change some of the fundamental attitudes the MNCs hold sacred, so that changes can be effected in MNC/Host Country (HC) relations.

Unless MNCs change their ways, their presence (at least in the developing countries) will go the way of the American Buffalo: once numerous, powerful, sweeping aside everything in their path; soon only a few, protected, more of an oddity than a challenge to the neighbors with which they come into contact.

Before commenting upon what actions I believe MNCs must adopt to retain their position(s) in the economic environment of tomorrow, let us review (1) the position of the MNC in today's economic world and in particular the developing nations, and (2) the strains/stresses that exist in relationships between the MNC and HC in the developing countries. (I shall limit this discussion to developing countries, since I believe that the challenges the MNCs face will first occur in the developing countries rather than the developed ones. In the longer range, however, these same strains/stresses will extend to the developed countries, with the same effect.)

The position of MNCs in today's world economy can be seen in the statistics of the top 40 companies in *Fortune* magazine's listing of the largest U.S.A./non-U.S.A. industrial enterprises. These companies are all MNCs.[1] By comparing the combined data on sales, assets, net income, and number of employees, we can gain some insight into the MNC's power and influence (see Attachment I).

The *combined sales* of these 40 companies is equal to about 350 billion (U.S.) dollars and is one and one-half times the GNP of Japan, two times the GNP of Communist China, and almost six times that of India. The comparison of *assets* is not much different from that of sales. The *combined net income* of these companies is 22 billion (U.S.) dollars, which is about three times the GNP of Indonesia (the fifth most populous country in the world)

ATTACHMENT I

Twenty Largest Multinational Companies—U.S.A. and Foreign

		Billion Dollars						100,000		
		Sales		Assets		Net Income		Employees		
	U.S.A.	USA	For.	USA	For.	USA	For.	USA	For.	Foreign
1.	General Motors	35.8	18.7	20.3	22.8	2.4	1.8	8.11	1.68	Royal Dutch Shell
2.	Exxon Corp.	25.7	11.0	25.1	5.7	2.4	.4	1.37	3.53	Unilever
3.	Ford	23.0	8.1	13.0	8.6	.9	.3	4.74	4.02	Philips Radio
4.	Chrysler	11.8	7.7	6.1	10.4	.3	.8	2.73	.69	British Petroleum
5.	General Electric	11.6	7.6	8.3	9.0	.6	.2	3.88	.97	Nippon Steel
6.	Texaco	11.4	6.4	13.6	4.8	1.3	.1	.75	2.15	Volkswagon
7.	Mobil	11.4	6.0	10.7	7.3	.8	.3	.74	1.51	Hitachi
8.	I.B.M.	11.0	5.6	12.3	5.9	1.6	.2	2.74	1.55	Farbwerke Hoechst
9.	Int. Tel. & Tel.	10.2	5.6	10.1	2.2	.5	.1	4.38	1.56	Daimler-Benz
10.	Gulf	8.4	5.5	10.1	3.7	.8	.3	.52	.57	Toyota
11.	Stand. Oil Calif.	7.8	5.5	9.1	6.2	.8	.2	.39	3.03	Siemens
12.	Western Electric	7.0	5.4	4.8	4.8	.3	.2	2.07	.52	BASF
13.	U.S. Steel	7.0	5.3	6.9	6.4	.3	.4	1.85	1.99	ICI
14.	Westinghouse	5.7	5.2	4.4	8.1	.2	.1	1.94	1.14	Mitsubishi
15.	Stan. Oil Ind.	5.4	5.2	7.0	3.8	.5	.2	.47	1.28	Nestle
16.	DuPont	5.3	4.9	4.8	5.1	.6	.2	1.18	.85	Nissan
17.	Gen. Tel. & Electric	5.1	4.7	10.8	1.8	.4	-	1.96	1.70	Renault
18.	Shell Oil (USA)	4.9	4.7	5.4	5.0	.3	.2	.32	1.10	Bayer
19.	Goodyear	4.7	4.6	3.9	5.7	.2	.1	1.53	1.57	Montedison
20.	RCA	4.2	4.4	3.3	3.9	.2	.3	1.26	.85	Matsushita
	Sub Total	217.4	132.1	190.6	131.2	15.4	6.4	42.92	32.26	
	Total	349.5		321.8		21.8		85.18		

Data from FORTUNE Magazine: May and August 1974

and almost one-half that of Brazil (a nation having one of the largest geographical areas in the world). The number of *people* employed by these 40 industrial enterprises is again significant: It is equivalent to about one-third of West German's employment, or about one and one-half times that of Canada's total number of workers.

While the above figures indicate that the MNCs are a significant factor in the world economy, the statistics apply primarily to developed countries, not developing nations. Since my discussion of MNC/HC relationships, attitudes, and "formula for change" will focus principally on experiences in developing countries, the MNC's economic position in this sphere should be outlined. (Unfortunately, I am unable to present definite statistics here on just how significant the MNCs are in the developing economies other than to cite my own experiences and observations.) In many of the countries in which I have worked, the local affiliates (wholly- or majority-owned) of MNCs are among the largest industrial enterprises and are responsible for a significant portion of the economic activity in the developing nation. In many cases the MNC's influence in the developing country is far more dominant than the MNC's influence worldwide. Let us assume therefore that the MNCs are a significant factor in the developing countries' economy —comparable to the MNC's influence worldwide.

This commanding economic position in the developing countries and the world in general is both a blessing and a burden to the MNC. It is a blessing because the MNC is a significant factor in the local economy and therefore has entry (and clout) with the highest echelons of government, labor, and influence makers. Also, the MNC's broad geographical diversification gives the MNC a substantial and broad financial base with the flexibility to transfer operations to those countries which will insure the MNC maximum efficiency and profitability. These blessings are also a burden because the HC resents the MNC's flexibility (and leverage), in that the MNC is not overly dependent upon the operations (and the laws) in one country for its economic well-being and existence. Unfortunately, the MNC compounds this resentment by seeking, on many occasions, special considerations —by pointing out to the host government that the economic incentive(s) in other countries are more attractive, and unless the HC meets these alternate conditions the MNC will make its investments elsewhere.

Another burden is that the MNC is highly visible. Usually among the best managed and hence among the more successful of business, the MNC becomes prone to attacks by "economic" nationalists. This resentment is reinforced since the MNC is usually foreign-owned[2]; and the locally-owned and less successful business interests, nationalists, and anti-business groups accuse the MNC of monopoly practices and behaving in less than the best interest of the HC. These critics cite foreign exchange drains on the country, high costs of materials parts and components which suppress local profits and raise taxes, and the less favorable cultural imports that the MNC introduces—such as drug abuse, hippie behavior, and permissiveness.

I could list a whole gamut of "anti" factors that have been hurled at the MNCs by many of the developing countries. However, it is sufficient here to recognize that they exist and to varying degrees. Why should this be so?

The one resource that all developing countries need is capital—in particular capital derived from foreign sorces. In the beginning, developing nations will woo foreign companies—MNCs—with all kinds of concessions in order to attract their capital. In the beginning of this relationship or marriage, the HC views the relationship favorably since the MNC is doing the following:

- Importing foreign capital to buy local goods and services.
- Importing capital goods at no immediate cost to the HC.
- Training a work force and transferring technological and managerial talents to local citizens.
- Building a viable and modern technological business base.
- Creating a middle class which is educated and paying taxes.
- Building up foreign reserves if it is export oriented or, conversely, saving foreign exchange if it is an import-substituting enterprise.
- Generating corporate income taxes to the government.

The above attractions are at their zenith immediately after the venture is in full production and all of the above elements are contributing to the growth and viability of the project. So long as the HC decides that the favorable elements are contributing significantly to the development of the nation, it (and the nation's public) will downplay the negative or "anti" factors that the MNC imports into the HC. Over a period of time, however, as the enterprise of the MNC matures in the HC, many of the inputs are no longer looked upon as plus factors. For instance, foreign capital no longer is imported to pay for goods and services since local funds are now generated and can be utilized. Also, local funds are converted to foreign exchange as depreciation and profits are remitted to the MNC's home office; in effect, the MNC becomes a "consumer" of foreign exchange.

The same argument holds for the transfer of technological and managerial talents. Once these have been transferred, the HC "forgets" the value of these assets, including the contribution in these areas that the MNC has made. As this situation begins to develop, the HC starts to question the value of the MNC to the development of its nation. At this point, the "anti" factors become more pronounced and begin to multiply in magnitude. Under these conditions the MNC and the HC are set on a collision course; it is only a matter of time before the rupture is announced.

While I have only used two of the many issues that can lead to the rupture of a supposedly viable MNC/HC relationship, a review of why a disassociation occurs reveals a pattern. When the MNC enters a country, it brings all the components that I mentioned previously (capital, expertise, jobs, markets, etc.) which over a period of time are either transferable or are generated from within the country. As the investment of the MNC matures, a situation develops different from that at the beginning of the project: The MNC begins to "export" the components it was previously importing or creating. At first, the HC will tolerate this reverse flow situation. In those relationships where the MNC is continuing to contribute something other than ownership to the MNC/HC partnership, the rupture will be somewhat delayed. It is important, therefore, that the MNC recognize that so long as it is contributing something that the HC cannot do itself, it will have a better chance to maintain the profitable MNC/HC relationship. Too many MNCs err in assuming that ownership is sacred and entitles them to perpetual life so long as its investment results in a successful venture; that all the MNC must do is to guide the business along its efficient and profitable path and in return will be assured of its dividends and profits.

The fact that the management itself, the market, the expertise, the capital, and the raw material are now indigenous to the HC does not seem to make much of an impression upon the MNC. It *does* to the HC, especially when it "discovers" that the return(s) to the MNC have usually been handsome. In these situations, the MNC is looked upon as a parasite; and in those developing nations where capital continues to remain the single most important factor in increasing economic development, the critics of the MNC begin to have an increasingly louder voice and the expropriation or buy-out stage can be anticipated.

In such a dismal situation, is there any future for MNCs in tomorrow's environment in the developing countries? Yes, there is, but not as MNC/HC relationships are structured today.

First of all, MNCs must recognize that their foreign investments have a limited life; after a period of time, they will revert to the HC. In effect, this is what is happening today, although both parties—the MNC and the HC—do not fully appreciate and recognize what is occurring. Let us review this "limited life" cycle:

Conception: Negotiation of a project; if successful, agreement is signed.

Birth: Start of enterprise. Both parties desire to see venture prosper and succeed.

Development: Enterprise attains its full potential; as it does expertise is transferred and capital flows begin to be reversed.

Maturity: Full potential attained and HC begins to see MNC as a "taker," contributing nothing new to development of the nation.

Decline: HC "anti" groups prominent and internal political and economic pressures override ownership argument of rights.

Termination: Buy out or expropriation. The point of no return has been reached.

This "limited life" cycle may take only a few years in some cases; in others, it may go on for years. What is definite is that the termination will occur; however, how long after conception it will happen will vary and be dependent upon whether the MNC is offering some economic service or value which is not easily transferable or which depends upon facilities or expertise outside of the HC. Two examples will illustrate this:

1. The "hotel conglomerate" type. The attraction for this kind of venture

is that the MNC offers something, a service, that cannot be duplicated by the HC. Also, without this service, the venture in the HC may not be viable or, alternatively, may be only marginally successful. A good example of this is a chain of hotels operated by an international organization (i.e., Hilton) which uses its worldwide reservation system to insure high occupancy rates. The international organization earns a service fee on the reservation and also, because of this reservation service, commands the right to operate and manage the hotel. This latter proviso ensures the hotel's clients minimum quality standards—conditions which can only be guaranteed if the international hotel chain is operating the hotel facilities. Naturally, the operating organization earns a fee or commission on the operation of the hotel, and this adds to the profits of the parent international organization. This relationship will remain a viable one as long as both parties believe they gain from the partnership. As soon as one begins to doubt this, a dissolution is imminent. The fact, however, that the MNC is doing a service that the HC can identify and which the HC cannot duplicate adds cement to the relationship and insures that this type of economic involvement will last.

2. The "highly technological" type, which usually involves rapid and frequent changes in technology requiring very large expenditures and large markets since an economy of scale is needed. These characteristics rule out operations in only one country because the needed resources (capital, materials, management) are larger than one or two developing countries can supply. Rather, the MNC, which is composed of many affiliates, can spread the costs (and benefits) of developing the technological advances among all the affiliates. Also, the markets in all the affiliates give the MNC the capital base and the required economy of scale. IBM would be an example of this type of venture.

While the above examples illustrate how MNCs can prolong their stay in HCs, one might say these are special examples and many MNCs do not have such operations; they have no "muscle" to blunt the HC's appetite to expropriate or buy them out once the ventures are mature and successful. Are these MNC's therefore not doomed to the loss of their business? I answer yes . . . and no. Let me explain.

In their lifetime, MNCs in developing (and developed) countries will approach the "decline" phase of their "limited life" cycle. This is a truism. But just as in human life, judicious (clean living) behavior over a period of time will mean longer life. How can this be achieved? By assisting the HC in attaining national planning and development goals. By this, I mean the MNC should attempt to assist the HC in the attainment of some of its social and economic goals: projects which are not directly related to the venture in which the MNC/HC is involved.

For instance, in most countries oil companies are facing much criticism and increasingly restrictive legislation on their activities; in a few countries they have been expropriated. Doesn't it make sense therefore for the oil companies to become involved with a national issue that requires a solution?

Would not the development of urban transportation systems (to choose an example) be a logical one since it touches the lives of so many citizens, and can add so much to the development of cities, states, and nations? All over the world this problem plagues the community, yet no economical, practical solutions are in sight. Could not the MNCs direct the released expatriate management people, who have finished training their local management replacements, into the study of these national social problems?

It is true that these released expatriate managers might not be "experts" in this new field; however, good managers are logical thinkers and using the team approach to the learning cycle for the released managers should not take too long. Also, the MNCs have the financial base to undertake some of this "research" (learning) which when developed can be used in similar situations in other HCs; this base can result in new attractive economic ventures in the HC (subject to the limitation of "limited life"), and may in fact prolong the existence of the MNC's existing business(es). It would indeed be a rare case where an HC would terminate an existing operating venture with an MNC when that party is trying to solve a difficult, expensive social problem for which the HC has given a high priority in its Development Plan.

The future of the MNCs therefore can be a bright one if they recognize that their presence in the developing country is a function of a "limited life"—a relationship which is dependent upon: (a) services which are not easily transferable and/or which depend upon facilities or assets outside of the developing country in question, and (b) services it renders in attaining social goals toward the nation's development objectives.

The "limited life" will be extended if one or both of the above conditions are prevalent. If the MNC, however, does not believe that its proposed venture in the HC has any of these "strengths," then the MNC should recognize the limitations to its corporate life. Its negotiations with the HC should take into account this "limited life" in the terms of the proposed venture. In this manner once a project is initiated both parties will recognize the conditions under which the venture is conceived, including the terms under which the MNC/HC relationship will be allowed to exist and be terminated.

If a venture is started in an HC under the constraints of a "limited life," there may develop an opportunity later on in which the MNC can assist the HC in the attainment of an established (but not yet achieved) national goal, which could be in the business sector (development of tourism, for example) or in the public domain (construction of inexpensive housing).

If situations such as these do develop and the MNC can participate in these new ventures, it should do so within the confines and limitations of the "limited life" strategy. By doing so, however, not only will the MNC open up new areas for profitable investment but will also prolong the "limited life" of its existing MNC/HC venture. This extension can be very profitable to the MNC and should be an attractive incentive to the MNC to try to innovate in ways that will enable it to remain a business entity in the developing countries.

In summary, it is important in MNC/HC relationships to recognize each party's strengths, weaknesses, concerns, and doubts at the initial negotiating stages so that these points can be included in the initial discussions and evaluated in the final agreement. If this is done, the venture can develop on a realistic schedule, and events in the life cycle will hold no surprises.

In addition, this new relationship between the MNC and HC will evidence a mutual dependency; it may lead to a situation where each party will attempt to continue this dependency and thus prove equally attractive to both parties. This equality should lead to a true partnership—one built on government/private-sector foundations. Possibly, this is the wave of the future. What is required is trust, truth, and most of all realism. Hopefully, the recognition of the "limited life" of a venture and the application of this concept to MNC/HC negotiations will bring about the much needed realism that can lead to better MNC/HC relationships.

NOTES

1. A multinational corporation is one that operates in many countries at different economic levels. Its local subsidiaries are managed by nationals and its central management is usually multinational.

2. All but two of the 40 largest MNCs in the *Fortune* listing are U.S., British, German, Japanese, or Dutch.

37

Coming Investment Wars?

C. Fred Bergsten

CANADA will now permit new foreign direct investments only when they bring "significant benefit" to Canada. The determination of "significant benefit" is explicitly to be a policy decision of the cabinet, based on five criteria: the contribution of the proposed investment to "the level and nature of economic activity in Canada," including employment, use of Canadian components, and exports; the degree and significance of Canadian participation in the enterprise; the effect on productivity, technological development and innovation in Canada; the effect on industrial competition; and the compatibility of the investment with the economic and industrial policies of the national and provincial governments.

The following scenario thus becomes almost inevitable. The Canadian cabinet will approve a large and controversial U.S. investment. Nationalist opposition will charge a sellout of Canadian interests. The government will respond that the investment brings "significant benefit" to Canada.

But Canadian politics will not permit the simple assertion of "national interest" by the governing party. Opponents of the investment (and of the governing party) will enumerate the alleged injury it brings to Canada. The government will be forced to counter by specifying the benefits which, in its view, outweigh the disadvantages. It will thus publicly reveal, for example, that the investment will bring *x* thousand additional jobs and *y* million dollars of additional exports to Canada.

International conflict becomes certain at this point. The AFL-CIO will charge that the *x* thousand jobs have been exported from the United States to Canada, validating its case against foreign investment by U.S. firms. The Treasury Department will charge that Canada has diverted the *y* million dollars of exports from the United States, weakening the U.S. balance of payments and the dollar. One virtually certain result is intensified U.S.-Canadian hostility. Another, which is a theme of this article, is an intensification of political pressure in the United States against all foreign investment by American firms.

Such overt efforts by Canada to capture an increasing share of the benefits of foreign investment would by themselves have a significant impact on U.S. policy, because Canada remains by far the largest single recipient of U.S. investment and because the rapid flow of communications between the two countries assures that adversely affected American interests will become aware of the situation. But the new Canadian policy is only illustrative of one of the basic global trends of the 1970s. Virtually every country in the world which receives direct investment—which means virtually every country in the world, big or small, industrialized or developing, Communist or non-Communist, Left or Right—is levying increasingly stringent requirements on foreign firms.

The objective of these policies of host countries is to tilt the benefits brought by multinational companies as far as possible in their favor and to minimize the costs to them which can be associated with such investments. Few countries any longer ask the simplistic question: "Do we want foreign investment?" The issue is how to get foreign investment on the terms which are best for them, and indeed to use the power of the firms to promote their own national goals.

Host countries are adopting a variety of strategies to achieve this objective. Most are applying much more sensible general economic policies, and thus removing such sources of windfall profits for the firms—and losses for the countries—as overvalued exchange rates and undervalued interest rates. In addition, most are seeking to position themselves as strongly as possible to negotiate better deals on the whole range of relevant issues with applicant firms. They list broad criteria for judging specific applications, require detailed statements from applicant firms on the effects of their proposals, and then seek the best mix of benefits they can achieve without deterring the investor. This effort of host countries to negotiate maximum benefits and minimum costs from foreign investors will shortly become the focus of the entire international debate about multinational firms.

II

Efforts by host countries to maximize their returns from foreign investors are, of course, nothing new. There are four features, however, which differentiate the present markedly from the past. First, virtually all host countries are now adopting such policies, whereas only a few did so before. Second, the policies themselves are becoming more evident and explicit and hence will attract increasing attention in the home countries of the firms, particularly the United States.

Third, host-country objectives are now much broader and deeper. Governments throughout the world are accepting responsibility for an increasing number of economic and social objectives—such as regional equity, better income distribution and the development of indigenous high-technology industries—in addition to the traditional macroeconomic goals of full employment, growth and price stability. Developing countries are also seeking to reduce unemployment directly rather than assuming that it will fall automatically with economic growth.

Thus governments are seeking additional policy instruments, to meet an increased number of policy targets. With the explosive acceleration of international economic interpenetration, external forces can hinder—or assist—the successful use of traditional domestic policy instruments. Multinational firms, as the chief engine of interpenetration, represent both a major threat to the success of internal policies and a major opportunity for help. Host countries are thus virtually compelled by their own political imperatives to seek to exert a maximum impact on the detailed behavior of almost all incoming direct investments.

Fourth, host-country efforts are now far more likely to succeed because of fundamental shifts in the world economic and political environment that have put many host countries in a far stronger position than before. They have large and rapidly growing markets, especially when they are members of regional arrangements, such as the European Community or the Andean Pact, which discriminate against imports from outsiders. Many represent highly productive, lower-cost "export platforms" from which multinational firms can substantially improve their global competitive positions. Those possessing key raw materials are in a particularly strong position, both with companies in the extractive industries themselves and with companies which use the materials;[1] producers of raw materials have now demonstrated the ability to get together to promote their common interests, rather than compete with each other to the benefit of outsiders. And the indigenous talent that has emerged in even the least developed, as the result of a generation of economic growth with heavy emphasis on advanced education, enables host countries both to perceive accurately their national interests and take

[1] See C. Fred Bergsten, "The New Era in World Commodity Markets," *Challenge,* Sept.–Oct. 1974.

maximum advantage of their stronger positions. Outside help in negotiating with the firms is also increasingly available for those countries which still need it. So the firms can no longer dictate, or even heavily influence, host-country policies as they may have done in the past; the *dependencia* syndrome, under which foreign and domestic elites collude against the national interests of host countries, is rapidly disappearing.

In addition, host countries now have a far wider array of options in pursuing their objectives. Not long ago the multinational firm was the only source of large-scale capital, advanced technology and superior management. Not long ago the United States was virtually the sole source of large chunks of investment capital, technological know-how and marketing skills. Not long ago security considerations devolving from the cold war enabled the United States to dominate its allies, most small countries, and the international rules and institutions which governed world economic relations.

Now, however, the multinationals have lost much of their power because the attributes which they once monopolized, and which could only be obtained in package form, can be increasingly "unbundled"—capital obtained in the private markets, technology licensed from a variety of sources, management hired directly. Increasing numbers of European and Japanese companies offer formidable competition for American multinationals —and are often willing to invest on terms more generous to host countries, to make up for their delayed emergence on the world scene. Capital, technology and other skills can be bought in Europe and elsewhere, as well as in America. With the onset of détente, host countries large and small no longer fear to cross the United States by challenging U.S.-based firms and the international economic environment which helped them flourish in the 1950s and 1960s. Multinational firms based in the United States, recognizing these basic changes and with their own international exposure greatly increased by virtue of their rapid global expansion, complete the circle by seeking in virtually all cases to accommodate to the new leverage of host countries and by eschewing the backing of the U.S. government.

In short, sovereignty is no longer at bay in host countries. To be sure, the degree of this shift in power differs from country to country, and from industry to industry. It is virtually complete in most industrial host countries and some developing countries as well, and is well underway in many other developing countries. Only in a few countries—industrial as well as developing, and indeed including the United States itself—have new host-country policies on foreign investment not yet begun to emerge.

The shift in power and resulting policy is further along in extractive than in manufacturing industries. Within manufacturing, it is further advanced for low-technology investments and those aimed at the local market than for high-technology investments and those which use the country as an "export platform." But the trend appears inexorable.

III

What about the effects of this trend on home countries—that is, the countries from which investment comes, via multinational firms based there—in particular the United States? Before addressing that question, we need to take a closer look at the specific requirements being levied on the multinational firms.

These requirements derive from the policy objectives of the host countries. They differ in degree from country to country, but fall into three broad categories: domestic economic objectives, foreign economic policy objectives, and national control over the local subsidiaries of the foreign-based firms.

In the first category, the most direct requirement is job quotas for nationals. This has both a quantitative and a qualitative aspect. Developing countries with high rates of aggregate unemployment simply impose overall job requirements. Indonesia requires that 75 percent of all employees of foreign-based firms be Indonesian within five to eight years; Nigeria and Morocco sharply limit the access to alien labor of such firms. In both industrial and developing countries, such job requirements are often part of "regional policies": Canada, France, Iran, the Netherlands, and the United Kingdom, among others, offer major incentives to enterprises to bring jobs to "depressed areas." (In some countries, regional authorities themselves add to the list of requirements.) In addition, layoffs may be forbidden (Italy, some recent cases in France) or made very costly (Germany, Belgium), so that the firm is locked tightly into any level of employment which it initially recruits.

Qualitative job requirements are prevalent in both industrial countries and the new middle class of semi-developed countries. Argentina requires at least 85 percent of management, scientific, technical and administrative personnel to be Argentine. Singapore judges investment applications partly by the ratio of skilled and technical workers to be included in the work force. An increasing number of industrialized countries, particularly in Europe, are requiring the firms to carry out locally both a significant share of their total research and development and some of their most advanced research. Training of local workers is another requirement, aimed at both more and better jobs.

Two measures used to pursue both domestic and foreign economic objectives are "value-added" and "anti-concentration" requirements. To avoid becoming mere entrepôts for foreign firms, developing countries will now often require domestic production of a certain share of final output. This promotes the employment objective, both in the new industry itself and in those local industries which supply it; and furthers its balance-of-payments objective by raising the net foreign exchange return from the investment.

To avoid excessive industrial concentration, which can lead both to higher prices at home and to an impaired competitive position in world markets, some countries—particularly more developed ones—either reject foreign investments (especially take-overs) which would create excessive market power or let them proceed only if steps are taken to guard against such an outcome. Germany, the United States and Canada are particularly concerned with this issue.

Many developing countries are pursuing a similar aim through different means. Some multinational firms have traditionally limited or excluded competition among their own subsidiaries (and the parent) by dividing up world markets for each of their products. One result is that subsidiaries in particular countries are barred completely from the export market, or limited to a particular region. Global competition may be reduced as a result, and the export (and hence total production) opportunities of the country hosting the hobbled subsidiary are certainly reduced. Led by the Andean Pact, developing host countries are banning any such limitations on the distribution of local production by the subsidiaries (and any other tie-in clauses that would restrict the subsidiaries' use of the parents' technology).

Host countries are now promoting balance-of-payments objectives in several ways. A special target has been the trend in most multinational firms toward local financing, a practice which both limits the inflow of capital and diverts scarce local capital.

From 1957–1965, for example, only 17 percent of the investments of U.S.-based firms in Latin America originated outside the host country.[2] From 1965 until early 1974, U.S. policy actually promoted the trend toward local financing by limiting (first voluntarily, then mandatorily from 1968) the capital outflows of U.S. firms—but not their actual investments. Now a reaction has set in. Australia was one of the first countries to require external capital to come with the firm, largely in retaliation against the U.S. capital controls. Many hosts now require external financing for foreign investments, and others achieve the same purpose by limiting subsidiaries' access to domestic capital. On the other side of the capital account, a widening array of countries (e.g., Brazil, India, the Andean Pact) limit tightly the repatriation of capital investment and even profits.

Requirements that the investing firm export a sizable share of output are even more important, because they go directly to the location of world production, jobs and the most sensitive aspects of each country's external position. Andean Pact countries will permit foreign investors to avoid divestiture only if they export more than 80 percent of their output outside the group. Mexico permits 100 percent foreign ownership only if the firm exports 100 percent of its output. India requires foreign investors to export 60 percent of output within three years. Practically every host developing country—and many host developed countries—attach very high priority to the export criterion.

As with jobs, the export requirement is qualitative as well as quantitative. Many countries are seeking to upgrade and diversify their export base, and so require foreign investors to push the processing of raw materials or the assembly of components a stage or two further than might otherwise occur. A particular objective is building high-technology exports.[3]

Some efforts are still being made to get foreign firms to replace imports as well. Canada recently barred a major U.S. computer company from competing for government contracts unless it helped Canada achieve balanced trade in that sector, by replac-

[2] Ronald Müller, "Poverty Is the Product," *Foreign Policy,* Winter 1973–74, pp. 85–88.

[3] This emphasis on high-technology exports may affect a country's balance of payments less than its industrial structure. In a country whose exchange rate is floating, such as Canada, any increase in the exports of the promoted sector will produce upward movement in the currency, which will tend to limit exports (and increase imports) in other sectors.

ing imports as well as exporting. However, host countries are increasingly emphasizing exports because such a focus permits larger-scale production, greater efficiency, and more jobs and growth for the longer run. The shift requires more explicit policies toward the foreign investor and more affirmative action by the firms (especially if the host country is to avoid the costs to its wider objectives of excessive export subsidies and undervalued exchange rates). In addition, larger production runs by the subsidiaries mean greater potential conflict with the economic interests of the home country. This issue well illustrates the increasing clashes among countries which may arise.

Finally, virtually all host countries are seeking majority (if not complete) ownership of local subsidiaries of foreign firms. Many are seeking a major share in day-to-day management as well. The objective is to increase the likelihood that the subsidiary will respond positively to the national policies of the host country rather than to the global strategy of the corporate family, headquartered in the United States or another home country, and perhaps to the global strategy of the government of the home country as well.

Some of these host-country policies treat the multinational firm differently from local companies, though many do not. The main point, however, is not whether the policies are discriminatory. The significance is their clear intent to shift toward the host country the package of benefits brought by the foreign firms. To the extent that they do so successfully to an important degree, they trigger a potentially important new source of international conflict. To the extent that they do so through measures which produce results different from market-determined outcomes, there is increased justification for such clashes and even greater likelihood that they will occur.

IV

The firms themselves may have little or no objection to these host-country policies. They may be relatively indifferent, within fairly broad limits, as to where to locate sizable portions of their production and how to finance it.[4] They may quite easily accom-

[4] For an excellent analysis of this range see Paul Streeten, "The Multinational Enterprise and the Theory of Development Policy," *World Development,* Vol. 1, No. 10 (October 1973). He counsels host developing countries to marry cost-benefit analysis of their own needs to bargaining-power analysis of how far they can push. However, he views many host countries as weaker in their relations with multinationals than do I.

modate to host-country requirements on a majority, if not all, of the issues raised. The alacrity with which many firms have accepted the exceptionally detailed and far-reaching conditions imposed by Communist host countries is the most dramatic example, but the phenomenon is common. If too many firms do not play, a host country will sense that it has pushed too hard and retreat on the least important of its concerns, until it finds the mix that will maximize its interests.

The cooperativeness of the firms is promoted by the newly powerful positions of the host countries, as outlined above. It is often further accelerated by specific inducements. Some of the most frequent are favored tax treatment, export subsidies, "location grants" within the context of regional policies, subsidized training of local labor, prohibitions of strikes, preferred access to local credit, and protection against imports.

These considerations round out the strategies of the host countries. To maximize their returns, they must not only harness the activities of the firms but assure that the investments actually proceed. Thus they utilize the traditional mix of carrot and stick. The greater the incentives, the further the firms will, of course, tilt toward complying with the requests of their hosts.

Thus, a second broad trend is toward collaboration between the multinational firms and their hosts, and greater distance between the firms and their home governments. Few firms any longer appeal to their home government for support against host governments even in cases of outright nationalization, let alone to deal with the growing array of economic and political requirements which they face. Some firms, particularly in the natural resources industries, seek to limit the leverage of host countries by blending together capital from a variety of countries and selling their output forward to buyers in a variety of countries, to increase the problems for the host if it takes extreme action.[5] But even this strategy does not deter the achievement of the host's primary objectives; indeed, it may promote them by enhancing the inflow of external capital and assuring a diversified export market. And most firms, in recognition of the current balance of power, are in fact cooperating fully with their hosts. The oil industry is the most obvious recent case in point, but the trend is

[5] See Theodore H. Moran, "Transnational Strategies of Protection and Defense by Multinational Corporations: Spreading the Risk and Raising the Cost for Nationalization in Natural Resources," *International Organization*, Vol. 27, No. 2 (Spring 1973).

certainly widespread.

This analysis differs sharply from the picture painted in the recent debates in the United Nations and elsewhere, where the developing countries (and even some developed countries) continue to attack the alleged alliance against them of multinational firms and home-country governments. The difference can be explained partly by the usual lag in perceptions of overall bargaining power by the bargainer who is catching up step by step; partly by the dominance of the rhetoric by politicians whose perceptions are shaped by images, rather than by the technocrats who are implementing the new policies; partly by the zeal of the developing countries to stick together, which requires them to adopt the position of the weakest among them; and perhaps mainly by the overwhelming tactical advantage of keeping the home countries tagged as defenders of the multinationals and aggressors against host-country interests. As in the case of raw material prices, some of the traditionally have-not countries suffer from intellectual lag and others find it highly convenient to maintain the rhetoric of the past though it no longer bears much relation to reality. Their tactics can succeed as long as the home countries fail to recognize what is really happening. But reality in the field of foreign direct investment cannot be submerged much longer.

V

The main impact of these new global trends is on the home countries of the multinational firms. It falls most heavily on the United States, the largest home country by far.

If host countries are achieving an increasing share of the benefits brought by multinational firms, someone else is receiving a decreasing share. As just outlined, this "loser" is seldom the firms themselves; indeed, they may gain more from the incentives than they lose from the requirements. In some cases, countries which are neither home nor host to the company may lose—as when a Brazilian subsidiary of a U.S. firm competes with German sales in the world automobile market.

But the United States, as the home country, may frequently be on the losing side of the new balance in two senses. Host-country inducements to American firms may attract economic activity and jobs away from the United States, in some cases without economic justification. Traditionally, the United States has forcefully opposed policies which discriminated against foreign investors; now it increasingly finds its national interests threatened by policies which discriminate in favor of those firms. And host-country requirements may skew the results of U.S. investments against the overall U.S. national interest.

To be sure, many foreign direct investments represent non-zero-sum games: as in all classical market behavior, world welfare improves. It is also conceivable that all parties benefit from some of those investments. Some host-country measures may also help home countries, such as the United States; if a host country breaks up the global allocation of markets by a multinational firm, the home country may benefit more from lower prices than it loses in oligopoly rents. And some host-country policies (such as placing a few directors on the boards of subsidiaries) essentially bring them psychic rather than financial income, and have no adverse impact on anyone.

However, there is always the issue of how to divide the benefits even when all parties do gain. Indeed, there may be losses to the United States (through the firms) even when more economically sensible host-country policies increase world welfare by eliminating or reducing market imperfections which profited the firms in the past. Most important, many investments are largely indifferent to location and hence are close to zero-sum games; in such cases a decision that is one party's gain *is* another party's loss. Furthermore, world welfare may actually decline as a result of some foreign investments, such as those induced primarily by host-country tax preferences and those which increase global market concentration, even though host countries gain from them. So there is great latitude for home countries to lose when host countries successfully tilt the benefits of the investment package in their own direction.

The balance-of-payments aspects are the clearest case in point. Existing world demand for a product may often be relatively fixed in the short run, especially for the processed goods and high-technology items which countries are avid to produce. Thus there is a limit to world exports. If Brazil requires General Motors to export a certain share of its production in order to remain in business (or to retain its favored tax treatment), U.S. automotive exports may decline even though no such shift was dictated by purely economic considerations. Similarly, the U.S. capital which Brazil requires General Motors to use to construct its plant may not be automatically offset by other capital inflows into the United States. Similar shifts in benefits can occur with respect to jobs, technology or other economic aspects of investment whose outcome is altered by host-country policies.

The effects of shifts in ownership and management control imposed by host countries are more subtle, and more difficult to trace. In the past, control of foreign natural resources by U.S. companies generally increased the likelihood that those resources would be available to the United States in a crisis; now, however, the seizure of effective control by most host countries has rendered the United States as uncertain as all other countries in this area. Increased host-country control renders the firms less susceptible to the extraterritorial reach of the U.S. government. And shifts in effective control reduce the likelihood that the United States will derive monopoly rents or other benefits from the overseas activities of U.S. firms.

Such shifts of investment-induced benefits from the United States to host countries may, from many points of view, be desirable. They may distribute world income more equitably. They may reduce some of the tensions which have clouded interstate relations heretofore, because host governments felt inferior to the firms and hence susceptible to ill treatment by them.

However, these shifts may not always be so benign from the standpoint of the home country. Indeed, the United States now finds itself in a most peculiar position. Negotiations between U.S.-based multinational firms and host countries are having an increasingly important bearing on the national interests of the United States. The interests of the host countries are represented through their governments. The interests of the firms are represented directly. But the third major actor in the drama is at present wholly unrepresented.

In the past, some observers would have brushed off this apparent asymmetry on three counts: that U.S.-based firms could be counted on to represent U.S. national interests explicitly, or at least advance them inadvertently; that the United States was so powerful economically that any costs to its economy would be easily absorbed (and perhaps welcomed officially in view of U.S. support for economic development elsewhere); and that any such costs would be quite small anyway in view of the insensitivity of the U.S. economy to external events and the marginal economic importance of foreign investment.

Each of these considerations has now changed dramatically,

as part of the change in the overall economic and political environment noted in Section III.[6] Many "U.S.-based" firms have become truly multinational and thus, quite logically and defensibly from their standpoints, pursue a set of interests which may not coincide closely with any of several concepts of U.S. national interests. Indeed, as discussed above, many firms now respond much more clearly to host-country interests, because those host countries have both achieved a much stronger position vis-à-vis the firms and articulated far more clearly than home countries what they expect the firms to do.[7] In their constant quest for legitimacy and acceptance, the firms will naturally slide toward those who care most about their activities and who direct policies at them most explicitly.

And it is obvious that the U.S. economy is not so healthy that it can blithely ignore the effects of a phenomenon as large as direct investment. Such investment now accounts for more than 20 percent of the annual plant and equipment expenditures and profits of U.S.-based firms, and both numbers are rising rapidly. The corporations and the AFL-CIO agree that the phenomenon has an important impact on U.S. jobs and the balance of payments (though they disagree whether that impact is positive or negative). The United States is increasingly affected by world commodity arrangements, the structure of world markets and changes in exchange rates, all of which are influenced importantly by multinational firms.

It is thus both undesirable and completely unrealistic, in both economic and political terms, to anticipate continued abstention by the U.S. government from involvement in the foreign direct investment activities of U.S.-based enterprises. The British government has for several years made foreign exchange available to U.K.-based firms only if they can demonstrate that their foreign investments will benefit Britain's balance of payments, through exports and profit remittances. The Swedish government has had similar restrictions, and has just passed legislation which will also enable it to block foreign investments

[6] And elaborated in C. Fred Bergsten, *The Future of the International Economic Order: An Agenda for Research,* Lexington, Mass.: D.C. Heath and Co., 1973, esp. pp. 1–8.

[7] This in turn reflects a far clearer appreciation by host than home countries of the effects on them of multinational firms, and thus a far clearer idea of the ends to which they might want to harness foreign investors. There has been much more extensive analysis of the effects of foreign investment on host countries than of the effects on home countries, a situation which a forthcoming book on U.S. policy toward such investment by the present author, Thomas Horst and Theodore Moran seeks to help balance.

by Swedish firms which hurt its economy or foreign policy. Japan and, to a lesser extent, France have also traditionally used a variety of government levers to try to assure benefits to the home country from the foreign activities of their firms. So the United States is virtually alone, among home countries, in not playing an active role toward foreign investment by national enterprises.

As in host countries, the issue will not be whether or not to permit foreign investment as a general rule. Nor will it primarily focus on the simplistic U.S. concerns of the past: "prompt, effective and adequate" compensation for nationalized properties, avoidance of barriers to U.S. investment or discrimination against it, codes of conduct to legitimize the firms. The issue will sometimes be whether to permit a specific investment. But it will primarily be the terms on which investments proceed, and the equitable sharing of the resulting impact on the national economies involved.

VI

As the United States seeks to fill the empty chair which currently marks most international discussion of its foreign direct investment, the likelihood of international conflict will rise sharply. For at stake is nothing less than the international division of production and the fruits thereof. Indeed, "the kinds of techniques used by governments both to attract and to constrain multinational firms sometimes look like the largest nontariff barriers of all."[8] Unless host countries cease their efforts to tilt the benefits of investment in their own direction, which is unlikely (and undesirable unless accompanied by other steps to help them achieve their legitimate objectives), the clash of these particular national interests could become a central problem of world economics and politics.

Over the coming decade, international investment policy could therefore replicate to an unfortunate degree the evolution of international trade policy in the interwar period. At that time, trade was the dominant source of international economic exchange. As governments accepted increasing responsibility for the economic and social welfare of their populations, particularly with the onset of the Depression, they sought to increase their national shares of the international benefits which resulted

[8] A. E. Safarian and Joel Bell, "Issues Raised by National Control of the Multinational Corporation," *Columbia Journal of World Business*, Winter 1973, p. 16.

from trade. Other governments would not accept such diversion, and either emulated the moves of the initiators of controls or retaliated against them. There were no international rules and institutions to deter and channel such conflict. The result was trade warfare, and the deepening and broadening of the Depression.

Some observers fear that another depression looms on our contemporary horizon. Others wonder whether a Great Inflation, which in my view is more likely, will similarly lead countries desperately to pursue nationalistic measures in an effort to export their problems and insulate themselves from external pressures. Either cataclysm would greatly intensify the problem under discussion. Indeed, the national clashes outlined here might already have arisen much more frequently had not the postwar world economy progressed so successfully until recently.

Even without such extreme underlying conditions, however, the struggle for the international location of production will almost certainly continue to grow in both magnitude and impact on all countries concerned. Foreign direct investment and multinational enterprises have now replaced traditional, arms-length trade as the primary source of international economic exchange. As indicated throughout, host countries are increasingly adopting explicit policies to tilt in their directions the benefits generated by those enterprises. The impact of these efforts may turn out to be even greater than their trade predecessors of the 1930s, both because the economic interpenetration of nations is now more advanced than in the 1920s and because governments now pursue so many more policy targets.

Indeed, the U.S. government has already begun to voice opposition in international forums to the tax subsidies and other incentives which artificially lure U.S. firms to invest abroad, and the changes in U.S. taxation of foreign income proposed by the Treasury Department in April 1973 were largely aimed at countervailing such practices. Much stronger U.S. reactions can be envisaged over the next few years. The original AFL-CIO attack against foreign investment by American firms, as embodied in the Burke-Hartke bill, was based on ambiguous aggregate data and a handful of unrepresentative individual cases. Hence it made little headway. The efforts of the Treasury Department to limit direct investment outflows in the middle 1960s were similarly stymied by ambiguities over the effect of the outflows on the balance of payments.

But now labor, those concerned with the balance of payments, and the many other opponents of multinational enterprises will have a much stronger case: the shifting of benefits from the United States to host countries *through the overt policy steps* of those host countries. Such groups will ask how the U.S. government can sit idly by and let such shifts occur, just as similar American groups have since the 1930s—correctly and usually successfully—insisted that the U.S. government retaliate against the efforts of other countries to tilt the benefits of trade through subsidizing exports to the United States, blocking imports from the United States, or other measures of commercial policy which injured U.S. economic interests. And there are no domestic or international rules and procedures through which to channel such protests, like those developed for trade after World War II to avoid a repetition of the interwar experience.

The problem is further exacerbated by the subtlety and variety of inducements offered, and requirements levied, by host countries. A tariff or import quota is easy to see, and is usually known publicly. But a regional investment grant can be negotiated privately with a firm, and portrayed as "purely domestic" in any event if exposed. Export or job quotas, which are by their nature negotiated on a case-by-case basis, are even less obvious. The universal call for "transparency" of the operations of multinational firms must be joined by a call for transparency of the policies of many host countries toward those firms.

VII

The scenario envisaged at the outset of this article can thus be concluded as follows. After the Canadian government approves the proposed investment, because it transferred x thousand jobs and y million dollars of exports from the United States to Canada, the U.S. government—under intense domestic political pressure—decides to retaliate. It seeks to bar the particular investment, either directly or by declaring that the foreign tax credit will not apply to its profits.

Either approach, however, requires legislation. Congress, probably supported by any Administration in power, properly decides that such legislation should cover the overall issue of foreign investment rather than a single case or even a single country. The legislation clearly derives from a foreign action to pull jobs and exports away from the United States, and more examples of such actions, by a growing list of host countries, are added to the debate each day. The whole discussion may even take place with unemployment rising and the trade balance slipping. Thus the new legislation slaps a licensing requirement on all foreign investment and eliminates the tax credit altogether, except perhaps for investments where host countries avoid levying any requirements on U.S.-based firms.

Canada and most other host countries of course stick to their guns, being unable politically to back down in favor of multinational firms and at the dictates of the U.S. government. Foreign-based multinationals quickly begin to fill the void, and the United States begins to lose the many advantages conferred on it by the foreign investments of U.S.-based firms. Many of these firms then seek to "leave the United States," but the Treasury pursues them. In the end, as in the trade wars of the interwar period, the results include open political hostility among nations, a severe blow to the world economy, and a shattering of investor confidence.

Hopefully, the world will learn from its past mistakes and prevent this scenario from ever occurring. To do so, host countries should limit their efforts to skew the activities of multinational firms, perhaps by following the Australian example of insisting on "no adverse effects" rather than the Canadian example of requiring "significant benefit." But many will not do so unless some other power countervails the power of the firms. Nor will many of them, particularly the developing countries, do so unless they find other ways to meet their legitimate national aspirations.

It follows that home countries, particularly the United States, should take steps to help developing host countries achieve their goals in less disruptive ways. Such measures should encompass trade policy, commodity arrangements, and foreign assistance.[9]

More narrowly, home countries will also need tools that can be used to counter efforts of host countries that go beyond reasonable norms. For example, legislation increasing taxation of the foreign income of American corporations to offset tax inducements offered by host countries would be a precise analogy to present laws, in the trade field, that provide for countervailing duties against export subsidies by foreign governments. And a mechanism is needed to deal with individual cases where problems arise, analogous to the present escape clause in the trade

[9] See C. Fred Bergsten, "The Threat From The Third World," *Foreign Policy*, Summer 1973.

area providing for temporary protection where U.S. interests are injured by particular import flows.

But such measures by home countries could simply lead to a series of retaliatory and counter-retaliatory steps between them and host countries. Thus international investment wars will be prevented only by the adoption of a truly new international economic order, just as the trade wars of the 1930s were prevented from recurring in the postwar period only by the creation of a new international order based on the GATT, the IMF, the World Bank and American leadership.

The new order will have to include international rules governing investment itself, to limit the jousting for benefits between home and host countries and to provide a channel for the disputes that will inevitably arise among them, however ambitious the preventive rules. It will have to limit the power of the firms in ways acceptable to host countries, and provide alternative means for the latter to reduce domestic unemployment and expand exports. Multinational enterprises have a vital interest in the creation of such a new order, because they will otherwise be caught increasingly in the struggle between host and home countries; it will no longer be possible for them to side with home countries due to the weakness of the hosts, as in the 1950s and early 1960s, nor with hosts due to the inattention of the home countries, as in the late 1960s and early 1970s.

There are already many reasons to begin the construction of a new international economic order to replace the order of the first postwar generation, which has collapsed: the globalization of inflation, international monetary instability, the growing use of export controls, the scrambles for oil and other natural resources, the dire needs of the resource-poor countries of the "Fourth World" and the abilities of the new "middle class" of semi-developed countries to help in assisting them.

The threat of investment wars adds another crucial issue to the list for global economic reform. Fortunately, this particular threat has not yet become acute. There is time to deal with it carefully and constructively, instead of waiting for a series of crises to force hasty reaction. To begin to do so would both defuse the emotional issues raised by the existence and spread of multinational enterprises, and begin to apply the tested principles of international rules and cooperation to one of the major new features of the postwar world economy.